Data Management

Databases and Organizations

Data Management

Databases and Organizations

Fifth edition

Richard T. Watson
Department of MIS
Terry College of Business
The University of Georgia

John Wiley & Sons, Inc.

ACQUISITIONS EDITOR	Beth Lang Golub
ASSOCIATE EDITOR	Lorraina Raccuia
EDITORIAL ASSISTANT	Jen Snyder
SENIOR PRODUCTION EDITOR	Ken Santor
MARKETING MANAGER	Jillian Rice
COVER DESIGNER	Madelyn Lesure

This book was set in 10/12 Garamond by Richard and Ned Watson and printed and bound by Malloy Lithographing. Brady Palmer Printing manufactured the cover.

This book was printed on acid-free paper. ∞

To order books or for customer service, please call 1-800-CALL-WILEY (225-5945).

ISBN-13   978-0-471-71536-8
ISBN   0-471-71536-0

Printed in the United States of America

10 9 8 7 6 5 4 3 2 1

To Clare

Preface

This is not your traditional database textbook. It differs in three fundamental ways.

First, it is deeper than most database books in its coverage of data modeling and SQL. The market seeks graduates who have these fundamental skills. Time and again, students who have completed my data management class have told me how these skills have been invaluable in their first job. The intention is to place great emphasis on the core skills of data management. The consequence is that there is a better match between the skills students develop and market needs. This means that students find this text highly relevant.

Second, the treatments of data modeling and SQL are intertwined because my database teaching experience indicates that students more readily understand the intent of data modeling when they grasp the long-term goal—querying a well-designed relational database. The double helix, upward, intertwined, spiraling of data modeling and SQL is a unique pedagogical feature. Classroom testing indicates it is a superior method of teaching compared to handling data modeling and SQL separately. Students quickly understand the reason for data modeling and appreciate why it is a valuable skill. Also, rapid exposure to SQL means students gain hands-on experience that much sooner.

Third, the book is broader than most database books. Databases are one component of an expansive organizational memory. Information systems professionals need to develop a wide perspective of data management if they are to comprehend fully the organizational role of information technology.

In essence, the book is deeper where it matters—data modeling and SQL—and broader to give students a managerial outlook.

Information is a key resource for modern organizations. It is a critical input to managerial tasks. Because managers need high-quality information to manage change in a turbulent, global environment, many organizations have established systems for storing and retrieving data, the raw material of information. These storage and retrieval systems are an organization's memory. The organization relies on them, just as individuals rely on their personal memory, to continue as a going concern.

The central concern of information systems management is to design, build, and maintain information delivery systems. Information systems management needs to discover its organization's information requirements so that it can design systems to serve these needs. It must merge a system's design and information technology to build an application that provides the organization with data in a timely manner, appropriate format, and at a convenient location. Furthermore, it must manage applications so they evolve to meet changing needs, continue to operate under adverse conditions, and are protected from unauthorized access.

An information delivery system has two components: data and processes. This book concentrates on data, which is customarily thought of as a database. I deliberately set out to extend this horizon, however, by including all forms of organizational data stores because I believe students need to understand the role of data management that is aligned with current practice. In my view, data management is the design and maintenance of computer-based organizational memory. Thus, you will find chapters on XML and organizational intelligence technologies.

The decision to start the book with a managerial perspective arises from the belief that successful information systems practice is based on matching managerial needs, social system constraints, and technical opportunities. I want readers to appreciate the *big picture* before they become immersed in the intricacies of data modeling and SQL. In line with this perspective, business stories are used to support and enhance the text. Many of these vignettes serve double duty because they also alert students to current economic trends such as the globalization of business and the growth of the service sector. To provide an international flavor, I selected organizational stories from a variety of nations. The broad, international, managerial approach is one of several innovative pedagogical features in a data management text.

The first chapter introduces the case study, *The Expeditioner*, which is used in most subsequent chapters to introduce the key themes discussed. Often it sets the scene for the ensuing material by presenting a common business problem. I hope the case study also injects a little humor.

The second section of the book provides in-depth coverage of data modeling and SQL. Data modeling is the foundation of database quality. A solid grounding in data modeling principles and extensive practice are necessary for successful database design. In addition, this book exposes students to the full power of SQL.

I intend this book to be a long-term investment for students. There are useful reference sections for data modeling and SQL. The data modeling section details the standard structures and their relational mappings. The SQL section contains an extensive list of queries that serves as a basis for developing other SQL queries. The purpose of these sections is to facilitate *pattern matching*. For example, a student with an SQL query that is similar to a previous problem can rapidly search the SQL reference section to find the closest match. The student can then use the model answer as a guide to formulating the SQL query for the problem at hand. These reference sections are another unique teaching feature that will serve students well during the course and in their subsequent careers.

Although I set out to cast data management in a new light, I have not ignored the traditional core of a database course. Section 3 presents database architectures and their implementation. Coverage includes data storage technologies, data and file structures, client/server models, distributed database, and object-oriented, spatial, and temporal data management. Naturally, this section reflects a managerial perspective and discusses the trade-offs for the various options facing the data manager.

In keeping with the organizational memory theme introduced in Chapter 1, Section 4 covers other information technologies, including organizational intelligence technologies (data warehousing, OLAP, and data mining), the Web, Java, and XML.

The final section examines the management of organizational data stores. The outstanding feature of this section is the rigorous treatment of data integrity and data administration. The section concludes with a discussion of future issues in data management by examining how u-commerce, the next stage in the evolution of commerce, will influence data management.

A student completing this text will

- ❖ have a broad, managerial perspective of an organization's need for a memory;
- ❖ be able to design and create a relational database;
- ❖ be able to formulate complex SQL queries;
- ❖ have a sound understanding of database architectures and their managerial implications;
- ❖ be familiar with the full range of information technologies available for organizational memory;
- ❖ understand the fundamentals of data administration;
- ❖ know about data management developments and their organizational implications.

My purpose is to create a data management text that is innovative, relevant, and lively. I trust that you will enjoy reading this book and learn a great deal about managing data in today's organization.

Supplements

Accompanying this book are an instructors' manual[1] and an extensive Web site[2] that provides

- ❖ Overhead slides in PowerPoint format
- ❖ All relational tables in the book in electronic format
- ❖ Code for Java and XML examples in the book
- ❖ Answers to many of the exercises
- ❖ Additional exercises
- ❖ Revisions and errata
- ❖ Links to useful Web sites

---

1. Instructors should contact the author at <rwatson@terry.uga.edu> for the instructors' manual.
2. www.wiley.com/college/watson

New in the fifth edition

This edition has the following improvements and additions

- ❖ Representation of weak entities via a '+' rather than '|' to avoid confusion with data modeling dialects that use '|' to represent mandatory
- ❖ Greater focus on MySQL
- ❖ Increased coverage of mandatory and optional elements in data modeling
- ❖ A section on multidimensional expressions (MDX)
- ❖ New material on content management systems (CMS) and wiki technology
- ❖ A new chapter on embedded SQL in Java and JDBC

Acknowledgments

The support of Beth Golub at John Wiley & Sons was much appreciated. I thank my son, Ned, for help with the typesetting and my wife, Clare, for indexing and proofreading the book.

I would like to thank the reviewers of this and prior editions for their many excellent suggestions and ideas for improving the quality of the content and presentation of the book.

I acknowledge the thoughtful comments of James Suleiman of the University of Southern Maine. He offered many good suggestions for improving this edition.

I thank Tore Ørvik of Agder College, Norway, for his major contribution to the chapter on object-oriented database. His experience and knowledge of the object-oriented approach were most valuable.

My mate and colleague, Bob Bostrom of The University of Georgia, provided many insights and suggestions and contributed extensively to two chapters in the first edition. His extremely thorough review of the first edition added considerable value. I am very grateful for his many contributions to this project.

Richard T. Watson
Athens, Georgia

Brief Table of Contents

Table of Contents

Organizational Memory Technologies 431

Managing Organizational Memory 527

Section 1

The Managerial Perspective

People only see what they are prepared to see.
   Ralph Waldo Emerson, *Journals*, 1863

Organizations are accumulating vast volumes of data because of the implementation of technology (e.g., bar codes and scanners) that makes it easier and cheaper to collect data. The world's data are estimated to be doubling every 20 months, and many large companies now routinely manage terabytes (10^{12} bytes) of data. Data management has become a key function for many organizations.

The first section prepares you to see the role of data and information in an organization. The managerial perspective on data management concentrates on why organizations design and maintain data management systems, or organizational memories. Chapter 1 examines this topic by detailing the components of organizational memory and then discussing some of its common problems. The intention is to make you aware of the scope of data management and its many facets. Chapter 2 discusses the relationship between information and organizational goals. Again, a very broad outlook is adopted in order to provide a sweeping perspective on the relationship of information to organizational change.

At this point, we want to give you some *maps* for understanding the territory you will explore. Since the territory is possibly very new, these maps initially may be hard to read, and so you may need to read them several times before you understand the terrain you are about to enter.

The first map (see Figure S1-1) is based on the Newell-Simon model[1] of the human information processing system, which shows that humans receive input, process it, and produce output. The processing is done by a processor, which is linked to a memory divided into data and processes. The processor retrieves both data and processes from memory.

To understand this model, consider a person receiving a message to telephone a close friend. The message is input to the human information processing system. The person re-

---

1.   Newell, A., and H. A. Simon. 1972. *Human problem solving*. Englewood Cliffs, NJ: Prentice-Hall.

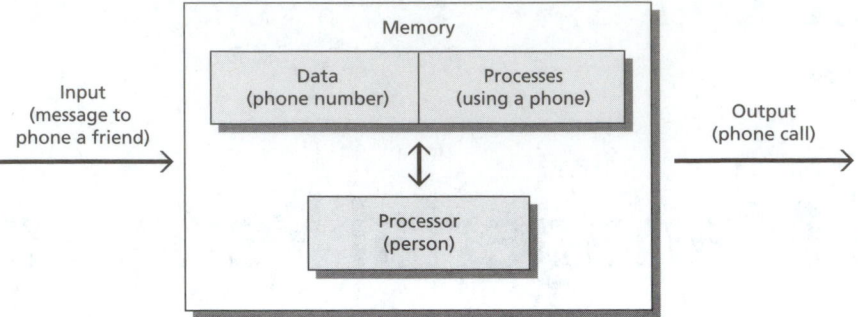

Figure S1-1. The Newell-Simon model of human information processing

trieves the friend's telephone number from memory and also retrieves the process, or instructions, for making a telephone call (e.g., pick up hand piece, press numbers, and so on). The person then makes the phone call, the processing of the input message. The phone call is the output. Sometimes these processes are so well ingrained in our memory that we never think about retrieving them. We just do them automatically.

Human information processing systems are easily overloaded. Our memory is limited, and our ability to process data is restricted; thus we use a variety of external tools to extend and augment our capacities. A telephone book is an example of external data memory. A recipe, a description of the process for preparing food, is an example of external process memory. Calculators and computers are examples of external processors we use to augment our limited processing capacity.

The original model of human information processing can be extended to include external memory, for storing data and processes, and external processors, for executing processes (see Figure S1-2).

This model of augmented human information processing translates directly to an organizational setting. Organizations collect inputs from the environment: market research, customer complaints, and competitor actions. They process these data and produce outputs: sales campaigns, new products, price changes, and so on. Figure S1-3 gives an example of how an organization might process data. As a result of some market research (input), a marketing analyst (an internal processor) retrieves sales data (data) and does a sales forecast (process). The analyst also requests a marketing consultant (an external processor) to analyze (process) some demographic data (data) before deciding to launch a new promotion (output).

An organization's memory comes in a variety of forms, as you will see in Chapter 1. This memory also can be divided into data and processes. The data part may contain information about customers. The process portion may store details of how to handle a customer order. Organizations use a variety of processors to handle data, including people and com-

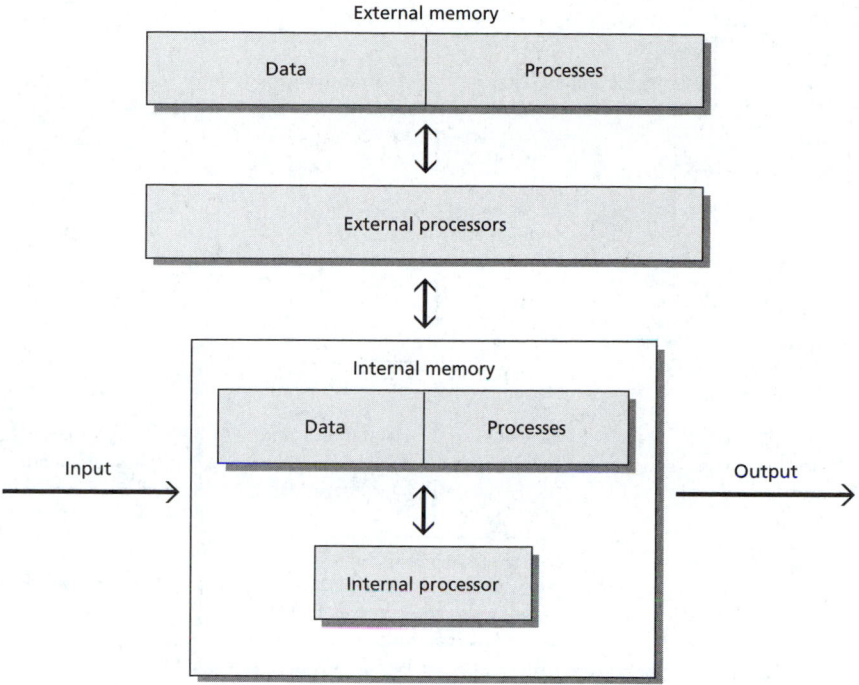

Figure S1-2. An augmented human information processing model

puters. Organizations also rely on external sources to extend their information processing capacity. For example, a business may use a specialist credit agency to check a customer's creditworthiness, or an engineering firm may buy time on a university's supercomputer for structural analysis of a bridge. Viewed this way, the augmented human information processing model becomes the pattern for an organizational information processing system.

This book focuses on the data side of organizational memory. While it is primarily concerned with data stored within the organization, there is also coverage of data in external memory. The process side of organizational memory is typically covered in a systems analysis and design course.

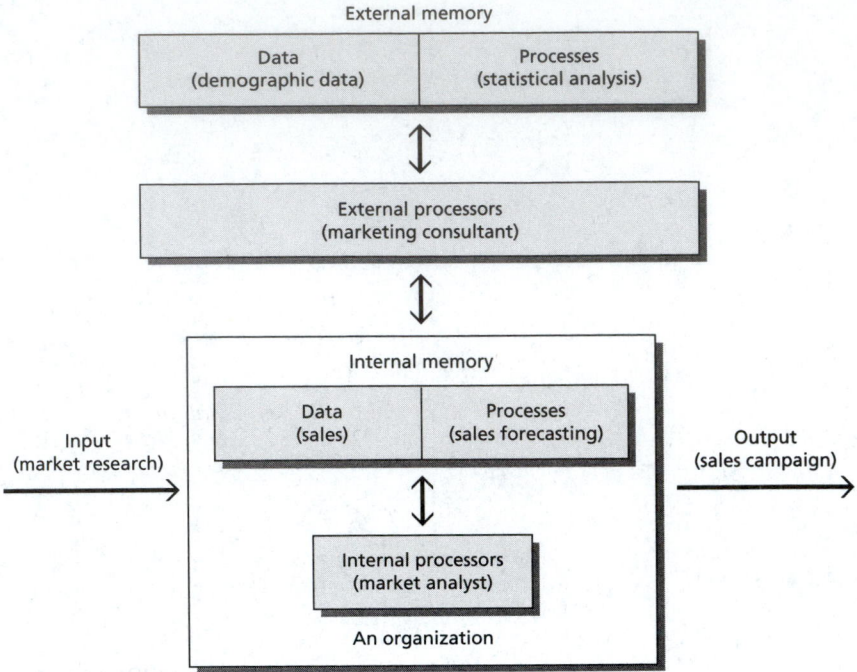

Figure S1-3. An organizational information processing model

1

Managing Data

All the value of this company is in its people. If you burned down all our plants, and we just kept our people and our information files, we should soon be as strong as ever.
Thomas Watson, Jr., former chairman of IBM[1]

Learning objectives

Students completing this chapter will

- ❖ understand the key concepts of data management;
- ❖ recognize that there are many components of an organization's memory;
- ❖ understand the problems with existing data management systems;
- ❖ realize that successful data management requires an integrated understanding of organizational behavior and information technology.

Introduction

Imagine what would happen to a bank that forgot who owed it money or a magazine that lost the names and addresses of its subscribers. Both would soon be in serious difficulty, if not out of business. Organizations have data management systems to record the myriad of details necessary for transacting business and making informed decisions. Societies and organizations have always recorded data. The system may be as simple as carving a notch in a stick to keep a tally, or as intricate as modern database technology. A memory system can be as personal as a to-do list or as public as a library.[2]

The management of organizational data, generally known as **data management**, requires skills in designing, using, and managing the memory systems of modern organizations. It requires multiple perspectives. Data managers need to see the organization as a social sys-

---

1. As reported in Quinn, J. B. 1992. *Intelligent enterprise: A knowledge and service based paradigm for industry*. New York, NY: Free Press, p. 244.
2. This text is written for an international audience. Measures are reported using the International System of Units (*Système internationale d'unités*) (SI) and U.S. units. Most monetary amounts are in U.S. dollars.

tem and to understand data management technology. The integration of these views, the sociotechnical perspective, is a prerequisite for successful data management.

Individuals also need to manage data. You undoubtedly are more familiar with individual memory management systems. They provide a convenient way of introducing some of the key concepts of data management.

Individual data management

As humans, we are well aware of our limited capacity to remember many things. The brain, our internal memory, can get overloaded with too much detail, and its memory decays with time. We store a few things internally: home and work telephone numbers, where we last parked our car, and faces of people we have met recently. We use external memory to keep track of those many things we know we should remember. External memory comes in a variety of forms.

We carry calendars to remind us of meetings and project deadlines. We have address books to record the addresses and phone numbers of those we contact frequently. We use to-do lists to remind us of the things we must do today or this week. The interesting thing about these aides-mémoire is that each has a unique way of storing data and supporting its rapid retrieval.

December 25, 1852	
9	Breakfast on the veranda
10	Read newspapers
11	Open gifts
12	Check lunch preparations
1	Pre-lunch drinks
2	Christmas lunch
3	
4	Afternoon nap
5	
6	Drive to club
7	Christmas dinner
8	
9	Port and cigars

© 1803, The Expeditioner, London

Figure 1-1. A calendar

Calendars (see Figure 1-1) come in many shapes and forms, but they are all based on the same organizing principle. A set amount of space is allocated for each day of the year, and the spaces are organized in date order, which supports rapid retrieval of any date. Some calendars have added features to speed up access. A bookmark can be used to mark the current date. Perforated tear-offs on the bottom right corner of the right-hand pages are often used to assist rapid location of current data.

Address books (see Figure 1-2) also have a standard format. They typically contain pre-printed spaces for storing address details (e.g., name, street, city, zip, and phone). Another common feature is the use of alphabetic tabs to separate the sections. For example, if we are searching for Jack London, we first locate the L tab to find the appropriate set of pages on which to check more closely.

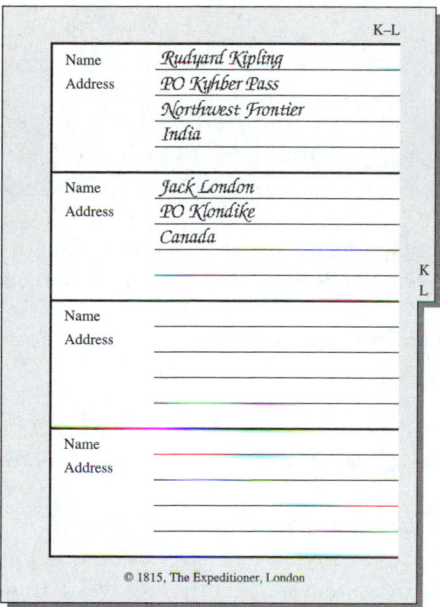

Figure 1-2. An address book

The structure of to-do lists (see Figure 1-3) tends to be fairly standard. They are often written on pads with ruled lines and a small left-hand margin. The idea is to write each item to be done on the right side of the page. The left side is used to check (✔) or mark those tasks that have been completed. The beauty of the check method is that you can quickly scan the left side to identify incomplete tasks.

Many people use some form of the individual memory systems just described. They are frequently marketed as "time management systems" in business magazines. Stationery stores devote considerable space to them. Some of these systems are conveniently packaged into wallets containing a calendar, address book, to-do list pad, and other forms for individual memory support. Packaging figures prominently in the buyer's decision because the buyer has to make a trade-off between the portability of pocket size and the spa-

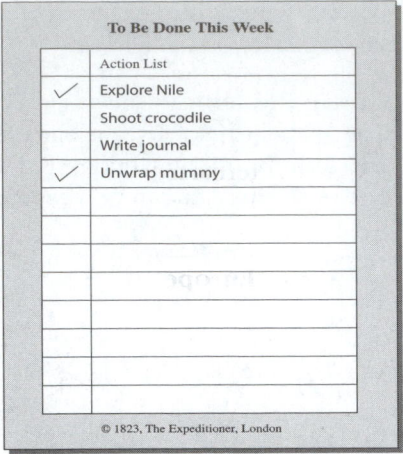

Figure 1-3. A to-do list

ciousness of desk size. Portability means reduced space for storing data. A spacious desk edition allows detailed record keeping but lacks the convenience of being easily portable.

These three examples of individual memory systems illustrate some features common to all data management systems:

- ❖ There is a storage medium. Data are written on paper in each of these examples.
- ❖ There is a structure for storing data. For instance, the address directory has labeled spaces for entering pertinent data.
- ❖ The storage device is organized for rapid data entry and retrieval. A calendar is in date sequence so that the data space for any date can be found quickly.
- ❖ The selection of a data management system frequently requires a trade-off decision. In this example, the trade-off is portability versus spaciousness.

Skill builder

Many people have multiple information appliances, such as a PDA, MP3 player, mobile phone, laptop computer, and desktop computer. A common data management problem for individuals is a lack of synchronization of files across these many devices. Visit the Web sites for SyncML and Apple's iSync.[3] Forecast what developments will emerge in individual data management in the next few years.

---

3.   www.syncml.com/ and www.apple.com/isync/

There are differences between internal and external memories. Our internal memory is small, fast, and convenient (our brain is always with us — well, most of the time). External memory is large, slow, and not as convenient. The two systems are interconnected. We rely on our internal memory to access external memory. We need to remember that appointments are stored in a calendar. Our internal memory and our brain's processing skills manage the use of external memories. Again, we see some trade-offs. Ideally, we would like to store everything in our fast and convenient internal memory, but its limited capacity means that we are forced to use the larger, slower external memory for many items.

No need to get lost in Europe

The Swedish firm Wayfinder Systems AB is the world's leading provider of mobile phone navigation for smartphones. In December 2004, it signed an agreement with mobilkom Austria to provide mobile navigation services to mobilkom's cell phone customers.

Customers pay €1.00 per day for route planning and navigation in Austria, or €1.90 per day for using the system anywhere in Western Europe. This one-day navigation package is especially valuable for customers who seldom need a navigation system but want to make certain they don't get lost when traveling to or around a strange city. Wayfinder's service covers more than 1,000 European cities and provides details of over 1,500,000 points of interest.

Wayfinder's EuroNavigator™ system computes the best route, any time of the day or night, no matter whether the customer is walking or driving. Moving maps, zoom functions, and pan-across directions guide customers to their destination. Voice-guidance gives turning instructions to keep a driver or pedestrian on track. The system works with more than a dozen high-end smartphones made by Nokia, SonyEricsson, and other technology leaders in the mobile business.

Source: www.wayfinder.com (Jan 2005).

Organizational data management

Organizations, like people, need to remember many things. If you look around any office, you will see examples of the apparatus of organizational memory: people, filing cabinets,[4] policy manuals, planning boards, and computers. The same principles found in individual memory systems apply to an organization's data management systems.

There is a storage medium. In the case of computers, the storage medium varies. Small files might be stored on a floppy disk and large, archival files on an optical disk. In Chapter 11, we discuss electronic storage media in more detail.

---

4. Melvil Dewey won a gold medal at the 1893 World's Fair for his invention of the filing cabinet (Gladwell, M. 2002. The social life of paper. *The New Yorker,* Mar. 25, 92–95).

A table is a common structure for storing data. For example, if we want to store details of customers, we can set up a table with each row containing individual details of a customer and each column containing data on a particular feature (e.g., customer code).

Storage devices are organized for rapid data entry and retrieval. Time is the manager's enemy: too many things to be done in too little time. Customers expect rapid responses to their questions and quick processing of their transactions. Rapid data access is a key goal of nearly all data management systems, but it always comes at a price. Fast access memories cost more, so there is nearly always a trade-off between access speed and cost.

As you will see, selecting *how* and *where* to store organizational data frequently involves a trade-off. Data managers need to know and understand what the trade-offs entail. They must know the key questions to ask when evaluating choices.

When we move from individual to organizational memory, some other factors come into play. To understand these factors, we need to review the different types of information systems. The automation of routine business transactions was the earliest application of information technology to business. A **transaction processing system** (TPS) handles common business tasks such as accounting, inventory, purchasing, and sales. The realization that the data collected by these systems could be sorted, summarized, and rearranged gave birth to the notion of a **management information system** (MIS). Furthermore, it was recognized that when internal data captured by a TPS is combined with appropriate external data, the raw material was available for a **decision support system** (DSS) or **executive information system** (EIS). Recently, **online analytical processing** (OLAP), **data mining,** and **business intelligence** (BI) have emerged as advanced data analysis techniques for data captured by business transactions and gathered from other sources (these systems are covered in detail in Chapter 15). The purpose of each of these systems is described in Table 1-1, and their interrelationship can be understood by examining the information systems cycle.

Table 1-1: Types of information systems

Type of information system	System's purpose
transaction processing system TPS	Collects and stores data from routine transactions
Management information system MIS	Converts data from a TPS into information for planning, controlling, and managing an organization
Decision support system DSS	Supports managerial decision making by providing models for processing and analyzing data
Executive information system EIS	Provides senior management with information necessary to monitor organizational performance and develop and implement strategies
Online analytical processing OLAP	Presents a multidimensional, logical view of data
Data mining	Uses statistical analysis and artificial intelligence techniques to identify hidden relationships in data

Table 1-1: Types of information systems (continued)

Type of information system	System's purpose
Business intelligence BI	Systems for gathering, storing, analyzing, and accessing data to improve decision making

The information systems cycle

The various systems and technologies found in an organization are linked in a cycle (see Figure 1-4). The routine ongoing business of the organization is processed by TPSs, the systems that handle the present. Data collected by TPSs are stored in databases, a record of the past, the history of the organization and its interaction with those with whom it conducts business. These data are converted into information by analysts using a variety of software (e.g., a DSS). These technologies are used by the organization to prepare for the future (e.g., sales in Finland have expanded, so we will build a new service center in Helsinki). The business systems created to prepare for the future determine the transactions the company will process and the data that will be collected. And the process continues. The entire cycle is driven by people using technology (e.g., sales personnel using point-of-sale [POS] terminals and data administrators designing databases).

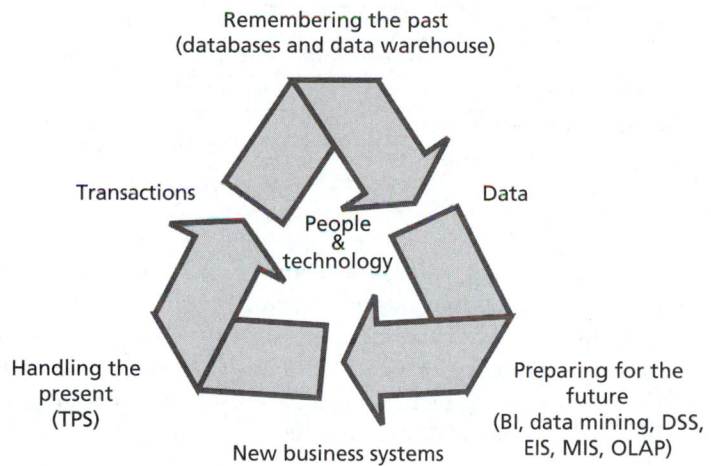

Figure 1-4. The information systems cycle

Decision making, or preparing for the future, is the central activity of modern organizations.[5] Today's organizations are busy turning out goods, services, and decisions. Knowledge and information workers, 55 percent of the U.S. labor force, produce 60 percent of

5. Huber, G. P., and R. R. McDaniel. 1986. The decision-making paradigm of organizational design. *Management Science* 32 (5):572–589.

the GNP.[6] Many of these people are decision makers. Their success and their organization's success depend on the quality of their decisions.

Industrial society was a producer of goods, and the hallmark of success was product quality. Japanese manufacturers convincingly demonstrated that focusing on product quality was the key to market leadership and profitability. The methods and the philosophy of quality gurus, such as W. Edwards Deming, have been internationally recognized and adopted by many providers of goods and services. As we make the transition from an industrial society to one based on knowledge and services, the key determinant of success is likely to shift from product quality to decision quality. In the turbulent environment of global business, successful organizations will be those able to make high-quality decisions quickly.

Attributes of data

Once we realize the critical importance of data to organizations, we can recognize some desirable attributes of data (see Table 1-2).

Table 1-2: Desirable attributes of data

Shareable	Readily accessed by more than one person at a time
Transportable	Easily moved to a decision maker
Secure	Protected from destruction and unauthorized use
Accurate	Reliable, precise records
Timely	Current and up-to-date
Relevant	Appropriate to the decision

Shareable

Organizations contain many decision makers. There are occasions when more than one person will require access to the same data at the same time. For example, in a large bank it would not be uncommon for two customer representatives simultaneously to want data on the latest rate for a three-year certificate of deposit. As data become more volatile, shareability becomes more of a problem. Consider a restaurant. The permanent menu is printed, today's special might be displayed on a blackboard, and the waiter tells you what is no longer available.

Transportable

Data should be transportable from their storage location to the decision maker. Technologies that transport data have a long history. Homing pigeons were used to relay messages by the Egyptians and Persians 3,000 years ago. The telephone revolutionized business and social life because it rapidly transmitted voice data. Fax machines accelerated organizational correspondence because they transported both text and visual data. Computers

---

6.   Laudon, K. C., and J. P. Laudon. 1998. *Management Information Systems: New approaches to organization and technology.* 5th ed. Upper Saddle River, NJ: Prentice-Hall. p. 552.

have changed the nature of many aspects of business because they enable the transport of text, visual, and voice data.

Today, transportability is more than just getting data to a decision maker's desk. It means getting product availability data to a salesperson in a client's office or advising a delivery driver, en route, of address details for an urgent parcel pickup. The general notion is that decision makers should have access to relevant data whenever and wherever required, although most organizations are some way from reaching this target.

Secure

In a postindustrial society, organizations highly value data as a resource. As you have already learned, data support day-to-day business transactions and decision making. Because the forgetful organization will soon be out of business, organizations are very vigilant in protecting their data. There are a number of actions that organizations take to protect data against loss, sabotage, and theft. A common approach is to duplicate data and store the copy, or copies, at other locations. This technique is popular for data stored in computer systems. Access to data is often restricted through the use of physical barriers (e.g., a vault) or electronic barriers (e.g., a password). Another approach, which is becoming popular with firms that employ knowledge workers, is a noncompetition contract. For example, some software companies legally restrain computer programmers from working for a competitor for two years after they leave, hoping to prevent the transfer of valuable data, in the form of the programmer's knowledge of software, to competitors.

Accurate

You probably remember students who excelled in exams because of their good memories. Similarly, organizations with an accurate memory will do better than their less precise competitors. Organizations need to remember many details accurately. For example, an airline needs accurate data to predict the demand for each of the many flights it flies in a year. The quality of decision making will drop dramatically if managers use a data management system riddled with errors.

Polluted data threatens a firm's profitability. One study[7] suggests that missing, wrong, and otherwise bad data cost U.S. firms billions of dollars annually. The consequences of bad data include improper billing, cost overruns, delivery delays, and product recalls. Because data accuracy is so critical, organizations need to be watchful when capturing data—the point at which data accuracy is most vulnerable.

Timely

The value of a collection of data is often determined by its age. You can fantasize about how rich you would be if you knew tomorrow's stock prices. Although decision makers are most interested in current data, the required currency of data can vary with the task. Operational managers often want real-time data. They want to tap the pulse of the produc-

---

7.   Knight, B. 1992. The data pollution problem. *Computerworld*, 81, 83.

tion line so that they can react quickly to machine breakdowns or quality slippages. In contrast, strategic planners might be content with data that are months old because they are more concerned with detecting long-term trends.

Relevant

Organizations must maintain data that are relevant to transaction processing and decision making. In processing a credit card application, the most relevant data might be the customer's credit history, current employment status, and income level. Hair color would be irrelevant. When assessing the success of a new product line, a marketing manager probably wants an aggregate report of sales by marketing region. A voluminous report detailing every sale would be irrelevant. Data are relevant when they pertain directly to the decision and are aggregated appropriately.

Relevance is a key concern in designing a data management system. Users have to decide what should be stored because it is pertinent now or could have future relevance. Of course, identifying data that might be relevant in the future is difficult, and there is a tendency to accumulate too much. Relevance is also an important consideration when extracting and processing data from a data management system. Provided the pertinent data are available, query languages can be used to aggregate data appropriately.

In the final years of the twentieth century, organizations started to move much of their data, both high and low volatility, to the Web. This move has increased shareability, timeliness, and availability and has lowered the cost of distributing data.

In summary, a data management system for maintaining an organization's memory supports transaction processing, remembering the past, and decision making. Its contents must be shareable, secure, and accurate. Ideally, users of a data management system must be able to get timely and relevant data when and where required. A major challenge for data management professionals is to create data management systems that meet these criteria. Unfortunately, many existing systems fail in this regard, though we can understand some of the reasons why by reviewing the components of existing organizational memory systems.

Components of organizational memory

An organization's memory[8] resides on a variety of media in a variety of ways. It is in people, standard operating procedures, roles, organizational culture, physical storage equipment, and electronic devices. It is scattered around the organization like pieces of a jigsaw puzzle designed by Salvador Dali.[9] The pieces don't fit together, they sometimes overlap, there are gaps, and there are no edge pieces to define the boundaries. Organizations struggle to design structures and use data management technology to link some of the pieces.

---

8.   For an advanced treatment of organizational memories, see Walsh, J. P., and G. R. Ungson. 1991. Organizational memory. *Academy of Management Review* 16 (1):57–91.

9.   The Spanish painter Salvador Dali (1904–1989) was a leader of surrealism with a declared ambition to *systemize confusion*.

To understand the complexity of this wicked puzzle, we need to examine some of the pieces (see Figure 1-5). Data managers have a particular need to understand the different forms of organizational memory because their activities often influence a number of the components.

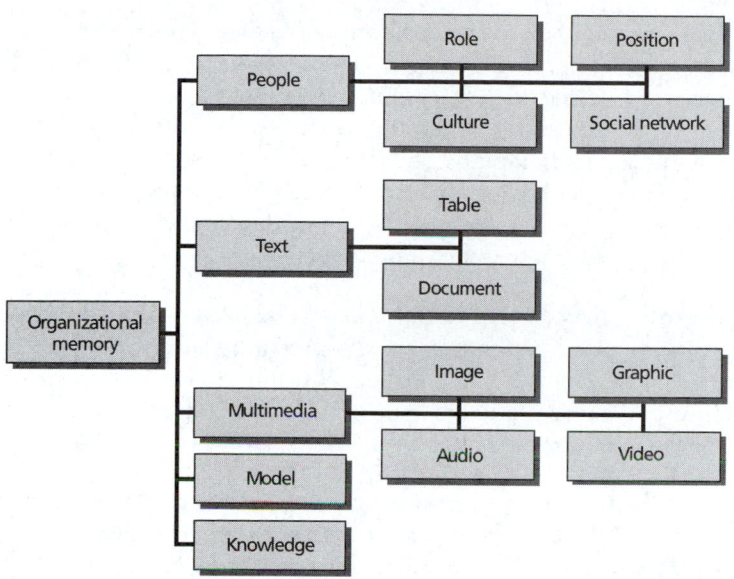

Figure 1-5. Components of organizational memory

People

People are the linchpin of an organization's memory. They recall previous decisions and business actions. They create, maintain, evolve, and use data management systems. They are the major component of an organization's memory because they know how to use all the other components. People extract data from the various components of organizational memory to provide as complete a picture of a situation as possible.

Each person in an organization has a **role** and a **position** in the hierarchy. Role and position are both devices for remembering how the organization functions and how to process data. By labeling people (e.g., Chief Information Officer) and placing their names on an organizational chart, the organization creates another form of organizational memory.

Organizational culture is the shared beliefs, values, attitudes, and norms that influence the behavior and expectations of each person in an organization. A long-lived, stable memory system, culture determines acceptable behavior and influences decision making.

People develop skills for doing their particular job—learning what to do, how to do it, and who can help them get things done. For example, they might discover someone in employee benefits who can handle personnel problems or a contact in a computer company who can answer questions promptly. These **social networks**, which often take years to develop, are used to make things happen and to learn about the business environment. Despite their high value, they are rarely documented, at least not beyond an address book or Rolodex, and they are typically lost when a person leaves an organization.

Conversations are an important method for knowledge workers to create, modify, and share organizational memory and to build relationships and social networks. Discussions with customers are a key device for learning how to improve an organization's products and services and learning about competitors. The *conversational company* can detect change faster and react more rapidly. The telephone, fax, e-mail, coffee machine, cocktail hour, and cafeteria are all devices for promoting conversation and creating networks. Some firms deliberately create structures for supporting conversations to make the people component of organizational memory more effective.

Standard operating procedures exist for many organizational tasks. Processing a credit application, selecting a marketing trainee, and preparing a departmental budget are typical procedures that are clearly defined by many organizations. They are described in office manuals, computer programs, and job specifications. They are the way an organization remembers to perform routine activities.

Successful people learn how to use organizational memory. They learn what data are stored where, how to retrieve them, and how to put them together. In promoting a new product, a salesperson might send the prospect a package containing some brochures and a copy of a product review in a trade journal, and supply the phone number and e-mail address of the firm's technical expert for that product. People's recall of how to use organizational memory is the core component of organizational memory. Academics call this **metamemory**; people in business call it *learning the ropes*. New employees spend a great deal of time building their metamemory so that they can use organizational memory effectively. Without this knowledge, organizational memory would have little value.

Tables

A table is a common form of storing organizational data. Table 1-3 shows a price list in tabular form. Often, the first row defines the meaning of data in subsequent rows.

Table 1-3: A price list

Product	Price
Pocket knife–Nile	4.50
Compass	10.00
Geopositioning system	500.00
Map measure	4.90

A table is a general form that describes a variety of other structures used to store data. Computer-based files are tables or can be transformed into tables; the same is true for general ledgers, worksheets, and spreadsheets. Accounting systems make frequent use of tables. Card files can be readily transformed into tables. Each card becomes one row, and each data value on the card (e.g., the item's name) becomes a column (see Figure 1-6). As you will discover in the next section, the table is the central structure of the relational database model.

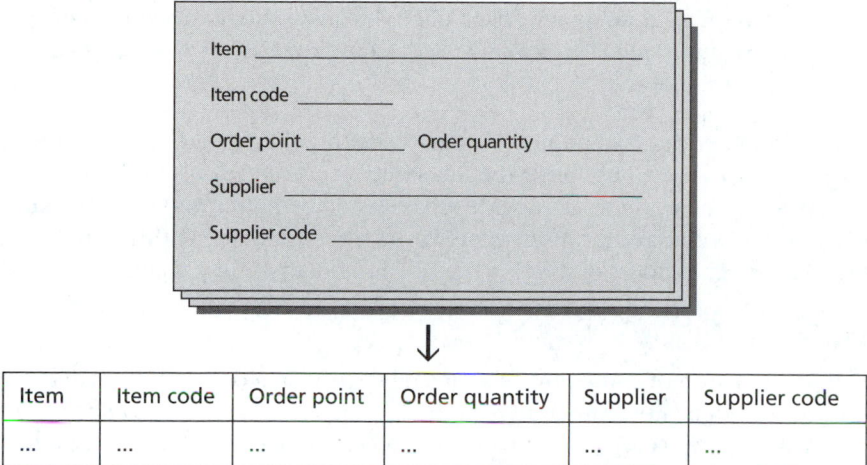

Figure 1-6. Transforming a card file to table format

Data stored in tables typically have certain characteristics:

* Data in one column are of the same type. For example, each cell of the column headed "Order point" contains a number. (Of course, the exception is the first row of each column, which contains the title of the column.)
* Data are limited by the width of available space.

Rapid searching is one of the prime advantages of a table. For example, if the price list is sorted by product name, you can quickly find the price of any product.

Tables are a common form of storing organizational data because their structure is readily understood. People learn to read and build tables in the early years of their schooling. Also, a great deal of the data that organizations want to remember can be stored in tabular form.

Documents

The **document**—of which reports, manuals, brochures, and memos are examples—is a common medium for storing organizational data. Although documents may be subdivided into chapters, sections, paragraphs, and sentences, they lack the regularity and discipline of a table. Each row of a table has the same number of columns, but each paragraph of a document does not have the same number of sentences.

Most documents are now stored electronically. Because of the widespread use of word processing, text files are a common means of storing documents. Typically, such files are read sequentially like a book. Although there is support for limited searching of the text, such as finding the next occurrence of a specified text string, text files are usually processed linearly.

Hypertext, the familiar linking technology of the Web, supports nonlinear document processing. A hypertext document has built-in linkages between sections of text that permit the reader to jump quickly from one part to another. As a result, readers can find data they require more rapidly.

Although hypertext is certainly more user-friendly than a flat, sequential text file, it takes time and expertise to establish the links between the various parts of the text. Someone familiar with the topic has to decide what should be linked and then establish these links. While it takes the author more time to prepare a document this way, the payoff is the speed at which readers of the document can find what they want.

Multimedia

The introduction of the Web has spurred interests in storing multimedia objects, such as sound and video clips. Automotive company Web sites have video clips of cars, music outlets provide sound clips of new releases, and clothing companies have online catalogs displaying photos of their latest products. Maintaining a Web site, because of the many multimedia objects that some sites contain, has become a significant data management problem for some organizations (see Chapter 16 for an in-depth coverage of this topic). Consider the different types of data that a news outfit such as CNN has to store to provide a timely, informative, and engaging Web site.

Images

Images are visual data: photographs and sketches. Image banks are maintained for several reasons. *First,* images are widely used for identification and security. Police departments keep fingerprints and mug shots. *Second*, images are used as evidence. Highly valuable items such as paintings and jewelry often are photographed for insurance records. *Third*, images are used for advertising and promotional campaigns, and organizations need to maintain records of material used in these ventures. Image archiving and retrieval are essential for mail-order companies, which often produce several photo-laden catalogs every year. *Fourth*, some organizations specialize in selling images and maintain extensive libraries of clip art and photographs.

Graphics

Maps and engineering drawings are examples of electronically stored graphics. An organization might maintain a map of sales territories and customers. Manufacturers have extensive libraries of engineering drawings that define the products they produce. Graphics often contain a high level of detail. An engineering drawing will define the dimensions of all parts and may refer to other drawings for finer detail about any components.

A graphic differs from an image in that it contains explicitly embedded data. Consider the difference between an engineering plan for a widget and a photograph of the same item. An engineering plan shows dimensional data and may describe the composition of the various components. The embedded data are used to manufacture the widget. A photograph of a widget does not have embedded data and contains insufficient data to manufacture the product. An industrial spy will receive far more for an engineering plan than for a photograph of a widget.

Geographic information systems (GISs) are specialized graphical storage systems for geographic data (see Figure 1-7). The underlying structure of a GIS is a map on which data are displayed. A power company can use a GIS to store and display data about its power grid and the location of transformers. Using a pointing device such as a mouse, an engineer can click on a transformer's location to display a window of data about the transformer (e.g., type, capacity, installation date, and repair history). GISs have found widespread use in governments and organizations that have geographically dispersed resources.

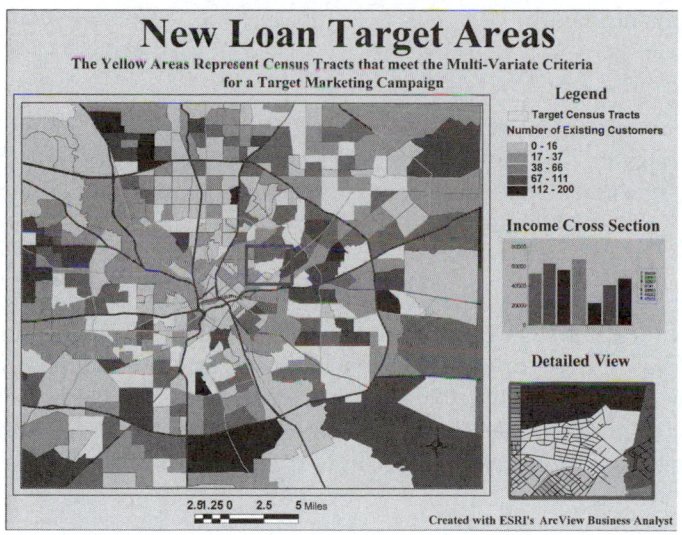

Figure 1-7. A geographic information system (GIS)

Audio

CD customers usually prefer to hear a sample of a CD prior to purchase. Music producers such as Sony enable prospective purchasers to hear audio clips of new CDs. News producers such as National Public Radio (NPR) store some of their special broadcasts in archives that are accessible via the Web.

Some firms conduct a great deal of their business by phone. In many cases, it is important to maintain a record of the conversation between the customer and the firm's representative. The Royal Hong Kong Jockey Club, which covers horse racing gambling in Hong Kong, records all conversations between its operators and customers. Phone calls are stored on a highly specialized voice recorder, which records the time of the call and other data necessary for rapid retrieval. In the case of a customer dispute, an operator can play back the original conversation.

Video

A video clip can give a potential customer additional detail that cannot be readily conveyed by text or a still image. Consequently, some auto companies now use video and virtual reality to promote their cars. Visit Honda's Web site and view a video clip of the Accord or rotate an image to view the car from all angles.

Models

Organizations build mathematical models to describe their business. These models, usually placed in the broader category of DSS, are then used to analyze existing problems and forecast future business conditions. A mathematical model can often produce substantial benefits to the organization.

Knowledge

Organizations build systems to capture the knowledge of their experienced decision makers and problem solvers. This expertise is typically represented as a set of rules, semantic nets, and frames in a knowledge base, another form of organizational memory.

Decisions

Decision making is the central activity of modern organizations. Very few organizations, however, have a formal system for recording decisions. Most keep the minutes of meetings, but these are often very brief and record only a meeting's outcome. Because they do not record details such as the objectives, criteria, assumptions, and alternatives that were considered prior to making a decision, there is no formal audit trail for decision making. As a result, most organizations rely on humans to remember the circumstances and details of prior decisions.

Specialized memories

Because of the particular nature of their business, some organizations maintain memories rarely found elsewhere. Perfume companies, for instance, maintain a library of scents, and paint manufacturers and dye makers catalog colors.[10]

---

10. For a fascinating story of one man's highly specialized memory, read Langewiesche, W. 2000. The million-dollar nose. *The Atlantic Monthly* 286 (6), www.theatlantic.com/issues/2000/12/langewiesche.htm.

External memories

Organizations are not limited to their own memory stores. There are firms whose business is to store data for resale to other organizations. Such businesses have existed for many years and are growing as the importance of data in a postindustrial society expands. Lawyers using Mead Data Central's LEXIS can access the laws and court decisions of all 50 American states and the U.S. federal government. Similar legal data services exist in many other nations. There is a range of other services that provide news, financial, business, scientific, and medical data.

Problems with data management systems

Successful management of data is a critical skill for nearly every organization. Yet, few have gained complete mastery, and there are a variety of problems that typically afflict data management in most firms (see Table 1-4).

Table 1-4: Problems with organizational data management systems

Redundancy	Same data are stored in different systems
Lack of data control	Data are poorly managed
Poor interface	Data are difficult to access
Delays	There are frequently long delays to requests for data
Lack of reality	Data management systems do not reflect the complexity of the real world
Lack of data integration	Data are dispersed across different systems

Redundancy

In many cases, data management systems have grown haphazardly. As a result, it is often the situation that the same data are stored in several different memories. The classic example is a customer's address, which might be stored in the sales reporting system, accounts receivable system, and the salesperson's telephone book. The danger is that when the customer changes address, the change is not recorded in all systems. Data redundancy causes additional work because the same item must be entered several times. Redundancy causes confusion when what is supposedly the same item has different values.

Lack of data control

Allied with the redundancy problem is poor data control. Although data are an important organizational resource, they frequently do not receive the same degree of management attention as other important organizational resources, such as people and money. Organizations have a personnel department to manage human resources and a treasury to handle cash. The IS department looks after data captured by the computer systems they operate, but there are many other data stores scattered around the organization. Data are stored everywhere in the organization (e.g., on personal computers and in departmental filing systems), but there is a general lack of data management. This lack is particularly surprising, since many pundits claim that data are a key competitive resource.

Poor interface

Too frequently, potential users of data management systems have been deterred by an unfriendly interface. The computer dialogue for accessing a data store is sometimes difficult to remember for the occasional user. People become frustrated and give up because their queries are rejected and error messages are unintelligible. Fortunately, the widespread adoption of the Web browser as the interface to many applications has alleviated the problem to some degree.

Delays

Globalization and technology have accelerated the pace of business in the last decade. Managers must make more decisions more rapidly. They cannot afford to wait for programmers to write special-purpose programs to retrieve data and format reports. They expect their questions to be answered rapidly, often within a day and sometimes more quickly. Managers, or their support personnel, need query languages that provide rapid access to the data they need, in a format that they want.

Lack of reality

Organizational data stores must reflect the reality and complexity of the real world. Consider a typical bank customer who might have a personal checking account, mortgage account, credit card account, and some certificates of deposit. When a customer requests an overdraft extension, the bank officer needs full details of the customer's relationship with the bank in order to make an informed decision. If customer data are scattered across unrelated data stores, then these data are not easily found, and in some cases important data might be overlooked. The request for full customer details is reasonable and realistic, and the bank officer should expect to be able to enter a single, simple query to obtain it. Unfortunately, this is not always the case, because data management systems do not always reflect reality.

In this example, the reality is that the personal checking, mortgage, and credit card accounts, and certificates of deposit all belong to one customer. If the bank's data management system does not record this relationship, then it does not mimic reality. This makes it impossible to retrieve a single customer's data with a single, simple query.

A data management system must meet the decision-making needs of managers, who must be able to request both routine and ad hoc reports. In order to do so effectively, a data management system must reflect the complexity of the real world. If it does not store required organizational data or record a real-world relationship between data elements, then many managerial queries cannot be answered quickly and efficiently.

Lack of data integration

There is a general lack of data integration in most organizations. Not only are data dispersed in different forms of organizational memory (e.g., files and image stores), but even within one storage format there is often a lack of integration. For example, many organizations maintain file systems that are not integrated. Appropriate files in the accounting system may not be linked to the production system.

This lack of integration will be a continuing problem for most organizations for two important reasons. *First,* early computer systems were not integrated, because of the limitations of available technology. Organizations created simple file systems to support a particular function. Many of these systems are still in use. *Second*, integration is a long-term goal. As new systems are developed and old ones rewritten, organizations can evolve integrated systems. It would be too costly and disruptive to try to solve the data integration problem in one step.

Many data management problems can be solved with present technology. Data modeling and relational database technology, topics covered in Section 2 of this book, help overcome many of the current problems.

First change the organization

Charlie Feld is an IT firefighter. He parachutes into a firm to become its CIO for two or three years to sort out major IT problems. He has spent time as acting CIO at large firms such as Delta Air Lines, Burlington Northern and Santa Fe Railway Company, and Westinghouse.

Mr. Feld does more than fix technology. His main task is to create the right organization for the new IT system. Unless you do that, he says, "the inertia of an organization makes you end up with just another ugly IT animal."

McKinsey & Co. believes both software vendors and their customers could save themselves a lot of money by paying more attention to the organizational aspects of introducing new technology. In a study of a clothing retailer's investment in supply-chain software, McKinsey found that the program yielded savings of $15 million a year, but that another $55 million of potential savings was left on the table because the firm did not make changes in its organizational structure, business processes, and incentives.

Source: Anonymous. 2001. Even the best software won't work without organizational change. *The Economist*, Apr. 12, www.economist.com/displayStory.cfm?Story_ID=568313.

A brief history of data management systems

Data management is not a new problem. It is an old problem that has become more significant, important, and critical because of the emergence of data as a critical resource for effective performance in the modern economy. Organizations have always needed to manage their data so that they could remember a wide variety of facts necessary to conduct business.

The recent history of data management systems is depicted in Figure 1-8. File systems were the earliest form of computer-based data management. Limited by the sequential nature of magnetic tape technology, it was very difficult to integrate data from different files. The advent of magnetic disk technology in the mid-1950s stimulated development of integrated file systems, and the hierarchical database management system (DBMS) emerged in the 1960s, followed some years later by the network DBMS. The spatial database, or geographic information system (GIS), appeared around 1970. Until the mid-1990s, the hierarchical DBMS, mainly in the form of IBM's DL/I product, was the predominant technology for managing data. It has now been replaced by the relational DBMS, a concept first discussed by Edgar Frank Codd in an academic paper in 1970 but not commercially available until the mid-1970s. In the late 1980s, the notion of an object-oriented DBMS, primed by the ideas of object-oriented programming, emerged as a solution to situations not handled well by the relational DBMS.

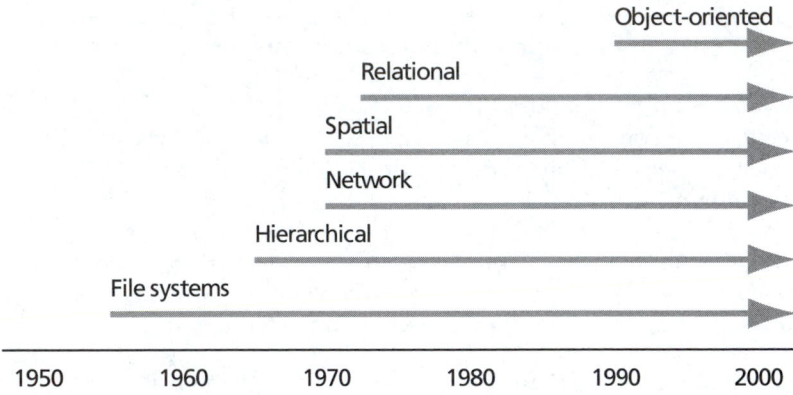

Figure 1-8. Data management systems timeline

This book concentrates on the relational model, currently the most widely used data management system. As mentioned, Section 2 is devoted to the development of the necessary skills for designing and using a relational database.

Data, information, and knowledge

Often the terms *data* and *information* are used interchangeably, but they are distinctly different. **Data** are raw, unsummarized, and unanalyzed facts. **Information** is data that have been processed into a meaningful form.

A list of a supermarket's daily receipts is data, but it is not information, because it is too detailed to be very useful. A summary of the data that gives daily departmental totals is information, because the store manager can use the report to monitor store performance. The same report would be only data for a regional manager, however, because, again, it is too detailed for meaningful decision making at the regional level. Information for a regional manager may be a weekly report of sales by department for each supermarket.

Data are always data, but one person's information can be another person's data. Information that is meaningful to one person can be too detailed for another person. A manager's notion of information can change quickly, however. If a problem is identified, a manager might request finer levels of detail to diagnose the problem's cause. Thus what was previously data suddenly becomes information because it helps solve the problem. When the problem is solved, the information reverts to data. There is a need for information systems that let managers customize the processing of data so that they always get information. As their needs change, they need to be able to adjust the detail of the reports they receive.

Knowledge is the capacity to use information. The education and experience that managers accumulate provide them with the expertise to make sense of the information they receive. Knowledge means that managers can interpret information and use it in decision making. In addition, knowledge is the capacity to recognize what information would be useful for making decisions. For example, a sales manager knows that requesting a report of profitability by product line is useful when she has to decide whether to employ a new product manager. Thus, when a new information system is delivered, managers need to be taught what information the system can deliver and what that information means.

The relationship between data, information, and knowledge is depicted in Figure 1-9. A knowledgeable person requests information to support decision making. To fulfill the request, data are converted into information. Personal knowledge is then applied to interpret the requested information and reach a conclusion. Of course, the cycle can be repeated several times if more information is needed before a decision can be made. Notice how knowledge is essential for grasping what information to request and interpreting that information in terms of the required decision.

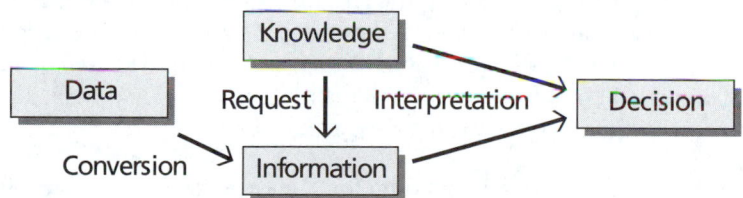

Figure 1-9. The relationship between data, information, and knowledge

The challenge

A major challenge facing organizations is to make effective use of the data currently stored in their diverse data management systems. This challenge exists because these various systems are not integrated and many potential users not only lack the training to access the systems but often are unaware that they exist. Before data managers can begin to address this problem, however, they must understand how organizational memories are used. In particular, they need to understand the relationship between information and managerial decision making. Data management is not a new problem. It has existed since the early days of civilization and will be an enduring problem for organizations and societies.

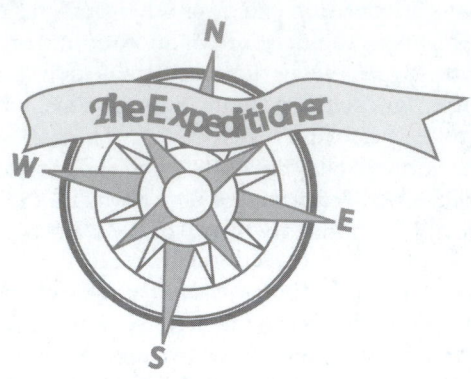

Alice Lindsay was enjoying the luxuries of first-class travel. It was quite a change from being an undergraduate student of business. She was enjoying her filet mignon and glass of shiraz. Good riddance to pizzas, hamburgers, and subs! Hello to fine food and gourmet restaurants. With her newly found wealth, she could travel in style and enjoy the very best restaurants. Alice, or Lady Alice to be more precise, had recently inherited a title, a valuable portfolio of stocks, and The Expeditioner. Her good fortune had coincided with the completion of her business degree. Now, instead of looking for a job, the job had found her: She was chairman and managing director of The Expeditioner.

The Expeditioner is in a nineteenth-century building in Explorer's Lane, opposite Kensington Gardens and just a stone's throw from the Royal Geographical Society. Founded in the Middle Ages, The Expeditioner has a long history of equipping explorers, adventurers, and travelers. Its initial success was due to its development of a light, flexible chain mail armor. It did very well during the Middle Ages, when highway robbery was a growth business and travelers sought protection from the arrows and slings aimed at their fortunes. The branch office at the entrance to Sherwood Forest had done exceptionally well, thanks to passing wealthy clientele. The resident company wit, one Ned Thomas, often claims that "The Expeditioner was the first mail order company."

The Expeditioner's customers included the famous and the legendary. Orders from Marco Polo, Columbus, Magellan, Cook, and Livingston can be found in the ledgers. The most long-lived customer is a Mr. Walker,[11] who for several hundred years has had a standing yearly order of one roll of purple, premium-quality, non-rip, jungle twill. The Expeditioner's hats are very popular with a Mr. I. Jones, an American.

The nineteenth century was one long boom for The Expeditioner, the supplier de rigueur for the guardians of the European colonies. Branch offices were opened in Bombay, Sydney, Cape Town, and Singapore. For a generous fee, cad and renowned adventurer Harry Flashman[12] assiduously promoted The Expeditioner's wares on his many trips. As a result, orders poured in from the four corners of the globe. The Expeditioner's catalog was found in polite society and clubs throughout the British Empire.

The founder of The Expeditioner was a venturesome Scot who sought his fortune in London. Carefully guarding the family business, The Expeditioner's proprietors were inclined to be closefisted and invested their massive profits wisely. Because of their close contacts with many explorers, they made some very canny investments in mining ventures in dis-

---

11. For Ghost Who Walks.
12. See the *Flashman* stories by George MacDonald Fraser.

tant lands. As a result, when business contracted during the twentieth century, the investment portfolio kept the company solvent. Traditionally, ownership of the firm was inherited by the eldest child. When the most recent owner, a bachelor, died, the firm's lawyers spent months on genealogical research to identify the legal heir.

Alice had vivid memories of the day when Mr. Mainwaring phoned her to request an appointment. Like most students, she was never home, and the message was left on her answering machine. She remembered listening to it several times because she was intrigued by both the unusual accent and the message. It sounded something like, "Good afternoon, Lady Alice, I am Nigel Mannering of Chumli, Crepiny, Marchbanks, and Sinjun. If you would like to hear news to your advantage, please contact me."

Two days later, Alice met with Nigel. This also had been most memorable. The opening conversation had been confusing. He started with the very same formal introduction, "Good afternoon, Lady Alice, I am Nigel Mannering of Chumli, Crepiny, Marchbanks, and Sinjun. I am pleased to meet you," and handed Alice his card. Alice quickly inspected the card, which read, "Nigel Mainwaring, LL. B., Cholmondeley, Crespigny, Majoribanks, and St. John," but he had said nothing like that. She thought, "What planet is this guy from?"

It took fifteen minutes for Alice to discover that British English was not quite the same as American English. She quickly learned—or should that be "learnt?"—that many proper English names have a traditional pronunciation not easily inferred from the spelling.[13] Once this names problem had been sorted out, Nigel told Alice of her good fortune. She was the new owner of The Expeditioner. She also inherited the title that had been conferred on a previous owner by a grateful monarch who had been equipped by The Expeditioner for traveling in the Australian outback. She was now entitled to be called "Lady Alice of Bullamakanka." Nigel was in a bit of a rush. He left Alice with a first-class ticket to London and an attaché case of folders, and with an effusive "Jolly good show," disappeared.

Summary

Organizations must maintain a memory to process transactions and make decisions. Organizational data should be shareable, transportable, secure, and accurate, and provide timely, relevant data. The essential components are people (the most important), text, multimedia data, models, and knowledge. A wide variety of technologies can be used to manage data. External memories enlarge the range of data available to an organization. Data management systems often have some major shortcomings: redundancy, poor data control, poor interfaces, long lead times for query resolution, an inability to supply answers for questions posed by managers, and poor data integration. Data are raw facts; information is data processed into a meaningful form. Knowledge is the capacity to use information.

---

13. For further insights into this interesting feature of British English, see an appendix in the *Concise Oxford Dictionary*.

Key terms and concepts

Data	Internal memory
Database management system (DBMS)	Knowledge
Data management	Management information system (MIS)
Data management system	Metamemory
Data mining	Online analytical processing (OLAP)
Data security	Organizational culture
Decision making	Organizational memory
Decision quality	Shareable data
Decision support system (DSS)	Social networks
Documents	Standard operating procedures
Executive information system (EIS)	Storage device
External memory	Storage medium
Geographic information system (GIS)	Storage structure
Graphics	Tables
Hypertext	Transaction processing
Images	transaction processing system (TPS)
Information	Voice data

References and additional readings

Drucker, P. F. 1991. The new productivity challenge. *Harvard Business Review* 69 (6):45–53.

Schenk, D. 1997. *Data smog: Surviving the information glut*. New York, NY: HarperCollins.

Exercises

1. What are the major differences between internal and external memory?
2. What is the difference between the things you remember and the things you write down?
3. What features are common to most individual memory systems?
4. What do you think organizations did before filing cabinets were invented?
5. Discuss the memory systems you use. How do they improve your performance? What are the shortcomings of your existing systems? How can you improve them?
6. Describe the most "organized" person you know. Why is that person so organized? Why haven't you adopted some of the same methods? Why do you think people differ in the extent to which they are organized?
7. Think about the last time you enrolled in a class. What data do you think were recorded for this transaction?
8. What roles do people play in organizational memory?
9. What do you think is the most important attribute of organizational memory? Justify your answer.
10. What is the difference between transaction processing and decision making?
11. When are data relevant?
12. Give some examples of specialized memories.

13. How can you measure the quality of a decision?

14. What is organizational culture? Can you name some organizations that have a distinctive culture?

15. What is hypertext? How does it differ from linear text? Why might hypertext be useful in an organizational memory system?

16. What is imaging? What are the characteristics of applications well suited for imaging?

17. What is an external memory? Why do organizations use external memories instead of building internal memories?

18. What is the common name used to refer to systems that help organizations remember knowledge?

19. What is a DSS? What is its role in organizational memory?

20. What are the major shortcomings of many data management systems? Which do you think is the most significant shortcoming?

21. What is the relationship between data, information, and knowledge?

22. Consider the following questions about The Expeditioner:

    a. What sort of data management systems would you expect to find at The Expeditioner?

    b. For each type of data management system that you identify, discuss it using the themes of data being shareable, transportable, secure, accurate, timely, and relevant.

    c. An organization's culture is the set of key values, beliefs, understandings, and norms that its members share. Discuss your ideas of the likely organizational culture of The Expeditioner.

    d. How difficult will it be to change the organizational culture of The Expeditioner? Do you anticipate that Alice will have problems making changes to the firm? If so, why?

23. Using the Web, find some stories about firms using data management systems. You might enter keywords such as "database" and "imaging" and access the Web sites of publications such as *Computerworld* and *PCWeek*. Identify the purpose of each system. How does the system improve organizational performance? What are the attributes of the technology that make it useful? Describe any trade-offs the organization might have made. Identify other organizations in which the same technology might be applied.

24. Make a list of the organizational memory systems identified in this chapter. Interview several people working in organizations. Ask them to indicate which organizational memory systems they use. Ask which system is most important and why. Write up your findings and your conclusion.

25. What is a personal digital assistant (PDA)? How do people use them? What do you think will happen with these products over the next few years?

2

Information

Effective information management must begin by thinking about how people use information — not with how people use machines.

Thomas Davenport[1]

Learning objectives

Students completing this chapter will

- ❖ understand the importance of information to society and organizations;
- ❖ be able to describe the various roles of information in organizational change;
- ❖ be able to distinguish between soft and hard information;
- ❖ know how managers use information;
- ❖ be able to describe the characteristics of common information delivery systems;
- ❖ distinguish the different types of knowledge.

Introduction

There are two key characteristics of the beginning of the twenty-first century: high-velocity global change and the emerging power of information organizations. Rapid changes in international relations, the globalization of business, the rise of China as a major economic power, and the creation of massive trading blocs are major forces contributing to global change. Organizations are undergoing large-scale restructuring as they attempt to reposition themselves to survive the threats and exploit the opportunities presented by this change.

In the last few years, some very powerful and highly profitable information-based organizations have emerged. Microsoft and Bill Gates are to the information age what Standard Oil and John Rockefeller were to the industrial era.[2] Google has become a well-known global brand as it fulfills its mission "to organize the world's information and make it univer-

---

1. Davenport, T. H. 1994. Saving IT's soul: Human-centered information management. *Harvard Business Review* 72 (2):119–131.
2. Cook, W. J. 1993. The new Rockefeller. *U.S. News & World Report* 114 (6):64–67.

sally accessible and useful." Founded in 1995, eBay rightly calls itself the "The World's Online Marketplace®." The German software firm, SAP,[3] markets the enterprise resource planning (ERP) software that is used by many of the world's largest organizations. Apple, with its combination of iPod and iTunes, has shown the power of a new information service to change an industry. Information products and information systems have become a major driver of organizational growth. We gain further insights into the value of information by considering its role in civilization.

A historical perspective

Three distinct phases of civilization have been identified, and recently a possible fourth phase has been suggested. Agriculture, the first phase, arose around 3000 B.C.E. It prospered through the use of iron and tools. Output was recorded in units of volume of grain harvested, such as the bushel. The pioneering cultures of the agricultural phase were China and Egypt. The industrial revolution, the second phase, commenced in Britain in the eighteenth century C.E. Its success was based on harnessing energy, initially in the form of the steam engine and later as the internal combustion engine. The third phase, the information society, was pioneered by the United .States., where it emerged in the late twentieth century. The integrated circuit, the driving force of this society, is the basis of computer and communication technologies that manipulate and transport data. The key word in the information society is *data*. It is predicted that the twenty-first century will witness the development of a society based on creation. The key word of this civilization will be *idea*. The technology will be *idea engineering* and productivity will be measured in terms of *creative output*.[4] The form of this technology will become clearer as the new phase emerges.

A constant across all of these eras is organizational memory, or in its larger form, social memory. Writing and paper manufacturing developed about the same time as agricultural societies. Limited writing systems appeared about 30,000 years ago. Full writing systems, which have evolved in the last 5,000 years, made possible the technological transfer that enabled humanity to move from hunting and gathering to farming. Writing enables the recording of knowledge, and information can accumulate from one generation to the next. Before writing, knowledge was confined by the limits of human memory.

There is a need for a technology that can store knowledge for extended periods and support transport of written information. The storage medium advanced from clay tablets (4000 B.C.E.), papyrus (3500 B.C.E.), and parchment (2000 B.C.E) to paper (100 C.E.). Written knowledge gained great impetus from Johannes Gutenberg, whose achievement was a printing system involving movable metal type, ink, paper, and press. In less than 50 years, printing technology diffused throughout most of Europe. In the last century, a range of new storage media appeared (e.g., photographic, magnetic, and optical).

---

3.   SAP is an abbreviation for Systeme, Anwendungen, Produkte in der Datenverarbeitung.
4.   Murakami, T., and T. Nishiwaki. 1991. *Strategy for creation*. Cambridge, UK: Woodhead Publishing.

An early writing system

Organizational memories emerged with the development of large organizations such as governments, armies, churches, and trading companies. The growth of organizations during the industrial revolution saw a massive increase in the number and size of organizational memories. This growth continued throughout the twentieth century.

The Web has demonstrated that we now live in a borderless world. There is a free flow of information, investment, and industry across borders. Customers ignore national boundaries to buy products and services. In the borderless information age, the old ways of creating wealth have been displaced by intelligence, marketing, global reach, and education (see Table 2-1). Excelling in the management of data, information, and knowledge has become a prerequisite to corporate and national wealth.

Table 2-1: Wealth creation

The old	The new
Military power	Intelligence
Natural resources	Marketing
Population	Global reach
Industry	Education

This brief history shows the increasing importance of information. Civilization was facilitated by the discovery of means for recording and disseminating information. In our society, organizations are the predominant keepers and transmitters of information.

A brief history of information systems[5]

Information systems has three significant eras (see Table 2-2). In the first era, information work was transported to the computer. For instance, a punched card deck was physically transported to a computer center, the information was processed, and the output physically returned to the worker as a printout.

Table 2-2: Eras of information systems

Era	Focus	Period	Technology	Networks
1	Take information work to the computer	1950s – mid-1970s	Batch	Few data networks
2	Take information work to the employee	Mid-1970s – mid-1990s	Host/terminal Client/server	Spread of private networks
3	Take information work to the customer and other stakeholders	Mid-1990s – present	Browser/server	Public networks (Internet)

In the second era, private networks were used to take information work to the employee. Initially, these were time-sharing and host/terminal systems (see page 361). IS departments were concerned primarily with creating systems for use by an organization's employees when interacting with customers (e.g., a hotel reservation system used by call center employees) or for the employees of another business to transact with the organization (e.g., clerks in a hospital ordering supplies).

Era 3 starts with the advent of the Web browser in the mid-1990s. The browser, which can be used on the public and global Internet, permits organizations to take information and information work to customers and other stakeholders. Now, the customer undertakes work previously done by the organization (e.g., making an airline reservation).

The scale and complexity of era 3 is at least an order of magnitude greater than those of era 2. Nearly every company has far more customers than employees. For example, UPS, with an annual investment of more than $1 billion in information technology and 359,000 employees, is one of the world's largest employers. However, there are 11 million customers, 30 times the number of employees, who are today electronically connected to UPS.

Era 3 introduced direct electronic links between a firm and its stakeholders, such as investors and citizens. In the earlier eras, intermediaries often communicated with stakeholders on behalf of the firm (e.g., a press release to the news media). These messages could be filtered and edited, or sometimes possibly ignored, by intermediaries. Now, organizations can communicate directly with their stakeholders via the Web and e-mail. Internet technologies offer firms a chance to rethink their goals vis-à-vis each stakeholder class and to use Internet technology to pursue these goals.

---

5.   This section is based on Watson, Richard T., and Detmar W. Straub. 2002. Brave new horizons for IS research in net-enhanced organizations (working paper): University of Georgia.

This brief history leads to the conclusion that the value IS creates is determined by whom an organization can reach, how it can reach them, and where and when it can reach them.

❖ **Whom.** Whom an organization can contact determines whom it can influence, inform, or transfer work to. For example, if a hotel can be contacted electronically by its customers, it can promote online reservations (transfer work to customers), and reduce its costs.

❖ **How.** How an organization reaches a stakeholder determines the potential success of the interaction. The higher the bandwidth of the connection, the richer the message (e.g., using video instead of text), the greater the amount of information that can be conveyed, and the more information work that can be transferred.

❖ **Where.** Value is created when customers get information directly related to their current location (e.g., a navigation system) and what local services they want to consume (e.g., the nearest Italian restaurant).

❖ **When.** When a firm delivers a service to a client can greatly determine its value. Stockbrokers, for instance, who can inform clients immediately of critical corporate news or stock market movements are likely to get more business.

Information characteristics

Three useful concepts for describing information are hardness, richness, and class. **Information hardness** is a subjective measure of the accuracy and reliability of an item of information. **Information richness** describes the concept that information can be *rich* or *lean* depending on the information delivery medium. **Information class** groups types of information by their key features.

Information hardness

In 1812, the Austrian mineralogist Friedrich Mohs proposed a scale of hardness, in order of increasing relative hardness, based on 10 common minerals. Each mineral can scratch those with the same or a lower number, but cannot scratch higher-numbered minerals.

A similar approach can be used to describe information (see Table 2-3).[6] Market information, such as the current price of gold, is the hardest because it is measured extremely accurately. There is no ambiguity, and its measurement is highly reliable. In contrast, the softest information, which comes from unidentified sources, is rife with uncertainty.

Audited financial statements are in the corundum zone. They are measured according to standard rules (known as "generally accepted accounting principles") that are promulgated by national accounting societies. External auditors monitor application of these standards, although there is generally some leeway in their application and sometimes multiple standards for the same item. The use of different accounting principles can lead to different profit and loss statements. As a result, the information in audited financial statements has some degree of uncertainty.

---

6.   This scale is an extension of work by colleagues at the University of Georgia.

Table 2-3: An information hardness scale

Minerals	Scale	Data
Talc	1	Unidentified source—rumors, gossip, and hearsay
Gypsum	2	Identified nonexpert source—opinions, feelings, ideas
Calcite	3	Identified expert source—predictions, speculations, forecasts, estimates
Fluorite	4	Unsworn testimony—explanations, justifications, assessments, interpretations
Apatite	5	Sworn testimony—explanations, justifications, assessments, interpretations
Orthoclase	6	Budgets, formal plans
Quartz	7	News reports, nonfinancial data, industry statistics, survey data
Topaz	8	Unaudited financial statements, government statistics
Corundum	9	Audited financial statements
Diamond	10	Stock exchange and commodity market data

There are degrees of hardness within accounting systems. The hardest data are counts, such as units sold or customers served. These are primary measures of organizational performance. Secondary measures, such as dollar sales and market share, are derived from counts. Managers vary in their preference for primary and secondary measures. Operational managers opt for counts for measuring productivity because they are uncontaminated by price changes and currency fluctuations. Senior managers, because their focus is on financial performance, select secondary measures.

The scratch test provides a convenient and reliable method of assessing the hardness of a mineral. Unfortunately, there is no scratch test for information. Managers must rely on their judgment to assess information hardness.

Although managers want hard information, there are many cases when it is not available. They compensate by seeking information from several different sources. Although this approach introduces redundancy, this is precisely what the manager seeks. Consistent information from different sources is reassuring.

Information richness

Information can be described as *rich* or *lean*. Information is richest when delivered face-to-face. Conversation permits immediate feedback for verification of meaning. You can always stop the other speaker and ask, "What do you mean?" Face-to-face information delivery is rich because you see the speaker's body language, hear the tone of voice, and natural language is used. A numeric document is the leanest form of information. There is no opportunity for questions, no additional information from body movements and vocal tone. The information richness of some communication media is shown in Table 2-4.

Managers seek rich information when they are trying to resolve equivocality. Equivocality means ambiguity. It means that managers cannot make sense of a situation because they arrive at multiple, conflicting interpretations of the information. An example of an equiv-

Table 2-4: Information richness and communication media[a]

Richest				Leanest
Face-to-face	Telephone	Personal documents (letters and memos)	Impersonal written documents	Numeric documents

a. Daft, R. L., and R. H. Lengel. 1986. Organizational information requirements, media richness, and structural design. *Management Science* 32 (5):554–571.

ocal situation is a class assignment where some of the instructions are missing and others are contradictory (of course, this example is an extremely rare event).

Equivocal situations cannot be resolved by collecting more information, because managers are uncertain about what questions to ask and often a clear answer is not possible. Managers reduce equivocality by sharing their interpretations of the available information and reaching a collective understanding of what the information means. By exchanging opinions and recalling their experiences, they try to make sense of an ambiguous situation.

Many of the situations that managers face each day involve a high degree of equivocality. Formal organizational memories, such as databases, are not much help, because the information they provide is lean. Managers rely far more on talking with colleagues and using informal organizational memories such as social networks.

Data management is almost exclusively concerned with administering the formal information systems that deliver lean information. Although this is their proper role, data managers must realize that they can deliver only a portion of the data required by decision makers.

Information classes

Information can be grouped into four classes: content, form, behavior, and action (see Table 2-5). Until recently, most organizational information fell into the first category.

Table 2-5: Information classes

Class	Description
Content	Quantity, location, and types of items
Form	Shape and composition of an object
Behavior	Simulation of a physical object
Action	Creation of action (e.g., industrial robots)

Content information records details about quantity, location, and types of items. It tends to be historical in nature and is traditionally the class of information collected and stored by organizations. The content information of a car would describe its model number, color, price, options, horsepower, and so forth. Hundreds of bytes of data may be required to record the full content information of a car. Typically, content data are captured by a TPS.

Form information describes the shape and composition of an object. For example, the form information of a car would define the dimensions and composition of every component in the car. Millions of bytes of data are needed to store the form of a car. CAD/CAM systems are used to create and store form information.

Behavior information is used to predict the behavior of a physical object using simulation techniques, which typically require form information as input. Massive numbers of calculations per second are required to simulate behavior. For example, simulating the flight of a new aircraft design may require trillions of computations. Behavior information is often presented visually because the vast volume of data generated cannot be easily processed by humans in other formats.

Action information enables the instantaneous creation of sophisticated action. Industrial robots take action information and manufacture parts, weld car bodies, or transport items. Antilock brakes are an example of action information in use.

A lifetime of information—every day

It is estimated that a single weekday issue of the *New York Times* contains more information than the average person in seventeenth-century England came across in a lifetime. Information, once rare, is now abundant and overflowing.

Roszak, T. 1986. *The cult of information: The folklore of computers and the true art of thinking*. New York, NY: Pantheon. p. 32.

Information and organizational change

Organizations are goal-directed. They undergo continual change as they use their resources, people, technology, and financial assets to reach some future desired outcome. Goals are often clearly stated, such as to make a profit of $100 million, win a football championship, or decrease the government deficit by 25 percent in five years. Goals are often not easily achieved, however, and organizations continually seek information that supports goal attainment. The information they seek falls into three categories: goal setting, gap, and change (see Figure 2-1).

The emergence of an information society also means that information provides dual possibilities for change. Information is used to plan change and information is a medium for change.

Goal-setting information

Organizations set goals or levels of desired performance. Managers need information to establish goals that are challenging but realistic. A common approach is to take the previ-

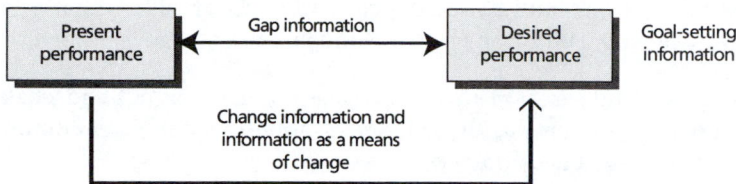

Figure 2-1. Organizational information categories

ous goal and stretch it. For example, a company that had a 15 percent return on investment (ROI) might set the new goal at 17 percent ROI. This technique is known as "anchoring and adjusting." Prior performance is used as a basis for setting the new performance standards. The problem with anchoring and adjusting is that it promotes incremental improvement rather than radical change because internal information is used to set performance standards.

Planning is a common approach to goal setting for many enterprises. Recently, some organizations have turned to external information and are using benchmarking as a source of information for goal setting.

Planning

Planning is an important task for senior managers. To set the direction for the company, they need information about consumers' potential demands and social, economic, technical, and political conditions. They use this information to determine the opportunities and threats facing the organization, thus permitting them to take advantage of opportunities and avoid threats.

Most of the information for long-term planning comes from sources external to the company. There are think tanks that analyze trends and publish reports on future conditions. Journal articles and books can be important sources of information about future events. There also will be a demand for some internal information. Major planning decisions, such as building a new plant, will be based on an analysis of internal data (use of existing capacity) and external data (projected customer demand).

Benchmarking

Benchmarking establishes goals based on best industry practices. It is founded on the Japanese concept of *dantotsu*, striving to be the *best of the best*. Benchmarking is externally directed. Information is sought on those companies, regardless of industry, that demonstrate outstanding performance in the areas to be benchmarked. Their methods are studied, documented, and used to set goals and redesign existing practices for superior performance.

Other forms of external information, such as demographic trends, economic forecasts, and competitors' actions can be used in goal setting. External information is valuable because it can force an organization to go beyond incremental goal setting.

Organizations need information to identify feasible, motivating, and challenging goals. Once these goals have been established, organizations need information on the extent to which these goals have been attained.

Gap information

Because goals are meant to be challenging, there is often a gap between actual and desired performance. Organizations use a number of mechanisms to detect a gap and gain some idea of its size. Problem identification and scorekeeping are two principal methods of providing gap information.

Problem identification

Business conditions are continually changing because of competitors' actions, trends in consumer demand, and government action. Often these changes are reflected in a gap between expectations and present performance. This gap is known as a *problem*.

To identify problems, managers use exception reports, which are generated only when conditions vary from the established standard. Once a potential problem has been identified, managers collect additional information to confirm that a problem really exists. Problem identification information can also be delivered by printed report or computer screen. Once management has been alerted, the information delivery system needs to shift into high gear. Managers will request rapid delivery of ad hoc reports from a variety of sources. The ideal organizational memory system can adapt smoothly to deliver appropriate information quickly.

Scorekeeping

Keeping track of the *score* provides gap information. Managers ask many questions: How many items did we make yesterday? What were the sales last week? Has our market share increased in the last year? They establish measurement systems to track variables that indicate whether organizational performance is on target. Keeping score is important; managers need to measure in order to manage. Also, measurement lets people know what is important. Once a manager starts to measure something, subordinates surmise that this variable must be important and pay more attention to the factors that influence it.

There are many aspects of the score that a manager can measure. The overwhelming variety of potentially available information is illustrated by the sales output information that a sales manager could track (see Table 2-6). Sales input information (e.g., number of service calls) can also be measured, and there is qualitative information to be considered. Because of time constraints, most managers are forced to limit their attention to 10 or fewer key variables singled out by the critical success factors (CSF) method.[7] Scorekeeping information is usually fairly stable.

Table 2-6: Sales output tracking information

Orders:	Number of current customers
	Average order size
	Batting average (orders to calls)
Sales volume:	Dollar sales volume
	Unit sales volume
	By customer type
	By product category
	Translated to market share
	Quota achieved
Margins:	Gross margin
	Net profit
	By customer type
	By product
Customers:	Number of new accounts
	Number of lost accounts
	Percentage of accounts sold
	Number of accounts overdue
	Dollar value of receivables
	Collections of receivables

Change information

Once a gap has been detected, managers take action to close it. Change information helps them determine which actions might successfully close the gap. Accurate change information is very valuable because it enables managers to predict the outcome of various actions with some certainty. Unfortunately, change information is usually not very precise, and there are many variables that can influence the effect of any planned change. Nevertheless, organizations spend a great deal of time collecting information to support problem solving and planning.

Problem solution

Managers collect information to support problem solution. Once a problem has been identified, a manager seeks to find its cause. A decrease in sales could be the result of competitors introducing a new product, an economic downturn, an ineffective advertising campaign, or many other reasons. Data can be collected to test each of these possible causes. Additional data are usually required to support analysis of each alternative. For example, if the sales decrease has been caused by an economic recession, the manager might use a decision support system (DSS) to analyze the effect of a price decrease or a range of promotional activities.

---

7.   Rockart, J. F. 1982. The changing role of the information systems executive: A critical success factors perspective. *Sloan Management Review* 24 (1):3–13.

> ### Norrath: the world's 77th wealthiest nation
>
> In March 1999, a small number of Californians founded Norrath, a virtual nation, with a population of around 410,000. The country grew rapidly through electronic migration from various places around the globe, but especially the United States. In 2001, based on online auction sales of avatars (a representation of a person in a shared virtual reality) and booty, its annual output was worth almost $1 billion. That made Norrath, a virtual world that existed entirely on 40 computers in San Diego, the 77th wealthiest nation. The nominal hourly wage was about $3.42 per hour.
>
> The original article by Edward Castanova describing Norrath has become one of the most popular downloads in the history of the Economics Research Network. It exceeds the popularity of the works of Nobel laureates.
>
> Sources: Castronova, Edward. 2001. Virtual worlds: a first-hand account of market and society on the cyberian frontier. *The Gruter Institute Working Papers on Law, Economics, and Evolutionary Biology* 2 (1). www.bepress.com/giwp/default/vol2/iss1/art1; and Shapiro, Robert. 2003. Fantasy economics: Why economists are obsessed with online role-playing games. *Slate*, Feb 4, slate.msn.com/id/2078053/.

Information as a means of change

The emergence of an information society means that information can be used as a means of changing an organization's performance. Corporations are creating information-based products and services, adding information to products, and using information to enhance existing performance or gain a competitive advantage. Further insights into the use of information as a change agent are gained by examining marketing, customer service, and empowerment.

Marketing

Marketing is a key strategy for changing organizational performance by increasing sales. Information has become an important component in marketing. Airlines and retailers have established frequent flyer and buyer programs to encourage customer loyalty and gain more information about customers. These systems are heavily dependent on database technology because of the massive volume of data that must be stored. Indeed, without database technology, some marketing strategies could never be implemented.

Database technology offers the opportunity to change the very nature of communications with customers. Broadcast media have been the traditional approach to communication. Advertisements are aired on television or radio or placed in newspapers or magazines. Database technology can be used to address customers directly. No longer just a mailing list, today's database is a memory of customer relationships, a record of every message and response between the firm and a customer. Some companies keep track of customers' preferences and customize advertisements to their needs. Leading catalog retailers now send customers only those catalogs for which they estimate there is a high probability of a purchase. For example, a customer with a history of buying jazz CDs is sent a catalog of jazz recordings instead of one featuring classical music.

The Web has significantly enhanced the value of database technology. Many firms now use a combination of a Web site and a DBMS to market products and service customers. Because this topic is so important, Chapter 16 provides extensive coverage of Web data management.

Customer Service

Customer service is a key competitive issue for nearly every organization. Many American business leaders rank customer service as their most important goal for organizational success. Many of the developed economies are service economies. In the United States, services account for approximately 75 percent of the gross national product and 9 out of 10 new jobs. Many companies now fight for customers by offering superior customer service. Information is frequently a key to this improved service.

Skill Builder

For many businesses, information is the key to high-quality customer service. Thus, some firms use information, and thus customer service, as a key differentiating factor, while others might compete on price. Compare the book component of Web sites Amazon[8] and Doublediscount.[9] Which site competes on price and which on information? What are the implications for data management if a firm uses information to compete?

Empowerment

Empowerment has attracted considerable attention in the business press because many high-performing businesses use empowerment. In general terms, empowerment means giving employees greater freedom to make decisions. More precisely, it is sharing with frontline employees[10]

❖ information about the organization's performance;
❖ rewards based on the organization's performance;
❖ knowledge and information that enable employees to understand and contribute to organizational performance;
❖ power to make decisions that influence organizational direction and performance.

---

8. www.amazon.com/
9. www.doublediscount.com/
10. Bowen, D. E., and E. E Lawler III. 1992. The empowerment of service workers: What, why, how, and when. *Sloan Management Review* 33 (3):31–39.

Notice that information features prominently in the process. A critical component is giving employees access to the information they need to perform their tasks with a high degree of independence and discretion. Information is empowerment. An important task for data managers is to develop and install systems that give employees ready access to the organization's memory. By linking employees to organizational memory, data managers play a pivotal role in empowering people.

Organizations believe that empowerment contributes to organizational performance by increasing the quality of products and services. Together, empowerment and information are mechanisms of planned change.

Information and managerial work

Managers are a key device for implementing organizational change. Because they frequently use data management systems in their normal activities as a source of information about change and as a means of implementing change, it is crucial for data management systems designers to understand how managers work. Failure to take account of managerial behavior can result in a system that is technically sound but rarely used because it does not fit the social system.

Studies over several decades reveal a very consistent pattern:[11] Managerial work is very fragmented. Managers spend an average of 10 minutes on any task, and their day is organized into brief periods of concentrated attention to a variety of tasks. They work unrelentingly and are frequently interrupted by unexpected disturbances. Managers are action oriented and rely on intuition and judgment far more than contemplative analysis of information.

Managers strongly prefer oral communication. They spend a great deal of time conversing directly or by telephone. Managers use interpersonal communication to establish networks, which they later use as a source of information and a way to make things happen. The continual flow of verbal information helps them make sense of events and lets them feel the organizational pulse.

Managers rarely use formal reporting systems. They do not spend their time analyzing computer reports or querying databases but resort to formal reports to confirm evidence, should interpersonal communications suggest there is a problem. Even when managers are provided with a purpose-built, ultra-friendly EIS, their behavior changes very little. They may access a few screens during the day, but oral communication is still their preferred method of data gathering and dissemination.

Managers' information requirements

Managers have certain requirements of the information they receive. These expectations should shape a data management system's content and how data are processed.

---

11. Mintzberg, H. 1973. *The nature of managerial work*. New York, NY: Harper & Row; and Kotter, J. P. 1982. *The general managers*. New York, NY: Free Press.

Managers expect to receive information that is useful for their current task under existing business conditions. Unfortunately, managerial tasks can change rapidly. The interlinked, global, economic environment is highly turbulent. Since managers' expectations are not stable, the information delivery system must be sufficiently flexible to meet changing requirements.

Managers' demands for information vary with their perception of its hardness; they require only one source that scores 10 on the information hardness scale. The Nikkei Index at the close of today's market is the same whether you read it in the *Asian Wall Street Journal* or *The Western Australian* or hear it on CNN. As perceived hardness decreases, managers demand more information (see Figure 2-2), hoping to resolve uncertainty and gain a more accurate assessment of the situation. When the reliability of a source is questionable, managers seek confirmation from other sources. If a number of different sources provide consistent information, a manager gains confidence in the information's accuracy.

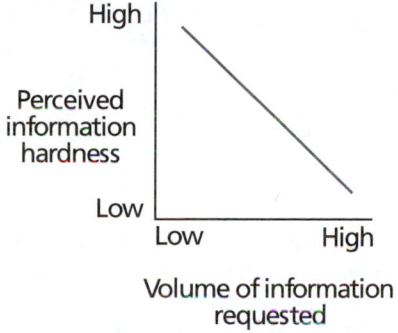

Figure 2-2. Relationship of perceived information hardness to volume of information requested

It is not unusual, therefore, to have a manager seek information from a database report, a conversation with a subordinate, and a contact in another organization. If a manager gets essentially the same information from each source, she or he has the confirmation she or he seeks. This means each data management system should be designed to minimize redundancy, but different components of organizational memory can supply overlapping information.

Managers' needs for information vary accordingly with responsibilities

Operational managers need detailed, short-term information to deal with well-defined problems in areas such as sales, service, and production. This information comes almost exclusively from internal sources that report recent performance in the manager's area. A sales manager may get weekly reports of sales by each person under that person's supervision.

As managers move up the organizational hierarchy, their information needs both expand and contract. They become responsible for a wider range of activities and are charged with planning the future of the organization, which requires information from external sources on long-term economic, demographic, political, and social trends. Despite this long-term focus, top-level managers also monitor short-term, operational performance. In this instance, they need less detail and more summary and exception reports on a small number of key indicators. To avoid information overload as new layers of information needs are added, the level of detail on the old layers naturally must decline, as illustrated in Figure 2-3.

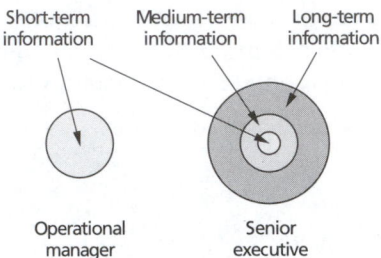

Figure 2-3. Management level and information need

Information satisficing

Because managers face making many decisions in a short period, most do not have the time or resources to collect and interpret all the information they need to make the best decision. Consequently, they are often forced to *satisfice*.[12] That is, they accept the first satisfactory decision they discover. They also satisfice in their information search, collecting only enough information to make a satisfactory decision.

Ultimately, information satisficing leads to lower-quality decision making. But if information technology can be used to accelerate delivery and processing of the right information, then managers should be able to move from selecting the first satisfactory decision to selecting the best of several satisfactory decisions.

Information delivery systems

Most organizations have a variety of delivery systems to provide information to managers. Developed over many years, these systems are being integrated to give managers better access to information. There are two aspects to information delivery. *First,* there is a need for software that accesses an organizational memory, extracts the required data, and formats it for presentation. We can use the categories of organizational memories introduced in Chapter 1 to describe the software side of information delivery systems (see Table 2-7).

---

12. Simon, H. A. 1976. *Administrative behavior: A study of decision-making processes in administrative organization.* 3rd ed. New York, NY: Free Press.

The *second* aspect of delivery is the hardware that gets information from a computer to the manager.

Table 2-7: Information delivery systems software

Organizational memory	Delivery systems
People	Conversation
	E-mail
	Meeting
	Report
	Groupware
Files	Management information system (MIS)
Documents	Web browser
	E-mail attachment
Images	Image processing system (IPS)
Graphics	Computer aided design (CAD)
	Geographic information system (GIS)
Voice	Voice mail
	Voice recording system
Mathematical model	Decision support system (DSS)
Knowledge	Expert system (ES)
Decisions	Conversation
	E-mail
	Meeting
	Report
	Groupware

Software is used to move data to and from organizational memory. There is usually tight coupling between software and the format of an organizational memory. For example, a relational database management system can access tables but not decision-support models. This tight coupling is particularly frustrating for managers who often want integrated information from several organizational memories. For example, a sales manager might expect a monthly report to include details of recent sales (from a relational database) to be combined with customer comments (from e-mail messages to a customer service system). A quick glance at Table 2-7 shows that there are many different information delivery systems. We will discuss each of these briefly to illustrate the lack of integration of organizational memories.

Verbal exchange

Conversations, meetings, and oral reporting are commonly used methods of information delivery. Indeed, managers show a strong preference for verbal exchange as a method for gathering information. This is not surprising because we are accustomed to oral information. This is the way we learned for thousands of years as a preliterate culture. Only recently have we learned to make decisions using spreadsheets and computer reports.

Voice mail

Voice mail is useful for people who are frequently away from their offices, because it supports asynchronous communication; that is, the two parties to the conversation are not simultaneously connected by a communication line. Voice-mail systems also can store many prerecorded messages that can be selectively replayed using the keypad of a Touch-Tone phone. Organizations use this feature to support standard customer queries.

Electronic mail

E-mail is an important system of information delivery. It too supports asynchronous messaging, and it is less costly than voice mail for communication. Many documents are exchanged as attachments to e-mail.

Written report

Formal, written reports have a long history in organizations. Before electronic communication, they were the main form of information delivery. They still have a role in organizations because they are an effective method of integrating information of varying hardness and from a variety of organizational memories. For example, a report can contain text, tables, graphics, and images.

Written reports are often supplemented by a verbal presentation of the key points in the report. Such a presentation enhances the information delivered, because the audience has an opportunity to ask questions and get an immediate response.

Meetings

Because managers spend between 30 and 80 percent of their time in meetings, these become a key source of information.

Groupware

Since meetings occupy so much managerial time and in many cases are poorly planned and managed, organizations are looking for improvements. *Groupware* is a general term applied to a range of software systems designed to improve some aspect of group work. It is excellent for tapping soft information and the informal side of organizational memory.

Management information system

Management information systems are a common method of delivering information from data management systems. A preplanned query is often used to extract the data. Managers who have developed some skills in using a query language might create their own custom reports as query languages become more powerful and easier to use.

Preplanned reports often contain too much or too detailed information, because they are written in anticipation of a manager's needs. Customized reports do not have these shortcomings, but they are more expensive and time consuming for programmers to write.

Web

Word processing, desktop publishing, or HTML editors are used for preparing documents that are disseminated by placing them on a Web server. Documents can be readily shared and accessed.

Image processing system

An image processing system (IPS) captures data using a scanner to digitize an image. Images in the form of letters, reports, illustrations, and graphics always have been an important type of organizational memory. An IPS permits these forms of information to be captured electronically and disseminated.

Computer-aided design

Computer-aided design (CAD) is used extensively to create graphics. For example, engineers use CAD in product design, and architects use it for building design. These plans are a part of organizational memory for designers and manufacturers.

Geographic information system

A geographic information system (GIS) stores graphical data about a geographic region. Many cities use a GIS to record details of roads, utilities, and services. This graphical information is another form of organizational memory. Again, special-purpose software is required to access and present the information stored in this memory.

Decision support system

A decision support system (DSS) is frequently a computer-based mathematical model of a problem. DSS software, available in a range of packages, permits the model and data to be retrieved and executed. Model parameters can be varied to investigate alternatives.

Expert system

An expert system (ES) has the captured knowledge of someone who is particularly skillful at solving a certain type of problem. It is convenient to think of an ES as a set of rules. An ES is typically used interactively, as it asks the decision-maker questions and uses the responses to determine the action to recommend.

Information integration

You can think of organizational memory as a vast, disorganized data dump. A fundamental problem for most organizations is that their memory is fragmented across a wide variety of formats and technologies. Too frequently, there is a one-to-one correspondence between an organizational memory for a particular functional area and the software delivery system. For example, sales information is delivered by the sales system and production information by the production system. This is not a very desirable situation because managers want all the information they need, regardless of its source or format, preferably on one screen or at least on as few screens as possible.

A response to providing access to the disorganized data dump has been the development of software, such as an EIS or Web application, that integrates information from a variety of delivery systems. This situation is shown in Figure 2-4. An important task of this software is to integrate and present information from multiple organizational memories. Recently, some organizations have created vast integrated data stores—data warehouses—that are organized repositories of organizational data (see Chapter 15 for more details).

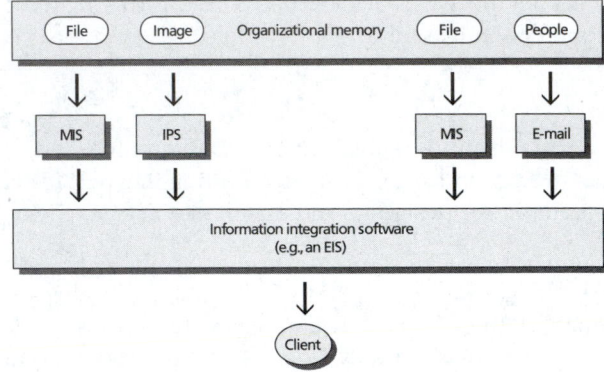

Figure 2-4. Information integration—the present situation

Information integration software is really a dirty (and not necessarily very quick) fix for a very critical need. The real requirement is to integrate *organizational memory* so that digital data (tables, images, graphics, and voice) can be stored together. The ideal situation is shown in Figure 2-5: The entire organizational memory is accessed as a single unit[13] via one information delivery system that meets all the client's requirements.

There is a long-term trend of data integration. Early information systems were based on independent files. As these systems were rewritten, designers integrated independent files to form databases. The next level of integration is to get all forms of data together. For example, the customer database might contain file data (e.g., customer name and address) and image data (e.g., photograph supporting an insurance claim).

Knowledge

The performance of many organizations is determined more by their intellectual capabilities and knowledge than their physical assets. A nation's wealth is increasingly a result of

---

13. Physically it might be multiple systems, but it appears to be one logical system.

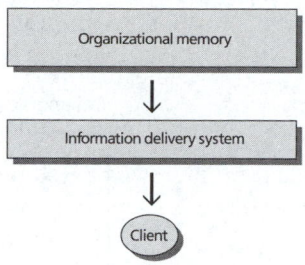

Figure 2-5. The ideal organizational memory and information delivery system

the knowledge and skills of its citizens, rather than its natural resources and industrial plant. Currently, about 85 percent of all jobs in America and 80 percent of those in Europe are knowledge-based.[14]

An organization's knowledge, in order of increasing importance, is

❖ cognitive knowledge (know what);
❖ advanced skills (know how);
❖ system understanding and trained intuition (know why);
❖ self-motivated creativity (care why).

This text illustrates the different types of knowledge. You will develop cognitive knowledge in Section 3, when you learn about data architectures and implementations. For example, *knowing what* storage devices can be used for archival data is cognitive knowledge. Section 2, which covers data modeling and SQL, develops advanced skills because, upon completion of that section, you will *know how* to model data and write SQL queries. The first two chapters are designed to expand your understanding of the influence of organizational memory on organizational performance. You need to *know why* you should learn data management skills. Managers know when and why to apply technology, whereas technicians know what to apply and how to apply it. Finally, you are probably an IS major, and your coursework is inculcating the values and norms of the IS profession so that you *care why* problems are solved using information technology.

Organizations tend to spend more on developing cognitive skills than they do on fostering creativity (see Figure 2-6). This is, unfortunately, the wrong priority. Returns are likely to be much greater when higher-level knowledge skills are developed. Well-managed organizations place more attention on creating *know why* and *care why* skills because they recognize that knowledge is a key competitive weapon. Furthermore, these firms have learned that knowledge grows, often exponentially, when shared. Knowledge is like a communication network, whose potential benefit grows exponentially as the nodes within the network grow arithmetically. When knowledge is shared within the organization,

---

14. This section is based on Quinn, B. J., P. Anderson, and S. Finkelstein. 1996. Leveraging intellect. *Academy of Management Executive* 10 (3):7–27.

or with customers and suppliers, it multiplies as each person receiving knowledge imparts it to someone else in the organization or to one of the business partners.

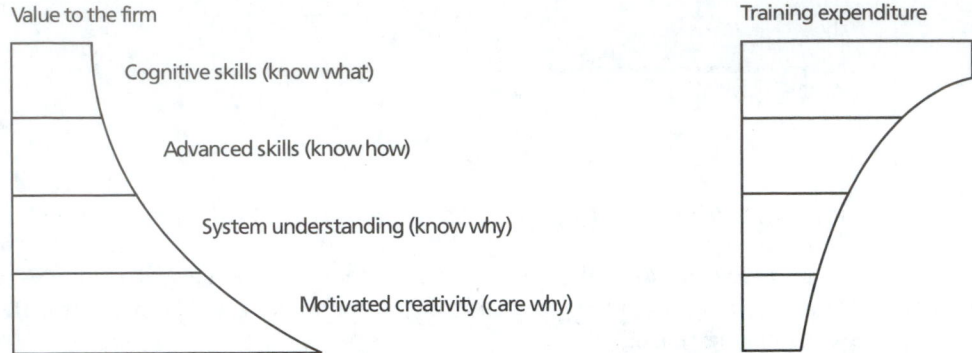

Figure 2-6. Skills values vs. training expenditures (source: Quinn et al., 1996)

There are two types of knowledge: explicit and tacit. **Explicit knowledge** is codified and transferable. This textbook is an example of explicit knowledge. Knowledge about how to design databases has been formalized and communicated with the intention of transferring it to you, the reader. **Tacit knowledge** is personal knowledge, experience, and judgment that is difficult to codify. It is more difficult to transfer tacit knowledge because it resides in people's minds. Usually, the transfer of tacit knowledge requires the sharing of experiences. In learning to model data, the subject of the next section, you will quickly learn how to represent an entity, because this knowledge is made explicit. However, you will find it much harder to model data, because this skill comes with practice. Ideally, you should develop several models under the guidance of an experienced modeler, such as your instructor, who can pass on his or her tacit knowledge.

Summary

Information has become a key foundation for organizational growth. The information society is founded on computer and communications technology. The accumulation of knowledge requires a capacity to encode and share information. Hard information is very exact. Soft information is extremely imprecise. Rich information exchange occurs in face-to-face conversation. Numeric reports are an example of lean information. Organizations use information to set goals, determine the gap between goals and achievements, determine actions to reach goals, and create new products and services to enhance organizational performance. Managers depend more on informal communication systems than on formal reporting systems. They expect to receive information that meets their current, everchanging needs. Operational managers need short-term information. Senior executives require mainly long-term information but still have a need for both short- and medium-term information. When managers face time constraints, they collect only enough information to make a satisfactory decision. Most organizations have a wide variety of poorly integrated information delivery systems. Organizational memory should be integrated to provide managers with one interface to an organization's information stores.

Key terms and concepts

Advanced skills (know how)	Information organization
Benchmarking	Information requirements
Change information	Information richness
Cognitive knowledge (know what)	Information satisficing
Empowerment	Information society
Explicit knowledge	Knowledge
Gap information	Managerial work
Global change	Organizational change
Goal-setting information	Phases of civilization
Information as a means of change	Self-motivated creativity (care why)
Information delivery systems	Social memory
Information hardness	System understanding (know why)
Information integration	Tacit knowledge

References and additional readings

Davenport, T. H. 1994. Saving IT's soul: Human-centered information management. *Harvard Business Review* 72 (2):119–131.

Evans, P. B., and T. S. Wurster. 1997. Strategy and the new economics of information. *Harvard Business Review* 75 (5):71–82.

Nonaka, I., and H. Takeuchi. 1995. *The knowledge-creating company: How Japanese companies create the dynamics of innovation*. New York, NY: Oxford University Press.

Ohmae, K. 1990. *The borderless world*. New York, NY: HarperCollins.

Quinn, J. B., P. Anderson, and S. Finkelstein. 1996. Leveraging intellect. *Academy of Management Executive* 10 (3):7-27.

Exercises

1. From an information perspective, what is different about the early years of the twenty-first century compared to the last years of the twentieth century?
2. Why did Intel and Microsoft grow so rapidly in the 1990s?
3. Why are paper and writing systems important?
4. What is the difference between soft and hard information?
5. What is the difference between rich and lean information exchange?
6. What are three major types of information connected with organizational change?
7. What is benchmarking? When might a business use benchmarking?
8. What is gap information?
9. Give some examples of how information is used as a means of change.
10. What sorts of information do senior managers want?
11. Describe the differences between the way managers handle hard and soft information.

12. What is information satisficing?
13. Describe an incident where you used information satisficing.
14. Give some examples of common information delivery systems.
15. Who uses an EIS?
16. What is a GIS? Who might use a GIS?
17. What is groupware?
18. Why is information integration a problem?
19. Select two public companies listed on the stock exchange in your country. One of these should be an information-based organization (e.g., Microsoft) and the other an industrial-era company (e.g., Ford). Compare the PE ratios, assets, revenues, and numbers of employees. What do you observe? What does this mean?
20. How "hard" is an exam grade?
21. Could you develop a test for the hardness of a piece of information?
22. Is very soft information worth storing in formal organizational memory? If not, where might you draw the line?
23. If you had just failed your database exam, would you use rich or lean media to tell a parent or spouse about the result?
24. Interview a businessperson to determine his or her firm's critical success factors (CSFs). Remember, a CSF is something the firm must do right to be successful. Generally a firm has about seven CSFs. For the firm's top three CSFs, identify the information that will measure whether the CSF is being achieved.
25. If you were managing a fast-food store, what information would you want to track store performance? Classify this information as short-, medium-, or long-term.
26. Interview a manager. Identify the information that person uses to manage the company. Classify this information as short-, medium-, or long-term information. Comment on your findings.
27. Why is organizational memory like a data warehouse? What needs to be done to make good use of this data warehouse?
28. What information are you collecting to help determine your career or find a job? What problems are you having collecting this information? Is the information mainly hard or soft?
29. What type of knowledge should you gain in a university class?
30. What type of knowledge is likely to make you most valuable?

Case questions

Imagine you are the new owner of The Expeditioner (see page 25).

1. What information would you request to determine the present performance of the organization?
2. What information would help you to establish goals for The Expeditioner? What goals would you set?
3. What information would you want to help you assist you in changing The Expeditioner?
4. How could you use information to achieve your goals?

Section 2

Data Modeling and SQL

It is a capital mistake to theorize before one has data.
Sir Arthur Conan Doyle, "A Scandal in Bohemia," *The Adventures of Sherlock Holmes*, 1891

The application backlog, a large number of requests for new information systems, has been a recurring problem in many organizations for decades. The demand for new information systems and the need to maintain existing systems have usually outstripped available information systems skills. The application backlog, unfortunately, is not a new problem. In the 1970s, Codd laid out a plan for improving programmer productivity and accelerating systems development by improving the management of data. Codd's **relational model**, designed to solve many of the shortcomings of earlier systems, is currently the most popular database model.

This section develops two key skills—data modeling and query formation—that are required to take advantage of the relational model. We concentrate on the design and use of relational databases. This very abrupt change in focus is part of our plan to give you a dual understanding of data management. Section 1 is the managerial perspective, whereas this section covers technical skills development. Competent data managers are able to accommodate both views and apply whichever (or some blend of the two) is appropriate.

In Chapter 1, many forms of organizational memory were identified, but in this section we focus on files and their components. Thus, only the files branch of organizational memory is detailed in Figure S2-1. A collection of related files is a **database**. Describing the collection of files as related means that it has a common purpose (e.g., data about students). Sometimes files are also called tables, and there are synonyms for some other terms (Figure S2-1 shows the alternative names in parentheses). Files contain **records** (or rows). Each record contains the data for one instance of the data the file stores. For example, if the file stores data about students, each record will contain data about a single student. Records have **fields** (or columns) that store the fine detail of each instance (e.g., student's first name, last name, and date of birth). Fields are composed of **characters** (a, b, c, . . , 1, 2, 3, . . . , %, $, #, . . . , A, B, etc.). A **byte**, a unit of storage sufficient to store a single letter (in English) or digit, consists of a string of eight contiguous **bits** or binary digits.

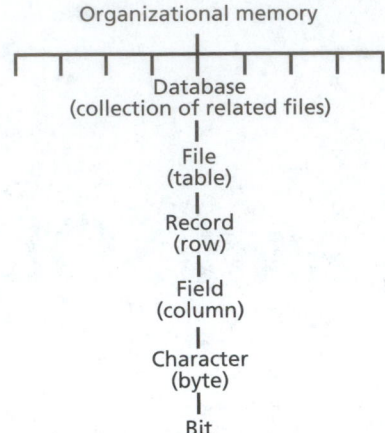

Figure S2-1. Data management hierarchy

The data management hierarchy stimulates three database design questions:

- ❖ What collection of files should the database contain?
- ❖ How are these files related?
- ❖ What fields should each record in the file contain?

The first objective of this section is to describe data modeling, a technique for answering the first two questions. Data modeling helps you to understand the structure and meaning of data, which is necessary before a database can be created. Once a database has been designed, built, and loaded with data, the aim is to deploy it to satisfy management's requests for information. Thus, the second objective is to teach you to query a relational database. The learning of modeling and querying will be intertwined, making it easier to grasp the intent of database design and to understand why data modeling is so critical to making a database an effective tool for managerial decision making.

Chapter 3 covers modeling a single entity and querying a single-table database. This is the simplest database that can be created. As you will soon discover, a **data model** is a graphical description of the components of a database. One of these components is an entity, some feature of the real world about which data must be stored. This section also introduces the notions of a **data definition language** (DDL), which is used to describe a database, and a **data manipulation language** (DML), which is used to maintain and query a database. Subsequent chapters in this section cover advanced data modeling concepts and querying capabilities.

3

The Single Entity

I want to be alone.
 Attributed to Greta Garbo

Learning objectives

Students completing this chapter will be able to

❖   model a single entity;
❖   define a single database;
❖   write queries for a single-table database.

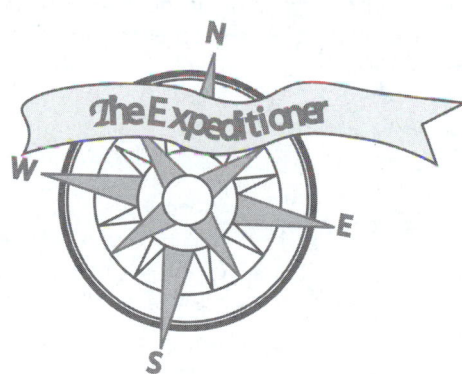

Alice pulled another folder out of the seemingly endless collection supplied by Mr. Mainwaring, the lawyer from Cholmondeley, Crespigny, Majoribanks, and St. John. She had certainly made one decision—to find a lawyer called Smith or Brown. It was most disconcerting to be unable to remember how to pronounce the man's name. The folder, boldly titled "Shares," contained a single sheet of paper on which were listed the names of 10 companies and the number of shares held in each company. Alice thought, "This is just a mass of data. What I really need to know is how much each of these shares is worth and its annual dividend." She forcefully pressed the call button to summon the attendant for a copy of the *Financial Times*.

The relational model

The relational model introduced by Codd in 1970 is the most popular technology for managing large collections of data. At this point, the major concepts of the relational model are introduced. Extensive coverage of the relational model is left until Chapter 9, by which time you will have sufficient practical experience to appreciate fully its usefulness, value, and elegance.

A **relation**, similar to the mathematical concept of a set, is a two-dimensional table arranged in rows and columns. This is a very familiar idea. You have been using tables for many years. A **relational database** is a collection of relations, where *relation* is a mathematical term for a table. One row of a table stores details of one observation, instance, or case of an item about which facts are retained—for example, one row for details of a particular student. All the rows in a table store data about the same type of item. Thus, a database might have one table for student data and another table for class data. Similarly, each column in the table contains the same type of data. For example, the first column might record a student's identification number (in the United States, this is often a social security number). A key database design question is to decide what to store in each table. What should the rows and columns contain?

In a relational database, each row must be uniquely identified. There must be a **primary key**, such as student identifier, so that a particular row can be designated. The use of unique identifiers is very common. Telephone numbers and e-mail addresses are examples of unique identifiers in common use. Selection of the primary key, or unique identifier, is another key issue of database design.

The tables in a relational database are *connected* or *related* by means of the data in the tables. You will learn, in the next chapter, that this connection is through a pair of values—a primary key and a foreign key. Consider a table of airlines serving a city. When examining this table, you may not recognize the code of an airline, so you then go to another table to find the name of the airline. For example, if you inspect Table 3-1, you find that AM is an international airline serving Atlanta.

Table 3-1: International airlines serving Atlanta

Airlines
AM
JL
KX
LM
MA
OS
RG
SN
SR
LH
LY

If you don't know which airline has the abbreviation AM, then you need to look at the table of airline codes (Table 3-2) to discover that AeroMexico, with code AM, serves Atlanta.

The two tables are *related* by airline code. Later, you will discover which is the primary key and which is the foreign key.

Table 3-2: A partial list of airline codes

Code	Airline
AA	American Airlines
AC	Air Canada
AD	Lone Star Airlines
AE	Mandarin Airlines
AF	Air France
AG	Interprovincial Airlines
AI	Air India
AM	AeroMexico
AQ	Aloha Airlines

When designing the relational model, Codd provided commands for processing multiple records at a time. His intention was to increase the productivity of programmers by moving beyond the record-at-a-time processing that is found in most programming languages. Consequently, the relational model supports set processing (multiple records-at-a-time), which is most frequently implemented as **Structured Query Language (SQL)**.

When writing applications for earlier data management systems, programmers usually had to consider the physical features (e.g., the track size) of the storage device. This made programming more complex and also often meant that when data were moved from one storage device to another, software modification was necessary. The relational model separates the logical design of a database and its physical storage. This notion of **data independence** simplifies data modeling and database programming. In this section, we focus on logical database design, and now that you have had a brief introduction to the relational model, you are ready to learn data modeling.

Getting started

As with most construction projects, building a relational database must be preceded by a design phase. Data modeling, our design technique, is a method for creating a plan or blueprint of a database. The data model must accurately mirror real-world relationships if it is to support processing business transactions and managerial decision making.

Rather than getting bogged down with a *theory first, application later* approach to database design and use, we will start with application. We will get back to theory when you have some experience in data modeling and database querying. After all, you did not learn to talk by first studying sentence formation; you just started by learning and using simple words. We start with the simplest data model, a single entity, and the simplest database, a single table (see Table 3-3).

Table 3-3: Share data

Firm's code	Firm's name	Price	Quantity	Dividend	PE ratio
FC	Freedonia Copper	27.50	10,529	1.84	16
PT	Patagonian Tea	55.25	12,635	2.50	10
AR	Abyssinian Ruby	31.82	22,010	1.32	13
SLG	Sri Lankan Gold	50.37	32,868	2.68	16
ILZ	Indian Lead & Zinc	37.75	6,390	3.00	12
BE	Burmese Elephant	.07	154,713	0.01	3
BS	Bolivian Sheep	12.75	231,678	1.78	11
NG	Nigerian Geese	35.00	12,323	1.68	10
CS	Canadian Sugar	52.78	4,716	2.50	15
ROF	Royal Ostrich Farms	33.75	1,234,923	3.00	6

Modeling a single-entity database

The simplest database contains information about one entity, which is some real-world thing. Some entities are physical — CUSTOMER,[1] ORDER, and STUDENT; others are conceptual — WORK ASSIGNMENT and AUTHORSHIP. We represent an entity by a rectangle: Figure 3-1 shows a representation of the entity SHARE.[2] The name of the entity is shown in singular form in uppercase in the top part of the rectangle.

SHARE

Figure 3-1. The entity SHARE

An entity has characteristics or attributes. An **attribute** is a discrete element of data; it is not usually broken down into smaller components. Attributes describe an entity and contain the entity's data we want to store. Some attributes of the entity SHARE are *identification code, firm name, price, quantity owned, dividend,* and *price-to-earnings ratio.*[3] Attributes are shown below the entity's name (Figure 3-2). Notice that we refer to *share price,* rather than *price,* to avoid confusion if there should be another entity with an attribute called *price.* Attribute names must be carefully selected so that they are self-explanatory and unique. For example, *share dividend* is easily recognized as belonging to the entity SHARE.

---

1. The convention in this book is to use uppercase for an entity's name.
2. SHARE could also be known as STOCK, EQUITY, or SECURITY.
3. Attributes are shown in italics within the text.

```
┌─────────────────┐
│     SHARE       │
│                 │
│   share code    │
│   share name    │
│   share price   │
│  share quantity │
│  share dividend │
│    share PE     │
└─────────────────┘
```

Figure 3-2. The entity SHARE and its attributes

An **instance** is a particular occurrence of an entity (e.g., facts about Freedonia Copper). To avoid confusion, each instance of an entity needs to be uniquely identified. Consider the case of customer billing. In most cases, a request to bill Smith $100 cannot be accurately processed because a firm typically has many customers called Smith. If a firm has carefully controlled procedures for ensuring that each customer has a unique means of identification, then a request to bill customer number 1789 $100 can be accurately processed. An attribute or collection of attributes that uniquely identifies an instance of an entity is called an **identifier**. The identifier for the entity SHARE is *share code*, a unique identifier assigned by the stock exchange.

There may be several attributes, or combinations of attributes, that are feasible identifiers for an instance of an entity. Attributes that are identifiers are prefixed by an asterisk. Figure 3-3 shows an example of a representation of an entity, its attributes, and identifier.

```
┌─────────────────┐
│     SHARE       │
│                 │
│   *share code   │
│   share name    │
│   share price   │
│  share quantity │
│  share dividend │
│    share PE     │
└─────────────────┘
```

Figure 3-3. The entity SHARE is uniquely identified by share code

Briefly, entities are things in the environment about which we wish to store information. Attributes describe an entity. An entity must have a unique identifier.

- -

Skill builder

A ship has a name, registration code, gross tonnage, and a year of construction. Ships are classified as cargo or passenger. Draw a data model for a ship.

- -

Data modeling

The modeling language used in this text is designed to record the essential details of a data model. The number of modeling symbols to learn is small, and they preserve all the fundamental concepts of data modeling. Since data modeling often occurs in a variety of settings, the symbols used have been selected so that they can be quickly drawn using pencil-and-paper, whiteboard, or a general-purpose drawing program (such as that built into PowerPoint). This also means that models can be quickly revised as parts can be readily erased and redrawn.

The symbols are distinct and visual clutter is minimized because only the absolutely essential information is recorded. This also makes the language easy for clients to learn so they can read and amend models.

Models can be rapidly translated to a set of tables for a relational database. More importantly, since this text implements the fundamental notions of all data modeling languages, you can quickly convert to another language (see page 223). Data modeling is a high-level skill, and the emphasis needs to be on learning to think like a data modeler rather than on learning a modeling language. This text's goal is to get you off to a fast start.

Creating a single-table database

The next stage is to translate the data model into a relational database. The translation rules are very direct:

- ❖ Each entity becomes a table.
- ❖ The entity name becomes the table name.
- ❖ Each attribute becomes a column.
- ❖ The identifier becomes the primary key.

The American National Standards Institute's (ANSI) recommended language for relational database definition and manipulation is SQL, which is both a data definition language (DDL) (to define a database), a data manipulation language (DML) (to query and maintain a database), and a data control language (DCL) (to control access). SQL is a common standard for describing and querying databases and is available with many commercial relational database products, including DB2, Oracle, and Microsoft Access, and open source products such as MySQL and PostgreSQL.

SQL uses the CREATE statement to define a table. It is not a particularly friendly command, and most products have easier methods for defining tables (e.g., see Figure 3-4), but it is the standard. Because some relational databases restrict table and column names to eight characters, it is often necessary to abbreviate a data model's attribute names, as has been done in this example for the data shown in Table 3-3.

Defining a table

The CREATE command to establish a table called shr[4] is as follows:

```
CREATE TABLE shr (
    shrcode         CHAR(3),
    shrfirm         VARCHAR(20) NOT NULL,
    shrprice        DECIMAL(6,2),
    shrqty          DECIMAL(8),
    shrdiv          DECIMAL(5,2),
    shrpe           DECIMAL(2),
       PRIMARY KEY (shrcode));
```

The first line of the command names the table; subsequent lines describe each of the columns in it. The first component is the name of the column (e.g., shrcode). The second component is the data type (e.g., CHAR), and its length is shown in parentheses. shrfirm is a variable-length character field of length 20, which means it can store up to 20 characters, including spaces. The column shrdiv stores a decimal number that can be as large as 999.99 because its total length is 5 digits and there are 2 digits to the right of the decimal point. Some examples of allowable data types are shown in Table 3-4. The third component (e.g., NOT NULL), which is optional, indicates any instance that cannot have null values. A column will have a null value when it is either unknown or not applicable. In the case of the share table, we specify that shrfirm must be defined for each instance in the database.

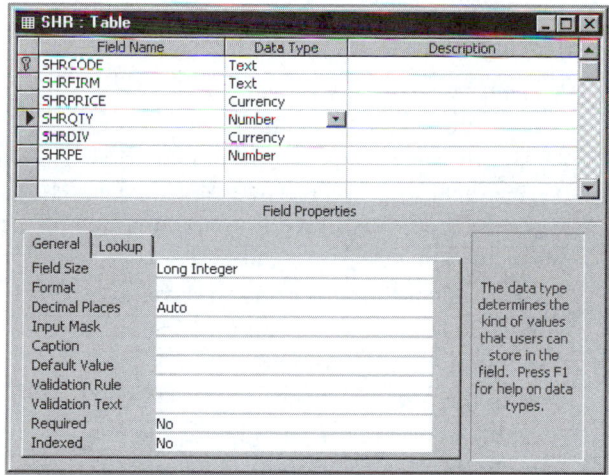

Figure 3-4. Table creation with MS Access

---

4. It is the usual practice to give the table the same name as the entity; however, this is not always possible. In this case, share is not permissible because it is a reserved word in SQL; thus we have used shr as the table name.

The final line of the CREATE statement defines shrcode as the primary key, the unique identifier for shr. When a primary key is defined, the relational database management system (RDBMS) will enforce the requirement that the primary key is unique and not null. Before any row is added to the table shr, the RDBMS will check that the value of shrcode is not null and that there does not already exist a duplicate value for shrcode in an existing row of shr. If either of these constraints is violated, the RDBMS will not permit the new row to be inserted. This constraint, the **entity integrity** rule, ensures that every row has a unique, non-null primary key. Allowing the primary key to take a null value would mean there could be a row of shr that is not uniquely identified. Note that each SQL statement is terminated by a semicolon.

SQL statements can be written in any mix of valid upper- and lowercase characters. To make it easier for you to learn the syntax, this book adopts the following conventions:

❖ SQL keywords are in uppercase.
❖ Table and column names are lowercase.

There are more elaborate layout styles, but we will bypass those because it is more important at this stage to learn SQL. You should lay out your SQL statements so that they are easily read by you and others.

Table 3-4 shows some of the data types supported by most relational databases. Other implementations of the relational model may support some of these data types and additional ones (see Table 3-5 for the data types supported by Microsoft Access). It is a good idea to review the available data types in your RDBMS before defining your first table.

Table 3-4: Some allowable data types

Numeric	SMALLINT	A 15-bit signed binary value
	INTEGER	A 31-bit signed binary value
	FLOAT(p)	A scientific format number of p binary digits precision
	DECIMAL(p,q)	A packed decimal number of p digits total length; q decimal spaces to the right of the decimal point may be specified.
String	CHAR(n)	A fixed-length string of n characters
	VARCHAR(n)	A variable-length string of up to n characters
	TEXT	A variable-length string of up to 65,535 characters
Date/time	DATE	Date in the form *yyyymmdd*
	TIME	Time in the form *hhmmss*
	TIMESTAMP	A combination of date and time to the nearest microsecond
	TIME WITH TIME ZONE	Same as time, with the addition of an offset from UTC of the specified time
	TIMESTAMP WITH TIME ZONE	Same as timestamp, with the addition of an offset from UTC of the specified time
Logical	BOOLEAN	A set of truth values: TRUE, FALSE, or UNKNOWN

Table 3-5: MS Access data types

TEXT		A variable-length character string of up to 255 characters
MEMO		A variable-length character string of up to 64,000 characters
Number	BYTE	An 8-bit unsigned binary value
	INTEGER	A 15-bit signed binary value
	LONG INTEGER	A 31-bit signed binary value
	SINGLE	A signed number with an exponent in the range –45 to +38
	DOUBLE	A signed number with an exponent in the range –324 to +308
DATE/TIME		A formatted date or time for the years 100 through 9999
CURRENCY		A monetary value
AUTONUMBER		A unique sequential number or random number assigned by Access whenever a new record is added to a table
YES/NO		A binary field that contains one of two values (Yes/No, True/False, or On/Off)
OLE OBJECT		An object, such as a spreadsheet, document, graphic, sound, or other binary data
HYPERLINK		A hyperlink address (e.g., a URL)

The CHAR and VARCHAR data types are similar but differ in the way character strings are stored and retrieved. Both can be up to 255 characters long. The length of a CHAR column is fixed to the declared length. When values are stored, they are right-padded with spaces to the specified length. When CHAR values are retrieved, trailing spaces are removed. VARCHAR columns store variable-length strings and use only as many characters as are needed to store the string. Values are not padded; instead, trailing spaces are removed. In this book, we use VARCHAR to define most character strings, unless they are short.[5]

- -

Skill builder

Create a relational database for the ship entity you modeled previously. Insert some rows.

- -

Inserting rows into a table

The rows of a table store instances of an entity. A particular shareholding (say, Freedonia Copper) is an example of an instance of the entity SHARE. The SQL statement INSERT is used to add rows to a table. Although most implementations of the relational model have an easier method of row insertion, the INSERT command is defined for completeness. The following command adds one row to the table shr:

---

5. For performance reasons, MySQL silently changes VARCHAR of length less than four to CHAR, and CHAR of length greater than 3 to VARCHAR.

```
INSERT INTO shr
    (shrcode,shrfirm,shrprice,shrqty,shrdiv,shrpe)
        VALUES ('FC','Freedonia Copper',27.5,10529,1.84,16);
```

There is a one-to-one correspondence between a column name in the first set of parentheses and a value in the second set of parentheses. That is, shrcode has the value "FC," shrfirm the value "Freedonia Copper," and so on. Notice that the value of a column that stores a character string (e.g., shrfirm) is contained within quotes.

The list of field names can be omitted when values are inserted in all fields of the table, so the preceding expression could be written

```
INSERT INTO shr
    VALUES ('FC','Freedonia Copper',27.5,10529,1.84,16);
```

The data for the shr table shown in Table 3-6 will be used in subsequent examples. If you have ready access to a relational database, it is a good idea to create a table and enter the data. Then you will be able to use these data to practice querying the table.

Table 3-6: Data for shr

shr					
shrcode	shrfirm	shrprice	shrqty	shrdiv	shrpe
FC	Freedonia Copper	27.50	10,529	1.84	16
PT	Patagonian Tea	55.25	12,635	2.50	10
AR	Abyssinian Ruby	31.82	22,010	1.32	13
SLG	Sri Lankan Gold	50.37	32,868	2.68	16
ILZ	Indian Lead & Zinc	37.75	6,390	3.00	12
BE	Burmese Elephant	.07	154,713	0.01	3
BS	Bolivian Sheep	12.75	231,678	1.78	11
NG	Nigerian Geese	35.00	12,323	1.68	10
CS	Canadian Sugar	52.78	4,716	2.50	15
ROF	Royal Ostrich Farms	33.75	1,234,923	3.00	6

Notice that shrcode is underlined in the relational table to show it is a primary key. In the data model it has an asterisk prefix to indicate it is an identifier. In the relational model it becomes a primary key, a column that guarantees that each row of the table can be uniquely addressed.

Query-by-example (QBE),[6] the other common method for working with a relational database, is easier to use than SQL because you make entries in a table rather than writing commands. There is no standard for QBE. Most implementations look similar, and once you have mastered one version, it is easy to use another. Using QBE for input is like entering

---

6.   Zloof, M. M. 1975. Query by example in *Proceedings of the NCC* 44, May 1975. Zloof invented QBE.

data in a spreadsheet, as inspection of Figure 3-5 quickly reveals. QBE can also be used for writing queries, but more powerful queries typically require SQL. Because IS professionals must be able to write complex queries, we will focus on learning the full power of SQL.

SHR : Table					
SHRCODE	**SHRFIRM**	**SHRPRICE**	**SHRQTY**	**SHRDIV**	**SHRPE**
AR	Abyssinian Ruby	31.82	22010	1.32	13
BE	Burmese Elephant	0.07	154713	0.01	3
BS	Bolivian Sheep	12.75	231678	1.78	11
CS	Canadian Sugar	52.78	4716	2.50	15
FC	Freedonia Copper	27.50	10529	1.84	16
ILZ	Indian Lead & Zinc	37.75	6390	3.00	12
NG	Nigerian Geese	35.00	12323	1.68	10
PT	Patagonian Tea	55.25	12635	2.50	10
ROF	Royal Ostrich Farms	33.75	1234923	3.00	6
SLG	Sri Lankan Gold	50.37	32868	2.68	16

Record: 11 of 11

Figure 3-5. Inserting rows with MS Access

The objective of developing a database is to make it easier to use the stored data to solve problems. Typically, a manager raises a question (e.g., How many shares have a PE ratio greater than 12?). A question or request for information, usually called a **query**, is then translated into a specific data manipulation or query language. The most widely used query languages for relational databases are SQL and some form of QBE. After the query has been executed, the resulting data are displayed. In the case of a relational database, the answer to a query is always a table.

There is also a query language called **relational algebra**, which describes a set of operations on tables. Sometimes it is useful to think of queries in terms of these operations. Where appropriate, we will introduce the corresponding relational algebra operation.

Generally we use a four-phase format for describing queries:

1. A brief explanation of the query's purpose
2. The query, prefixed by ○ and in bold, as it might be phrased by a manager
3. The SQL version of the query
4. The results of the query.

Displaying an entire table

All the data in a table can be displayed using the SELECT statement. In SQL, the *all* part is indicated by an asterisk (*).

○ **List all data in the share table.**

```
SELECT * FROM shr;
```

shrcode	shrfirm	shrprice	shrqty	shrdiv	shrpe
FC	Freedonia Copper	27.50	10529	1.84	16
PT	Patagonian Tea	55.25	12635	2.50	10
AR	Abyssinian Ruby	31.82	22010	1.32	13
SLG	Sri Lankan Gold	50.37	32868	2.68	16
ILZ	Indian Lead & Zinc	37.75	6390	3.00	12
BE	Burmese Elephant	.07	154713	0.01	3
BS	Bolivian Sheep	12.75	231678	1.78	11
NG	Nigerian Geese	35.00	12323	1.68	10
CS	Canadian Sugar	52.78	4716	2.50	15
ROF	Royal Ostrich Farms	33.75	1234923	3.00	6

More identifying stripes

In 2005, the 12-digit UPC bar codes assigned by the Universal Code Council in the United States and Canada increased to 13 digits. Incorporating the additional number into current retail systems required significant investments in time and capital. There are two reasons for expanding the 12-digit bar code: a shortage of available UPC numbers and the use of 13-digit bar codes almost everywhere else in the world

Source: Murphy, Kate. 2002. Bigger bar code inches up on retailers. *The New York Times*, Aug 12, www.nytimes.com/2002/08/12/technology/12CODE.html ?ex=1030153578&ei=1&en=d60a709cee524b42.

Project—choosing columns

The relational algebra operation **project** creates a new table from the columns of an existing table. Project takes a vertical slice through a table by selecting all the values in specified columns. The projection of shr on columns shrfirm and shrpe produces a new table with 10 rows and 2 columns. These columns are shaded in Table 3-7.

Table 3-7: Projection of shrfirm and shrpe

shr					
shrcode	shrfirm	shrprice	shrqty	shrdiv	shrpe
FC	Freedonia Copper	27.50	10,529	1.84	16
PT	Patagonian Tea	55.25	12,635	2.50	10
AR	Abyssinian Ruby	31.82	22,010	1.32	13
SLG	Sri Lankan Gold	50.37	32,868	2.68	16
ILZ	Indian Lead & Zinc	37.75	6,390	3.00	12
BE	Burmese Elephant	.07	154,713	0.01	3
BS	Bolivian Sheep	12.75	231,678	1.78	11
NG	Nigerian Geese	35.00	12,323	1.68	10
CS	Canadian Sugar	52.78	4,716	2.50	15
ROF	Royal Ostrich Farms	33.75	1,234,923	3.00	6

The SQL syntax for the project operation simply lists the columns to be displayed.

○   **Report a firm's name and price-earnings ratio.**

```
SELECT shrfirm, shrpe FROM shr;
```

shrfirm	shrpe
Freedonia Copper	16
Patagonian Tea	10
Abyssinian Ruby	13
Sri Lankan Gold	16
Indian Lead & Zinc	12
Burmese Elephant	3
Bolivian Sheep	11
Nigerian Geese	10
Canadian Sugar	15
Royal Ostrich Farms	6

Restrict—choosing rows

The relational algebra operation **restrict** creates a new table from the rows of an existing table. The operation restricts the new table to those rows that satisfy a specified condition. Restrict takes all columns of an existing table but only those rows that meet the specified condition. The restriction of shr to those rows where the PE ratio is less than 12 will give a new table with five rows and six columns. These rows are shaded in Table 3-8.

Table 3-8: Restriction of shr

shr					
shrcode	shrfirm	shrprice	shrqty	shrdiv	shrpe
FC	Freedonia Copper	27.50	10,529	1.84	16
PT	Patagonian Tea	55.25	12,635	2.50	10
AR	Abyssinian Ruby	31.82	22,010	1.32	13
SLG	Sri Lankan Gold	50.37	32,868	2.68	16
ILZ	Indian Lead & Zinc	37.75	6,390	3.00	12
BE	Burmese Elephant	.07	154,713	0.01	3
BS	Bolivian Sheep	12.75	231,678	1.78	11
NG	Nigerian Geese	35.00	12,323	1.68	10
CS	Canadian Sugar	52.78	4,716	2.50	15
ROF	Royal Ostrich Farms	33.75	1,234,923	3.00	6

Restrict is implemented in SQL using the WHERE clause to specify the condition on which rows are restricted.

○ **Get all firms with a price-earnings ratio less than 12.**

```
SELECT * FROM shr WHERE shrpe < 12;
```

shrcode	shrfirm	shrprice	shrqty	shrdiv	shrpe
PT	Patagonian Tea	55.25	12,635	2.50	10
BE	Burmese Elephant	0.07	154,713	0.01	3
BS	Bolivian Sheep	12.75	231,678	1.78	11
NG	Nigerian Geese	35.00	12,323	1.68	10
ROF	Royal Ostrich Farms	33.75	1,234,923	3.00	6

In this example, we have a *less than* condition for the WHERE clause. All permissible comparison operators are listed in Table 3-9.

Table 3-9: Comparison operators

Comparison operator	Meaning
=	Equal to
<	Less than
<=	Less than or equal to
>	Greater than
>=	Greater than or equal to
<>	Not equal to

In addition to the comparison operators, the BETWEEN construct is available.

a BETWEEN x AND y is equivalent to a >= x AND a <= y

Combining project and restrict—choosing rows and columns

SQL permits project and restrict to be combined. A single SQL SELECT statement can specify which columns to project and which rows to restrict.

○ **List the name, price, quantity, and dividend of each firm where the share holding is at least 100,000.**

```
SELECT shrfirm, shrprice, shrqty, shrdiv FROM shr
   WHERE shrqty >= 100000;
```

shrfirm	shrprice	shrqty	shrdiv
Burmese Elephant	0.07	154,713	0.01
Bolivian Sheep	12.75	231,678	1.78
Royal Ostrich Farms	33.75	1,234,923	3.00

More about WHERE

The WHERE clause can contain several conditions linked by AND or OR. A clause containing AND means all specified conditions must be true for a row to be selected. In the case of OR, at least one of the conditions must be true for a row to be selected.

○ **Find all firms where the PE is 12 or higher and the share holding is less than 10,000.**

```
SELECT * FROM shr
    WHERE shrpe >= 12 AND shrqty < 10000;
```

shrcode	shrfirm	shrprice	shrqty	shrdiv	shrpe
ILZ	Indian Lead & Zinc	37.75	6390	3	12
CS	Canadian Sugar	52.78	4716	2.5	15

The power of the primary key

The purpose of a primary key is to guarantee that any row in a table can be uniquely addressed. In this example, we use shrcode to return a single row because shrcode is unique for each instance of shr. The sought code (AR) must be specified in quotes because shrcode was defined as a character string when the table was created.

○ **Report firms whose code is AR.**

```
SELECT * FROM shr WHERE shrcode = 'AR';
```

shrcode	shrfirm	shrprice	shrqty	shrdiv	shrpe
AR	Abyssinian Ruby	31.82	22010	1.32	13

A query based on a non-primary-key column cannot guarantee that a single row is accessed, as the following illustrates.

○ **Report firms with a dividend of 2.50.**

```
SELECT * FROM shr WHERE shrdiv = 2.5;
```

shrcode	shrfirm	shrprice	shrqty	shrdiv	shrpe
PT	Patagonian Tea	55.25	12,635	2.50	10
CS	Canadian Sugar	52.78	4,716	2.50	15

The IN crowd

The keyword IN is used with a list to specify a set of values. IN is always paired with a column name. All rows for which a value in the specified column has a match in the list are selected. It is a simpler way of writing a series of OR statements.

○ **Report data on firms with codes of FC, AR, or SLG.**

```
SELECT * FROM shr WHERE shrcode IN ('FC','AR','SLG');
```

The foregoing query could have also been written as

```
SELECT * FROM shr
    WHERE shrcode = 'FC' OR shrcode = 'AR' OR shrcode = 'SLG';
```

shrcode	shrfirm	shrprice	shrqty	shrdiv	shrpe
FC	Freedonia Copper	27.50	10,529	1.84	16
AR	Abyssinian Ruby	31.82	22,010	1.32	13
SLG	Sri Lankan Gold	50.37	32,868	2.68	16

The NOT IN crowd

A NOT IN list is used to report instances that do not match any of the values.

○ **Report all firms other than those with the code CS or PT.**

```
SELECT * FROM shr WHERE shrcode NOT IN ('CS','PT');
```

is equivalent to

```
SELECT * FROM shr WHERE shrcode <> 'CS' AND shrcode <> 'PT';
```

shrcode	shrfirm	shrprice	shrqty	shrdiv	shrpe
FC	Freedonia Copper	27.50	10,529	1.84	16
AR	Abyssinian Ruby	31.82	22,010	1.32	13
SLG	Sri Lankan Gold	50.37	32,868	2.68	16
ILZ	Indian Lead & Zinc	37.75	6,390	3.00	12
BE	Burmese Elephant	0.07	154,713	0.01	3
BS	Bolivian Sheep	12.75	231,678	1.78	11
NG	Nigerian Geese	35.00	12,323	1.68	10
ROF	Royal Ostrich Farms	33.75	1,234,923	3.00	6

Skill builder

List those shares where the value of the holding exceeds one million.

Ordering columns

The order of reporting columns is identical to their order in the SQL command. For instance, compare the output of the following queries.

```
SELECT shrcode, shrfirm FROM shr WHERE shrpe = 10;
```

shrcode	shrfirm
PT	Patagonian Tea
NG	Nigerian Geese

```
SELECT shrfirm, shrcode FROM shr WHERE shrpe = 10;
```

shrfirm	shrcode
Patagonian Tea	PT
Nigerian Geese	NG

Ordering rows

People can process an ordered report faster than an unordered one. Imagine trying to find a name in a phone book that was not sorted by last name. That's why telephone books are ordered alphabetically by last name and then, within the same last name, by first name. (Actually, this is not true in Iceland where the telephone book is ordered alphabetically by first name. Because of Icelandic naming traditions, it is easier to search the telephone book on the basis of first name than last name.[7])

In SQL, the ORDER BY clause specifies the row order in a report. The default ordering sequence is ascending (A before B, 1 before 2). Descending is specified by adding DESC after the column name.

○ **List all firms where PE is at least 10, and order the report in descending PE. Where PE ratios are identical, list firms in alphabetical order.**

```
SELECT * FROM shr WHERE shrpe >= 10
    ORDER BY shrpe DESC, shrfirm;
```

shrcode	shrfirm	shrprice	shrqty	shrdiv	shrpe
FC	Freedonia Copper	27.50	10529	1.84	16
SLG	Sri Lankan Gold	50.37	32868	2.68	16
CS	Canadian Sugar	52.78	4716	2.50	15
AR	Abyssinian Ruby	31.82	22010	1.32	13
ILZ	Indian Lead & Zinc	37.75	6390	3.00	12
BS	Bolivian Sheep	12.75	231678	1.78	11
NG	Nigerian Geese	35.00	12323	1.68	10
PT	Patagonian Tea	55.25	12635	2.50	10

---

7. If an Icelandic man with the first name Ragnar has a daughter named Inga, her full name will be Inga Ragnarsdottir (literally daughter of Ragnar). If he has a son, the son's last name will be Ragnarsson.

Numeric versus character sorting

Numeric data in character fields (e.g., a product code) do not always sort the way you initially expect. The difference arises from the way data are stored:

- ❖ Numeric fields are right justified and have leading zeros.
- ❖ Character fields are left justified and have trailing spaces.

For example, the value 1066 stored in a character field of four bytes would be stored as '1066' and the value 45 would be stored as '45 '. If the column containing these data is sorted in ascending order, then '1066' precedes '45 ' because '1' is less than '4'. You can avoid this problem by always storing numeric values as numeric data types (e.g., integer or decimal) or preceding numeric values with zeros when they are stored as character data. Alternatively, start numbering at 1,000 so that all values are four digits.

Derived data

One of the important principles of database design is to avoid redundancy. One form of redundancy is including a column in a table when these data can be derived from other columns. For example, we do not need a column for yield because it can be calculated by dividing dividend by price and multiplying by 100 to obtain the yield as a percentage. This means that the query language does the calculation when the value is required.

○ **Get firm name, price, quantity, and firm yield.**

```
SELECT shrfirm, shrprice, shrqty, shrdiv/shrprice*100 AS yield FROM shr;
```

shrfirm	shrprice	shrqty	yield
Freedonia Copper	27.50	10,529	6.69
Patagonian Tea	55.25	12,635	4.52
Abyssinian Ruby	31.82	22,010	4.15
Sri Lankan Gold	50.37	32,868	5.32
Indian Lead & Zinc	37.75	6,390	7.95
Burmese Elephant	0.07	154,713	14.29
Bolivian Sheep	12.75	231,678	13.96
Nigerian Geese	35.00	12,323	4.80
Canadian Sugar	52.78	4,716	4.74
Royal Ostrich Farms	33.75	1,234,923	8.89

You can give the results of the calculation a column name. In this case, a good choice is yield. Note the use of AS to indicate the name of the column in which the results of the calculation are displayed.

In the preceding query, the keyword AS is introduced to specify an **alias**, or temporary name. The statement specifies that the result of the calculation is to be reported under the column heading `yield`. You can rename any column or specify a name for the results of an expression using an alias.

Aggregate functions

SQL has built-in functions to enhance its retrieval power and handle many common aggregation queries, such as computing the total value of a column. Four of these functions (AVG, SUM, MIN, and MAX) work very similarly. COUNT is a little different.

COUNT

COUNT computes the number of rows in a table. Rows are counted even if they contain null values. Count can be used with a WHERE clause to specify a condition.

○ **How many firms are there in the portfolio?**

```
SELECT COUNT(*) AS investments FROM shr;
```

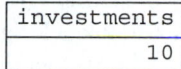

investments
10

○ **How many firms have a holding greater than 50,000?**

```
SELECT COUNT(*) AS bigholdings FROM shr WHERE shrqty > 50000;
```

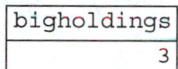

bigholdings
3

AVG—averaging

AVG computes the average of the values in a column of numeric data. Null values in the column are not included in the calculation.

○ **Find the average dividend.**

```
SELECT AVG(shrdiv) AS avgdiv FROM shr;
```

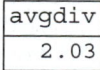

avgdiv
2.03

○ **What is the average yield for the portfolio?**

```
SELECT AVG(shrdiv/shrprice*100) AS avgyield FROM shr;
```

avgyield
7.53

SUM, MIN, and MAX

SUM, MIN, and MAX differ in the statistic they calculate but are used similarly to AVG. As with AVG, null values in a column are not included in the calculation. SUM computes the sum of a column of values. MIN finds the smallest value in a column; MAX finds the largest.

Subqueries

Sometimes we need the answer to another query before we can write the query of ultimate interest. For example, to list all shares with a PE ratio greater than the portfolio average, you first must find the average PE ratio for the portfolio. You could do the query in two stages:

A. SELECT AVG(shrpe) FROM shr;
B. SELECT shrfirm, shrpe FROM shr WHERE shrpe > x;

where x is the value returned from the first query.

Unfortunately, the two-stage method introduces the possibility of errors. You might forget the value returned by the first query or enter it incorrectly. It also takes longer to get the results of the query. We can solve these problems by using parentheses to indicate the first query is nested within the second one. As a result, the value returned by the inner or nested subquery, the one in parentheses, is used in the outer query. In the following example, the nested query returns 11.20, which is then automatically substituted in the outer query.

❍ **Report all firms with a PE ratio greater than the average for the portfolio.**

```
SELECT shrfirm, shrpe FROM shr
   WHERE shrpe > (SELECT AVG(shrpe) FROM shr);
```

shrfirm	shrpe
Freedonia Copper	16
Abyssinian Ruby	13
Sri Lankan Gold	16
Indian Lead & Zinc	12
Canadian Sugar	15

Warning: The preceding query is often mistakenly written as

```
SELECT shrfirm, shrpe FROM shr
   WHERE shrpe > AVG(shrpe);
```

China's new smart ID cards

With a population of 1.3 billion, China needs to track population changes and movements, which have increased in the past two decades of economic reform, when the government started allowing freer movement of families, especially from the rural areas to the cities.

China is issuing new intelligent ID cards that it hopes will prevent the prolific forging of the old ID cards. The new card contains a special chip containing information on the cardholder. Police can cross-check the information stored in a new ID card. The information stored includes digital data for management and anti-counterfeiting.

The chip-module was jointly developed by the Institute of Microelectronics under Tsinghua University and Tsinghua Tongfang Microelectronics Co. Ltd., a subsidiary controlled by Tsinghua University.

The replacement program of 1 billion cards should be completed by the end of 2008.

Source: Anonymous. 2004. China to issue smart ID cards. *China Daily*, Jan 28. www.china-daily.com.cn/en/doc/2004-01/28/content_301237.htm.

Skill builder

Find the name of the firm for which the value of the holding is greatest.

LIKE—pattern matching

Have you ever searched a major city's phone book for someone whose last name and street address you can recall but whose first name you just cannot remember? If you are looking for a Ms. Smith in Sydney, you will spend a lot of time sequentially searching through the Smiths, looking for the matching street name. LIKE solves these types of problems when you are searching a table because it searches for a specified pattern in a nominated column. LIKE uses two symbols for specifying a search pattern:

❖ The percentage sign (%) is the symbol for any number of characters, or none.
❖ The underscore (_) is the symbol for any single character.[8]

These examples illustrate the use of LIKE.

---

8. With MS Access, use * and ? in place of % and _ , respectively.

○   **List all firms with a name starting with "F."**

```
SELECT shrfirm FROM shr WHERE shrfirm LIKE 'F%';
```

shrfirm
Freedonia Copper

○   **List all firms containing "Ruby" in their names.**

```
SELECT shrfirm FROM shr WHERE shrfirm LIKE '%Ruby%';
```

shrfirm
Abyssinian Ruby

○   **Find firms with "t" as the third letter of their names.**

```
SELECT shrfirm FROM shr WHERE shrfirm LIKE '__t%'; 9
```

shrfirm
Patagonian Tea

○   **Find firms not containing an "s" in their names.**

This query is a little vague, even for academic work. Do you assume that it refers to the lowercase *s*, uppercase *S*, or both? In the business world, you would ask the manager who requested the data. We assume it means neither uppercase nor lowercase.

```
SELECT shrfirm FROM shr
   WHERE shrfirm NOT LIKE '%S%'
   AND shrfirm NOT LIKE '%s%';
```

shrfirm
Freedonia Copper
Patagonian Tea
Indian Lead & Zinc

DISTINCT—eliminating duplicate rows

The DISTINCT clause is used to eliminate duplicate rows. It can be used with the column functions or before a column name. When used with a column function, it ignores duplicate values.

---

9.   There are two underscores before the t in '__t%'

○ **Report the different values of the PE ratio.**

```
SELECT DISTINCT shrpe FROM shr;
```

shrpe
3
6
10
11
12
13
15
16

○ **Find the number of different PE ratios.**

```
SELECT COUNT(DISTINCT shrpe) AS 'Different PEs' FROM shr; 10
```

Different PEs
8

When used before a column name, DISTINCT prevents the selection of duplicate rows. Notice a slightly different use of the keyword AS. In this case, because the alias includes a space, the entire alias is enclosed in quotes.

DELETE

Rows in a table can be deleted using the DELETE clause in an SQL statement. DELETE is typically used with a WHERE clause to specify the rows to be deleted. If there is no WHERE clause, all rows are deleted.

○ **Erase the data for Burmese Elephant. All the shares have been sold.**

```
DELETE FROM shr WHERE shrfirm = 'Burmese Elephant';
```

In the preceding statement, shrfirm is used to indicate the row to be deleted.

UPDATE

Rows can be modified using SQL's UPDATE clause, which is used with a WHERE clause to specify the rows to be updated.

---

10. This code does not work with MS Access. Once you have learned how to create a virtual table, you will be able to write appropriate SQL for MS Access (see page 103).

○ **Change the share price of FC to 31.50.**

```
UPDATE shr
   SET shrprice = 31.50
   WHERE shrcode = 'FC';
```

○ **Increase the total number of shares for Nigerian Geese by 10% because of the recent bonus issue.**

```
UPDATE shr
   SET shrqty = shrqty*1.1
   WHERE shrfirm = 'Nigerian Geese';
```

Skill builder

List the firms containing "ian" in their name.

Debriefing

Now that you have learned how to model a single entity, create a table, and specify queries, you are on the way to mastering the fundamental skills of database design, implementation, and use. Remember, planning occurs before action. A data model is a plan for a database. The action side of a database is inserting rows and running queries.

Summary

The relational database model is an effective means of representing real-world relationships. Data modeling is used to determine what data must be stored and how data are related. An entity is something in the environment. An entity has attributes, which describe it, and an identifier, which uniquely marks an instance of an entity. Every entity must have a unique identifier. A relational database consists of tables with rows and columns. A data model is readily translated to a relational database. The SQL statement CREATE is used to define a table. Rows are added to a table using INSERT. In SQL, queries are written using the SELECT statement. QBE is an alternative to SQL. Project (choosing columns) and restrict (choosing rows) are common table operations. The WHERE clause is used to specify row selection criteria. WHERE can be combined with IN and NOT IN, which specify values for a single column. The rows of a report are sorted using the ORDER BY clause. Arithmetic expressions can appear in SQL statements, and SQL has built-in functions for common arithmetic operations. A subquery is a query within a query. The LIKE clause is used for pattern matching of character strings. Duplicate rows are eliminated with the DISTINCT clause. Rows can be erased using DELETE or modified with UPDATE.

Key terms and concepts

Alias	LIKE
AS	MAX
Attribute	MIN
AVG	NOT IN
Column	ORDER BY
COUNT	Primary key
CREATE	Project
Data modeling	Query-By-Example (QBE)
Data type	Relational database
Database	Restrict
DELETE	Row
DISTINCT	SELECT
Entity	SQL
Entity integrity rule	Subquery
Identifier	SUM
IN	Table
INSERT	UPDATE
Instance	WHERE

Exercises

1. Draw data models for the following entities. In each case, make certain that you show the attributes and identifiers:
   a. Aircraft: An aircraft has a manufacturer, model number, call sign (e.g., N123D), payload, and a year of construction. Aircraft are classified as civilian or military.
   b. Car: A car has a manufacturer, range name, and style code (e.g., a Honda Accord DX, where Honda is the manufacturer, Accord is the range, and DX is the style). A car also has a vehicle identification code, registration code, and color.
   c. Restaurant: A restaurant has an address, seating capacity, phone number, and style of food (e.g., French, Russian, Chinese).
   d. Cow: A dairy cow has a name, date of birth, breed (e.g., Holstein), and a numbered plastic ear tag.
2. Take each of the entities you have modeled, create a relational database, and insert some rows.
3. Do the following queries using SQL:
   a. List a share's name and its code.
   b. List full details for all shares with a price less than $1.
   c. List the names and prices of all shares with a price of at least $10.
   d. Create a report showing firm name, share price, share holding, and total value of shares held. (Value of shares held is price times quantity.)
   e. List the names of all shares with a yield exceeding 5 percent.
   f. Report the total dividend payment of Patagonian Tea. (The total dividend payment is dividend times quantity.)
   g. Find all shares where the price is less than 20 times the dividend.

h. Find the share with the minimum yield.

i. Find the total value of all shares with a PE ratio > 10.

j. Find the share with the maximum total dividend payment.

k. Find the value of the holdings in Abyssinian Ruby and Sri Lankan Gold.

l. Find the yield of all firms except Bolivian Sheep and Canadian Sugar.

m. Find the total value of the portfolio.

n. List firm name and value in descending order of value.

o. List shares with a firm name containing "Gold."

p. Find shares with a code starting with "B."

4. Run the following queries and explain the differences in output. Write each query as a manager might state it.

a. `SELECT shrfirm FROM shr WHERE shrfirm NOT LIKE '%s%';`

b. `SELECT shrfirm FROM shr WHERE shrfirm NOT LIKE '%S%';`

c. `SELECT shrfirm FROM shr WHERE shrfirm NOT LIKE '%s%' AND shrfirm NOT LIKE '%S%';`

d. `SELECT shrfirm FROM shr WHERE shrfirm NOT LIKE '%s%' OR shrfirm NOT LIKE '%S%';`

e. `SELECT shrfirm FROM shr WHERE (shrfirm NOT LIKE '%s%' AND shrfirm NOT LIKE '%S%') OR shrfirm LIKE 'S%';`

5. A weekly newspaper, sold at supermarket checkouts, frequently reports stories of aliens visiting Earth and taking humans on short trips. Sometimes a captured human sees Elvis commanding the spaceship. Well, to keep track of all these reports, the newspaper has created the following data model.

ALIEN

*al#
alname
alheads
alcolor
alsmell

The paper has also supplied some data for the last few sightings and asked you to create the database, add details of these aliens, and answer the following queries:

a. What's the average number of heads of an alien?

b. Which alien has the most heads?

c. Are there any aliens with a double *o* in their names?

d. How many aliens are chartreuse?

e. Report details of all aliens sorted by smell and color.

6. If you have a database system on your personal computer, create the `shr` table and insert some rows. Compare the approach of standard SQL to your database system. Which was easier to use for defining a table and inserting some rows? Next, do some queries. How do the two systems compare?

7. Eduardo, a bibliophile, has a collection of several hundred books. Being a little disorganized, he has his books scattered around his den. They are piled on the floor, some are in bookcases, and others sit on top of his desk. Because he has so many books, he finds it difficult to remember what he has, and sometimes he cannot find the book he wants. Eduardo has a simple personal computer file system that is fine for a single entity or file. He has decided that he would like to list each book by author(s)' name and type of book (e.g., literature, travel, reference). Draw a data model for this problem, create a single entity table, and write some SQL queries.
   a. How do you identify each instance of a book? (It might help to look at a few books.)
   b. How should Eduardo physically organize his books to permit fast retrieval of a particular one?
   c. Are there any shortcomings with the data model you have created?
8. What is an identifier? Why does a data model have an identifier?
9. What are entities?
10. What is the entity integrity rule?

CD library case[11]

Ajay, who is a DJ in the student-operated radio station at his university, is impressed by the station's large collection of CDs but is frustrated by the time he spends searching for a particular piece of music. Recently, when preparing his weekly jazz session, he spent more than half an hour searching for a recording of Duke Ellington's "Creole Blues." An IS major, Ajay had recently commenced a data management class. He quickly realized that a relational database, storing details of all the CDs owned by the radio station, would enable him to find quickly any piece of music.

Having just learned how to model a single entity, Ajay decided to start building a CD database. He took one of his favorite CDs, John Coltrane's *Giant Steps*, and drew a model to record details of the tracks on this CD (see Figure 3-6).

```
TRACK

*trkid
trknum
trktitle
trklength
```

Figure 3-6. CD library V1.0

---

11. This case extends your skills in data modeling and SQL. Gradually, you will design and implement a database for storing details of CDs. This case continues through to Chapter 6.

Ajay pondered using *track number* as the identifier since each track on a CD is uniquely numbered, but he quickly realized that *track number* was not suitable because it uniquely identifies only those tracks on a specific CD. So, he introduced *trackid* to identify uniquely each track irrespective of the CD on which it is found.

He also recorded the name of the track and its length. He had originally thought that he would record the track's length in minutes and seconds (e.g., 4:43) but soon discovered that the TIME data type of his DBMS is designed to store time of day rather than the length of time of an event. Thus, he concluded that he should store the length of a track in minutes as a decimal (i.e., 4:43 is stored as 4.72).

Table 3-10: Giant Steps

Trkid	Trknum	Trktitle	Trklength
1	1	Giant Steps	4.72
2	2	Cousin Mary	5.75
3	3	Countdown	2.35
4	4	Spiral	5.93
5	5	Syeeda's Song Flute	7.00
6	6	Naima	4.35
7	7	Mr. P.C.	6.95
8	8	Giant Steps	3.67
9	9	Naima	4.45
10	10	Cousin Mary	5.90
11	11	Countdown	4.55
12	12	Syeeda's Song Flute	7.03

- -

Skill builder

1. Create a single table database using the data in Table 3-10.
2. Justify your choice of data type for each of the attributes.

- -

Ajay ran a few queries on his single table database.

○ **On what track is "Giant Steps"?**

```
SELECT trknum, trktitle FROM track
   WHERE trktitle = 'Giant Steps';
```

trknum	trktitle
1	Giant Steps
8	Giant Steps

Observe that there are two tracks with the title "Giant Steps."

○ **Report all recordings longer than 5 minutes.**

```
SELECT trknum, trktitle, trklength FROM track
   WHERE trklength > 5;
```

trknum	trktitle	trklength
2	Cousin Mary	5.75
4	Spiral	5.93
5	Syeeda's Song Flute	7.00
7	Mr. P.C.	6.95
10	Cousin Mary	5.90
12	Syeeda's song flute	7.03

○ **What is the total length of recordings on the CD?**

This query makes use of the function SUM to total the length of tracks on the CD.

```
SELECT SUM(trklength) AS sumtrklen FROM track;
```

sumtrklen
62.65

When you run the preceding query, the value reported may not be exactly 62.65. Why?

○ **Find the longest track on the CD.**

```
SELECT trknum, trktitle, trklength FROM track
   WHERE trklength = (SELECT MAX(trklength) FROM track);
```

This query follows the model described previously in this chapter. First determine the longest track (i.e., 7.03 minutes) and then find the track, or tracks, that are this length.

trknum	trktitle	trklength
12	Syeeda's Song Flute	7.03

○ **How many tracks are there on the CD?**

```
SELECT COUNT(*) AS tracks FROM track;
```

tracks
12

○ **Sort the different titles on the CD by their name.**

```
SELECT DISTINCT(trktitle) FROM track
   ORDER BY trktitle;
```

trktitle
Countdown
Cousin Mary
Giant Steps
Mr. P.C.
Naima
Spiral
Syeeda's Song Flute

○ **List the shortest track containing "song" in its title.**

```
SELECT trknum, trktitle, trklength FROM track
   WHERE trktitle LIKE '%song%'
   AND trklength = (SELECT MIN(trklength) FROM track
      WHERE trktitle LIKE '%song%');
```

The subquery determines the length of the shortest track with "song" in its title. Then any track with a length equal to the minimum and also containing "song" in its title (just in case there is another without "song" in its title that is the same length) is reported.[12]

trknum	trktitle	trklength
5	Syeeda's Song Flute	7.00

○ **Report details of tracks 1 and 5.**

```
SELECT trknum, trktitle, trklength FROM track
   WHERE trknum IN (1,5);
```

trknum	trktitle	trklength
1	Giant Steps	4.72
5	Syeeda's Song Flute	7.00

- -

Skill builder

1. Write SQL commands for the following queries:
   a. Report all tracks between 4 and 5 minutes long.
   b. On what track is "Naima"?
   c. Sort the tracks by descending length.
   d. What tracks are longer than the average length of tracks on the CD?
   e. How many tracks are less than 5 minutes?
   f. What tracks start with "Cou"?

---

12. If you are using MS Access, use * in place of %.

2. Add the 13 tracks from The Manhattan Transfer's *Swing* CD in the following table to the `track` table:

Track	Title	Length
1	Stomp of King Porter	3.20
2	Sing a Study in Brown	2.85
3	Sing Moten's Swing	3.60
4	A-tisket, A-tasket	2.95
5	I Know Why	3.57
6	Sing You Sinners	2.75
7	Java Jive	2.85
8	Down South Camp Meetin'	3.25
9	Topsy	3.23
10	Clouds	7.20
11	Skyliner	3.18
12	It's Good Enough to Keep	3.18
13	Choo Choo Ch' Boogie	3.00

3. Write SQL to answer the following queries:
    a. What is the longest track on *Swing*?
    b. What tracks on *Swing* include the word *Java*?
4. What is the data model missing?

4

The One-to-Many Relationship

Cow of many — well milked and badly fed.
Spanish proverb

Learning objectives

Students completing this chapter will be able to

❖ model a one-to-many relationship between two entities;
❖ define a database with a one-to-many relationship;
❖ write queries for a database with a one-to-many relationship.

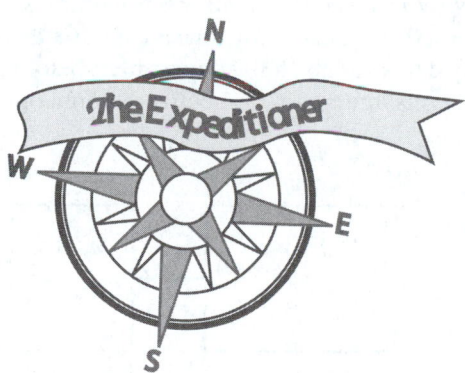

Alice sat with a self-satisfied smirk on her face. Her previous foray into her attaché case had revealed the extent of her considerable stock holdings. She was wealthy beyond her dreams. What else was there in this marvelous, magic attaché case? She rummaged further into the case and retrieved a folder labeled "Stocks — foreign." More shares!

On the inside cover of the folder was a note stating that the stocks in this folder were not listed in the United Kingdom. The folder contained three sheets of paper. Each was headed by the name of a country and followed by a list of stocks and the number of shares. The smirk became the cattiest of Cheshire grins. Alice ordered another bottle of champagne and turned to the *Financial Times* page that listed foreign stock prices. She wanted to calculate the current value of each stock and then use current exchange rates to convert the values into British currency.

Relationships

Entities are not isolated; they are related to other entities. When we move beyond the single entity, we need to identify the relationships between entities to accurately represent the real world. Once we recognize that all stocks in our case study are not listed in the United Kingdom, we need to introduce an entity called NATION. We now have two entities, STOCK[1] and NATION. Consider the relationship between them. A NATION can have many listed stocks. A stock, in this case, is listed in only one nation. There is a 1:m (one-to-many)[2] relationship between NATION and STOCK.

A 1:m relationship between two entities is depicted by a line connecting the two with a crow's foot or chicken foot at the many end of the relationship. Figure 4-1 shows the 1:m relationship between STOCK and NATION. This can be read as: "a nation can have many stocks, but a stock belongs to only one nation." The entity NATION is identified by a *nation code* and has attributes *nation name* and *exchange rate*.

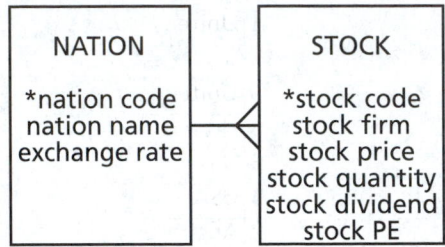

Figure 4-1. A 1:m relationship between NATION and STOCK

The 1:m relationship occurs frequently in business situations. Sometimes it occurs in a tree or hierarchical fashion. Consider a firm. It has many divisions, but a division belongs to only one firm. A division has many departments, but a department belongs to only one division. A department has many sections, but a section belongs to only one department (see Figure 4-2).

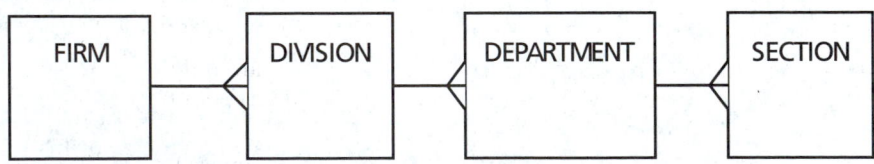

Figure 4-2. A series of 1:m relationships

---

1. Why have we changed the label to STOCK when it seems to be the same as SHR? Because, as you will see shortly, STOCK is related to another entity, whereas SHR stands alone.
2. One-to-many is the common interpretation of 1:m. You can also think of it as one-and-many because there are two relationships — STOCK is related to one NATION, and NATION is related to many STOCKs. While we believe one-and-many is more precise, we have adopted the common usage.

Why did we create an additional entity?

Another approach to adding data about listing nation and exchange rate is to add two attributes to STOCK: *nation name* and *exchange rate*. At first glance, this seems a very workable solution; however, this will introduce considerable redundancy, as Table 4-1 illustrates.

Table 4-1: The table STOCK with additional columns

stock							
stkcode	stkfirm	stkprice	stkqty	stkdiv	stkpe	natname	exchrate
FC	Freedonia Copper	27.50	10,529	1.84	16	United Kingdom	1.00
PT	Patagonian Tea	55.25	12,635	2.50	10	United Kingdom	1.00
AR	Abyssinian Ruby	31.82	22,010	1.32	13	United Kingdom	1.00
SLG	Sri Lankan Gold	50.37	32,868	2.68	16	United Kingdom	1.00
ILZ	Indian Lead & Zinc	37.75	6,390	3.00	12	United Kingdom	1.00
BE	Burmese Elephant	.07	154,713	0.01	3	United Kingdom	1.00
BS	Bolivian Sheep	12.75	231,678	1.78	11	United Kingdom	1.00
NG	Nigerian Geese	35.00	12,323	1.68	10	United Kingdom	1.00
CS	Canadian Sugar	52.78	4,716	2.50	15	United Kingdom	1.00
ROF	Royal Ostrich Farms	33.75	1,234,923	3.00	6	United Kingdom	1.00
MG	Minnesota Gold	53.87	816,122	1.00	25	USA	0.67
GP	Georgia Peach	2.35	387,333	.20	5	USA	0.67
NE	Narembeen Emu	12.34	45,619	1.00	8	Australia	0.46
QD	Queensland Diamond	6.73	89,251	.50	7	Australia	0.46
IR	Indooroopilly Ruby	15.92	56,147	.50	20	Australia	0.46
BD	Bombay Duck	25.55	167,382	1.00	12	India	0.0228

The same *nation name* and *exchange rate* pair occurs 10 times for stocks listed in the United Kingdom. Redundancy presents problems when we want to insert, delete, or update data. These problems, generally known as *update anomalies*, occur with these three basic operations.

Insert anomalies

We cannot insert a fact about a nation's exchange rate unless we first buy a stock that is listed in that nation. Consider the case where we want to keep a record of France's exchange rate and we have no French stocks. We cannot skirt this problem by putting in a null entry for stock details because `stkcode`, the primary key, would be null, and this is not allowed. If we have a separate table for facts about a nation, then we can easily add new nations without having to buy stocks. This is particularly useful when other parts of the organization, say International Trading, also need access to exchange rates.

Delete anomalies

If we delete data about a particular stock, we might also lose a fact about exchange rates. For example, if we delete details of Bombay Duck, we also erase the Indian exchange rate.

Update anomalies

Exchange rates are volatile. Many companies need to update them every day. What happens when the Australian exchange rate changes? Every row in `stock` with `nation` = `'Australia'` will have to be updated. In a large portfolio, many rows will be changed. There is also the danger of someone forgetting to update all the instances of the nation and exchange rate pair. As a result, there could be two exchange rates for the one nation. If exchange rate is stored in `nation`, however, only one change is necessary, there is no redundancy, and there is no danger of inconsistent exchange rates.

Vein-recognition security system

Fujitsu Ltd. has commercialized a biometric security system based on vein pattern recognition technology. A scanner takes a snapshot of the customer's palm using infrared light so that the veins illuminated under the skin appear as dark patterns. The snapshot data is compared to data previously stored on the customer's ATM card. Comparison takes about the same time as inserting a card and punching in a personal identification number but is more secure.

This method eliminates the current problem of ATM cards, where criminals watch the customer punching in a PIN and then steal the card and withdraw cash. This system is less secure but more convenient than iris recognition, which takes much longer. However, many people are concerned about hygiene issues with the palm scanner.

Suruga Bank and The Bank of Tokyo-Mitsubishi started using the system in 2004.

Source: Kallender, Paul. 2004. Japanese banks choose vein-recognition security system. *Computerworld*, Aug 27. www.computerworld.com/securitytopics/security/story/ 0,10801,95545,00.html.

Creating a database with a 1:m relationship

As before, each entity becomes a table in a relational database, the entity name becomes the table name, each attribute becomes a column, and each identifier becomes a primary key. The 1:m relationship is mapped by adding a column to the entity at the many end of the relationship. The additional column contains the identifier of the one end of the relationship.

Consider the relationship between the entities STOCK and NATION (see Figure 4-1). The database (see Figure 4-3) has two tables: `stock` and `nation`. The table `stock` has an additional column, `natcode`, which contains the identifier of `nation`. If `natcode` is not stored in `stock`, then there is no way of knowing the identity of the nation where the stock is listed.

nation		
natcode	natname	exchrate
UK	United Kingdom	1.00
USA	United States	0.67
AUS	Australia	0.46
IND	India	0.0228

stock						
stkcode	stkfirm	stkprice	stkqty	stkdiv	stkpe	natcode
FC	Freedonia Copper	27.50	10,529	1.84	16	UK
PT	Patagonian Tea	55.25	12,635	2.50	10	UK
AR	Abyssinian Ruby	31.82	22,010	1.32	13	UK
SLG	Sri Lankan Gold	50.37	32,868	2.68	16	UK
ILZ	Indian Lead &Zinc	37.75	6,390	3.00	12	UK
BE	Burmese Elephant	.07	154,713	0.01	3	UK
BS	Bolivian Sheep	12.75	231,678	1.78	11	UK
NG	Nigerian Geese	35.00	12,323	1.68	10	UK
CS	Canadian Sugar	52.78	4,716	2.50	15	UK
ROF	Royal Ostrich Farms	33.75	1,234,923	3.00	6	UK
MG	Minnesota Gold	53.87	816,122	1.00	25	USA
GP	Georgia Peach	2.35	387,333	.20	5	USA
NE	Narembeen Emu	12.34	45,619	1.00	8	AUS
QD	Queensland Diamond	6.73	89,251	.50	7	AUS
IR	Indooroopilly Ruby	15.92	56,147	.50	20	AUS
BD	Bombay Duck	25.55	167,382	1.00	12	IND

Figure 4-3. A relational database with tables nation and stock

Notice `natcode` appears in both the `stock` and `nation` tables. In `nation`, `natcode` is the primary key; it is unique for each instance of nation. In `stock`, `natcode` is a foreign key because it is the primary key of `nation`, the one end of the 1:m relationship. The column `natcode` is a foreign key in `stock` because it is a primary key in `nation`. A matched primary key–foreign key pair is the method for recording the 1:m relationship between the two tables. This method of representing a relationship is graphically illustrated in Figure 4-3 for the two USA stocks. In the `stock` table, `natcode` is italicized to indicate that it is a foreign key. This method, like underlining a primary key, is a useful reminder.

Although the same name has been used for the primary key and the foreign key in this example, it is not mandatory. The two columns can have different names, and in some cases you are forced to use different names. When possible, we find it convenient to use identical column names to help us remember that the tables are related.

Although a nation can have many stocks, it is not mandatory to have any. That is, in data modeling terminology, many can be zero, one, or more, but it is mandatory to have a value for `natcode` in `nation` for every value of `natcode` in `stock`. This requirement, known as the **referential integrity constraint**, maintains the accuracy of a database. Its application means that every foreign key in a table has an identical primary key in that same table or another table. In this example, it means that for every value of `natcode` in `stock`, there is a corresponding entry in `nation`. As a result, a primary key row must be created before its corresponding foreign key row. Thus, details for a `nation` must be added before any data about its listed stocks are entered.

Every foreign key must have a matching primary key (referential integrity rule), and every primary key must be non-null (entity integrity rule). Thus, a foreign key cannot be null.[3]

Why is the foreign key in the table at the "many" end of the relationship? Because each instance of `stock` is associated with exactly one instance of `nation`. The rule is that a stock must be listed in one and only one nation. Thus, the foreign key field is single-valued when it is at the "many" end of a relationship. The foreign key is not at the "one" end of the relationship because each instance of `nation` can be associated with more than one instance of `stock`, and this implies a multivalued foreign key. The relational model does not support multivalued fields because of the processing problems they can cause.

Using SQL, the two tables are defined in a similar manner to the way we created a single table in Chapter 3. Here are the SQL statements:

```
CREATE TABLE nation (
    natcode         CHAR(3),
    natname         VARCHAR(20),
    exchrate        DECIMAL(9,5),
        PRIMARY KEY(natcode));

CREATE TABLE stock (
    stkcode         CHAR(3),
    stkfirm         VARCHAR(20),
    stkprice        DECIMAL(6,2),
    stkqty          DECIMAL(8),
    stkdiv          DECIMAL(5,2),
    stkpe           DECIMAL(5),
    natcode         CHAR(3),
        PRIMARY KEY(stkcode),
        CONSTRAINT fk_has_nation FOREIGN KEY(natcode)
            REFERENCES nation(natcode) ON DELETE RESTRICT);
```

---

3.   As you will discover, this statement needs some further explanation (see page 137) because there are situations where the foreign key column can have a null value. For your present stage of skill development, this explanation is best put aside until later.

Notice that the definition of stock includes additional information to specify the foreign key and the referential integrity constraint. The CONSTRAINT clause defines the column or columns in the table being created that constitute the foreign key. A referential integrity constraint can be named, and in this case, its name is fk_has_nation.[4] The foreign key is the column natcode in stock, and it references the primary key of nation.

The ON DELETE clause specifies what processing should occur if an attempt is made to delete a row in nation with a primary key that is a foreign key in stock. In this case, the ON DELETE clause specifies that it is not permissible (the meaning of RESTRICT) to delete a primary key row in nation while a corresponding foreign key in stock exists. In other words, the system will not execute the delete. The user must first delete all corresponding rows in stock before attempting to delete the row containing the primary key. ON DELETE is the default clause for most RDBMSs, so we will dispense with specifying it for future foreign key constraints.

Observe that both the primary and foreign keys are defined as CHAR(3). The relational model requires that a primary key–foreign key pair have the same data type and are the same length. Later, you will learn that this means they must be defined on the same domain (page 232).

In MS Access, a 1:m relationship is represented in a similar manner to the method you have just learned. Instead of a crow's foot, an infinity sign (∞) is used to signify the "many" end of the relationship (see Figure 4-4). Also, note that the foreign key is shown in the "many" end. We omit the foreign key when data modeling because it can be inferred. In the case of MS Access, the foreign key is recorded because MS Access is an RDBMS, and what you see is an implementation of a database model.

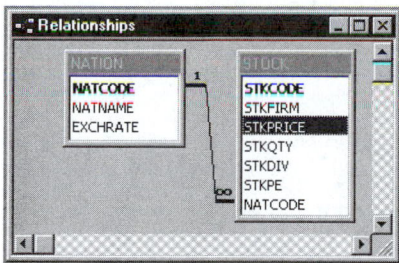

Figure 4-4. Specifying a 1:m relationship in MS Access

---

4. If a referential integrity constraint is named (fk_stock_nation in this case), then it can be turned on or off. Processing will be faster if referential integrity constraints are turned off, and this is desirable during a large database change with data that have been previously checked to ensure referential integrity is obeyed (e.g., converting from one DBMS to another).

Skill Builder

The university architect has asked you to develop a data model to record details of the campus buildings. A building can have many rooms, but a room can be in only one building. Buildings have names, and rooms have a size and purpose (e.g., lecture, laboratory, seminar). Draw a data model for this situation and create the matching relational database.

Querying a two-table database

A two-table database offers the opportunity to learn more SQL and another relational algebra operation: join.

Join

Join creates a new table from two existing tables by matching on a column common to both tables. Usually the common column is a primary key – foreign key pair: The primary key of one table is matched with the foreign key of another table. Join is frequently used to get the data for a query into a single row. Consider the tables `nation` and `stock`. If we want to calculate the value — in British pounds — of a stock, we multiply stock price by stock quantity and then exchange rate. To find the appropriate exchange rate for a stock, get its `natcode` from `stock` and then find the exchange rate in the matching row in `nation`, the one with the same value for `natcode`. For example, to calculate the value of Georgia Peach, which has `natcode = 'US'`, find the row in `nation` that also has `natcode = 'US'`. In this case, the stock's value is 2.35*387333*0.67 = £609,855.81.

Calculation of stock value is very easy once a join is used to get the three values in one row. The SQL command for joining the two tables is:

```
SELECT * FROM stock, nation
   WHERE stock.natcode = nation.natcode;
```

and the result is shown in Table 4-2.

There are several things to notice about the SQL command and the result:

❖ To avoid confusion because `natcode` is a column name in both `stock` and `nation`, it needs to be *qualified*. Qualification means that a column name is preceded by its table name, separated from it by a period (e.g., `nation.natcode`). If `natcode` is not qualified, the system will reject the query because it cannot distinguish between the two columns titled `natcode`.

❖ The new table has the `natcode` column replicated. It is called both `natcode` and `natcode1`. The naming convention for the replicated column varies with the RDBMS. In some, for example, the columns will be labeled `stock.natcode` and `nation.natcode`.

Table 4-2: The join of stock and nation

stkcode	stkfirm	stkprice	stkqty	stkdiv	stkpe	natcode	natcode1	natname	exchrate
NE	Narembeen Emu	12.34	45619	1.00	8	AUS	AUS	Australia	0.46000
IR	Indooroopilly Ruby	15.92	56147	0.50	20	AUS	AUS	Australia	0.46000
QD	Queensland Diamond	6.73	89251	0.50	7	AUS	AUS	Australia	0.46000
BD	Bombay Duck	25.55	167382	1.00	12	IND	IND	India	0.02280
ROF	Royal Ostrich Farms	33.75	1234923	3.00	6	UK	UK	United Kingdom	1.00000
CS	Canadian Sugar	52.78	4716	2.50	15	UK	UK	United Kingdom	1.00000
FC	Freedonia Copper	27.50	10529	1.84	16	UK	UK	United Kingdom	1.00000
BS	Bolivian Sheep	12.75	231678	1.78	11	UK	UK	United Kingdom	1.00000
BE	Burmese Elephant	0.07	154713	0.01	3	UK	UK	United Kingdom	1.00000
ILZ	Indian Lead & Zinc	37.75	6390	3.00	12	UK	UK	United Kingdom	1.00000
SLG	Sri Lankan Gold	50.37	32868	2.68	16	UK	UK	United Kingdom	1.00000
AR	Abyssinian Ruby	31.82	22010	1.32	13	UK	UK	United Kingdom	1.00000
PT	Patagonian Tea	55.25	12635	2.50	10	UK	UK	United Kingdom	1.00000
NG	Nigerian Geese	35.00	12323	1.68	10	UK	UK	United Kingdom	1.00000
MG	Minnesota Gold	53.87	816122	1.00	25	US	US	United States	0.67000
GP	Georgia Peach	2.35	387333	0.20	5	US	US	United States	0.67000

❖ The SQL command specifies the names of the tables to be joined, the columns to be used for matching, and the condition for the match (equality in this case).

❖ The number of columns in the new table is the sum of the columns in the two tables.

❖ The stock value calculation is now easily specified in an SQL command because all the data are in one row.

Remember that during data modeling we created two entities, STOCK and NATION, and defined the relationship between them. We showed that if the information was stored in one table, there could be updating problems. Now, with a join, we have combined these data. So why separate the data only to put them back together later? There are two reasons. *First*, we want to avoid update anomalies. *Second*, as you will discover, we do not join the same tables every time.

Join comes in several flavors. The matching condition can be =, <>, <=, <, >=, and >. This generalized version is called a *theta-join*. Generally, when people refer to a join, however, they mean an *equijoin*, when the matching condition is equality.

A join can be combined with other SQL commands.

○ **Report the value of each stockholding in UK pounds. Sort the report by nation and firm.**

```
SELECT natname, stkfirm, stkprice, stkqty, exchrate,
    stkprice*stkqty*exchrate AS stkvalue
        FROM stock,nation
            WHERE stock.natcode = nation.natcode
                ORDER BY natname, stkfirm;
```

natname	stkfirm	stkprice	stkqty	exchrate	stkvalue
Australia	Indooroopilly Ruby	15.92	56147	0.46000	411175.71
Australia	Narembeen Emu	12.34	45619	0.46000	258951.69
Australia	Queensland Diamond	6.73	89251	0.46000	276303.25
India	Bombay Duck	25.55	167382	0.02280	97506.71
United Kingdom	Abyssinian Ruby	31.82	22010	1.00000	700358.20
United Kingdom	Bolivian Sheep	12.75	231678	1.00000	2953894.50
United Kingdom	Burmese Elephant	0.07	154713	1.00000	10829.91
United Kingdom	Canadian Sugar	52.78	4716	1.00000	248910.48
United Kingdom	Freedonia Copper	27.50	10529	1.00000	289547.50
United Kingdom	Indian Lead & Zinc	37.75	6390	1.00000	241222.50
United Kingdom	Nigerian Geese	35.00	12323	1.00000	431305.00
United Kingdom	Patagonian Tea	55.25	12635	1.00000	698083.75
United Kingdom	Royal Ostrich Farms	33.75	1234923	1.00000	41678651.25
United Kingdom	Sri Lankan Gold	50.37	32868	1.00000	1655561.16
United States	Georgia Peach	2.35	387333	0.67000	609855.81
United States	Minnesota Gold	53.87	816122	0.67000	29456209.73

Control break reporting

The purpose of a join is to collect the necessary data for a report. When two tables in a 1:m relationship are joined, the report will contain repetitive data. If you re-examine the report from the join, you will see that `nation` and `exchrate` are often repeated because the same values apply to many stocks. A more appropriate format is shown in Figure 4-5, an example of a *control break report*.

Nation Firm	Exchange rate	Price	Quantity	Value
Australia	0.4600			
Indooroopilly Ruby		15.92	56,147	411,175.71
Narembeen Emu		12.34	45,619	258,951.69
Queensland Diamond		6.73	89,251	276,303.25
India	0.0228			
Bombay Duck		25.55	167,382	97,506.71
United Kingdom	1.0000			
Abyssinian Ruby		31.82	22,010	700,358.20
Bolivian Sheep		12.75	231,678	2,953,894.50
Burmese Elephant		0.07	154,713	10,829.91
Canadian Sugar		52.78	4,716	248,910.48
Freedonia Copper		27.50	10,529	289,547.50
Indian Lead & Zinc		37.75	6,390	241,222.50
Nigerian Geese		35.00	12,323	431,305.00
Patagonian Tea		55.25	12,635	698,083.75
Royal Ostrich Farms		33.75	1,234,923	41,678,651.25
Sri Lankan Gold		50.37	32,868	1,655,561.16
United States	0.6700			
Georgia Peach		2.35	387,333	609,855.81
Minnesota Gold		53.87	816,122	29,456,209.73

Figure 4-5. A control break report

A control break report recognizes that the values in a particular column or columns seldom change. In this case, `natname` and `exchrate` are often the same from one row to the next, so it makes sense to report these data only when they change. The report is also easier to read. The column `natname` is known as a *control field*. Notice that there are four groups of data, because `natname` has four different values.

Many RDBMS packages have report-writing languages to facilitate creating a control break report. These languages typically support summary reporting for each group of rows having the same value for the control field(s). A table must be sorted on the control break field(s) before the report is created.

GROUP BY—reporting by groups

The GROUP BY clause is an elementary form of control break reporting. It permits grouping of rows that have the same value for a specified column or columns, and it produces one row for each different value of the grouping column(s).

○ **Report by nation the total value of stockholdings.**

```
SELECT natname, sum(stkprice*stkqty*exchrate) AS stkvalue
    FROM stock, nation WHERE stock.natcode = nation.natcode
        GROUP BY natname;
```

natname	stkvalue
Australia	946430.65
India	97506.71
United Kingdom	48908364.25
United States	30066065.54

SQL's built-in functions (COUNT, SUM, AVERAGE, MIN, and MAX) can be used with the GROUP BY clause. They are applied to a group of rows having the same value for a specified column. You can specify more than one function in a select statement. For example, we can compute total value and number of different stocks and group by nation using:

○ **Report the number of stocks and their total value by nation.**

```
SELECT natname, COUNT(*), SUM(stkprice*stkqty*exchrate) AS stkvalue
        FROM stock, nation WHERE stock.natcode = nation.natcode
            GROUP BY natname;
```

natname	count	stkvalue
Australia	3	946430.65
India	1	97506.71
United Kingdom	10	48908364.25
United States	2	30066065.54

You can group by more than one column name; however, all column names appearing in the SELECT clause must be associated with a built-in function or be in a GROUP BY clause.

○ **List stocks by nation, and for each nation show the number of stocks for each PE ratio and the total value of those stock holdings in UK pounds.**

```
SELECT natname,stkpe,COUNT(*),
    SUM(stkprice*stkqty*exchrate) AS stkvalue
      FROM stock, nation WHERE stock.natcode = nation.natcode
        GROUP BY natname, stkpe;
```

natname	stkpe	count	stkvalue
Australia	7	1	276303.25
Australia	8	1	258951.69
Australia	20	1	411175.71
India	12	1	97506.71
United Kingdom	3	1	10829.91
United Kingdom	6	1	41678651.25
United Kingdom	10	2	1129388.75
United Kingdom	11	1	2953894.50
United Kingdom	12	1	241222.50
United Kingdom	13	1	700358.20
United Kingdom	15	1	248910.48
United Kingdom	16	2	1945108.66
United States	5	1	609855.81
United States	25	1	29456209.73

In this example, stocks are grouped by both natname and stkpe. In most cases, there is only one stock for each pair of natname and stkpe; however, there are two situations (U.K. stocks with PEs of 10 and 16) where details of multiple stocks are grouped into one report line. Examining the values in the COUNT column helps you to identify these stocks.

HAVING—the WHERE clause of groups

HAVING does in the GROUP BY what the WHERE clause does in a SELECT. It restricts the number of groups reported, whereas WHERE restricts the number of rows reported. Used with built-in functions, HAVING is always preceded by GROUP BY and is always followed by a function (SUM, AVG, MAX, MIN, or COUNT).

○ **Report the total value of stocks for nations with two or more listed stocks.**

```
SELECT natname, SUM(stkprice*stkqty*exchrate) AS stkvalue
    FROM stock, nation WHERE stock.natcode = nation.natcode
      GROUP BY natname
```

```
        HAVING COUNT(*) >= 2;
```

natname	stkvalue
Australia	946430.65
United Kingdom	48908364.25
United States	30066065.54

Skill Builder

Report by nation the total value of dividends.

Subqueries

A subquery, or nested SELECT, is a SELECT nested within another SELECT. A subquery can be used to return a list of values subsequently searched with an IN clause.

○ **Report the names of all Australian stocks.**

```
SELECT stkfirm FROM stock
   WHERE natcode IN
      (SELECT natcode FROM nation
         WHERE natname = 'Australia');
```

stkfirm
Narembeen Emu
Queensland Diamond
Indooroopilly Ruby

Conceptually, the subquery is evaluated first. It returns a list of natcodes ('AUS') so that the query then is the same as:

```
SELECT stkfirm FROM stock
   WHERE natcode IN ('AUS');
```

When discussing subqueries, sometimes a subquery is also called an *inner query*. The term *outer query* is applied to the SQL preceding the inner query. In this case, the outer and inner queries are:

Outer query	SELECT stkfirm FROM stock WHERE natcode IN
Inner query	(SELECT natcode FROM nation WHERE natname = 'Australia');

Note that in this case we do not have to qualify natcode. There is no identity crisis, because natcode in the inner query is implicitly qualified as nation.natcode and natcode in the outer query is understood to be stock.natcode.

This query also can be run as a join by writing:

```
SELECT stkfirm FROM stock, nation
   WHERE stock.natcode = nation.natcode
   AND natname = 'Australia';
```

Correlated subquery

In a correlated subquery, the subquery cannot be evaluated independently of the outer query. It depends on the outer query for the values it needs to resolve the subquery. The subquery is evaluated for each value passed to it by the outer query. An example illustrates when you might use a correlated subquery and how it operates.

○ **Find those stocks where the quantity is greater than the average for that country.**

An approach to this query is to examine the rows of stock one a time, and each time compare the quantity of stock to the average for that country. This means that for each row, the subquery must receive the outer query's country code so it can compute the average for that country.

```
SELECT natname, stkfirm, stkqty FROM stock, nation
WHERE stock.natcode = nation.natcode
AND stkqty >
   (SELECT AVG(stkqty) FROM stock
      WHERE stock.natcode = nation.natcode);
```

natname	stkfirm	stkqty
Australia	Queensland Diamond	89251
United Kingdom	Bolivian Sheep	231678
United Kingdom	Royal Ostrich Farms	1234923
United States	Minnesota Gold	816122

Conceptually, think of this query as stepping through the join of stock and nation one row at a time and executing the subquery each time. The first row has natcode = 'AUS' so the subquery becomes

```
SELECT AVG(stkqty) FROM stock
   WHERE stock.natcode = 'AUS';
```

Since the average stock quantity for Australian stocks is 63,672.33, the first row in the join, Narembeen Emu, is not reported. Neither is the second row reported, but the third is.

The term *correlated subquery* is used because the subquery's execution depends on receiving a value for a variable (`nation.natcode` in this instance) from the outer query. A correlated subquery thus cannot be evaluated once and for all. It must be evaluated repeatedly — once for each value of the variable received from the outer query. In this respect, a correlated subquery is different from a subquery, which only needs to be evaluated once. The requirement to compare each row of a table against a function (e.g., average or count) for some rows of a column is usually a clue that you need to write a corrected subquery.

Skill builder

1. Why are no Indian stocks reported in the correlated subquery example? How would you change the query to report an Indian stock?
2. Report only the three stocks with the largest quantities (i.e., do the query without using ORDER BY).

Views—virtual tables[5]

You have noticed that in these examples we repeated the join and stock value calculation for each query. Ideally, we should do this once, store the result, and be able to use it with other queries. We can do so if we create a *view*, a virtual table. A view does not physically exist as stored data; it is an imaginary table constructed from existing tables as required. You can treat a view as if it were a table and write SQL to query it. In MS Access, any saved query is a view.

A view contains selected columns from one or more tables. The selected columns can be renamed and rearranged. New columns based on arithmetic expressions can be created. GROUP BY can also be used to create a view. Remember, a view contains no actual data. It is a virtual table.

This SQL command does the join, calculates stock value, and saves the result as a view:

```
CREATE VIEW stkvalue
   (nation, firm, price, qty, exchrate, value)
   AS SELECT natname, stkfirm, stkprice, stkqty, exchrate,
      stkprice*stkqty*exchrate
         FROM stock, nation
         WHERE stock.natcode = nation.natcode;
```

There are several things to notice about creating a view:

❖ The six names enclosed by parentheses are the column names for the view.

_____

5. Support for views was added to MySQL 5.0.1.

❖ There is a one-to-one correspondence between the names in parentheses and the names or expressions in the SELECT clause. Thus the view column named value contains the result of the arithmetic expression specified in the view creation statement stkprice*stkqty*exchrate.

A view can be used in a query, such as:

○ **Find stocks with a value greater than £100,000.**

```
SELECT nation, firm, value FROM stkvalue WHERE value > 100000;
```

nation	firm	value
United Kingdom	Freedonia Copper	289547.50
United Kingdom	Patagonian Tea	698083.75
United Kingdom	Abyssinian Ruby	700358.20
United Kingdom	Sri Lankan Gold	1655561.16
United Kingdom	Indian Lead & Zinc	241222.50
United Kingdom	Bolivian Sheep	2953894.50
United Kingdom	Nigerian Geese	431305.00
United Kingdom	Canadian Sugar	248910.48
United Kingdom	Royal Ostrich Farms	41678651.25
United States	Minnesota Gold	29456209.73
United States	Georgia Peach	609855.80
Australia	Narembeen Emu	258951.69
Australia	Queensland Diamond	276303.24
Australia	Indooroopilly Ruby	411175.71

There are two main reasons for creating a view. *First,* as we have seen, query writing can be simplified. If you find that you are frequently writing the same section of code for a variety of queries, then isolate the common section and put it in a view. This means that you will usually create a view when a fact, such as stock value, is derived from other facts in the table.

The *second* reason is to restrict access to certain columns or rows. For example, the person who updates stock could be given a view that excludes stkqty. In this case, changes in stock prices could be updated without revealing confidential information, such as the value of the stock portfolio.

Skill builder

How could you use a view to solve the following query that was used when discussing the correlated subquery?

Find those stocks where the quantity is greater than the average for that country.

Summary

Entities are related to other entities by relationships. The 1:m (one-to-many) relationship occurs frequently in data models. An additional entity is required to represent a 1:m relationship to avoid update anomalies. In a relational database, a 1:m relationship is represented by an additional column, the foreign key, in the table at the many end of the relationship. The referential integrity constraint insists that a foreign key must always exist as a primary key in a table. A foreign key constraint is specified in a CREATE statement.

Join creates a new table from two existing tables by matching on a column common to both tables. Often the common column is a primary key – foreign key combination. A theta-join can have matching conditions of =, <>, <=, <, >=, and >. An equijoin describes the situation where the matching condition is equality. The GROUP BY clause is used to create an elementary control break report. The HAVING clause of GROUP BY is like the WHERE clause of SELECT. A subquery, which has a SELECT statement within another SELECT statement, causes two SELECT statements to be executed—one for the inner query and one for the outer query. A correlated subquery is executed as many times as there are rows selected by the outer query. A view is a virtual table that is created when required. Views can simplify report writing and restrict access to specified columns or rows.

Key terms and concepts

Constraint	Join
Control break reporting	One-to-many (1:m) relationship
Correlated subquery	Referential integrity
Delete anomalies	Relationship
Equijoin	Theta-join
Foreign key	Update anomalies
GROUP BY	Views
HAVING	Virtual table
Insert anomalies	

Exercises

1. Draw data models for the following situations. In each case, make certain that you show the attributes and feasible identifiers:

   a. A farmer can have many cows, but a cow belongs to only one farmer.

b. A university has many students, and a student can attend at most one university.

c. An aircraft can have many passengers, but a passenger can be on only one flight at a time.

d. A nation can have many states and a state many cities.

e. An art researcher has asked you to design a database to record details of artists and the museums in which their paintings are displayed. For each painting, the researcher wants to know the size of the canvas, year painted, title, and style. The nationality, date of birth, and death of each artist must be recorded. For each museum, record details of its location and specialty, if it has one.

2. Report all values in British pounds:

a. Report the value of stocks listed in Australia.

b. Report the dividend payment of all stocks.

c. Report the total dividend payment by nation.

d. Create a view containing nation, firm, price, quantity, exchange rate, value, and yield.

e. Report the average yield by nation.

f. Report the minimum and maximum yield for each nation.

g. Report the nations where the average yield of stocks exceeds the average yield of all stocks.

3. How would you change the queries in exercise 4-2 if you were required to report the values in American dollars, Australian dollars, or Indian rupees?

4. What is a foreign key and what role does it serve?

5. What is the referential integrity constraint? Why should it be enforced?

6. Kisha, against the advice of her friends, is simultaneously studying data management and Shakespearean drama. She thought the two subjects would be an interesting contrast. However, the classes are very demanding and often enter her midsummer dreams. Last night, she dreamed that William Shakespeare wanted her to draw a data model. He explained, before she woke up in a cold sweat, that a play had many characters but the same character never appeared in more than one play. "Methinks," he said, "the same name may have appeareth more than the once, but 'twas always a person of a different ilk." He then, she hazily recollects, went on to spout about the quality of data dropping like the gentle rain.

Draw a data model to keep old Bill quiet and help Kisha get some sleep.

7. An orchestra has four broad classes of instruments (strings, woodwinds, brass, and percussion). Each class contains musicians who play different instruments. For example, the strings section of a full symphonic orchestra contains 2 harps, 16 to 18 first violins, 14 to 16 second violins, 12 violas, 10 cellos, and 8 double basses. A city has asked you to develop a database to store details of the musicians in its three orchestras. All the musicians are specialists and play only one instrument for one orchestra.

8. Answer the following queries based on the following database for a car dealer:

a. What is the personid of Sheila O'Hara?

b. List sales personnel sorted by last name and within last name, first name.

c. List details of the sales made by Bruce Bush.

d. List details of all sales showing the gross profit (selling price minus cost price).

e. Report the number of cars sold of each type.
f. What is the average selling price of cars sold by Sue Lim?
g. Report details of all sales where the gross profit is less than the average.
h. What was the maximum selling price of any car?
i. What is the total gross profit?
j. Report the gross profit made by each salesperson who sold at least three cars.
k. Create a view containing all the details in the `car` table and the gross profit.

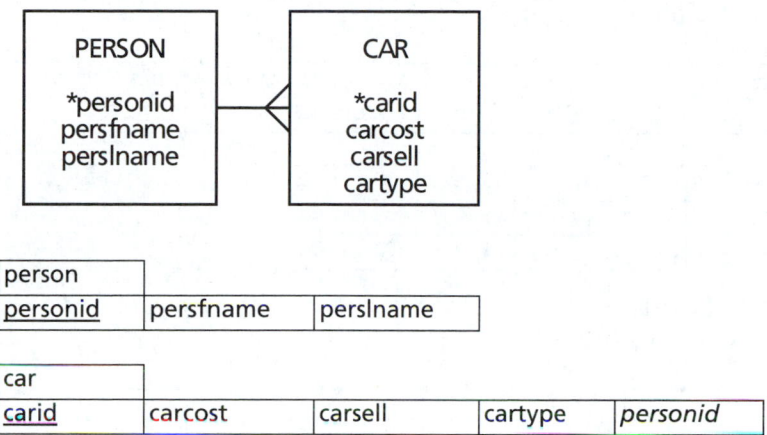

person		
personid	persfname	perslname

car				
carid	carcost	carsell	cartype	personid

9. Find the number of different PE ratios in `stock` using a virtual table (a stored query in MS Access). (See page 76 for the original discussion of this query.)

CD library case

Ajay soon realized that a CD contains far more data that just a list of track titles and their length. Now that he had learned about the 1:m relationship, he was ready to add some more detail. He recognized that a CD contains many tracks, and a label (e.g., Atlantic) releases many CDs. He revised his data model to include these additional entities (CD and LABEL) and their relationships (see Figure 4-6).

Giant Steps and *Swing* are both on the Atlantic label; the data are

The `cd` data, where *lbltitle* is the foreign key, are

The `track` data, where *cdid* is the foreign key, are

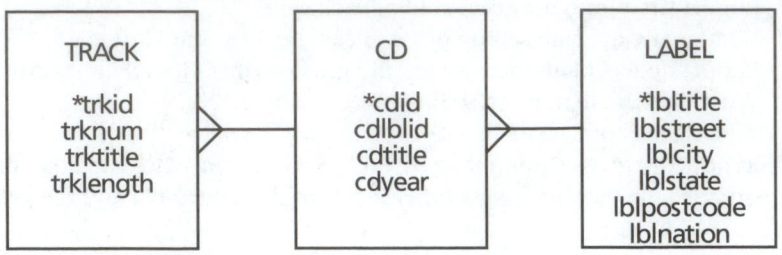

Figure 4-6. CD library V2.0

lbltitle	lblstreet	lblcity	lblstate	lblpostcode	lblnation
Atlantic	75 Rockefeller Plaza	New York	NY	10019	USA

cdid	cdlblid	cdtitle	cdyear	lbltitle
1	A2 1311	Giant Steps	1960	Atlantic
2	83012-2	Swing	1977	Atlantic

trkid	trknum	trktitle	trklength	cdid
1	1	Giant Steps	4.72	1
2	2	Cousin Mary	5.75	1
3	3	Countdown	2.35	1
4	4	Spiral	5.93	1
5	5	Syeeda's Song Flute	7.00	1
6	6	Naima	4.35	1
7	7	Mr. P.C.	6.95	1
8	8	Giant Steps	3.67	1
9	9	Naima	4.45	1
10	10	Cousin Mary	5.90	1
11	11	Countdown	4.55	1
12	12	Syeeda's Song Flute	7.03	1
13	1	Stomp of King Porter	3.20	2
14	2	Sing a Study in Brown	2.85	2
15	3	Sing Moten's Swing	3.60	2
16	4	A-tisket, A-tasket	2.95	2
17	5	I Know Why	3.57	2
18	6	Sing You Sinners	2.75	2
19	7	Java Jive	2.85	2
20	8	Down South Camp Meetin'	3.25	2
21	9	Topsy	3.23	2
22	10	Clouds	7.20	2
23	11	Skyliner	3.18	2
24	12	It's Good Enough to Keep	3.18	2
25	13	Choo Choo Ch' Boogie	3.00	2

Skill builder

1. Create tables to store the label and CD data. Add a column to `track` to store the foreign key.[6] Then, either enter the new data or download it from the web site. Define `lbltitle` as a foreign key in `cd` and `cdid` as a foreign key in `track`.

Ajay ran a few queries on his revised database.

○ **What are the tracks on *Swing*?**

This query requires joining `track` and `cd` because the name of a CD (*Swing* in this case) is stored in `cd` and track data are stored in `track`. The foreign key of `track` is matched to the primary key of `cd` (i.e., `track.cdid = cd.cdid`).

```
SELECT trknum, trktitle, trklength FROM track, cd
   WHERE track.cdid = cd.cdid
   AND cdtitle = 'Swing';
```

trknum	trktitle	trklength
1	Stomp of King Porter	3.20
2	Sing a Study in Brown	2.85
3	Sing Moten's Swing	3.60
4	A-tisket, A-tasket	2.95
5	I Know Why	3.57
6	Sing You Sinners	2.75
7	Java Jive	2.85
8	Down South Camp Meetin'	3.25
9	Topsy	3.23
10	Clouds	7.20
11	Skyliner	3.18
12	It's Good Enough to Keep	3.18
13	Choo Choo Ch' Boogie	3.00

○ **What is the longest track on *Swing*?**

Like the prior query, this one requires joining `track` and `cd`. The inner query isolates the tracks on *Swing* and then selects the longest of these using the MAX function. The outer query also isolates the tracks on *Swing* and selects the track equal to the maximum length. The outer query must restrict attention to tracks on *Swing* in case there are other tracks in the `track` table with a time equal to the value returned by the inner query.

---

6. Adding a column is easy in MS Access. With other systems you might have to use ALTER TABLE (see page 259).

```
SELECT trknum, trktitle, trklength FROM track, cd
   WHERE track.cdid = cd.cdid
   AND cdtitle = 'Swing'
   AND trklength =
      (SELECT MAX(trklength) FROM track, cd
          WHERE track.cdid = cd.cdid
          AND cdtitle = 'Swing');
```

trknum	trktitle	trklength
10	Clouds	7.20

O **What are the titles of CDs containing some tracks less than 3 minutes long and on U.S.-based labels? List details of these tracks as well.**

This is a three-table join since resolution of the query requires data from cd (cdtitle), track (trktitle), and LABEL (lblnation).

```
SELECT cdtitle, trktitle, trklength FROM track, cd, label
   WHERE track.cdid = cd.cdid
   AND cd.lbltitle = label.lbltitle
   AND trklength < 3
   AND lblnation = 'USA';
```

cdtitle	trktitle	trklength
Giant Steps	Countdown	2.35
Swing	Sing a Study in Brown	2.85
Swing	A-tisket, A-tasket	2.95
Swing	Sing You Sinners	2.75
Swing	Java Jive	2.85

O **Report the number of tracks on each CD.**

This query requires GROUP BY because the number of tracks on each CD is totaled by using the aggregate function COUNT.

```
SELECT cdtitle, COUNT(*) AS tracks FROM track, cd
   WHERE track.cdid = cd.cdid
      GROUP BY cdtitle;
```

cdtitle	tracks
Giant Steps	12
Swing	13

○ **Report, in ascending order, the total length of tracks on each CD.**

This is another example of GROUP BY. In this case, SUM is used to accumulate track length, and ORDER BY is used for sorting in ascending order, the default sort order.

```
SELECT cdtitle, SUM(trklength) AS sumtrklen FROM track, cd
   WHERE track.cdid = cd.cdid
      GROUP BY cdtitle
      ORDER BY SUM(trklength);
```

cdtitle	sumtrklen
Swing	44.81
Giant Steps	62.65

○ **Does either CD have more than 60 minutes of music?**

This query uses the HAVING clause to limit the CDs reported based on their total length.

```
SELECT cdtitle, SUM(trklength) AS sumtrklen FROM track, cd
   WHERE track.cdid = cd.cdid
      GROUP BY cdtitle HAVING SUM(trklength) > 60;
```

cdtitle	sumtrklen
Giant Steps	62.65

Skill builder

1. Write SQL for the following queries:
   a. List the tracks by CD in order of track length.
   b. What is the longest track on each CD?
2. What is wrong with the current data model?
3. Could *cdlblid* be used as an identifier for CD?

5

The Many-to-Many Relationship

Learning objectives

Students completing this chapter will be able to

❖ model a many-to-many relationship between two entities;
❖ define a database with a many-to-many relationship;
❖ write queries for a database with a many-to-many relationship.

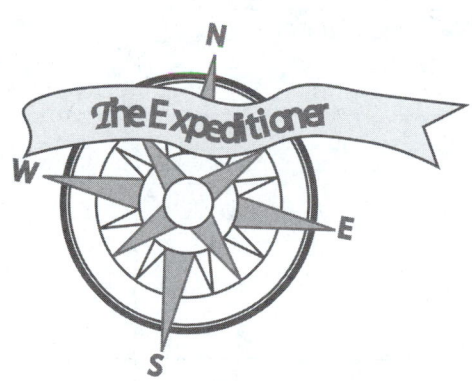

Alice was deeply involved in uncovering the workings of her firm. She spent hours talking to the staff, wanting to know everything about the products sold. She engaged many a customer in conversation to find out why they shopped at The Expeditioner, what they were looking for, and how they thought the business could be improved. She examined all the products herself and pestered the staff to tell her who bought them, how they were used, how many were sold, who supplied them, and a host of other questions. She plowed (or should that be "ploughed") through accounting journals, sales reports, and market forecasts. She was more than a new broom; she was a giant vacuum cleaner sucking up data about the firm so that she would be prepared to manage it successfully.

Ned, the marketing manager, was a Jekyll and Hyde character. By day he was a charming, savvy, marketing executive. Walking to work in his three-piece suit, bowler hat, and furled umbrella, he was the epitome of the conservative English businessman. By night he became a computer nerd with ragged jeans, a T-shirt, black-framed glasses, and unruly hair. Ned had been desperate to introduce computers to The Expeditioner for years, but he knew that he could never reveal his second nature. The other staff at The Expeditioner just would not accept such a radical change in technology. Why, they had not even switched to fountain pens until their personal stock of quill pens was finally depleted. Ned was just not prepared to face the indignant silence and contempt that would greet his mere mention of computers. It was better to continue a secret double life than admit to being a cyber punk.

But times were changing, and Ned saw the opportunity. He furtively suggested to Lady Alice that perhaps she needed a database of sales facts. Her response was instantaneous: "Yes, and do it as soon as possible." Ned was ecstatic. This was truly a wonderful woman.

The many-to-many relationship

Consider the case when items are sold. We can immediately identify two entities: SALE and ITEM. A sale can consist of many items, and an item can appear in many sales. We are not saying the same item can be sold many times, but the particular type of item (e.g., a compass) can be sold many times; thus we have a many-to-many (m:m) relationship between SALE and ITEM. When we get an m:m relationship, we create a third entity to link the entities through two 1:m relationships. Usually, it is fairly easy to name this third entity. In this case, this third entity, typically known as an **associative entity**, is called LINE ITEM. A typical sales form (see Figure 5-1 for an example) lists the items purchased by a customer. Each of the lines appearing on the order form is generally known in retailing as a line item, which links an item and a sale.

The Expeditioner					
Sale of Goods					
Sale# 123456			Date:		
	Item#	Description	Quantity	Unit price	Total
1					
2					
3					
4					
5					
6					
Grand Total					

Figure 5-1. A sales form

The representation of this m:m relationship is shown in Figure 5-2. We say many-to-many because there are two relationships — ITEM is related to many SALEs, and SALE is related to many ITEMs. This data model can also be read as: "a sale has many line items, but a line item refers to only one sale. Similarly, an item can appear as many line items, but a line item references only one item."

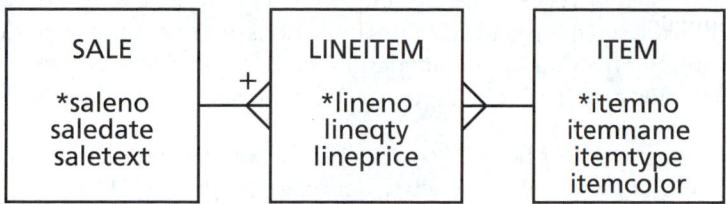

Figure 5-2. An m:m relationship

The entity SALE is identified by *saleno* and has the attributes *saledate* and *saletext* (a brief comment on the customer — soft information[1]). LINEITEM is partially identified by *lineno* and has attributes *lineqty* (the number of units sold) and *lineprice* (the unit selling price for this sale). ITEM is identified by *itemno* and has attributes *itemname*, *itemtype* (e.g., clothing, equipment, navigation aids, furniture, and so on), and *itemcolor*.

If you look carefully at Figure 5-2, you will notice that there is a plus sign (+) above the crow's foot at the "many" end of the 1:m relationship between SALE and LINEITEM. This plus sign provides information about the identifier of LINEITEM. As you know, every entity must have a unique identifier. A sales order (see Figure 5-1) is a series of lines, and *lineno* is unique only within a particular order. If we just use *lineno* as the identifier, we cannot guarantee that every instance of LINEITEM is unique. If we use *saleno* and *lineno* together, however, we have a unique identifier for every instance of LINEITEM. *Saleno* is unique for every sale, and *lineno* is unique within any sale. The plus indicates that LINEITEM's unique identifier is the concatenation of *saleno* and *lineno*.

LINEITEM is termed a **weak entity**[2] (see page 179) because it relies on another entity for its existence and identification.

Why did we create a third entity?

When we have an m:m relationship, we create an associative entity to store data about the relationship. In this case, we have to store data about the items sold. We cannot store the data with SALE because a sale can be many items, and an entity stores only single-value facts. Similarly, we cannot store data with ITEM because an item can appear in many sales. Since we cannot store data in SALE or ITEM, we must create another entity to store data about the m:m relationship.

---

1. Remember, we discussed information hardness on page 35.
2. Sometimes called a dependent entity.

You might find it useful to think of the m:m relationship as two 1:m relationships. An item can appear on many line item listings, and a line item entry refers to only one item. A sale has many line items, and each line item entry refers to only one sale.

Social Security number is not unique!

Two girls named Sarah Lee Ferguson were born on May 3, 1959. The U.S. government considered them one and the same and issued both the same Social Security number (SSN), a nine-digit identifier of U.S. residents. Now Sarah Lee Ferguson Boles and Sarah Lee Ferguson Johnson share the same SSN.

Mrs. Boles became aware of her SSN twin in 1987 when the Internal Revenue Service claimed there was a discrepancy in her reported income. Because SSN is widely used as an attribute or identifier in many computer systems, Mrs. Boles encountered other incidents of mistaken identity. Some of Mrs. Johnson's purchases appeared on Mrs. Boles' credit reports.

In late 1989, the Social Security Administration notified Mrs. Boles that her original number was given to her in error and she had to provide evidence of her age, identity, and citizenship to get a new number. When Mrs. Boles got her new SSN, it is likely she had to also get a new driver's license and establish a new credit history.

Adapted from: "Two women share a name, birthday, and S.S. number!" *Athens [Georgia] Daily News*, January 29 1990, 7A.

Creating a relational database with an m:m relationship

As before, each entity becomes a table in a relational database, the entity name becomes the table name, each attribute becomes a column, and each identifier becomes a primary key. Remember, a 1:m relationship is mapped by adding a column to the entity of the many end of the relationship. The new column contains the identifier of the one end of the relationship.

Conversion of the foregoing data model results in the three tables shown in Table 5-1. Note the one-to-one correspondence between attributes and columns for `sale` and `item`. Observe the `lineitem` has two additional columns, `saleno` and `itemno`. Both of these columns are foreign keys in `lineitem` (remember the use of italics to signify foreign keys). Two foreign keys are required to record the two 1:m relationships. Notice in `lineitem` that `saleno` is both part of the primary key and a foreign key.

The SQL commands to create the three tables are as follows:

```
CREATE TABLE sale (
   saleno        INTEGER,
   saledate      DATE,
   saletext      VARCHAR(50),
      PRIMARY KEY(saleno));

CREATE TABLE item (
   itemno        INTEGER,
   itemname      VARCHAR(30),
   itemtype      CHAR(1),
   itemcolor     VARCHAR(10),
      PRIMARY KEY(itemno));

CREATE TABLE lineitem (
   lineno        INTEGER,
   lineqty       INTEGER,
   lineprice     DECIMAL(7,2),
   saleno        INTEGER,
   itemno        INTEGER,
      PRIMARY KEY(lineno,saleno),
      CONSTRAINT fk_has_sale FOREIGN KEY(saleno)
         REFERENCES sale(saleno),
      CONSTRAINT fk_has_item_item FOREIGN KEY(itemno)
         REFERENCES item(itemno));
```

Although the `sale` and `item` tables are created in a similar fashion to previous examples, there are two things to note about the definition of `lineitem`. *First,* the primary key is a composite of `lineno` and `saleno`, because together they uniquely identify an instance of `lineitem`. *Second,* there are two foreign keys, because `lineno` is at the "many" end of two 1:m relationships.

Table 5-1: Tables sale, lineitem, and item

sale		
saleno	saledate	saletext
1	2003-01-15	Scruffy Australian—called himself Bruce.
2	2003-01-15	Man. Rather fond of hats.
3	2003-01-15	Woman. Planning to row Atlantic—lengthwise!
4	2003-01-15	Man. Trip to New York—thinks NY is a jungle!
5	2003-01-16	Expedition leader for African safari.

lineitem

lineno	lineqty	lineprice	*saleno*	*itemno*
1	1	4.50	1	2
1	1	25.00	2	6
2	1	20.00	2	16
3	1	25.00	2	19
4	1	2.25	2	2
1	1	500.00	3	4
2	1	2.25	3	2
1	1	500.00	4	4
2	1	65.00	4	9
3	1	60.00	4	13
4	1	75.00	4	14
5	1	10.00	4	3
6	1	2.25	4	2
1	50	36.00	5	10
2	50	40.50	5	11
3	8	153.00	5	12
4	1	60.00	5	13
5	1	0.00	5	2

item

itemno	itemname	itemtype	itemcolor
1	Pocket knife—Nile	E	Brown
2	Pocket knife—Avon	E	Brown
3	Compass	N	—
4	Geopositioning system	N	—
5	Map measure	N	—
6	Hat—Polar Explorer	C	Red
7	Hat—Polar Explorer	C	White
8	Boots—snake proof	C	Green
9	Boots—snake proof	C	Black
10	Safari chair	F	Khaki
11	Hammock	F	Khaki
12	Tent—8 person	F	Khaki
13	Tent—2 person	F	Khaki
14	Safari cooking kit	E	—
15	Pith helmet	C	Khaki
16	Pith helmet	C	White
17	Map case	N	Brown
18	Sextant	N	—
19	Stetson	C	Black
20	Stetson	C	Brown

Skill builder

A hamburger shop makes several types of hamburgers, and the same type of ingredient can be used with several types of hamburgers. This does not literally mean the same piece of lettuce is used many times, but lettuce is used with several types of hamburgers. Draw the data model for this situation. What is a good name for the associative entity?

Querying an m:m relationship

A three-table join

The join operation can be easily extended from two tables to three or more merely by specifying the tables to be joined and the matching conditions. For example:

```
SELECT * FROM sale, lineitem, item
   WHERE sale.saleno = lineitem.saleno
   AND item.itemno = lineitem.itemno;
```

The three tables to be joined are listed after the FROM clause. There are two matching conditions: one for sale and lineitem (sales.saleno = lineitem.saleno) and one for the item and lineitem tables (item.itemno = lineitem.itemno). The table lineitem is the link between sale and item and must be referenced in both matching conditions.

You can tailor the join to be more precise and report some columns rather than all.

○ **List the name, quantity, price, and value of items sold on January 16, 2003.**

```
SELECT itemname, lineqty, lineprice, lineqty*lineprice AS total
   FROM sale, lineitem, item
      WHERE lineitem.saleno = sale.saleno
      AND item.itemno = lineitem.itemno
      AND saledate = '2003-01-16';
```

itemname	lineqty	lineprice	total
Pocket knife—Avon	1	0.00	0.00
Safari chair	50	36.00	1800.00
Hammock	50	40.50	2025.00
Tent—8 person	8	153.00	1224.00
Tent—2 person	1	60.00	60.00

EXISTS—does a value exist

EXISTS is used in a WHERE clause to test whether a table contains at least one row satisfying a specified condition. It returns the value *true* if and only if some row satisfies the condition; otherwise it returns *false*. EXISTS represents the **existential quantifier** of formal logic. The best way to get a feel for EXISTS is to examine a query.

⭕ **Report all clothing items (type "C") for which a sale is recorded.**

```
SELECT itemname, itemcolor FROM item
    WHERE itemtype = 'C'
    AND EXISTS (SELECT * FROM lineitem
        WHERE lineitem.itemno = item.itemno);
```

itemname	itemcolor
Hat—Polar Explorer	Red
Boots—snake proof	Black
Pith helmet	White
Stetson	Black

Conceptually, we can think of this query as evaluating the subquery for each row of item. The first item with itemtype = 'C', Hat—Polar Explorer (red), in item has itemno = 6. Thus, the query becomes

```
SELECT itemname, itemcolor FROM item
    WHERE itemtype = 'C'
    AND EXISTS (SELECT * FROM lineitem
        WHERE lineitem.itemno = 6);
```

Because there is at least one row in lineitem with itemno = 6, the subquery returns *true*. The item has been sold and should be reported. The second clothing item, Hat—Polar Explorer (white), in item has itemno = 7. There are no rows in lineitem with itemno = 7, so the subquery returns *false*. That item has not been sold and should not be reported.

You can also think of the query as, "Select clothing items for which a sale exists." Remember, for EXISTS to return *true*, there needs to be only one row for which the condition is *true*.

■ ■

Skill builder

Report all red items that have been sold. Write the query twice, once using EXISTS and once without EXISTS.

■ ■

NOT EXISTS—select a value if it does not exist

NOT EXISTS is the negative of EXISTS. It is used in a WHERE clause to test whether all rows in a table fail to satisfy a specified condition. It returns the value *true* if there are no rows satisfying the condition; otherwise it returns *false*.

○ **Report all clothing items that have not been sold.**

```
SELECT itemname, itemcolor FROM item
   WHERE itemtype = 'C'
    AND NOT EXISTS
       (SELECT * FROM lineitem
           WHERE item.itemno = lineitem.itemno);
```

If we consider this query as the opposite of that used to illustrate EXISTS, it seems logical to use NOT EXISTS. Conceptually, we can also think of this query as evaluating the sub-query for each row of item. The first item with itemtype = 'C', Hat−Polar Explorer (red), in item has itemno = 6. Thus, the query becomes

```
SELECT itemname, itemcolor FROM item
   WHERE itemtype = 'C'
       AND NOT EXISTS
           (SELECT * FROM lineitem
               WHERE lineitem.itemno = 6);
```

There is at least one row in lineitem with itemno = 6, so the subquery returns *true*. The NOT before EXISTS then negates the *true* to give *false*; the item will not be reported because it has been sold.

The second item with itemtype = 'C', Hat−Polar Explorer (white), in item has itemno = 7. The query becomes

```
SELECT itemname, itemcolor FROM item
   WHERE itemtype = 'C'
   AND NOT EXISTS
       (SELECT * FROM lineitem
           WHERE lineitem.itemno = 7);
```

Because there are no rows in lineitem with itemno = 7, the subquery returns *false*, and this is negated by the NOT before EXISTS to give *true*. The item has not been sold and should be reported.

itemname	itemcolor
Hat−Polar Explorer	White
Boots−snake proof	Green
Pith helmet	Khaki
Stetson	Brown

You can also think of the query as, "Select clothing items for which no sales exist." Also remember, for NOT EXISTS to return *true*, no rows should satisfy the condition.

Skill builder

Report all red items that have not been sold. Write the query twice, once using EXISTS and once without EXISTS.

Divide (and be conquered)

In addition to the existential quantifier that you have already encountered, formal logic has a **universal quantifier** known as *forall* that is necessary for queries such as

○   **Find the items that have appeared in all sales.**

If a universal qualifier were supported by SQL, this query could be phrased as, "Select item names where *forall* sales there *exists* a lineitem row recording that this item was sold." A quick inspection of Table 5-1 shows that one item satisfies this condition (itemno = 2).

While SQL does not directly support the universal qualifier, formal logic shows that *forall* can be expressed using EXISTS. The query becomes, "Find items such that there does not exist a sale in which this item does not appear." The equivalent SQL expression is

```
SELECT itemno, itemname FROM item
   WHERE NOT EXISTS
      (SELECT * FROM sale
         WHERE NOT EXISTS
            (SELECT * FROM lineitem
                WHERE lineitem.itemno = item.itemno
                AND lineitem.saleno = sale.saleno));
```

```
itemno itemname
     2 Pocket knife-Avon
```

If you are interested in learning the inner workings of the preceding SQL for divide, see the additional material for Chapter 5 on the book's Web site.

Relational algebra (Chapter 9) has the divide operation, which makes divide queries easy to write. Be careful: Not all queries containing the *all* are divides. With experience, you will learn to recognize and conquer divide.

To save the tedium of formulating this query from scratch, we have developed a template (see Figure 5-3) for dealing with these sorts of queries. Divide queries typically occur with m:m relationships.

An appropriate generic query and template SQL command are

Figure 5-3. A template for divide

○ **Find the target1 that have appeared in all sources.**

```
SELECT target1 FROM target
   WHERE NOT EXISTS
      (SELECT * FROM source
          WHERE NOT EXISTS
             (SELECT * FROM target-source
                 WHERE target-source.target# = target.target#
                 AND target-source.source# = source.source#));
```

Skill builder

Find the brown items that have appeared in all sales.

Beyond the great divide[3]

Divide proves troublesome to most people because of the double negative—we just don't think that way. If divide sends your neurons into knots, then try the following approach.

The query, "Find the items that have appeared in all sales" can be rephrased as "Find all the items for which the number of sales that include this item is equal to the total number of sales." This is an easier query to write than "Find items such that there does not exist a sale in which this item does not appear." The rephrased query has two parts. *First,* determine the total number of sales. Here we mean distinct sales (i.e., the number of rows with a distinct value for saleno). The SQL is

```
SELECT COUNT(DISTINCT saleno) FROM sale;
```

Second, group the items sold by itemno and itemname and use a HAVING clause with COUNT to calculate the number of sales in which the item has occurred. Forcing the count in the HAVING clause to equal the result of the first query, which becomes an inner query, results in a list of items appearing in all sales.

---

3. Thanks to Dr. Gert Jan Hofstede of Wageningen University, The Netherlands, for pointing out this approach.

```
SELECT item.itemno, item.itemname
   FROM item, lineitem
      WHERE item.itemno = lineitem.itemno
         GROUP BY item.itemno, item.itemname
            HAVING COUNT(DISTINCT saleno)
               = (SELECT COUNT(DISTINCT saleno) FROM sale);
```

Set operations

Set operators are useful for combining the values derived from two or more SQL queries. The UNION operation is equivalent to *or*, and INTERSECT is equivalent to *and*.

○ **List items that were sold on January 16, 2003, or are brown.**

Resolution of this query requires two tables: one to report items sold on January 16, 2003, and one to report the brown items. UNION (i.e., or) then combines the results of the tables, including *any* rows in both tables and excluding duplicate rows.

```
SELECT itemname FROM item, lineitem, sale
   WHERE item.itemno = lineitem.itemno
   AND lineitem.saleno = sale.saleno
   AND saledate = '2003-01-16'
UNION
   SELECT itemname FROM item WHERE itemcolor = 'Brown';
```

itemname
Hammock
Map case
Pocket knife—Avon
Pocket knife—Nile
Safari chair
Stetson
Tent—2 person
Tent—8 person

○ **List items that were sold on January 16, 2003, and are brown.**

This query uses the same two tables as the previous query. In this case, INTERSECT (i.e., and) then combines the results of the tables including *only* rows in both tables and excluding duplicates.

```
SELECT itemname FROM item, lineitem, sale
   WHERE item.itemno = lineitem.itemno
   AND lineitem.saleno = sale.saleno
   AND saledate = '2003-01-16'
INTERSECT
   SELECT itemname FROM item WHERE itemcolor = 'Brown';
```

```
itemname
Pocket knife—Avon
```

- -

Skill builder

List the items that contain the words "Hat", "Helmet", or "Stetson" in their names. Write the query twice, once using `IN` and once using `UNION`.

- -

Summary

There can be a many-to-many (m:m) relationship between entities, which is represented by creating an associative entity and two 1:m relationships. An associative entity stores data about an m:m relationship. The join operation can be extended from two tables to three or more tables. `EXISTS` tests whether a table has at least one row that meets a specified condition. `NOT EXISTS` tests whether all rows in a table do not satisfy a specified condition. Both `EXISTS` and `NOT EXISTS` return *true* or *false*. The relational operation divide, also known as *forall*, can be translated into a double negative. It is represented in SQL by a query containing two `NOT EXISTS` statements. Set operations enable the results of queries to be combined.

Key terms and concepts

Associative entity	Many-to-many (m:m) relationship
Divide	`NOT EXISTS`
Existential quantifier	`UNION`
`EXISTS`	Universal quantifier
`INTERSECT`	

Exercises

1. Draw data models for the following situations. In each case, think about the names you give each entity:
   a. Farmers can own cows or share cows with other farmers.
   b. A track and field meet can have many competitors, and a competitor can participate in more than one event.
   c. A patient can have many physicians, and a physician can have many patients.
   d. A student can attend more than one class, and the same class can have many students.
   e. *The Marathoner*, a monthly magazine, regularly reports the performance of professional marathon runners. It has asked you to design a database to record the details of all major marathons (e.g., Boston, London, and Paris). Professional marathon runners compete in several races each year. A race may have thousands of competitors, but only about 200 or so are professional runners, the ones *The Marathoner* tracks. For each race, the magazine reports a runner's

time and finishing position and some personal details such as name, gender, and age.

2. The data model shown was designed by a golf statistician. Write SQL statements to create the corresponding relational database.

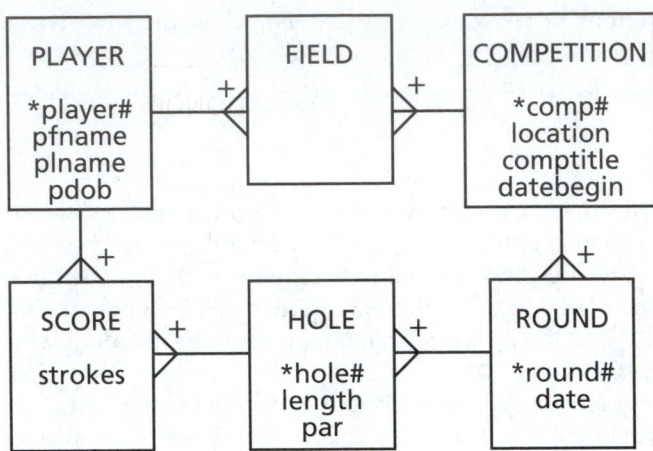

3. Write the following SQL queries for the database described in this chapter:
    a. List the names of items for which the quantity sold is greater than one for any sale.
    b. Compute the total value of sales for each item by date.
    c. Report all items of type "F" that have been sold.
    d. List all items of type "F" that have not been sold.
    e. Compute the total value of each sale.
4. Write SQL statements to create a relational database described by the following data model.

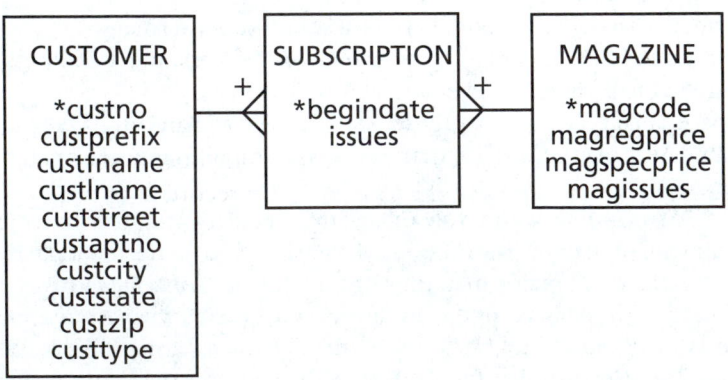

5. Why do you have to create a third entity when you have an m:m relationship?
6. What does a plus sign near a relationship arc mean?
7. How does EXISTS differ from other clauses in an SQL statement?
8. How is the relational algebra divide statement implemented in SQL? What do you think of this approach?
9. Answer the following queries based on the described relational database.

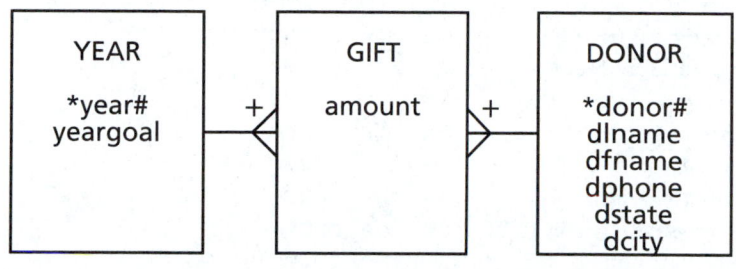

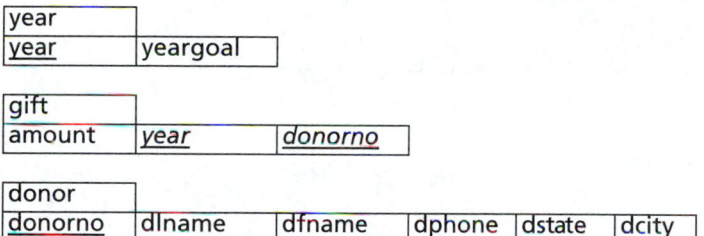

   a. List the phone numbers of donors 106 and 125.
   b. How many donors are there in the donor table?
   c. How many people made donations in 1999?
   d. What is the name of the person who made the largest donation in 1999?
   e. What was the total amount donated in 2000?
   f. List the donors who have made a donation every year.
   g. List the donors who give twice the average.
   h. List the total amount given by each person across all years; sort the report by the donor's name.
   i. Report the total donations in 2001 by state.
   j. In which years did the total donated exceed the goal for the year?

10. The following table records data found on the side of a breakfast cereal carton. Use these data as a guide to develop a data model to record nutrition facts for a meal. In this case, a meal is a cup of cereal and 1/2 cup of skim milk.

Nutrition facts		
Serving size 1 cup (30g)		
Servings per container about 17		
Amount per serving	Cereal	with 1/2 cup of skim milk
Calories	110	150
Calories from Fat	10	10
Total Fat 1g	1%	2%
Saturated Fat 0g	0%	0%
Polyunsaturated Fat 0g		
Monounsaturated Fat 0g		
Cholesterol 0mg	0%	1%
Sodium 220mg	9%	12%
Potassium 105 mg	3%	9%
Total Carbohydrate 24g	8%	10%
Dietary Fiber 3g	13%	13%
Sugars 4g		
Other Carbohydrate 17g		
Protein 3g		
Vitamin A	10%	15%
Vitamin C	10%	10%
Calcium	2%	15%
Iron	45%	45%
Vitamin D	10%	25%
Thiamin	50%	50%
Riboflavin	50%	50%
Niacin	50%	50%
Vitamin B12	50%	60%
Phosphorus	10%	20%
Magnesium	8%	10%
Zinc	50%	50%
Copper	4%	4%

CD library case

After learning how to model m:m relationships, Ajay realized he could now model a number of situations that had bothered him. He had been puzzling over some relationships that he had recognized but was unsure how to model:

❖ A person can appear on many tracks, and a track can have many persons (e.g., The Manhattan Transfer, a quartet, has recorded many tracks).

❖ A person can compose many songs, and a song can have multiple composers (e.g., Rodgers and Hammerstein collaborated many times with Rodgers composing the music and Hammerstein writing the lyrics).

❖ An artist can release many CDs, and a CD can feature several artists (e.g., John Coltrane, who has many CDs, has a CD, *Miles & Coltrane,* with Miles Davis).

Ajay revised his data model to include the m:m relationships he had recognized. He wrestled with what to call the entity that stored details of people. Sometimes these people are musicians; other times singers, composers, and so forth. He decided that the most general approach was to call the entity PERSON. The extended data model is shown in Figure 5-4.

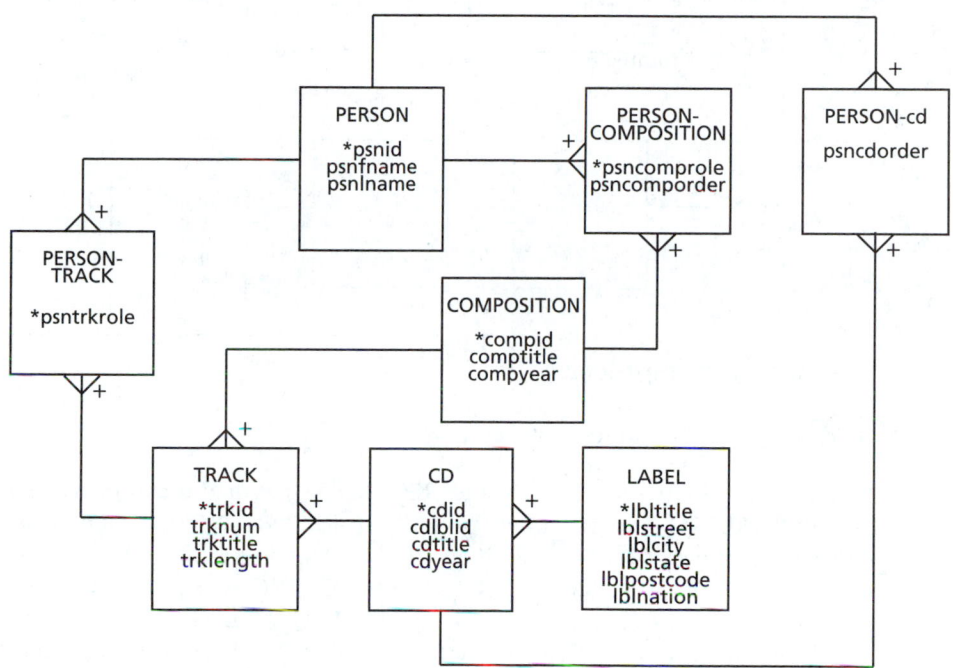

Figure 5-4. CD library V3.0

In version 3.0, Ajay introduced several new entities, including COMPOSITION to record details of a composition. He initially linked COMPOSITION to TRACK with a 1:m relationship. In other words, a composition can have many tracks, but a track is of one composition. This did not seem right.

After further thought, he realized there was a missing entity—RECORDING. A composition has many recordings (e.g., multiple recordings of John Coltrane's composition "Giant Steps"), and a recording can appear as a track on different CDs (typically those whose title begins with *The Best of* ... feature tracks on earlier CDs). Also, because a recording is a performance of a composition, it is a composition that has a title, not recording or track. So, he revised version 3.0 of the data model to produce version 4.0 (see Figure 5-5).

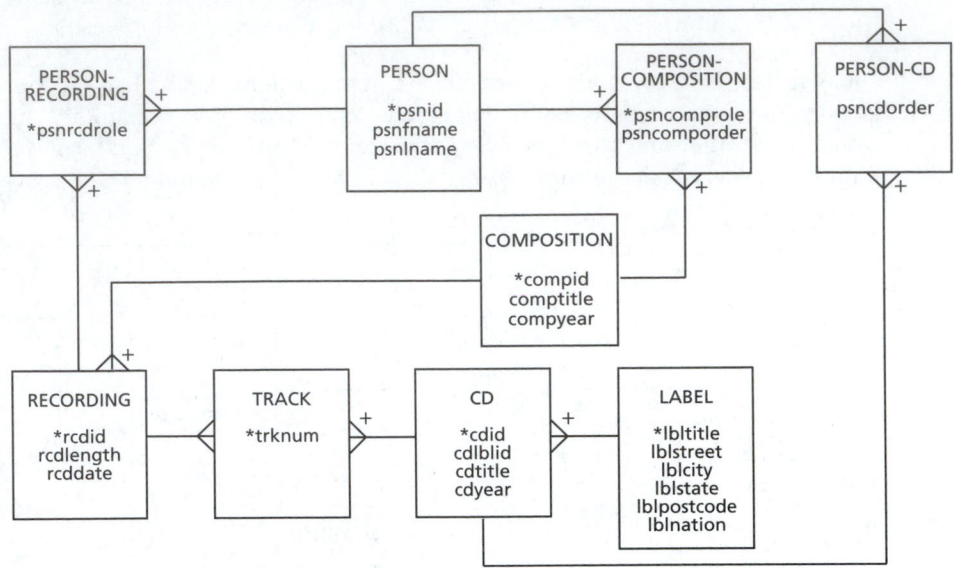

Figure 5-5. CD library V4.0

Version 4.0 of the model captures:

❖ the m:m between PERSON and RECORDING with the associative entity PERSON-RECORDING. The identifier for PERSON-RECORDING is a composite key (*psnid, rcdid, psnrcdrole*). The identifiers of PERSON and RECORDING are required to identify uniquely an instance of PERSON-RECORDING, which is why there are plus signs on the crow's feet attached to PERSON-RECORDING. Also, because a person can have multiple roles on a recording, (e.g., play the piano and sing), then *psnrcdrole* is required to uniquely identify these situations.

❖ the m:m between PERSON and COMPOSITION with the associative entity PERSON-COMPOSITION. The identifier is a composite key (*psnid, compid, psncomprole*). The attribute *psncomporder* is for remembering the correct sequence in those cases where there are multiple people involved in a composition. That is, the database needs to record that it is Rodgers and Hammerstein, not Hammerstein and Rodgers.

❖ the m:m between PERSON and CD with the associative entity PERSON-CD. Again the identifier is a composite key (*psnid, cdid*) of the identifiers of entities in the m:m relationship, and there is an attribute (*psncdorder*) to record the order of the people featured on the CD.

❖ the 1:m between RECORDING and TRACK. A recording can appear on many tracks, but a track has only one recording.

❖ the 1:m between CD and TRACK. A CD can have many tracks, but a track appears on only one CD. You can also think of TRACK as the name for the associative entity of the m:m relationship between RECORDING and CD. A recording can appear on many CDs, and a CD has many recordings.

After creating the new tables, Ajay was ready to add some data. He decided first to correct the errors introduced by his initial, incorrect modeling of TRACK by inserting data for RECORDING and revising TRACK. He realized that because RECORDING contains a foreign key to record the 1:m relationship with COMPOSITION, he needed to start by entering the data for COMPOSITION, shown in Table 5-2.[4]

Table 5-2: The table composition

compid	comptitle	compyear
1	Giant Steps	
2	Cousin Mary	
3	Countdown	
4	Spiral	
5	Syeeda's Song Flute	
6	Naima	
7	Mr. P.C.	
8	Stomp of King Porter	1924
9	Sing a Study in Brown	1937
10	Sing Moten's Swing	1997
11	A-tisket, A-tasket	1938
12	I Know Why	1941
13	Sing You Sinners	1930
14	Java Jive	1940
15	Down South Camp Meetin'	1997
16	Topsy	1936
17	Clouds	
18	Skyliner	1944
19	It's Good Enough to Keep	1997
20	Choo Choo Ch' Boogie	1945

Once `composition` was entered, Ajay moved on to the `recording` table, Table 5-3.

Table 5-3: The table recording

rcdid	compid	rcdlength	rcddate
1	1	4.72	1959-May-04
2	2	5.75	1959-May-04
3	3	2.35	1959-May-04
4	4	5.93	1959-May-04
5	5	7.00	1959-May-04
6	6	4.35	1959-Dec-02
7	7	2.95	1959-May-04
8	1	5.93	1959-Apr-01
9	6	7.00	1959-Apr-01
10	2	6.95	1959-May-04
11	3	3.67	1959-May-04
12	2	4.45	1959-May-04

---

4.   When the text accompanying a CD does not include the year of composition, make it NULL.

Table 5-3: The table recording (continued)

rcdid	compid	rcdlength	rcddate
13	8	3.20	
14	9	2.85	
15	10	3.60	
16	11	2.95	
17	12	3.57	
18	13	2.75	
19	14	2.85	
20	15	3.25	
21	16	3.23	
22	17	7.20	
23	18	3.18	
24	19	3.18	
25	20	3.00	

The last row of the recording table (Table 5-3) indicates a recording of the composition "Choo Choo Ch' Boogie," which has compid = 20.

Next, the data for track could be entered, as illustrated by Table 5-4.

Table 5-4: The table track

CDid	trknum	rcdid
1	1	1
1	2	2
1	3	3
1	4	4
1	5	5
1	6	6
1	7	7
1	8	1
1	9	6
1	10	2
1	11	3
1	12	5
2	1	13
2	2	14
2	3	15
2	4	16
2	5	17
2	6	18
2	7	19
2	8	20
2	9	21
2	10	22
2	11	23
2	12	24
2	13	25

The last row of the `track` data indicates that track 13 of *Swing* (`cdid = 2`) is a recording of "Choo Choo Ch' Boogie" (`rcdid = 25 and compid = 20`).

The table `person-recording` stores details of the people involved in each recording. Referring to the accompanying notes for the CD *Giant Steps*, Ajay learned that the composition "Giants Steps," recorded on May 4, 1959, included the following personnel: John Coltrane on tenor sax, Tommy Flanagan on piano, Paul Chambers on bass, and Art Taylor on drums. Using the following data, he inserted four rows in the `person` table (Table 5-5).

Table 5-5: The table person

psnid	psnfname	psnlname
1	John	Coltrane
2	Tommy	Flanagan
3	Paul	Chamber
4	Art	Taylor

Then, he linked these people to the particular recording of "Giant Steps" by entering the following data in Table 5-6, `person-recording`.

Table 5-6: The table person-recording

psnid	rcdid	psncdrole
1	1	tenor sax
2	1	piano
3	1	bass
4	1	drums

Skill builder

1. What data will you enter in `person-cd` to relate John Coltrane to the *Giant Steps* CD?
2. Enter appropriate values in `person-composition` to relate John Coltrane to compositions with compid 1 through 7. You should indicate he wrote the music by entering a value of "music" for the person's role in the composition.
3. Use SQL to solve the following queries:
    a. List the tracks on *Swing*.
    b. Who composed the music for "Spiral"?
    c. Who played which instruments for the May 4, 1959 recording of "Giant Steps"?
    d. List the composers who write music and play the tenor sax.
4. What is the data model missing?

6

One-to-One and Recursive Relationships

Self-reflection is the school of wisdom.
Baltasar Gracián, *The Art of Worldly Wisdom*, 1647

Learning objectives

Students completing this chapter will be able to

❖ model one-to-one and recursive relationships;
❖ define a database with one-to-one and recursive relationships;
❖ write queries for a database with one-to-one and recursive relationships.

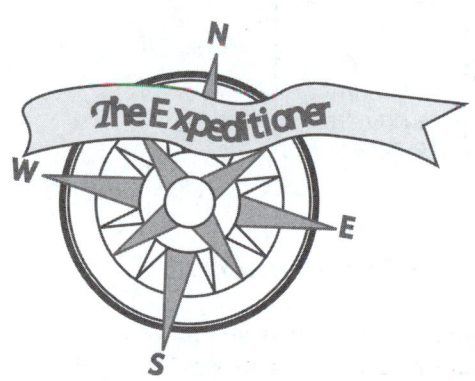

Alice was convinced that a database of business facts would speed up decision making. Her initial experience with the sales database had reinforced this conviction. She decided that employee data should be computerized next. When she arrived at The Expeditioner, she found the company lacked an organization chart and job descriptions for employees. One of her first tasks had been to draw an organization chart (see Figure 6-1).

She divided the firm into four departments and appointed a boss for each department. The first person listed in each department was its boss; of course, Alice was paramount.

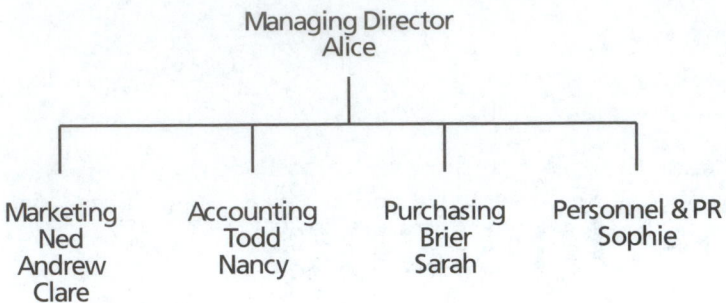

Figure 6-1. The Expeditioner's organization chart

Ned had finished the sales database, so the time was right to create an employee database. Ned seemed to be enjoying his new role, though his dress standard had slipped. Maybe Alice would have to move him out of Marketing. In fact, he sometimes reminded her of fellows who used to hang around the computer lab all day playing weird games. She wasn't quite ready to sound a "nerd alert," but it was getting close.

Modeling a one-to-one relationship

Initially, the organization chart appears to record two relationships. *First,* a department has one or more employees, and an employee belongs to one department. *Second*, a department has one boss, and a person is boss of only one department. That is, boss is a 1:1 relationship between DEPT and EMP. The data model for this situation is shown in Figure 6-2.

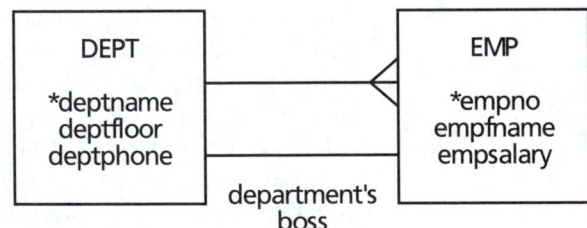

Figure 6-2. A data model illustrating a 1:1 relationship

As a general rule, the 1:1 relationship is labeled to avoid confusion because the meaning of such a relationship cannot always be inferred. This label is called a *relationship descriptor*. The 1:m relationship between DEPT and EMP is not labeled because its meaning is readily understood by reading the model. Use a relationship descriptor when there is more than one relationship between entities or when the meaning of the relationship is not readily inferred from the model.

If we think about this problem, we realize there is more to boss than just a department. People also have a boss. Thus, Alice is the boss of all the other employees. In this case, we are mainly interested in who directly bosses someone else. So, Alice is the direct boss of Ned, Todd, Brier, and Sophie. We need to record the person-boss relationship as well as the department-boss relationship.

The person-boss relationship is a 1:m **recursive relationship** because it is a relationship between employees — an employee has one boss and a boss can have many employees. The data model is shown in Figure 6-3.

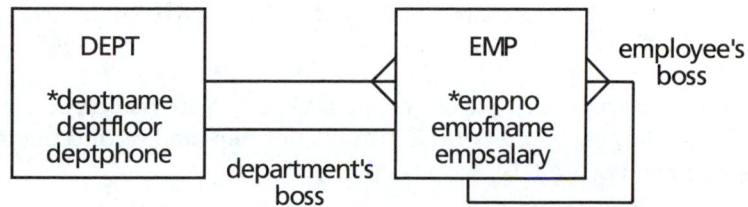

Figure 6-3. A data model illustrating a recursive1:m relationship

It is a good idea to label the recursive relationship, because its meaning is often not obvious from the data model.

Mapping a one-to-one relationship

Since mapping a 1:1 relationship follows the same rules as for any other data model, the major consideration is where to place the foreign key(s). There are three alternatives:

1. Put the foreign key in dept.
    Doing so means that every instance of dept will record empno of the employee who is boss. Because all departments in this case have a boss, the foreign key will always be non-null.
2. Put the foreign key in emp.
    Choosing this alternative means that every instance of emp should record dept-name of the department this employee bosses. Since many employees are not bosses, the value of the foreign key column will generally be null.[1]
3. Put a foreign key in both dept and emp.
    The consequence of putting a foreign key in both tables in the 1:1 relationship is the combination of points 1 and 2.

---

1. Earlier, you learned that a foreign key cannot be null. This can cause confusion, because "null" can mean several things, as explained on page 276. A null value in the foreign key column will typically mean that there is no relationship, in which case there is no foreign key because there is no related primary key. Thus, a null value for the foreign key in emp would indicate there is no relationship with dept. In other words, the person is not a department boss. If there is a relationship and the foreign key is null, then there is a violation of the entity integrity rule, which implies that all primary keys are not null.

Although it does not matter where you put the foreign key, a sound approach is to select the entity that results in the fewest nulls, since this tends to be less confusing to users. In this case, the simplest approach is to put the foreign key in dept.

Mapping a one-to-many recursive relationship

A 1:m recursive relationship is mapped like a standard 1:m relationship. An additional column, for the foreign key, is created for the entity at the "many" end of the relationship. Of course, in this case the "one" and "many" ends are the same entity, so an additional column is added to emp. This column contains the key empno of the "one" end of the relationship. Since empno is already used as a column name, a different name needs to be selected. In this case, it makes sense to call the foreign key column bossno because it stores the boss's employee number.

The mapping of the data model is shown in Table 6-1. Note that deptname becomes a column in emp, the "many" end of the 1:m relationship, and empno becomes a foreign key in dept, an end of the 1:1 relationship.

Table 6-1: The tables dept and emp

dept

deptname	deptfloor	deptphone	empno
Management	5	2001	1
Marketing	1	2002	2
Accounting	4	2003	5
Purchasing	4	2004	7
Personnel & PR	1	2005	9

emp

empno	empfname	empsalary	deptname	bossno
1	Alice	75000	Management	
2	Ned	45000	Marketing	1
3	Andrew	25000	Marketing	2
4	Clare	22000	Marketing	2
5	Todd	38000	Accounting	1
6	Nancy	22000	Accounting	5
7	Brier	43000	Purchasing	1
8	Sarah	56000	Purchasing	7
9	Sophie	35000	Personnel & PR	1

If you examine emp, you will see that the boss of the employee with empno = 2 (Ned) has bossno = 1. You can then look up the row with empno = 1 to find that Ned's boss is Alice. This "double lookup" is frequently used when manually interrogating a table that represents a recursive relationship. Soon you will discover how this is handled with SQL.

Here is the SQL to create the two tables:

```
CREATE TABLE dept (
    deptname        VARCHAR(15),
    deptfloor       SMALLINT    NOT NULL,
    deptphone       SMALLINT    NOT NULL,
    empno           SMALLINT    NOT NULL,
        PRIMARY KEY(deptname));

CREATE TABlE emp (
    empno           SMALLINT,
    empfname        VARCHAR(10),
    empsalary       DECIMAL(7,0),
    deptname        VARCHAR(15),
    bossno          SMALLINT,
        PRIMARY KEY(empno),
        CONSTRAINT fk_belong_dept FOREIGN KEY(deptname)
            REFERENCES dept(deptname),
        CONSTRAINT fk_has_boss FOREIGN KEY (bossno)
            REFERENCES emp(empno));
```

You will notice that there is no foreign key definition for empno in dept and for bossno in emp (the recursive boss relationship). Why? Observe that deptname is a foreign key in emp. If we make empno a foreign key in dept, then we have a *deadly embrace*. A new department cannot be added to the dept table until there is a boss for that department (i.e., there is a person in the emp table with the empno of the boss); however, the other constraint states that an employee cannot be added to the emp table unless there is a department to which that person is assigned. If we have both foreign key constraints, we cannot add a new department until we have added a boss, and we cannot add a boss until we have added a department for that person. Nothing, under these circumstances, can happen if both foreign key constraints are in place. Thus, only one of them is specified.

In the case of the recursive employee relationship, we can create a constraint to ensure that bossno exists for each employee, except of course the person, Alice, who is top of the pyramid. This form of constraint is known as a *self-referential* foreign key. However, we must make certain that the first person inserted into emp is Alice. The following statements illustrate that we must always insert a person's boss before we insert the person.

```
INSERT INTO emp (empno, empfname, empsalary, deptname)
    VALUES (1,'Alice',75000,'Management');
INSERT INTO emp VALUES (2,'Ned',45000,'Marketing',1);
INSERT INTO emp VALUES (3,'Andrew',25000,'Marketing',2);
INSERT INTO emp VALUES (4,'Clare',22000,'Marketing',2);
INSERT INTO emp VALUES (5,'Todd',38000,'Accounting',1);
INSERT INTO emp VALUES (6,'Nancy',22000,'Accounting',5);
INSERT INTO emp VALUES (7,'Brier',43000,'Purchasing',1);
INSERT INTO emp VALUES (8,'Sarah',56000,'Purchasing',7);
INSERT INTO emp VALUES (9,'Sophie',35000,'Personnel',1);
```

In more complex modeling situations, such as when there are multiple relationships between a pair of entities, use of a FOREIGN KEY clause may result in a deadlock. Always consider the consequences of using a FOREIGN KEY clause before applying it.

Skill builder

A consulting company has assigned each of its employees to a specialist group (e.g., database management). Each specialist group has a team leader. When employees join the company, they are assigned a mentor for the first year. One person might mentor several employees, but an employee has at most one mentor.

Querying a one-to-one relationship

Querying presents no special difficulties but does allow us to see additional SQL features.

○   **List the salary of each department's boss.**

```
SELECT empfname, deptname, empsalary FROM emp
    WHERE empno IN (SELECT empno FROM dept);
```

or

```
SELECT empfname, dept.deptname, empsalary
    FROM emp, dept
        WHERE dept.empno = emp.empno;
```

empfname	deptname	empsalary
Alice	Management	75000
Ned	Marketing	45000
Todd	Accounting	38000
Brier	Purchasing	43000
Sophie	Personnel & PR	35000

Querying a recursive relationship

Querying a recursive relationship is puzzling until you realize that you can join a table to itself by creating two copies of the table. In SQL, you create a temporary copy, a **table alias**, by following the table's name with the alias (e.g., emp wrk creates a temporary copy, called wrk, of the permanent table emp).[2] Table aliases are always required so that SQL can distinguish which copy of the table is being referenced. To demonstrate:

---

2.   In MS Access, the equivalent expression is emp AS wrk.

○ **Find the salary of Nancy's boss.**

```
SELECT wrk.empfname, wrk.empsalary,boss.empfname, boss.empsalary
   FROM emp wrk, emp boss
      WHERE wrk.empfname = 'Nancy'
      AND wrk.bossno = boss.empno;
```

Many queries are solved by getting all the data you need to answer the request in one row. In this case, the query is easy to answer once the data for Nancy and her boss are in the one row. Thus, think of this query as joining two copies of the table emp to get the worker and her boss's data in one row.[3] Notice that there is a suffix (wrk and boss) for each copy of the table to distinguish between them. It helps to use a suffix that makes sense. In this case, the wrk and boss suffixes can be thought of as referring to the worker and boss tables, respectively. You can understand how the query works by examining Table 6-2.

Table 6-2: Joining a table with itself (self-join)

emp wrk				
empno	empfname	empsalary	deptname	bossno
1	Alice	75000	Management	
2	Ned	45000	Marketing	1
3	Andrew	25000	Marketing	2
4	Clare	22000	Marketing	2
5	Todd	38000	Accounting	1
6	Nancy	22000	Accounting	5
7	Brier	43000	Purchasing	1
8	Sarah	56000	Purchasing	7
9	Sophie	35000	Personnel & PR	1

emp boss				
empno	empfname	empsalary	deptname	bossno
1	Alice	75000	Management	
2	Ned	45000	Marketing	1
3	Andrew	25000	Marketing	2
4	Clare	22000	Marketing	2
5	Todd	38000	Accounting	1
6	Nancy	22000	Accounting	5
7	Brier	43000	Purchasing	1
8	Sarah	56000	Purchasing	7
9	Sophie	35000	Personnel & PR	1

---

3.   This is called a *self-join*.

The first step is to find the row in `wrk` where the employee's name is "Nancy." This row is shaded in `wrk`. The `bossno` column of this row contains 5. The second step is to join this row to the row in the `boss` table with `empno` = 5. This row is also shaded. The result of the SQL query is:

wrk.empfname	wrk.empsalary	boss.empfname	boss.empsalary
Nancy	22000	Todd	38000

○ **Find the names of employees who earn more than their boss.**

```
SELECT wrk.empfname
   FROM emp wrk, emp boss
      WHERE wrk.bossno = boss.empno
      AND wrk.empsalary > boss.empsalary;
```

This would be very easy if the employee and boss data were in the same row. We could simply compare the salaries of the two people. To get the data in the one row, we join by matching `bossno` in `wrk` with `empno` in `boss`. The result is as follows:

wrk					boss				
empno	empfname	empsalary	deptname	bossno	empno	empfname	empsalary	deptname	bossno
2	Ned	45000	Marketing	1	1	Alice	75000	Management	
3	Andrew	25000	Marketing	2	2	Ned	45000	Marketing	1
4	Clare	22000	Marketing	2	2	Ned	45000	Marketing	1
5	Todd	38000	Accounting	1	1	Alice	75000	Management	
6	Nancy	22000	Accounting	5	5	Todd	38000	Accounting	1
7	Brier	43000	Purchasing	1	1	Alice	75000	Management	
8	Sarah	56000	Purchasing	7	7	Brier	43000	Purchasing	1
9	Sophie	35000	Personnel & PR	1	1	Alice	75000	Management	

Now the rest of the query is very straightforward. It is easy to compare the salaries of employees and their boss. The result is as follows:

empfname
Sarah

- -

Skill builder

Find the name of Sophie's boss.

- -

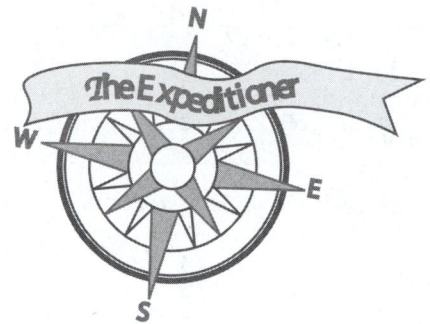

Alice has found several histories of The Expeditioner from a variety of eras. Because many expeditions they outfitted were conducted under royal patronage, it was not uncommon for these histories to refer to British monarchs. Alice could remember very little about British history, let alone when various kings and queens reigned. This sounded like another database problem. She would ask Ned to create a database that recorded details of each monarch. She thought it also would be useful to record details of royal succession.

Modeling a one-to-one recursive relationship

The British monarchy can be represented by a simple one-entity model. A monarch has one direct successor and one direct predecessor. The sequencing of monarchs can be modeled by a 1:1 recursive relationship, shown in Figure 6-4.

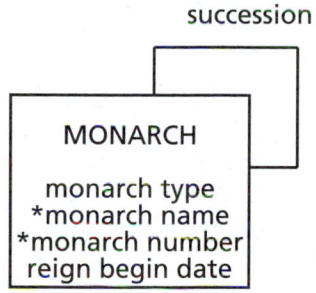

Figure 6-4. A data model illustrating a 1:1 recursive relationship

Mapping a one-to-one recursive relationship

The 1:1 recursive relationship is mapped by adding a foreign key to monarch. You can add a foreign key to represent either the successor or predecessor relationship. In this case, for no particular reason, the preceding relationship is selected. Because each instance of a monarch is identified by a composite key, two columns are added to monarch for the foreign key. Data for recent monarchs are shown in Table 6-3.

Table 6-3: The table monarch

monarch montype	monname	monnum	rgnbeg	premonname	premonnum
King	William	IV	1830/6/26		
Queen	Victoria	I	1837/6/20	William	IV
King	Edward	VII	1901/1/22	Victoria	I

Table 6-3: The table monarch (continued)

King	George	V	1910/5/6	Edward	VII
King	Edward	VIII	1936/1/20	George	V
King	George	VI	1936/12/11	Edward	VII
Queen	Elizabeth	II	1952/02/06	George	VI

The SQL statements to create the table are very straightforward.

```
CREATE TABLE monarch (
     montype      CHAR(5) nOT NULL,
     monname      VARCHAR(15),
     monnum       VARCHAR(5),
     rgnbeg       DATE,
     premonname   VARCHAR(15),
     premonnum    VARCHAR(5),
        PRIMARY KEY(monname,monnum),
        CONSTRAINT fk_monarch FOREIGN KEY (premonname, premonnum)
           REFERENCES monarch(monname, monnum);⁴
```

Because the 1:1 relationship is recursive, you cannot insert Queen Victoria without first inserting King William IV. What you can do is first insert King William, without any reference to the preceding monarch (i.e., a null foreign key). The following code illustrates the order of record insertion so that the referential integrity constraint is obeyed.

```
INSERT INTO monarch (montype,monname, monnum,rgnbeg)
   values ('King','William','IV','1830-06-26');
INSERT INTO monarch
   values ('Queen','Victoria','I','1837-06-20','William','IV');
INSERT INTO monarch
   values ('King','Edward','VII','1901-01-22','Victoria','I');
INSERT INTO monarch
   values ('King','George','V','1910-05-06','Edward','VII');
INSERT INTO monarch
   values ('King','Edward','VIII','1936-01-20','George','V');
INSERT INTO monarch
   values('King','George','VI','1936-12-11','Edward','VIII');
INSERT INTO monarch
   values('Queen','Elizabeth','II','1952-02-06','George','VI');
```

---

4.   A self-referential foreign key constraint might not work with some relational systems. In which case, delete the constraint.

Sharing check images

Viewpointe Archive Services LLC was founded in 2000 by Bank of America Corp., J.P. Morgan Chase & Co., and IBM. Its check archive and ImageShare exchange service enables members to load check images to a central repository, where they are archived and can be accessed by individual banks rather than exchanged from one bank to another. This also reduces the number of paper checks that are handled.

Wells Fargo & Co., the San Francisco-based bank, had previously been sharing check images with the Federal Reserve Bank and The Clearing House in New York through its own data warehouse. Now, it will set up a network to transmit the 4.5 billion check images it captures each year. It is currently installing check-image scanners at the teller windows in its 6,000 U.S. branch offices. This could also mean that banks that regularly do business with Wells Fargo will become Viewpointe customers as well.

The Check Clearing for the 21st Century Act, or Check 21, took effect October 28, 2004, thus allowing banks to substitute image-replacement documents for original paper checks, which can then be destroyed.

SunTrust Banks Inc. in Atlanta and First Horizon National Corp. in Memphis claim to be the first banks in the United States to agree to share check images.

Source: Mearian, Lucas. 2005. Wells Fargo Buys Into Check-Image Sharing. *Computerworld*, Jan 17. www.computerworld.com/databasetopics/data/story/0,10801,98970,00.html.

Skill builder

In a competitive bridge[5] competition, the same pair of players play together for the entire tournament. Draw a data model to record details of all the players and the pairs of players.

Querying a one-to-one recursive relationship

Some queries on the MONARCH table demonstrate querying a 1:1 recursive relationship.

○ **Who preceded Elizabeth II?**

```
SELECT premonname, premonnum FROM monarch
    WHERE monname = 'Elizabeth' AND monnum = 'II';
```

premonname	premonnum
George	VI

---

5. Bridge is a card game played by two teams each of two players.

This is simple because all the data are in one row. A more complex query is:

○   **Was Elizabeth II's predecessor a king or queen?**

```
SELECT pre.montype FROM monarch cur, monarch pre
   WHERE cur.premonname = pre.monname
   AND cur.premonnum = pre.monnum
   AND cur.monname = 'Elizabeth' AND cur.monnum = 'II';
```

montype
King

This is very similar to the query to find the salary of Nancy's boss. The monarch table is joined with itself to create a row that contains all the details to answer the query.

○   **List the kings and queens of England in ascending chronological order.**

```
SELECT montype, monname, monnum, rgnbeg
   FROM monarch ORDER BY rgnbeg;
```

montype	monname	monnum	rgnbeg
Queen	Victoria	I	1837-06-20
King	Edward	VII	1901-01-22
King	George	V	1910-05-06
King	Edward	VIII	1936-01-20
King	George	VI	1936-12-11
Queen	Elizabeth	II	1952-02-06

This is a simple query because rgnbeg is like a ranking column. It would not be enough to store just the year in rgnbeg, because two kings started their reigns in 1936; hence, the full date is required.

■ ━ ━ ━ ■ ━ ━ ■ ━ ━ ■ ━ ━ ■ ━ ━ ■ ━ ━ ■ ━ ━ ■

Skill builder

Who succeeded Queen Victoria?

■ ━ ━ ━ ■ ━ ━ ■ ━ ━ ■ ━ ━ ■ ━ ━ ■ ━ ━ ■ ━ ━ ■

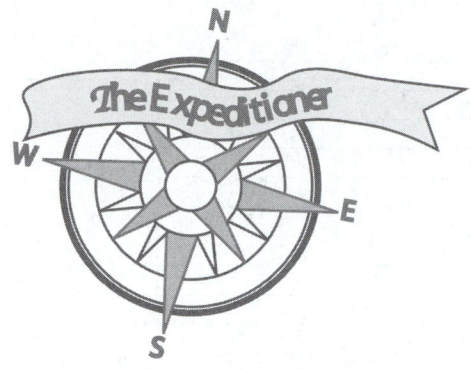

Of course, Alice soon had another project for Ned. The Expeditioner keeps a wide range of products that are sometimes assembled into kits to make other products. For example, the animal photography kit is made up of eight items that The Expeditioner also sells separately. In addition, some kits became part of much larger kits. The animal photography kit is included as one of 45 items in the East African Safari package. All of the various items are considered products, and each has its own product code. Ned was now required to create a product database that would keep track of all the items in The Expeditioner's stock.

Modeling a many-to-many recursive relationship

The assembly of products to create other products is very common in business. Manufacturing even has a special term to describe it: a *bill of materials*. Data modeling is relatively simple once you realize that a product can appear as part of many other products and can be composed of many other products; that is, we have a **many-to-many (m:m) recursive relationship** for product. As usual, we turn an m:m relationship into two one-to-many (1:m) relationships. Thus, we get the data model displayed in Figure 6-5.

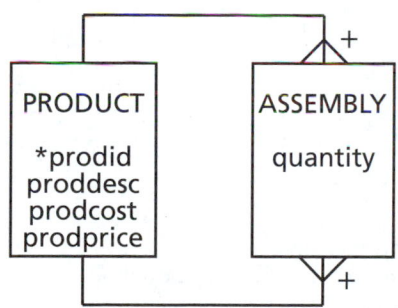

Figure 6-5. A data model illustrating an m:m recursive relationship

Mapping a many-to-many recursive relationship

Mapping follows the same procedure described previously, producing the two tables shown in Table 6-4. The SQL statements to create the tables are shown next. Observe that `assembly` has a composite key, and there are two foreign key constraints.

Table 6-4: Tables product and assembly

product

prodid	proddesc	prodcost	prodprice
1000	Animal photography kit		725
101	35mm camera	150	300
102	Camera case	10	15
103	70-210 zoom lens	125	200
104	28-85 zoom lens	115	185
105	Photographer's vest	25	40
106	Lens cleaning cloth	1	1.25
107	Tripod	35	45
108	24 exp. 100ASA 35mm col neg	.85	1

assembly

quantity	*prodid*	*subprodid*
1	1000	101
1	1000	102
1	1000	103
1	1000	104
1	1000	105
2	1000	106
1	1000	107
10	1000	108

```
CREATE TABLE product (
    prodid        INTEGER,
    proddesc      VARCHAR(30),
    prodcost      DECIMAL(9,2),
    prodprice     DECIMAL(9,2),
      PRIMARY KEY(prodid));

CREATE TABLE assembly (
    quantity        INTEGER  NOT NULL,
    prodid          INTEGER,
    subprodid       INTEGER,
      PRIMARY KEY(prodid, subprodid),
      CONSTRAINT fk_assembly_product FOREIGN KEY(prodid)
        REFERENCES product(prodid),
      CONSTRAINT fk_assembly_subproduct FOREIGN KEY(subprodid)
        REFERENCES product(prodid));
```

Skill builder

An army is broken up into many administrative units (e.g., army, brigade, platoon). A unit can contain many other units (e.g., a regiment contains two or more battalions), and a unit can be part of a larger unit (e.g., a squad is a member of a platoon).

Querying a many-to-many recursive relationship

○ **List the product identifier of each component of the animal photography kit.**

```
SELECT subprodid FROM product, assembly
   WHERE proddesc = 'Animal photography kit'
      AND product.prodid = assembly.prodid;
```

subprodid
101
106
107
105
104
103
102
108

Why are the values for subprodid listed in no apparent order? Remember, there is no implied ordering of rows in a table, and it is quite possible, as this example illustrates, for the rows to have what appears to be an unusual ordering. If you want to order rows, use the ORDER BY clause.

○ **List the product description and cost of each component of the animal photography kit.**

```
SELECT proddesc, prodcost FROM product
   WHERE prodid IN
      (SELECT subprodid FROM product, assembly
         WHERE proddesc = 'Animal photography kit'
         AND product.prodid = assembly.prodid);
```

In this case, first determine the prodid of those products in the animal photography kit (the inner query), and then report the description of these products. Alternatively, a three-way join can be done using two copies of product.

```
SELECT b.proddesc, b.prodcost FROM product a, assembly, product b
   WHERE a.proddesc = 'Animal photography kit'
   AND a.prodid = assembly.prodid
   AND assembly.subprodid = b.prodid;
```

proddesc	prodcost
35mm camera	150.00
Camera case	10.00
70-210 zoom lens	125.00
28-85 zoom lens	115.00
Photographer's vest	25.00
Lens cleaning cloth	1.00
Tripod	35.00
24 exp. 100ASA 35mm col neg	0.85

Skill builder

How many lens cleaning cloths are there in the animal photography kit?

Summary

Relationships can be one-to-one and recursive. A recursive relationship is within a single entity rather than between entities. Recursive relationships are mapped to the relational model in the same way as other relationships. A self-referential foreign key constraint permits a foreign key reference to a key within the same table. Resolution of queries involving recursive relationships often requires a table to be joined with itself. Many-to-many recursive relationships occur in business in the form of a bill of materials.

Key terms and concepts

Many-to-many (m:m) recursive relationship	Recursive relationship
One-to-many (1:m) recursive relationship	Relationship descriptor
One-to-one (1:1) recursive relationship	Self-join
One-to-one (1:1) relationship	Self-referential foreign key

Exercises

1. Draw data models for the following two problems:
   a. (i) A dairy farmer, who is also a part-time cartoonist, has several herds of cows. He has assigned each cow to a particular herd. In each herd, the farmer has one cow that is his favorite — often that cow is featured in a cartoon.

   (ii) A few malcontents in each herd, mainly those who feel they should have appeared in the cartoon, disagree with the farmer's choice of a favorite cow, whom they disparagingly refer to as the *sacred* cow. As a result, each herd now has elected a herd leader.
   b. The originator of a pyramid marketing scheme has a system for selling ethnic jewelry. The pyramid has three levels — gold, silver, and bronze. New associates join the pyramid at the bronze level. They contribute 30 percent of the revenue of their sales of jewelry to the silver chief in charge of their clan. In turn, silver

chiefs contribute 30 percent of what they receive from bronze associates to the gold master in command of their tribe. Finally, gold masters pass on 30 percent of what they receive to the originator of the scheme.

c. The legion, the basic combat unit of the ancient Roman army, contained 3,000 to 6,000 men, consisting primarily of heavy infantry (hoplites), supported by light infantry (velites), and sometimes by cavalry. The hoplites were drawn up in three lines. The hastati (youngest men) were in the first, the principes (seasoned troops) in the second, and the triarii (oldest men) behind them, reinforced by velites. Each line was divided into 10 maniples, consisting of two centuries (60 to 80 men per century) each. Each legion had a commander, and a century was commanded by a centurion. Julius Caesar, through one of his Californian channelers, has asked you to design a database to maintain details of soldiers. Of course, Julius is a little forgetful at times, and he has not supplied the titles of the officers who command maniples, lines, and hoplites, but he expects that you can handle this lack of fine detail.

d. A travel agency is frequently asked questions about tourist destinations. For example, customers want to know details of the climate for a particular month, the population of the city, and other geographic facts. Sometimes they request the flying time and distance between two cities. The manager has asked you to create a database to maintain these facts.

e. The Center for the Study of World Trade keeps track of trade treaties between nations. For each treaty, it records details of the countries signing the treaty and where and when it was signed.

f. Design a database to store details about U.S. presidents and their terms in office. Also, record details of their date and place of birth, gender, and political party affiliation (e.g., Caluthumpian Progress Party). You are required to record the sequence of presidents so that the predecessor and successor of any president can be identified. How will you model the case of Grover Cleveland, who served nonconsecutive terms as president? Is it feasible that political party affiliation may change? If so, how will you handle it?

g. The IS department of a large organization makes extensive use of software modules. New applications are built, where possible, from existing modules. Software modules can also contain other modules. The IS manager realizes that she now needs a database to keep track of which modules are used in which applications or other modules. (*Hint:* It is helpful to think of an application as a module.)

h. Data modeling is finally getting to you. Last night you dreamed you were asked by Noah to design a database to store data about the animals on the ark. All you can remember from Sunday school is the bit about the animals entering the ark two-by-two, so you thought you should check the real thing.
Take with you seven pairs of every kind of clean animal, a male and its mate, and two of every kind of unclean animal, a male and its mate, and also seven pair of every kind of bird, male and female. Genesis 7:2
Next time Noah disturbs your sleep, you want to be ready. So, draw a data model and make certain you record the two-by-two relationship.

2. Write SQL to answer the following queries using the DEPT and EMP tables described in this chapter:
   a. Find the departments where all the employees earn less than their boss.
   b. Find the names of employees who are in the same department as their boss (as an employee).
   c. List the departments having an average salary greater than $25,000.
   d. List the departments where the average salary of the employees, excluding the boss, is greater than $25,000.
   e. List the names and manager of the employees of the Marketing department who have a salary greater than $25,000.
   f. List the names of the employees who earn more than any employee in the Marketing department.
3. Write SQL to answer the following queries using the monarch table described in this chapter:
   a. Who succeeded Victoria I?
   b. How many days did Victoria I reign?
   c. How many kings are there in the table?
   d. Which monarch had the shortest reign?
4. Write SQL to answer the following queries using the product and assembly tables:
   a. How many different items are there in the animal photography kit?
   b. What is the most expensive item in the animal photography kit?
   c. What is the total cost of the components of the animal photography kit?
   d. Compute the total quantity of all items required to assemble 15 animal photography kits.

CD Library case

Ajay had some more time to work on this CD Library database. He picked up The Manhattan Transfer's *Swing* CD to enter its data. Very quickly he recognized the need for yet another entity if he was going to store details of the people in a group. A group can contain many people (there are four artists in The Manhattan Transfer), and also it is feasible that over time a person could be a member of multiple groups. So, there is an m:m between PERSON and GROUP. Building on his understanding of the relationship between PERSON and RECORDING and CD, Ajay realized there are two other required relationships: an m:m between GROUP and RECORDING, and between GROUP and CD. This led to version 5.0, shown in Figure 6-6.

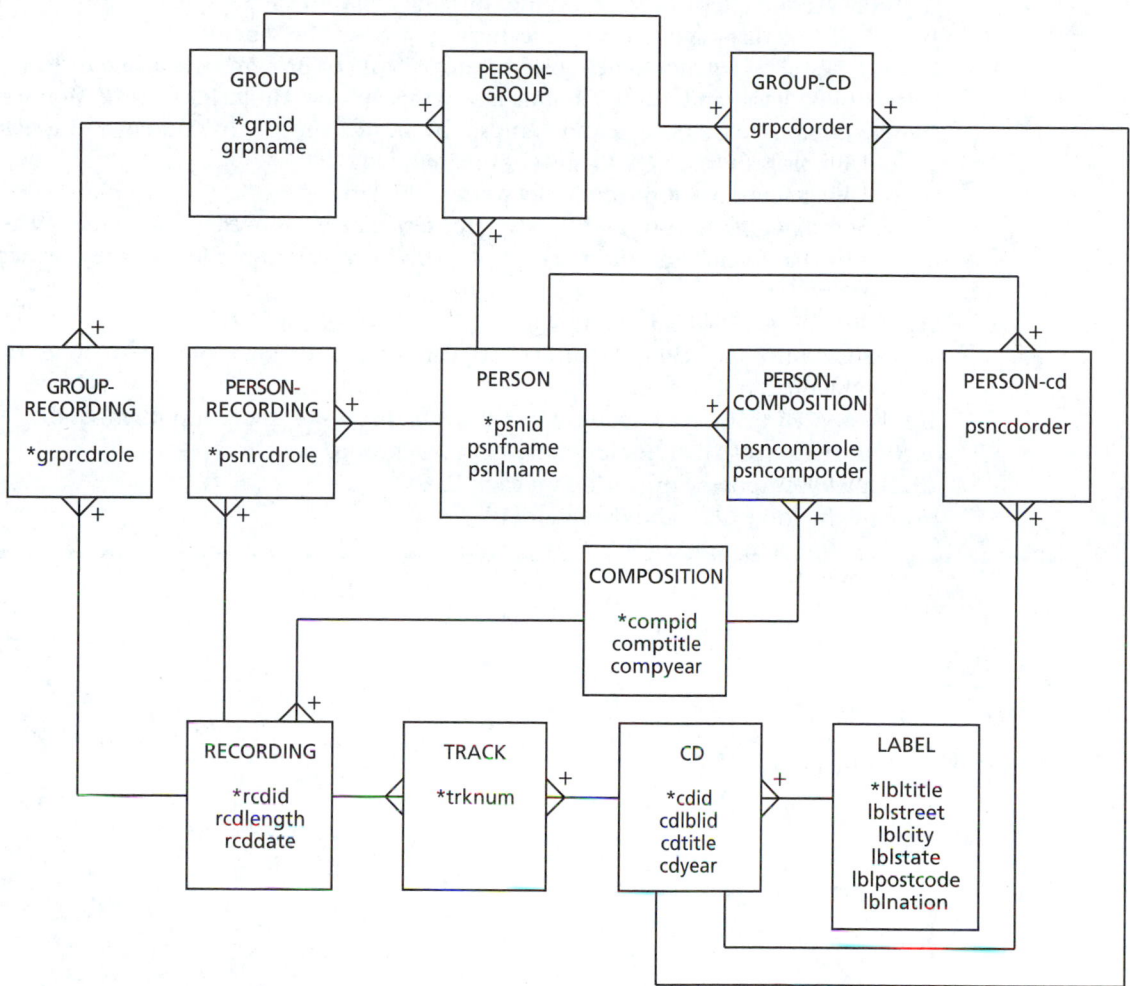

Figure 6-6. CD library V5.0

- -

Skill builder

1. The members of The Manhattan Transfer are Cheryl Bentyne, Janis Siegel, Tim Hauser, and Alan Paul. Update the database with this information, and write SQL to answer the following:
   a. Who are the members of The Manhattan Transfer?
   b. What CDs have been released by The Manhattan Transfer?
   c. What CDs feature Cheryl Bentyne as an individual or member of a group?
2. The group known as Asleep at the Wheel is featured on tracks 3, 4, and 7 of *Swing*. Record these data and write SQL to answer the following:

      a. What are the titles of the recordings on which Asleep at the Wheel appear?

      b. List all CDs that have any tracks featuring Asleep at the Wheel.

3.   Record the following facts. The music of "Sing a Song of Brown," composed in 1937, is by Count Basie and Larry Clinton and lyrics by Jon Hendricks. "Sing Moten's Swing," composed in 1932, features music by Buster and Benny Moten, and lyrics by Jon Hendricks. Write SQL to answer the following:

      a. For what songs has Jon Hendricks written the lyrics?

      b. Report all compositions and their composers where more than one person was involved in composing the music. Make certain you report them in the correct order.

4.   Test your SQL skills with the following:

      a. List the tracks on which Alan Paul appears as an individual or as a member of The Manhattan Transfer.

      b. List all CDs featuring a group, and report the names of the group members.

      c. Report all tracks that feature more than one group.

      d. List the composers appearing on each CD.

5.   How might you extend the data model?

7

Data Modeling

Man is a knot, a web, a mesh into which relationships are tied. Only those relationships matter.

Antoine de Saint-Exupéry in *Flight to Arras*

Learning objectives

Students completing this chapter will be able to create a well-formed, high-fidelity data model.

Modeling

Modeling is widely used within business to learn about organizational problems and design solutions. To understand where data modeling fits within the broader context, it is useful to review the full range of modeling activities, as illustrated in Table 7-1.[1]

Table 7-1: A broad perspective on modeling

		Scope	Model	Technology
Motivation	Why	Goals	Business plan	Groupware
People	Who	Business units	Organization chart	System interface
Time	When	Key events	PERT chart	Scheduling
Data	What	Key entities	Data model	Relational database
Function	How	Key processes	Process model	Application software
Network	Where	Locations	Logistics network	System architecture

Modeling occurs at multiple levels. At the highest level, an organization needs to determine the scope of its business by identifying the major elements of its environment, such as its goals, business units, where it operates, and critical events, entities, and processes. At the top level, textual models are frequently used. For example, an organization might

---

1. Adapted from Zachman, J. A. 1982. Business systems planning and business information control study: A comparison. *IBM Systems Journal* 21(1):31–53, and Bruce, T. A. 1992. *Designing quality databases with IDEF1X information models*. New York, NY: Dorset House.

list its major goals and business processes. A map will be typically used to display where the business operates.

Once senior managers have clarified the scope of a business, models can be constructed for each of the major elements. Goals will be converted into a business plan, business units will become an organizational chart, and so on. The key models, from an IS perspective, are the data, process, and logistics models. The required courses in most IS programs cover these models in data management (data modeling), systems analysis and design (process modeling), and telecommunications (network modeling).

Technology, the final stage, converts models into operational systems to support the organization. Many organizations now rely extensively on e-mail and Web technology for communicating business decisions. People connect to systems through an interface, such as a Web browser. Ensuring that events occur at the right time is managed by scheduling software. This could be implemented with operating system procedures that schedule the execution of applications. In some database management systems (DBMSs), triggers can be established. A **trigger** is a database procedure that is automatically executed when some event is recognized. For example, U.S. banks are required to report all deposits exceeding $10,000, and a trigger could be coded for this event.

From your IS studies, you should know that data models are typically converted into relational databases, and process models become computer programs. The logistic network, which handles the physical flow of goods, is typically mirrored by a telecommunications network to handle the electronic flow of data that supports the physical flow (e.g., invoices and payments) and enables the flow of other communication between dispersed business units.

Thus, you can see that data modeling is one element of a comprehensive modeling activity that is often required to design business systems. When a business undergoes major change, such as a reengineering project, many dimensions can be altered, and it may be appropriate to rethink many elements of the business, starting with its goals. Because such major change is very disruptive and costly, it occurs less frequently. It is more likely that data modeling is conducted as a stand-alone activity or part of process modeling to create a new business application.

Data modeling

You were introduced to the basic building blocks of data modeling in Chapters 3 through 6. Now it is time to learn how to assemble blocks to build a data model. Data modeling is a method for determining what data and relationships should be stored in the database. It is also a way of communicating a database design.

The goal of data modeling is to identify the facts that must be stored in a database. A data model is not concerned with how the data will be stored. This is the concern of those who implement the database. A data model is not concerned with how the data will be processed. This is the province of process modeling, which is generally taught in systems analysis and design courses. The goal is to create a data model that is an accurate representation of data needs and real-world data relationships.

Building a data model is a partnership between a client, a representative of the eventual users of the database, and a designer. Of course, there can be a team of clients and designers. For simplicity, we assume there is one client and one designer.

Drawing a data model is an iterative process of trial and revision. A data model is a working document that will change as you learn more about the client's needs and world. Your early versions are likely to be quite different from the final product. Draw your diagrams with a pencil and keep an extra-large eraser handy. Better still, use software for drawing and revising the data model.

The building blocks

The purpose of a database is to store data about things. These things can include facts (e.g., an exchange rate), plans (e.g., scheduled production of two-person tents for June), estimates (e.g., forecast of demand for geopositioning systems), and a variety of other data. A data model describes these things and their relationships with other things using four components: entity, attribute, relationship, and identifier.

Entity

The entity is the basic building block of a data model. An entity is a thing about which data should be stored, something we need to describe. Each entity in a data model has a unique name that we write in singular form. Why singular? Because we want to emphasize that an entity describes an instance of a thing. Thus, we previously used the word SHARE to define an entity because it describes each instance of a share rather than shares in general.

We have already introduced the convention that an entity is represented by a rectangle, and the name of the entity is shown in uppercase letters (see Figure 7-1).

Figure 7-1. The entity SHARE

A data model will typically have less than 100 entities. A database can easily contain millions of instances (rows) for any one entity (table). Imagine the number of instances in a national tax department's database.

How do you begin to identify entities? One approach is to underline any *nouns* in the problem description. Most nouns are possible entities, and underlining ensures that you do not overlook any potential entities. Start by selecting an entity that seems central to the problem. If you were designing a student database, you might start with the student. Once you have picked a central entity, describe it. Then move to the others.

Attribute

An attribute describes an entity. When an entity has been identified, the next step is to determine its attributes, that is, the data that should be kept to describe the entity realistically. An attribute name is singular and unique within the data model. You may need to use a modifier to make an attribute name unique (e.g., "hire date" and "sale date" rather than just "date").

Our convention is that the name of an attribute is recorded in lowercase letters within the entity rectangle. Figure 7-2 illustrates that SHARE has attributes share code, share name, share price, share quantity, share dividend, and share PE. Notice the frequent use of the modifier "share". It is possible that other entities in the database might also have a price and quantity, so we use a modifier to create unique attribute names.

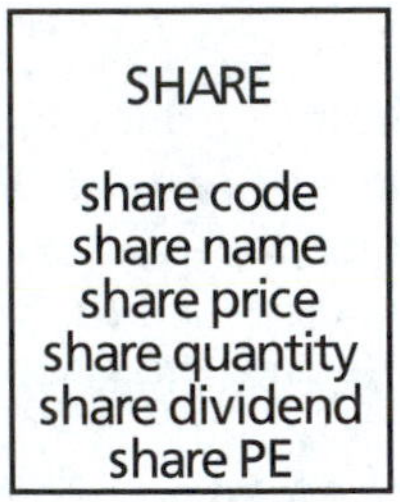

```
SHARE

share code
share name
share price
share quantity
share dividend
share PE
```

Figure 7-2. The entity SHARE with its attributes

Defining attributes generally takes considerable discussion with the client. You should include any attribute that is likely to be required for present or future decision making. But don't get carried away. Avoid storing unnecessary data. For example, to describe the entity STUDENT you usually record date of birth, but it is unlikely that you would store height. If you were describing an entity PATIENT, on the other hand, it might be necessary to record height, because that is sometimes relevant to medical decision making.

An attribute has a single value, which may be null. Multiple values are not allowed. If you need to store multiple values, it is a signal that you have a one-to-many (1:m) relationship and need to define another entity.

Relationship

Entities are related to other entities. If there were no relationships between entities, there would be no need for a data model and no need for a relational database. A simple, flat file (a single-entity database) would be sufficient. A relationship is binary. It describes a linkage between two entities and is represented by an arc between them.

Because a relationship is binary, strictly speaking it has two relationship descriptors, one for each entity. Each relationship descriptor has a degree stating how many instances of the other entity may be related to each instance of the described entity. Consider the entities STOCK and NATION and their 1:m relationship (see Figure 7-3). We have two relationship descriptors: *stocks of nation* for NATION and *nation of stock* for STOCK. The relationship descriptor *stocks of nation* has a degree of m because a nation may have zero or more listed stocks. The relationship descriptor *nation of stock* has a degree of 1 because a stock is listed in at most one nation. To reduce data model clutter, we will use a single label for the pair of relationship descriptors. Experience shows this approach captures the meaning of the relationship and improves readability.

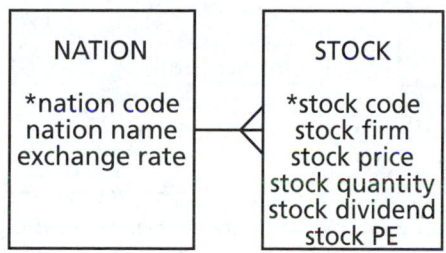

Figure 7-3. A 1:m relationship between STOCK and NATION

Because the meaning of relationships frequently can be inferred, there is no need to label every one; however, each additional arc between two entities must be labeled to clarify meaning. Also, it is a good idea to label one-to-one (1:1) relationships, because the label is not always obvious.

Consider the fragment in Figure 7-4. The descriptors of the 1:m relationship can be inferred as a firm has employees and an employee belongs to a firm. The 1:1 relationship is clarified by labeling the 1:1 arc as firm's boss.

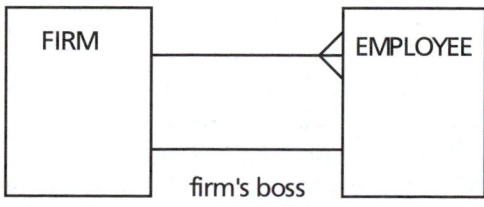

Figure 7-4. Relationship labeling

Identifier

An identifier uniquely distinguishes an instance of an entity. An identifier is one or more attributes and may include the identifier of a related entity. When a related entity's identifier is part of an identifier, a plus sign is placed on the arc closest to the entity being identified. In Figure 7-5, an instance of the entity LINEITEM is identified by the composite of *lineno* and *saleno*, the identifier of SALE. *Lineno* does not uniquely identify an instance of LINEITEM, because it is simply a number that appears on the sales form. Thus, the identifier must include *saleno* (the identifier of SALE). So, any instance of LINEITEM is uniquely identified by the composite *saleno* and *lineno*.

Figure 7-5. A related entity's identifier as part of the identifier

Occasionally, there will be several possible identifiers, and these are each given a different symbol. Our convention is to prefix an identifier with an asterisk (*). If there are multiple identifiers, use other symbols such as #, !, or &. Be careful: If you have too many possible identifiers, your model will look like comic book swearing. In most cases, you will have only one identifier.

No part of an identifier can be null. If this were permitted, there would be no guarantee that the other parts of the identifier were sufficiently unique to distinguish all instances in the database.

Data model quality

There are two criteria for judging the quality of a data model. It must be well-formed and have high fidelity.

A well-formed data model

A well-formed data model (see Table 7-2) clearly communicates information to the client. Being well-formed means the construction rules have been obeyed. There is no ambiguity; all entities are named, and all entities have identifiers. If identifiers are missing, the client may make incorrect inferences about the data model. All relationships are recorded using the proper notation and labeled whenever there is a possibility of confusion.

All the attributes of an entity are listed because missing attributes create two types of problems. *First*, it is unclear what data will be stored about each instance. *Second*, the data model may be missing some relationships. Attributes that can have multiple values be-

---

A data model for retailing

The Association for Retail Technology Standards (ARTS) of the National Retail Federation is a retailer-driven membership organization dedicated to creating an international, barrier-free technology environment for retailers. ARTS was established in 1993 to ensure that technology works to enhance a retailer's ability to develop store level business solutions and avoid situations that limit a retailer's ability to implement change while providing industry standards designed to provide greater value at lower costs.

ARTS has created a Retail Data Model, which is distributed to ARTS members via the ARTS web site. The ARTS Data Model facilitates a high degree of plug-and-play compatibility for retail applications, which was previously difficult, or in many cases impossible, to achieve. On March 31, 2003, release 4.0 of the data model was announced. The data model has 78 diagrams, which each show the entities and relationships for a particular retail subject area,

ARTS claims the model is comprehensive and applies to both food and general merchandise retailing. Also, because ARTS is an international organization, care was taken to include input from members around the world to ensure that the data model is valid on a global basis. More than 50 of the leading European retailers and their vendor partners are involved in ARTS European Consortium. Adopters include Marks and Spencer, The Gap, Home Depot, Target, and Nordstrom.

Source: www.nrf-arts.org.

---

come entities. It is only by listing all of an entity's attributes that these additional entities are recognized.

In a well-formed data model, all attribute names are meaningful and unique. The names of entities, identifiers, attributes, and relationships must be meaningful to the client because they are meant to describe the client's world. Indeed, in nearly all cases they are the client's everyday names. Take care in selecting words because they are critical to communicating meaning. The acid test for comprehension is to get the client to read the data model to other potential users. Names need to be unique to avoid confusion.

A high-fidelity image

Music lovers aspire to own a high-fidelity stereo system — one that faithfully reproduces the original performance with minimal or no distortion. A data model is a high-fidelity image when it faithfully describes the world it is supposed to represent. All relationships are recorded and are of the correct degree. There are no compromises or distortions. If the real-world relationship is many-to-many (m:m), then so is the relationship shown in the data model. A well-formed, high-fidelity data model is complete, understandable, accurate, and syntactically correct.

Table 7-2: Characteristics of a well-formed data model

All construction rules are obeyed.
There is no ambiguity.
All entities are named.
Every entity has an identifier.
All relationships are represented, using the correct notation.
Relationships are labeled to avoid misunderstanding.
All attributes of each entity are listed.
All attribute names are meaningful and unique.

Quality improvement

A data model is an evolving representation. Each change should be an incremental improvement in quality. Occasionally, you will find a major quality problem at the data model's core and have to change the data model dramatically.

Detail and context

The quality of a data model can be determined only by understanding the context in which it will be used. Consider the data model (see Figure 7-6) used in Chapter 4 to discuss the 1:m relationship. This fragment says a nation has many stocks. But is that really what we want to represent? Stocks are listed on a stock exchange, and a nation may have several stock exchanges. For example, each Australian state's capital city has a stock exchange. Australian stocks can be listed on multiple exchanges but have a single home exchange. Furthermore, some Australian stocks are listed on the New York Stock Exchange. If this is the world we have to describe, the data model is likely to differ from that shown in Figure 7-6. Try drawing the revised data model.

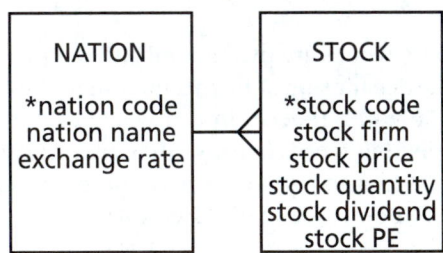

Figure 7-6. A 1:m relationship between STOCK and NATION

As you can see, the data model in Figure 7-7 is quite different from the initial data model of Figure 7-6. Which one is better? They both can be valid models; it just depends on the world you are trying to represent and possible future queries. In the first case, the purpose was to determine the value of a portfolio. There was no interest in where stocks were listed or their home exchange. So the first model has high fidelity for the described situation.

The second data model would be appropriate if the client needed to know the home exchange of stocks and their price on the various exchanges where they were listed. The second data model is an improvement on the first if it incorporates the additional facts and relationships required. If it does not, then the additional detail is not worth the extra cost.

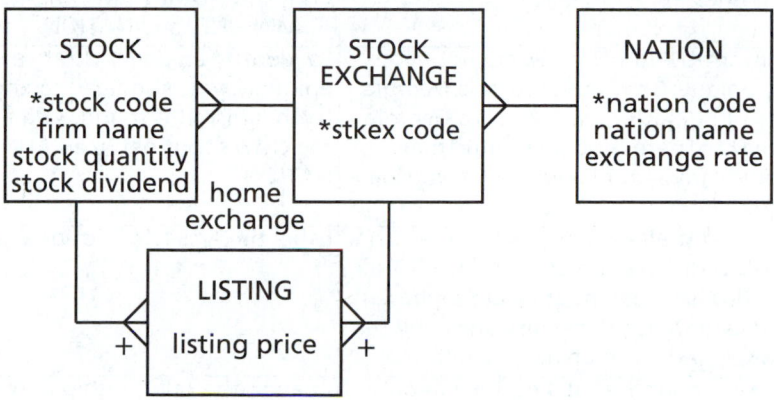

Figure 7-7. Revised NATION-STOCK data model

A lesson in pure geography

A data model must be an accurate representation of the world you want to model. The data model must account for all the exceptions — there should be no impurities. Let's say you want to establish a database to store details of the world's cities. You might start with the data model depicted in Figure 7-8.

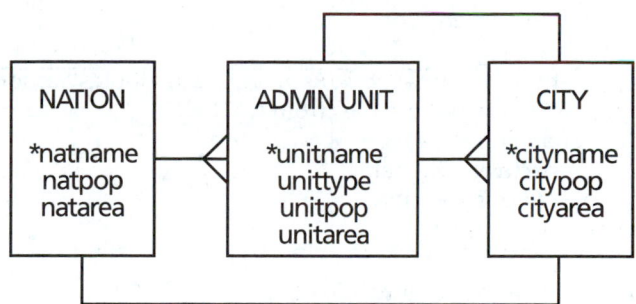

Figure 7-8. A world's cities data model

Before looking more closely at the data model, let's clarify the meaning of *unittype*. Because most countries are divided into administrative units that are variously called states, provinces, territories, and so forth, *unittype* indicates the type of administrative unit (e.g., state). How many errors can you find in the initial data model (see Table 7-3)?

Table 7-3: Problems and solutions for the initial world's cities data model

	Problem	Solution
1.	City names are not unique. There is an Athens in Greece and the U.S. has an Athens in Georgia, Alabama, Ohio, Pennsylvania, Tennessee, and Texas.	To identify a city uniquely, you need to specify its administrative unit and country. Add a plus sign to the crow's feet between CITY and ADMIN UNIT and between ADMIN UNIT and NATION.
2.	Administrative unit names are not necessarily unique. There used to be a Georgia in the old U.S.S.R., and there is a Georgia in the U.S. There is no guarantee that administrative unit names will always be unique.	To identify an administrative unit uniquely, you also need to know the country in which it is found. Add a plus sign to the crow's foot between ADMIN UNIT and NATION.
3.	There are unlabeled 1:1 arcs between CITY and ADMIN UNIT and CITY and NATION. What do these mean? They are supposed to indicate that an administrative unit has a capital, and a nation has a capital.	Label the arcs (e.g., national capital city).
4.	The assumption is that a nation has only one capital, but there are exceptions. South Africa has three capitals: Cape Town (legislative), Pretoria (administrative), and Bloemfontein (judicial). You only need one exception to lower the fidelity of a data model significantly.	Change the relationship between NATION and CITY to 1:m. Add an attribute *natcaptype* to CITY to distinguish between types of capitals.
5	The assumption is that an administrative unit has only one capital, but there are exceptions. Chandigarh is the capital of two Indian states, Punjab and Haryana. The Indian state of Jammu & Kashmir has two capitals: Jammu (summer) and Srinagar (winter).	Change the relationship between ADMIN UNIT and CITY to m:m by creating an associative entity and include a distinguishing attribute of *unitcaptype*.
6.	Some values can be derived. National population, *natpop*, and area, *natarea*, are the sum of the regional populations, *regpop*, and areas, *regarea*, respectively. The same rule does not apply to regions and cities because not everyone lives in a city.	Remove the attributes *natpop* and *natarea* from NATION.

The revised data model is shown in Figure 7-9.

This geography lesson demonstrates how you often start with a simple model of low fidelity. Additional thinking about relationships and consideration of exceptions gradually create a high-fidelity data model.

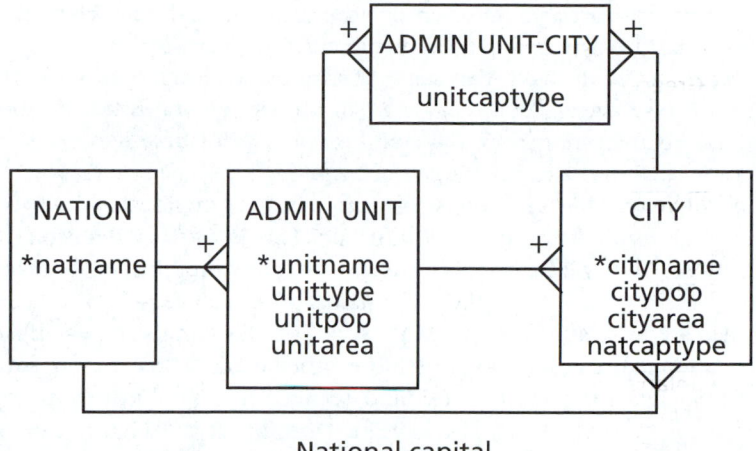

National capital

Figure 7-9. A revised world's cities data model

Skill Builder

1. Write SQL to determine which administrative units have two capitals and which have a shared capital.

Family matters

Families can be very complicated. It can be tricky to keep track of all those relations — maybe you need a relational database (this is the worst joke in the book; they improve after this). We start with a very limited view of marriage and gradually ease the restrictions to demonstrate how any and all aspects of a relationship can be modeled. An initial fragment of the data model is shown in Figure 7-10. There are several things to notice about it.

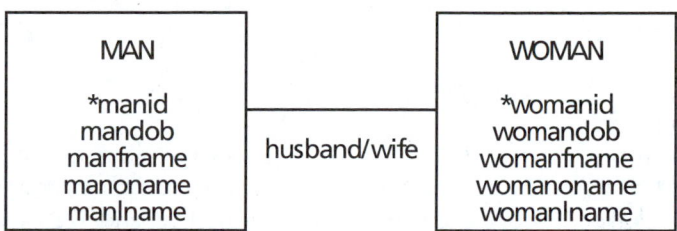

Figure 7-10. A MAN-WOMAN data model

1. There is a 1:1 relationship between man and woman. The labels indicate that this relationship is marriage, but there is no indication of the marriage date. We are left to infer that the data model records the current marriage.

2. MAN and WOMAN have the same attributes. A modifier is used to make them unique. Both have an identifier (*...id*, in the United States this would probably be a Social Security number), date of birth (*...dob*), first name (*...fname*), other names (*...oname*), and last name (*...lname*).

3. Other names (*...oname*) looks like a multivalued attribute, which is not allowed. Should *...oname* be single or multivalue? This is a tricky decision. It depends on how these data will be used. If queries such as "find all men whose other names include Herbert" are likely, then a person's other names — kept as a separate entity that has a 1:m relationship for MAN and WOMAN — must be established. That is, a man or woman can have one or more other names. However, if you just want to store the data for completeness and retrieve it in its entirety, then *...oname* is fine. It is just a text string. The key question to ask is, "What is the lowest level of detail possibly required for future queries?" Also, remember that SQL's LIKE clause can be used to search for values within a text string.

The use of a modifier to distinguish attribute names in different entities suggests you should consider combining the entities. In this case, we could combine the entities MAN and WOMAN to create an entity called PERSON. Usually when entities are combined, you have to create a new attribute to distinguish between the different types. In this example, the attribute *gender* is added. We can also generalize the relationship label to *spouse*. The revised data model appears in Figure 7-11.

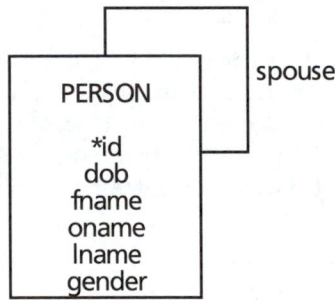

Figure 7-11. A PERSON data model

Now for a bit of marriage counseling. Marriage normally is a relationship between two people. Is that so? Well, some societies permit polygamy (one man can have many wives), and others allow polyandry (one woman can have many husbands). So marriage, if we consider all the possibilities, is an m:m relationship. Also, a person can be married more than once. To distinguish between different marriages, we really need to record the start and end date of each relationship and who was involved (see Figure 7-12).

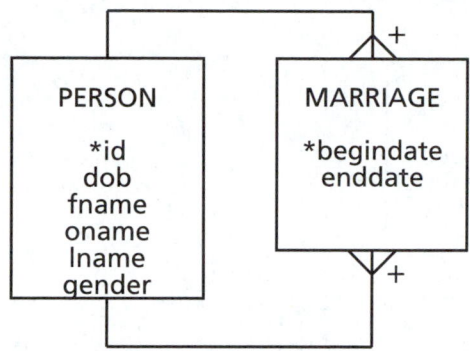

Figure 7-12. A marriage data model

Marriage is an m:m relationship between two persons. It has attributes *begindate* and *enddate*. An instance of marriage is uniquely identified by a composite identifier: the two spouse identifiers and *begindate*. This means any marriage is uniquely identified by the composite of two person identifiers and the beginning date of the marriage. We need *begindate* as part of the identifier because the same couple might have more than one marriage (e.g., get divorced and remarry each other later). Furthermore, we can safely assume that it is impossible for a couple to get married, divorced, and remarried all on the one day. *Begindate* and *enddate* can be used to determine the current state of a marriage. If *enddate* is null, the marriage is current; otherwise, the couple has divorced.

This data model assumes a couple goes through some formal process to get married or divorced, and there is an official date for both of these events. What happens if they just gradually drift into cohabitation, and there is no official beginning date? Think about it. (The data model problem, that is—not cohabitation!) Many countries recognize this situation as a common-law marriage, so the data model needs to recognize it. The present data model cannot handle this situation because *begindate* cannot be null—it is an identifier. Instead, a new identifier is needed, and *begindate* should become an attribute.

Two new attributes can handle a common-law marriage. *Marriageno* for marriage number can count the number of times a couple has been married to each other. In the great majority of cases, *marriageno* will be 1. *Marriagestatus* can record whether a marriage is current or ended. Now we have a data model that can also handle common-law marriages. This is also a high-quality data model in that the client does not have to remember to examine *enddate* to determine a marriage's current status. It is easier to remember to examine *marriagestatus* to check status. Also, we can allow a couple to be married, divorced, and remarried as many times as they like on the one day — which means we can now use the database in Las Vegas. The latest version of the data model is shown in Figure 7-13.

All right, now that we have the couple successfully married, we need to start thinking about children. A marriage has zero or more children, and let's start with the assumption

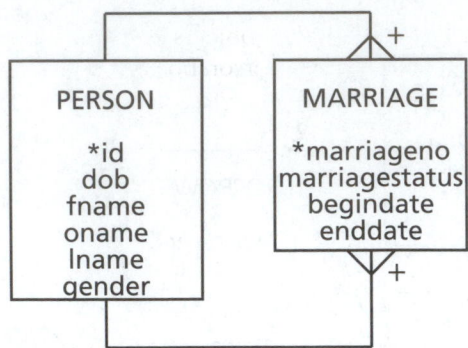

Figure 7-13. A revised marriage data model

a child belongs to only one marriage. Therefore, we have a 1:m relationship between marriage and person to represent the children of a marriage (see Figure 7-14).

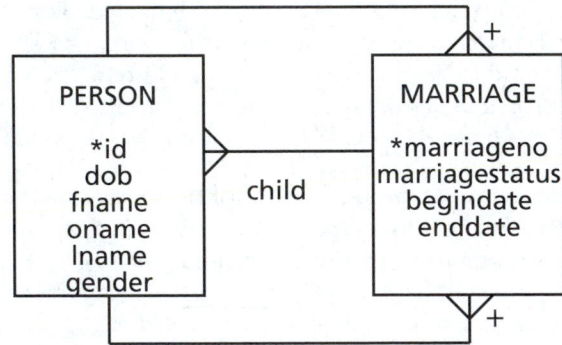

Figure 7-14. A marriage with children data model

You might want to consider how the model would change to handle single-parent families, adopted children, and other aspects of human relationships.

Skill builder

The International Commission for Border Resolution Disputes requires a database to record details of which countries have common borders. Design the database. Incidentally, which country borders the most other countries?

When's a book not a book?

Sometimes we have to rethink our ideas of physical objects. Consider a data model for a library. The fragment (Figure 7-15) assumes that a person borrows a book. What happens

Figure 7-15. A library data model fragment

if the library has two copies of the book? Do we add an attribute to BOOK called *copy number*? No, because we would introduce redundancy by repeating the same information for each book. What you need to recognize is that in the realm of data modeling, a book is not really a physical thing, but the copy is, because it is what you borrow. The revised data model fragment is illustrated in Figure 7-16.

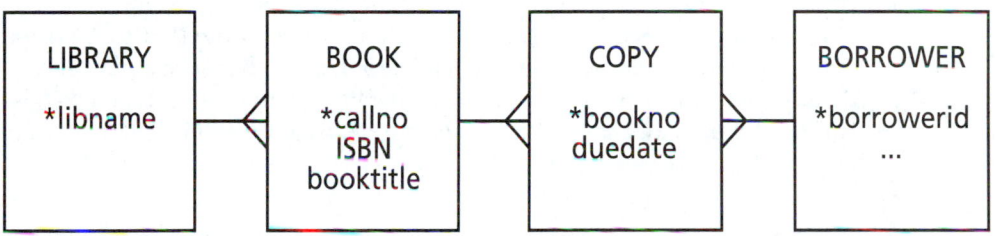

Figure 7-16. A revised library data model fragment

As you can see, a book has many copies, and a copy is of one book. A book can be identified by *callno*, which is usually a Library of Congress number or Dewey number. A copy is identified by a *bookno*. This is a unique number allocated by the library to the copy of the book. If you look in a library book, you will generally find it pasted on the inside back cover and shown in numeric and bar code format. Notice that it is called *book number* despite the fact that it really identifies a copy of a book. This is because most people, including librarians, think of the copy as a book.

The International Standard Book Number (ISBN) uniquely identifies any instance of a book (not copy). Although it sounds like a potential identifier for BOOK, it is not. ISBNs were introduced in the second half of the twentieth century, and books published before then do not have an ISBN.

A history lesson

Many organizations maintain historical data (e.g., a person's job history or a student's enrollment record). A data model can depict historical data relationships just as readily as current data relationships.

Consider the case of an employee who works for a firm that consists of divisions (e.g., production) and departments (e.g., quality control). The firm contains many departments, but a department belongs to only one division. At any one time, an employee belongs to only one department. If we were modeling the current situation, the data model fragment would look like that shown in Figure 7-17.

Figure 7-17. Employment history—take 1

The fragment in Figure 7-17 can be amended to keep track of the divisions and departments in which a person works. While employed with a firm, a person can work in more than one department. Since a department can have many employees, we have an m:m relationship between DEPARTMENT and EMPLOYEE. We might call the resulting associative entity POSITION (see Figure 7-18).

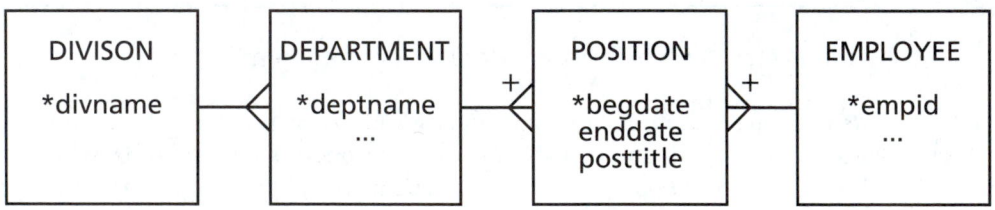

Figure 7-18. Employment history—take 2

The revised fragment records employee work history. Note that any instance of POSITION is identified by *begdate* and the identifiers for EMPLOYEE and DEPARTMENT. The fragment is typical of what happens when you move from just keeping current data to recording history. A 1:m becomes an m:m relationship to record history.

People who work get paid. How do we keep track of an employee's pay data? An employee has many pay slips, but a pay slip belongs to one employee. When you look at a pay slip, you will find it contains many items: gross pay and a series of deductions for tax, medical insurance, and so on. Think of a pay slip as containing many lines, analogous to a sales form. Now look at the revised data model in Figure 7-19.

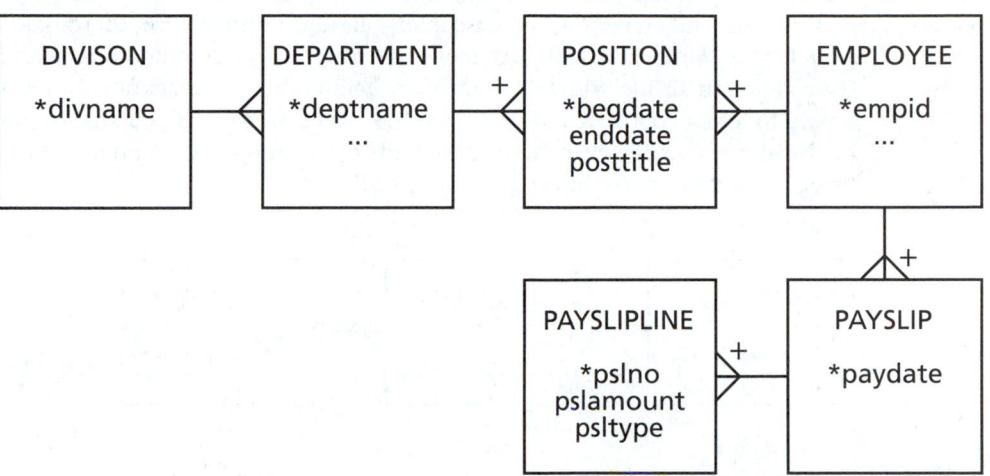

Figure 7-19. Employment history—take 3

Typically, an amount shown on a pay slip is identified by a short text field (e.g., gross pay). PAYSLIPLINE contains an attribute *psltype* to identify the text that should accompany an amount, but where is the text? When dealing with codes like *psltype* and their associated text, the fidelity of a data model is improved by creating a separate entity, PSLTEXT, for the code and its text (Figure 7-20).

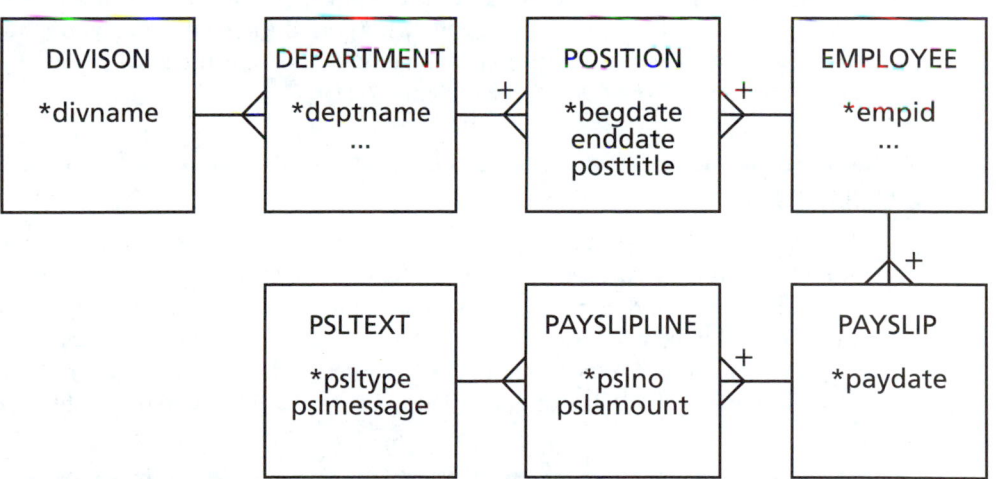

Figure 7-20. Employment history—take 4

171

A ménage à trois for entities[2]

Consider aircraft leasing. A plane is leased to an airline for a specific period of time. When a lease expires, the plane can be leased to another airline. So, an aircraft can be leased many times, and an airline can lease many aircraft. Furthermore, there is an agent responsible for handling each deal. An agent can lease many aircraft and deal with many airlines. Over time, an airline will deal with many agents. When an agent reaches a deal with an airline to lease a particular aircraft, you have a transaction. If you analyze the aircraft leasing business, you discover there are three m:m relationships. You might think of these as three separate relationships (see Figure 7-21).

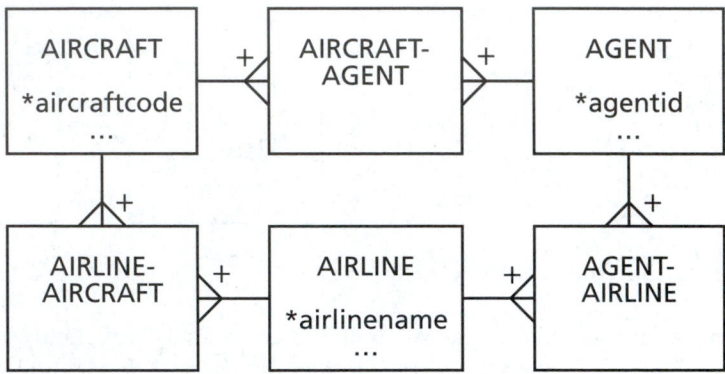

Figure 7-21. An AIRCRAFT-AIRLINE-AGENT data model

The problem with three separate m:m relationships is that it is unclear where to store data about the lease. Is it stored in AIRLINE-AIRCRAFT? If you store the information there, what do you do about recording the agent who closed the deal? After you read the fine print and do some more thinking, you discover that a lease is the association of these three entities in an m:m relationship (see Figure 7-22).

Skill builder

Horse racing is a popular sport in some parts of the world. A horse competes in at most one race on a course at a particular date. Over time, a horse can compete in many races on many courses. A horse's rider is called a jockey, and a jockey can ride many horses and a horse can have many jockeys. Of course, there is only ever one jockey riding a horse at a particular time. Courses vary in their features, such as the length of the course and the type of surface (e.g., dirt or grass). Design a database to keep track of the results of horse races.

---

2.   Also known as a ternary relationship, but its life is less interesting.

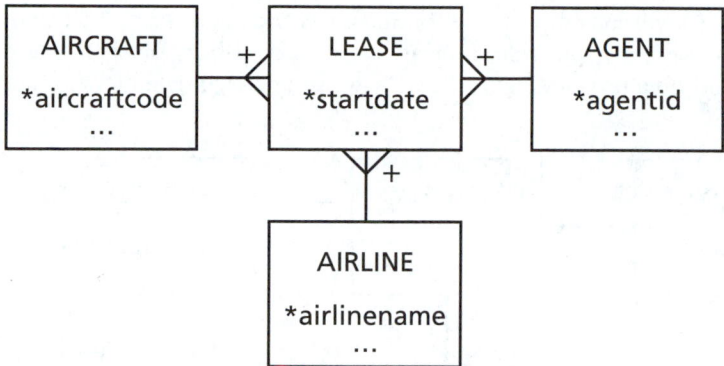

Figure 7-22. A revised AIRCRAFT-AIRLINE-AGENT data model

Project management—planning and doing

Project management involves both planned and actual data. A project is divided into a number of activities that use resources. Planning includes estimation of the resources to be consumed. When a project is being executed, managers keep track of the resources actually used in order to monitor progress and keep the project on budget. Planning data may not be as detailed as actual data and is typically fairly broad, such as an estimate of the number of hours that an activity will take. Actual data will be more detailed because they are usually collected by getting those assigned to the project to log a daily account of how they spent their time. Also, resources used on a project are allocated to a particular activity. For the purposes of this data model, we will focus only on recording time and nothing else (see Figure 7-23).

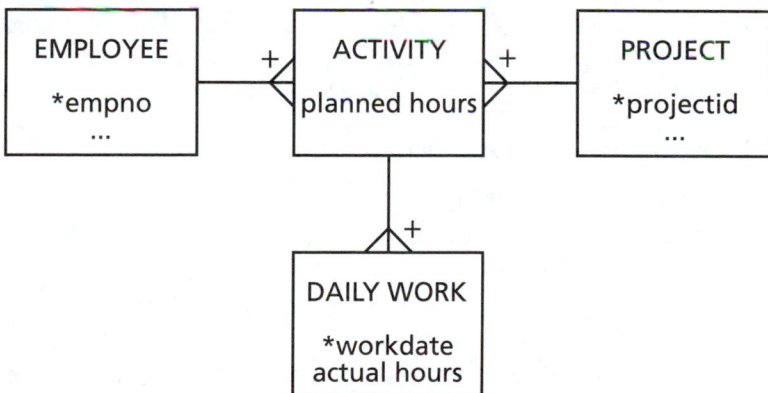

Figure 7-23. A project management data model

Notice that *planned hours* is an attribute of ACTIVITY, and *actual hours* is an attribute of DAILY WORK. The hours spent on an activity are derived by summing *actual hours* in

173

the associated DAILY WORK entity. This is a high-fidelity data model if planning is done at the activity level and employees submit daily worksheets. Planning can be done in greater detail, however, if planners indicate how many hours of each day each employee should spend on a project. Figure 7-24 shows the revised data model fragment.

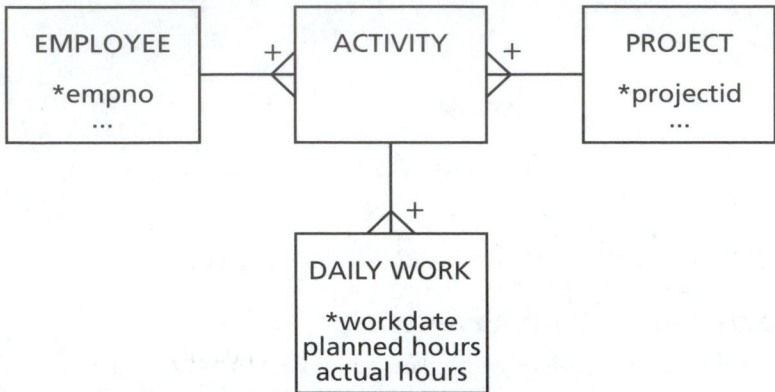

Figure 7-24. A revised project management data model

Now you see that *planned hours* and *actual hours* are both attributes of DAILY WORK. The message of this example, therefore, is not to assume that planned and actual data have the same level of detail, but do not be surprised if they do.

Cardinality

Some data modeling languages are quite precise in specifying the cardinality, or multiplicity, of a relationship (see Table 7-4). Thus, in a 1:m relationship, you might see additional information on the diagram. For example, the "many" end of the relationship might contain notation (such as 0,n) to indicate zero or more instances of the entity at the "many" end of the relationship.

Table 7-4: Cardinality and modality options

Cardinality	Modality	Meaning
0,1	Optional	There can be zero or one instances of the entity relative to the other entity.
0,n		There can be zero or many instances of the entity relative to the other entity.
1,1	Mandatory	There is exactly one instance of the entity relative to the other entity.
1,n		The entity must have at least one and can have many instances relative to the other entity.

The data modeling method of this text, as you now realize, has taken a broad approach to cardinality (is it 1:1 or 1:m?). We have not been concerned with greater precision (is it 0,1 or 1,1?) because the focus has been on acquiring basic data modeling skills. Once you know how to model, you can add more detail. When learning to model, too much detail and too much terminology can get in the way of mastering this difficult skill. Also, it is far easier to sketch models on a whiteboard or paper when you have less to draw. Once you switch to a data modeling tool, then adding cardinality precision is easier and appropriate.

Modality

Modality, also known as optionality, specifies whether an instance of an entity must participate in a relationship. Cardinality indicates the range of instances of an entity participating in a relationship, while modality defines the minimum number of instances. Cardinality and modality are linked, as shown in Table 7-4. If an entity is optional, the minimum cardinality will be 0, and if mandatory, the minimum cardinality is 1.

By asking the question, "Does an occurrence of this entity require an occurrence of the other entity?" you can assess whether an entity is mandatory. The usual practice is to use "O" for optional and place it near the entity that is optional. Mandatory relationships are often indicated by a short line (or bar) at right angles to the arc for the relationship between the entities.

In Figure 7-25, it is mandatory for an instance of STOCK to have an instance of NATION, and optional for an instance of NATION to have an instance of STOCK, which means we can record details of a nation for which stocks have not yet been purchased. During conversion of the data model to a relational database, the mandatory requirement (i.e., each stock must have a nation) is enforced by the foreign key constraint.

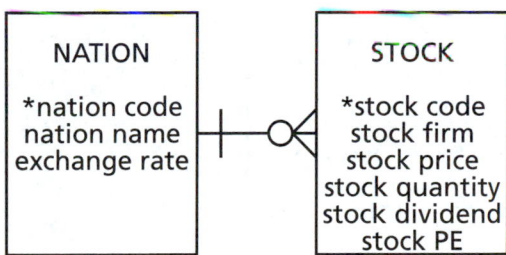

Figure 7-25. 1:m relationship showing modality

Now consider an example of an m:m relationship (see Figure 7-26). A SALE can have many LINEITEMs, and a LINEITEM has only one SALE. An instance of LINEITEM must be related to an instance of SALE, otherwise it can't exist. Similarly, it is mandatory for an instance of SALE to have an instance of LINEITEM, because it makes no sense to have a sale without any items being sold.

In a relational database, the foreign key constraint handles the mandatory relationship between instances of LINEITEM and SALE, The mandatory requirement between SALE and LINEITEM has to be built into the processing logic of the application that processes a sales transaction. Basic business logic requires that a sale include some items, so a sales transaction creates one instance of SALE and multiple instances of LINEITEM. It does not make sense to have a sale that does not sell something.

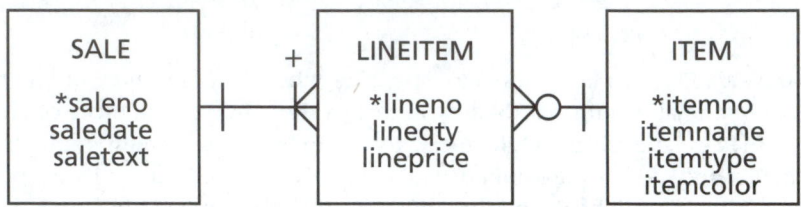

Figure 7-26. An m:m relationship showing modality

The relationship between ITEM and LINEITEM is similar in structure to that of NATION and STOCK, which we saw in the previous example. An instance of a LINEITEM has a mandatory requirement for an instance of ITEM. An instance of an ITEM can exist without the need for an instance of a LINEITEM (i.e., the items that have not been sold).

We gain further understanding of modality by considering a 1:1 relationship (Figure 7-27).We focus attention on the 1:1 because the 1:m relationship has been covered. The 1:1 implies that it is mandatory for an instance of DEPT to be related to one instance of EMP (i.e., a department must have a person who is the boss), and an instance of EMP is optionally related to one instance of DEPT (i.e., an employee can be a boss, but not all employees are departmental bosses).

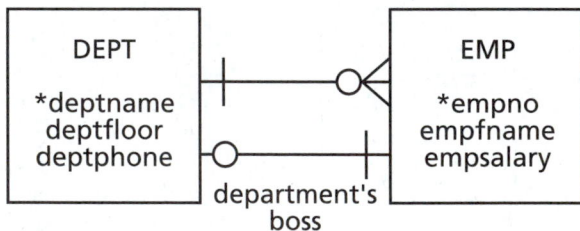

Figure 7-27. A 1:1 relationship showing modality

When deciding where to store the foreign key for the 1:1 relationship, we considered three options (see page 137). We settled on placing the foreign key in DEPT, because all departments have a boss. Now we have a rule. The foreign key goes with the entity for which the relationship is mandatory. When specifying the create statements, you will need to be aware of the chicken-and-egg connection between DEPT and EMP. We cannot insert an employee in EMP unless we know that person's department, and we cannot insert a department unless we have already inserted the boss for that department in EMP. We can get around this problem with some logic in the application that inserts departments and employees and by using a **deferrable** foreign key constraint.[3]

Let's now consider recursive relationships. Figure 7-27 shows a recursive 1:m between employees, representing that one employee can be the boss of many other employees and a person has one boss. It is optional that a person is a boss, and also optional that everyone has a boss, mainly because there has to be one person who is the boss of everyone. However, we can get around this one exception by inserting employees in a particular order (see page 138). By inserting the biggest boss first, we effectively make it mandatory that all employees have a boss. Nevertheless, data models cover every situation and exception, so we still show the relationship as optional.

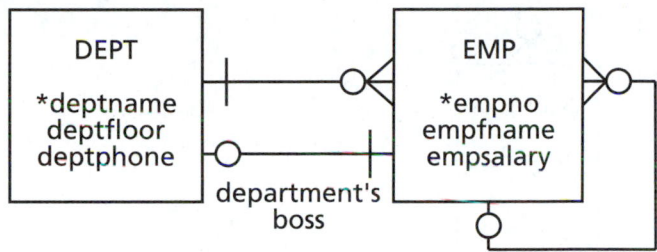

Figure 7-28. 1:m recursive with modality

We rely again on the British monarchy.[4] This time we use it to illustrate modality with a 1:1 recursive relationship. As Figure 7-29 shows, it is optional for a monarch to have a successor. We are not talking about the end of a monarchy, but rather how we address the data modeling issue of not knowing who succeeds the current monarch. Similarly, there must be a monarch who did not succeed someone (i.e., the first king or queen). Thus, both ends of the succession relationship have optional modality.

Finally, in our exploration of modality, we examine the m:m recursive (see Figure 7-30). The model indicates that it is optional for a product to have components and optional for a product to be a component in other products. However, every assembly must have associated products.

Summary

Modality adds additional information to a data model, and once you have grasped the fundamental ideas of entities and relationships, it is quite straightforward to consider whether a relationship is optional or mandatory. When a relationship is mandatory, you need to

---

3. Deferrable constraints are outside the scope of this text.
4. Royalty still has some value in the 21st century.

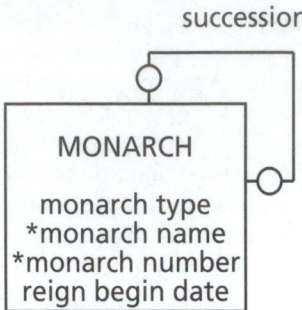

Figure 7-29. 1:1 recursive with modality

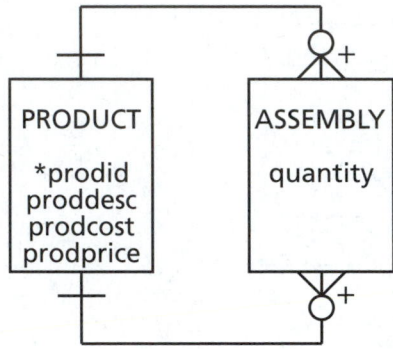

Figure 7-30. m:m recursive with modality

consider what constraint you can add to a table's definition to enforce the relationship. As we have seen, in some cases the foreign key constraint handles mandatory relationships. In other cases, the logic for enforcing a requirement will be built into the application.

Entity types

A data model contains different kinds of entities, which are distinguished by the format of their identifiers. Labeling each of these entities by type will help you to determine what questions to ask.

Independent entity

An independent entity is often central to a data model and foremost in the client's mind. Independent entities are frequently the starting points of a data model. Remember that in the investment database, the independent entities are STOCK and NATION. Independent entities typically have clearly distinguishable names because they occur so frequently in the client's world. In addition, they usually have a single, arbitrary identifier, such as *stock code* or *nation code*.

Independent entities are often connected to other independent entities in a 1:m or m:m relationship. The data model in Figure 7-31 shows two independent entities linked in a 1:m relationship.

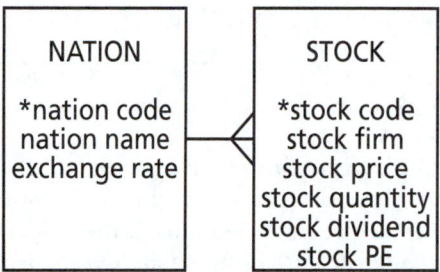

Figure 7-31. NATION and STOCK—independent entities

Weak or dependent entity

A weak entity (also known as a dependent entity) relies on another entity for its existence and identification. It is recognized by a plus on the weak entity's end of the arc (see Figure 7-32). CITY cannot exist without REGION. A CITY is uniquely identified by *cityname* and *regname*. If the composite identifier becomes unwieldy, creating an arbitrary identifier (e.g., cityno) will change the weak entity into an independent one.

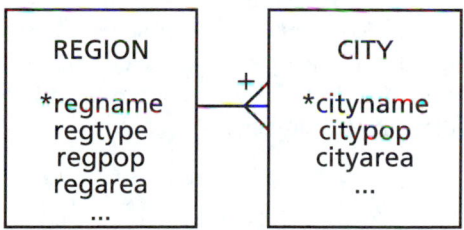

Figure 7-32. CITY—a weak entity

Associative entity[5]

Associative entities are by-products of m:m relationships. They are typically found between independent entities. Associative entities sometimes have obvious names because they occur in the real world. For instance, the associative entity for the m:m relationship between DEPARTMENT and EMPLOYEE is usually called POSITION (see Figure 7-33). If the associative entity does not have a common name, the two entity names are generally hyphenated (e.g., DEPARTMENT-EMPLOYEE). Always search for the appropriate name, because it will improve the quality of the data model. Hyphenated names are a last resort.

---

5. Also known as an *intersection entity* in some data modeling dialects.

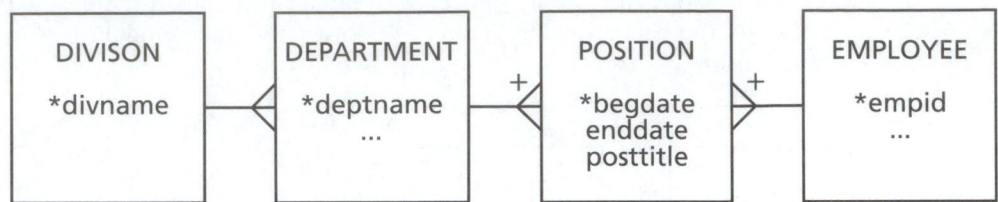

Figure 7-33. POSITION is an associative entity

Associative entities can show either the current or the historic relationship between two entities. If an associative entity's only identifiers are the two related entities' identifiers, then it records the current relationship between the entities. If the associative entity has some time measure as a partial identifier (e.g., date or hour), then it records the history of the relationship. Whenever you find an associative entity, ask the client whether the history of the relationship should be recorded.

Creating a single, arbitrary identifier for an associative entity will change it to an independent one. This is likely to happen if the associative entity becomes central to an application. For example, if a personnel department does a lot of work with POSITION, it may find it more expedient to give it a separate identifier (e.g., *position number*).

Aggregate entity

An aggregate entity is created when several different entities have similar attributes that are distinguished by a preceding or following modifier to keep their names unique. For example, because components of an address might occur in several entities (e.g., CUSTOMER and SUPPLIER), an aggregate address entity can be created to store details of all addresses. Aggregate entities usually become independent entities. In this case, we could use *address number* to identify an instance of address uniquely.

Subordinate entity

A subordinate entity stores data about an entity that can vary among instances. A subordinate entity is useful when an entity consists of mutually exclusive classes that have different descriptions. The farm animal database shown in Figure 7-34 indicates that the farmer requires different data for sheep and horses. Notice that each of the subordinate entities is identified by the related entity's identifier. You could avoid subordinate entities by placing all the attributes in ANIMAL, but then you make it incumbent on the client to remember which attributes apply to horses and which to sheep. This becomes an important issue for null fields. For example, is the attribute *hay consumption* null because it does not apply to sheep, or is it null because the value is unknown?

If a subordinate entity becomes important, it is likely to evolve to an independent entity. The framing of a problem often determines whether subordinate entities are created. Stating the problem as, "A farmer has many animals, and these animals can be horses or

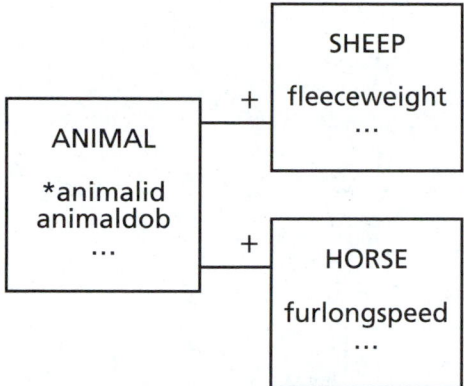

Figure 7-34. SHEEP and HORSE are subordinate entities

sheep," might lead to the creation of subordinate entities. Alternatively, saying that "a farmer has many sheep and horses" might lead to setting up SHEEP and HORSE as independent entities.

Generalization and aggregation

Generalization and aggregation are common ideas in many modeling languages, particularly object-oriented modeling languages such as the Unified Modeling Language (UML), which is discussed further in Chapter 13.

Generalization

A generalization[6] is a relationship between a more general element and a more specific element. In Figure 7-35, the general element is *animal*, and the specific elements are *sheep* and *horse*. A horse is a subtype of animal. A generalization is often called an "is a" relationship because the subtype element *is a* member of the generalization.

A generalization is directly mapped to the relational model with one table for each entity. For each of the subtype entities (i.e., SHEEP and HORSE), the primary key is that of the supertype entity (i.e., ANIMAL). You must also make this column a foreign key so that a subtype cannot be inserted without the presence of the matching supertype. A generalization is represented by a series of 1:1 relationships to weak entities (see Figure 7-34).

Aggregation

Aggregation is a part-whole relationship between two entities. Common phrases used to describe an aggregation are "consists of," "contains," and "is part of." Figure 7-36 shows an aggregation where a herd consists of many cows.[7] Cows can be removed or added, but

---

6.   UML notation is used to represent the generalization structure.
7.   An asterisk (*) indicates many in UML.

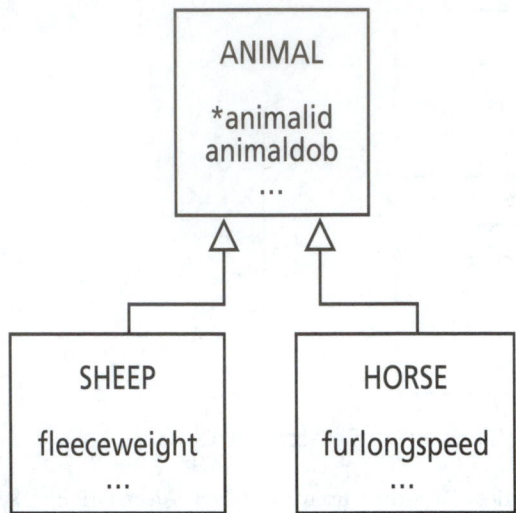

Figure 7-35. A generalization hierarchy

it is still a herd. An open diamond next to the whole denotes an aggregation. In data modeling terms, there is a 1:m relationship between herd and cow.

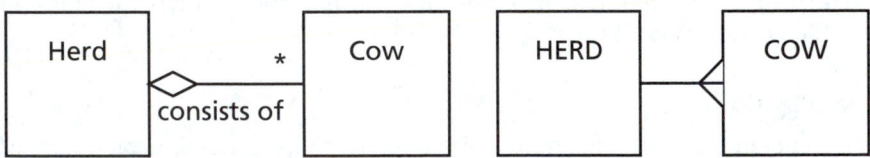

Figure 7-36. An aggregation in UML and data modeling

There are two special types of aggregation: shared and composition. With **shared aggregation**, one entity owns another entity, but other entities can own that entity as well. A sample shared aggregation is displayed in Figure 7-37, which shows that a class has many students, and a student can be a member of many classes. Students, the parts in this case, can be part of many classes. An open diamond next to the whole denotes a shared aggregation, which we represent in data modeling as an m:m relationship.

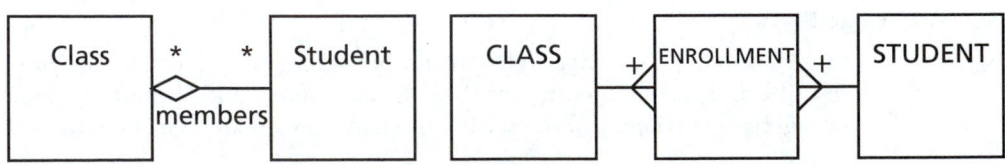

Figure 7-37. Shared aggregation in UML and data modeling

In a **composition aggregation,** one entity exclusively owns the other entity. A solid diamond at the whole end of the relationship denotes composition aggregation. The appropriate data model is a weak entity, as shown in Figure 7-38.

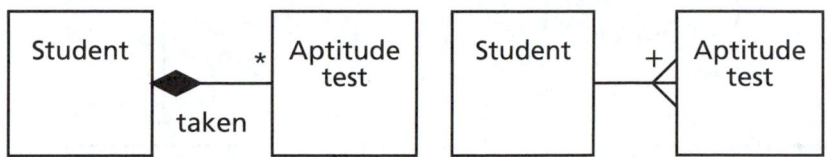

Figure 7-38. Composition aggregation in UML and data modeling

Data modeling hints

A high-fidelity data model takes time to develop. The client must explain the problem fully so that the database designer can understand the client's requirements and translate them into a data model. Data modeling is like prototyping; the database designer gradually creates a model of the database as a result of interaction with the client. Some issues will frequently arise in this progressive creation, and the following hints should help you resolve many of the common problems you will encounter.

The rise and fall of a data model

Expect your data model to both expand and contract. Your initial data model will expand as you extend the boundaries of the application. You will discover some attributes will evolve into entities, and some 1:m relationships will become m:m relationships. It will grow because you will add entities, attributes, and relationships to allow for exceptions. Your data model will grow because you are representing the complexity of the real world. Do not try to constrain growth. Let the data model be as large as is necessary. As a rough rule, expect your final data model to grow to about two to three times the number of entities of your initial data model.

Expect your data model to contract as you generalize structures. Consider the abbreviated data model shown in Figure 7-39.

This fragment is typical of the models produced by novice data modelers. It can be reduced by recognizing that CD, LP, and TAPE are all types of audio recordings. A more general entity, AUDIO RECORDING, could be used to represent the same data. Of course, it would need an additional attribute to distinguish the different types of audio recordings (see Figure 7-40).

As you discover new entities, your data model will grow. As you generalize, your data model will shrink.

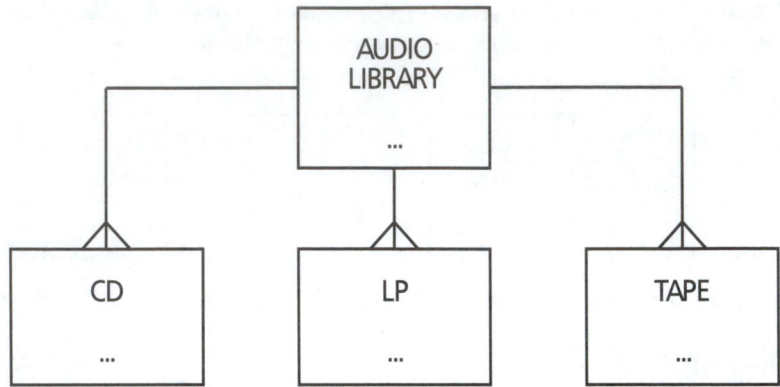

Figure 7-39. A data model that can shrink

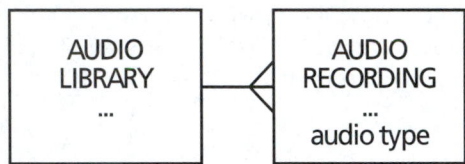

Figure 7-40. The shrunken data model

Identifier

If there is no obvious simple identifier, invent one. The simplest is a meaningless code (e.g., *person number* or *order number*). If you create an identifier, you can also guarantee its uniqueness.

Don't overwork an identifier. The worst case we have seen is a 22-character product code used by a plastics company that supposedly not only uniquely identified an item but told you its color, its manufacturing process, and type of plastic used to make it! Color, manufacturing process, and type of plastic are all attributes. This product code was unwieldy. Data entry error rates were extremely high, and very few people could remember how to decipher the code.

An identifier has to do only one thing: uniquely identify every instance of the entity. Sometimes trying to make it do double, or even triple, duty only creates more work for the client.

Position and order

There is no ordering in a data model. Entities can appear anywhere. You will usually find a central entity near the middle of the data model only because you tend to start with prominent entities (e.g., starting with STUDENT when modeling a student information system). What really matters is that you identify all relevant entities.

Attributes are in no order. You find that you will tend to list them as they are identified. For readability, it is a good idea to list some attributes sequentially. For example, first name, other names, and last name are usually together. This is not necessary, but it speeds up verification of a data model's completeness.

Instances are also assumed to have no ordering. There is no first instance, next instance, or last instance. If you must recognize a particular order, create an attribute to record the order. For example, if ranking of potential investment projects must be recorded, include an attribute (*projrank*) to store this data. This does not mean the instances will be stored in *projrank* order, but it does allow you to use the ORDER BY clause of SQL to report the projects in rank order.

If you need to store details of a precedence relationship (i.e., there is an ordering of instances and a need to know the successor and predecessor of any instance), then use a 1:1 recursive relationship. This is illustrated by the Monarch data model in Figure 7-41.

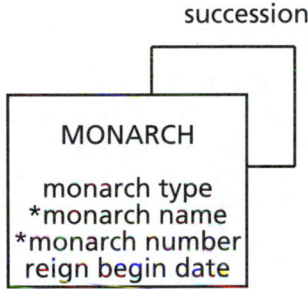

Figure 7-41. Using an attribute to record an ordering of instances

Attributes and consistency

Attributes must be consistent, retaining the same meaning for every instance. An example of an inconsistent attribute would be an attribute *stock info* that contains a stock's PE ratio or its ROI (return on investment). Another attribute, say *stock info code*, is required to decipher which meaning applies to any particular instance. The code could be "1" for PE and "2" for ROI. If one attribute determines the meaning of another, you have inconsistency. Writing SQL queries will be extremely challenging because inconsistent data increases query complexity. It is better to create separate attributes for PE and ROI.

Names and addresses

An attribute is the smallest piece of data that will conceivably form part of a query. If an attribute has segments (e.g., a person's name), determine whether these could form part of a query. If so, then make them separate attributes and reapply the query test. When you apply the query test to *person name*, you will usually decide to create three attributes: *first name*, *other name*, and *last name*.

What about titles? There are two sorts of modifier titles: preceding titles (e.g., Mr., Mrs., Ms., and Dr.) and following titles (e.g., Jr. and III). These should be separate attributes, especially if you have divided *name* into separate attributes.

Addresses seem to cause more concern than names because they are more variant. Business addresses tend to be the most complicated, and foreign addresses add a few more twists. The data model fragment in Figure 7-42 works in most cases.

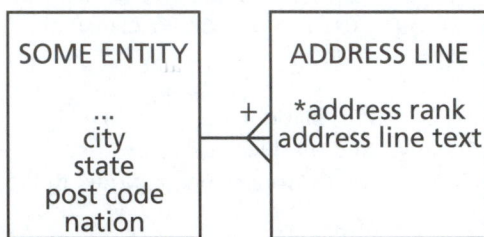

Figure 7-42. Handling addresses

Common features of every address are city, state (province in Canada, county in Eire), postal code (ZIP code in the United States), and nation. Some of these can be null. For example, Singapore does not have any units corresponding to states. In the United States, city and state can be derived from the ZIP code, but this is not necessarily true for other countries. Furthermore, even if this were true for every nation, you would need a different derivation rule for each country, which could be beyond the scope of some RDBMSs. If there is a lifetime guarantee that every address in the database will be for one country, then examine the possibility of reducing redundancy by just storing *post code*.

Notice that the problem of multiple address lines is represented by a 1:m relationship. An address line is a text string that appears as one line of an address. There is often a set sequence in which these are displayed. The attribute *address rank* records this order.

How do you address students? First names may be all right for class, but it is not adequate enough for student records. Students typically have multiple addresses: a home address, a school address, and maybe a summer address. The following data model fragment (see Figure 7-43) shows how to handle this situation. Any instance of ADDRESS LINE is identified by the composite of *studentid, addresstype*, and *address rank*.

The identifier *address type* is used to distinguish among the different types of addresses. The same data model fragment works in situations where a business has different mailing and shipping addresses.

When data modeling, can you take a shortcut with names and addresses? It is time consuming to write out all the components of name and address. It creates clutter and does not add much fidelity. Our practical advice is to do two things. *First,* create a policy for all names and addresses (e.g., all names will be stored as three parts: first name, other names,

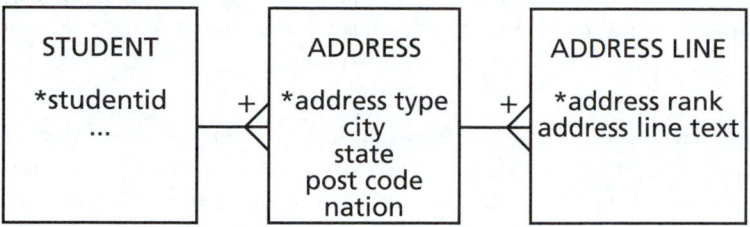

Figure 7-43. Students with multiple addresses

last name). *Second*, use shorthand forms of attributes for names and addresses when they obey the policy. So from now on, we will use name and address as attributes with the understanding that when the database is created, the parts will become separate columns.

Single-instance entities

Do not be afraid of creating an entity with a single instance. Consider the data model fragment in Figure 7-44 which describes a single fast-food chain. Because the data model describes only one firm, the entity FIRM will have only one instance. The inclusion of this single-instance entity permits facts about the firm to be maintained. Furthermore, it provides flexibility for expansion. If two fast-food chains combine, the data model needs no amendment.

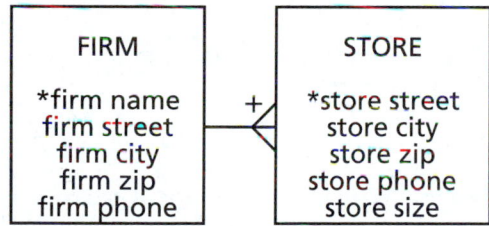

Figure 7-44. FIRM—a single-instance entity

Picking words

Words are very important. They are all we have to make ourselves understood. Let the client choose the words, because the data model belongs to the client and describes the client's world. If you try to impose your words on the client, you are likely to create a misunderstanding.

Synonyms

Synonyms are words that have the same meaning. For example, task, assignment, and project might all refer to the same real-world object. One of these terms, maybe the one in most common use, needs to be selected for naming the entity. Clients need to be told the official name for the entity and encouraged to adopt this term for describing it. Alternatively, create views that enable clients to use their own term. Synonyms are not a technical problem. It is a social problem of getting clients to agree on one word.

Homonyms

Homonyms are words that sound the same but have different meanings. Homonyms can create real confusion. *Sale date* is a classic example. In business it can have several meanings. To the salespeople, it is the day that the customer shakes hands and says, "We have a deal." For the lawyers, it is the day when the contract is signed, and for production, it is the day the customer takes delivery. In this case, the solution is reasonably obvious; redefine *sale date* to be separate terms for each area (e.g., *sales date*, *contract date*, and *delivery date* for sales, legal, and production departments, respectively).

Homonyms cause real confusion when clients do not realize that they are using the same word for different entities or attributes. Hunt down homonyms by asking lots of questions and querying a range of clients.

Exception hunting

Go hunting for exceptions. Keep asking the client questions such as

❖   Is it always like this?
❖   Would there be any situations where this could be an m:m relationship?
❖   Have there ever been any exceptions?
❖   Are things likely to change in the future?

Always probe for exceptions and look for them in the examples the client uses. Redesigning the data model to handle exceptions increases fidelity.

Relationship labeling

Relationship labeling clutters a data model. In most cases, labels can be correctly inferred, so use labels only when there is a possibility of ambiguity.

Keeping the data model in shape

As you add to a data model, maintain fidelity. Do not add entities without also completing details of the identifier and attributes. By keeping the data model well formed, you avoid ambiguity, which frequently leads to miscommunication.

Used entities

Would you buy a used data model? Certainly, because a used data model is more likely to have higher fidelity than a brand new one. A used data model has been subjected to much scrutiny and revision and should be a more accurate representation of the real world.

Meaningful identifiers

An identifier is said to be meaningful when some attributes of the entity can be inferred from the identifier's value (e.g., a code of B78 for an item informs a clerk that the item is black). The word "meaningful" in everyday speech usually connotes something desirable, but many data managers agree that meaningful identifiers or codes create problems. While avoiding meaningful identifiers is generally accepted as good data management practice, they are still widely used. After a short description of some examples of meaningful identifiers, this section discusses the pros and cons of meaningful identifiers.[8]

The invoice number "98dec0001" is a meaningful identifier. The first five positions indicate in which period the invoice was generated. The last four digits of the invoice number have a meaning. The 0001 indicates it was the first invoice sent in December. In addition, e-mail addresses, like mvdpas@bizzo.nl, have a meaning.

When coding a person's gender, some systems use the codes "m" and "f" and others "1" and "2." The pair (m, f) is meaningful, but (1, 2) is not and puts the onus on the user to remember the meaning. The codes "m" and "f" are derived from the reality that they represent. They are the first letters of the words male and female. The "1" and "2" are not abstracted from reality, and therefore they do not have a meaning. This observation is reiterated by the following quote from the International Organization for Standardization (ISO) information interchange standard for the representation of human sexes (ISO 5218):

No significance is to be placed on the fact that "Male" is coded "1" and "Female" is coded "2." This standard was developed based upon predominant practices of the countries involved and does not convey any meaning of importance, ranking or any other basis that could imply discrimination.

In determining whether an identifier is meaningful, one can look at the way new values of that identifier are generated. If the creation takes place on the basis of characteristics that appear in reality, the identifier is meaningful. That is why the identifier of the invoice "98dec0002," which is the identifier assigned to the second invoice generated in December 1998, is meaningful. It is also why the e-mail address rwatson@terry.uga.edu is meaningful.

Meaningful identifiers clearly have some advantages and disadvantages, and these are now considered. Also see the summary in Table 7-5.

Table 7-5: Advantages and disadvantages of meaningful identifiers

Advantages	Disadvantages
Recognizable and rememberable Administrative simplicity	Identifier exhaustion Reality changes Loss of meaningfulness

---

8. This section is based on the work of Mark Van der Pas <postmaster@markvanderpas.nl>, Information Manager, Libertel <www.libertel.com>.

Advantages of meaningful identifiers

Recognizable and rememberable

People can often recognize and remember the significance of meaningful identifiers. If, for example, someone receives an e-mail from rwatson@terry.uga.edu, this person can probably deduce the sender's name and workplace. If a manufacturer, for instance, uses the last two digits of its furniture code to indicate the color (e.g., 08 = beech), employees can then quickly determine the color of a packed piece of furniture. Of course, the firm could also show the color of the furniture on the label, in which case customers, who are most unlikely to know the coding scheme, can quickly determine the color of the enclosed product.

Administrative simplicity

By using meaningful identifiers, administration can be relatively easily decentralized. Administering e-mail addresses, for instance, can be handled at the domain level. This way, one can avoid the process of synchronizing with other domains whenever a new e-mail address is created.

A second example is the EAN[9] (European article number), the bar code on European products. Issuing EANs can be administered per country, since each country has a unique number in the EAN. When issuing a new number, a country need only issue a code that is not yet in use in that country. The method of contacting all countries to ask whether an EAN has already been issued is time consuming and open to error. On the other hand, creating a central database of issued EAN codes is an option. If every issuer of EAN codes can access such a database, alignment among countries is created and duplicates are prevented.

Disadvantages of meaningful identifiers

Identifier exhaustion

Suppose a company with a six-digit item identifier decides to use the first three digits to specify the product group (e.g., stationery) uniquely. Within this group, the remaining three digits are used to define the item (e.g., yellow lined pad). As a consequence, only one thousand items can be specified per product group. This problem remains even when some numbers in a specific product group, or even when entire product groups, are not used.

Consider the case when product group "010" is exhausted and is supplemented by the still unused product group code "940." What seems to be a simple quick fix causes problems, because a particular product group is not uniquely identified by a single identifier. Clients have to remember there is an exception.

---

9.   UPC (universal product code) in the U.S.

A real-world example of identifier exhaustion is a holding company that identifies its subsidiaries by using a code, where the first character is the first letter of the subsidiary's name. When the holding company acquired its seventh subsidiary, the meaningfulness of the coding system failed. The newly acquired subsidiary name started with the same letter as one of the existing subsidiaries. The system had already run out of identifiers.

When existing identifiers have to be converted because of exhaustion, printed codes on labels, packages, shelves, and catalogs will have to be redone. Recoding is an expensive process and should be avoided.

Exhaustion is not only a problem with meaningful identifiers. It can happen with non-meaningful identifiers. The problem is that meaningful identifier systems tend to exhaust sooner. To avoid identifier exhaustion and maintain meaningful identifiers, some designers increase identifier lengths (e.g., four digits for product group). Consequently, more disk space will be required to store the longer identifiers.

Reality changes

The second problem of meaningful identifiers is that the reality they record changes. For example, a company changes its name. The College of Business at the University of Georgia was renamed the Terry College of Business. E-mail addresses changed (e.g., rwatson@cba.uga.edu became rwatson@terry.uga.edu). An identifier can remain meaningful over a long period only if the meaningful part rarely or never changes.

Nonmeaningful identifiers avoid reality changes. Consider the case of most telephone billing systems, which use an account ID to identify a customer rather than a telephone number. This means a customer can change telephone numbers without causing any coding problems because telephone number is not the unique identifier of each customer.

A meaningful identifier can lose its meaningfulness

Consider the problems that can occur with the identifier that records both the color and the material of an article. Chipboard with a beech wood veneer is coded BW. A black product, on the other hand, is coded BL. Problems arise whenever there is an overlap between these characteristics. What happens with a product that is finished with a black veneer on beech wood? Should the code be BW or BL? And what about a black-painted product that is made out of beech wood? Maybe a new code, BB for black beech wood, is required. There will always be employees and customers who do not know the meaning of these not-so-meaningful identifiers and attribute the wrong meaning to them.

The solution—nonmeaningful identifiers

Most people are initially inclined to try to make identifiers meaningful. There is a sense that something is lost by using a simple numeric to identify a product or customer. Nothing, however, is lost and much is gained. Nonmeaningful identifiers serve their sole purpose well—to identify an entity uniquely. Attributes are used to describe the characteristics of the entity (e.g., color, type of wood). A clear distinction between the role of identifiers and attributes creates fewer data management problems now and in the future.

Vehicle identification

In most countries, every road vehicle is uniquely identified. The Vehicle Identification Number (VIN) was originally described in ISO Standard 3779 in February 1977 and last revised in 1983. It is designed to identify motor vehicles, trailers, motorcycles, and mopeds. A VIN is 17 characters, A through Z and 0 through 9.

The European Union and the United States have different implementations of the standard. The U.S. VIN is divided into four parts

- ❖ World Manufacturer's Identification (WMI) - three characters
- ❖ Vehicle Description Section (VDS) - five characters
- ❖ Check digit
- ❖ Vehicle Identification Section (VIS) - eight characters

When decoded, a VIN specifies the country and year of manufacture; make, model, and serial number; assembly plant; and even some equipment specifications.

VINs are normally located in several locations on a car, but the most common places are in the door frame of the front doors, on the engine itself, around the steering wheel, or on the dash near the window.

What do you think of the VIN as a method of vehicle identification? How do you reconcile it with the recommendation to use meaningless identifiers? If you were consulted on a new VIN system, what would advise?

The seven habits of highly effective data modelers

There is often a large gap between the performance of *average* and *expert* data modelers. An insight into the characteristics that make some data modelers more skillful than others should improve your data modeling capabilities.[10]

Immerse

Find out what the client wants by immersing yourself in the task environment. Spend some time following the client around and participate in daily business. Firsthand experience of the problem will give you a greater understanding of the client's requirements. Observe, ask questions, reflect, and talk to a wide variety of people (e.g., managers, operations personnel, customers, and suppliers). The more you learn about the problem, the better equipped you are to create a high-fidelity data model.

---

10. Based on Moody, D. 1996. The seven habits of highly effective data modelers. *Database programming and design* 9 (10):57–64.

Challenge

Challenge existing assumptions; dig out the exceptions. Test the boundaries of the data model. Try to think about the business problem from different perspectives (e.g., how might the industry leader tackle this problem?). Run a brainstorming session with the client to stimulate the search for breakthrough solutions.

Generalize

Reduce the number of entities whenever possible by using generalized structures (remember the Audio Library model) to simplify the data model. Simpler data models are usually easier to understand and less costly to implement. Expert data modelers can see beyond surface differences to discern the underlying similarities of seemingly different entities.

Test

Test the data model by reading it to yourself and several people intimately familiar with the problem. Test both directions of every relationship (e.g., a farmer has many cows and a cow belongs to only one farmer). Build a prototype so that the client can experiment and learn with a concrete model. Testing is very important because it costs very little to fix a data model but a great deal to repair a system based on an incorrect data model.

Limit

Set reasonable limits to the time and scope of data modeling. Don't let the data modeling phase continue forever. Discover the boundaries early in the project and stick to these unless there are compelling reasons to extend the project. Too many projects are allowed to expand because it is easier to say *yes* than *no*. In the long run, however, you do the client a disservice by promising too much and extending the life of the project. Determine the core entities and attributes that will solve most of the problem, and confine the data model to this core. Keep sight of the time and budget constraints of the project.

Integrate

Step back and reflect on how your project fits with the organization's information architecture. Integrate with existing systems where feasible and avoid duplication. How does your data model fit with the corporate data model and those of other projects? Can you use part of an existing data model? A skilled data modeler has to see both the fine-grained detail of a project data model and the big picture of the corporate data resource.

Complete

Good data modelers don't leave data models ill-defined. All entities, attributes, and relationships are carefully defined, ambiguities are resolved, and exceptions are handled. Because the full value of a data model is realized only when the system is complete, the data modeler should stay involved with the project until the system is implemented. The data modeler, who generally gets involved in the project from its earliest days, can provide continuity through the various phases and ensure the system solves the problem.

Summary

Data modeling is both a technique for modeling data and its relationships and a graphical representation of a database. It communicates a database's design. The goal is to identify the facts that must be stored in a database. Building a data model is a partnership between a client, a representative of the eventual users of the database, and a designer. The building blocks are an entity, attribute, identifier, and relationship. A well-formed data model, which means the construction rules have been obeyed, clearly communicates information to the client. A high-fidelity data model faithfully describes the world it represents.

A data model is an evolving representation. Each change should be an incremental improvement in quality. The quality of a data model can be determined only by understanding the context in which it will be used. A data model can model historical data relationships just as readily as current ones. Cardinality specifies the precise multiplicity of a relationship. Modality indicates whether a relationship is optional or mandatory. The five different types of entities are independent, dependent, associative, aggregate, and subordinate. Expect a data model to expand and contract. A data model has no ordering. Introduce an attribute if ordering is required. An attribute must have the same meaning for every instance. An attribute is the smallest piece of data that will conceivably form part of a query. Synonyms are words that have the same meaning; homonyms are words that sound the same but have different meanings. Identifiers should generally have no meaning. Highly effective data modelers immerse, challenge, generalize, test, limit, integrate, and complete.

Key terms and concepts

Aggregate entity	Homonym
Aggregation	Identifier
Associative entity	Independent entity
Attribute	Instance
Cardinality	Mandatory
Composite aggregation	Modality
Data model	Modeling
Data model quality	Optional
Dependent entity	Relationship
Determinant	Relationship descriptor
Domain	Relationship label
Entity	Shared aggregation
Generalization	Synonym

References and additional readings

Carlis, J. V. 1991. *Logical data structures*. Minneapolis, MN: University of Minnesota.

Hammer, M. 1990. Reengineering work: Don't automate, obliterate. *Harvard Business Review* 68 (4):104–112.

Wetherbe, J. C. 1991. Executive information requirements: Getting it right. *MIS Quarterly* 15 (1):51–65.

Exercises

Short answers

1. What is data modeling?
2. What is a useful technique for identifying entities in a written description of a data modeling problem?
3. When do you label arcs?
4. When is a data model well formed, and when is it high-fidelity?
5. How do you handle exceptions when data modeling?
6. Describe the different types of entities.
7. Why might a data model grow?
8. Why might a data model contract?
9. How do you indicate ordering of instances in a data model?
10. What is the difference between a synonym and a homonym?

Data modeling

Create a data model from the following narratives, which are sometimes intentionally incomplete. You will have to make some assumptions. Make certain you state these alongside your data model. Define the identifier(s) and attributes of each entity.

1. The president of a book wholesaler has told you that she wants information about publishers, authors, and books.
2. A university has many subject areas (e.g., MIS, Romance languages). Professors teach in only one subject area, but the same subject area can have many professors. Professors can teach many different courses in their subject area. An offering of a course (e.g., Data Management 457, French 101) is taught by only one professor at a particular time.
3. Kids'n'Vans retails minivans for a number of manufacturers. Each manufacturer offers several models of its minivan (e.g., SE, LE, GT). Each model comes with a standard set of equipment (e.g., the Acme SE comes with wheels, seats, and an engine). Minivans can have a variety of additional equipment or accessories (radio, air-conditioning, automatic transmission, airbag, etc.), but not all accessories are available for all minivans (e.g., not all manufacturers offer a driver's side airbag). Some sets of accessories are sold as packages (e.g., the luxury package might include stereo, six speakers, cocktail bar, and twin overhead foxtails).
4. Steve operates a cinema chain and has given you the following information:
"I have many cinemas. Each cinema can have multiple theaters. Movies are shown throughout the day starting at 11 A.M. and finishing at 1 A.M. Each movie is given a two-hour time slot. We never show a movie in more than one theater at a time, but we do shift movies among theaters because seating capacity varies. I am interested in knowing how many people, classified by adults and children, attended each showing of a movie. I vary ticket prices by movie and time slot. For instance, *Lassie Get Lost* is 50 cents for everyone at 11 A.M. but is 75 cents at 11 P.M."

5. A university gymnastics team can have as many as 10 gymnasts. The team competes many times during the season. A meet can have one or more opponents and consists of four events: vault, uneven bars, beam, and floor routine. A gymnast can participate in all or some of these events though the team is limited to five participants in any event.

6. A famous Greek shipping magnate, Stell, owns many container ships. Containers are collected at one port and delivered to another port. Customers pay a negotiated fee for the delivery of each container. Each ship has a sailing schedule that lists the ports the ship will visit over the next six months. The schedule shows the expected arrival and departure dates. The daily charge for use of each port is also recorded.

7. A medical center employs several physicians. A physician can see many patients, and a patient can be seen by many physicians, though not always on the one visit. On any particular visit, a patient may be diagnosed to have one or more illnesses.

8. A telephone company offers a 10 percent discount to any customer who phones another person who is also a customer of the company. To be eligible for the discount, the pairing of the two phone numbers must be registered with the telephone company. Furthermore, for billing purposes, the company records both phone numbers, start time, end time, and date of call.

9. Global Trading (GT), Inc. is a conglomerate. It buys and sells businesses frequently and has difficulty keeping track of what strategic business units (SBUs) it owns, in what nations it operates, and what markets it serves. For example, the CEO was recently surprised to find that GT owns 25 percent of Dundee's Wild Adventures, headquartered in Zaire, that has subsidiaries operating tours of Australia, Zaire, and New York. You have been commissioned to design a database to keep track of GT's businesses. The CEO has provided you with the following information:

   SBUs are headquartered in one country, not necessarily the United States. Each SBU has subsidiaries or foreign agents, depending on local legal requirements, in a number of countries. Each subsidiary or foreign agent operates in only one country but can operate in more than one market. GT uses the standard industrial code (SIC) to identify a market (e.g., newspaper publishing). The SIC is a unique four-digit code.

   While foreign agents operate as separate legal entities, GT needs to know in what countries and markets they operate. On the other hand, subsidiaries are fully or partly owned by GT, and it is important for GT to know who are the other owners of any subsidiary and what percentage of the subsidiary they own. It is not unusual for a corporation to have shares in several of GT's subsidiary companies and for several corporations to own a portion of a subsidiary. Multiple ownership can also occur at the SBU level.

10. A real estate investment company owns many shopping malls. Each mall contains many shops. To encourage rental of its shops, the company gives a negotiated discount to retailers who have shops in more than one mall. Each shop generates an income stream that can vary from month to month because rental is based on a flat rental charge and a negotiated percentage of sales revenue. Also, each shop has monthly expenses for scheduled and unscheduled maintenance. The company uses

the data to compute its monthly net income per square meter for each shop and for ad hoc querying.

11. Draw a data model for the following table taken from a magazine that evaluates consumer goods. The reports follow a standard fashion of listing a brand and model, price, overall score, and then an evaluation of a series of attributes, which can vary with the product. For example, the sample table evaluates stereo systems. A table for evaluating microwave ovens would have a similar layout, but different features would be reported (e.g., cooking quality).

Brand and model	Price	Overall score	Sound quality	Taping quality	FM tuning	CD handling	Ease of use
Phillips SC-AK103	140	62	Very good	Good	Very good	Excellent	Fair
Panasonic MC-50	215	55	Good	Good	Very good	Very good	Good
Rio G300	165	38	Good	Good	Fair	Very good	Poor

12. Draw a data model for the following freight table taken from a mail order catalog.

Merchandise subtotals	Regular delivery 7–10 days	Rush delivery 4–5 business days	Express delivery 1–2 business days
Up to $30.00	$4.95	$9.95	$12.45
$30.01–$65.00	$6.95	$11.95	$15.45
$65.01–$125.00	$8.95	$13.95	$20.45
$125.01+	$9.95	$15.95	$25.45

Reference 1

Basic Structures

Few things are harder to put up with than the annoyance of a good example.
Mark Twain, *Pudd'nhead Wilson*, 1894

Every data model is composed of the same basic structures. This is a major advantage because you can focus on a small part of a full data model without being concerned about the rest of it. As a result, translation to a relational database is very easy because you systematically translate each basic structure. This section describes each of the basic structures and shows how they are mapped to a relational database. Because the mapping is shown as a diagram and SQL CREATE statements, you will use this section frequently.

One entity

No relationships

The unrelated entity was introduced in Chapter 3. This is simply a flat file, and the mapping is very simple (see Figure R1-1). Although it is unlikely that you will have a data model with a single entity, the single entity is covered for completeness.

```
PERSON

*personid
attribute1
attribute 2
   ...
```

person			
<u>personid</u>	attribute1	attribute2	...

```
CREATE TABLE person (
    personid    INTEGER,
    attribute1 … ,
    attribute2 … ,
    …
        PRIMARY KEY(personid));
```

Figure R1-1. A single entity with no relationships

A 1:1 recursive relationship

A recursive one-to-one (1:1) relationship is used to describe situations like current marriage (see Figure R1-2). A person can have zero or one current spouse. The relationship should be labeled to avoid misunderstandings. Mapping to the relational database requires that the identifier of one end of the relationship becomes a foreign key. It does not matter which one you select. Notice that when `personid` is used as a foreign key, it must be given an alias — in this case `spouse` — because two columns in the same table cannot have the same name. The foreign key constraint is not defined, because this constraint cannot refer to the table being created.

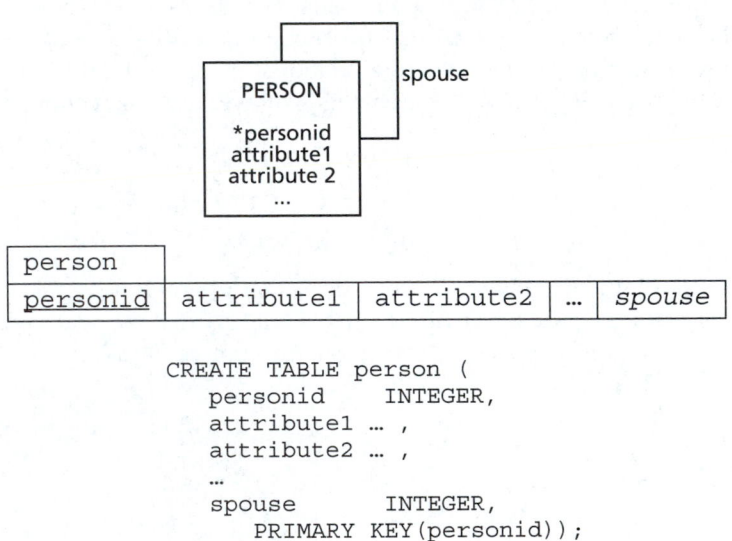

```
CREATE TABLE person (
    personid    INTEGER,
    attribute1 … ,
    attribute2 … ,
    …
    spouse        INTEGER,
        PRIMARY KEY(personid));
```

Figure R1-2. A single entity with a 1:1 recursive relationship

A recursive 1:m relationship

A recursive one-to-many (1:m) relationship describes situations like fatherhood or motherhood. Figure R1-3 maps fatherhood. A father may have many biological children, but a child has only one biological father. The relationship is mapped like any other 1:m relationship. The identifier of the one end becomes a foreign key in the many end. Again, we must rename the identifier when it becomes a foreign key in the same row. Also, again the foreign key constraint is not defined because it cannot refer to the table being created.

It is possible to have more than one 1:m recursive relationship. For example, details of a mother-child relationship would be represented in the same manner and result in the data model having a second 1:m recursive relationship. The mapping to the relational model would result in an additional column to contain a foreign key MOTHER, the PERSONID of a person's mother.

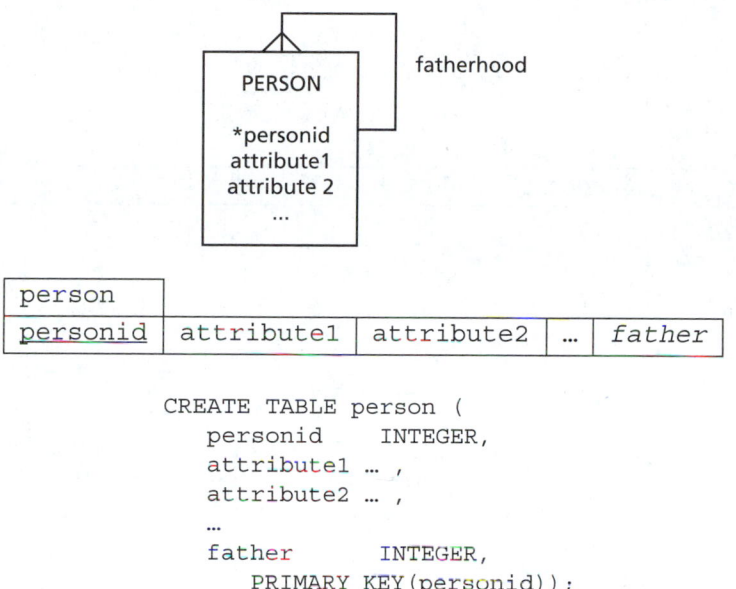

```
CREATE TABLE person (
    personid      INTEGER,
    attribute1 … ,
    attribute2 … ,
    …
    father        INTEGER,
      PRIMARY KEY(personid));
```

Figure R1-3. A single entity with a 1:m recursive relationship

A recursive m:m relationship

A recursive many-to-many (m:m) relationship can describe a situation like friendship (see Figure R1-4). A person can have many friends and be a friend to many persons. As with m:m relationships between a pair of entities, we convert this relationship to two 1:m relationships and create an associative entity.

The resulting table `friendship` has a composite primary key based on the identifier of `person`, which in effect means the two components are based on `personid`. To distinguish between them, these components are called `personid1` and `personid2`, so you can think of `friendship` as a pair of `personids`. You will see the same pattern occurring with other m:m recursive relationships. Notice both person identifiers are independent foreign keys, because they are used to map the two 1:m relationships between `person` and `friendship`.

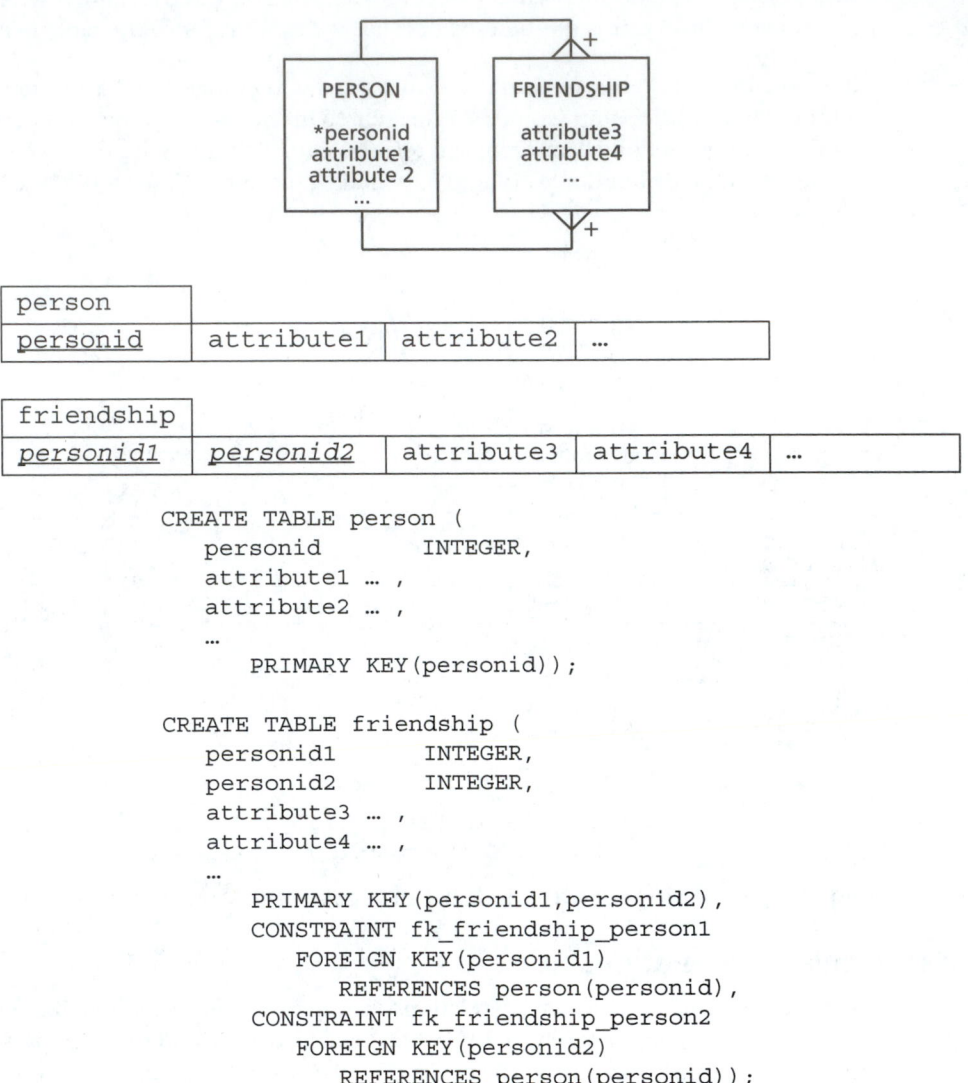

Figure R1-4. A single entity with an m:m recursive relationship

A single entity can have multiple m:m recursive relationships. Relationships such as enmity (not enemyship) and siblinghood are m:m recursive on person. The approach to recording these relationships is the same as that outlined previously.

Two entities

No relationship

When there is no arc between two entities, the client has decided there is no need to record a relationship between the two entities. When you are reading the data model with the client, be sure that you check whether this assumption is correct both now and for the foreseeable future. When there is no relationship between two entities, map them each as you would a single entity with no relationships.

A 1:1 relationship

A 1:1 relationship usually occurs in parallel with a 1:m relationship between two entities. It signifies some instances of an entity that have an additional role. For example, a department has many employees (the 1:m relationship), and a department has one boss (the 1:1). The data model fragment shown in Figure R1-5 represents the 1:1 relationship.

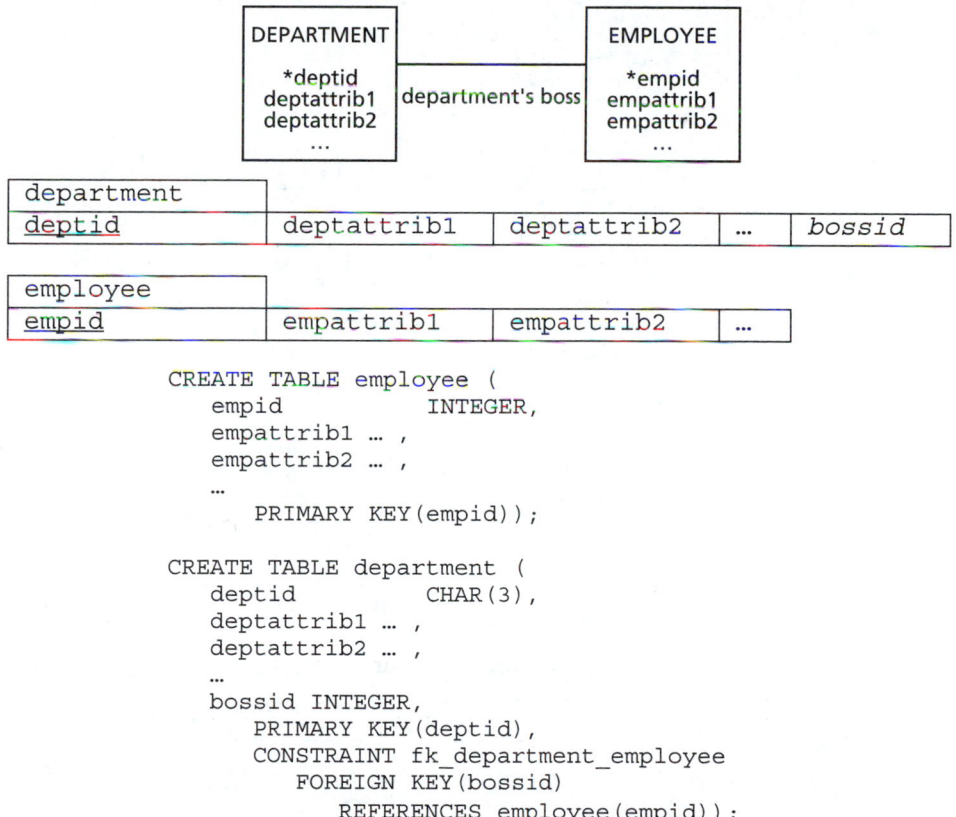

```
CREATE TABLE employee (
    empid            INTEGER,
    empattrib1 … ,
    empattrib2 … ,
    …
        PRIMARY KEY (empid));

CREATE TABLE department (
    deptid           CHAR(3),
    deptattrib1 … ,
    deptattrib2 … ,
    …
    bossid INTEGER,
        PRIMARY KEY (deptid),
        CONSTRAINT fk_department_employee
            FOREIGN KEY (bossid)
                REFERENCES employee (empid));
```

Figure R1-5. A 1:1 relationship between two entities

The guideline, as explained in Chapter 6, is to map the relationship to the relational model by placing the foreign key to minimize the number of instances when it will have a null value. In this case, we place the foreign key in `department`.

A 1:m relationship

The 1:m relationship is possibly the easiest to understand and map (see Figure R1-6). The mapping to the relational model is very simple. The primary key of the "one" end becomes a foreign key in the "many" end.

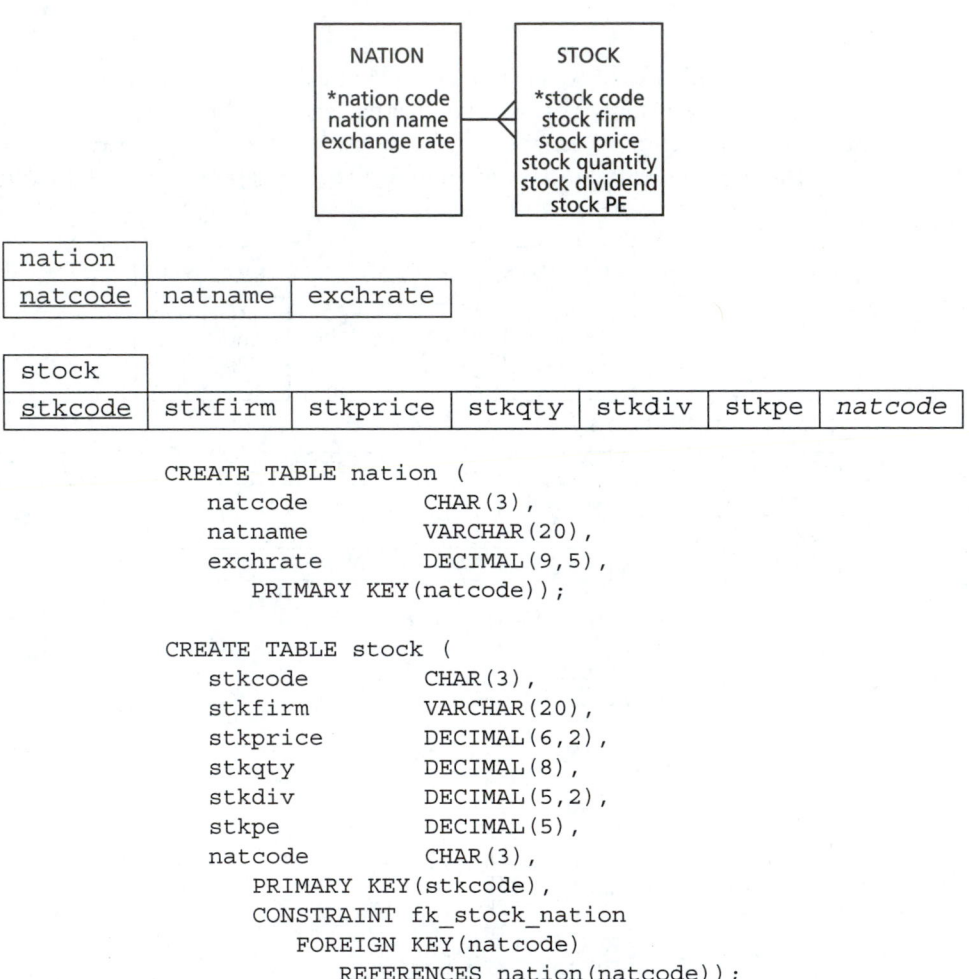

```
CREATE TABLE nation (
    natcode         CHAR(3),
    natname         VARCHAR(20),
    exchrate        DECIMAL(9,5),
      PRIMARY KEY(natcode));

CREATE TABLE stock (
    stkcode         CHAR(3),
    stkfirm         VARCHAR(20),
    stkprice        DECIMAL(6,2),
    stkqty          DECIMAL(8),
    stkdiv          DECIMAL(5,2),
    stkpe           DECIMAL(5),
    natcode         CHAR(3),
      PRIMARY KEY(stkcode),
      CONSTRAINT fk_stock_nation
        FOREIGN KEY(natcode)
            REFERENCES nation(natcode));
```

Figure R1-6. A 1:m relationship between two entities

An m:m relationship

An m:m relationship is transformed into two 1:m relationships. The mapping is then a two-fold application of the 1:m rule (see Figure R1-7).

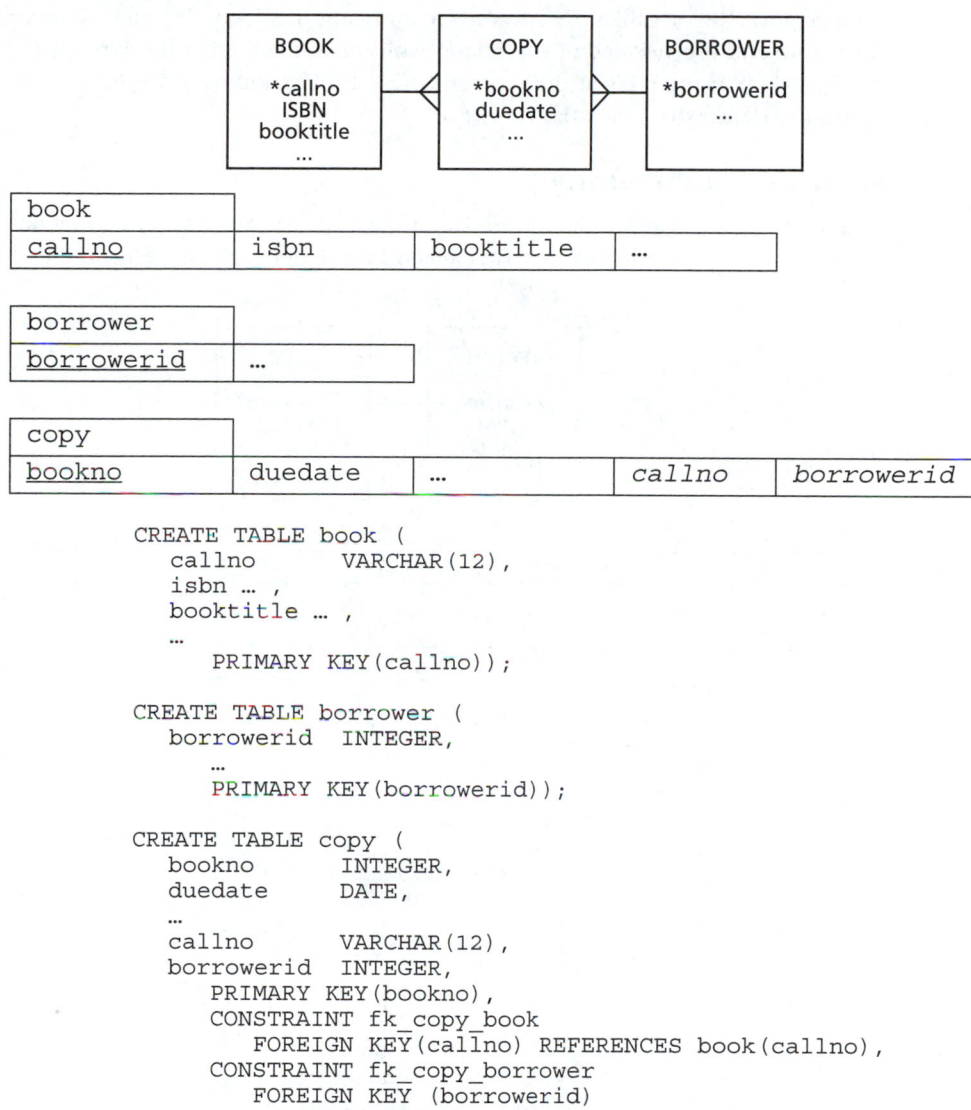

Figure R1-7. An m:m relationship between two entities

The book and borrower tables must be created first because copy contains foreign key constraints that refer to book and borrower. The column borrowerid can be null because a book need not be borrowed; if it's sitting on the shelf, there is no borrower.

Another entity's identifier as part of the identifier

Using one entity's identifier as part of another entity's identifier tends to cause the most problems for novice data modelers. (One entity's identifier is part of another identifier when there is a plus sign on an arc. The plus is almost always at the crow's foot end of a 1:m relationship.) Tables are formed by applying the following rule: The primary key of the table at the other end of the relationship becomes both a foreign key and part of the primary key in the table at the plus end. The application of this rule is shown for several common data model fragments.

A weak or dependent entity

In Figure R1-8, `regname` is part of the primary key (signified by the plus near the crow's foot) and a foreign key of `city` (because of the 1:m between `region` and `city`).

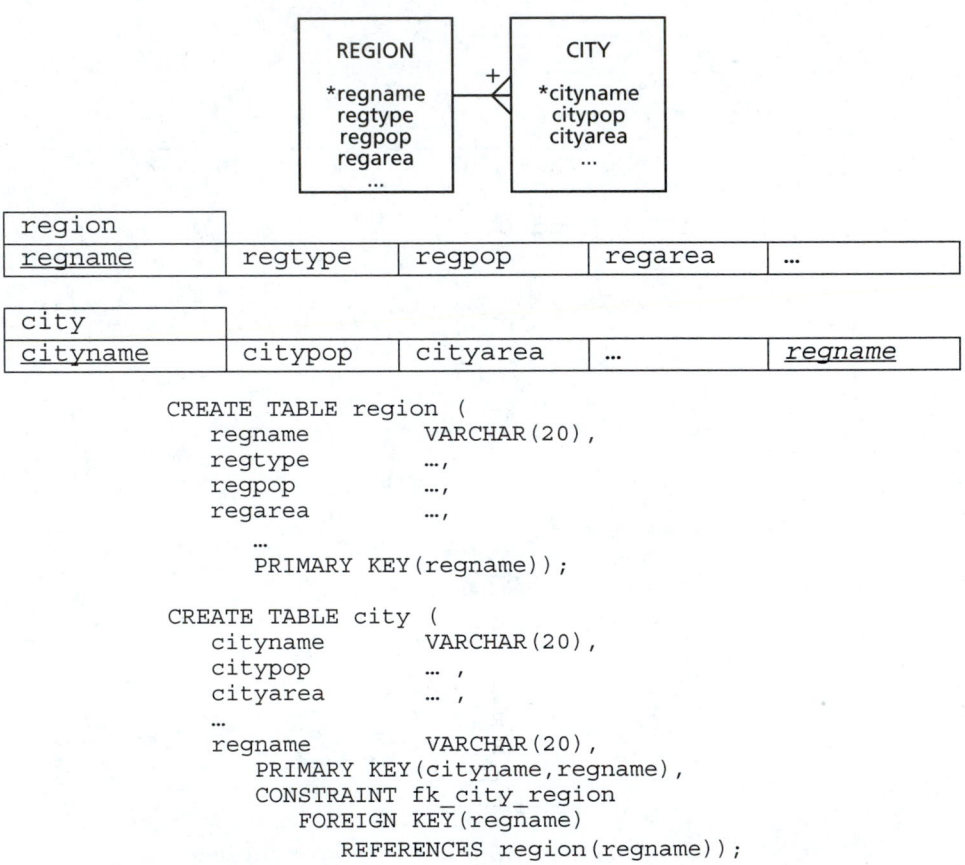

region				
<u>regname</u>	regtype	regpop	regarea	...

city				
<u>cityname</u>	citypop	cityarea	...	*<u>regname</u>*

```
CREATE TABLE region (
    regname          VARCHAR(20),
    regtype          ...,
    regpop           ...,
    regarea          ...,
    ...
        PRIMARY KEY(regname));

CREATE TABLE city (
    cityname         VARCHAR(20),
    citypop          ... ,
    cityarea         ... ,
    ...
    regname          VARCHAR(20),
        PRIMARY KEY(cityname,regname),
        CONSTRAINT fk_city_region
            FOREIGN KEY(regname)
                REFERENCES region(regname));
```

Figure R1-8. A weak entity

An associative entity

In Figure R1-9, observe that `cityname` and `firmname` are both part of the primary key (signified by the plus near the crow's foot) and foreign keys (because of the two 1:m relationships) of `store`.

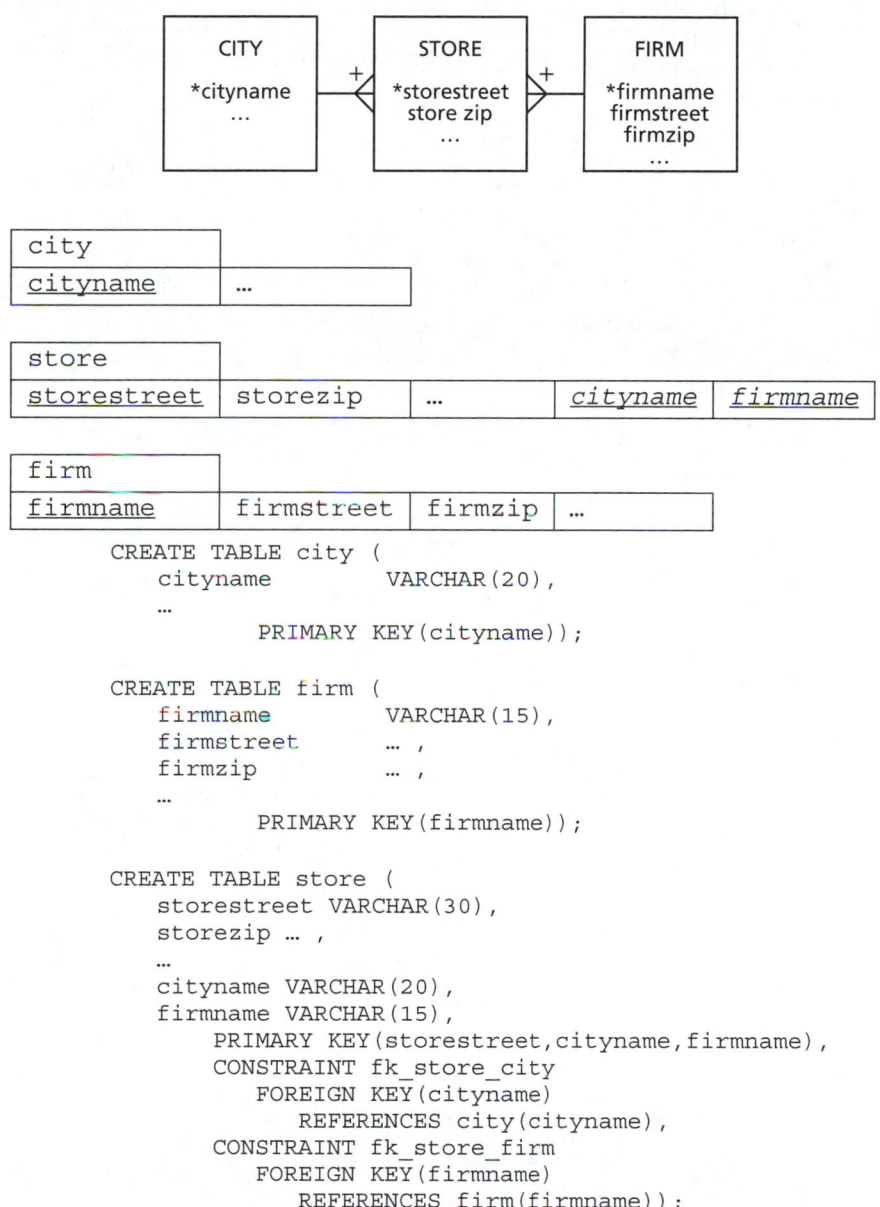

```
CREATE TABLE city (
    cityname        VARCHAR(20),
    ...
            PRIMARY KEY(cityname));

CREATE TABLE firm (
    firmname        VARCHAR(15),
    firmstreet      ... ,
    firmzip         ... ,
    ...
            PRIMARY KEY(firmname));

CREATE TABLE store (
    storestreet VARCHAR(30),
    storezip ... ,
    ...
    cityname VARCHAR(20),
    firmname VARCHAR(15),
        PRIMARY KEY(storestreet,cityname,firmname),
        CONSTRAINT fk_store_city
            FOREIGN KEY(cityname)
                REFERENCES city(cityname),
        CONSTRAINT fk_store_firm
            FOREIGN KEY(firmname)
                REFERENCES firm(firmname));
```

Figure R1-9. An associative entity

A tree structure

The interesting feature of Figure R1-10 is the primary key. Notice that the primary key of a lower level of the tree is a composite of its partial identifier and the primary key of the immediate higher level. The primary key of department is a composite of deptname, divname, and firmname. Novice modelers often forget to make this translation.

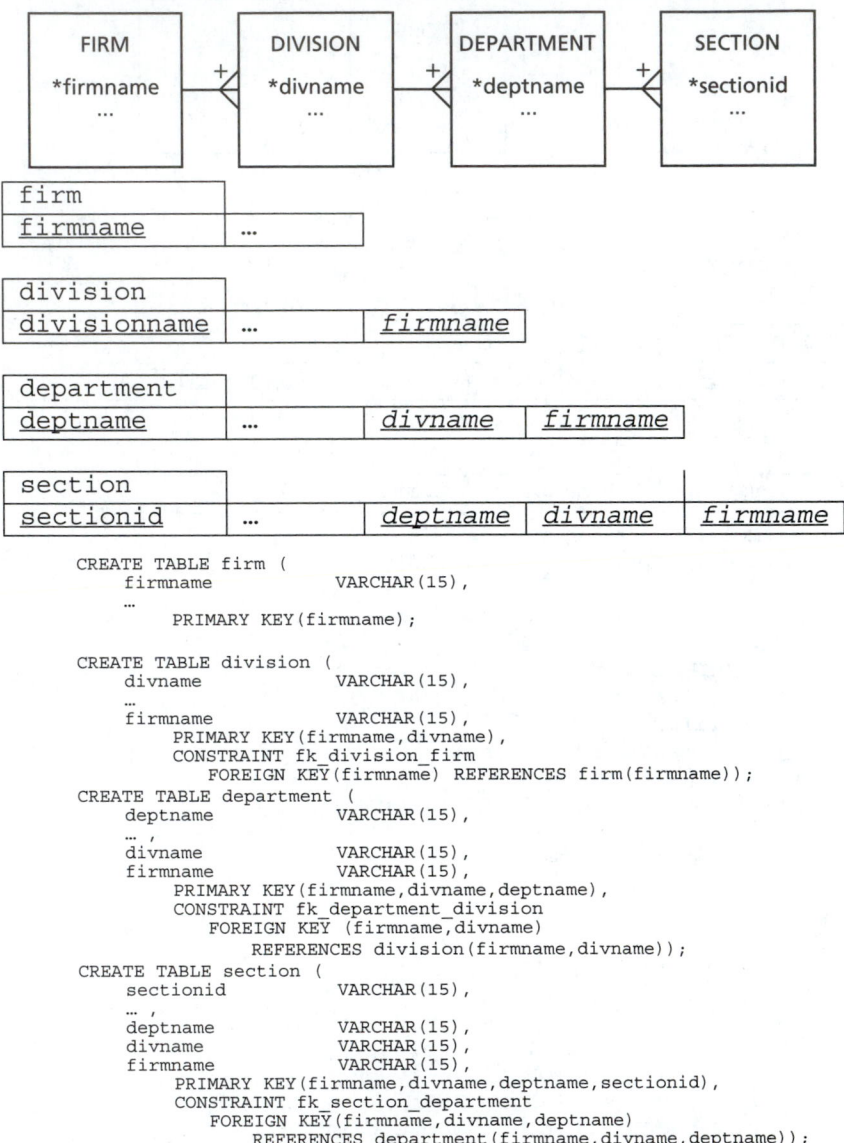

```
        CREATE TABLE firm (
            firmname            VARCHAR(15),
            ...
                PRIMARY KEY(firmname);


        CREATE TABLE division (
            divname             VARCHAR(15),
            ...
            firmname            VARCHAR(15),
                PRIMARY KEY(firmname,divname),
                CONSTRAINT fk_division_firm
                    FOREIGN KEY(firmname) REFERENCES firm(firmname));
        CREATE TABLE department (
            deptname            VARCHAR(15),
            ... ,
            divname             VARCHAR(15),
            firmname            VARCHAR(15),
                PRIMARY KEY(firmname,divname,deptname),
                CONSTRAINT fk_department_division
                    FOREIGN KEY (firmname,divname)
                        REFERENCES division(firmname,divname));
        CREATE TABLE section (
            sectionid           VARCHAR(15),
            ... ,
            deptname            VARCHAR(15),
            divname             VARCHAR(15),
            firmname            VARCHAR(15),
                PRIMARY KEY(firmname,divname,deptname,sectionid),
                CONSTRAINT fk_section_department
                    FOREIGN KEY(firmname,divname,deptname)
                        REFERENCES department(firmname,divname,deptname));
```

Figure R1-10. A tree structure

Another approach to a tree structure

A more general approach to modeling a tree structure is to recognize that it is a series of 1:m recursive relationships. Thus, it can be modeled as shown in Figure R1-11. This model is identical in structure to that of Figure R1-3 and converted to a table in the same manner. Notice that we label the relationship *superunit*, and this would be a good choice of name for the foreign key.

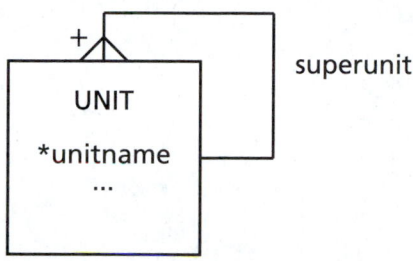

Figure R1-11. A more flexible model of a tree structure

Exercises

Write the SQL CREATE statements for the following data models.

a.

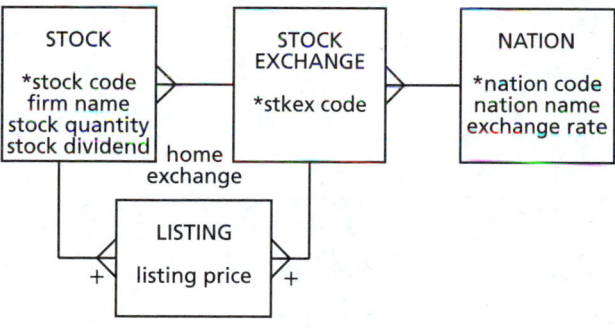

b.

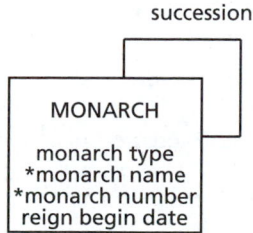

c.

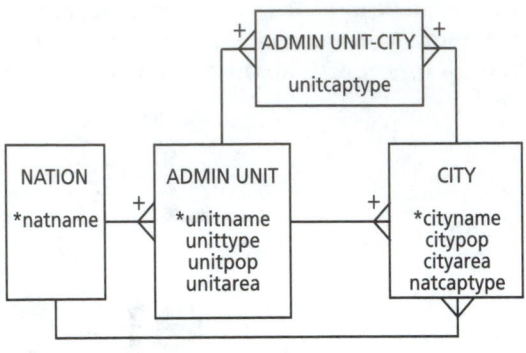

National capital

d.

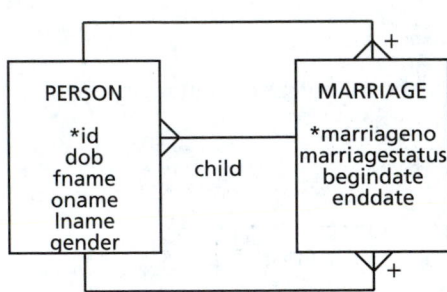

e.

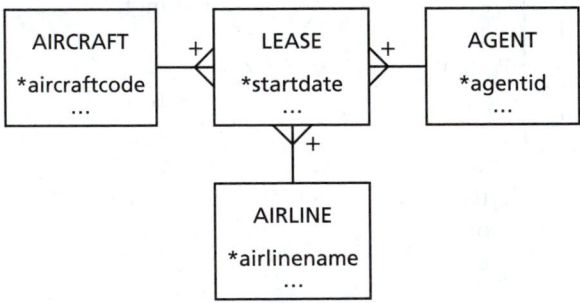

f. Under what circumstances might you use choose a fixed tree over a 1:m recursive data model?

8

Normalization and Other Data Modeling Methods

There are many paths to the top of the mountain, but the view is always the same.
Chinese Proverb

Learning objectives

Students completing this chapter will

❖ understand the process of normalization;
❖ be able to distinguish between different normal forms;
❖ recognize that different data modeling approaches, while they differ in representation methods, are essentially identical.

Introduction

There are often many ways to solve a problem, and different methods frequently produce essentially the same solution. When this is the case, the goal is to find the most efficient path. We believe that data modeling, as you have learned in the preceding chapters, is an efficient and easily learned approach to database design. There are, however, other paths to consider. One of these methods, normalization, was the initial approach to database design. It was developed as part of the theoretical foundation of the relational data model. It is useful to understand the key theoretical ideas of normalization because they advance your understanding of the relational model. Experience and research indicate, however, that normalization is more difficult to master than data modeling.

Data modeling first emerged as entity-relationship (E-R) modeling in a paper by Peter Pin-Shan Chen.[1] He introduced two key database design concepts:

---

1. Chen, P. 1976. The entity-relationship model—toward a unified view of data. *ACM Transactions on Database Systems,* 1 (1):9–36.

❖   Identify entities and the relationships between them.
❖   A graphical representation improves design communication.

Chen's core concepts spawned many species of data modeling. To give you an appreciation of the variation in data modeling approaches, we briefly review, later in this chapter, Chen's E-R approach and IDEF1X, an approach used by the Department of Defense.

Normalization

Normalization is a method for increasing the quality of database design. It is also a theoretical base for defining the properties of relations. The theory gradually developed to create an understanding of the desirable properties of a relation. The goal of normalization is identical to that of data modeling—a high-fidelity design. The need for normalization seems to have arisen from the conversion of file systems into database format. Often, analysts started with the old file design and used normalization to design the new database. Now, designers are more likely to start with a clean slate and use data modeling.

Normal forms can be arrived at in several ways. The recommended approach is data modeling, as experience strongly indicates people find it is an easier approach to database design. If the principles of data modeling are followed faithfully, then the outcome should be a high-fidelity model and a normalized database. In other words, if you model data correctly, you create a normalized design. Nevertheless, modeling mistakes can occur, and normalization is a useful crosscheck for ensuring the soundness of a data model. Normalization also provides a theoretical underpinning to data modeling.

Normalization gradually converts a file design into normal form by the successive application of rules to move the design from first to fifth normal form. But before we look at these steps, it is useful to learn about functional dependency.[2]

Functional dependency

A functional dependency is a relationship between attributes in an entity. It simply means that one or more attributes determine the value of another. For example, given a stock's code, you can determine its current PE ratio. In other words, PE ratio is functionally dependent on stock code. In addition, stock name, stock price, stock quantity, and stock dividend are functionally dependent on stock code. The notation for indicating that stock code functionally determines stock name is

stock code → stock name

An identifier functionally determines all the attributes in an entity. That is, if we know the value of stock code, then we can determine the value of stock name, stock price, and so on.

---

2.   This section is mainly based on Kent, W. 1983. A simple guide to five normal forms in relational database theory. *Communications of the ACM* 26 (2):120–125 and Date, C. J. 1995. *An introduction to database systems*. 6th ed. Reading, MA: Addison-Wesley.

Formulae, such as yield = stock dividend/stock price*100, are a form of functional dependency. In this case, we have

(stock dividend, stock price) $\rightarrow$ yield

This is an example of **full functional dependency** because yield can be determined only from both attributes.

An attribute, or set of attributes, that fully functionally determines another attribute is called a **determinant**. Thus, stock code is a determinant because it fully functionally determines stock PE. An identifier, usually called a key when discussing normalization, is a determinant. Unlike a key, a determinant need not be unique. For example, a university could have a simple fee structure where undergraduate courses are $500 and graduate courses are $750. Thus, course type $\rightarrow$ fee. Since there are many undergraduate and graduate courses, course type is not unique for all records.

There are situations where a given value determines multiple values. This **multidetermination** property is denoted as A $\rightarrow$ $\rightarrow$ B and reads "A multidetermines B." For instance, a department multidetermines a course. If you know the department, you can determine the set of courses it offers. **Multivalued dependency** means that functional dependencies are multivalued.

Functional dependency is a property of a relation's data. We cannot determine functional dependency from the names of attributes or the current values. Sometimes, examination of a relation's data will indicate that a functional dependency does not exist, but it is by understanding the relationships between data elements that we determine functional dependency.

Functional dependency is a theoretical avenue for understanding relationships between attributes. If we have two attributes, say A and B, then three relations are possible, as shown in Table 8-1.

Table 8-1: Functional dependencies of two attributes

Relationship	Functional dependency	Relationship
They determine each other	A $\rightarrow$ B and B $\rightarrow$ A	1:1
One determines the other	A $\rightarrow$ B	1:m
They do not determine each other	A not$\rightarrow$ B and B not$\rightarrow$ A	m:m

One-to-one attribute relationship

Consider two attributes that determine each other (A $\rightarrow$ B and B $\rightarrow$ A), for instance a country's code and its name. Using the example of Switzerland, there is a one-to-one (1:1) relationship between CH and Switzerland: CH $\rightarrow$ Switzerland and Switzerland $\rightarrow$ CH. When two attributes have a 1:1 relationship, they must occur together in at least one table in a database so that their equivalence is a recorded fact.

One-to-many attribute relationship

Examine the situation where one attribute determines another (i.e., A → B), but the reverse is not true (i.e., A not→ B), as is the case with country name and its currency unit. If you know a country's name, you can determine its currency, but if you know the currency unit (e.g., the euro), you cannot always determine the country (e.g., both Italy and Portugal use the euro). As a result, if A and B occur in the same table, then A must be the key. In our example, country name would be the key, and currency unit would be a nonkey column.

Many-to-many attribute relationship

The final case to investigate is when neither attribute determines the other (i.e., A not→ B and B not→ A). The relationship between country name and language is many-to-many (m:m). For example, Belgium has two languages (French and Flemish), and French is spoken in many countries. To record the m:m relationship between these attributes, a table containing both attributes as a composite key is required. This is essentially the associative entity created during data modeling when there is an m:m relationship between entities.

As you can understand from the preceding discussion, functional dependency is an explicit form of presenting some of the ideas you gained implicitly in earlier chapters on data modeling. The next step is to delve into another theoretical concepts underlying the relational model: normal forms.

Normal forms

Normal forms describe a classification of relations. Initial work by Codd identified first (1NF), second (2NF), and third (3NF) normal forms. Later researchers added Boyce-Codd (BCNF), fourth (4NF), and fifth (5NF) normal forms. Normal forms are nested like a set of Russian dolls, with the innermost doll, 1NF, contained within all other normal forms. The hierarchy of normal forms is 5NF, 4NF, BCNF, 3NF, 2NF, and 1NF. Thus, 5NF is the outermost doll.

A new normal form, domain-key normal form (DK/NF), appeared in 1981. When a relation is in DK/NF, there are no modification anomalies. Conversely, any relation that is free of anomalies must be in DK/NF. The difficult part is discovering how to convert a relation to DK/NF.

First normal form

A relation is in first normal form if and only if all columns are single-valued. In other words, 1NF states that all occurrences of a row must have the same number of columns. In data modeling terms, this means that an attribute must have a single value. An attribute that can have multiple values must be represented as a one-to-many (1:m) relationship at a minimum, a data model will be in 1NF because all attributes of an entity are required to be single-valued.

Second normal form

Second normal form is violated when a nonkey column is dependent on only a component of the primary key. This can also be stated as *a relation is in second normal form if and only if it is in first normal form, and all nonkey columns are dependent on the key*.

Consider Table 8-2. The primary key of order is a composite of itemno and customerid. The problem is that customer-credit is a fact about customerid (part of the composite key) rather than the full key (itemno+customerid), or in other words, it is not fully functionally dependent on the primary key. An insert anomaly arises when you try to add a new customer to order. You cannot add a customer until that person places an order, because until then you have no value for item number, and part of the primary key will be null. Clearly, this is neither an acceptable business practice nor an acceptable data management procedure.

Analyzing this problem, you realize an item can be in many orders, and a customer can order many items — an m:m relationship. By drawing the data model in Figure 8-1, you realize that *customer-credit* is an attribute of CUSTOMER, and you get the correct relational mapping.

Table 8-2: Second normal form violation

order			
itemno	customerid	quantity	customer-credit
12	57	25	OK
34	679	3	POOR

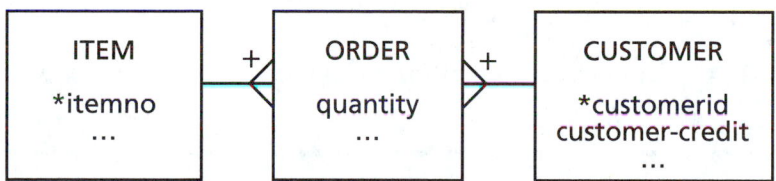

Figure 8-1. Resolving second normal form violation

Third normal form

Third normal form is violated when a nonkey column is a fact about another nonkey column. Alternatively, *a relation is in third normal form if and only if it is in second normal form and has no transitive dependencies*.

The problem in Table 8-3 is that exchange rate is a fact about nation, a nonkey field. In the language of functional dependency, exchange rate is not fully functionally dependent on stockcode, the primary key.

The functional dependencies are stockcode → nation → exchange rate. In other words, exchange rate is transitively[3] dependent on stock, since exchange rate is dependent on nation and nation is dependent on stockcode. The fundamental problem becomes very apparent when you try to add a new nation to the stock table. Until you buy at least one stock for that nation, you cannot insert the nation, because you do not have a primary key. Similarly, if you delete MG from the stock table, details of the USA exchange rate are lost. There are modification anomalies.

When you think about the data relationships, you realize that a nation has many stocks and a stock belongs to only one nation. Now the data model and relational map can be created readily (see Figure 8-2).

Table 8-3: Third normal form violation

stock		
stockcode	nation	exchange rate
MG	USA	0.67
IR	AUS	0.46

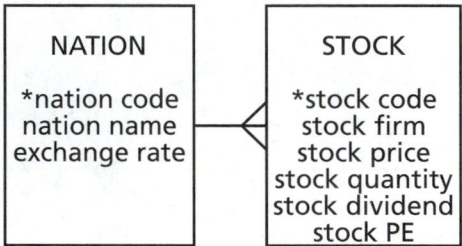

Figure 8-2. Resolving third normal form violation

Skill builder

You have been given a spreadsheet that contains details of invoices. The column headers for the spreadsheet are *date, invoice number, invoice amount, invoice tax, invoice total, cust number, cust name, cust street, cust city, cust state, cust postal code, cust nation, product code, product price, product quantity, salesrep number, salesrep first name, salesrep last name, salesrep district, district name,* and *district size.* Normalize this spreadsheet so that it can be converted to a high-fidelity relational database.

---

3.   Transitivity means that if one object bears a relation to a second object that bears the same relationship to a third object, then the first object bears this relationship to the third. For example, if $x = y$ and $y = z$, then $x = z$.

Boyce-Codd normal form

The original definition of 3NF did not cover a situation that, although rare, can occur. So Boyce-Codd normal form, a stronger version of 3NF, was developed. BCNF is necessary because 3NF does not cover the cases when

❖ A relation has multiple candidate keys.
❖ Those candidate keys are composite.
❖ The candidate keys overlap because they have at least one column in common.

Before considering an example, **candidate key** needs to be defined. Earlier we introduced the idea that an entity could have more than one unique identifier. These identifiers become candidate keys when the data model is mapped to a relational database. One of these candidates is selected as the primary key.

Consider the following case from a management consulting firm. A client can have many types of problems (e.g., finance, personnel), and the same problem type can be an issue for many clients. Consultants specialize and advise on only one problem type, but several consultants can advise on one problem type. A consultant advises a client. Furthermore, for each problem type, the client is advised by only one consultant. If you did not use data modeling, you might be tempted to create Table 8-4.

Table 8-4: Boyce-Codd normal form violation

advisor		
client	probtype	consultant
Alpha	Marketing	Gomez
Alpha	Production	Raginiski

The column `client` cannot be the primary key because a client can have several problem types; however, a client is advised by only one consultant for a specific problem type, so the composite key `client+probtype` determines `consultant`. Also, because a consultant handles only one type of problem, the composite key `client+consultant` determines `probtype`. So, both of these composites are candidate keys. Either one can be selected as the primary key, and in this case `client+probtype` was selected. Notice that all the previously stated conditions are satisfied — there are multiple, composite candidate keys that overlap. This means the table is 3NF, but not BCNF. This can be easily verified by considering what happens if the firm adds a new consultant. A new consultant cannot be added until there is a client — an insertion anomaly. The problem is that `consultant` is a determinant, `consultant → probtype`, but is not a candidate key. In terms of the phrasing used earlier, the problem is that part of the key column is a fact about a nonkey column. The precise definition is *a relation is in Boyce-Codd normal form if and only if every determinant is a candidate key*.

This problem is avoided by creating the correct data model (see Figure 8-3) and then mapping to a relational model.

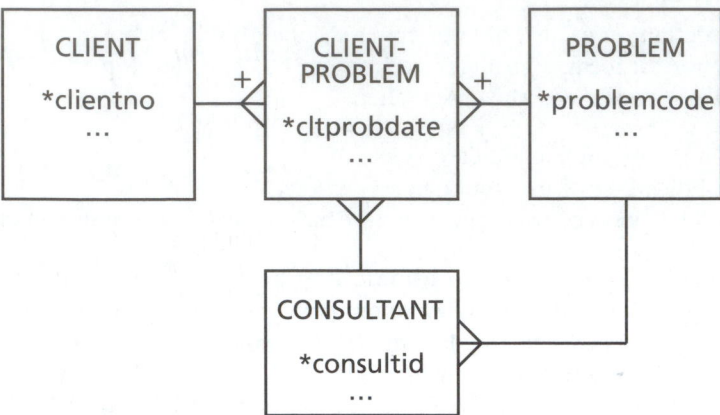

Figure 8-3. Resolving Boyce-Codd normal form violation

Fourth normal form

Fourth normal form requires that a row should not contain two or more independent multivalued facts about an entity. This requirement is more readily understood after investigating an example.

Consider students who play sports and study subjects. One way of representing this information is shown in Table 8-5. Consider the consequence of trying to insert a student who did not play a sport. Sport would be null, and this is not permissible because part of the composite primary key would then be null — a violation of the entity integrity rule. You cannot add a new student until you know her sport and her subject. Modification anomalies are very apparent.

Table 8-5: Fourth normal form violation

student			
studentid	sport	subject	...
50	Football	English	...
50	Football	Music	...
50	Tennis	Botany	...
50	Karate	Botany	...

This table is not in 4NF because sport and subject are independent multivalued facts about a student. There is no relationship between sport and subject. There is an indirect connection because sport and subject are associated with a student. In other words, a student can play many sports, and the same sport can be played by many students — a many-to-many (m:m) relationship between student and sport. Similarly, there is an m:m relationship between student and subject. It makes no sense to store information about a student's sports and subjects in the same table because sport and subject are not related. The problem arises because sport and subject are multivalued dependencies of student. The solution is to convert multivalued dependencies to functional dependencies. More formally, *a relation is in fourth normal form if it is in Boyce-Codd normal form and all multivalued dependencies on the relation are functional dependencies.* A data model (see Figure 8-4) sorts out this problem, although the correct relational mapping requires five tables.

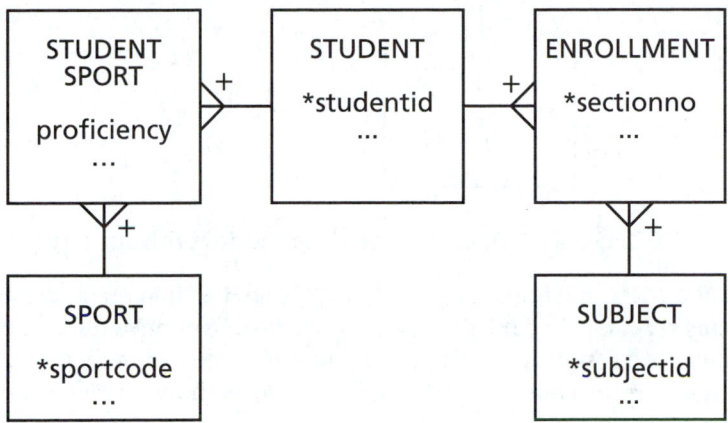

Figure 8-4. Resolving fourth normal form violation

Fifth normal form

Fifth normal form deals with the case where a table can be reconstructed from other tables. The reconstruction approach is preferred, because it means less redundancy and fewer maintenance problems.

The consultants, firms, and skills problem is used to illustrate the concept of 5NF. The problem is that consultants provide skills to one or more firms and firms can use many consultants; a consultant has many skills and a skill can be used by many firms; and a firm can have a need for many skills and the same skill can be required by many firms. The data model (see Figure 8-5) for this problem has the ménage-à-trois structure introduced in Chapter 7.

The relational mapping of the three-way relationships results in four tables, with the associative entity ASSIGNMENT mapping shown in Table 8-6.

The table is in 5NF because the combination of all three columns is required to identify which consultants supply which firms with which skills. For example, we see that Tan advises IBM on database and Apple on data communications. The data in this table cannot be reconstructed from other tables.

Table 8-6 is not in 5NF if there is a rule of the following form: If a consultant has a certain skill (e.g., database) and has a contract with a firm that requires that skill (e.g., IBM), then

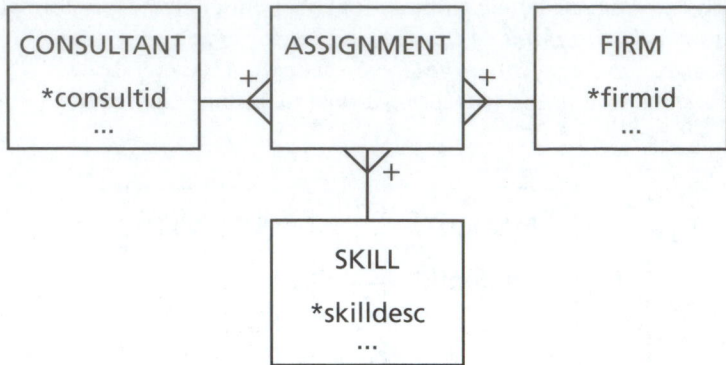

Figure 8-5. The CONSULTANT-FIRM-SKILL data model without a rule

the consultant advises that firm on that skill (i.e., he advises IBM on database). Notice that this rule means we can infer a relationship, and we no longer need the combination of the three columns. As a result, we break the single three-entity m:m relationship into three two-entity m:m relationships. The revised data model is shown in Figure 8-6.

Table 8-6: Relation table assignment

assignment		
consultid	firmid	skilldesc
Tan	IBM	Database
Tan	Apple	Data comm

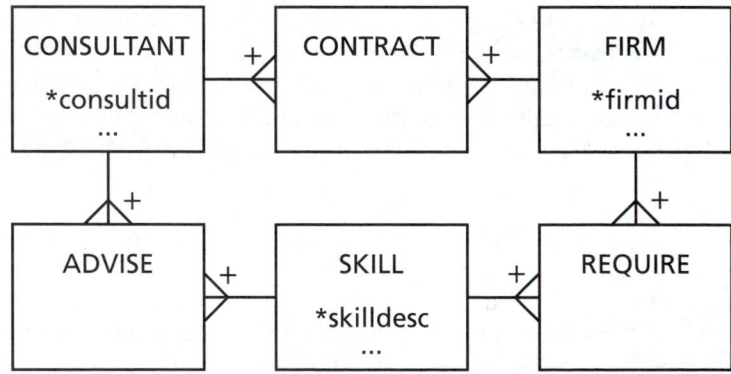

Figure 8-6. Revised data model after the introduction of the rule

Further understanding of 5NF is gained by examining the relational tables resulting from these three associative entities. Notice the names given to each of the associative entities.

contract records data about the firms a consultant advises; advise describes the skills a consultant has; and require stores data about the types of skills each firm requires. To help understand this problem, examine Table 8-7, Table 8-8, and Table 8-9.

Table 8-7: Relational table contract

contract	
consultid	firmid
Gonzales	Apple
Gonzales	IBM
Gonzales	NEC
Tan	IBM
Tan	NEC
Wood	Apple

Table 8-8: Relational table advise

advise	
consultid	skilldesc
Gonzales	Database
Gonzales	Data comm
Gonzales	Groupware
Tan	Database
Tan	Data comm
Wood	Data comm

Table 8-9: Relational table require

require	
firmid	skilldesc
IBM	Data comm
IBM	Groupware
NEC	Data comm
NEC	Database
NEC	Groupware
Apple	Data comm

Consider joining contract and advise, the result of which we call could advise (see Table 8-10) because it lists skills the consultant could provide if the firm required them. For example, Tan has skills in database and data communications, and Tan has a contract with IBM. If IBM required database skills, Tan could handle it. We need to look at require to determine whether IBM requires advice on database; it does not.

The join of could advise with require gives details of a firm's skill needs that a consultant can provide. The table can advise (see Table 8-11) is constructed by directly joining `contract`, `advise`, and `require`. Because we can construct `can advise` from three other tables, the data are in 5NF.

Table 8-10: Relational table could advise

could advise		
consultid	firmid	skilldesc
Gonzales	Apple	Database
Gonzales	Apple	Data comm
Gonzales	Apple	Groupware
Gonzales	IBM	Database
Gonzales	IBM	Data comm
Gonzales	IBM	Groupware
Gonzales	NEC	Database
Gonzales	NEC	Data comm
Gonzales	NEC	Groupware
Tan	IBM	Database
Tan	IBM	Data comm
Tan	NEC	Database
Tan	NEC	Data comm
Wood	Apple	Data comm

Table 8-11: Relational table can advise

can advise		
consultid	firmid	skilldesc
Gonzales	IBM	Data comm
Gonzales	IBM	Groupware
Gonzales	NEC	Database
Gonzales	NEC	Data comm
Gonzales	NEC	Groupware
Tan	IBM	Data comm
Tan	NEC	Database
Tan	NEC	Data comm
Wood	Apple	Data comm

Since data are stored in three separate tables, updating is easier. Consider the case where IBM requires database skills. We only need to add one row to `require` to record this fact. In the case of `can advise`, we would have to add two rows, one for Gonzales and one for Tan.

Now we can give 5NF a more precise definition: *A relation is in fifth normal form if and only if every join dependency of the relation is a consequence of the candidate keys of the relation.*

Up to this point, data modeling has enabled you to easily avoid normalization problems. Fifth normal form introduces a complication, however. How can you tell when to use a single three-way associative entity or three two-way associative entities? If there is a constraint or rule that is applied to the relationships between entities, consider the possibility of three two-way associative entities. Question the client carefully whenever you find a ménage à trois. Check to see that there are no rules or special conditions.

Domain-key normal form

The definition of DK/NF builds on three terms: key, constraint, and domain.[4] You already know a key is a unique identifier. A **constraint** is a rule governing attribute values. It must be sufficiently well-defined so that its truth can be readily evaluated. Referential integrity constraints, functional dependencies, and data validation rules are examples of constraints. A **domain** is a set of all values of the same data type (see page 232 for more detail). With the help of these terms, the concept of DK/NF is easily stated. *A relation is in domain-key normal form if and only if every constraint on the relation is a logical consequence of the domain constraints and the key constraints that apply to the relation.*

Note that DK/NF does not involve ideas of dependency; it just relies on the concepts of key, constraint, and domain. The problem with DK/NF is that while it is conceptually simple, no algorithm has been developed for converting relations to DK/NF. Hence, database designers must rely on their skills to create relations that are in DK/NF.

Conclusion

Normalization provides designers with a theoretical basis for understanding what they are doing when modeling data. It also alerts them to be aware of problems that they might not ordinarily detect when modeling. For example, 5NF cautions designers to investigate situations carefully (i.e., look for special rules), when their data model contains a ménage-à-trois.

Other data modeling methods

As mentioned previously, there are many species of data modeling. Here we consider two methods.

The E-R model

One of the most widely known data modeling methods is the E-R model developed by Chen.[5] There is no standard for the E-R model, and it has been extended and modified in a number of ways.

---

4. Fagin, R. 1981. A normal form for relational databases that is based on domains and keys. *ACM Transactions of Database Systems* 6 (3):387–415.
5. Chen, P. 1976. The entity-relationship model—toward a unified view of data. *ACM Transactions on Database Systems* 1 (1):9–36.

Sensor networks

Sensor networks can provide important tracking information and also report the physical attributes of the environment being monitored such as weight, temperature, and pressure. Unlike traditional wired networks, where each point connects to a central computer, a sensor network works more like a mesh, passing data from unit to unit.

Passing data to the next sensor is much cheaper than sending the data back to a central location and can cover a far greater area without the complexity and cost of stringing wires. The more nodes, the stronger the network.

For a hotel owner, this could mean cutting costs on heat and electricity by wiring up hotel rooms that sense when a guest has left his or her room. For manufacturing, it could mean replacing parts in a machine before it breaks down. For firefighters, it could mean locating one another in hazardous situations when radios fail.

Source: Anonymous. 2004. Sensor networks make early inroads. *CIO Insight*, Dec 1, www.cioinsight.com/article2/0,1397,1743159,00.asp.

As Figure 8-7 shows, an E-R model looks like the data models with which you are now familiar. Entities are shown by rectangles, and relationships are depicted by diamonds within which the cardinality of the relationship is indicated (e.g., there is a 1:m relationship between NATION and STOCK EXCHANGE). Cardinality can be 1:1, 1:m (conventionally shown as 1:N in E-R diagrams), and m:m (shown as M:N). Recursive relationships are also readily modeled. One important difference is that an m:m relationship is not shown as an associative entity; thus the database designer must convert this relationship to a table.

Attributes are shown as ellipses connected to the entity or relationship to which they belong (e.g., *stock name* is an attribute of STOCK). Relationships are named, and the name is shown above or below the relationship symbol. For example, LISTING is the name of the m:m relationship between STOCK and STOCK EXCHANGE. The method of recording attributes consumes space, particularly for large data models. It is more efficient to record attributes within a entity rectangle, as in the data modeling method you have learned.

IDEF1X

IDEF1X (Integrated DEFinition 1X)[6] was conceived in the late 1970s and refined in the early 1980s. It is based on the work of Codd and Chen. A quick look at some of the fundamental ideas of IDEF1X will show you how similar it is to the method you have learned. Entities are represented in a similar manner, as Figure 8-8 shows. The representation is a little different (e.g., the name of the entity is outside the rectangle), but the information is the same.

---

6.   Bruce, T. A. 1992. *Designing quality databases with IDEF1X information models*. New York, NY: Dorset House.

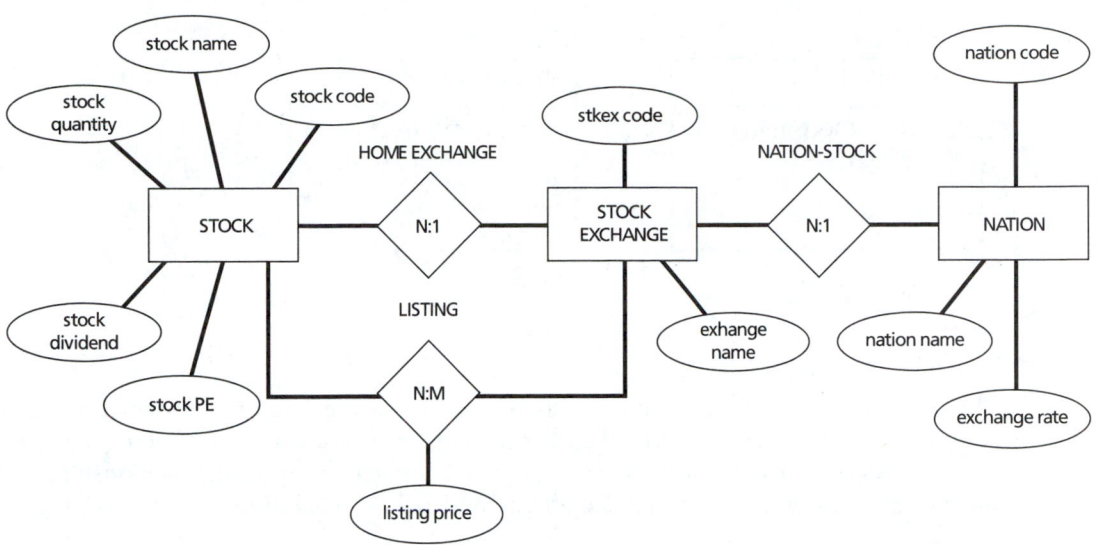

Figure 8-7. An E-R diagram

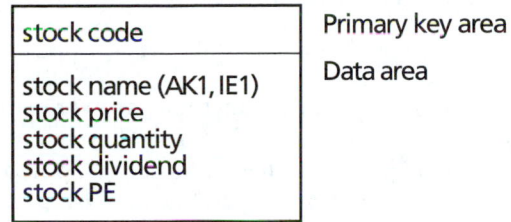

Figure 8-8. An entity

IDEF1X adds additional notation to an attribute to indicate whether it is an alternate key or inversion entry. An **alternate key** is a possible primary key (identifier) that was not selected as the primary key. *Stock name*, assuming it is unique, is an alternate key. An **inversion entry** indicates a likely frequent way of accessing the entity, so it should become an index (page 330). For instance, the entity may be accessed frequently via *stock name*. Alternate keys are shown as AK1, AK2, . . . and inversion entries as IE1, IE2, ... Thus, *stock name* is both an alternate key and an inversion entry.

The representation of relationships is also similar. A dot is used rather than a crow's foot, as illustrated in Figure 8-9. Also, notice that relationships are described, whereas you learned to describe only relationships when they are not readily inferred.

IDEF1X also incorporates a generalization hierarchy (see page 181).

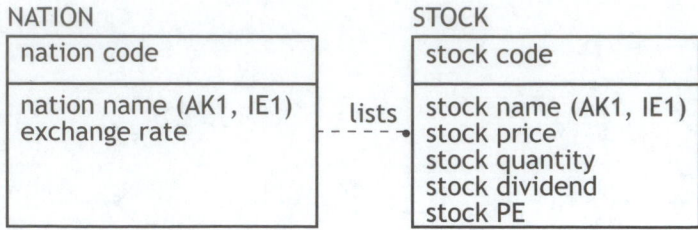

Figure 8-9. A relationship

Representing relationships

The various dialects of data modeling are most distinctive in the ways in which relationships are represented (see Table 8-12). Entities are almost always shown as rectangles. Before considering how different variations of data modeling represent relationships, we need to examine two extensions that add more detail to a data model.

As Table 8-12 clearly illustrates, there is a lack of consistency across various data modeling diagramming techniques, particularly for weak entities. However, you should have few problems adapting to another approach, since the fundamental concepts of data modeling do not vary—only the method of representing these concepts changes.

Conclusion

The underlying concepts of different data modeling methods are very similar. They all have the same goal: improving the quality of database design. They share common concepts, such as entity and relationship mapping. We have adopted an approach that is simple and effective. The method can be learned rapidly, and novice users can create high-quality models. Also, if you have learned one data modeling method, you can quickly adapt to the nuances of other methods. Interestingly, Microsoft uses a method very similar to ours in documentation of its database package, Access.

Tsunami warning system for the average beach Joe

Following the devastating tsunami that struck on December 26, 2004, there is great interest in building a sensor network capable of detecting an oceanic earthquake and a possible tsunami in the Indian Ocean. However, this will be useless unless communication systems are improved in the countries likely to be affected. As one expert noted, "If it's a tsunami, you've got to get the information down to the last Joe on the beach. This is the stuff that is really very hard."

Source: Knight, Wes. 2005. Tsunami warning system is not simply sensors. *New Scientist*, Jan 4, www.newscientist.com/channel/earth/tsunami/dn6839.

Table 8-12: Data modeling dialects

Relationship	Dialect	Diagram	Comments or alternate form
1:1	This text		
	E-R	1:1	1 ◇ 1
	IDEF1X	----Z●	A "Z" placed beside the dot indicates a cardinality of 0 or 1.
1:m	This text		
	E-R	1:M	1 ◇ M
	IDEF1X	-------●	
m:m	This text		Convert to an associative entity.
	E-R	M:N	M ◇ N
	IDEF1X		Convert to an associative entity.
weak entity (1:m)	This text	+/	
	E-R	▭	A weak entity is shown as a boxed rectangle.
	IDEF1X	●	A solid line indicates the entity at the dot end is weak.

Summary

Normalization gradually converts a file design into normal form by successive application of rules to move the design from first to fifth normal form. Functional dependency means that one or more attributes determine the value of another. An attribute, or set of attributes, that fully functionally determines another attribute is called a *determinant*. First normal form states that all occurrences of a row must have the same number of columns. Second normal form is violated when a nonkey column is a fact about a component of the prime key. Third normal form is violated when a nonkey column is a fact about another nonkey column. Boyce-Codd normal form is a stronger version of third normal form. Fourth normal form requires that a row should not contain two or more independent multivalued facts about an entity. Fifth normal form deals with the case where a table can be reconstructed from data in other tables. Fifth normal form arises when there are special rules or conditions. A high-fidelity data model will be of high normal form.

One of the most widely known methods of data modeling is the E-R model. The basic concepts of most data modeling methods are very similar. All aim to improve database design.

Key terms and concepts

Alternate key	Generalization hierarchy
Boyce-Codd normal form (BCNF)	IDEF1X
Constraint	Inversion entry
Data model	Many-to-many (m:m) attribute relationship
Determinant	Multidetermination
Domain	Multivalued dependency
Domain-key normal form (DK/NF)	Normalization
Entity	One-to-many (1:m) attribute relationship
Entity-relationship (E-R) model	One-to-one (1:1) attribute relationship
Fifth normal form (5NF)	Relationship
First normal form (1NF)	Second normal form (2NF)
Fourth normal form (1NF)	Third normal form (3NF)
Full functional dependency	Trigger
Functional dependency	

References and additional readings

Bruce, T. A. 1992. *Designing quality databases with IDEF1X information models*. New York, NY: Dorset House.

Chen, P. 1976. The entity-relationship model—toward a unified view of data. *ACM Transactions on Database Systems* 1 (1):9–36.

Hammer, M. 1990. Reengineering work: Don't automate, obliterate. *Harvard Business Review* 68 (4):104–112.

Kent, W. 1983. A simple guide to five normal forms in relational database theory. *Communications of the ACM* 26 (2):120–125.

Wetherbe, J. C. 1991. Executive information requirements: Getting it right. *MIS Quarterly* 15 (1):51–65.

Exercises

Short answers

1. What is normalization, and what is its goal?
2. How does DK/NF differ from earlier normal forms?
3. How do E-R and IDEF1X differ from the data modeling method of this text?

Normalization and modeling

Using normalization, E-R, or IDEF1X, create data models from the following narratives, which are sometimes intentionally incomplete. You will have to make some assumptions.

Make certain you state these assumptions alongside your data model. Define the identifier(s) and attributes of each entity.

1. The president of a book wholesaler has told you that she wants information about publishers, authors, and books.

2. A university has many subject areas (e.g., MIS, Romance languages). Professors teach in only one subject area, but the same subject area can have many professors. Professors can teach many different courses in their subject area. An offering of a course (e.g., Data Management 457, French 101) is taught by only one professor at a particular time.

3. Kids'n'Vans retails minivans for a number of manufacturers. Each manufacturer offers several models of its minivan (e.g., SE, LE, GT). Each model comes with a standard set of equipment (e.g., the Acme SE comes with wheels, seats, and an engine). Minivans can have a variety of additional equipment or accessories (radio, air conditioning, automatic transmission, airbag, etc.), but not all accessories are available for all minivans (e.g., not all manufacturers offer a driver's side airbag). Some sets of accessories are sold as packages (e.g., the luxury package might include stereo, six speakers, cocktail bar, and twin overhead foxtails).

4. Steve operates a cinema chain and has given you the following information:
"I have many cinemas. Each cinema can have multiple theaters. Movies are shown throughout the day starting at 11 A.M. and finishing at 1 A.M. Each movie is given a two-hour time slot. We never show a movie in more than one theater at a time, but we do shift movies among theaters because seating capacity varies. I am interested in knowing how many people, classified by adults and children, attended each showing of a movie. I vary ticket prices by movie and time slot. For instance, *Lassie Get Lost* is 50 cents for everyone at 11 A.M. but is 75 cents at 11 P.M."

5. A telephone company offers a 10 percent discount to any customer who phones another person who is also a customer of the company. To be eligible for the discount, the pairing of the two phone numbers must be registered with the telephone company. Furthermore, for billing purposes, the company records both phone numbers, start time, end time, and date of call.

9

The Relational Model and Relational Algebra

Nothing is so practical as a good theory.
K. Lewin, 1945

Learning objectives

Students completing this chapter will

❖ know the structures of the relational model;
❖ understand relational algebra commands;
❖ be able to determine whether a DBMS is completely relational.

Background

The relational model,[1] developed as a result of recognized shortcomings of hierarchical and network DBMSs, was introduced by Codd in 1970.[2] As the major developer, Codd believed that a sound theoretical model would solve most practical problems that could potentially arise.

In another article,[3] Codd expounds the case for adopting the relational over other database models. There is a threefold thrust to his argument. *First,* other models force the programmer to code at a low level of structural detail. As a result, application programs are more complex and take longer to write and debug. *Second*, no commands are provided

---

1. Under the spiral approach to teaching data modeling and SQL, many aspects of the relational model were introduced earlier. This chapter consolidates and extends the earlier work to provide formal coverage of this most widely used database technology.
2. Codd, E. F. 1970. A relational model for large shared data banks. *Communications of the ACM* 13 (6):377–387.
3. Codd, E. F. 1982. Relational database: A practical foundation for productivity. *Communications of the ACM* 25 (2):109–117.

for processing multiple records at one time. Other models do not provide the set-processing capability of the relational model. The set-processing feature means that queries can be more concisely expressed. *Third*, only the relational model, through a query language such as structured query language (SQL), recognizes the clients' need to make ad hoc queries. Adoption of the relational model and SQL permits an IS department to respond far more rapidly to unanticipated requests. It can also mean that clients can write their own queries. Thus, Codd's assertion that the relational model is a practical tool for increasing the productivity of IS departments is well founded.

The productivity increase arises from three of the objectives that drove Codd's research. The *first* was to provide a clearly delineated boundary between the logical and physical aspects of database management.[4] Programming could then be divorced from considerations of the physical representation of data. Codd labels this the **data independence objective**. The *second* objective was to create a simple model that was readily understood by a wide range of users and programmers. This **communicability objective** promotes effective and efficient communication between users and IS personnel. The *third* objective was to increase processing capabilities from record-at-a-time to multiple-records-at-a-time—the **set-processing objective**. Achievement of these objectives means fewer lines of code are required to write an application program, and there is less ambiguity in client-analyst communication.

The relational model has three major components:

❖ Data structures
❖ Integrity rules
❖ Operators used to retrieve, derive, or modify data

Data structures

Like most theories, the relational model is based on some key structures or concepts. We need to understand these in order to understand the theory.

Domain

A domain is a set of values all of the same data type. For example, the domain of nation name is the set of all possible nation names. The domain of all stock prices is the set of all currency values in, say, the range $0 to $10,000,000. You can think of a domain as all the legal values of an attribute.

In specifying a domain, you need to think about the smallest unit of data for an attribute defined on that domain. In Chapter 8, we discussed how a candidate attribute should be examined to see whether it should be segmented (e.g., we divide name into first name, other name, and last name, and maybe more). While it is unlikely that name will be a domain, it is likely that there will be a domain for first name, last name, and so on. Thus, a domain contains values that are in their *atomic* state; they cannot be decomposed further.

---

4.   This topic is covered in Section 3.

The practical value of a domain is to define what comparisons are permissible. Only attributes drawn from the same domain should be compared; otherwise it is a bit like comparing bananas and strawberries. For example, it makes no sense to compare a stock's PE ratio to its price. They do not measure the same thing; they belong to different domains. Although the domain concept is useful, it is rarely supported by relational model implementations.

Relations

A relation is a table of *n* columns (or *attributes*) and *m* rows (or *tuples*). Each column has a unique name, and all the values in a column are drawn from the same domain. Each row of the relation is uniquely identified. The order of columns and rows is immaterial.

The **cardinality** of a relation is its number of rows. The **degree** of a relation is the number of columns. For example, the relation NATION (see Figure 9-1) is of degree 3 and has a cardinality of 4. Because the cardinality of a relation changes every time a row is added or deleted, you can expect cardinality to change frequently. The degree changes if a column is added to a relation, but in terms of relational theory, it is considered to be a new relation. So, only a relation's cardinality changes.

Relational database

A relational database is a collection of relations or tables. The distinguishing feature of the relational model, when compared to the hierarchical and network models, is that there are no explicit linkages between tables. Tables are linked by common columns drawn on the same domain; thus, the portfolio database (see Figure 9-1) consists of tables stock and nation. The 1:m relationship between the two tables is represented by the column natcode that is common to both tables. Note that the two columns need not have the same name, but they must be drawn on the same domain so that comparison is possible. In the case of an m:m relationship, while a new table must be created to represent the relationship, the principle of linking tables through common columns on the same domain remains in force.

Primary key

A relation's primary key is its unique identifier; for example, the primary key of nation is natcode. As you already know, a primary key can be a composite of several columns. The primary key guarantees that each row of a relation can be uniquely addressed. A primary key need not be indexed, though it often is.

Candidate key

In some situations, there may be several attributes, known as candidate keys, that are potential primary keys. Column natcode is unique in the nation relation, for example. We also can be fairly certain that two nations will not have the same name. Therefore, nation has multiple candidate keys: natcode and natname.

nation

natcode	natname	exchrate
UK	United Kingdom	1.00
USA	United States	0.67
AUS	Australia	0.46
IND	India	0.0228

stock

stkcode	stkfirm	stkprice	stkqty	stkdiv	stkpe	natcode
FC	Freedonia Copper	27.50	10,529	1.84	16	UK
PT	Patagonian Tea	55.25	12,635	2.50	10	UK
AR	Abyssinian Ruby	31.82	22,010	1.32	13	UK
SLG	Sri Lankan Gold	50.37	32,868	2.68	16	UK
ILZ	Indian Lead & Zinc	37.75	6,390	3.00	12	UK
BE	Burmese Elephant	.07	154,713	0.01	3	UK
BS	Bolivian Sheep	12.75	231,678	1.78	11	UK
NG	Nigerian Geese	35.00	12,323	1.68	10	UK
CS	Canadian Sugar	52.78	4,716	2.50	15	UK
ROF	Royal Ostrich Farms	33.75	1,234,923	3.00	6	UK
MG	Minnesota Gold	53.87	816,122	1.00	25	USA
GP	Georgia Peach	2.35	387,333	.20	5	USA
NE	Narembeen Emu	12.34	45,619	1.00	8	AUS
QD	Queensland Diamond	6.73	89,251	.50	7	AUS
IR	Indooroopilly Ruby	15.92	56,147	.50	20	AUS
BD	Bombay Duck	25.55	167,382	1.00	12	IND

Figure 9-1. A relational database with tables NATION and STOCK

Alternate key

When there are multiple candidate keys, one is chosen as the primary key, and the remainder are known as alternate keys. In this case, we selected natcode as the primary key, and natname is an alternate key.

Foreign key

The foreign key is an important concept of the relational model. It is the way relationships are represented and can be thought of as the glue that holds a set of tables together to form a relational database. A foreign key is an attribute (possibly composite) of a relation that is also a primary key of a relation. The foreign key and primary key may be in different relations or the same relation, but both keys must be drawn from the same domain.

Integrity rules

The integrity section of the relational model consists of two rules. The **entity integrity rule** ensures that each instance of an entity described by a relation is identifiable in some way. Its implementation means that each row in a relation can be uniquely distinguished. The rule is

No component of the primary key of a relation may be null.

Null in this case means that the component cannot be undefined or unknown; it must have a value. Notice that the rule says "component of a primary key." This means every part of the primary key must be known. If a part cannot be defined, it implies that the particular entity it describes cannot be defined. In practical terms, it means you cannot add a nation to `nation` unless you also define a value for `natcode`.

The definition of a foreign key implies that there is a corresponding primary key. The **referential integrity rule** ensures that this is the case. It states

A database must not contain any unmatched foreign key values.

Simply, this rule means that you cannot define a foreign key without first defining its matching primary key. In practical terms, it would mean you could not add a Canadian stock to the `stock` relation without first creating a row in `nation` for Canada.

Notice that the concepts of foreign key and referential integrity are intertwined. There is not much sense in having foreign keys without having the referential integrity rule. Permitting a foreign key without a corresponding primary key means the relationship cannot be determined. Note that the referential integrity rule does not imply a foreign key cannot be null. There can be circumstances where a relationship does not exist for a particular instance, in which case the foreign key is null.

Manipulation languages

There are four approaches to manipulating relational tables, and you are already familiar with SQL and query-by-example (QBE). Less widely used manipulation languages are relational algebra and relational calculus. These languages are briefly discussed, with some attention given to relational algebra in the next section and SQL in the following chapter.

Relational algebra has a set of operations similar to traditional algebra (e.g., add and multiply) for manipulating tables. Although relational algebra can be used to resolve queries, it is seldom employed, because it requires you to specify both what you want and how to get it. That is, you have to specify the operations on each table. This makes relational algebra more difficult to use than SQL, where the focus is on specifying what is wanted.

Relational calculus overcomes some of the shortcomings of relational algebra by concentrating on what is required. In other words, there is less need to specify how the query will operate. Relational calculus is classified as a nonprocedural language, because you do not have to be overly concerned with the procedures by which a result is determined.

Unfortunately, relational calculus can be difficult to learn, and as a result, language designers developed **SQL** and **QBE**, which are nonprocedural and more readily mastered. You have already gained some skills in SQL and have had some exposure to QBE. Although QBE is generally easier to use than SQL, IS professionals need to master SQL for two reasons. *First,* SQL is frequently embedded in other programming languages, a feature not available with QBE. *Second*, it is very difficult, or impossible, to express some queries in QBE (e.g., divide). Because SQL is important, it is the focus of the next chapter.

QBE commands are translated to SQL prior to execution, and many systems allow you to view the generated SQL. This can be handy. You can use QBE to generate a portion of the SQL for a complex query and then edit the generated code to fine-tune the query.

Relational algebra

The relational model includes a set of operations (see Table 9-1), known as relational algebra, for manipulating relations. Relational algebra is a standard for judging data retrieval languages. If a retrieval language, such as SQL, can be used to express every relational algebra operator, it is said to be **relationally complete**.

Table 9-1: Relational algebra operators

Restrict	Creates a new table from specified rows of an existing table
Project	Creates a new table from specified columns of an existing table
Product	Creates a new table from all the possible combinations of rows of two existing tables
Union	Creates a new table containing rows appearing in one or both tables of two existing tables
Intersect	Creates a new table containing rows appearing in both tables of two existing tables
Difference	Creates a new table containing rows appearing in one table but not in the other of two existing tables
Join	Creates a new table containing all possible combinations of rows of two existing tables satisfying the join condition
Divide	Creates a new table containing x_i such that the pair (x_i, y_i) exists in the first table for every y_i in the second table

There are eight relational algebra operations that can be used with either one or two relations to create a new relation. The assignment operator (:=) indicates the name of the new relation. The relational algebra statement to create relation A, the union of relations B and C, is expressed as

```
A := B UNION C
```

Before we begin our discussion of each of the eight operators, note that the first two, restrict and project, operate on a single relation and the rest require two relations.

Restrict

Restrict extracts specified rows from a single relation. As the shaded rows in Figure 9-2 depict, restrict takes a horizontal slice through a relation.

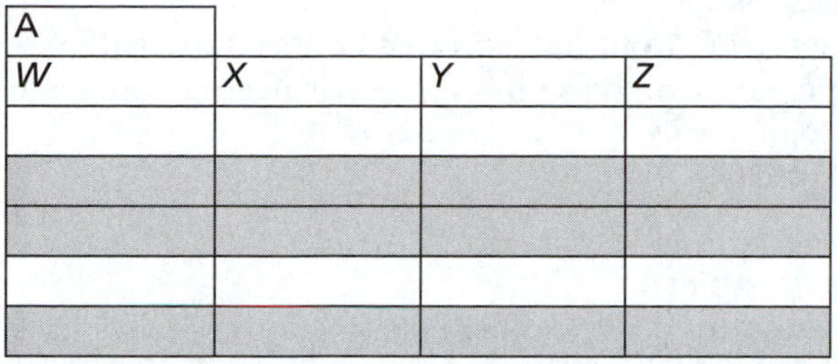

Figure 9-2. Relational operation restrict—a horizontal slice

The relational algebra command to create the new relation using restrict is

```
tablename WHERE column1 theta column2
```

or

```
tablename WHERE column1 theta literal
```

where theta can be =, <>, >, >=, <, or <=.

For example, the following relational algebra command creates a new table from STOCK containing all rows with a nation code of US:

```
usstock := stock WHERE natcode = 'US'
```

You will sometimes see restrict referred to as select. Nowadays, to avoid confusion with SQL's SELECT statement, "restrict" is the preferred term.

Project

Project extracts specified columns from a table. As Figure 9-3 shows, project takes a vertical slice through a table.

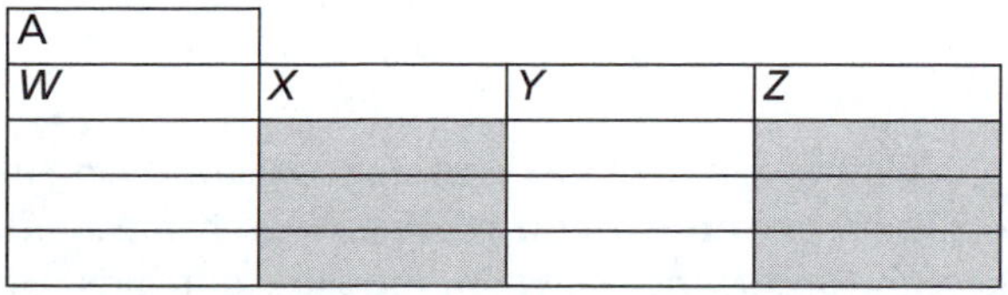

Figure 9-3. Relational operator project—a vertical slice

Figure 9-3. Relational operator project—a vertical slice

The relational algebra command to create the new relation using project is

```
tablename [columnname, …]
```

So, in order to create a new table from `nation` that contains the nation's name and its exchange rate, for example, you would use this relational algebra command:

```
rates := nation[natname, exchrate]
```

Product

Product creates a new relation from all possible combinations of rows in two other relations. It is sometimes called `TIMES` or `MULTIPLY`. The relational command to create the product of two tables is

```
tablename1 TIMES tablename2
```

The operation of product is illustrated in Figure 9-4, which shows the result of A TIMES B.

A	
V	W
v_1	w_1
v_2	w_2
v_3	w_3

B		
X	Y	Z
x_1	y_1	z_1
x_2	y_2	z_2

A TIMES B				
V	W	X	Y	Z
v_1	w_1	x_1	y_1	z_1
v_1	w_1	x_2	y_2	z_2
v_2	w_2	x_1	y_1	z_1
v_2	w_2	x_2	y_2	z_2
v_3	w_3	x_1	y_1	z_1
v_3	w_3	x_2	y_2	z_2

Figure 9-4. Relational operator product

Union

The union of two relations is a new relation containing all rows appearing in one or both relations. The two relations must be **union compatible,** which means they have the same column names, in the same order, and drawn on the same domains. Duplicate rows are automatically eliminated—they must be, or the relational model is no longer satisfied. The relational command to create the union of two tables is

```
tablename1 UNION tablename2
```

Union is illustrated in Figure 9-5. Notice that corresponding columns in tables A and B have the same names. While the sum of the number of rows in relations A and B is five, the union contains four rows, because one row (x_2, y_2) is common to both relations.

A	
X	Y
x_1	y_1
x_2	y_2
x_3	y_3

B	
X	Y
x_2	y_2
x_4	y_4

A UNION B	
X	Y
x_1	y_1
x_2	y_2
x_3	y_3
x_4	y_4

Figure 9-5. Relational operator union

Intersect

The intersection of two relations is a new relation containing all rows appearing in both relations. The two relations must be union compatible. The relational command to create the intersection of two tables is

```
tablename1 INTERSECT tablename2
```

The result of A INTERSECT B is one row, because only one row (x_2, y_2) is common to both relations A and B (see Figure 9-6).

A	
X	Y
x_1	y_1
x_2	y_2
x_3	y_3

B	
X	Y
x_2	y_2
x_4	y_4

A INTERSECT B	
X	Y
x_2	y_2

Figure 9-6. Relational operator intersect

Difference

The difference between two relations is a new relation containing all rows appearing in the first relation but not in the second. The two relations must be union compatible. The relational command to create the difference between two tables is

```
tablename1 MINUS tablename2
```

The result of A MINUS B is two rows (see Figure 9-7). Both of these rows are in relation A but not in relation B. The row containing (x_2, y_2) appears in both A and B and thus is not in A MINUS B.

A	
X	Y
x_1	y_1
x_2	y_2
x_3	y_3

B	
X	Y
x_2	y_2
x_4	y_4

A minus B	
X	Y
x_1	y_1
x_3	y_3

Figure 9-7. Relational operator difference

Join

Join creates a new relation from two relations for all combinations of rows satisfying the join condition. The general format of join is

```
tablename1 JOIN tablename2 WHERE tablename1.columnname1 theta
    tablename2.columnname2
```

where theta can be =, <>, >, >=, <, or <=.

Figure 9-8 illustrates A JOIN B where $W = Z$, which is an equijoin because theta is an equals sign. Tables A and B are matched when values in columns W and Z in each relation are equal. The matching columns should be drawn from the same domain. You can also think of join as a product followed by restrict on the resulting relation. So the join can be written

```
(A TIMES B) WHERE W THETA Z
```

Divide

Divide is the hardest relational operator to understand. Divide requires that A and B have a set of attributes, in this case Y, that are common to both relations. Conceptually, A divided by B asks the question, "Is there a value in the X column of A (e.g., x_1) that has a

A	
V	*W*
v_1	wz_1
v_2	wz_2
v_3	wz_3

B		
X	*Y*	*Z*
x_1	y_1	wz_1
x_2	y_2	wz_3

A EQUIJOIN B				
V	*W*	*X*	*Y*	*Z*
v_1	wz_1	x_1	y_1	wz_1
v_3	wz_3	x_2	y_2	wz_3

Figure 9-8. Relational operator join

value in the Y column of A for every value of y in the Y column of B?" Look first at B, where the Y column has values y_1 and y_2. When you examine the X column of A, you find there are rows (x_1, y_1) and (x_1, y_2). That is, for x_1, there is a value in the Y column of A for every value of y in the Y column of B. Thus, the result of the division is a new relation with a single row and column containing the value x_1 (see Figure 9-9).

A	
X	*Y*
x_1	y_1
x_1	y_3
x_1	y_2
x_2	y_1
x_3	y_3

B
Y
y_1
y_2

A DIVIDE B
X
x_1

Figure 9-9. Relational operator divide

Querying with relational algebra

A few queries will give you a taste of how you might use relational algebra. To assist in understanding these queries, the answer is expressed, side-by-side, in both relational algebra (on the left) and SQL (on the right).

○ **List all data in** SHARE.

A very simple report of all columns in the table `shr`.

shr	SELECT * FROM shr

○ **Report a firm's name and price-earnings ratio.**

A projection of two columns from shr.

shr [shrfirm, shrpe]	SELECT shrfirm, shrpe FROM shr

○ **Get all shares with a price-earnings ratio less than 12.**

A restriction of shr on column shrpe.

shr WHERE shrpe < 12	SELECT * FROM shr WHERE shrpe < 12

○ **List details of firms where the share holding is at least 100,000.**

A restriction and projection combined. Notice that the restriction is expressed within parentheses.

(shr WHERE shrqty >= 100000)
[shrfirm, shrprice, shrqty,
shrdiv]
	SELECT shrfirm, shrprice,
	  shrqty, shrdiv FROM shr
	  WHERE shrqty >= 100000

○ **Find all shares where the PE is 12 or higher and the share holding is less than 10,000.**

Intersect is used with two restrictions to identify shares satisfying both conditions.

(shr WHERE shrpe >= 12)
INTERSECT
(shr WHERE shrqty < 10000)
	SELECT * FROM shr
	  WHERE shrpe >= 12
	  AND shrqty < 10000

○ **Report all shares other than those with the code CS or PT.**

Difference is used to subtract those shares with the specified codes. Notice the use of union to identify shares satisfying either condition.

shr MINUS
  ((shr WHERE shrcode = 'CS')
UNION
  (shr WHERE shrcode = 'PT'))
	SELECT * FROM shr WHERE shrcode
	NOT IN ('CS','PT')

○ **Report the value of each stock holding in UK pounds.**

A join of STOCK and NATION and projection of specified attributes.

| ```
(STOCK JOIN nation
 WHERE stock.natcode =
  nation.natcode)
[natname, stkfirm,
 stkprice, stkqty, exchrate,
 stkprice*stkqty*exchrate]
``` | ```
SELECT natname, stkfirm,
 stkprice, stkqty, exchrate,
 stkprice*stkqty*exchrate
 FROM stock,nation
 WHERE stock.natcode =
  nation.natcode
``` |

○ **Find the items that have appeared in all sales.**

Divide reports the ITEMNO of items appearing in all sales, and this result is then joined with ITEM to report the items.

| ```
((lineitem[itemno, saleno]
 DIVIDEBY sale[saleno])
 JOIN item) [itemno, itemname]
``` | ```
SELECT itemno, itemname FROM
item
 WHERE NOT EXISTS
  (SELECT * FROM sale
   WHERE NOT EXISTS
    (SELECT * FROM lineitem
     WHERE lineitem.itemno =
      item.itemno
     AND lineitem.saleno =
      sale.saleno))
``` |

Skill builder

Write relational algebra statements for the following queries:

1. Report a firm's name and dividend.
2. Find the names of firms where the holding is greater than 10,000.

A primitive set of relational operators

The full set of eight relational operators is not required. As you have already seen, JOIN can be defined in terms of product and restrict. Intersection and divide can also be defined in terms of other commands. Indeed, only five operators are required: restrict, project, product, union, and difference. These five are known as *primitives* because these are the minimal set of relational operators. None of the primitive operators can be defined in terms of the other operators. Table 9-2 illustrates how each primitive can be expressed as an SQL command, which implies that SQL is relationally complete.

Table 9-2: Comparison of relational algebra primitive operators and SQL

Operator	Relational algebra	SQL
Restrict	A where condition	`SELECT * FROM A WHERE condition`
Project	A [X]	`SELECT X FROM A`
Product	A TIMES B	`SELECT * FROM A, B`
Union	A UNION B	`SELECT * FROM A UNION SELECT * FROM B`

Difference	A MINUS B	`SELECT * FROM A`
		`   WHERE NOT EXISTS`
		`   (SELECT * FROM B WHERE`
		`       A.X = B.X AND A.Y = B.Y AND ...`[a]

a. Essentially, where all columns of A are equal to all columns of B.

A fully relational database

The three components of a relational database system are structures (domains and relations), integrity rules (primary and foreign keys), and a manipulation language (relational algebra). A **fully relational database** system provides complete support for each of these components. Many commercial systems support SQL but do not provide support for domains or integrity rules. Such systems are not fully relational but are relationally complete.

In 1985, Codd[5] established the 12 commandments of relational database systems (see Table 9-3). In addition to providing some insights into Codd's thinking about the management of data, these rules can also be used to judge how well a database fits the relational model. The major impetus for these rules was uncertainty in the marketplace about the meaning of "relational DBMS". Codd's rules are a checklist for establishing the authenticity of a DBMS that claims to be relational.

Table 9-3: Codd's rules for a relational DBMS

The information rule
The guaranteed access rule
Systematic treatment of null values
Active online catalog of the relational model
The comprehensive data sublanguage rule
The view updating rule
High-level insert, update, and delete
Physical data independence
Logical data independence
Integrity independence
Distribution independence
The nonsubversion rule

---

5.   Codd, E. F. 1985. Is your DBMS really relational? *Computerworld*, October 14, and Does your DBMS run by the rules? *Computerworld*, October 21.

The information rule

This rule stipulates that there is only one logical representation of data in a database. All data must appear to be stored as values in a table.

The guaranteed access rule

Every value in a database must be addressable by specifying its table name, column name, and the primary key of the row in which it is stored.

Systematic treatment of null values

There must be a distinct representation for unknown or inappropriate data.[6] This must be unique and independent of data type. The DBMS should handle null data in a systematic way. For example, a zero or a blank cannot be used to represent a null. This is one of the more troublesome areas because null can have several meanings (e.g., missing or inappropriate).

Active online catalog of the relational model

There should be an online catalog that describes the relational model (see page 279 for details of the system catalog). Authorized users should be able to access this catalog using the DBMS's query language (e.g., SQL).

The comprehensive data sublanguage rule

There must be a relational language that supports data definition, data manipulation, security and integrity constraints, and transaction processing operations. Furthermore, this language must support both interactive querying and application programming and be expressible in text format. SQL fits these requirements.

The view updating rule

The DBMS must be able to update any view that is theoretically updatable.

High-level insert, update, and delete

The system must support set-at-a-time operations. For example, multiple rows must be updatable with a single command.

Physical data independence

Changes to storage representation or access methods will not affect application programs. For example, application programs should remain unimpaired even if a database is moved to a different storage device or an index is created for a table.

---

6. In DB2, each column has an associated 1-byte field that denotes whether the column is null.

Logical data independence

Information-preserving changes to base tables will not affect application programs. For instance, no applications should be affected when a new table is added to a database.

Integrity independence

Integrity constraints should be part of a database's definition rather than embedded within application programs. It must be possible to change these constraints without affecting any existing application programs.

Distribution independence

Introduction of a distributed DBMS or redistribution of existing distributed data should have no impact on existing applications (see the discussion of distributed databases starting on page 368).

The nonsubversion rule

It must not be possible to use a record-at-a-time interface to subvert security or integrity constraints. You should not be able, for example, to write a PHP program with embedded SQL commands to bypass security features.

Codd issued an additional higher-level rule, rule 0, which states that a relational DBMS must be able to manage databases entirely through its relational capacities. In other words, a DBMS is either totally relational or it is not relational.

Summary

The relational model developed as a result of recognized shortcomings of hierarchical and network DBMSs. Codd created a strong theoretical base for the relational model. Three objectives drove relational database research: data independence, communicability, and set processing. The relational model has domain structures, integrity rules, and operators used to retrieve, derive, or modify data. A domain is a set of values all of the same data type. The practical value of a domain is to define what comparisons are permissible. A relation is a table of n columns and m rows. The cardinality of a relation is its number of rows. The degree of a relation is the number of columns.

A relational database is a collection of relations. The distinguishing feature of the relational model is that there are no explicit linkages between tables. A relation's primary key is its unique identifier. When there are multiple candidates for the primary key, one is chosen as the primary key and the remainder are known as alternate keys. The foreign key is the way relationships are represented and can be thought of as the glue that binds a set of tables together to form a relational database. The purpose of the entity integrity rule is to ensure that each entity described by a relation is identifiable in some way. The referential integrity rule ensures that you cannot define a foreign key without first defining its matching primary key.

The relational model includes a set of operations, known as relational algebra, for manipulating relations. There are eight operations that can be used with either one or two relations to create a new relation. These operations are restrict, project, product, union, intersect, difference, join, and divide. Only five operators, known as primitives, are required to define all eight relational operations. An SQL statement can be translated to relational algebra and vice versa. If a retrieval language can be used to express every relational algebra operator, it is said to be relationally complete. A fully relational database system provides complete support for domains, integrity rules, and a manipulation language. Codd set forth 12 rules that can be used to judge how well a database fits the relational model. He also added rule 0—a DBMS is either totally relational or it is not relational.

Key terms and concepts

Alternate key	Join
Candidate key	Logical data independence
Cardinality	Nonsubversion rule
Catalog	Null
Communicability objective	Operators
Data independence	Physical data independence
Data structures	Primary key
Data sublanguage rule	Product
Degree	Project
Difference	Query-by-example (QBE)
Distribution independence	Referential integrity
Divide	Relational algebra
Domain	Relational calculus
Entity integrity	Relational database
Foreign key	Relational model
Fully relational database	Relationally complete
Guaranteed access rule	Relations
Information rule	Restrict
Integrity independence	Set processing objective
Integrity rules	Union
Intersect	View updating rule

References and additional readings

Bustamente, G. G., and K. Sorenson. 1994. Decision support at Lands' End—An evolution. *IBM Systems Journal* 33 (2):228–238.

Codd, E. F. 1982. Relational database: A practical foundation for productivity. *Communications of the ACM* 25 (2):109–117.

Codd, E. F. 1985. Is your DBMS really relational? *Computerworld*, October 14.

Codd, E. F. 1985. Does your DBMS run by the rules? *Computerworld*, October 21.

Codd, E. F. 1988. Fatal flaws in SQL. *Datamation*, August 15 and September 1.

Exercises

1. What reasons does Codd give for adopting the relational model?
2. What are the major components of the relational model?
3. What is a domain? Why is it useful?
4. What are the meanings of cardinality and degree?
5. What is a simple relational database?
6. What is the difference between a primary key and an alternate key?
7. Why do we need an entity integrity rule and referential integrity rule?
8. What is the meaning of "union compatible"? Which relational operations require union compatibility?
9. What is meant by the term "a primitive set of operations?"
10. What is a fully relational database?
11. Take a microcomputer relational database package and examine how well it satisfies Codd's rules.
12. Use relational algebra to solve the following queries:

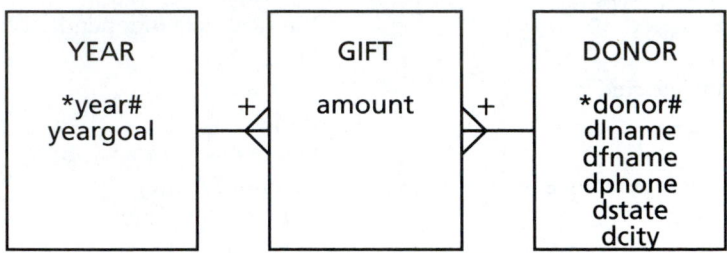

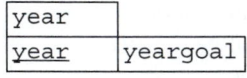

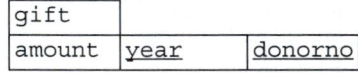

a. List all donors.
b. List the first and last names of all donors.
c. List the phone numbers of donors number 106 and 125.
d. List the amount given by each donor for each year.
e. List the donors who have made a donation every year.
f. List the names of donors who live in Georgia or North Carolina.
g. List the names of donors whose last name is Watson and who live in Athens, GA.

10

SQL

The questing beast.
   Sir Thomas Malory, *Le Morte D'Arthur,* 1470

Learning objectives

Students completing this chapter will have a detailed knowledge of SQL.

Introduction

Structured query language (SQL) is widely used as a relational database language, and SQL skills are essential for data management in a world that is increasingly reliant on relational technology. SQL originated in the IBM Research Laboratory in San Jose, California. Versions have since been implemented by commercial database vendors and open source teams for a wide range of operating systems. Both the American National Standards Institute (ANSI) and the International Organization for Standardization (ISO) have designated SQL as a standard language for relational database systems. ANSI SQL standards were released in 1986, 1989, 1992, and 1999. The most recent standard added object-oriented data management extensions.

SQL is a **complete database language**. It is used for defining a relational database, creating views, and specifying queries. In addition, it allows for rows to be inserted, updated, and deleted. In database terminology, it is both a **data definition language** (DDL), a **data manipulation language** (DML), and a **data control language** (DCL). SQL, however, is not a complete programming language like PHP and Java. Because SQL statements can be embedded into general-purpose programming languages, SQL is often used in conjunction with such languages to create application programs. The **embedded SQL** statements handle the database processing, and the statements in the general-purpose language perform the necessary tasks to complete the application.

SQL is a declarative language, because you declare the desired results. Languages such as Java and Visual Basic are procedural languages, because the programmer specifies each step the computer must execute. The SQL programmer can focus on defining what is required rather than detailing the process to achieve what is required. Thus, SQL programs are much shorter than their procedural equivalents.

You were introduced to SQL in Chapters 3 through 6. This chapter provides an integrated coverage of the language, pulling together the various pieces presented previously.

Data definition

One of the major advantages of relational database management systems (RDBMSs) is that DDL statements can be executed at any time. Earlier DBMSs often require halting the entire system to perform maintenance operations such as adding a new table or creating an index. In many cases, this is extremely difficult to do because some systems are now in use 24 hours per day. Relational DBMSs greatly alleviate this problem because new tables, views, and indexes can be created without interfering with current operational use.

The DDL part of SQL encompasses statements to operate on tables, views, and indexes. Before we proceed, however, the term "base table" must be defined. A **base table** is an autonomous, named table. It is autonomous because it exists in its own right; it is physically stored within the database. In contrast, a view is not autonomous because it is derived from one or more base tables and does not exist independently. A view is a virtual table. A base table has a name by which it can be referenced. This name is chosen when the base table is generated using the CREATE statement. Short-lived temporary tables, such as those formed as the result of a query, are not named.

Keys

The concept of a **key** occurs several times within SQL. In general, a key is one or more columns identified as such in the description of a table, an index, or a referential constraint. The same column can be part of more than one key. For example, it can be part of a primary key and a foreign key. A **composite key** is an ordered set of columns of the same table. In other words, the primary key of lineitem is always the composite of (saleno, lineno) in that order. The order cannot be changed.

Comparing composite keys actually means that corresponding components of the keys are compared. Thus, application of the referential integrity rule—*the value of a foreign key must be equal to a value of the primary key*—means that each component of the foreign key must be equal to a corresponding component of a composite primary key.

So far, you have met primary and foreign keys. A **unique key** is another type of key. Its purpose is to ensure that no two values of a key are equal. This constraint is enforced by the DBMS during the execution of INSERT and UPDATE statements. A unique key is part of the index mechanism.

Indexes

Indexes are used to accelerate data access and ensure uniqueness. An **index** is an ordered set of pointers to rows of a base table. Think of an index as a table that contains two columns (see Figure 10-1). The first column contains values for the index key, and the second contains a list of addresses of rows in the table. Since the values in the first column are ordered (i.e., in ascending or descending sequence), the index table can be searched quickly. It's like searching a phone book by a person's last name. This is easy because the phone book is in last name sequence. In contrast, searching by phone number is extremely time consuming because the phone book is not in this sequence. Once the required key has been found in the table, the row's address in the second column can be used to retrieve the data quickly. An index can be specified as being unique, in which case the DBMS ensures that the corresponding table does not have rows with identical index keys.[1]

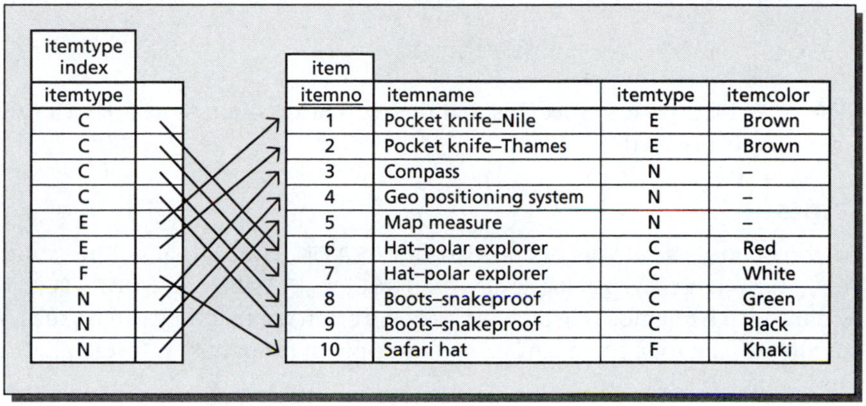

itemtype index			item			
itemtype			itemno	itemname	itemtype	itemcolor
C			1	Pocket knife–Nile	E	Brown
C			2	Pocket knife–Thames	E	Brown
C			3	Compass	N	–
C			4	Geo positioning system	N	–
E			5	Map measure	N	–
E			6	Hat–polar explorer	C	Red
F			7	Hat–polar explorer	C	White
N			8	Boots–snakeproof	C	Green
N			9	Boots–snakeproof	C	Black
N			10	Safari hat	F	Khaki

Figure 10-1. An example of an index

Notation

A short primer on notation is required before we examine SQL commands.

1. Text in uppercase is required as is.
2. Text in lowercase denotes values to be selected by the user.
3. Statements enclosed within square brackets are optional.
4. | indicates a choice.
5. An ellipsis (…) indicates that the immediate syntactic unit may be repeated optionally more than once.

Creating a table

CREATE TABLE is used to define a new base table, either interactively or by embedding the statement in a host language. The statement specifies a table's name, provides details of its columns, and provides integrity checks. The syntax of the command is

```
CREATE TABLE base-table
   column-definition-block
   [primary-key-block]
   [referential-constraint-block]
   [unique-block];
```

---

1. Indexes are covered in depth in Chapter 11.

Column definition

The column definition block defines the columns in a table. Each column definition consists of a column name, data type, and optionally the specification that the column cannot contain null values. The general form is

```
(column-definition [, …])
```

where column-definition is of the form

```
column-name data-type [NOT NULL]
```

The NOT NULL clause specifies that the particular column must have a value whenever a new row is inserted.

Constraints

A constraint is a rule defined as part of CREATE TABLE that defines valid sets of values for a base table by placing limits on INSERT, UPDATE, and DELETE operations. Constraints can be named (e.g., fk_stock_nation) so that they can be turned on or off and modified. The four constraint variations apply to primary key, foreign key, unique values, and range checks.

Primary key constraint

The primary key constraint block specifies a set of columns that constitute the primary key. Once a primary key is defined, the system enforces its uniqueness by checking that the primary key of any new row does not already exist in the table. A table can have only one primary key. While it is not mandatory to define a primary key, it is good practice always to define a table's primary key, though it is not that common to name the constraint. The general form of the constraint is

```
[primary-key-name] PRIMARY KEY(column-name [ASC|DESC] [, …])
```

The optional ASC or DESC clause specifies whether the values from this key are arranged in ascending or descending order, respectively.

For example:

```
pk_stock PRIMARY KEY(stkcode)
```

Foreign key constraint

The referential constraint block defines a foreign key, which consists of one or more columns in the table that together must match a primary key of the specified table (or else be null). A foreign key value is null when any one of the columns in the row constituting the foreign key is null. Once the foreign key constraint is defined, the DBMS will check every insert and update to ensure that the constraint is observed. The general form is

```
CONSTRAINT constraint-name FOREIGN KEY(column-name [,…])
   REFERENCES table-name(column-name [,…])
      [ON DELETE (RESTRICT | CASCADE | SET NULL)]
```

The constraint-name defines a referential constraint. You cannot use the same constraint-name more than once in the same table. Column-name identifies the column or columns that comprise the foreign key. The data type and length of foreign key columns must match exactly the data type and length of the primary key columns. The clause REFERENCES table-name specifies the name of the existing table, and its primary key, that contains the primary key, which cannot be the name of the table being created.

The ON DELETE clause defines the action taken when a row is deleted from the table containing the primary key. There are three options:

1. RESTRICT prevents deletion of the primary key row until all corresponding rows in the related table, the one containing the foreign key, have been deleted. RESTRICT is the default and the cautious approach for preserving data integrity.
2. CASCADE causes all the corresponding rows in the related table also to be deleted.
3. SET NULLS sets the foreign key to null for all corresponding rows in the related table.

For example:

```
CONSTRAINT fk_stock_nation FOREIGN KEY(natcode)
   REFERENCES nation(natcode)
```

Unique constraint

A unique constraint creates a unique index for the specified column or columns. A unique key is constrained so that no two of its values are equal. Columns appearing in a unique constraint must be defined as NOT NULL. Also, these columns should not be the same as those of the table's primary key, which is guaranteed uniqueness by its primary key definition. The constraint is enforced by the DBMS during execution of INSERT and UPDATE statements. The general format is

```
UNIQUE constraint-name (column-name [ASC|DESC] [, …])
```

An example follows:

```
CONSTRAINT unq_stock_stkname UNIQUE(stkname)
```

Check constraint

A check constraint defines a set of valid values and comes in three forms: table, column, or domain constraint.

Table constraints are defined in CREATE TABLE and ALTER TABLE statements. They can be set for one or more columns. A table constraint, for example, might limit item-code to values less than 500.

```
CREATE TABLE item (
    itemcode INTEGER,
    CONSTRAINT chk_item_itemcode CHECK(itemcode <500));
```

A **column constraint** is defined in a CREATE TABLE statement and must be for a single column. Once created, a column constraint is, in effect, a table constraint. The following example shows that there is little difference between defining a table and column constraint. In the following case, itemcode is again limited to values less than 500.

```
CREATE TABLE item (
    itemcode INTEGER
        CONSTRAINT chk_item_itemcode CHECK(itemcode <500),
    itemcolor VARCHAR(10));
```

A **domain constraint**[2] defines the legal values for a type of object (e.g., an item's color) that can be defined in one or more tables. The following example sets legal values of color.

```
CREATE DOMAIN valid_color AS CHAR(10)
CONSTRAINT chk_qitem_color CHECK(
    VALUE IN ('Bamboo','Black','Brown','Green','Khaki','White'));
```

In a CREATE TABLE statement, instead of defining a column's data type, you specify the domain on which the column is defined. The following example shows that itemcolor is defined on the domain VALID_COLOR.

```
CREATE TABLE item (
    itemcode INTEGER,
    itemcolor VALID_COLOR);
```

Data types

Some of the variety of data types that can be used are depicted in Figure 10-2 and described in more detail in the following pages.

BOOLEAN

BOOLEAN data types can have the values true or false.

SMALLINT and INTEGER

Most commercial computers have a 32-bit word, where a word is a unit of storage. An integer can be stored in a full word or half a word. If it is stored in a full word

---

2. The domain constraint is not available for some RDBMS implementations.

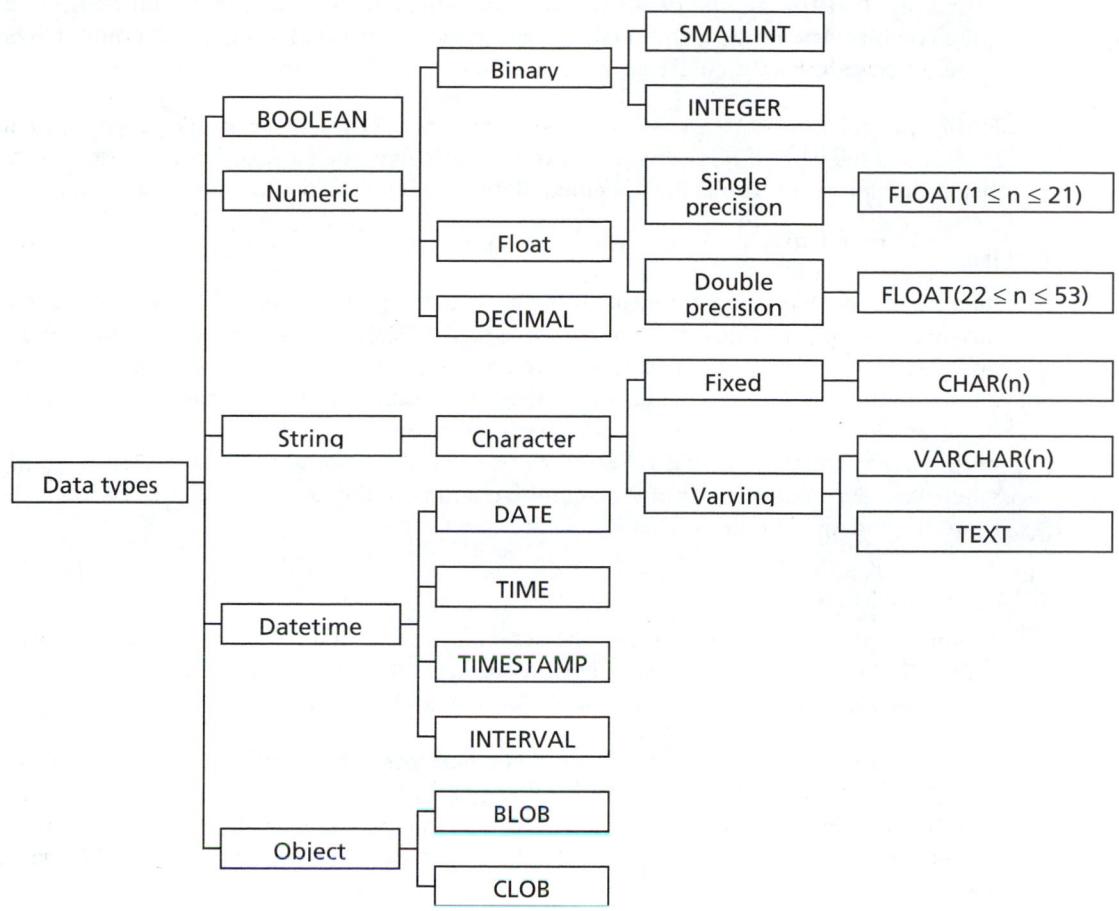

Figure 10-2. Data types

(INTEGER), then it can be 31 binary digits in length. If half-word storage is used (SMALLINT), then it can be 15 binary digits long. In each case, one bit is used for the sign of the number. A column defined as INTEGER can store a number in the range -2^{31} to $2^{31}-1$ or $-2,147,483,648$ to $2,147,483,647$. A column defined as SMALLINT can store a number in the range -2^{15} to $2^{15}-1$ or $-32,768$ to $32,767$. Just remember that INTEGER is good for ±2 billion and SMALLINT for $\pm32,000$.

FLOAT

Scientists often deal with numbers that are very large (e.g., Avogadro's number is 6.02252×10^{23}) or very small (e.g., Planck's constant is 6.6262×10^{-34} joule sec). The FLOAT data type is used for storing such numbers, often referred to as *floating-point* numbers. A single -precision floating-point number requires 32 bits of storage and can represent numbers in the range -7.2×10^{75} to -5.4×10^{-79}, 0, 5.4×10^{-79} to 7.2×10^{75}

with a precision of about 7 decimal digits. A double-precision floating-point number requires 64 bits. The range is the same as for a single-precision floating-point number. The extra 32 bits are used to increase precision to about 15 decimal digits.

In the specification FLOAT(n), if n is between 1 and 21 inclusive, single-precision floating-point is selected. If n is between 22 and 53 inclusive, the storage format is double-precision floating-point. If n is not specified, double-precision floating-point is assumed.

DECIMAL

Binary is the most convenient form of storing data from a computer's perspective. People, however, work with a decimal number system. The DECIMAL data type is convenient for business applications because data storage requirements are defined in terms of the maximum number of places to the left and right of the decimal point. To store the current value of an ounce of gold, you would possibly use DECIMAL(6,2) because this would permit a maximum value of $9,999.99. Notice that the general form is DECIMAL(p,q), where p is the total number of digits in the column, and q is the number of digits to the right of the decimal point.

CHAR and VARCHAR

Nonnumeric columns are stored as character strings. A person's family name is an example of a column that is stored as a character string. CHAR(n) defines a column that has a fixed length of n characters, where n can be a maximum of 255.

When a column's length can vary greatly, it makes sense to define the field as VARCHAR or TEXT. A column defined as VARCHAR consists of two parts: a header indicating the length of the character string and the string. If a table contains a column that occasionally stores a long string of text (e.g., a message field), then defining it as VARCHAR makes sense. TEXT can store strings up to 65,535 characters long.

Why not store all character columns as VARCHAR and save space? There is a price for using VARCHAR with some relational systems. *First,* additional space is required for the header to indicate the length of the string. *Second*, additional processing time is required to handle a variable-length string compared to a fixed-length string. Depending on the RDBMS and processor speed, these might be important considerations, and some systems will automatically make an appropriate choice. For example, MySQL converts VARCHAR of length less than 4 to CHAR, and CHAR of length greater than 3 to VARCHAR.

There are some columns where there is no trade-off decision because all possible entries are always the same length. U.S. Social Security numbers are always nine characters.

Data compression is another approach to the *space wars* problem. A database can be defined with generous allowances for fixed-length character columns so that few values are truncated. Data compression can be used to compress the file to remove *wasted* space. Data compression, however, is slow and will increase the time to process queries. You save space at the cost of time, and save time at the cost of space. When dealing with character fields, the database designer has to decide whether time or space is more important.

Times and dates

Columns that have a data type of DATE are stored as *yyyymmdd* (e.g., 2005-11-04 for November 4, 2005). There are two reasons for this format. *First,* it is convenient for sorting in chronological order. The common American way of writing dates (*mmddyy*) requires processing before chronological sorting. *Second*, the full form of the year should be recorded to avoid end-of-century problems.

For similar reasons, it makes sense to store times in the form *hhmmss* with the understanding that this is 24-hour time (also known as European time and military time). This is the format used for data type TIME.

Some applications require precise recording of events. For example, transaction processing systems typically record the time a transaction was processed by the system. Because computers operate at high speed, the TIMESTAMP data type records date and time with microsecond accuracy. A timestamp has seven parts — year, month, day, hour, minute, second, and microsecond. Date and time are defined as previously described (i.e., *yyyymmdd* and *hhmmss*, respectively). The range of the microsecond part is 000000 to 999999.

Although times and dates are stored in a particular format, the formatting facilities that generally come with an RDBMS usually allow tailoring of time and date output to suit local standards. Thus for a U.S. firm, date might appear on a report in the form *mm/dd/yy*; for a European firm following the ISO standard, date would appear as *yyyy-mm-dd*.

SQL-99 introduced the INTERVAL data type, which is a single value expressed in some unit or units of time (e.g., 6 years, 5 days, 7 hours). For an example, see page 426.

BLOB (binary large object)

BLOB is a large-object data type that stores any kind of binary data. Binary data typically consists of a saved spreadsheet, graph, fax, satellite image, voice pattern, or any digitized data. The BLOB data type has no maximum size.

CLOB (character large object)

CLOB is a large-object data type that stores any kind of character data. Text data typically consists of reports, correspondence, chapters of a manual, or contracts. The CLOB data type has no maximum size.

Special registers

Some implementations of SQL have special registers for commonly required data values (e.g., today's date). Some that you might like to use are CURRENT DATE, CURRENT TIME, and CURRENT TIMESTAMP. For example,

```
INSERT INTO sale
   (saleno, saledate, saletext)
   VALUES (6, CURRENT_DATE, 'Brazilian tourist');
```

■ ▬ ▬ ■ ▬ ■ ▬ ■ ▬ ■ ▬ ■ ▬ ■ ▬ ■ ▬ ■ ▬ ■

Skill builder

What data types would you recommend for the following?

1.   A book's ISBN[3]
2.   A photo of a product
3.   The speed of light (2.9979×10^8 meters per second)
4.   A short description of an animal's habitat
5.   The title of a Japanese book
6.   A legal contract
7.   The status of an electrical switch
8.   The date and time a reservation was made
9.   An item's value in euros
10.   The number of children in a family

■ ▬ ▬ ■ ▬ ■ ▬ ■ ▬ ■ ▬ ■ ▬ ■ ▬ ■ ▬ ■ ▬ ■

Scalar functions

Most implementations of SQL include functions that can be used in arithmetic expressions, and for data conversion or data extraction. A sampling of these functions will give you an idea of what is available (see Table 10-1). You will need to consult the documentation for your version of SQL to determine the functions it supports. For example, Microsoft SQL Server has more than 100 additional functions.

Table 10-1: Some examples of SQL3's built-in scalar functions

Function	Description
CURRENT_DATE	Retrieves the current date
EXTRACT(date_time_part FROM expression)	Retrieves part of a time or date (e.g., YEAR, MONTH, DAY, HOUR, MINUTE, or SECOND)
SUBSTRING(str, pos, len)	Retrieves a string of length *len* starting at position *pos* from string *str*

Some examples:

```
SELECT EXTRACT(day FROM CURRENT_DATE);

SELECT SUBSTRING(persfname, 1,1), perslname FROM person;
```

---

3.   Check the back cover of the text.

A vendor's additional functions can be very useful. Remember, though, that use of a vendor's extensions might limit portability.

○ **How many days' sales are stored in the sale table?**

This sounds like a simple query, but you have to do a self-join and also know that there is a function, DATEDIFF,[4] to determine the number of days between any two dates. Consult your RDBMS manual to learn about other functions for dealing with dates and times.

```
SELECT DATEDIFF(late.saledate,early.saledate) as difference
   FROM sale late, sale early
      WHERE late.saledate =
         (SELECT MAX(saledate) FROM sale)
      AND early.saledate =
         (SELECT MIN(saledate) FROM sale);
```

difference
1

The preceding query is based on the idea of joining sale with a copy of itself. The matching column from late is the latest sale's date (or MAX), and the matching column from early is the earliest sale's date (or MIN). As a result of the join, each row of the new table has both the earliest and latest dates.

Skill builder

Consult the documentation for the RDBMS you are using to determine how you report a numeric value with a defined number of decimal places.

Altering a table

The ALTER TABLE statement has two purposes. *First,* it can add a single column to an existing table. *Second*, it can add, drop, activate, or deactivate primary and foreign key constraints. A base table can be altered by adding one new column, which appears to the right of existing columns. The format of the command is

```
ALTER TABLE base-table ADD column data-type;
```

Notice that there is no optional NOT NULL clause for column-definition with ALTER TABLE. It is not allowed because the ALTER TABLE statement automatically fills the additional column with null in every case.[5] If you want to add multiple columns, you repeat

---

4. A MySQL extension.
5. This may not be what happens physically, but it is a good way of visualizing why NOT NULL is an inappropriate clause.

the command. ALTER TABLE does not permit changing the width of a column or amending a column's data type. It can be used for deleting an unwanted column. The following example illustrates the use of ALTER TABLE.

```
ALTER TABLE stock ADD stkrating CHAR(3);
```

ALTER TABLE is also used to change the status of referential constraints. You can deactivate constraints on a table's primary key or any of its foreign keys. Deactivation also makes the relevant tables unavailable to all users except the table's owner or someone possessing database management authority. After the data are loaded, referential constraints must be reactivated before they can be automatically enforced again. Activating the constraints enables the DBMS to validate the references in the data.

Dropping a table

A base table can be deleted at any time by using the DROP statement. The format is

```
DROP TABLE base-table;
```

The table is deleted, and any views or indexes defined on the table are also deleted.

Creating a view

A view is a virtual table. It has no physical counterpart but appears to the user as if it really exists. A view is defined in terms of other tables that exist in the database. The syntax is

```
CREATE VIEW view [column [,column] ...)]
    AS subquery;
```

There are several reasons for creating a view. *First,* a view can be used to restrict access to certain rows or columns. This is particularly important for sensitive data. An organization's person table can contain both private data (e.g., annual salary) and public data (office phone number). A view consisting of public data (e.g., person's name, department, and office telephone number) might be provided to many people. Access to all columns in the table, however, might be confined to a small number of people. Here is a sample view that restricts access to a table.

```
CREATE VIEW stklist
    AS SELECT stkfirm, stkprice FROM stock;
```

Handling derived data is a *second* reason for creating a view. A column that can be computed from one or more other columns should always be defined by a view. Thus, a stock's yield would be computed by a view rather than defined as a column in a base table.

```
CREATE VIEW stk
    (stkfirm, stkprice, stkqty, stkyield)
    AS SELECT stkfirm, stkprice, stkqty, stkdiv/stkprice*100
        FROM stock;
```

A *third* reason for defining a view is to avoid writing common SQL queries. For example, there may be some joins that are frequently part of an SQL query. Productivity can be increased by defining these joins as views. Here is an example:

```
CREATE VIEW stkvalue
   (nation, firm, price, qty, value)
   AS SELECT natname, stkfirm, stkprice*exchrate, stkqty,
      stkprice*exchrate*stkqty FROM stock, nation
         WHERE stock.natcode = nation.natcode;
```

The preceding example demonstrates how CREATE VIEW can be used to rename columns, create new columns, and involve more than one table. The column nation corresponds to natname, firm to stkfirm, and so forth. A new column, price, is created that converts all share prices from the local currency to British pounds.

Data conversion is a *fourth* useful reason for a view. The United States is one of the few countries that does not use the metric system, and reports for American managers often display weights and measures in pounds and feet, respectively. The database of an international company could record all measurements in metric format (e.g., weight in kilograms) and use a view to convert these measures for American reports.

When a CREATE VIEW statement is executed, the definition of the view is entered in the systems catalog. The subquery following AS, the view definition, is executed only when the view is referenced in an SQL command. For example, the following command would enable the subquery to be executed and the view created:

```
SELECT * FROM stkvalue WHERE price > 10;
```

In effect, the following query is executed:

```
SELECT natname, stkfirm, stkprice*exchrate, stkqty,
   stkprice*exchrate*stkqty
      FROM stock, nation
         WHERE stock.natcode = nation.natcode
         AND stkprice*exchrate > 10;
```

Any table that can be defined with a SELECT statement is a potential view. Thus, it is possible to have a view that is defined by another view.

Dropping a view

DROP VIEW is used to delete a view from the system catalog. A view might be dropped because it needs to be redefined or is no longer used. It must be dropped first before a revised version of the view is created. The syntax is

```
DROP VIEW view;
```

Remember, if a base table is dropped, all views based on that table are also dropped.

Creating an index

An index helps speed up retrieval (see Chapter 11 for a complete discussion of indexing). A column that is frequently referred to in a WHERE clause is a possible candidate for indexing. For example, if data on stocks were frequently retrieved using stkfirm, then this column should be considered for an index. The format for CREATE INDEX is

```
CREATE [UNIQUE] INDEX indexname
   ON base-table (column [order] [,column, [order]] …)
   [CLUSTER];
```

This next example illustrates use of CREATE INDEX.

```
CREATE UNIQUE INDEX stkfirmindx
   ON stock(stkfirm);
```

In the preceding example, an index called stkfirmindx is created for the table stock. Index entries are ordered by ascending (the default order) values of stkfirm. The optional clause UNIQUE specifies that no two rows in the base table can have the same value for stkfirm, the indexed column. Specifying UNIQUE means that the DBMS will reject any insert or update operation that would create a duplicate value for stkfirm.

A composite index can be created from several columns, which is often necessary for an associative entity. The following example illustrates the creation of a composite index.

```
CREATE INDEX lineitemindx
   ON lineitem (lineno, saleno);
```

Dropping an index

Indexes can be dropped at any time by using the DROP INDEX statement. The general form of this statement is

```
DROP INDEX index;
```

Data manipulation

SQL supports four DML statements — SELECT, INSERT, UPDATE, and DELETE. Each of these will be discussed in turn, with most attention focusing on SELECT because of the variety of ways in which it can be used. First, we need to understand why we must qualify column names and temporary names.

Qualifying column names

Ambiguous references to column names are avoided by qualifying a column name with its table name, especially when the same column name is used in several tables. Clarity is maintained by prefixing the column name with the table name. The following example demonstrates qualification of the natcode, which appears in both stock and nation.

```
SELECT * FROM stock, nation
    WHERE stock.natcode = nation.natcode;
```

Temporary names

A table or view can be given a temporary name, or alias, that remains current for a query. Temporary names are used in a self-join to distinguish the copies of the table. For example:

```
SELECT wrk.empfname
    FROM emp wrk, emp boss
        WHERE wrk.bossno = boss.empno;
```

A temporary name also can be used as a shortened form of a long table name. For example, l might have been used merely to avoid having to enter lineitem more than once. If a temporary name is specified for a table or view, any qualified reference to a column of the table or view must also use that temporary name.

SELECT

The SELECT statement is by far the most interesting and challenging of the four DML statements. It reveals a major benefit of the relational model — powerful interrogation capabilities. It is challenging because mastering the power of SELECT requires considerable practice with a wide range of queries. The major varieties of SELECT are presented in this section. The SQL Playbook (page 289) reveals the full power of the command.

The general format of SELECT is

```
SELECT [DISTINCT] item(s) FROM table(s)
    [WHERE condition]
    [GROUP BY column(s)]  [HAVING condition]
    [ORDER BY column(s)];
```

Product

Product, or more strictly Cartesian product, is a fundamental operation of relational algebra. It is rarely used by itself in a query; however, understanding its effect helps in comprehending join. The product of two tables is a new table consisting of all rows of the first table concatenated with all possible rows of the second table. For example:

○ **Form the product of stock and nation.**

```
SELECT * FROM stock, nation;
```

The new table contains 64 rows (16*4), where stock has 16 rows and nation has 4 rows. It has 10 columns (7 + 3), where stock has 7 columns and nation has 3 columns. The result of the operation is shown in Table 10-2. Note that each row in stock is concatenated with each row in nation.

Table 10-2: Product of stock and nation

stkcode	stkfirm	stkprice	stkqty	stkdiv	stkpe	natcode	natcode1	natname	exchrate
FC	Freedonia Copper	27.50	10529	1.84	16	UK	UK	United Kingdom	1.00000
FC	Freedonia Copper	27.50	10529	1.84	16	UK	US	United States	0.67000
FC	Freedonia Copper	27.50	10529	1.84	16	UK	AUS	Australia	0.46000
FC	Freedonia Copper	27.50	10529	1.84	16	UK	IND	India	0.02280
PT	Patagonian Tea	55.25	12635	2.50	10	UK	UK	United Kingdom	1.00000
PT	Patagonian Tea	55.25	12635	2.50	10	UK	US	United States	0.67000
PT	Patagonian Tea	55.25	12635	2.50	10	UK	AUS	Australia	0.46000
PT	Patagonian Tea	55.25	12635	2.50	10	UK	IND	India	0.02280
AR	Abyssinian Ruby	31.82	22010	1.32	13	UK	UK	United Kingdom	1.00000
AR	Abyssinian Ruby	31.82	22010	1.32	13	UK	US	United States	0.67000
AR	Abyssinian Ruby	31.82	22010	1.32	13	UK	AUS	Australia	0.46000
AR	Abyssinian Ruby	31.82	22010	1.32	13	UK	IND	India	0.02280
SLG	Sri Lankan Gold	50.37	32868	2.68	16	UK	UK	United Kingdom	1.00000
SLG	Sri Lankan Gold	50.37	32868	2.68	16	UK	US	United States	0.67000
SLG	Sri Lankan Gold	50.37	32868	2.68	16	UK	AUS	Australia	0.46000
SLG	Sri Lankan Gold	50.37	32868	2.68	16	UK	IND	India	0.02280
ILZ	Indian Lead & Zinc	37.75	6390	3.00	12	UK	UK	United Kingdom	1.00000
ILZ	Indian Lead & Zinc	37.75	6390	3.00	12	UK	US	United States	0.67000
ILZ	Indian Lead & Zinc	37.75	6390	3.00	12	UK	AUS	Australia	0.46000
ILZ	Indian Lead & Zinc	37.75	6390	3.00	12	UK	IND	India	0.02280
BE	Burmese Elephant	0.07	154713	0.01	3	UK	UK	United Kingdom	1.00000
BE	Burmese Elephant	0.07	154713	0.01	3	UK	US	United States	0.67000
BE	Burmese Elephant	0.07	154713	0.01	3	UK	AUS	Australia	0.46000
BE	Burmese Elephant	0.07	154713	0.01	3	UK	IND	India	0.02280
BS	Bolivian Sheep	12.75	231678	1.78	11	UK	UK	United Kingdom	1.00000
BS	Bolivian Sheep	12.75	231678	1.78	11	UK	US	United States	0.67000
BS	Bolivian Sheep	12.75	231678	1.78	11	UK	AUS	Australia	0.46000
BS	Bolivian Sheep	12.75	231678	1.78	11	UK	IND	India	0.02280
NG	Nigerian Geese	35.00	12323	1.68	10	UK	UK	United Kingdom	1.00000
NG	Nigerian Geese	35.00	12323	1.68	10	UK	US	United States	0.67000
NG	Nigerian Geese	35.00	12323	1.68	10	UK	AUS	Australia	0.46000
NG	Nigerian Geese	35.00	12323	1.68	10	UK	IND	India	0.02280
CS	Canadian Sugar	52.78	4716	2.50	15	UK	UK	United Kingdom	1.00000
CS	Canadian Sugar	52.78	4716	2.50	15	UK	US	United States	0.67000
CS	Canadian Sugar	52.78	4716	2.50	15	UK	AUS	Australia	0.46000
CS	Canadian Sugar	52.78	4716	2.50	15	UK	IND	India	0.02280
ROF	Royal Ostrich Farms	33.75	1234923	3.00	6	UK	UK	United Kingdom	1.00000
ROF	Royal Ostrich Farms	33.75	1234923	3.00	6	UK	US	United States	0.67000
ROF	Royal Ostrich Farms	33.75	1234923	3.00	6	UK	AUS	Australia	0.46000
ROF	Royal Ostrich Farms	33.75	1234923	3.00	6	UK	IND	India	0.02280
MG	Minnesota Gold	53.87	816122	1.00	25	US	UK	United Kingdom	1.00000
MG	Minnesota Gold	53.87	816122	1.00	25	US	US	United States	0.67000
MG	Minnesota Gold	53.87	816122	1.00	25	US	AUS	Australia	0.46000
MG	Minnesota Gold	53.87	816122	1.00	25	US	IND	India	0.02280
GP	Georgia Peach	2.35	387333	0.20	5	US	UK	United Kingdom	1.00000
GP	Georgia Peach	2.35	387333	0.20	5	US	US	United States	0.67000
GP	Georgia Peach	2.35	387333	0.20	5	US	AUS	Australia	0.46000
GP	Georgia Peach	2.35	387333	0.20	5	US	IND	India	0.02280
NE	Narembeen Emu	12.34	45619	1.00	8	AUS	UK	United Kingdom	1.00000
NE	Narembeen Emu	12.34	45619	1.00	8	AUS	US	United States	0.67000
NE	Narembeen Emu	12.34	45619	1.00	8	AUS	AUS	Australia	0.46000
NE	Narembeen Emu	12.34	45619	1.00	8	AUS	IND	India	0.02280
QD	Queensland Diamond	6.73	89251	0.50	7	AUS	UK	United Kingdom	1.00000
QD	Queensland Diamond	6.73	89251	0.50	7	AUS	US	United States	0.67000
QD	Queensland Diamond	6.73	89251	0.50	7	AUS	AUS	Australia	0.46000
QD	Queensland Diamond	6.73	89251	0.50	7	AUS	IND	India	0.02280
IR	Indooroopilly Ruby	15.92	56147	0.50	20	AUS	UK	United Kingdom	1.00000
IR	Indooroopilly Ruby	15.92	56147	0.50	20	AUS	US	United States	0.67000
IR	Indooroopilly Ruby	15.92	56147	0.50	20	AUS	AUS	Australia	0.46000
IR	Indooroopilly Ruby	15.92	56147	0.50	20	AUS	IND	India	0.02280
BD	Bombay Duck	25.55	167382	1.00	12	IND	UK	United Kingdom	1.00000
BD	Bombay Duck	25.55	167382	1.00	12	IND	US	United States	0.67000
BD	Bombay Duck	25.55	167382	1.00	12	IND	AUS	Australia	0.46000
BD	Bombay Duck	25.55	167382	1.00	12	IND	IND	India	0.02280

○ **Find the percentage of Australian stocks in the portfolio.**

To answer this query, you need to count the number of Australian stocks, count the total number of stocks in the portfolio, and then compute the percentage. Computing each of the totals is a straightforward application of COUNT. If we save the results of the two counts as views, then we have the necessary data to compute the percentage. The two views each consist of a single-cell table (i.e., one row and one column). We create the product of these two views to get the data needed for computing the percentage in one row. The SQL is

```
CREATE VIEW austotal (auscount) AS
   SELECT COUNT(*) FROM stock WHERE natcode = 'AUS';

CREATE VIEW total (totalcount) AS
   SELECT COUNT(*) FROM stock;

SELECT auscount*100/totalcount AS Percentage
   FROM austotal, total;
```

The result of a COUNT is always an integer, and SQL will typically create an integer data type in which to store the results. When two variables have a data type of integer, SQL will likely use integer arithmetic for all computations, and all results will be integer. To get around the issue of integer arithmetic, we first multiply the number of Australian stocks by 100 before dividing by the total number of stocks. Because of integer arithmetic, you might get a different answer if you used the following SQL.

```
SELECT auscount/totalcount*100 AS Percentage
   FROM austotal, total;
```

The preceding example was use to show when you might find product useful. You can also write the query as

```
SELECT (SELECT COUNT(*) FROM stock WHERE natcode = 'AUS')*100/
   (SELECT COUNT(*) FROM stock) AS Percentage;
```

Join

Join, a very powerful and frequently used operation, creates a new table from two existing tables by matching on a column common to both tables. An **equijoin** is the simplest form of join; in this case, columns are matched on equality. The shaded rows in Table 10-2 indicate the result of the following join example.

```
SELECT * FROM stock, nation
   WHERE stock.natcode = nation.natcode;
```

There are other ways of expressing join that are more concise. For example, we can write

```
SELECT * FROM stock INNER JOIN nation USING (natcode);
```

The preceding syntax makes the join easier to detect when reading SQL and implicitly recognizes the frequent use of the same column name for matching primary and foreign keys.

A further simplification is to rely on the primary and foreign key definitions to determine the join condition, so we can write

```
SELECT * FROM stock NATURAL JOIN nation;
```

An equijoin creates a new table that contains two identical columns. If one of these is dropped, then the remaining table is called a natural join.

Decision Support at Lands' End

Lands' End uses direct mailing of catalogs to market clothing for adults and children. One of the largest apparel brands in the United States, it needs to target its mailing precisely to reach the customers who are most likely to buy. Variables such as lifetime customer value, geographic location, and recent purchases can be used to determine who should receive a catalog. To assist in making such decisions, Lands' End developed a decision support system (DSS) based on IBM's DB2. Prior to implementing the DSS, Lands' End staff first used data modeling to identify data items and their descriptions.

A typical business question might be: What was the return rate for the women's division, grouped by category, in our Christmas catalog? Compare this year to last year.

The SQL query is

```
SELECT    catalog-year,
          catalog-desc,
          product-category-desc,
          SUM(returns)/SUM(shipments)
FROM      shipment_tbl d,
          return_tbl r
WHERE     d.order = r.order
AND       division = 'Womens'
AND       catalog_year IN (1992,1993)
AND       catalog_id = 'Xmas'
GROUP BY  category_year
          catalog_desc,
          product_category_desc;
```

The new DSS means that queries that would have taken hours are now satisfied in minutes. Lands' End can use its DSS to market its products more effectively.

Adapted from Bustamente, G. G., and K. Sorenson. 1994. Decision support at Lands' End—an evolution. *IBM Systems Journal* 33 (2):228–238.

As you now realize, join is really product with a condition clause. There is no reason why this condition needs to be restricted to equality. There could easily be another comparison operator between the two columns. This general version is called a theta-join because theta is a variable that can take any value from the set [=, <>, >, >=, <, <=].

As you discovered in Chapter 6, there are occasions when you need to join a table to itself. To do this, make two copies of the table first and give each of these copies a unique name.

○ **Find the names of employees who earn more than their boss.**

```
SELECT wrk.empfname
    FROM emp wrk, emp boss
        WHERE wrk.bossno = boss.empno
        AND wrk.empsalary > boss.empsalary;
```

Outer join

A traditional join, more formally known as an **inner join**, reports those rows where the primary and foreign keys match. An **outer join** reports these matching rows and others depending on which form is used, as the following examples illustrate for the sample table.

t1		t2	
id	col1	id	col2
1	a	1	x
2	b	3	y
3	c	5	z

A **left outer join** is an inner join plus those rows from t1 not included in the inner join.

```
SELECT * FROM t1 LEFT JOIN t2 USING (id);
```

t1.id	col1	t2.id	col2
1	a	1	x
2	b	null	null
3	c	3	y

Here is an example to illustrate the use of a left join.

○ **For all brown items, report each sale. Include in the report those brown items that have appeared in no sales.**

```
SELECT itemname, saleno, lineqty FROM item
    LEFT JOIN lineitem USING ( itemno )
        WHERE itemcolor = 'Brown'
        ORDER BY itemname;
```

itemname	saleno	lineqty
Map case	NULL	NULL
Pocket knife - Avon	1	1
Pocket knife - Avon	3	1
Pocket knife - Avon	2	1
Pocket knife - Avon	5	1
Pocket knife - Avon	4	1
Pocket knife - Nile	NULL	NULL
Stetson	NULL	NULL

A **right outer join** is an inner join plus those rows from t2 not included in the inner join.

```
SELECT * FROM t1 RIGHT JOIN t2 USING (id);
```

t1.id	col1	t2.id	col2
1	a	1	x
3	c	3	y
null	null	5	z

A **full outer join** is an inner join plus those rows from t1 and t2 not included in the inner join.

```
SELECT * FROM t1 FULL JOIN t2 USING (id);
```

t1.id	col1	t2.id	col2
1	a	1	x
2	b	null	null
3	c	3	y
null	null	5	z

Simple subquery

A subquery is a query within a query. There is a SELECT statement nested inside another SELECT statement. Simple subqueries were used extensively in Chapters 3 and 4. For reference, here is a simple subquery used in Chapter 4:

```
SELECT stkfirm FROM stock
   WHERE natcode IN
      (SELECT natcode FROM nation
         WHERE natname = 'Australia');
```

Correlated subquery

A correlated subquery differs from a simple subquery in that the inner query must be evaluated more than once. Consider the following example described previously in Chapter 4:

○ **Find those stocks where the quantity is greater than the average for that country.**

```
SELECT natname, stkfirm, stkqty FROM stock, nation
WHERE stock.natcode = nation.natcode
AND stkqty >
   (SELECT AVG(stkqty) FROM stock
      WHERE stock.natcode = nation.natcode);
```

The requirement to compare a column against a function (e.g., average or count) of some column of specified rows of is usually a clue that you need to write a correlated subquery. In the preceding example, the stock quantity for each row is compared with the average stock quantity for that row's country.

Aggregate functions

SQL's aggregate functions increase its retrieval power. These functions are covered in Chapter 3 and are only mentioned briefly here for completeness. The five aggregate functions are shown in Table 10-3. Nulls in the column are ignored in the case of SUM, AVG, MAX, and MIN. However, COUNT does not distinguish between null and non-null values in a column.

Table 10-3: Aggregate functions

COUNT	Counts the number of values in a column
SUM	Sums the values in a column
AVG	Determines the average of the values in a column
MAX	Determines the largest value of a column
MIN	Determines the smallest value of a column

GROUP BY and HAVING

The GROUP BY clause is an elementary form of control break reporting and supports grouping of rows that have the same value for a specified column and produces one row for each different value of the grouping column. For example,

○ **Report by nation the total value of stockholdings.**

```
SELECT natname, SUM(stkprice*stkqty*exchrate) as total
   FROM stock, nation WHERE stock.natcode = nation.natcode
      GROUP BY natname;
```

gives the following results:

natname	total
Australia	946430.65
India	97506.71
United Kingdom	48908364.25
United States	30066065.54

The HAVING clause is often associated with GROUP BY. It can be thought of as the WHERE clause of GROUP BY because it is used to eliminate rows for a GROUP BY condition. Both GROUP BY and HAVING are dealt with in-depth in Chapter 4.

LIKE

The LIKE clause supports pattern matching to find a defined set of strings in a character column (CHAR or VARCHAR). Refer to Chapter 3 for more details.

INSERT

There are two formats for INSERT. The first format is used to insert one row into a table.

Inserting a single record

The general form is

```
INSERT INTO table [(column [,column] …)]
    VALUES (literal [,literal] …);
```

For example,

```
INSERT INTO stock
    (stkcode,stkfirm,stkprice,stkqty,stkdiv,stkpe)
    VALUES ('FC','Freedonia Copper',27.5,10529,1.84,16);
```

In this example, stkcode is given the value "FC," stkfirm is "Freedonia Copper," and so on. In general, the nth column in the table is the nth value in the list.

When the value list refers to all field names in the left-to-right order in which they appear in the table, then the columns list can be omitted. So, it is possible to write the following:

```
INSERT INTO stock
    VALUES ('FC','Freedonia Copper',27.5,10529,1.84,16);
```

If some values are unknown, then the INSERT can omit these from the list. Undefined columns will have nulls. For example, if a new stock is to be added for which the price, dividend, and PE ratio are unknown, the following INSERT statement would be used:

```
INSERT INTO stock
    (stkcode, stkfirm, stkqty)
    VALUES ('EE','Elysian Emeralds',0);
```

Inserting multiple records using a query

The second form of INSERT operates in conjunction with a subquery. The resulting rows then are inserted into a table. Imagine the situation where stock price information is downloaded from an information service into a table. This table could contain information about all stocks and may contain additional columns that are not required for the stock table. The following INSERT statement could be used:

```
INSERT INTO stock
    (stkcode, stkfirm, stkprice, stkdiv, stkpe)
    SELECT code, firm, price, div, pe
    FROM download WHERE code IN
    ('FC','PT','AR','SLG','ILZ','BE','BS','NG','CS','ROF');
```

Think of INSERT with a subquery as a way of copying a table. You can select the rows and columns of a particular table that you want to copy into an existing or new table.

UPDATE

The UPDATE command is used to modify values in a table. The general format is

```
UPDATE table
    SET column = scalar expression
        [, column = scalar expression] …
    [WHERE condition];
```

Permissible scalar expressions involve columns, scalar functions (see the section on scalar functions in this chapter), or constants. No aggregate functions are allowable.

Updating a single row

UPDATE can be used to modify a single row in a table. Suppose you need to revise your data after 200,000 shares of Minnesota Gold are sold. You would code the following:

```
UPDATE stock
    SET stkqty = stkqty - 200000
    WHERE stkcode = 'MG';
```

Updating multiple rows

Multiple rows in a table can be updated as well. Imagine the situation where several stocks change their dividend to £2.50. Then the following statement could be used:

```
UPDATE stock
    SET stkdiv = 2.50
    WHERE stkcode IN ('FC','BS','NG');
```

Updating all rows

All rows in a table can be updated by simply omitting the WHERE clause. To give everyone at The Expeditioner a 5 percent raise, use

```
UPDATE emp
   SET empsalary = empsalary*1.05;
```

Updating with a subquery

A subquery can also be used to specify which rows should be changed. Consider the following example. The employees in the departments on the fourth floor of The Expeditioner have won a productivity improvement bonus of 10 percent. The following SQL statement would update their salaries:

```
UPDATE emp
   SET empsalary = empsalary*1.10
   WHERE deptname IN
      (SELECT deptname FROM dept WHERE deptfloor = 4);
```

DELETE

The DELETE statement erases one or more rows in a table. The general format is

```
DELETE FROM table
   [WHERE condition];
```

Delete a single record

If all stocks with stkcode "BE" were sold, then this row can be deleted using

```
DELETE FROM stock WHERE stkcode = 'BE';
```

Delete multiple records

If all Australian stocks were liquidated, then the following command would delete all the relevant rows:

```
DELETE FROM stock
   WHERE natcode IN
   (SELECT natcode FROM nation WHERE natname = 'Australia');
```

Delete all records

All records in a table can be deleted by omitting the WHERE clause. The following statement would delete all rows if the entire portfolio were sold:

```
DELETE FROM stock;
```

This command is not the same as DROP TABLE because, although the table is empty, it still exists.

Delete with a subquery

Despite their sterling efforts in the recent productivity drive, all the employees on the fourth floor of The Expeditioner have been fired (the rumor is that they were fiddling the tea money). Their records can be deleted using

```
DELETE FROM emp
    WHERE deptname IN
        (SELECT deptname FROM dept WHERE deptfloor = 4);
```

SQL routines

SQL provides two types of routines—functions and procedures—that are created, altered, and dropped using standard SQL. Until SQL-99, there were no standards for defining routines, and some vendors have still not brought their RDBMS into line. Routines add flexibility, improve programmer productivity, and facilitate the enforcement of business rules and standard operating procedures across applications.

SQL function

A function is SQL code that returns a value when invoked within an SQL statement. It is used in a similar fashion to SQL's built-in functions. Consider the case of an Austrian firm with a database in which all measurements are in SI units (e.g., meters). Because its U.S. staff are not familiar with SI, it decides to implement a series of user-defined functions to handle the conversion. Here is the function for converting from kilometers to miles.

```
CREATE FUNCTION km_to_miles()
    RETURNS REAL
    RETURN 0.6213712;
```

The preceding function can be used within any SQL statement to make the conversion. For example:

```
SELECT 100*km_to_miles();
```

- -

Skill builder

Create a table containing the average daily temperature in Tromsø, Norway,[6] then write a function to convert Celsius to Fahrenheit (F = C*1.8 + 32), and test the function by reporting temperatures in C and F.

Month	Jan	Feb	Mar	Apr	May	Jun	Jul	Aug	Sep	Oct	Nov	Dec
°C	-4.7	-4.1	-1.9	1.1	5.6	10.1	12.7	11.8	7.7	2.9	-1.5	-3.7

- -

---

6.   Tromsø, at 69°41' N, is the home of the University of Tromsø, the world's northernmost university.

SQL procedure

A procedure is SQL code that is dynamically loaded and executed by a CALL statement, usually within a database application. We use an accounting system to demonstrate the features of a stored procedure, in which a single accounting transaction results in two entries (one debit and one credit). In other words, a transaction has multiple entries, but an entry is related to only one transaction. An account (e.g., your bank account) has multiple entries, but an entry is for only one account. Considering this situation results in the following data model, Figure 10-3.

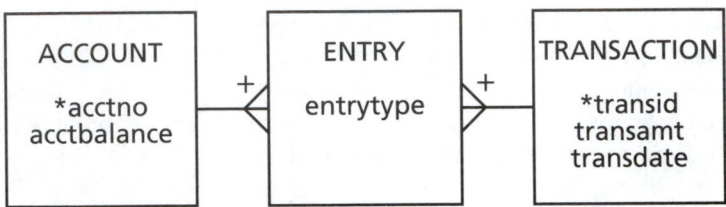

Figure 10-3. A simple accounting system

The following are a set of steps for processing a transaction (e.g., transferring money from a checking account to a money market account):

1. Write the transaction to the `transaction` table so you have a record of the transaction.
2. Update the account to be credited by incrementing its balance in the `account` table.
3. Insert a row in the `entry` table to record the credit.
4. Update the account to be debited by decrementing its balance in the `account` table.
5. Insert a row in the `entry` table to record the debit.

Here is the code for a stored procedure to execute these steps.

```
CREATE PROCEDURE transfer (
IN cracct INTEGER,
IN dbacct INTEGER,
IN amt DECIMAL(9,2),
IN transno INTEGER)
LANGUAGE SQL
BEGIN
INSERT INTO transaction VALUES (transno, amt, current_date);
UPDATE account
SET acctbalance = acctbalance + amt
WHERE acctno = cracct;
INSERT INTO entry VALUES(transno, cracct, 'cr');
```

```
UPDATE account
SET acctbalance = acctbalance - amt
WHERE acctno = dbacct;
INSERT INTO entry VALUES (transno, dbacct, 'db');
END;
```

A CALL statement executes a stored procedure. The generic CALL statement for the preceding procedure is

```
CALL transfer(cracct, dbacct, amt, transno);
```

Thus, imagine that transaction 1005 transfers $100 to account 1 (the credit account) from account 2 (the debit account). The specific call is

```
CALL transfer(1,2,100,1005);
```

- -

Skill builder

1. After verifying that the system you use for learning SQL supports stored procedures, create the tables for the preceding data model and enter the code for the stored procedure. Now, test the stored procedure and query the tables to verify that the procedure has worked.
2. Write a stored procedure to add details of a gift to the donation database (see exercises in Chapter 5).

- -

Triggers

Triggers are a form of stored procedure that execute automatically when a table's rows are modified. Triggers can be defined to execute either before or after rows are inserted into a table, when rows are deleted from a table, and when columns are updated in the rows of a table. Triggers include virtual tables that reflect the row image before and after the operation, as appropriate. Triggers can be used to enforce business rules or requirements, integrity checking, and automatic transaction logging.

Consider the case of recording all updates to the stock table (see Chapter 4). First, you must define a table in which to record details of the change.

```
CREATE TABLE stock_log (
stkcode       CHAR(3),
old_stkprice  DECIMAL(6,2),
new_stkprice  DECIMAL(6,2),
old_stkqty    DECIMAL(8),
new_stkqty    DECIMAL(8),
update_stktime TIMESTAMP not null,
    PRIMARY KEY(update_stktime));
```

The trigger (see the following SQL) writes a record to `stock_log` every time an update is made to `stock`. Use is made of two virtual tables (`old` and `new`) to access the prior and current values of stock price (`old_row.stkprice` and `new_row.stkprice` and stock quantity (`old_row.stkprice` and `new_row.stkprice`). The INSERT statement also writes the stock's identifying code and the time of the transaction.

```
CREATE TRIGGER stock_update
AFTER UPDATE ON stock
REFERENCING old AS old_row new AS new_row
FOR EACH ROW MODE db2sql
INSERT INTO stock_log VALUES
    (old_row.stkcode, old_row.stkprice, new_row.stkprice,
    old_row.stkqty, new_row.stkqty, current timestamp);
```

--- --- --- --- --- --- --- --- ---

Skill builder

Why is the primary key of `stock_log` not the same as that of `stock`?

--- --- --- --- --- --- --- --- ---

Nulls—much ado about missing information

Nulls are overworked in SQL because they can represent several situations. Null can represent unknown information. For example, you might add a new stock to the database, but lacking details of its latest dividend, you leave the field null. Null can be used to represent a value that is inapplicable. For instance, the `employee` table contains a null value in `bossno` for Alice because she has no boss. The value is not unknown; it is not applicable for that field. In other cases, null might mean "no value supplied" or "value undefined." Because null can have multiple meanings, the user must infer which meaning is appropriate to the circumstances.

Do not confuse null with blank or zero, which are values. In fact, null is a marker that specifies that the value for the particular column is null. Thus, null represents no value.

The well-known database expert Chris Date[7] has been outspoken in his concern about the confusion caused by nulls. His advice is that nulls should be explicitly avoided by specifying NOT NULL for all columns and by using codes to make the meaning of a value clear (e.g., "U" means "unknown," "I" means "inapplicable," "N" means "not supplied").

Security

Data are a valuable resource for nearly every organization. Just as an organization takes measures to protect its physical assets, it also needs to safeguard its electronic assets — its organizational memory, including databases. Furthermore, it often wants to limit the ac-

---

7.   Date, C. J. 1992. *Relational database: Writings, 1989–1991*. Reading, MA: Addison-Wesley.

cess of authorized users to particular parts of a database and restrict their actions to particular operations.

Two SQL features are used to administer security procedures. A view, discussed earlier in this chapter, can restrict a user's access to specified columns or rows in a table, and authorization commands can establish a user's privileges.

The authorization subsystem is based on the concept of a privilege — the authority to perform an operation. For example, a user cannot update a table unless she has been granted the appropriate update privilege. The database administrator (DBA) is king of the heap and has the highest privilege. The DBA can perform any legal operation. The creator of an object, say a base table, has full privileges for that object. Those with privileges can then use GRANT and REVOKE, commands included in SQL's data control language (DCL) to extend privileges to or rescind them from other users.

GRANT

The GRANT command defines a user's privileges. The general format of the statement is

```
GRANT privileges ON object TO users [WITH GRANT OPTION];
```

where "privileges" can be a list of privileges or the keyword ALL PRIVILEGES, and "users" is a list of user identifiers or the keyword PUBLIC. An "object" can be a base table or a view.

The following privileges can be granted for tables and views: SELECT, UPDATE, DELETE, and INSERT.

The UPDATE privilege specifies the particular columns in a base table or view that may be updated. Some privileges apply *only* to base tables. These are ALTER and INDEX.

The following examples illustrate the use of GRANT:

○ **Give Alice all rights to the stock table.**

```
GRANT ALL PRIVILEGES ON stock TO alice;
```

○ **Permit the accounting staff, Todd and Nancy, to update the price of a stock.**

```
GRANT UPDATE (stkprice) ON stock TO todd, nancy;
```

○ **Give all staff the privilege to select rows from item.**

```
GRANT SELECT ON item TO PUBLIC;
```

○ **Give Alice all rights to view stk.**

```
GRANT SELECT, UPDATE, DELETE, INSERT ON stk TO alice;[8]
```

The WITH GRANT OPTION clause

The `WITH GRANT OPTION` command allows a user to transfer his privileges to another user, as this next example illustrates:

○ **Give Ned all privileges for the item table and permit him to grant any of these to other staff members who may need to work with item.**

```
GRANT ALL PRIVILEGES ON item TO ned WITH GRANT OPTION;
```

This means that Ned can now use the `GRANT` command to give other staff privileges. To give Andrew permission for select and insert on `item`, for example, Ned would enter

```
GRANT SELECT, INSERT ON item TO andrew;
```

REVOKE

What `GRANT` granteth, `REVOKE` revoketh. Privileges are removed using the `REVOKE` statement. The general format of this statement is

```
REVOKE privileges ON object FROM users;
```

These examples illustrate the use of `REVOKE`.

○ **Remove Sophie's ability to select from item.**

```
REVOKE SELECT ON item FROM sophie;
```

○ **Nancy is no longer permitted to update stock prices.**

```
REVOKE UPDATE ON stock FROM nancy;[9]
```

Cascading revoke

When a `REVOKE` statement removes a privilege, it can result in more than one revocation. An earlier example illustrated how Ned used his `WITH GRANT OPTION` right to authorize Andrew to select and insert rows on `item`. The following `REVOKE` command

```
REVOKE INSERT ON item FROM ned;
```

automatically revokes Andrew's insert privilege.

---

8. In this case, since `stk` is a view, we cannot use `ALL PRIVILEGES` because **ALL** includes `ALTER` and `INDEX` privileges, which apply only to base tables and not views.
9. A revoked `UPDATE` privilege is not column specific.

The catalog

The catalog[10] describes a relational database. It contains the definitions of base tables, views, indexes, and so on. The catalog itself is a relational database and can be interrogated using SQL. Tables in the catalog are called *system tables* to distinguish them from base tables, though, conceptually, these tables are the same. In DB2, some important system tables are `syscatalog`, `syscolumns`, and `sysindexes`, and these are used in the following examples. Note that the names of the system catalog tables vary with RDBMS implementations, so while the following examples illustrate use of system catalog tables, it is likely that you will have to change the table names for other RDBMSs.

The table `syscatalog` contains details of all tables in the database. There is one row for each table in the database and the attributes of the rows are table name (`tname`), creator (`creator`), number of columns (`ncols`), and other data. `syscatalog` can be queried using `SELECT` on the qualified name `system.syscatalog`.

○ **Find the table(s) with the most columns.**

```
SELECT tname FROM system.syscatalog
    WHERE ncols = (select max(ncols) from system.syscatalog);
```

The column `syscolumns` stores details about each column in the database. Each row of `syscolumns` contains data such as column name (`cname`), the table in which the column appears (`tname`), type of data in the column (`coltype`), column length (`length`), column creator (`creator`), and other items.

○ **I've forgotten the length of a field in table sale.**

```
SELECT colno, cname, coltype, length FROM system.syscolumns
    WHERE tname = 'sale' and creator = 'userid'
        ORDER BY colno;
```

colno	cname	coltype	length
1	saleno	INTEGER	
2	saledate	DATE	
3	saletext	VARCHAR	50

Sometimes you forget parts of a table definition, such as the length of a text field. The preceding query recalls details of all the columns in a specified table. Notice that you must indicate the userid of the table's creator because others may use the same table name.

○ **What columns in which tables store dates?**

```
SELECT tname, cname FROM system.syscolumns
    WHERE coltype = 'date'
```

---

10. A catalog is similar to a data dictionary, which is discussed in Chapter 20.

The table `sysindexes` contains details of indexes. There is one row for each index. The attributes of `sysindexes` include index name (`iname`), the name of table indexed (`tname`), and other data.

○ **Find all tables that have indexes.**

```
SELECT tname FROM system.sysindexes;
```

As you can see, querying the catalog is the same as querying a database. This is a useful feature because you can use SQL queries on the catalog to find out more about a database.

Natural language processing

Infrequent inquirers of a relational database may be reluctant to use SQL because they don't use it often enough to remain familiar with the language. While the QBE approach can make querying easier, a more natural approach is to use standard English. In this case, natural language processing (NLP) is used to convert ordinary English into SQL so the query can be passed to the relational database. The example in Table 10-4 shows the successful translation of a query to SQL. However, when *reported* was used in place of *sorted*, the natural language processor asked for clarification because it did not understand the meaning of *reported*. Thus, NLP must translate a request to SQL and request clarification where necessary.

Table 10-4: An example of natural language processing

English	SQL generated for MS Access
Which movies have won best foreign film sorted by year?	`SELECT DISTINCT [Year], [Title] FROM [Awards] INNER JOIN [Movies] ON [Movies].[Movie ID] = [Awards].[Movie ID] WHERE [Category]='Best Foreign Film' and [Status]='Winner' ORDER BY [Year] ASC;`

Connectivity and ODBC

Over time and because of differing needs, an organization is likely to purchase DBMS software from a variety of vendors. Also, in some situations, mergers and acquisitions can create a multivendor DBMS environment. Consequently, the SQL Access Group developed SQL Call-Level Interface (CLI), a unified standard for remote database access. The intention of CLI is to provide programmers with a generic approach for writing software that accesses a database. With the appropriate CLI database driver, any DBMS server can provide access to client programs that use the CLI. On the server side, the DBMS CLI driver is responsible for translating the CLI call into the server's access language. On the client side, there must be a CLI driver for each database to which it connects. CLI is not a query language but a way of wrapping SQL so it can be understood by a DBMS. In 1996, CLI was adopted as an international standard and renamed X/Open CLI.

Open database connectivity (ODBC)

The de facto standard for database connectivity is **Open Database Connectivity** (ODBC), an extended implementation of CLI developed by Microsoft. This application programming interface (API) is cross-platform and can be used to access any DBMS or DBMS server that has an ODBC driver.This enables a software developer to build and distribute a client/server application without targeting a specific DBMS. Database drivers are then added to link the application to the client's choice of DBMS. For example, a microcomputer running under Windows can use ODBC to access an Oracle DBMS running on a Unix box. Major DBMS vendors support the ODBC API.

There is considerable support for ODBC. Application vendors like it because they do not have to write and maintain code for each DBMS; they can write one API. DBMS vendors support ODBC because they do not have to convince application vendors to support their product. For database systems managers, ODBC provides vendor and platform independence. For end-users, it provides access to corporate data from the desktop. Although the ODBC API was originally developed to provide database access from MS Windows products, many ODBC driver vendors support Linux and Macintosh clients.

Most vendors also have their own SQL APIs. For example, IBM's DB2 family's native protocol is ESQL/DRDA, but it also supports ODBC and X/Open CLI. The problem is that most vendors, as a means of differentiating their DBMS, have a more extensive native API protocol and also add extensions to standard ODBC. The developer who is tempted to use these extensions threatens the portability of the database.

ODBC introduces greater complexity and a processing overhead because it adds two layers of software. As Figure 10-4 illustrates, an ODBC-compliant application has additional layers for the ODBC API and ODBC driver. As a result, ODBC APIs can never be as fast as native APIs.

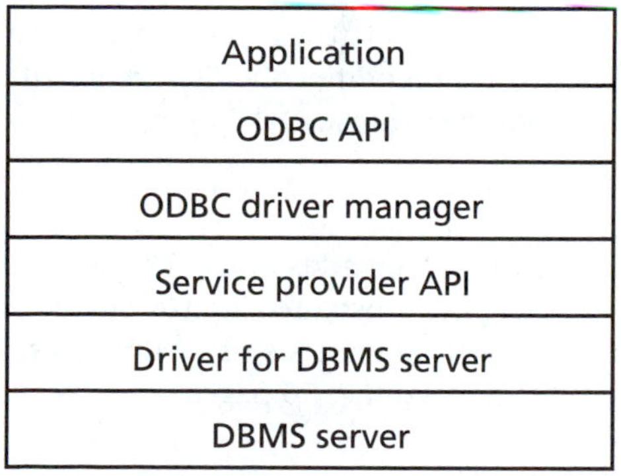

Application
ODBC API
ODBC driver manager
Service provider API
Driver for DBMS server
DBMS server

Figure 10-4. ODBC layers

Embedded SQL

SQL can be used in two modes. *First,* SQL is an interactive query language and database programming language. SELECT defines queries; INSERT, UPDATE, and DELETE maintain a database. *Second*, any interactive SQL statement can be embedded in an application program.

This dual-mode principle is a very useful feature. It means that programmers need to learn only one database query language, because the same SQL statements apply for both interactive queries and application statements. Programmers can also interactively examine SQL commands before embedding them in a program, a feature that can substantially reduce the time to write an application program.

Because SQL is not a complete programming language, however, it must be used with a traditional programming language to create applications. Common complete programming languages, such as PHP and Java, support embedded SQL. If you are to write application programs using embedded SQL, you will need considerable training in both the application language and the finer details of how it communicates with SQL.[11]

The future of SQL

Since 1986, developers of database applications have benefited from an SQL standard, one of the most successful standardization stories in the software industry. Most current implementations of SQL follow International Standard Database Language SQL-92. Also, known as SQL2, it is both a national standard for the United States and an international standard.

Although most database vendors have implemented their own proprietary extensions of SQL, standardization has kept the language consistent, and SQL code is highly portable. Standardization was relatively easy when focused on the storage and retrieval of numbers and characters. Objects have made standardization more difficult.

If SQL is to continue to thrive, it needs to accommodate the major force in current systems development, object orientation (OO). SQL-99 modifies the SQL standard to handle objects. SQLJ simplifies the interface between the popular OO language Java and an RDBMS.

SQL-99

The **SQL-99** (also known as SQL3) standard, which adds object-handling extensions, is a major development. The level of change is quite substantial, and it took considerable time to reach consensus on the new standard. SQL-99 consists of 2,100 pages of definitions, syntax, and usage rules. In contrast, SQL-89 was only 150 pages.

The SQL-99 standard meets three market needs:

---

11. To see a sample COBOL program with embedded SQL, see *Additions* on the book's web site.

❖ It provides better support for Java and other object-oriented languages.
❖ It supports multimedia extensions.
❖ It retains portability by defining standards for object-oriented extensions to the relational model. Vendors have made extensions, and the strength and value of the relational model are severely curtailed if a vendor's extensions are incompatible.

There are two major issues for SQL-99. *First,* will vendors release products that are compatible with the standard? Some vendors have already moved ahead of the standard and added features that may not be in the standard or vary somewhat from the standard. If major vendors go their own way, then considerable cross-platform compatibility will be lost. *Second*, will SQL-99 retain the simplicity, power, and elegance of the current SQL standard? One of the strengths of SQL is that the language is readily learned and deployed. Enhancements always have a cost because they increase complexity.

User-defined types

Versions of SQL prior to the SQL-99 specification had predefined data types, and programmers were limited to selecting the data type and defining the length of character strings. One of the basic ideas behind the object extensions is that, in addition to the normal built-in data types defined by SQL, user-defined data types (UDTs) are available.

A UDT is used like a predefined type, but it must be set up before it can be used. In order to define a UDT, the database designer must specify 12 pieces of information. In SQL-99, a UDT is defined by specifying a set of declarations of the stored attributes that represent the value of the UDT, the operations that define the equality and ordering relationships of the UDT, and the operations and derived attributes that represent the behavior of the UDT.

SQLJ

In 1997, some leading DBMS and software vendors formed a consortium to define standardization of Java development for database applications. In December 1998, the specification of SQLJ was accepted as an ANSI standard. SQLJ provides integration of SQL and Java, thus reinforcing the adoption and use of Java for enterprise data-intensive applications.

SQLJ gives Java developers a quick and easy way to use SQL directly in their Java applications without having to do database programming. This means that applications involving a very large quantity of data manipulation can be written in Java. SQLJ is a good choice for static SQL programming tasks, and many SQL applications are static in nature. SQLJ does not handle dynamic SQL actions determined at run time by the application, in which case JDBC (see page 490) must be used.

Summary

Structured Query Language (SQL), a widely used relational database language, has been adopted as a standard by ANSI and ISO. It is a data definition language (DDL), data manipulation language (DML), and data control language (DCL). A base table is an autonomous, named table. A view is a virtual table. A key is one or more columns identified as such in the description of a table, an index, or a referential constraint. SQL supports primary, foreign, and unique keys. Indexes accelerate data access and ensure uniqueness. CREATE TABLE defines a new base table and specifies primary, foreign, and unique key constraints. Numeric, string, date, or graphic data can be stored in a column. BLOB and CLOB are data types for large fields. ALTER TABLE adds one new column to a table or changes the status of a constraint. DROP TABLE removes a table from a database. CREATE VIEW defines a view, which can be used to restrict access to data, report derived data, store commonly executed queries, and convert data. A view is created dynamically. DROP VIEW deletes a view. CREATE INDEX defines an index, and DROP INDEX deletes one.

Ambiguous references to column names are avoided by qualifying a column name with its table name. A table or view can be given a temporary name that remains current for a query. SQL has four data manipulation statements — SELECT, INSERT, UPDATE, and DELETE. INSERT adds one or more rows to a table. UPDATE modifies a table by changing one or more rows. DELETE removes one or more rows from a table. SELECT provides powerful interrogation facilities. The product of two tables is a new table consisting of all rows of the first table concatenated with all possible rows of the second table. Join creates a new table from two existing tables by matching on a column common to both tables. A subquery is a query within a query. A correlated subquery differs from a simple subquery in that the inner query is evaluated multiple times rather than once.

SQL's aggregate functions increase its retrieval power. GROUP BY supports grouping of rows that have the same value for a specified column. The LIKE clause supports pattern matching. SQL includes scalar functions that can be used in arithmetic expressions, data conversion, or data extraction. Nulls cause problems because they can represent several situations — unknown information, inapplicable information, no value supplied, or value undefined. Remember, a null is not a blank or zero. The SQL commands GRANT and REVOKE support data security. GRANT authorizes a user to perform certain SQL operations, and REVOKE removes a user's authority. The table, syscatalog, which describes a relational database, can be queried using SELECT. SQL can be used as an interactive query language and as embedded commands within an application programming language.

Natural language processing (NLP), open database connectivity (ODBC), and SQL-99 are extensions to relational technology that enhance its usefulness in terms of query writing, compatibility, and handling objects, respectively. SQL-99 and SQLJ are part of the trend of linking the dominant programming model, object orientation, to the dominant data management model, relational technology.

Key terms and concepts

Aggregate functions	INSERT
ALTER TABLE	ISO
ANSI	Join
Base table	Key
Complete database language	Natural language processing (NLP)
Complete programming language	Null
Composite key	Open database connectivity (ODBC)
Connectivity	Primary key
Correlated subquery	Product
CREATE FUNCTION	Qualified name
CREATE INDEX	Referential integrity rule
CREATE PROCEDURE	REVOKE
CREATE TABLE	Routine
CREATE TRIGGER	Scalar functions
CREATE VIEW	Security
Cursor	SELECT
Data control language (DCL)	Special registers
Data definition language (DDL)	SQL
Data manipulation language (DML)	SQLJ
Data types	Subquery
DELETE	Synonym
DROP INDEX	syscatalog
DROP TABLE	syscolumns
DROP VIEW	sysindexes
Embedded SQL	Temporary names
Foreign key	Unique key
GRANT	UPDATE
GROUP BY	View
Index	

References and additional readings

Date, C. J. 2000. *An introduction to database systems*. 7th ed. Reading, MA: Addison-Wesley.

Date, C. J. 1993. *A guide to the SQL Standard: A user's guide to the standard relational language SQL*. 3rd ed. Reading, MA: Addison-Wesley.

Gulutzan, P., and T. Pelzer. 1999. *SQL-99 complete, really*. Lawrence, KS: R & D Books.

Exercises

1. Why is it important that SQL was adopted as a standard by ANSI and ISO?
2. What does it mean to say "SQL is a complete database language"?
3. Is SQL a complete programming language? What are the implications of your answer?
4. List some operational advantages of an RDBMS.

5. What is the difference between a base table and a view?
6. What is the difference between a primary key and a unique key?
7. What is the purpose of an index?
8. Consider the three choices for the ON DELETE clause associated with the foreign key constraint. What are the pros and cons of each option?
9. Specify the data type (e.g., DECIMAL(6,2)) you would use for the following columns:
    a. The selling price of a house
    b. A telephone number with area code
    c. Hourly temperatures in Antarctica
    d. A numeric customer code
    e. A credit card number
    f. The distance between two cities
    g. A sentence using Chinese characters
    h. The number of kilometers from the Earth to a given star
    i. The text of an advertisement in the classified section of a newspaper
    j. A basketball score
    k. The title of a CD
    l. The X-ray of a patient
    m. A U.S. ZIP code
    n. A British or Canadian postal code
    o. The photo of a customer
    p. The date a person purchased a car
    q. The time of arrival of an e-mail message
    r. The number of full-time employees in a small business
    s. The text of a speech
    t. The thickness of a layer on a silicon chip
10. How could you add two columns to an existing table? Precisely describe the steps you would take.
11. What is the difference between DROP TABLE and deleting all the rows in a table?
12. Give some reasons for creating a view.
13. When is a view created?
14. Write SQL codes to create a unique index on firm name for the shr table defined in Chapter 3. Would it make sense to create a unique index for PE ratio in the same table?
15. What is the difference between product and join?
16. What is the difference between an equijoin and a natural join?
17. You have a choice between executing two queries that will both give the same result. One is written as a simple subquery and the other as a correlated subquery. Which one would you use and why?
18. What function would you use for the following situations?
    a. Computing the total value of a column
    b. Finding the minimum value of a column
    c. Counting the number of customers in the customer table
    d. Displaying a number with specified precision

    e. Reporting the month part of a date

    f. Displaying the second part of a time

    g. Retrieving the first five characters of a city's name

    h. Reporting the distance to the sun in feet

19. A student database records a home and school term phone number for each student. Some students have a null value for school term phone number. What does this mean?

20. Write SQL statements for the following:

    a. Let Hui-Tze query and add to the `nation` table.

    b. Give Lana permission to update the phone number column in the `customer` table.

    c. Remove all of William's privileges.

    d. Give Chris permission to grant other users authority to select from the `address` table.

    e. Find the name of all tables that include the word `sale`.

    f. List all the tables owned by user CMS5432.

    g. What is the length of the column `streetname`?

    h. Find all columns that have a data type of `SMALLINT`.

21. What are the two modes in which you can use SQL?

22. How do procedural programming languages and SQL differ in the way they process data? How is this difference handled in an application program? What is embedded SQL?

Reference 2

SQL Playbook

Play so that you may be serious.
Anacharsis (c. 600 B.C.E.)

The power of SQL

SQL is a very powerful retrieval language, and most novices underestimate its capability. Furthermore, mastery of SQL takes considerable practice and exposure to a wide variety of problems. This reference serves the dual purpose of revealing the full power of SQL and providing an extensive set of diverse queries. To make this reference easier to use, we have named each of the queries to make them easy to remember.

Lacroix and Pirotte[1] have defined 66 queries for testing a query language's power, and their work is the foundation of this chapter. Not all their queries are included; some have been kept for the end-of-chapter exercises. Also, many of the queries have been reworded to various extents. Because these queries are more difficult than those normally used in business decision making, they provide a good test of your SQL skills. If you can answer all of them, then you are a proficient SQL programmer. The set of queries also can be used as a test package for evaluating the capability of an implementation of SQL.

You are encouraged to formulate and test your answer to a query before reading the suggested solution.[2] A *q* has been prefixed to all entity and table names to distinguish them from entities and tables used in earlier problems. The going gets tough after the first few queries, and you can expect to spend some time formulating and testing each one, but remember, this is still considerably faster than using a procedural programming language to write the same queries.

---

1. Lacroix, M., and A. Pirotte. 1976. *Example queries in relational languages.* Brussels, M.B.L.E, Technical note no. 107.
2. The author is indebted to Dr. Mohammad Dadashzadeh of Wichita State University in Kansas, who provided valuable assistance by checking each query. Dr. Gert Jan Hofstede of Wageningen University in the Netherlands also willingly contributed some improvements. Many of their suggestions for the SQL code to answer these queries have been incorporated. All the queries have been tested with a small database. If you discover a problem with a query or a better way of expressing it, please send an e-mail message to rwatson@terry.uga.edu.

The data model accompanying Lacroix and Pirotte's queries is shown in Figure R2-1. You will notice that the complexity of the real world has been reduced; a sale and a delivery are assumed to have only one item. The corresponding relational model is shown in Table R2-1, and some data that can be used to test your SQL queries appear at the end of this chapter (see page 317).

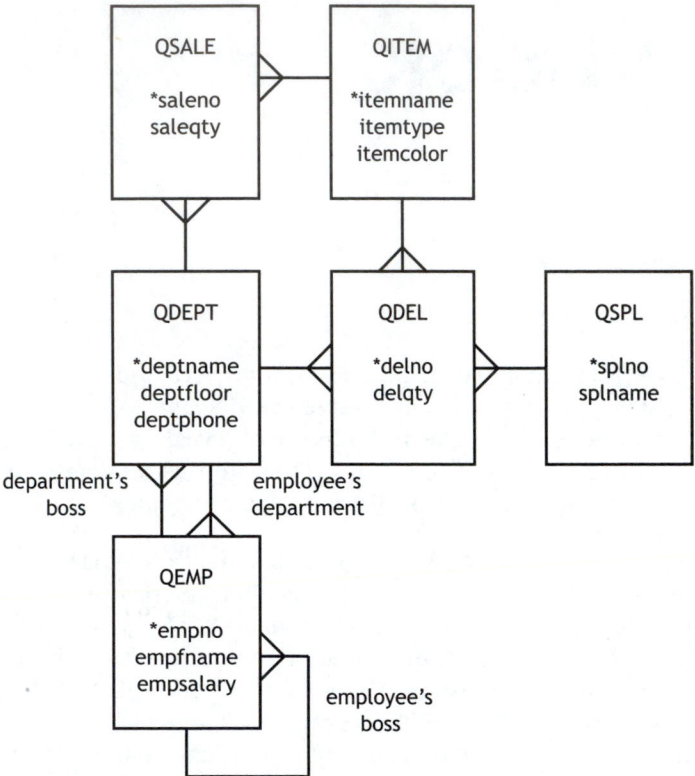

Figure R2-1. Data model

Table R2-1. Relational tables

qsale			
saleno	saleqty	*itemname*	*deptname*

qitem		
itemname	itemtype	itemcolor

qdel				
delno	delqty	*itemname*	*deptname*	*splno*

qspl	
splno	splname

qdept			
deptname	deptfloor	deptphone	*empno*

qemp				
empno	empfname	empsalary	*deptname*	*bossno*

1. A slow full toss

In cricket, a slow full toss is the easiest ball to hit. The same applies to this simple query.

○ **Find the names of employees in the Marketing department.**

```
SELECT empfname FROM qemp WHERE deptname = 'Marketing';
```

2. Skinning a cat

Queries often can be solved in several ways. For this query, four possible solutions are presented. Also, we indicate the resource units required to answer the query when using SQL/VM.

○ **Find the items sold by a department on the second floor.**

2.1 Join (545 units)

```
SELECT DISTINCT itemname FROM qsale, qdept
   WHERE qdept.deptname = qsale.deptname
   AND deptfloor = 2;
```

A join of `qsale` and `qdept` is possibly the most obvious way to answer this query.

2.2 In (8)

```
SELECT DISTINCT itemname FROM qsale
    WHERE deptname IN
        (SELECT deptname FROM qdept WHERE deptfloor = 2);
```

Another simple approach is to use an IN clause. First find all the departments on the second floor, and then find a match in qsale. The subquery returns a list of all departments on the second floor. Then use the IN clause to find a match on department name in qsale. Notice that this is the most efficient form of the query.

2.3 Correlated subquery (7,780)

```
SELECT DISTINCT itemname FROM qsale
    WHERE deptname IN
        (SELECT deptname FROM qdept
            WHERE qdept.deptname = qsale.deptname
            AND deptfloor = 2);
```

Conceptually, you can think of this correlated query as stepping through qsale one row at a time. The subquery is executed for each row of qsale, and if there is a match for the current value of qsale.deptname, the current value of itemname is listed.

2.4 Exists (8,080)

```
SELECT DISTINCT itemname FROM qsale
    WHERE EXISTS
        (SELECT * FROM qdept
            WHERE qsale.deptname = qdept.deptname
            AND deptfloor = 2);
```

Conceptually, think of this query as stepping through each row of qsale and evaluating whether the existence test is true. Remember, EXISTS returns *true* if there is at least one row in the inner query for which the condition is true.

The difference between a correlated subquery and existence testing is that a correlated subquery returns either the value of a column or an empty table, while EXISTS returns either *true* or *false*. It may help to think of this version of the query as, "Select item names from sale such that there exists a department relating them to the second floor."

3. Another full toss

○   **Find the names of items sold on floors other than the second floor.**

This query is a slight adaptation of the second. Just change the equals to a not equals.

```
SELECT DISTINCT itemname FROM qsale, qdept
    WHERE qsale.deptname = qdept.deptname
    AND deptfloor <> 2;
```

4. Subtracting from all

○ **Find the items sold by no department on the second floor.**

You may first think this query is the same as the preceding. However, the prior query does not exclude an item that is sold on some other floor in addition to the second floor. For example, if polo sticks are sold on both the third and second floors, they will be reported by the preceding query because they are sold on a floor other than the second floor.

The correct way to approach this is to first get a list of all items sold on the second floor (the second query) and then subtract this result from all items sold. Clearly, the difference must be all items not sold on the second floor.

```
SELECT DISTINCT itemname FROM qsale
    WHERE itemname NOT IN
        (SELECT DISTINCT itemname FROM qsale, qdept
            WHERE qsale.deptname = qdept.deptname
            AND deptfloor = 2);
```

5. Dividing

○ **Find the items sold by all departments on the second floor.**

This is the relational algebra divide or the SQL double NOT EXISTS encountered in Chapter 5. You can think of this query as

Select items from sales such that there does not exist a department on the second floor that does not sell this item.

However, it is easier to apply the SQL template described in Chapter 5, which is

```
SELECT target1 FROM target
    WHERE NOT EXISTS
        (SELECT * FROM source
            WHERE NOT EXISTS
                (SELECT * FROM target-source
                    WHERE target-source.target# = target.target#
                    AND target-source.source# = source.source#));
```

The substitutions are straightforward.

```
target1         =   itemname
target          =   qitem
source          =   qdept
target-source   =   qsale
target#         =   itemname
source#         =   deptname
```

Some additional code needs to be added to handle the restriction to items on the second floor. The query becomes

```
SELECT DISTINCT itemname FROM qitem
    WHERE NOT EXISTS
        (SELECT * FROM qdept WHERE deptfloor = 2
        AND NOT EXISTS
            (SELECT * FROM qsale
                WHERE qsale.itemname = qitem.itemname
                AND qsale.deptname = qdept.deptname));
```

Here is an alternative approach to formulating the problem:

Find all the items for which the number of second-floor departments that sell them is equal to the total number of departments on the second floor.

```
SELECT qsale.itemname FROM qsale, qdept
    WHERE qsale.deptname = qdept.deptname
    AND qdept.deptfloor = 2
        GROUP BY qsale.itemname
            HAVING COUNT(DISTINCT qdept.deptname) =
                (SELECT COUNT(DISTINCT deptname)
                    FROM qdept WHERE deptfloor = 2);
```

6. At least some number

○ **Find the items sold by at least two departments on the second floor.**

The GROUP BY and HAVING clauses make it easy for you to count the number of rows that meet some condition.

```
SELECT itemname FROM qsale, qdept
    WHERE qsale.deptname = qdept.deptname AND deptfloor = 2
        GROUP BY itemname
            HAVING COUNT(DISTINCT qdept.deptname) > 1;
```

7. A friendly IN for an SQL traveler

○ **Find the salary of Clare's manager.**

This query is readily handled with the IN clause. The inner query gets the employee number of Clare's manager, and this locates the row containing that person's salary.

```
SELECT empfname, empsalary FROM qemp
    WHERE empno IN
        (SELECT bossno FROM qemp WHERE empfname = 'Clare');
```

8. Joining a table with itself

○ **Find numbers and names of those employees who make more than their manager.**

This query is a simple play once you realize that you can conceptually create two copies of a table and join them. This type of query is discussed in more depth in Chapter 6.

```
SELECT wrk.empno, wrk.empfname FROM qemp wrk, qemp boss
   WHERE wrk.bossno = boss.empno
   AND boss.empsalary < wrk.empsalary;
```

9. A combination of subtract from all and a self-join

○ **Find the departments where all the employees earn less than their manager.**

The key is to first find the departments where at least one employee earns more than or the same as the manager, and then subtract these departments from the set of all departments. Also, we exclude Management because it has no boss. What is left must be the departments where no employee earns more than the manager. This query is a combination, conceptually, of queries 4 and 8.

```
SELECT DISTINCT deptname FROM qemp
   WHERE deptname <> 'Management'
   AND deptname NOT IN
      (SELECT wrk.deptname FROM qemp wrk, qemp boss
         WHERE wrk.bossno = boss.empno
         AND wrk.empsalary >= boss.empsalary);
```

10. Self-join with GROUP BY

○ **Count the number of direct employees of each manager.**

Join the table with itself by matching employees and their managers and then group by manager's name with a count. Just in case two bosses have the same first name, employee number is included in the selection and grouping clauses.

```
SELECT boss.empno, boss.empfname, COUNT(*)
   FROM qemp wrk, qemp boss
      WHERE wrk.bossno = boss.empno
         GROUP BY boss.empno, boss.empfname;
```

11. A self-join with two matching conditions

○ **Find the names of employees who are in the same department as their manager (as an employee). Report the name of the employee, the department, and the boss's name.**

There is no reason why a join cannot have matching on more than one common column. Here we have two conditions: one for employee number and one for department name.

```
SELECT wrk.empfname, wrk.deptname, boss.empfname
    FROM qemp wrk, qemp boss
        WHERE wrk.bossno = boss.empno
        AND wrk.deptname = boss.deptname;
```

12. Averaging with GROUP BY

○ **List the departments having an average salary over $25,000.**

A gimme for any half-decent SQL programmer.

```
SELECT deptname, AVG(empsalary) FROM qemp
    GROUP BY deptname
        HAVING AVG(empsalary) > 25000;
```

13. Inner query GROUP BY and HAVING

○ **List the departments where the average salary of the employees of each manager is more than $25,000.**

This query is more challenging than simple averaging. Note that the query implies that you should exclude the manager's salary from the calculation. An employee is the manager of a particular department if that person's employee number and the department name are in the same row in qdept (i.e., wrk.empno = qdept.empno AND wrk.deptname = qdept.deptname). Once the department manager has been excluded, then use grouping to get the employee data by department.

```
SELECT wrk.deptname, AVG(wrk.empsalary)
    FROM qemp wrk
        WHERE wrk.empno NOT IN
            (SELECT qdept.empno FROM qdept
                WHERE wrk.empno = qdept.empno
                AND wrk.deptname = qdept.deptname)
                    GROUP BY wrk.deptname
                        HAVING AVG(wrk.empsalary) > 25000;
```

14. An IN with GROUP BY and COUNT

○ **List the name and salary of the managers with more than two employees.**

The inner query uses grouping with counting to identify the employee numbers of managers with more than two employees. The outer query reports details of these managers.

```
SELECT empfname, empsalary FROM qemp
    WHERE empno IN
        (SELECT bossno FROM qemp
            GROUP BY bossno HAVING COUNT(*) > 2);
```

15. A self-join with some conditions

○ **List the name, salary, and manager of the employees of the Marketing department who have a salary over $25,000.**

A join gets workers and bosses together in the same row, and then the various conditions are applied to restrict the rows reported.

```
SELECT wrk.empfname, wrk.empsalary, boss.empfname
    FROM qemp wrk, qemp boss
        WHERE wrk.bossno = boss.empno
        AND wrk.deptname = 'Marketing'
        AND wrk.empsalary > 25000;
```

16. Making comparisons

○ **List the names of the employees who earn more than any employee in the Marketing department.**

The first step is to determine the maximum salary of anyone in the Marketing department. Then, find anyone with a larger salary.

```
SELECT empfname, empsalary FROM qemp
    WHERE empsalary >
        (SELECT MAX(empsalary) FROM qemp
            WHERE deptname = 'Marketing');
```

17. An IN with GROUP BY and SUM

○ **Among all the departments with total salary greater than $25,000, find the departments that sell Stetsons.**

This is very similar to query 16. First, find the departments that satisfy the condition, and then select from that list any departments that sell Stetsons.

```
SELECT DISTINCT deptname FROM qsale
    WHERE itemname = 'Stetson'
    AND deptname IN
        (SELECT deptname FROM qemp
            GROUP BY deptname HAVING SUM(empsalary) > 25000);
```

18. A double divide!

○   **List the items delivered by every supplier that delivers all items of type N.**

SQL programmers who tackle this query without blinking an eye are superheroes. This is a genuinely true-blue, tough query because it is two divides. There is an inner divide that determines the suppliers that deliver all items of type N. The SQL for this query is

```
SELECT * FROM qspl
   WHERE NOT EXISTS
      (SELECT * FROM qitem WHERE itemtype = 'N'
      AND NOT EXISTS
         (SELECT * FROM qdel
            WHERE qdel.itemname = qitem.itemname
            AND qdel.splno = qspl.splno));
```

Then there is an outer divide that determines which of the suppliers (returned by the inner divide) provide all these items. If we call the result of the inner query qspn, the SQL for the outer query is

```
SELECT DISTINCT itemname FROM qdel del
   WHERE NOT EXISTS
      (SELECT * FROM qspn
         WHERE NOT EXISTS
            (SELECT * FROM qdel
               WHERE qdel.itemname = del.itemname
               AND qdel.splno = qspn.splno));
```

The complete query is

```
SELECT DISTINCT itemname FROM qdel del
   WHERE NOT EXISTS
      (SELECT * FROM qspl
         WHERE NOT EXISTS
            (SELECT * FROM qitem WHERE itemtype = 'N'
            AND NOT EXISTS
               (SELECT * FROM qdel
                  WHERE qdel.itemname = qitem.itemname
                  AND qdel.splno = qspl.splno))
         AND NOT EXISTS
            (SELECT * FROM qdel
               WHERE qdel.itemname = del.itemname
               AND qdel.splno = qspl.splno));
```

19. A slam dunk

○ **Find the suppliers that deliver compasses.**

A simple query to recover from the double divide. It is a good idea to include supplier number since `splname` could possibly be nonunique.

```
SELECT DISTINCT qspl.splno, splname FROM qspl, qdel
    WHERE qspl.splno = qdel.splno AND itemname = 'Compass';
```

20. A 6-inch putt for a birdie

○ **Find the suppliers that do not deliver compasses.**

This is a relatively straightforward subtract (and take one off par for a birdie).

```
SELECT splno, splname FROM qspl
    WHERE splno NOT IN
        (SELECT splno FROM qdel WHERE itemname = 'Compass');
```

21. Making the count

○ **Find the suppliers that deliver both compasses and an item other than compasses.**

A simple approach is to find those suppliers that supply items other than compasses (i.e., `itemname <> 'Compass'`) and also supply compasses (the subquery).

```
SELECT DISTINCT qdel.splno, splname FROM qspl, qdel
    WHERE qdel.splno = qspl.splno
    AND itemname <> 'Compass'
    AND qdel.splno IN
        (SELECT splno FROM qdel WHERE itemname = 'Compass');
```

A more general approach is to find suppliers that have delivered compasses and more than one item (i.e., `COUNT(DISTINCT itemname) > 1`). This means they deliver at least an item other than compasses. Note that the `GROUP BY` clause includes supplier number to cope with the situation where two suppliers have the same name. The `DISTINCT itemname` clause must be used to guard against multiple deliveries of compasses from the same supplier.

```
SELECT DISTINCT qdel.splno, splname FROM qspl, qdel
    WHERE qdel.splno = qspl.splno
    AND qdel.splno IN
        (SELECT splno FROM qdel WHERE itemname = 'Compass')
    GROUP BY qdel.splno, splname HAVING COUNT(DISTINCT itemname) > 1;
```

The more general approach enables you to solve queries, such as *Find suppliers that deliver three items other than compasses,* by changing the `HAVING` clause to `COUNT(DISTINCT itemname > 3)`.

Because `DISTINCT colname` is not supported by MS Access, for that DBMS you must first create a view containing distinct `splno, itemname` pairs and then substitute the name of the view for `qdel` and drop the `DISTINCT` clause in the `COUNT` statement.

22. Minus and divide

○ **List the departments that have not recorded a sale for all the items of type N.**

This query has two parts: an inner divide and an outer minus. The inner query finds departments that have sold all items of type N. These are then subtracted from all departments to leave only those that have not sold all items of type N.

```
SELECT deptname FROM qdept WHERE deptname NOT IN
    (SELECT deptname FROM qdept
        WHERE NOT EXISTS
            (SELECT * FROM qitem WHERE itemtype = 'N'
            AND NOT EXISTS
                (SELECT * FROM qsale
                    WHERE qsale.deptname = qdept.deptname AND
                    qsale.itemname = qitem.itemname)));
```

23. Division with copies

○ **List the departments that have at least one sale of all the items delivered to them.**

This is a variation on the divide concept. Normally with a divide, you have three tables representing a many-to-many (m:m) relationship. In this case, you only have two tables: `qdel` and `qsale`. You can still construct the query, however, by creating two copies of `qdel` (`del1` and `del2` in this case) and then proceeding as if you had three different tables. Also, you must match on `deptname` so that you get the correct (`deptname, itemname`) pair for comparing with `qsale`.

```
SELECT DISTINCT deptname FROM qdel del1
    WHERE NOT EXISTS
        (SELECT * FROM qdel del2
            WHERE del2.deptname = del1.deptname
            AND NOT EXISTS
                (SELECT * FROM qsale
                    WHERE del2.itemname = qsale.itemname
                    AND del1.deptname = qsale.deptname));
```

This query can also be written as shown next. Observe how `NOT IN` functions like `NOT EXISTS`. We will use this variation on divide with some of the upcoming queries.

```
SELECT DISTINCT deptname FROM qdel del1
   WHERE NOT EXISTS
      (SELECT * FROM qdel del2
         WHERE del2.deptname = del1.deptname
         AND itemname NOT IN
            (SELECT itemname FROM qsale
               WHERE deptname = del1.deptname));
```

24. A difficult pairing

○ **List the supplier-department pairs where the department sells all items delivered to it by the supplier.**

This query is yet another variation on divide. An additional complication is that you have to match the department name and item name of sales and deliveries.

```
SELECT splname, deptname FROM qdel del1, qspl
   WHERE del1.splno = qspl.splno
   AND NOT EXISTS
      (SELECT * FROM qdel
         WHERE qdel.deptname = del1.deptname
         AND qdel.splno = del1.splno
         AND itemname NOT IN
            (SELECT itemname FROM qsale
               WHERE qsale.deptname = del1.deptname));
```

25. Two divides and an intersection

○ **List the items delivered to all departments by all suppliers.**

This query has three parts. First, find the items delivered by all suppliers (the first divide); then find the items delivered to all departments (the second divide). Finally, find the items that satisfy both conditions—the function of the AND connection between the two divides. The items reported must be the ones both delivered by all suppliers and delivered to all departments. The administrative departments (Management, Marketing, Personnel, Accounting, and Purchasing) should be excluded because they do not sell items.

```
SELECT itemname FROM qitem
   WHERE NOT EXISTS
      (SELECT * FROM qspl
         WHERE NOT EXISTS
            (SELECT * FROM qdel
               WHERE qdel.itemname = qitem.itemname
               AND qdel.splno = qspl.splno))
   AND NOT EXISTS
      (SELECT * FROM qdept WHERE deptname
         NOT IN ('Management', 'Marketing', 'Personnel',
            'Accounting', 'Purchasing')
         AND NOT EXISTS
            (SELECT * FROM qdel
               WHERE qdel.itemname = qitem.itemname
               AND qdel.deptname = qdept.deptname));
```

26. A divide with a matching condition

○ **List the items sold only by departments that sell all the items delivered to them.**

Yet another variation on divide — which is why you needed a break. There are two parts to this query. First, look for items sold by departments that sell all items delivered to them, and then make sure that no other department sells the same item.

```
SELECT DISTINCT itemname FROM qsale sale
   WHERE deptname IN
      (SELECT deptname FROM qdept dept1
         WHERE NOT EXISTS
            (SELECT * FROM qdel
               WHERE qdel.deptname = dept1.deptname
               AND itemname NOT IN
                  (SELECT itemname FROM qsale
                     WHERE qsale.deptname = dept1.deptname)))
   AND NOT EXISTS
      (SELECT * FROM qsale
         WHERE itemname = sale.itemname
         AND deptname NOT IN
            (SELECT deptname FROM qdept dept2
               WHERE NOT EXISTS
                  (SELECT * FROM qdel
                     WHERE qdel.deptname = dept2.deptname
                     AND itemname NOT IN
                        (SELECT itemname FROM qsale
                        WHERE qsale.deptname = dept2.deptname))));
```

27. Restricted divide

○ **Who are the suppliers that deliver all the items of type N?**

A slight variation on the standard divide to restrict consideration to the type N items.

```
SELECT splno, splname FROM qspl
   WHERE NOT EXISTS
      (SELECT * FROM qitem WHERE itemtype = 'N'
      AND NOT EXISTS
         (SELECT * FROM qdel
            WHERE qdel.splno = qspl.splno
            AND qdel.itemname = qitem.itemname));
```

28. A NOT IN variation on divide

○ **List the suppliers that deliver only the items sold by the Books department.**

This query may be rewritten as, *Select suppliers for which there does not exist a delivery that does not include the items sold by the Books department*. Note the use of the IN clause to limit consideration to those suppliers that have made a delivery. Otherwise, a supplier that has never delivered an item will be reported as delivering only the items sold by the Books department.

```
SELECT splname FROM qspl
    WHERE splno IN (SELECT splno FROM qdel)
    AND NOT EXISTS
        (SELECT * FROM qdel
            WHERE qdel.splno = qspl.splno
            AND itemname NOT IN
                (SELECT itemname FROM qsale
                    WHERE deptname = 'Books'));
```

29. All and only

○ **List the suppliers that deliver all and only the items sold by the Equipment department.**

This is a query with three parts. The first part identifies suppliers that deliver all items sold by the Equipment department (they could also deliver other items, but these are not sold in the Equipment department). The second part identifies suppliers that deliver only items sold by the Equipment department (i.e., they do not deliver any other items). This part is similar to the previous query. The third part is the intersection of the first two queries to indicate suppliers that satisfy both conditions.

```
SELECT splname FROM qspl
    WHERE NOT EXISTS
        (SELECT * FROM qsale
            WHERE deptname = 'Equipment'
            AND itemname NOT IN
                (SELECT itemname FROM qdel
                    WHERE qdel.splno = qspl.splno))
                AND NOT EXISTS
                    (SELECT * FROM qdel
                        WHERE qdel.splno = qspl.splno
                        AND itemname NOT IN
                            (SELECT itemname FROM qsale
                                WHERE deptname = 'Equipment'));
```

30. Divide with an extra condition

○   **List the suppliers that deliver every item of type C to the same department on the second floor.**

This is a divide in which there are three WHERE conditions in the innermost query. The extra condition handles the "same department" requirement.

```
SELECT splname FROM qspl
   WHERE EXISTS (SELECT * FROM qdept
      WHERE deptfloor = 2
      AND NOT EXISTS (SELECT * FROM qitem
         WHERE itemtype = 'C'
         AND NOT EXISTS (SELECT * FROM qdel
            WHERE qdel.splno = qspl.splno
            AND qdel.itemname = qitem.itemname
            AND qdel.deptname = qdept.deptname)));
```

31. At least some COUNT

○   **List the suppliers that deliver at least two items of type N to departments.**

First, do a three-way join to get the data for deliveries, suppliers, and items. Then, group with a COUNT condition. This can be easily extended to a variety of conditions based on counts.

```
SELECT qspl.splno, splname FROM qdel, qspl, qitem
   WHERE itemtype = 'N'
   AND qdel.splno = qspl.splno
   AND qdel.itemname = qitem.itemname
      GROUP BY qspl.splno, splname
         HAVING COUNT(DISTINCT qdel.itemname) > 1;
```

32. Double divide with a restriction

○   **List the suppliers that deliver all the items of type B to departments on the second floor who sell all the items of type R.**

Break this query into two parts. First, create a view of departments on the second floor that sell all items of type R.

```
CREATE VIEW v32 AS
   (SELECT deptname FROM qdept
      WHERE deptfloor = 2
      AND NOT EXISTS (SELECT * FROM qitem
         WHERE itemtype = 'R'
         AND NOT EXISTS (SELECT * FROM qsale
            WHERE qsale.itemname = qitem.itemname
            AND qsale.deptname = qdept.deptname)));
```

Second, report all the suppliers that deliver all the items of type B to the departments designated in the previously created view.

```
SELECT splname FROM qspl
    WHERE NOT EXISTS (SELECT * FROM qitem
        WHERE itemtype = 'B'
        AND NOT EXISTS (SELECT * FROM qdel
            WHERE qdel.itemname = qitem.itemname
            AND qdel.splno = qspl.splno
            AND deptname IN (SELECT deptname FROM v32)));
```

33. Triple divide with an intersection

○ **List the suppliers that deliver all the items of type B to the departments that also sell all the items of type N.**

Defeat this by dividing — *that* word again — the query into parts. First, identify the departments that sell all items of type N, and save as a view.

```
CREATE VIEW v33a AS
    (SELECT deptname FROM qdept
        WHERE NOT EXISTS (SELECT * FROM qitem
            WHERE itemtype = 'N'
            AND NOT EXISTS (SELECT * FROM qsale
                WHERE qsale.deptname = qdept.deptname
                AND qsale.itemname = qitem.itemname)));
```

Next, select the departments to which all items of type B are delivered, and save as a view.

```
CREATE VIEW v33b AS
    (SELECT deptname FROM qdept
        WHERE NOT EXISTS (SELECT * FROM qitem
            WHERE itemtype = 'B'
            AND NOT EXISTS (SELECT * FROM qdel
                WHERE qdel.deptname = qdept.deptname
                AND qdel.itemname = qitem.itemname)));
```

Now, find the suppliers that supply all items of type B to the departments that appear in both views.

```
SELECT splname FROM qspl
    WHERE NOT EXISTS (SELECT * FROM qitem
        WHERE itemtype = 'B'
        AND NOT EXISTS (SELECT * FROM qdel
            WHERE qdel.splno = qspl.splno
            AND qdel.itemname = qitem.itemname
            AND EXISTS
                (SELECT * FROM v33a
                    WHERE qdel.deptname = v33a.deptname)
                AND EXISTS
                    (SELECT * FROM v33b
                        WHERE qdel.deptname = v33b.deptname)));
```

34. An easy one COUNT

O **List the items delivered by exactly one supplier (i.e., list the items always delivered by the same supplier).**

A reasonably straightforward GROUP BY with an exact count.

```
SELECT itemname FROM qdel
   GROUP BY itemname HAVING COUNT(DISTINCT splno) = 1;
```

35. The only one

O **List the supplier and the item, where the supplier is the only deliverer of some item.**

For each item delivered, check to see whether there is no other delivery of this item by another supplier.

```
SELECT DISTINCT qspl.splno, splname, itemname
   FROM qspl, qdel del1
      WHERE qspl.splno = del1.splno
      AND itemname NOT IN
         (SELECT itemname FROM qdel
            WHERE qdel.splno <> del1.splno);
```

36. At least some number

O **List the suppliers that deliver at least 10 items.**

This is an easy GROUP BY with a count condition.

```
SELECT qspl.splno, splname FROM qdel, qspl
   WHERE qdel.splno = qspl.splno
      GROUP BY qspl.splno, splname
         HAVING COUNT(DISTINCT qdel.itemname) >= 10;
```

37. A three-table join

O **For each item, give its type, the departments that sell the item, and the floor locations of these departments.**

A three-table join is rather easy after all the divides.

```
SELECT qitem.itemname, itemtype, qdept.deptname, deptfloor
   FROM qitem, qsale, qdept
      WHERE qsale.itemname = qitem.itemname
      AND qsale.deptname = qdept.deptname;
```

38. Using NOT IN like NOT EXISTS

○ **List the departments for which each item delivered to the department is delivered to some other department as well.**

This is another variation on double negative logic. The query can be rewritten as, *Find departments where there is not a delivery where a supplier does not deliver the item to some other department*. In this situation, the NOT IN clause is like a NOT EXISTS.

```
SELECT DISTINCT deptname FROM qdel del1
    WHERE NOT EXISTS
        (SELECT * FROM qdel del2
            WHERE del2.deptname = del1.deptname
            AND itemname NOT IN
                (SELECT itemname FROM qdel del3
                    WHERE del3.deptname <> del1.deptname));
```

39. Minus after GROUP BY

○ **List each item delivered to at least two departments by each supplier that delivers it.**

The inner query uses grouping to identify items delivered by the same supplier to one department at most. The remaining items must be delivered by the same supplier to more than one department.

```
SELECT DISTINCT itemname FROM qdel
    WHERE itemname NOT IN
        (SELECT itemname FROM qdel
            GROUP BY itemname, splno
                HAVING COUNT(DISTINCT deptname) < 2);
```

40. Something to all

○ **List the items that are delivered only by the suppliers that deliver something to all the departments.**

This is a variation on query 25 with the additional requirement, handled by the innermost query, that the supplier delivers to all departments. Specifying that all departments get a delivery means that the number of departments to which a supplier delivers (GROUP BY splno HAVING COUNT (DISTINCT deptname)) must equal the number of departments that sell items (SELECT COUNT(*) FROM qdept WHERE deptname NOT IN ('Management', 'Marketing', 'Personnel', 'Accounting', 'Purchasing')).

```
SELECT DISTINCT itemname FROM qdel del1
   WHERE NOT EXISTS
      (SELECT * FROM qdel del2
         WHERE del2.itemname = del1.itemname
         AND splno NOT IN
            (SELECT splno FROM qdel
               GROUP BY splno HAVING COUNT(DISTINCT deptname) =
                  (SELECT COUNT(*) FROM qdept
                     WHERE deptname NOT IN ('Management',
                        'Marketing', 'Personnel',
                        'Accounting', 'Purchasing'))));
```

41. Intersection (AND)

❍ **List the items delivered by Nepalese Corp. and sold in the Navigation department.**

The two parts to the query — the delivery and the sale — are intersected using AND.

```
SELECT DISTINCT itemname FROM qdel, qspl
   WHERE qdel.splno = qspl.splno
      AND splname = 'Nepalese Corp.'
AND itemname IN
   (SELECT itemname FROM qsale
      WHERE deptname = 'Navigation');
```

42. Union (OR)

❍ **List the items delivered by Nepalese Corp. or sold in the Navigation department.**

The two parts are the same as query 41, but the condition is OR rather than AND.

```
SELECT DISTINCT itemname FROM qdel, qspl
   WHERE qdel.splno = qspl.splno
      AND splname = 'Nepalese Corp.'
OR itemname IN
   (SELECT itemname FROM qsale
      WHERE deptname = 'Navigation');
```

43. Intersection/union

❍ **List the departments selling items of type E that are delivered by Nepalese Corp. and/or are sold by the Navigation department.**

The inner query handles the and/or with OR. Remember OR can mean that the items are in both tables or one table. The outer query identifies the departments that receive the delivered items, which satisfy the inner query.

```
SELECT DISTINCT deptname FROM qsale
   WHERE itemname IN
   (SELECT qitem.itemname FROM qitem, qdel, qspl
      WHERE qitem.itemname = qdel.itemname
      AND qdel.splno = qspl.splno
      AND splname = 'Nepalese Corp.'
      AND itemtype = 'E')
   OR itemname IN
      (SELECT itemname FROM qsale
         WHERE deptname = 'Navigation');
```

44. Averaging with a condition

○ **Find the average salary of the employees in the Clothes department.**

This is very easy, especially after conquering the divides.

```
SELECT AVG(empsalary) FROM qemp
   WHERE deptname = 'Clothes';
```

45. Averaging with grouping

○ **Find, for each department, the average salary of the employees.**

Another straightforward averaging query.

```
SELECT deptname, AVG(empsalary) FROM qemp
   GROUP BY deptname;
```

46. Average with a join, condition, and grouping

○ **Find, for each department on the second floor, the average salary of the employees.**

A combination of several averaging queries.

```
SELECT qdept.deptname, AVG(empsalary) FROM qemp, qdept
   WHERE qemp.deptname = qdept.deptname
      AND deptfloor = 2
         GROUP BY qdept.deptname;
```

47. Averaging with multiple joins

○ **Find, for each department that sells items of type E, the average salary of the employees.**

Four joins, a condition, and grouping—this is not a particularly challenging query. The multiple joins are needed to get the data required for the answer into a single row.

```
SELECT qdept.deptname, AVG(empsalary)
   FROM qemp, qdept, qsale, qitem
      WHERE qemp.deptname = qdept.deptname
      AND qdept.deptname = qsale.deptname
      AND qsale.itemname = qitem.itemname
      AND itemtype = 'E'
         GROUP BY qdept.deptname;
```

48. Complex counting

○ **What is the number of different items delivered by each supplier that delivers to all departments?**

First, determine the suppliers that deliver to each department, excluding administrative departments. The inner query handles this part of the main query. Second, count the number of different items delivered by the suppliers identified by the inner query.

```
SELECT splname, COUNT(DISTINCT itemname)
   FROM qdel del1, qspl
      WHERE del1.splno = qspl.splno
      AND NOT EXISTS
         (SELECT * FROM qdept
            WHERE deptname NOT IN
               (SELECT deptname FROM qdel
                  WHERE qdel.splno = del1.splno)
                  AND deptname NOT IN
                     ('Management', 'Marketing', 'Personnel',
                      'Accounting', 'Purchasing'))
                  GROUP BY splname;
```

49. Summing with joins and conditions

○ **Find the total number of items of type E sold by the departments on the second floor.**

Summing is very similar to averaging (see query 47).

```
SELECT SUM(saleqty) FROM qitem, qsale, qdept
   WHERE qitem.itemname = qsale.itemname
   AND qdept.deptname = qsale.deptname
   AND itemtype = 'E'
   AND deptfloor = 2;
```

50. Summing with joins, conditions, and grouping

○ **Find, for each item, the total quantity sold by the departments on the second floor.**

Conceptually, this query is similar to query 47.

```
SELECT itemname, SUM(saleqty) FROM qsale, qdept
   WHERE qsale.deptname = qdept.deptname
   AND deptfloor = 2
      GROUP BY itemname;
```

51. Advanced summing

○ **List suppliers that deliver a total quantity of items of types C and N that is altogether greater than 100.**

The difficult part of this query, and it is not too difficult, is to write the condition for selecting items of type C and N. Notice that the query says C and N,[3] but don't translate this to (`itemtype = 'C' AND itemtype = 'N'`) because an item cannot be both types simultaneously. The query means that for any delivery, the item should be type C or type N.

```
SELECT qdel.splno, splname FROM qspl, qdel, qitem
   WHERE qspl.splno = qdel.splno
   AND qitem.itemname = qdel.itemname
   AND (itemtype = 'C' OR itemtype = 'N')
      GROUP BY qdel.splno, splname HAVING SUM(delqty) > 100;
```

52. Comparing to the average with a join

○ **List the employees in the Accounting department and the difference between their salaries and the average salary of the department.**

The key to solving this query is placing the average salary for Accounting employees in the same row as the department salary data. This is a two-stage process. You first need to determine the average salary of the employees in all departments and save this as a view. Then, join this view to the qemp table matching the Accounting department's name. Once the average departmental salary has been concatenated to each row, the query is straightforward.

```
CREATE VIEW v52(deptname, dpavgsal) AS
   SELECT deptname, AVG(empsalary) FROM qemp
      GROUP BY deptname;

SELECT empfname, (empsalary - dpavgsal) FROM v52, qemp
   WHERE v52.deptname = qemp.deptname
   AND qemp.deptname = 'Accounting';
```

---

3.   Aren't you glad that this isn't a bad pun about a TV network?

53. Comparing to the average with a product

O **List the employees in the Accounting department and the difference between their salaries and the average salary of all the departments.**

This is a slight variation on the previous query except that a join is not used to combine the data from the view with the employee table. The view is a single-row-and-column table containing the average salary for the organization. To concatenate this row with the data for employees in the Accounting department, we use a product instead of a join. Remember, a product is specified by simply listing the names of the two tables.

```
CREATE VIEW v53(allavgsal) AS
    SELECT AVG(empsalary) FROM qemp;

SELECT empfname, (empsalary - allavgsal) FROM v53, qemp
    WHERE deptname = 'Accounting';
```

54. Averaging with multiple grouping

O **What is, for each supplier, the average number of items per department that the supplier delivers?**

Here, the averaging is broken into two levels: department within supplier.

```
SELECT qdel.splno, splname, deptname, AVG(delqty)
    FROM qspl, qdel
        WHERE qspl.splno = qdel.splno
            GROUP BY qdel.splno, splname, deptname;
```

55. More than the average with grouping

O **For each department, find the average salary of the employees who earn more than the average salary of the department.**

The inner query determines the average salary of each department. Look carefully at how it handles matching departments.

```
SELECT deptname, AVG(empsalary) FROM qemp out
        WHERE empsalary > (SELECT AVG(empsalary) FROM qemp inn
            WHERE out.deptname = inn.deptname)
                GROUP BY deptname;
```

56. The simplest average

O **Give the overall average of the salaries in all departments.**

This is a very simple query.

```
SELECT AVG(empsalary) FROM qemp;
```

Another possible interpretation is that you have to find the total average salary after you determine the average salary for each department. To do this, you would first create a view containing the average salary for each department (see query 52) and then find the average of these average salaries.[4]

```
SELECT AVG(dpavgsal) FROM v52;
```

57. Difference from the average

○ **List each employee's salary, the average salary within that person's department, and the difference between the employees' salaries and the average salary of the department.**

This is reasonably easy once you have created a view of departmental average salaries.

```
SELECT empfname, empsalary,
    dpavgsal, (empsalary - dpavgsal)
        FROM v52, qemp
            WHERE v52.deptname = qemp.deptname;
```

58. Averaging with multiple joins, multiple grouping, and a condition

○ **What is the average delivery quantity of items of type N delivered by each company who delivers them?**

This is similar to query 54.

```
SELECT qdel.splno, splname, qdel.itemname, AVG(delqty)
    FROM qdel, qspl, qitem
        WHERE qdel.splno = qspl.splno
        AND qdel.itemname = qitem.itemname
        AND itemtype = 'N'
            GROUP BY qdel.splno, splname, qdel.itemname;
```

59. Detailed averaging

○ **What is the average delivery quantity of items of type N delivered by each supplier to each department (given that the supplier delivers items of type N to the department)?**

Now we take averaging to three levels — supplier, department, item. You can take averaging to as many levels as you like.

---

4. Some implementations of SQL do not permit scalar operations on views; so, you may not be able to execute this query.

```
SELECT qdel.splno, splname, deptname, qdel.itemname, AVG(delqty)
    FROM qdel, qspl, qitem
        WHERE qdel.splno = qspl.splno
        AND qdel.itemname = qitem.itemname
        AND itemtype = 'N'
            GROUP BY qdel.splno, splname, deptname, qdel.itemname;
```

60. Counting pairs

○ **What is the number of supplier-department pairs in which the supplier delivers at least one item of type E to the department?**

First, find all the supplier-department pairs. Without DISTINCT, you would get duplicates, which would make the subsequent count wrong.

```
CREATE VIEW v60 AS
    (SELECT DISTINCT splno, deptname FROM qdel, qitem
        WHERE qdel.itemname = qitem.itemname
        AND itemtype = 'E');
```

Now, it is a simple count.

```
SELECT COUNT(*) FROM v60;
```

61. No Booleans

○ **Is it true that all the departments that sell items of type C are located on the third floor? (The result can be a Boolean 1 or 0, meaning yes or no.)**

SQL cannot return *true* or *false*; it always returns a table. But you can get close to Boolean results by using counts. If we get a count of zero for the following query, there are no departments that are not on the third floor that sell items of type C.

```
SELECT COUNT(*) FROM qdept
    WHERE deptfloor <> 3
    AND EXISTS
        (SELECT * FROM qsale, qitem
            WHERE qsale.itemname = qitem.itemname
            AND qsale.deptname = qdept.deptname
            AND itemtype = 'C');
```

Then you need to check that departments on the third floor sell items of type C. If the second query returns a nonzero value, then it is true that departments that sell items of type C are located on the third floor.

```
SELECT COUNT(*) FROM qdept
   WHERE deptfloor = 3
   AND EXISTS
      (SELECT * FROM qsale, qitem
          WHERE qsale.itemname = qitem.itemname
          AND qsale.deptname = qdept.deptname
          AND itemtype = 'C');
```

Summary

Although SQL is a powerful retrieval language, alas, formulation of common business queries is not always trivial.

Key terms and concepts

SELECT

Exercises

Here is an opportunity to display your SQL mastery.

1. List the green items of type C.
2. Find the names of green items sold by the Recreation department.
3. Of those items delivered, find the items not delivered to the Books department.
4. Find the departments that have never sold a geopositioning system.
5. Find the departments that have sold compasses and at least two other items.
6. Find the departments that sell at least four items.
7. Find the employees who are in a different department from their manager's department.
8. Find the employees whose salary is less than half that of their manager's.
9. Find the green items sold by no department on the second floor.
10. Find the items delivered by all suppliers.
11. Find the items delivered by at least two suppliers.
12. Find the items not delivered by Nepalese Corp.
13. Find the items sold by at least two departments.
14. Find the items delivered for which there have been no sales.
15. Find the items delivered to all departments except Administration.
16. Find the name of the highest-paid employee in the Marketing department.
17. Find the names of employees who make 10 percent less than the average salary.
18. Find the names of employees with a salary greater than the minimum salary paid to a manager.
19. Find the names of suppliers that do not supply compasses or geopositioning systems.
20. Find the number of employees with a salary under $10,000.
21. Find the number of items of type A sold by the departments on the third floor.
22. Find the number of units sold of each item.
23. Find the green items delivered by all suppliers.
24. Find the supplier that delivers no more than one item.

25. Find the suppliers that deliver to all departments.
26. Find the suppliers that deliver to all the departments that also receive deliveries from supplier 102.
27. Find the suppliers that have never delivered a compass.
28. Find the type A items delivered by São Paulo Manufacturing.
29. Find, for each department, its floor and the average salary in the department.
30. If Nancy's boss has a boss, who is it?
31. List each employee and the difference between his or her salary and the average salary of his or her department.
32. List the departments on the second floor that contain more than one employee.
33. List the departments on the second floor.
34. List the names of employees who earn more than the average salary of employees in the Shoe department.
35. List the names of items delivered by each supplier. Arrange the report by supplier name, and within supplier name, list the items in alphabetical order.
36. List the names of managers who supervise only one person.
37. List the number of employees in each department.
38. List the green items delivered by exactly one supplier.
39. Whom does Todd manage?
40. List the departments that have not sold all green items.
41. Find the first name of Sophie's boss.
42. Find the names of employees who make less than half their manager's salary.
43. List the names of each manager and their employees arranged by manager's name and employee's name within manager.
44. Who earns the lowest salary?
45. List the names of employees who earn less than the minimum salary of the Marketing department.
46. List the items sold by every department to which all brown items have been delivered.
47. List the department and the item where the department is the only seller of that item.
48. List the brown items sold by the Books department and delivered by All Seasons.
49. Which department has the highest average salary?
50. List the supplier that delivers all and only brown items.

Data for tables

QSALE

saleno	saleqty	*itemname*	*deptname*
1001	2	Boots—snakeproof	Clothes
1002	1	Pith helmet	Clothes
1003	1	Sextant	Navigation
1004	3	Hat—polar explorer	Clothes
1005	5	Pith helmet	Equipment
1006	1	Pocket knife—Nile	Clothes
1007	1	Pocket knife—Nile	Recreation
1008	1	Compass	Navigation
1009	1	Geopositioning system	Navigation
1010	5	Map measure	Navigation
1011	1	Geopositioning system	Books
1012	1	Sextant	Books
1013	3	Pocket knife—Nile	Books
1014	1	Pocket knife—Nile	Navigation
1015	1	Pocket knife—Nile	Equipment
1016	1	Sextant	Clothes
1017	1	Sextant	Equipment
1018	1	Sextant	Recreation
1019	1	Sextant	Furniture
1020	1	Pocket knife—Nile	Furniture
1021	1	Exploring in 10 Easy Lessons	Books
1022	1	How to Win Foreign Friends	Books
1023	1	Compass	Books
1024	1	Pith helmet	Books
1025	1	Elephant polo stick	Recreation
1026	1	Camel saddle	Recreation

QSPL

splno	splname
101	Global Books & Maps
102	Nepalese Corp.
103	All Sports Manufacturing
104	Sweatshops Unlimited
105	All Points, Inc.
106	São Paulo Manufacturing

QITEM

itemname	itemtype	itemcolor
Boots—snakeproof	C	Green
Camel saddle	R	Brown
Compass	N	—
Elephant polo stick	R	Bamboo
Exploring in 10 Easy Lessons	B	—
Geopositioning system	N	—
Hammock	F	Khaki
Hat—polar explorer	C	White
How to Win Foreign Friends	B	—
Map case	E	Brown
Map measure	N	—
Pith helmet	C	Khaki
Pocket knife—Avon	E	Brown
Pocket knife—Nile	E	Brown
Safari chair	F	Khaki
Safari cooking kit	F	—
Sextant	N	—
Stetson	C	Black
Tent—2 person	F	Khaki
Tent—8 person	F	Khaki

QDEPT

deptname	deptfloor	deptphone	empno
Management	5	34	1
Books	1	81	4
Clothes	2	24	4
Equipment	3	57	3
Furniture	4	14	3
Navigation	1	41	3
Recreation	2	29	4
Accounting	5	35	5
Purchasing	5	36	7
Personnel	5	37	9
Marketing	5	38	2

QDEL

delno	delqty	itemname	deptname	splno
51	50	Pocket knife—Nile	Navigation	105
52	10	Pocket knife—Nile	Books	105
53	10	Pocket knife—Nile	Clothes	105
54	10	Pocket knife—Nile	Equipment	105
55	10	Pocket knife—Nile	Furniture	105
56	10	Pocket knife—Nile	Recreation	105
57	50	Compass	Navigation	101
58	10	Geopositioning system	Navigation	101
59	10	Map measure	Navigation	101
60	25	Map case	Navigation	101
61	2	Sextant	Navigation	101
62	1	Sextant	Equipment	105
63	20	Compass	Equipment	103
64	1	Geopositioning system	Books	103
65	15	Map measure	Navigation	103
66	1	Sextant	Books	103
67	5	Sextant	Recreation	102
68	3	Sextant	Navigation	104
69	5	Boots—snakeproof	Clothes	105
70	15	Pith helmet	Clothes	105
71	1	Pith helmet	Clothes	101
72	1	Pith helmet	Clothes	102
73	1	Pith helmet	Clothes	103
74	1	Pith helmet	Clothes	104
75	5	Pith helmet	Navigation	105
76	5	Pith helmet	Books	105
77	5	Pith helmet	Equipment	105
78	5	Pith helmet	Furniture	105
79	5	Pith helmet	Recreation	105
80	10	Pocket knife—Nile	Navigation	102
81	1	Compass	Navigation	102
82	1	Geopositioning system	Navigation	102
83	10	Map measure	Navigation	102
84	5	Map case	Navigation	102
85	5	Compass	Books	102
86	5	Pocket knife—Avon	Recreation	102
87	5	Tent—2 person	Recreation	102
88	2	Tent—8 person	Recreation	102
89	5	Exploring in 10 Easy Lessons	Navigation	102
90	5	How to Win Foreign Friends	Navigation	102
91	10	Exploring in 10 Easy Lessons	Books	102
92	10	How to Win Foreign Friends	Books	102

93	2	Exploring in 10 Easy Lessons	Recreation	102
94	2	How to Win Foreign Friends	Recreation	102
95	5	Compass	Equipment	105
96	2	Boots—snakeproof	Equipment	105
97	20	Pith helmet	Equipment	106
98	20	Pocket knife—Nile	Equipment	106
99	1	Sextant	Equipment	106
100	3	Hat—polar explorer	Clothes	105
101	3	Stetson	Clothes	105

QEMP

empno	empfname	empsalary	deptname	bossno
1	Alice	75000	Management	
2	Ned	45000	Marketing	1
3	Andrew	25000	Marketing	2
4	Clare	22000	Marketing	2
5	Todd	38000	Accounting	1
6	Nancy	22000	Accounting	5
7	Brier	43000	Purchasing	1
8	Sarah	56000	Purchasing	7
9	Sophie	35000	Personnel	1
10	Sanjay	15000	Navigation	3
11	Rita	15000	Books	4
12	Gigi	16000	Clothes	4
13	Maggie	16000	Clothes	4
14	Paul	11000	Equipment	3
15	James	15000	Equipment	3
16	Pat	15000	Furniture	3
17	Mark	15000	Recreation	3

Section 3

Database Architectures and Implementations

We shape our buildings: thereafter they shape us.
Winston Churchill, *Time*, 12 September 1960

A database architecture is a design for the storage and processing of data. Organizations strive to find an architecture that simultaneously achieves multiple goals:

1. It responds to queries in a timely manner.
2. It minimizes the cost of processing data.
3. It minimizes the cost of storing data.
4. It minimizes the cost of data delivery.

This section deals with the approaches that can be used to achieve each of these goals. We begin by tracing the development of schema architectures and conclude with a description of the American National Standards Institute/Standards Planning and Requirements Committee (ANSI/SPARC) architecture.

Development of data architectures

Remember that first program you wrote? It was probably very simple—something that added two numbers and printed the result. More than likely, the two numbers to be added were *hard coded* into the program. If you wanted to add a different pair of numbers, you had to edit the program and rerun it. Most beginners' programs exemplify the situation where programs and data are not separated—also known as a no-schema architecture (see Figure S3-1). A schema is a representation of the data's structure.

As your programming skills advanced, you learned it was more efficient to separate a program and its data. Instead of hard-coding data, you used variable names to represent data values, and your program read data from a file or asked the user to input values. Although

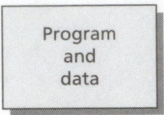

Figure S3-1. No-schema architecture

you had separated the program and the data, essentially you still saw the data exactly as the program saw it. Your internal schemas were identical: This approach is known as a one-schema architecture (see Figure S3-2). One advantage of separating the data from a program is that the same data can be used by several different programs, or the same program can run several different sets of data.

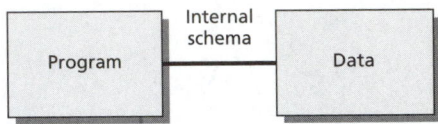

Figure S3-2. One-schema architecture

Many users, however, do not want to know how data are represented in a program or a file. They simply want a view of the data that matches their needs. As a result, the idea of an external schema emerged—charting the users' view of the data. Thus we have a two-schema architecture (see Figure S3-3), which separates the user from the data. Most word processors have a two-schema architecture; your view of the words you type is quite different from what is actually stored.

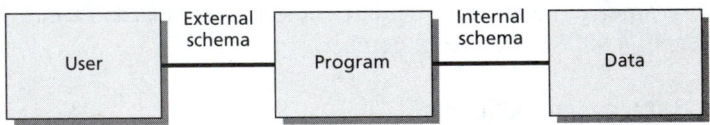

Figure S3-3. Two-schema architecture

The major shortcoming of a two-schema architecture is that every time a physical data structure is changed, programs have to be changed.[1] This problem is overcome by introducing a conceptual schema and three-level architecture to separate a program further from the data.

---

1. You may notice that some word-processing files are not compatible across different versions of the same product. This is an example of how changing the internal schema—the data storage structures—requires the program to change. Of course, conversion programs are usually provided to bridge the gap.

ANSI/SPARC

In 1972, ANSI established a committee to examine standardization of database technology. This study group, officially known as the ANSI/X3/SPARC Study Group on Data Base Management, produced a general architecture for describing a database and its various interfaces, the only area that it concluded was suitable for standardization. Its framework for database interfaces is known as the ANSI/SPARC architecture.[2]

The ANSI/SPARC architecture consists of three schemas or levels (the word favored by the group): internal, conceptual, and external (see Figure S3-4).

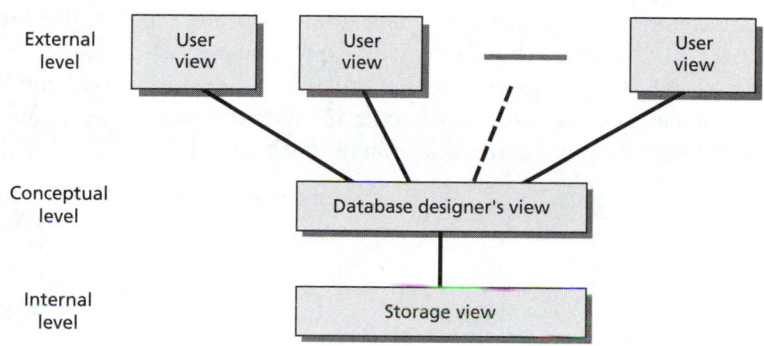

Figure S3-4. The ANSI/SPARC architecture

The external level

The external level represents a user's view of the system. As the diagram shows, there can be many user views, and, as we learned previously, multiple views can be defined for a single SQL table by using CREATE VIEW. These views can be tailored to the needs and data access privileges of any authorized user.

The conceptual level

The conceptual level is the database designer's view, which is completely unrestricted and includes all the files and all the fields in each file. The database designer sees everything.

The conceptual level is the mapping of the data model to the database management system's data definition language (DDL). In the case of SQL, CREATE TABLE specifies the conceptual level. Because data independence is a key goal of data administration, the selected DDL should not require any consideration of storage structure or data access mech-

2. Tsichritzis, D. C., and A. Klug. 1978. The ANSI/X3/SPARC DBMS framework: Report of the study group on data base management systems. *Information Systems* 3.
    Rosen, Bruce K., and Margaret Henderson Law. 1989. *Guide to data administration*. Gaithersburg, MD: Information Technology Laboratory; Washington, D.C.: U.S. Dept. of Commerce.

anisms. The conceptual level may also include definitions of security and integrity level checks (e.g., GRANT and foreign key constraints). Ideally, this level completely describes the database without taking physical considerations into account.

The internal level

As the chapters in this section will discuss, the internal level—the lowest-level description of a database—is concerned with the way data are stored. Although it describes attributes such as types of records stored, indexes, and record sequencing, the internal level does not deal with the device-specific attributes.

Chapter 11 covers database structure and storage alternatives. It provides the knowledge necessary to determine an appropriate data storage structure and device for a given situation. Chapter 12 addresses the fundamental questions of where to store the data and where they should be processed. An alternative to the relational data model, the object-oriented database, is considered in Chapter 13. We conclude this section with a discussion of spatial and temporal data management in Chapter 14.

11

Data Structure and Storage

The modern age has a false sense of superiority because it relies on the mass of knowledge that it can use, but what is important is the extent to which knowledge is organized and mastered.

Goethe, 1810

Learning objectives

Students completing this chapter will, for a given situation, be able to recommend

- ❖ a data storage structure;
- ❖ a storage device.

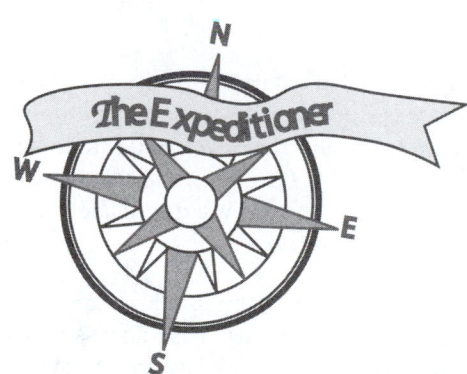

Every quarter, The Expeditioner's IS group measures the quality of its service. It asks users to assess whether their hardware and software are adequate for their jobs, whether IS service is reliable and responsive, and whether they thought the IS staff were helpful and knowledgeable.[1] The most recent survey revealed that some were experiencing unreasonably long delays for what were relatively simple queries. How could the IS group *tune* the database to reduce response time?

As though some grumpy users were not enough, Alice dumped another problem on Ned's desk. The Marketing department had

---

1. For more details, see Watson, R. T., L. F. Pitt, and C. B. Kavan. 1998. Information systems service quality: Lessons from two longitudinal case studies. *MIS Quarterly* 23 (1):61–79.

complained to her that the product database had been down for 30 minutes during a peak selling period. What was Ned going to do to prevent such an occurrence in the future?

Ned had just finished reading Alice's memo about the database problem when the Chief Accountant poked his head in the door. Somewhat agitated, he was waving an article from his favorite accounting journal that claimed that data stored on magnetic tape decayed with time. So what was he to do with all those financial records on magnetic tapes stored in the fireproof safe in his office? Were the magnetic bits likely to disappear tonight, tomorrow, or next week? "This business had lasted for centuries with paper ledgers. Why, you can still read the financial transactions for 1527," which he did whenever he had a few moments to spare. "But, if what I read is true, I soon won't be able to read the balance sheet from last year!"

It was just after 10 A.M. on a Monday, and Ned was faced with finding a way to improve response time, ensure that databases were continually available during business hours, and protect the long-term existence of financial records. It was going to be a long week.

Introduction

The following pages explore territory that is not normally the concern of application programmers or database users. Fortunately, the relational model keeps data structures and data access methods hidden. Nevertheless, an overview of what happens *under the hood* is part of a well-rounded education in data management.

Data structures and access methods are the province of the person responsible for physically designing the database so that it responds in a timely manner to both queries and maintenance operations. Of course, there may be installations where application programmers have such responsibilities, and in these situations you will need to know physical database design.

Data structures

An in-depth consideration of the internal level of database architecture provides an understanding of the basic structures and access mechanisms underlying database technology. As you will see, the overriding concern of the internal level is to minimize disk access. In dealing with this level, we will speak in terms of files, records, and fields rather than the relational database terms of tables, rows, and columns. We do this because the discussion extends beyond the relational model to file structures in general.

The time required to access data on a magnetic disk, the usual storage device for databases, is relatively long compared to that for main memory. Disk access times are measured in milliseconds (10^{-3}), and main memory access times are referred to in nanoseconds (10^{-9}). There are generally around five orders of magnitude difference between disk and main memory access— it takes about 10^5 times longer. This distinction is more meaningful if placed in an everyday context; it is like asking someone a question by phone or writing them a letter. The phone response takes seconds, and the written response takes days.

For many business applications, slow disk drives are a bottleneck. The computer often must wait for a disk to retrieve data before it can continue processing a request for information. This delay means that customers are also kept waiting. Appropriate selection of data structures and data access methods can considerably reduce delays. Database designers have two options: decrease disk read/write head movement or reduce disk accesses. Before considering these options, we need a general model of database access.

Database access

A three-layer model provides a framework for thinking about minimization of data access (see Figure 11-1). This is a generic model, and a particular database management system (DBMS) may implement the approach using a different number of layers. For simplicity, the discussion is based on retrieving a single record in a file, although the principles also apply to the retrieval of multiple records or an entire file.

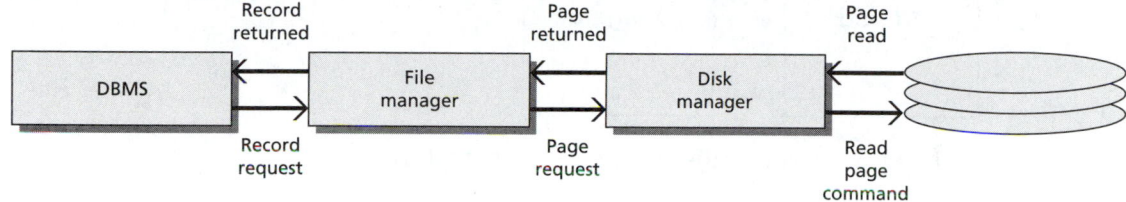

Figure 11-1. Database access layers

1. The DBMS determines which record is required and passes a request to the file manager to retrieve a particular record in a file.

2. The **file manager** converts this request into the address of the unit of storage (usually called a page) containing the specified record. A **page** is the minimum amount of storage accessed at one time and is typically around 1–4 kbytes. A page will often contain several short records (e.g., 200 bytes), but a long record (e.g., 10 kbytes) might be spread over several pages. In this example, we assume that records are shorter than a page.

3. The **disk manager** determines the physical location of the page, issues the retrieval instructions, and passes the page to the file manager.

4. The file manager extracts the requested record from the page and passes it to the DBMS.

The disk manager

The disk manager is that part of the operating system responsible for physical I/O. It maintains a directory of the location of each page on the disk with all pages identified by a unique page number. The disk manager's main functions are to retrieve pages, replace pages, and keep track of free pages.

Page retrieval requires the disk manager to convert the page number to a physical address and issue the command to read the physical location. Since a page can contain multiple records, when a record is updated, the disk manager must retrieve the relevant page, update the appropriate portion containing the record, and then replace the page without changing any of the other data on it.

The disk manager thinks of the disk as a collection of uniquely numbered pages (see Figure 11-2). Some of these pages are allocated to the storage of data, and others are unused. When additional storage space is required, the disk manager allocates a page address from the set of unused page addresses. When a page becomes free because a file or some records are deleted, the disk manager moves that page's address to the unallocated set.

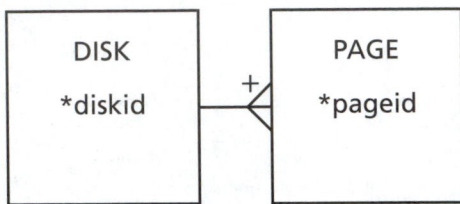

Figure 11-2. Disk manager's view of the world

The file manager

The file manager, a level above the disk manager, is concerned with the storage of files. It thinks of the disk as a set of stored files (see Figure 11-3). Each file has a unique file identifier, and each record within a file has a record identifier that is unique within that file.

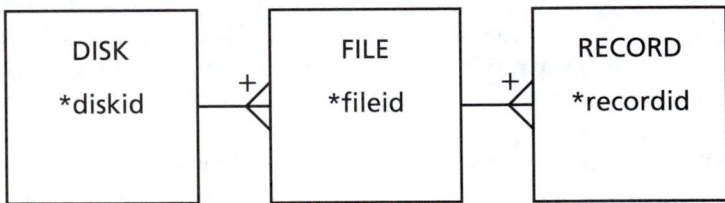

Figure 11-3. File manager's view of the world

The file manager can

❖   Create a file
❖   Delete a file
❖   Retrieve a record from a file
❖   Update a record in a file
❖   Add a new record to a file
❖   Delete a record from a file

Techniques for reducing head movement

All disk storage devices have some common features. They have one or more recording surfaces. Typically, a magnetic disk drive has multiple recording surfaces, and a removable magneto-optical disk has two surfaces. Data are stored on tracks on each surface.

The key characteristics of disk storage devices that affect database access are **rotational speed** and **access arm speed**. All disks spin at high speed. The rotational speed of a magnetic disk is in the range of 4,200 to 15,000 rpm. Reading or writing a page to disk requires moving the read/write head to the destination track and waiting for the storage address to come under the head. Because moving the head usually takes more time (e.g., about 9 msec) than waiting for the storage address to appear under it (e.g., about 4 msec), data access times can be reduced by minimizing the movement of the read/write head or by rotating the disk faster. Since rotational speed is set by the disk manufacturer, minimizing read/write head movement is the only option available to database designers.

Cylinders

Head movement is reduced by storing data that are likely to be accessed at the same time, such as records in a file, on the same track on a single surface. When a file is too large to fit on one track, then it can be stored on the same track on different surfaces; such a collection of tracks is called a cylinder. The advantage of cylinder storage is that all tracks can be accessed without moving the read/write head. When a cylinder is full, remaining data are stored on adjacent cylinders. Adjacent cylinders are ideal for sequential file storage because the record retrieval pattern is predefined — the first record is read, then the second, and so on.

Clustering

Cylinder storage can also be used when the record retrieval pattern has some degree of regularity to it. Consider the following familiar data model of Figure 11-4. Converting this data model to a relational database creates two tables. Conceptually, we may think of the data in each of the tables as being stored in adjacent cylinders. If, however, you frequently need to retrieve one row of `nation` and all the corresponding rows of `stock`, then `nation` and `stock` rows should be intermingled to minimize access time.

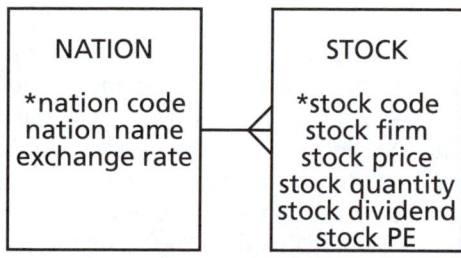

Figure 11-4. Data model for `nation` and `stock`

The term **clustering** denotes the concept that records that are frequently used together should be physically close together on a disk. Some DBMSs permit the database designer to specify clustering of different files to tune the database to reduce average access times. If usage patterns change, clustering specifications should be altered. Of course, clustering should be totally transparent to application programs and users.

Techniques for reducing disk accesses

Several techniques are used to accelerate retrieval by reducing disk accesses. The ideal situation is when the required record is obtained with a single disk access. In special circumstances, it may be possible to create a file where the primary key can convert directly to a unique disk address (e.g., the record with primary key 1 is stored at address 1001, the record with primary key 2 is stored at address 1002, and so on). If possible, this method of **direct addressing** should be used because it is the fastest form of data access; however, it is most unusual to find such a direct mapping between the primary key and a disk address. For example, it would not be feasible to use direct addressing with a student file that has a Social Security number as the primary, key because so many disk addresses would be wasted. Furthermore, direct addressing can work only for the primary key. What happens if there is a need for rapid retrieval on another field?

In most cases, database designers use features such as indexing, hashing, and linked lists. **Indexing**, a flexible and commonly used method of reducing disk accesses when searching for data, centers on the creation of a compact file containing the index field and the address of its corresponding record. The **B-tree** is a particular form of index structure that is widely used as the storage structure of relational DBMSs. **Hashing** is a direct access method based on using an arithmetic function to compute a disk address from a field within a file. A **linked list** is a data structure that accelerates data access by using pointers to show relationships existing between records.

Indexing

Consider the `item` file partially shown in Table 11-1. Let's assume that this file has 10,000 records and each record requires 1 kbyte, which is a page on the particular disk system used. Suppose a common query is to request all the items of a particular type. Such a query might be

○   **Find all items of type E.**

Regardless of the number of records with `itemtype = 'E'`, this query will require 10,000 disk accesses. Every record has to be retrieved and examined to determine the value of `itemtype`. For instance, if 20 percent of the items are of type E, then 8,000 of the disk accesses are wasted because they retrieve a record that is not required. The ideal situation would be to retrieve only those 2,000 records that contain an item of type E. We get closer to this ideal situation by creating a small file containing just the value of `itemtype` for each record and the address of the full record. This small file is called an index. Part of the `itemtype` index for `item` and the `item` table are shown in Figure 11-5.

Table 11-1: Portion of a 10,000 Record File

itemno	itemname	itemtype	itemcolor
1	Pocket knife—Nile	E	Brown
2	Pocket knife—Thames	E	Brown
3	Compass	N	—
4	Geopositioning system	N	—
5	Map measure	N	—
6	Hat—polar explorer	C	Red
7	Hat—polar explorer	C	White
8	Boots—snake proof	C	Green
9	Boots—snake proof	C	Black
10	Safari chair	F	Khaki

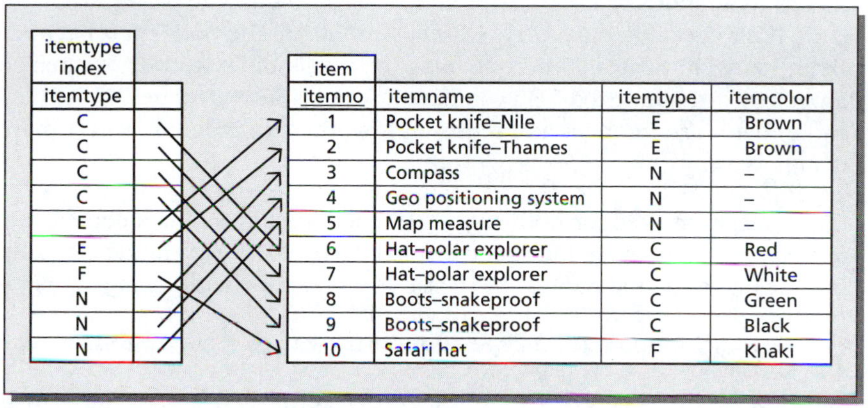

Figure 11-5. Part of the `itemtype` index

The `itemtype` index is a file. It contains 10,000 records and two fields. There is one record in the index for each record in `item`. The first field contains a value of `itemtype` and the second contains a pointer, an address, to the matching record of `item`. Notice that the index is in `itemtype` sequence. Storing the index in a particular order is another means of reducing disk accesses, as we will see shortly. The index is quite small. One byte is required for `itemtype` and four bytes for the pointer. So the total size of the index is 50 kbytes, which in this case is 50 pages of disk space.

Now consider finding all records with an item type of E. One approach is to read the entire index into memory, search it for type E items, and then use the pointers to retrieve the required records from `item`. This method requires 2,050 disk accesses — 50 to load the index and 2,000 accesses of `item`. Creating an index for `item` results in substantial savings in disk accesses for this example. Here, we assume that 20 percent of the records in `item` contained `itemtype = 'E'`. The number of disk accesses saved varies with the proportion of records meeting the query's criteria. If there are no records meeting the criteria, 9,950 disk accesses are avoided. At the other extreme, when all records meet the criteria, it takes 50 extra disk accesses to load the index.

The SQL (see page 250 for a detailed discussion of the syntax of the command) for creating the index is

```
CREATE INDEX itemtypeindx
   ON item (itemtype);
```

The entire index need not be read into memory. As you will see when we discuss tree structures, we can take advantage of the index's ordering to reduce disk accesses further. Nevertheless, the clear advantage of an index is evident: It speeds up retrieval by reducing disk accesses. Like many aspects of database management, however, indexes have a drawback. Adding a record to a file without an index requires a single disk write. Adding a record to an indexed file requires at least two, and maybe more, disk writes, because an entry has to be added to both the file and its index. The trade-off is between faster retrievals and slower updates. If there are many retrievals and few updates, then opt for an index, especially if the indexed field can have a wide variety of values. If the file is very volatile and updates are frequent and retrievals few, then an index may cost more disk accesses than it saves.

Indexes can be used for both sequential and direct access. Sequential access means that records are retrieved in the sequence defined by the values in the index. In our example, this means retrieving records in `itemtype` sequence with a range query such as

○   **Find all items with a type code in the range E through K.**

Direct access means records are retrieved according to one or more specified values. A sample query requiring direct access would be

○   **Find all items with a type code of E or N.**

Indexes are also handy for existence testing. Remember, the `EXISTS` clause of SQL returns *true* or *false* and not a value. An index can be searched to check whether the indexed field takes a particular value, but there is no need to access the file because no data are returned. The following query can be answered by an index search:

○   **Are there any items with a code of R?**

Multiple indexes

Multiple indexes can be created for a file. The `item` file could have an index defined on `itemcolor` or any other field. Multiple indexes may be used independently, as in this query:

○　**List red items.**

or jointly, with a query such as

○　**Find red items of type C.**

The preceding query can be solved by using the indexes for `itemtype` and `itemcolor` (see Figure 11-6).

itemtype index		itemcolor index	
itemtype	Disk address	itemcolor	Disk address
C	d6	Black	d9
C	d7	Brown	d1
C	d8	Brown	d2
C	d9	Green	d8
E	d1	Khaki	d10
E	d2	Red	d6
F	d10	White	d7
N	d3	–	d3
N	d4	–	d4
N	d5	–	d5

Figure 11-6. Indexes for fields `itemtype` and `itemcolor`

Examination of the `itemtype` index indicates that items of type C are stored at addresses d6, d7, d8, and d9. The only red item recorded in the `itemcolor` index is stored at address d6, and since it is the only record satisfying the query, it is the only record that needs to be retrieved.

Multiple indexes, as you would expect, involve a trade-off. Whenever a record is added or updated, each index must also be updated. Savings in disk accesses for retrieval are exchanged for additional disk accesses in maintenance. Again, you must consider the balance between retrieval and maintenance operations.

Indexes are not restricted to a single field. It is possible to specify an index that is a combination of several fields. For instance, if item type and color queries were very common, then an index based on the concatenation of both fields could be created. As a result, such queries could be answered with a search of a single index rather than scanning two indexes as in the preceding example. The SQL for creating the combined index is

```
CREATE INDEX typecolorindx
   ON item (itemtype, itemcolor);
```

Sparse indexes

Indexes are used to reduce disk accesses to accelerate retrieval. The simple model of an index introduced earlier suggests that the index contains an entry for each record of the file. If we can shrink the index to eliminate an entry for each record, we can save more disk accesses. Indeed, if an index is small enough, it, or key parts of it, can be retained continuously in primary memory.

There is a physical sequence to the records in a file. Records within a page are in a physical sequence, and pages on a disk are in a physical sequence. A file can also have a logical sequence, the ordering of the file on some field within a record. For instance, the `item` file could be ordered on `itemno`. Making the physical and logical sequences correspond is a way to save disk accesses. Remember that the `item` file was assumed to have a record size of 1,024 bytes, the same size as a page, and one record was stored per page. If we now assume the record size is 512 bytes, then two records are stored per page. Furthermore, suppose that `item` is physically stored in `itemno` sequence. The index can be compressed by storing `itemno` for the second record on each page and that page's address. The new index is shown in Figure 11-7.

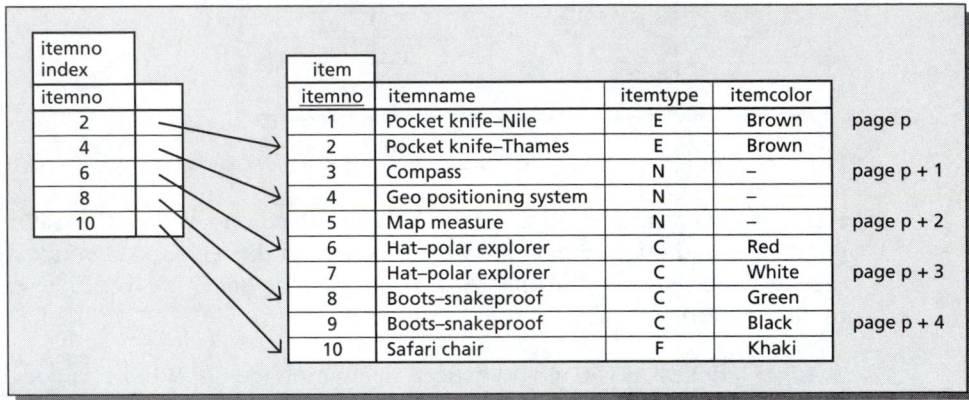

Figure 11-7. A sparse index for `item`

Consider the process of finding the record with `itemno = 7`. *First*, the index is scanned to find the first value for `itemno` that is greater than or equal to 7—the entry for `itemno = 8`. *Second*, the page on which this record is stored (page $p + 3$) is loaded into memory. *Third*, the required record is extracted from the page.

Indexes that take advantage of the physical sequencing of a file are known as *sparse* or nondense because they do not contain an entry for every value of the indexed field. (A *dense* index is one that contains an entry for every value of the indexed field.)

As you would expect, a sparse index has pros and cons. One major advantage is that it takes less storage space and so requires fewer disk accesses for reading. One disadvantage is that it can no longer be used for existence tests because it does not contain a value for every record in the file.

A file can have only one sparse index because it can have only one physical sequence. This field on which a sparse index is based is often called the **primary key**. Other indexes, which must be dense, are called *secondary indexes*.

In SQL, a sparse index is created using the CLUSTER option. For example, to define a sparse index on item the command is

```
CREATE INDEX itemnoindx
   ON item (itemno) CLUSTER;
```

B-trees

The B-tree is a particular form of index structure that is frequently the main storage structure for relational systems. It is also the basis for IBM's VSAM (Virtual Storage Access Method), the file structure underlying DB2. A B-tree is an efficient structure for both sequential and direct accessing of a file. It consists of two parts: the sequence set and the index set.

The **sequence set** is a single-level index to the file with pointers to the records (the vertical arrows in the lower part of Figure 11-8). It can be sparse or dense, but is normally dense. Entries in the sequence set are grouped into pages, and these pages are linked together (the horizontal arrows in Figure 11-8) so that the logical ordering of the sequence set is the physical ordering of the file. Thus, the file can be processed sequentially by processing the records pointed to by the first page (records with identifiers 1, 4, and 5), the records pointed to by the next logical page (6, 19, and 20), and so on.

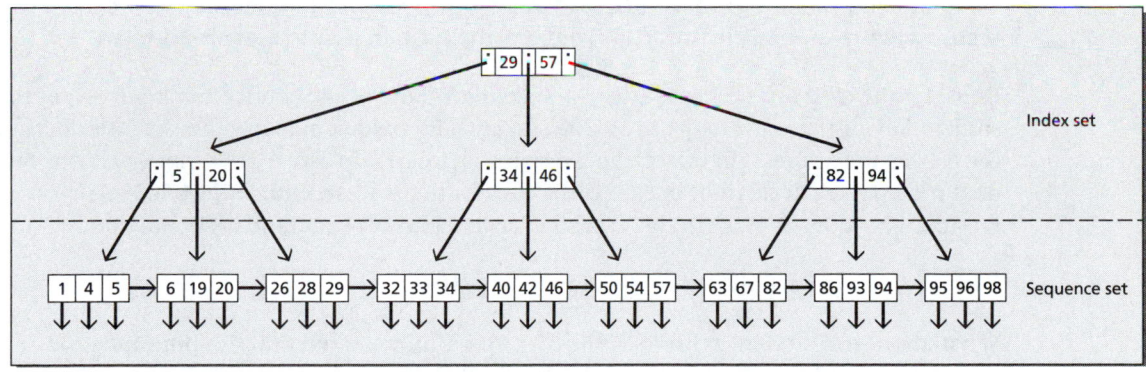

Figure 11-8. Structure of a simple B-tree

The **index set** is a tree-structured index to the sequence set. The top of the index set is a single node called the **root**. In this example, it contains two values (29 and 57) and three pointers. Records with an identifier less than or equal to 29 are found in the left branch, records with an identifier greater than 29 and less than or equal to 57 are found in the middle branch, and records with an identifier greater than 57 are found in the right branch. The three pointers are the page numbers of the left, middle, and right branches. The nodes at the next level have similar interpretations. The pointer to a particular record is found by moving down the tree until a node entry points to a value in the sequence set; this value can be used to retrieve the record. Thus, the index set provides direct access to the sequence set and then the data.

The index set is a B-tree. The combination of index set and sequence set is generally known as a B+ tree (**B-plus tree**). The B-tree shown in Figure 11-8 simplifies the concept in two ways. *First,* the number of data values and pointers for any given node is not restricted to 2 and 3, respectively. In its general form, a B-tree of order n can have at least n and no more than $2n$ data values. If it has k values, the B-tree will have $k + 1$ pointers (in the example tree, nodes have two data values, $k = 2$, and there are three, $k + 1 = 3$, pointers). *Second*, B-trees typically have free space to permit rapid insertion of data values and possible updating of pointers when a new record is added.

As usual, there is a trade-off with B-trees. Retrieval will be fastest when each node occupies one page and is packed with data values and pointers. This lack of free space will slow down the addition of new records, however. Most implementations of the B+ tree permit a specified portion of free space to be defined for both the index and sequence set.

Hashing

Hashing reduces disk accesses by allowing direct access to a file. As you know, direct accessing via an index requires at least two or more accesses. The index must be loaded and searched, and then the record retrieved. For some applications, direct accessing via an index is too slow. Hashing can reduce the number of accesses to almost one by using the value in some field (the **hash field**, which is usually the primary key) to compute a record's address. A **hash function** converts the hash field into a **hash address**.

Consider the case of a university that uses the nine-digit Social Security number (SSN) as the student key. If the university has 10,000 students, it could simply use the last four digits of the SSN as the address. In effect, the file space is broken up into 10,000 slots with one student record in each slot. For example, the data for the student with SSN 417-03-4356 would be stored at address 4356. In this case, the hash field is SSN, and the hash function is

hash address = remainder after dividing SSN by 10,000.

What about the student with SSN 532-67-4356? Unfortunately, the hashing function will give the same address because most hashing schemes cannot guarantee a unique hash address for every record. When two hash fields have the same address, they are called **synonyms**, and a **collision** is said to have occurred.

There are techniques for handling synonyms. Essentially, you store the colliding record in an overflow area and point to it from the hash address. Of course, more than two records can have the same hash address, which in turn creates a synonym chain. Figure 11-9 shows an example of hashing with a synonym chain. Three SSNs hash to the same address. The first record (417-03-4356) is stored at the hash address. The second record (532-67-4356) is stored in the overflow area and is connected by a pointer to the first record. The third record (891-55-4356) is also stored in the overflow area and connected by a pointer from the second record. Because each record contains the full key (SSN in this case), during retrieval the system can determine whether it has the correct record or should follow the chain to the next record.

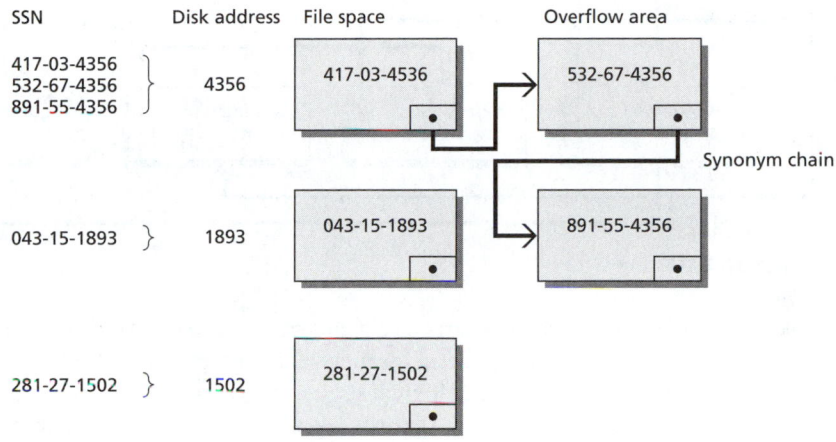

Figure 11-9. An example of hashing

If there are no synonyms, hashing gives very fast direct retrieval, taking only one disk access to retrieve a record. Even with a small percentage of synonyms, retrieval via hashing is very fast. Access time degrades, however, if there are long synonym chains.

There are a number of different approaches to defining hashing functions. The most common method is to divide by a prime and use the remainder as the address. Before adopting a particular hashing function, test several functions on a representative sample of the hash field. Compute the percentage of synonyms and the length of synonym chains for each potential hashing function and compare the results.

Of course, hashing has trade-offs. There can be only one hashing field. In contrast, a file can have many indexed fields. The file can no longer be processed sequentially because its physical sequence loses any logical meaning if the records are not in primary key sequence or are sequenced on any other field.

Linked lists

A **linked list** is a useful data structure for interfile clustering. Suppose that the query, *Find all stocks of country X,* is a frequent request. Disk accesses can be reduced by storing a nation and its corresponding stocks together in a linked list (see Figure 11-10).

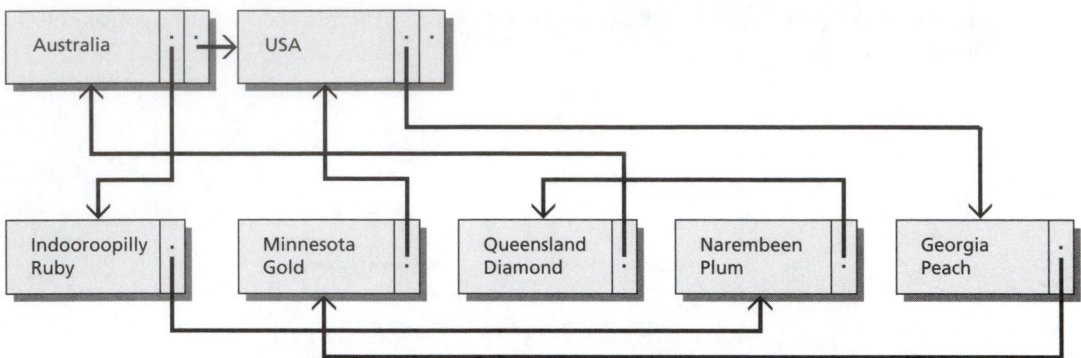

Figure 11-10. A linked list

In this example, we have two files: `nation` and `stock`. Records in `nation` are connected by pointers (e.g., the horizontal arrow between Australia and USA). The pointers are used to maintain the `nation` file in logical sequence (by nation, in this case). Each record in `nation` is linked to its `stock` records by a forward-pointing chain. The `nation` record for Australia points to the first `stock` record (Indooroopilly Ruby), which points to the next (Narembeen Plum), which points to the final record in the chain (Queensland Diamond). Notice that the last record in this `stock` chain points to the `stock` record to which the chain belongs (i.e., Australia). Similarly, there is a chain for the two USA stocks. In any chain, the records are maintained in logical sequence (by firm name, in this case).

This linked-list structure is also known as a parent/child structure. (The parent in this case is `nation` and the child is `stock`.) Although it is a suitable structure for representing a one-to-many (1:m) relationship, it is possible to depict more than one parent/child relationship. For example, stocks could be grouped into classes (e.g., high, medium, and low risk). A second chain linking all stocks of the same risk class can run through the file. Interfile clustering of a nation and its corresponding stocks will speed up access; so, the record for the parent Australia and its three children should be stored on one page. Similarly, all American stocks could be clustered with the USA record and so on for all other nations.

Of course, you expect some trade-offs. What happens with a query such as *Find the country in which Minnesota Gold is listed?* There is no quick way to find Minnesota Gold except by sequentially searching the `stock` file until the record is found and then following the chain to the parent `nation` record. This could take many disk accesses. One way to circumvent this is to build an index or hashing scheme for `stock` so that any record can be found directly. Building an index for the parent, `nation`, will speed up access as well.

Linked lists come in a variety of flavors:

❖ Lists that have two-way pointers, both forward and backward, speed up deletion.
❖ For some lists, every child record has a parent pointer. This helps prevent chain traversal when the query is concerned with finding the parent of a particular child.

Bitmap index

A **bitmap index** uses a single bit, rather than multiple bytes, to indicate the specific value of a field. For example, instead of using three bytes to represent *red* as an item's color, the color red is represented by a single bit. The relative position of the bit within a string of bits is then mapped to a record address.

Conceptually, you can think of a bitmap as a matrix. Figure 11-11 shows a bitmap containing details of an item's color and code. An item can have three possible colors; so, three bits are required, and two bits are needed for the two codes for the item. Thus, you can see that, in general, n bits are required if a field can have n possible values.

itemcode	color			code		Disk address
	Red	Green	Blue	A	N	
1001	0	0	1	0	1	d1
1002	1	0	0	1	0	d2
1003	1	0	0	1	0	d3
1004	0	1	0	1	0	d4

Figure 11-11. A bitmap index

When an item has a large number of values (i.e., n is large), the bitmap for that field will be very sparse, containing a large number of zeros. Thus, a bitmap is typically useful when the value of n is relatively small. When is n small or large? There is no simple answer; rather, database designers have to simulate alternative designs and evaluate the trade-offs.

In some situations, the bit string for a field can have multiple bits set to *on* (set to 1). A location field, for instance, may have two bits *on* to represent an item that can be found in Atlanta and New York.

The advantage of a bitmap is that it usually requires little storage. For example, we can recast the bitmap index as a conventional index (see Figure 11-12). The core of the bitmap in Figure 11-11 (i.e., the cells storing data about the color and code) requires 5 bits for each record, but the core of the traditional index requires 9 bytes, or 72 bits, for each record.

itemcode	color char(8)	code char(1)	Disk address
1001	Blue	N	d1
1002	Red	A	d2
1003	Red	A	d3
1004	Green	A	d4

Figure 11-12. An index

Bitmaps have been used for some time and were a feature of some prerelational databases. Recently, some vendors of relational database management systems (RDBMSs) have introduced bitmaps into their products to accelerate complex queries.

Join index

Many RDBMS queries frequently require two or more tables to be joined. Indeed, some people refer to the RDBMS as a join machine. A join index can be used to improve the execution speed of joins by creating indexes based on the matching columns of tables that are highly likely to be joined. For example, natcode is the common column used to join nation and stock, and each of these tables can be indexed on natcode (see Figure 11-13).

nation index	
natcode	Disk address
UK	d1
USA	d2

stock index	
natcode	Disk address
UK	d101
UK	d102
UK	d103
USA	d104
USA	d105

Figure 11-13. Indexes for natcode for the nation and stock tables

A join index is a list of the disk addresses of the rows for matching columns (see Figure 11-14). All indexes, including the join index, must be updated whenever a row is inserted into or deleted from the nation or stock tables. When a join of the two tables on the matching column is made, the join index is used to retrieve only those records that will be joined. This example demonstrates the advantage of a join index. If you think of a join as a product with a WHERE clause, then without a join index, 10 (2*5) rows have to be retrieved, but with the join index only 5 rows are retrieved. Join indexes can also be created for joins involving several tables. As usual, there is a trade-off. Joins will be faster, but insertions and deletions will be slower because of the need to update the indexes.

join index	
nation disk address	stock disk address
d1	d101
d1	d102
d1	d103
d2	d104
d2	d105

Figure 11-14. Join index

Data coding standards

The successful exchange of data between two computers requires agreement on how information is coded. American Standard Code for Information Interchange (ASCII) and Unicode are two widely used data coding standards.

ASCII

ASCII is the most common format for digital text files. In an ASCII file, each alphabetic, numeric, or special character is represented by a 7-bit code. Thus, 128 (2^7) possible characters are defined. Because most computers process data in eight-bit bytes or multiples thereof, an ASCII code usually occupies one byte.

Unicode

Unicode, officially the Unicode Worldwide Character Standard, is a system for the interchange, processing, and display of the written texts of the diverse languages of the modern world. Unicode provides a unique binary code for every character, no matter what the platform, program, or language. The Unicode standard currently contains 34,168 distinct coded characters derived from 24 supported language scripts. These characters cover the principal written languages of the world.

Unicode provides for two encoding forms: a default 16-bit form, and a byte (8-bit) form called UTF-8 that has been designed for ease of use with existing ASCII-based systems. As the default encoding of HTML and XML, Unicode is required for new Internet protocols. It is implemented in all modern operating systems and computer languages such as Java. Unicode is the basis of software that must function globally.

- -

Skill builder

Create indexes on `empfname` in `qemp` and `splname` in `qspl` (see page 290).

- -

Data storage devices

Corporations double the amount of data they need to store every three to four years. So the selection of data storage devices is a key consideration for data managers. When evaluating data storage options, data managers need to consider possible uses, which include:[2]

1. Online data
2. Backup files
3. Archival storage

Many systems require data to be online — continually available. Here the prime concerns are usually access speed and capacity, because many firms require rapid response to large volumes of data. Backup files are required to provide security against data loss. Ideally, backup storage is high volume capacity at low cost. Archived data may need to be stored for many years; so the archival medium should be highly reliable, with no data decay over extended periods, and low-cost.

In deciding what data will be stored where, database designers need to consider a number of variables:

1. Volume of data
2. Volatility of data
3. Required speed of access to data
4. Cost of data storage
5. Reliability of the data storage medium
6. Legal standing of stored data

The design options are discussed and considered in terms of the variables just identified.

Magnetic technology

Billions are spent annually on magnetic storage devices. Between one-third and one-half of IS hardware budgets are consumed by magnetic storage. Magnetic technology, the backbone of data storage for five decades, is based on magnetization and demagnetization of spots on a magnetic recording surface. The same spot can be magnetized and demagnetized repeatedly. Magnetic recording materials may be coated on rigid platters (hard disks), thin ribbons of material (magnetic tapes), or rectangular sheets (magnetic cards).

The main advantages of magnetic technology are its relative maturity, widespread use, and rapidly declining cost.[3] A major disadvantage is susceptibility to strong magnetic fields, which can corrupt data stored on a disk. Another shortcoming is data storage life; magnetization decays with time.

---

2. Caveat: This section details characteristics of various devices such as storage capacity, access time, and transfer speed, but technological change can quickly date this information. Use the figures as comparative measures rather than absolute values.
3. The cost of a megabyte of storage declines roughly 40 percent a year (Burrows, Peter. 2003. Santa brought a lot of disk drives. *BusinessWeek*, Jan 27, 40,42.)

As organizations convert paper to images, they need a very long-term, unalterable storage medium for documents that could be demanded in legal proceedings (e.g., a customer's handwritten insurance claim or a client's completed form for a mutual fund investment). Because data resident on magnetic media can be readily changed and decay with time, magnetic storage is not a good medium for storing archival data or legal documents.

U.S. National Medal of Technology

The U.S. National Medal of Technology was presented to IBM for its invention of the magnetic hard disk drive in the mid-1950s and also for its major breakthroughs in disk storage technology over that period. Over the past 20 years, the storage density of disk drives has increased more than 4,000-fold. Today, the total worldwide production of hard disk drives exceeds 170 million units each year. IBM has also played an important role in the development of magnetic tape and optical disk storage technologies.

Who would have believed that the size and capacity of those huge, expensive disk drives used during the 1970s and 1980s could be reduced to the matchbook-size, featherweight devices of today? IBM's first 1 Gbyte disk drive was the size of a refrigerator, weighed 550 pounds (250 kg), and cost US$40,000. Today, the 20 Gbyte IBM MicroDrive costs less than US$500 and can hold around 12 days of digital music. This miniaturization has paved the way for the units used in handheld electronic products, including digital cameras, PDAs, portable music players, and video cameras. In the future, we are likely to witness wearable computers, electronic books, global positioning system (GPS) receivers, and electronic wallets.

This award is the highest honor the U.S. president can bestow on leading innovators. It is an annual award presented to individuals, teams, or companies for the invention, development, or management of technology, as demonstrated by the introduction of new or significantly improved products, processes, or services.

Source: Anonymous. 2000. Hard disk drive inventor awarded medal. *Computing Canada*, Dec. 1, 15.

Fixed magnetic disk

A fixed magnetic disk containing one or more recording surfaces is permanently mounted in the disk drive and cannot be removed (see Figure 11-15). The recording surfaces and access mechanism are assembled in a clean room and then sealed to eliminate contaminants, making the device more reliable and permitting higher recording density and transfer rates. Access time is typically between 4 and 10 ms, and transfer rates can be as high as 1,300 Mbytes per second. Disk unit capacities range from gigabytes to terabytes. Magnetic disk units are often called direct-access storage devices or **DASD** (pronounced *das-dee*). At one time personal computers typically had a drive for a removable flexible, or *floppy*, disk, and the fixed disk became known as the *hard disk* by contrast.

Fixed disk is the medium of choice for most systems, from personal computers to super-computers. It gives rapid, direct access to large volumes of data and is ideal for highly volatile files. The major disadvantage of magnetic disk is the possibility of a head crash, which destroys the disk surface and data. With the read/write head of a disk just 15 millionths of an inch (40 millionths of a centimeter) above the surface of the disk, there is little margin for error. Hence, it is crucial to make backup copies of hard disk files regularly.

Figure 11-15. A disk storage unit

RAID

RAID (redundant array of independent, or inexpensive, disks) takes advantage of the economies of scale in manufacturing disks for the personal computing market. The cost of hard drives increases with their capacity and speed. RAID's idea is to use several cheaper drives whose total cost is less than one high-capacity drive. In addition to lower cost, RAID offers greater data security. All RAID levels (except level 0) can reconstruct the data on any single disk from the data stored on the remaining disks in the array in a manner that is quite transparent to the user.

RAID uses a combination of mirroring and striping to provide greater data protection. When a file is written to a mirrored array (see Figure 11-16), the disk controller writes identical copies of each record to each drive in the array. When a file is read from a mirrored array, the controller reads alternate pages simultaneously from each of the drives. It then puts these pages together in the correct sequence before delivering them to the computer. Mirroring reduces data access time by approximately the number of drives in the array because it interleaves the reading of records. During the time a conventional disk drive takes to read one page, a RAID system can read two or more pages (one from each drive). It is simply a case of moving from sequential to parallel retrieval of pages. Access times are halved for a two-drive array, quartered for a four-drive array, and so on.

If a read error occurs on a particular disk, the controller can always read the required page from another drive in the array because each drive has a full copy of the file. Mirroring, which requires at least two drives, improves response time and data security; however, it does take considerably more space to store a file because multiple copies are created.

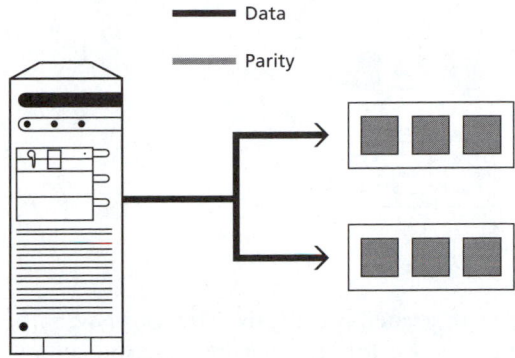

Figure 11-16. Mirroring

When a file is written to a striping array of three drives (see Figure 11-17), for instance, one half of the file is written to the first drive and the second half to the second drive. The third drive is used for error correction. A parity bit is constructed for each corresponding pair of bits written to drives one and two, and this parity bit is written to the third drive. When a file is read by a striping array, portions are retrieved from each drive and assembled in the correct sequence by the controller. If a read error occurs, the lost bits can be reconstructed by using the parity data on the third drive. If a drive fails, it can be replaced, and the missing data restored on the new drive. Striping requires at least three drives. Normally data are written to every drive but one, and that remaining drive is used for the parity bit. Striping gives added data security without requiring considerably more storage, but it does not have the same response time increase as mirroring.

RAID subsystems are divided into six levels, labeled 0 through 5. All RAID levels, except level 0, have common features:

- ❖ There is a set of physical disk drives viewed by the operating system as a single, logical drive.
- ❖ Data are distributed across corresponding physical drives.
- ❖ Parity information is used to recover data in the event of a disk failure.

Level 0 has been in use for many years. Data are broken into blocks that are interleaved or *striped* across disks. By spreading data over multiple drives, read and write operations can occur in parallel. As a result, I/O rates are higher, which makes level 0 ideal for I/O intensive applications such as recording video. There is no additional parity information and thus no data recovery when a drive failure occurs.

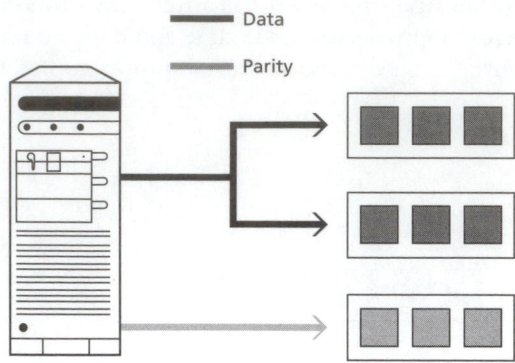

Figure 11-17. Striping

Level 1 implements mirroring, as described previously. This is possibly the most popular form of RAID because of its effectiveness for critical nonstop applications, although high levels of data availability and I/O rates are counteracted by higher storage costs. Another disadvantage is that every write command must be executed twice (assuming a two-drive array), and thus level 1 is inappropriate for applications that have a high ratio of writes to reads.

Level 2 implements striping by interleaving blocks of data on each disk and maintaining parity on the check disk. This is a poor choice when an application has frequent, short random disk accesses, because every disk in the array is accessed for each read operation. However, RAID 2 provides excellent data transfer rates for large sequential data requests. It is therefore suitable for computer-aided drafting and computer-aided manufacturing (CAD/CAM) and multimedia applications, which typically use large sequential files. RAID 2 is rarely used, however, because the same effect can be achieved with level 3 at lower cost.

Level 3 utilizes striping at the bit or byte level, so only one I/O operation can be executed at a time. Compared to level 1, RAID level 3 gives lower-cost data storage at lower I/O rates and tends to be most useful for the storage of large amounts of data, common with CAD/CAM and imaging applications.

Level 4 uses sector-level striping; thus, only a single disk needs to be accessed for a read request. Write requests are slower, however, because there is only one parity drive.

Level 5 (see Figure 11-18), a variation of striping, reads and writes data to separate disks independently and permits simultaneous reading and writing of data. Data and parity are written on the same drive. Spreading parity data evenly across several drives avoids the bottleneck that can occur when there is only one parity drive. RAID 5 is well designed for the high I/O rates required by transaction processing systems and servers, particularly e-mail servers. It is the most balanced implementation of the RAID concept in terms of price, reliability, and performance. It requires less capacity than mirroring with level 1 and higher I/O rates than striping with level 3, although performance can decrease with update-intensive operations. RAID 5 is frequently found in local-area network (LAN) environments.

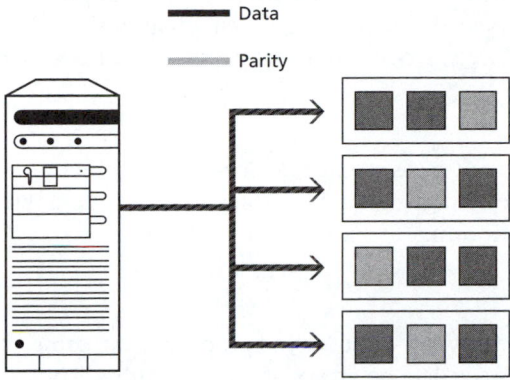

Figure 11-18. RAID level 5

RAID does have drawbacks. It often lowers a system's performance in return for greater reliability and increased protection against data loss. Extra disk space is required to store redundant information. Extra disk accesses are required to access and update redundant information. You should remember that RAID is not a replacement for standard backup procedures; it is a technology for increasing the fault tolerance of critical online systems. RAID systems offer terabytes of storage.

Removable magnetic disk

A removable disk comes in two formats: single-disk and disk pack. Disk packs consist of multiple disks mounted together on a common spindle in a stack, usually on a disk drive with retractable read/write heads. Because they are unsealed and exposed to possible contamination, storage densities and transfer rates are considerably lower than with fixed disks. Capacity is around 50 Gbytes.

The disk's removability is its primary advantage, making it ideal for backup. For example, an organization may regularly copy its fixed disk storage to multiple disk packs. Removable disk is also useful when applications need not be continuously online. For instance, the monthly payroll system can be stored on a removable pack and mounted as required.

Magnetic tape

A magnetic tape is a thin ribbon of plastic coated with ferric oxide. The once commonly used nine-track 2,400-foot (730 m) tape has a capacity of about 160 Mbytes and a data transfer rate of 2 Mbytes per second. The designation **nine-track** means nine bits are stored across the tape (8 bits plus one parity bit). Magnetic tape was used extensively for archiving and backup in early database systems; however, its limited capacity and sequential nature have resulted in its replacement by other media.

Magnetic tape cartridges

Tape cartridges, with a capacity measured in Gbytes and transfer rates of up to 6 Mbytes per second, have replaced magnetic tape. Easier handling is another feature favoring them over magnetic tape reels. Drives are usually less than $1,000 per unit.

Mass storage

There exists a variety of mass storage devices that automate labor-intensive tape and cartridge handling. The storage medium, with capacities of terabytes, is typically located and mounted by a robotic arm.

Solid-state memory

Solid-state storage devices connect to computers the same way regular magnetic disk drives do, but they store data on arrays of memory chips. These units can be 50 times faster than RAID but cost around $1,400 per Gbyte, compared to magnetic disks, which are around $1 per Gbyte. Solid-state storage is mainly used for stock-trading, video-editing, and video-streaming applications.

A **flash drive**, also known as a keydrive or jump drive, is a small, removable storage device with a Universal Serial Bus (USB) connector. It contains solid-state memory and is useful for transporting small amounts of data. Capacity is in the range 128 Mbytes to 2 Gbytes.

Table 11-2: A byte size table

Prefix		Factor	Equivalent to
k	kilo	10^3	
M	mega	10^6	
G	giga	10^9	A digital audio recording of a symphony
T	tera	10^{12}	
P	peta	10^{15}	50 percent of all books in U.S. academic libraries
E	exa	10^{18}	5 times all the world's printed material
Z	zetta	10^{21}	
Y	yotta	10^{24}	

Optical technology

Optical technology is a more recent development than magnetic. Its advantages are high-storage densities, low-cost media, and direct access. Optical storage systems work by reflecting beams of laser light off a rotating disk with a minutely pitted surface. As the disk rotates, the amount of light reflected back to a sensor varies, generating a stream of ones and zeros. A tiny change in the wavelength of the laser translates into as much as a tenfold increase in the amount of information that can be stored.

There are three storage media based on optical technology: CD-ROM, magneto-optical, and DVD (see Figure 11-19). All use a laser for reading and writing data, but because the methods of recording data differ, media are not typically interchangeable. For instance, a CD-ROM drive cannot read a magneto-optical disk.

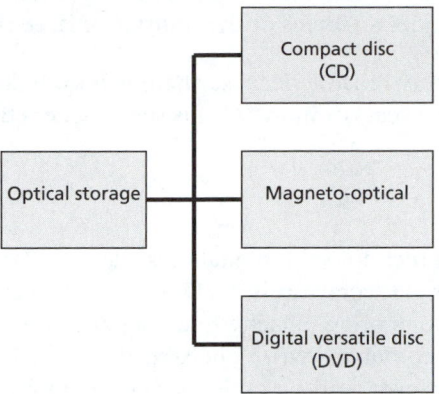

Figure 11-19. Optical storage media

Most optical disks can reliably store records for at least 10 years under prescribed conditions of humidity and temperature. Actual storage life may be in the region of 30 to 50 years. Optical technology is highly reliable because it is not susceptible to head crashes.

CD-ROM

In the early 1980s, engineers at Philips and Sony independently recognized that compact discs (CDs) could store data as well as sound. In 1986, these two companies introduced the CD-ROM format (ROM stands for read-only memory). Measuring approximately 5 inches (12 cm) in diameter, a CD-ROM stores some 650 Mbytes of data. CD-ROM drives are relatively slow devices.

CD-ROM is a compact, robust, high-capacity medium for the storage of permanent data. Data stored on CD-ROMs possibly have the highest legal standing of any of the forms discussed because once written, the data cannot be altered. Thus, it is ideal for storage of documents that potentially may be used in court.

CD-R (recordable) and CD-RW (read/writable) are extensions of the original CD-ROM technology. They will soon be displaced by their DVD equivalents when most machines have DVD drives.

Magneto-optical disk

Magneto-optical disks are a high-capacity read-write medium. Drives and media come in two sizes —3.5 inch (9 cm) and 5.25 inch (13.5 cm)—and the disks can store up to 9

Gbytes. An ISO standard for both sizes makes for a free exchange of disks across same size drives of manufacturers that follow this standard.

Magneto-optical disks are a compact, high-capacity, and reliable, data transfer and archival storage medium. The smaller disks are suitable for personal computer storage and backup. Also, they can be used to distribute data within an organization. The 5.25-inch disks are useful for the backup of databases under 9 Gbytes or the transfer of large files.

Magneto-optical technology is also very reliable because there is no possibility of a head crash, and stored data have a life of 30 years or more. At this stage, access times are somewhat longer than for magnetic disk.

Digital versatile disc

The most recently developed optical technology is digital versatile disc (DVD). A replacement for CD technology, DVD comes in several forms. DVD-Video and DVD-ROM are read-only versions designed respectively for storing full-length movies and computer software. DVD-Audio stores songs. DVD-R (recordable—write once, read many), DVD-RW (read/writable), and DVD-RAM (random access, read/writable) are designed for the computer industry.

Table 11-3: DVD formats used in the computer industry

Format	Description	Capacity in Gbytes (max)
DVD-ROM	Read only, manufactured by a press	17.1
DVD-R	Recordable	4.7
DVD-RW	Read/writable	4.7
DVD-RAM	random access read/writable	9.4

The future

HD-DVD (high-density DVD), likely to enter the market in 2005, offers capacities up to 30 Gbytes (over four hours of HDTV audio and video). It is designed for high-definition movies. The Chinese government has supported development of enhanced versatile disk (EVD) as a lower-cost alternative to HD-DVD. EVD disks and players entered the market in 2004. Another alternative is Blu-ray disc, which has a capacity of up to 50 Gbytes. Blu-ray recorders were introduced in 2003. These alternatives have a variety of supporters, and the next few years will see which emerge as enduring media.

Storage-area networks

A storage-area network (SAN) is a high-speed network for connecting and sharing different kinds of storage devices, such as tape libraries and disk arrays. In the typical LAN, the storage device (usually a disk) is closely coupled to a server and communicates through a bus connection. Communication among storage devices occurs through servers and over the LAN, which can lead to network congestion.

A SAN creates a pool of storage that can be shared by multiple servers. A SAN supports dynamic sharing of large amounts of data, regardless of operating system or application. Generally, a SAN communicates via pipelines that consist of an interface called Fibre Channel, a high-speed data connection between computer devices. Fibre Channel extends the possible distance between two connected devices. Where SCSI copper cables can extend up to 55 yards (50 m), Fibre Channels can run up to 6 miles (10 km).

SANs support disk mirroring, backup and restore, archival and retrieval of archived data, data migration from one storage device to another, and the sharing of data among different servers in a network. Typically, a SAN is part of the overall network of computing resources for an enterprise. SANs are likely to be a critical element for supporting e-commerce and applications requiring large volumes of data.

A SAN with a couple of servers could cost between $20,000 and $30,000. A high-end SAN could cost millions depending upon the capacity and nature of the system. SAN is part of the overall network of computing resources for an enterprise.

Long-term storage

Long-term data storage has always been of concern to societies and organizations. Some data, such as the location of toxic-waste sites, must be stored for thousands of years. Increasingly, governments are converting their records to electronic format. Unlike paper, magnetic media do not show degradation until it is too late to recover the data. Magnetic tapes can become so brittle that the magnetic coating separates from the backing. In addition, computer hardware and software rapidly become obsolete. The medium may be readable, but there could be no hardware to read it and no software to decode it.

Paper, it seems, is still the best medium for long-term storage (see Figure 11-20), and research is being conducted to create extra-long-life paper that can store information for hundreds of years. This paper, resistant to damage from heat, cold, and magnetism, will store data in a highly compact format but, obviously, nowhere near optical disk densities.

Data compression

Data compression is a method for encoding digital data so that they require less storage space and thus less communication bandwidth. There are two basic types of compression: lossless methods, in which no data are lost when the files are restored to their original format, and lossy methods, in which some data are lost when the files are decompressed.

Lossless compression

During lossless compression, the data-compression software searches for redundant or repetitive data and encodes it. For example, a string of 100 asterisks (*) can be stored more compactly by a compression system that records the repeated character (i.e., *) and the length of the repetition (i.e., 100). The same principle can be applied to a photo that contains a string of horizontal pixels of the same color. Clearly, you want to use lossless compression with text file (e.g., a business report or spreadsheet).

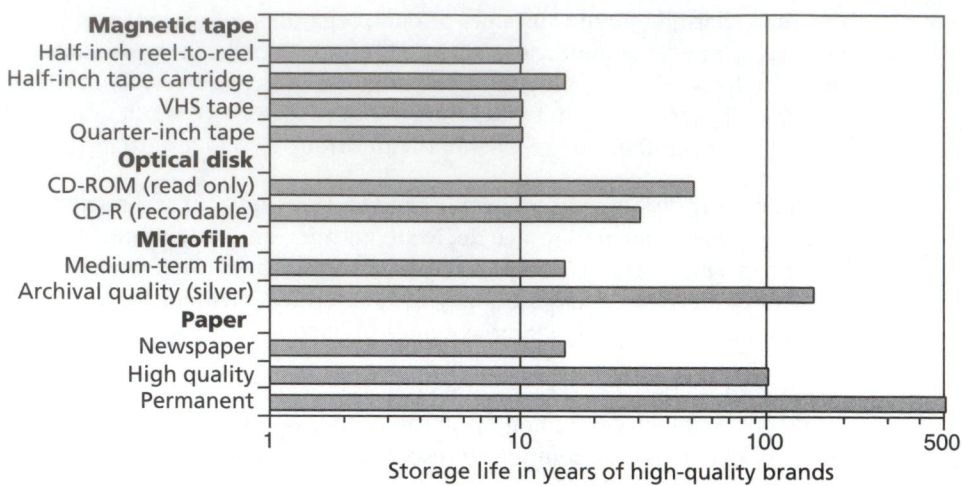

Figure 11-20. The life expectancy of various media at 20°C (68°F) and 40 percent relative humidity (source: National Media Lab)

Lossy compression

Lossy compression is used for graphics, video, and audio files because humans are often unable to detect minor data losses in these formats. Audio files can often be compressed to 10 percent of their original size (e.g., an MP3 version of a CD recording).

Skill builder

An IS department in a major public university records the lectures for 10 of its classes for video streaming to its partner universities in India and China. Each twice-weekly lecture runs for 1.25 hours and a semester is 15 weeks long. A video streaming expert estimates that one minute of digital video requires 6.5 Mbytes using MPEG-4[4] and Apple's Quick-Time software. What is MPEG-4? Calculate how much storage space will be required and recommend a storage device for the department.

Comparative analysis

Details of the various storage devices are summarized in Table 11-4. A simple three-star rating system has been used for each device—the more stars, the better. In regard to access speed, RAID gets more stars than DVD-RAM because it retrieves a stored record more quickly. Similarly, magneto-optical rates three stars because it costs less per megabyte to

---

4.   See www.apple.com/mpeg4/

store data on a magneto-optical disk than a fixed disk. The scoring system is relative. The fact that removable disk gets two stars for reliability does not mean it is an unreliable storage medium; it simply means that it is not as reliable as some other media.

Table 11-4: Relative merits of data storage devices

Device	Access speed	Volume	Volatility	Cost per megabyte	Reliability	Legal standing
Solid state	***	*	***	*	***	*
Fixed disk	***	***	***	**	**	*
RAID	***	***	***	**	***	*
Removable disk	**	**	***	**	**	*
Flash memory	**	*	***	*	***	*
Tape	*	**	*	***	**	*
Cartridge	**	***	*	***	**	*
Mass Storage	**	***	*	***	**	*
SAN	***	***	***	**	***	*
CD-ROM	*	**	*	**	***	***
Magneto-optical	**	***	**	***	***	*
DVD-ROM	*	***	*	***	***	***
DVD-R	*	***	*	***	***	**
DVD-RW	*	***	**	***	***	*
DVD-RAM	*	***	**	***	***	*

Legend

Characteristic	More stars mean ...
Access speed	Faster access to data
Volume	Device more suitable for large files
Volatility	Device more suitable for files that change frequently
Cost per megabyte	Less costly form of storage
Reliability	Device less susceptible to an unrecoverable read error
Legal standing	Media more acceptable as evidence in court

Conclusion

The internal and physical aspects of database design are a key determinant of system performance. Selection of appropriate data structures can substantially curtail disk accesses and reduce response times. In making data structure decisions, the database administrator needs to weigh the pros and cons of each choice. Similarly, in selecting data storage devices, the designer needs to be aware of the trade-offs. Various devices and media have both strengths and weaknesses, and these need to be considered.

Compressing XML

Although Extensible Markup Language (XML) has become a nearly universal way to share information online, the downside is its sluggish performance. Performance problems arise because XML stores information as text, creating very large files, which take a long time to download (e.g., images to cell phones). XML-based protocols, called Web Services, also generate a great deal of XML traffic. So far, there has been no agreement on what technology and standards are required to speed up XML traffic.

The move is toward a technology called binary XML, which uses a format for compressing the XML transmissions. Sun Microsystems' Fast Infoset plan proposes that XML documents get shrunk down into a binary format in order to speed up transmission of files over the Internet. Its compression method is already a standard for the telecommunications industry. Initial tests showed that applications performed two or three times faster using the software. The goal is to generate interest among developers and eventually create a standardized binary format.

However, the primary concern is with interoperability, especially if different binary formats for specific services are developed that are not universally understood. ZapThink, a research firm specializing in XML and Web services, echoes concerns over binary XML, notably the possibility of proprietary implementations.

One ZapThink analyst suggested that binary XML may be limited to niche uses such as high-volume applications, which demand the best performance. Also, others say that the ongoing advances in networking and processing power will alleviate performance concerns.

Source: LaMonica, M. 2005. Putting XML in the fast lane. Jan 13 [cited Mar 27, 2005]. Available from news.com.com/Putting+XML+in+the+fast+lane/2100-7345_3-5534249.html.

Summary

It takes considerably longer to retrieve data from a magnetic disk than from main memory. Appropriate selection of data structures and data access methods can considerably reduce delays by reducing disk accesses. The key characteristics of disk storage devices that affect database access are rotational speed and access arm speed. Access arm movement can be minimized by storing frequently used data on the same track on a single surface or on the same track on different surfaces. Records that are frequently used together should be clustered together. Intrafile clustering applies to the records within a single file. Interfile clustering applies to multiple files. The disk manager, the part of the operating system responsible for physical I/O, maintains a directory of pages. The file manager, a level above the disk manager, contains a directory of files.

Indexes are used to speed up retrieval by reducing disk accesses. An index is a file containing the value of the index field and the address of its full record. The use of indexes involves a trade-off between faster retrievals and slower updates. Indexes can be used for both sequential and direct access. A file can have multiple indexes. A sparse index does not contain an entry for every value of the indexed field. The B-tree, a particular form of index structure, consists of two parts: the sequence set and the index set. Hashing is a technique for reducing disk accesses that allows direct access to a file. There can be only one hashing field. A hashed file can no longer be processed sequentially because its physical sequence has lost any logical meaning. A linked list is a useful data structure for inter-file clustering. It is a suitable structure for representing a 1:m relationship. Pointers between records are used to maintain a logical sequence. Lists can have forward, backward, and parent pointers.

Systems designers have to decide what data storage devices will be used for online data, backup files, and archival storage. In making this decision, they must consider the volume of data, volatility of data, required speed of access to data, cost of data storage, reliability of the data storage medium, and the legal standing of the stored data. Magnetic technology, the backbone of data storage for five decades, is based on magnetization and demagnetization of spots on a magnetic recording surface. Fixed disk, removable disk, magnetic tape, tape cartridge, and mass storage are examples of magnetic technology. RAID uses several cheaper drives whose total cost is less than one high-capacity drive. RAID uses a combination of mirroring or striping to provide greater data protection. RAID subsystems are divided into six levels labeled 0 through 5. A storage-area network (SAN) is a high-speed network for connecting and sharing different kinds of storage devices, such as tape libraries and disk arrays.

Optical technology offers high storage densities, low-cost medium, and direct access. CD-ROM, magneto-optical, and DVD are examples of optical technology. Optical disks can reliably store records for at least 10 years and possibly up to 30 years. Optical technology is not susceptible to head crashes.

Data compression techniques reduce the need for storage capacity and bandwidth. Lossless methods result in no data loss, whereas with lossy techniques some data are lost during compression.

Key terms and concepts

Access time	Interfile clustering
Archival file	Internal schema
ASCII	Intrafile clustering
B-tree	Join index
Backup file	Linked list
Bitmap index	Lossless compression
CD-R	Lossy compression
CD-ROM	Magnetic disk
CD-RW	Magnetic tape
Clustering	Magneto-optical disk
Conceptual schema	Mass storage
Cylinder	Mirroring
Data compression	Page
Data storage device	Parity
Database architecture	Pointer
Digital versatile disc (DVD)	Redundant arrays of inexpensive or inde-
Disk manager	pendent drives (RAID)
External schema	Sequence set
File manager	Solid-state storage
Hash address	Sparse index
Hash field	Storage-area network (SAN)
Hash function	Striping
Hashing	Track
Index	Unicode
Index set	VSAM

Exercises

1. Why is a disk drive considered a bottleneck?
2. What is the difference between a record and a page?
3. Describe the two types of delay that can occur prior to reading a record from a disk. What can be done to reduce these delays?
4. What is clustering? What is the difference between intrafile and interfile clustering?
5. Describe the differences between a file manager and a disk manager.
6. What is an index?
7. What are the advantages and disadvantages of indexing?
8. Write the SQL to create an index on the column `natcode` in the `nation` table.
9. Is MP3 a lossless or lossy compression standard?
10. A Paris insurance firm keeps paper records of all policies and claims made on it. The firm now has a vault containing 100 filing cabinets full of forms. Because Paris rental costs are so high, the CEO has asked you to recommend a more compact medium for long-term storage of these documents. Because some insurance claims are contested, she is very concerned with ensuring that documents, once stored, cannot be altered. What would you recommend and why?

11. The national weather research center of a large South American country has asked you to recommend a data storage strategy for its historical weather data. The center electronically collects hourly weather information from 2,000 sites around the country. This database must be maintained indefinitely. Periodically, weather researchers extract a portion of these data for their use. A researcher must submit a written request detailing what data are required and the purpose of the study. After review of the request, the center sets up a data file on a file server. The center's director is very concerned with cost and wants to minimize the cost of data storage. What would you recommend and why?

12. The national aviation authority in your country has asked you to recommend a data storage device for its air traffic control system. The specification states that the file is relatively small (around 500 Mbytes) and system reliability is the foremost criterion. What would you recommend and why?

13. A magazine subscription service has a toll-free number for customers who may dial the company to place orders, inquire about existing orders, or check subscription rates. All customers are uniquely identified by an 11-digit numeric code. All magazines are identified by a 2- to 4-character code. The company has approximately 10 million customers who subscribe to an average of four magazines. Subscriptions are available to 126 magazines. Draw a data model for this situation. Decide what data structures you would recommend for the storage of the data for each entity. The management of the company prides itself on its customer service and strives to answer customer queries as rapidly as possible.

14. A German consumer research company collects scanning data from supermarkets throughout central Europe. The scanned data include product code identifier, price, quantity purchased, time, date, supermarket location, and supermarket name, and in some cases where the supermarket has a frequent buyer plan, it collects a consumer identification code. It has also created a table containing details of the manufacturer of each product. The database is very large and contains nearly 1 Tbyte of data. The data are used by market researchers in consumer product companies. A researcher will typically request access to a slice of the database (e.g., sales of all detergents) and analyze these data for trends and patterns. The consumer research company promises rapid access to its data. Its goal is to give clients access to requested data within one to two minutes. Once clients have access to the data, they expect very rapid response to queries. What data storage and retrieval strategy would you recommend?

15. The navy of a large industrial power has many modern ships. Because of the technology and complexity of these ships, many thick paper manuals are required to describe how to operate, maintain, and repair the many shipboard electronic and mechanical devices. In fact, because there are so many manuals, sailors quip that ships could be 10 percent smaller if they did not have to carry so much paper. What advice do you have for this navy?

16. A video producer has asked for your advice on a data storage device. She has specified that she must be able to record video at 5 to 7 Mbytes per second. What would you recommend and why?

17.   A firm is planning to offer a satellite-based digital radio service to the continental U.S. market. It will broadcast music, sports, and talk-radio programs from a library of 1.5 million digital audio files, which will be sent to a satellite uplink and then beamed to car radios equipped to accept the service. Consumers will pay $9.95 per month to access 100 channels.

    a. Assuming the average size of a digital audio file is 5 Mbytes (~4 minutes of music), how much storage space is required?

    b. What storage technology would you recommend?

18.   An airline plans to install remote diagnostic systems in its aircraft that will allow physicians on the ground to monitor an ill passenger remotely. The doctors will then be able to communicate with flight personnel on appropriate treatment. The system will send real-time electrocardiogram information, temperature (via an ear probe), blood pressure information (via a wrist cuff), blood oxygen levels, respiration rates, and other vital signs to computers at a hospital in Phoenix, Arizona. A built-in modem connected to a seat-back satellite phone will be used for data transmission. Graphical help screens will guide flight personnel through every step of the process. Since the satellite phone operates at only 2.4 Kbps, what technology can be used to support this system?

12

Data Processing Architectures

The difficulty in life is the choice.
George Moore, *The Bending of the Bough,* 1900

Learning Objectives

Students completing this chapter will be able to

- ❖ recommend a data architecture for a given situation;
- ❖ understand the differences between two- and three-tier client/server architecture;
- ❖ discuss the fundamental principles that a hybrid architecture should satisfy;
- ❖ demonstrate the general principles of distributed database design.

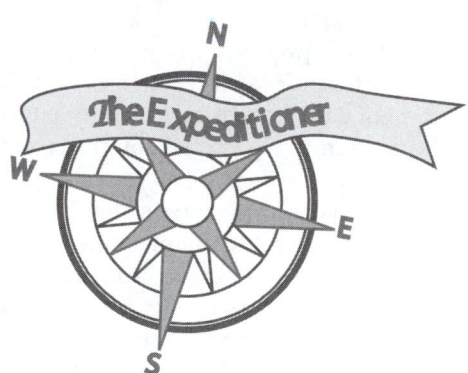

On a recent transatlantic flight, Sophie, the Personnel and PR manager, had been seated next to a very charming young man who had tried to impress her with his knowledge of computing. He worked for a large systems consulting firm, and his speech was sprinkled with words like "browser," "XML," "server," "client," and "distributed database." In return, Sophie responded with some "ums," "aahs," and an occasional "that's interesting." Of course, this was before the third glass of champagne. After that, he was more intent on finding out how long Sophie would be in New York and what restaurants and shows piqued her curiosity.

After an extremely pleasant week of wining, dining, and seeing the town — amid, of course, many hours of valuable work for The Expeditioner — Sophie returned to London. Now, she must ask Ned what all these weird terms meant. After all, it was difficult to carry on a conversation when she did not understand the language. That's the problem with IS, she thought, new words and technologies were always being invented. It makes it very hard for the rest of us to make sense of what's being said.

Introduction

In the mainframe era, all data were stored and processed on the mainframe. The advent of personal computers on users' desks provided a choice for separating data storage and processing. In general terms, data can be stored and processed locally or remotely. Combinations of these two options provide four basic architectures (see Figure 12-1). Client/ server, which is not exclusively local data processing and remote storage, is shown as overlapping adjacent quadrants.

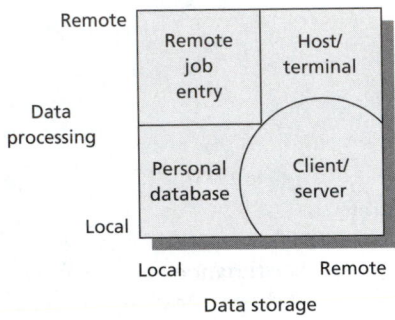

Figure 12-1. Basic architectures

Remote job entry

In remote job entry, data are stored locally and processed remotely. Data are sent over a communication link to a remote computer for processing, and the output is returned the same way. This once fairly common form of data processing is still used today because remote job entry can overcome three shortcomings of personal computers. *First,* a personal computer may be too slow. Scientists and engineers need occasional access to a supercomputer for computationally intensive applications, such as simulating global climate change. *Second*, a personal computer may have insufficient main memory. Supercomputers typically have larger amounts of main memory and can handle larger problems more easily. *Third*, the process may require highly specialized software that is not available on the user's personal computer because it only makes sense to run the software on a supercomputer.

Local storage is used for several reasons. *First*, it may be cheaper than storing on a supercomputer, whose management will charge for storage space. *Second*, the user may be able to do some local processing and preparation of the data before sending them to the supercomputer. Supercomputing time can be expensive; where possible, local processing is used for tasks such as data entry, validation, and reporting. *Third*, users may feel that local data storage is more secure for particularly sensitive data.

Personal database

Users can store and process their data locally when they have their own computers. Many personal computer database systems (e.g., MS Access and FileMaker) now permit users to develop their own applications, and there are many programs available for common applications that require database facilities.

There are a number of reasons favoring personal databases. *First,* the competitiveness and economies of scale of the microcomputer market make personal computers a low-cost alternative for data storage and processing. *Second*, users are independent of the information systems department. They have greater control and can develop their own software. The application backlog of most IS departments means that users often have a very long wait for IS department-developed systems. *Third*, desktop operating systems make personal computers easier to use. *Fourth*, the size of the personal computing market has attracted many software companies, and many leading-edge applications are written for personal computers. Thus, personal computer users have an extensive choice of user-friendly software for a wide range of applications.

Of course, there is a downside to personal databases. *First,* there is a great danger of repetition and redundancy. The same application gets developed in a slightly different way by many users. The same data get stored on many different systems. (It is not always the same, however, because data entry errors or maintenance inconsistencies result in discrepancies between personal databases.) *Second*, data are not readily shared because various users are not aware of what is available or find it inconvenient to share data. Personal databases are exactly that; but much of the data may be of corporate value and should be shared. *Third*, data integrity procedures are often quite lax for personal databases. Users might not make regular backups, databases are often not secured from unauthorized access, and data validation procedures are often ignored. *Fourth*, often when the employee leaves the organization or moves to another role, the application and data are lost because they are not documented and the organization is unaware of their existence. *Fifth*, there is a danger that users get addicted to developing software and ignore their assigned work. The job of managers is to manage, not write software or build personal databases. Personal databases are clearly very important for many organizations — when used appropriately. Data that are shared require a different processing architecture.

Host/terminal

The host/terminal approach was the initial solution to making data accessible to many users. Under this architecture, data storage and processing occur at one location, typically a mainframe. Users have terminals (also called network stations) linked to the central computer by communication lines. These terminals have minimal processing capability; they are used to display data and may do some limited formatting. Nowadays, personal computers have been substituted for terminals, but they are usually emulating a terminal and so have the same restricted processing capabilities. Host/terminal architecture was the basis of IBM's success for many years. Its mainframe computers, terminals, communication system, and supporting software were well suited to handling large volumes of data and high transaction processing rates.

A generic host/terminal architecture consists of several key components (see Figure 12-2). Requirements include the operating system, a data communications manager (usually abbreviated to DC manager), and database management system (DBMS). The DC manager handles the transfer of data between application programs and terminals. This is sometimes called a transaction processing (TP) monitor. For example, when a user enters a query at a terminal, the DC manager handles its transmission from the terminal to the relevant application program. Next, after some processing (e.g., validating the query), the application program passes the query to the DBMS, which retrieves the required data and returns it to the application program. The application program may then do some additional processing of the data before passing it to the DC manager for transmission to the user's terminal. As you can see from this example, mainframe-resident software does all the work.

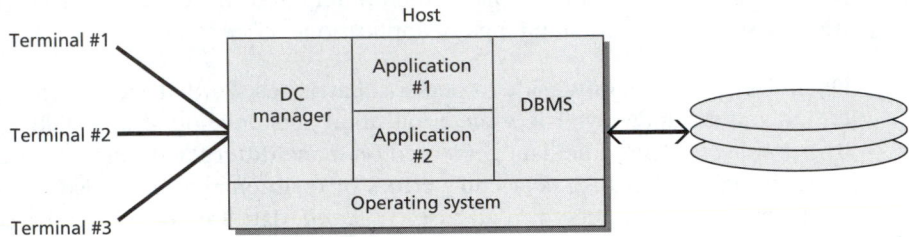

Figure 12-2. Host/terminal architecture

In a host/terminal setting, all shared resources are managed by the host. When additional processing capacity is required, the host must be upgraded or replaced. As a result, capacity changes tend to be very lumpy, and required capacity is often out of balance with actual needs.

LAN-based architectures

File server and DBMS server systems are variations on client/server found on a local area network (LAN). Before we delve into these architectures, however, you need a brief overview of LANs. A **LAN** connects computers and devices within the same limited geographic area (e.g., a building). High-performance communication connections enable data to be transferred on a LAN at speeds of up to 1,000 Mbits per second. A LAN enables users to share devices (e.g., laser printers), access shared files, and transfer files to others on the LAN. Its basic components include cabling to connect computers and devices, a card for each computer or device to connect it to the network, a file server for storing shared data, a network operating system (e.g., Novell's NetWare), and the computer and devices.

> **Big Macs**
>
> In 2003, Apple and scientists at Virginia Polytechnic Institute & State University collaborated to build a world-class cluster supercomputer using 1,100 PowerMac G5 desktop computers. Prior to this, UCLA researchers had discovered how easy a bunch of Macs could be roped together and developed software to do the setup in hours, not the days or even weeks typically needed to create a Linux cluster of PCs.
>
> Later that year, Virginia Tech's system ranked as the world's third-fastest supercomputer, notching a peak speed of 17.6 teraflops (trillion floating-point operations per second). Flops are the calculations at which supercomputers excel. Later, those PowerMacs were replaced with Apple's newer Xserve G5 servers.
>
> The supercomputing community was surprised and impressed by what this collaboration accomplished so quickly. It didn't take long for others to follow.
>
> The Mach 5 being built by Colsa Corp. will use 1,566 G5 Xserve units and will have a theoretical peak speed of more than 25 teraflops. Mach 5 will go into service at the Army R & D Command's Aviation & Missile Research, Development & Engineering Center in Huntsville, Alabama and will run just one job: simulating hypersonic flight. Currently, each simulation on the center's aging IBM supercomputer with 284 processors chews up a solid month of computing time. With Mach 5, they'll be able to do a new run every day, overnight.
>
> Apple's price/performance ratio is way ahead of other competitors. Also, the G5 servers are very effective in dissipating heat, whereas heat problems in the other systems prevented them from running their chips at maximum speed.
>
> Source: Anonymous. 2004. The "Big Mac" supercomputer biz. *BusinessWeek*, Aug. 3, www.businessweek.com/technology/content/aug2004/tc2004083_7126_tc153.htm.

LAN technology is a direct result of the massive influx of personal computers into organizations. People with personal computers soon discovered they wanted to access corporate databases, share data with colleagues, and share devices, such as a laser printer, within a workgroup.

A **server** is a general-purpose computer that provides and controls access to shareable resources such as applications, files, printers, communication lines, and databases. A server must be able to support multiple, simultaneous requests for shared resources. A server can have a single purpose (e.g., a database server and nothing else) or manage multiple shared resources (e.g., a server that handles sharing of a printer and multiple files).

In a client/server environment, shared resources are often managed by several servers. Capacity increases can be very gradual as additional servers are added or some servers are upgraded. Compared to a host/terminal architecture, it is far easier to keep required and actual capacity in balance.

File server

A file server is a LAN computer with a large disk file (see Figure 12-3). It is a central data store for the network's users. Files are kept on the file server, and processing occurs at the user's personal computer. This means that entire files are transferred on the LAN to an application running on a personal computer. For example, updating a file requires transfer of the file to the personal computer running the application, processing the update, and transferring the revised file to the file server. Also, when a file is retrieved for update, it is locked. Other users cannot access the file until the changes have been made and the file rewritten to the server. Clearly, this approach is limited to small files and low demand. Network congestion occurs when file sizes are large, and there are multiple, active users.

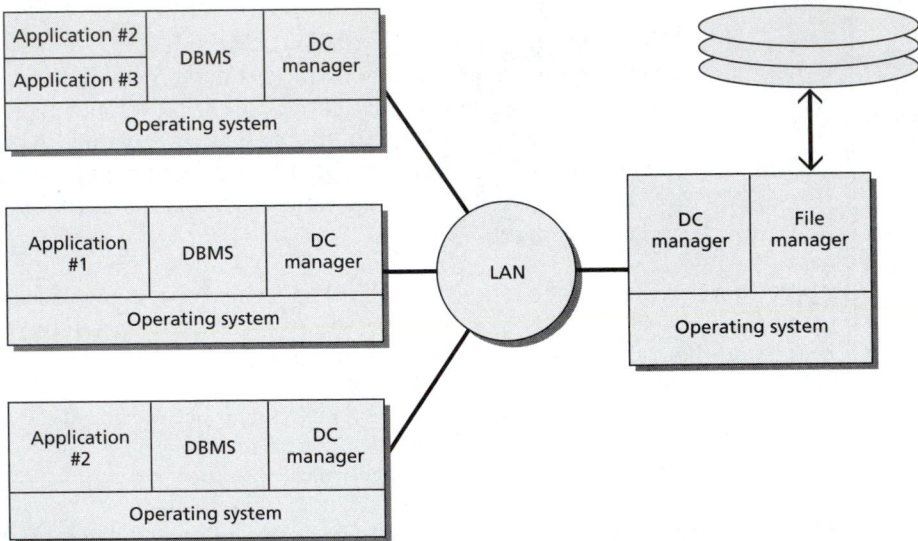

Figure 12-3. File server architecture

File server architecture is a relatively simple solution to data sharing on a local area network. Its shortcomings are addressed by DBMS server architecture.

DBMS server

Another LAN approach to client/server architecture operates a DBMS on the server, which can run on the file server or a separate computer. It does most of the DBMS processing so that only necessary records are transferred across the network, thus reducing network traffic substantially. In addition, with a DBMS server, locking can take place at the record rather than file level (see page 534 for a more detailed discussion of locking).

There are two separate programs: the DBMS server, sometimes known as the *back end,* and the client part, the *front end,* which resides on the user's personal computer. The following example illustrates how the processing load can be shared in a DBMS server environment (see Figure 12-4). When a user enters a query at a personal computer, it is handled by the resident application program, which will do local processing such as query validation. The application program then hands, for example, an SQL query to the client DC manager for transmission to the server. At the server, the server DC manager picks up the query and passes it to the DBMS, which executes the query. The result of the query is passed to the server's DC manager for transmission to the client's DC manager. The client's DC manager then passes the result to the client application program for processing. Finally, the result of the query appears on the user's personal computer.

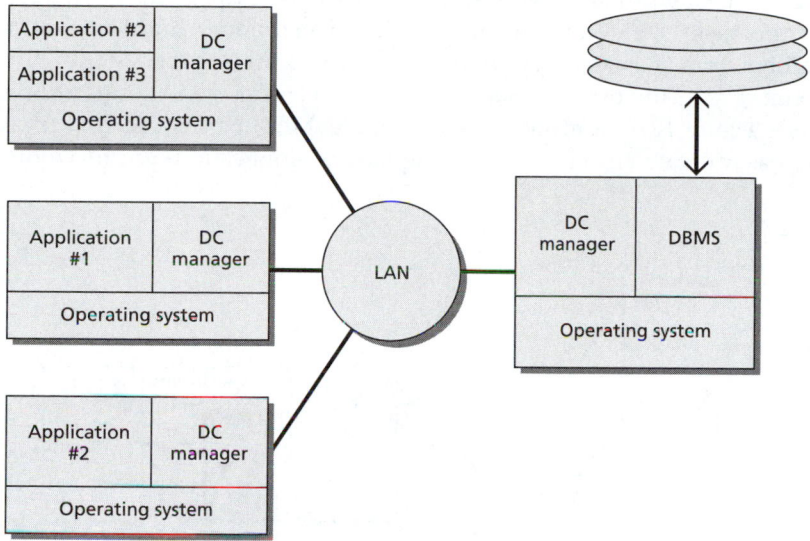

Figure 12-4. DBMS/server architecture

Client/server fundamentals

File servers and DBMS servers are examples of client/server architecture, in which two processes interact as superior and subordinate. The client process initiates requests and the server responds. The client is the dominant partner because it initiates a request. Client and server processes can run on the same computer, but generally they run on separate, linked computers. Typically, the client is a desktop computer and the server is a more powerful machine.

Most data management decisions require a trade-off. The costs and benefits of different architectures need to be closely investigated (see Table 12-1 for a summary).

Table 12-1: Architecture summary

Architecture	Main use
Remote job entry	Large-scale scientific or engineering work
Personal	Stand-alone, small, personal systems
Host/terminal	Large-scale transaction processing
Client/server	Flexible, friendly decision support and workflow

Client/server—the second generation

The client/server idea, as presented in the previous section, is a simple, two-tiered client/database model. By now, the client/server concept has evolved to describe a widely distributed, data-rich, cooperative environment. The second-generation model embraces servers dedicated to applications, data, transaction management, systems management, and other tasks. It extends the database side to incorporate nonrelational systems, such as multidimensional databases, multimedia databases, and legacy systems. A three-tier model has emerged as the predominant incarnation of second-generation client/server computing (see Figure 12-5). A major advantage of the three-tier model is that applications can be more easily created from reusable components. Applications are also more scalable.

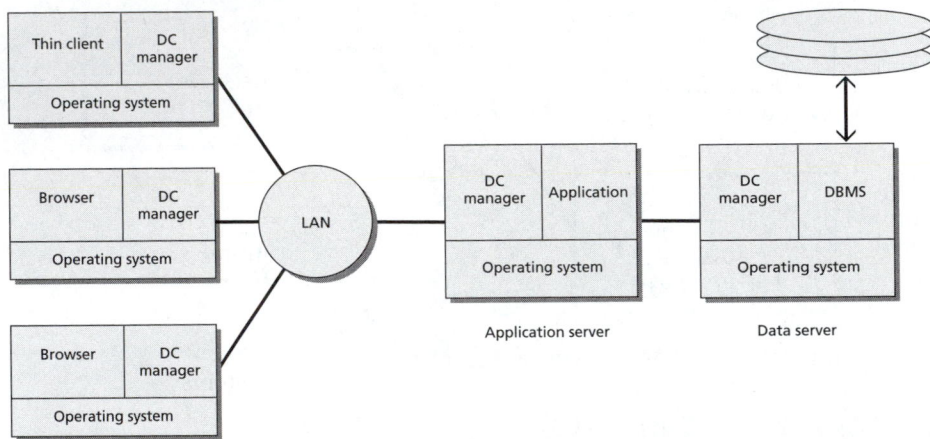

Figure 12-5. Three-tier client/server computing

The three-tier model consists of three types of systems:

❖ **Clients** perform presentation functions, manage the graphical user interface (GUI), and execute communication software that provides network access. In addition, the client may run code to access client-resident databases. The trend is toward the client being a browser (e.g., Firefox or Internet Explorer) or so-called *thin* client.

❖ **Application servers** are where the majority of the business and data logic are processed. Tasks handled by an application server include providing workgroup functions, assisting in network management, and supporting messaging. The application servers for many enterprise systems are Java 2 Platform Enterprise Edition (J2EE)-compliant (e.g., JBoss).

❖ **Data servers** provide support for relational and other DBMSs. They usually also provide backup and recovery services and transaction management control.

Under the three-tier model, the client requests a service from an application server, and the application server requests data from a data server. The computing environment is a complex array of clients, application servers, and data servers. An organization can spread its processing load across many servers. This enables it to scale up the data processing workload more easily. For example, if a server running several applications is overloaded, another server can be purchased and some of the workload moved to the new server.

Two-tier versus three-tier

The client in the two-tier model of client/server is also called a **thick client**, because most of the processing runs on the client side. Three-tier moves the application logic to the server, known as a **thin-client** or **thick-server** architecture. The main differences between thick and thin clients are summarized in Table 12-2.

Table 12-2: Thick and thin clients

Type of client	Thick	Thin
Technology	LAN	Web
Application logic	Mostly on the client	Mostly on the server
Network load	Medium	Low
Data storage	Server	Server
Server intelligence	Medium	High

Two-tier is good for building departmental applications, such as decision support and groupware. However, two-tier does not scale well. Three-tier is superior for handling large-scale Internet and intranet applications. Many Web-based applications are based on the three-tier model. The client is a browser, the application is a Web server, and the data server is an RDBMS. We will investigate Web-based systems in more detail in Chapter 16.

From a data management perspective, the three-tier model provides several advantages:

❖ Data security is higher because the data schema is not exposed to the client but hidden in the application server.

❖ Performance is better because only service requests and responses are transmitted between the client and the application server. With two-tier logic, many SQL statements are sent across the network, and selected data must be downloaded to the client for analysis.

❖ Access to legacy data systems and heterogeneous databases is supported via gateways.

❖ Application software is easier to implement and maintain because it is installed on a small number of servers rather than a large number of clients.

The rise of three-tier client/server can be attributed to the benefits of adopting a component-based architecture. The goal is to build quickly scalable systems by plugging together existing components. On the client side, the Web browser is a readily available component that makes deployment of new systems very simple. When everyone in the corporation has a browser installed on their PC, rolling out a new application is just a case of e-mailing the URL to the concerned people. Under a two-tier system, software has to be installed on each PC.

On the data server side, many data management systems already exist, either in relational format or some other data model. Middle-tier server applications can make these data available to customers through a Web client. For example, UPS was able to make its parcel tracking system available via the Web because the database already existed. A middle-tier was written to connect customers using a browser to the database.

The move to client/server architecture is part of the general move toward distributing data and *n*-tier client/server (see Table 12-3), where there are multiple servers and databases. Thus, it is appropriate at this point to consider the topic of distributed database.

Table 12-3: Evolution of client/server computing

Architecture	Description
Two-tier	Processing is split between client PC and server, which also runs the DBMS.
Three-tier	Client PC does presentation, processing is done by the server, and the DBMS is on a separate server.
N-tier	Client PC does presentation, and processing and DBMS can be spread across multiple servers. This is a distributed-resources environment.

Skill builder

A European city plans to establish a fleet of two-person hybrid cars that can be rented for short periods (e.g., less than a day) for one-way trips. Potential renters first register online and then receive via the postal system a smart card that is used to gain entry to the car and pay automatically for its rental. The city also plans to have an online reservation system that renters can use to find the nearest car and reserve it. Reservations can be held for up to 30 minutes, after which time the car is released for use by other renters. Discuss the data processing architecture that you would recommend to support this venture. What technology would you need to install in each car? What technology would renters need? What features would the smart card require? Are there alternatives to a smart card?

Distributed database

Client/server architecture is concerned with minimizing processing costs by distributing processing between the server and multiple clients. Another factor in the total processing cost equation is communication. The cost of transmitting data usually increases with distance, and there can be substantial savings by locating a database close to those most likely to use it. The trade-off for a distributed database is lowered communication costs versus increased complexity.

Distributed database architecture describes the situation where a database is in more than one location but still accessible as if it were centrally located. For example, a multinational organization might locate its Indonesian data in Jakarta, its Japanese data in Tokyo, and its Australian data in Sydney. If most queries deal with the local situation, communication costs are substantially lower than if the database were centrally located. Furthermore, since the database is still treated as one logical entity, queries that require access to different physical locations can be processed. For example, the query "Find total sales of red hats in Australia" is likely to originate in Australia and be processed using the Sydney part of the database. A query of the form "Find total sales of red hats" is more likely to come from a headquarters user and is resolved by accessing each of the local databases, though the user need not be aware of where the data are stored because the database appears as a single logical entity.

A distributed database management system (DDBMS) is a federation of individual DBMSs. Each site has a local DBMS and DC manager. In many respects, each site acts semi-independently. Each site also contains additional software that enables it to be part of the federation and act as a single database. It is this additional software that creates the DDBMS and enables the multiple databases to appear as one.

A DDBMS introduces a need for a data store containing details of the entire system. Information must be recorded about the structure and location of every database, table, row, and column and their possible replicas. The traditional system catalog is extended to include such information. The system catalog must also be distributed; otherwise, every request for information would have to be routed through some central point. For instance, if the systems catalog were stored in Tokyo, a query on Sydney data would first have to access the Tokyo-based catalog. This would create an expensive bottleneck.

A hybrid, distributed architecture

Any organization of a reasonable size is likely to have a mix of the data processing architectures previously described. Databases will exist on stand-alone personal computers, multiple client/server networks, distributed mainframes, and so on. Architectures continue to evolve because information technology is so dynamic. Today's best solutions for database processing can become obsolete very quickly. Yet, organizations have invested large sums in existing systems that meet their current needs and do not warrant replacement. As a result, organizations evolve a hybrid architecture — a mix of the various forms. The concern of the IS department is to patch this hybrid together so that users see it as a seamless system that readily provides needed information. In creating this ideal system, there are some underlying key concepts that should be observed. These fundamental principles (see Table 12-4) were initially stated in terms of a distributed database.[1] However, they can be considered to apply broadly to the evolving, hybrid architecture that organizations must continually fashion.

Table 12-4: The fundamental principles of a hybrid architecture

Principle
Transparency
No reliance on a central site
Local autonomy
Continuous operation
Distributed query processing
Distributed transaction processing
Fragmentation independence
Replication independence
Hardware independence
Operating system independence
Network independence
DBMS independence

Transparency

The user should not have to know where data are stored and how they are processed. The location of data, its storage format, and access method should be invisible to the user. The system should accept queries and resolve them expeditiously. Of course, the system should check that the user is authorized to access the requested data. Transparency is also known as **location independence**—the system can be used independently of the location of data.

No reliance on a central site

Reliance on a central site for management of a hybrid architecture creates two major problems. *First*, because all requests are routed through the central site, bottlenecks develop during peak periods. *Second*, if the central site fails, the entire system fails. A controlling central site is too vulnerable, and control should be distributed throughout the system.

Local autonomy

A high degree of local autonomy avoids dependence on a central site. Data are locally owned and managed. The local site is responsible for the security, integrity, and storage of local data. There cannot be absolute local autonomy because the various sites must cooperate in order for transparency to be feasible. Cooperation always requires relinquishing some autonomy.

---

1. Date, C. J. 1990. What is a distributed database system? In *Relational database writings 1985–1989*, edited by C. J. Date. Reading, MA: Addison-Wesley.

Continuous operation

The system must be accessible when required. Since business is increasingly global and users are geographically dispersed, the system must be continuously available. Many data centers now describe their operations as "24/7" (24 hours a day and 7 days a week).

Distributed query processing

The time taken to execute a query should be generally independent of the location from which it is submitted. Deciding the most efficient way to process the query is the system's responsibility, not the user's. For example, a Sydney user could submit the query, "Find sales of wombat coats in Japan." The system is responsible for deciding which messages and data to send between the various sites where tables are located.

Distributed transaction processing

In a hybrid system, a single transaction can require updating of multiple files at multiple sites. The system must ensure that a transaction is successfully executed for all sites. Partial updating of files will cause inconsistencies.

Fragmentation independence

Fragmentation independence means that any table can be broken into fragments and then stored in separate physical locations. For example, the sales table could be fragmented so that Indonesian data are stored in Jakarta, Japanese data in Tokyo, and so on. A fragment is any piece of a table that can be created by applying restriction and projection operations. Using join and union, fragments can be assembled to create the full table. Fragmentation is the key to a distributed database. Without fragmentation independence, data cannot be distributed.

Replication independence

Fragmentation is good when local data are mainly processed locally, but there are some applications that also frequently process remote data. For example, the New York office of an international airline may need both American (local) and European (remote) data, and its London office may need American (remote) and European (local) data. In this case, fragmentation into American and European data may not substantially reduce communication costs.

Replication means that a fragment of data can be copied and physically stored at multiple sites; thus the European fragment could be replicated and stored in New York, and the American fragment replicated and stored in London. As a result, applications in both New York and London will reduce their communication costs. Of course, the trade-off is that when a replicated fragment is updated, all copies also must be updated. Reduced communication costs are exchanged for increased update complexity.

Replication independence implies that replication happens behind the scenes. The user is oblivious to replication and requires no knowledge of this activity.

There are two major approaches to replication: synchronous or asynchronous updates. **Synchronous replication** means all databases are updated at the same time. Although this is ideal, it is not a simple task and is resource intensive. **Asynchronous replication** occurs when changes made to one database are relayed to other databases within a certain period established by the database administrator. It does not provide real-time updating, but it takes fewer IS resources. Asynchronous replication is a compromise strategy for distributed DBMS replication. When real-time updating is not absolutely necessary, asynchronous replication can save scarce IS resources.

Hardware independence

A hybrid architecture should support hardware from multiple suppliers without affecting the users' capacity to query files. Hardware independence is a long-term goal of many IS managers.

Operating system independence

Operating system independence is another goal much sought after by IS executives. Ideally, the various DBMSs and applications of the hybrid system should work on a range of operating systems on a variety of hardware.

Network independence

Clearly, network independence is desired by organizations that wish to avoid the electronic shackles of being committed to any single hardware or software supplier.

DBMS independence

The drive for independence is contagious and has been caught by the DBMS as well. Since SQL is a standard for relational databases, organizations may well be able to achieve DBMS independence. By settling on the relational model as the organizational standard, ensuring that all DBMSs installed conform to this model, and using only standard SQL, an organization may approach DBMS independence. Nevertheless, do not forget all those old systems from the prerelational days—a legacy that must be supported in a hybrid architecture.

Organizations can gain considerable DBMS independence by using Open Database Connectivity (ODBC) technology (see page 280). An application that uses the ODBC interface can access any ODBC-compliant DBMS. In a distributed environment, such as three-tier client/server, ODBC enables application servers to access a variety of vendors' databases on different data servers.

Conclusion—paradise postponed

For data managers, the 12 principles just outlined are ideal goals. In the hurly-burly of everyday business, incomplete information, and an uncertain future, data managers struggle valiantly to meet clients' needs with a hybrid architecture that is an imperfect interpretation of IS paradise. It is unlikely that these principles will ever be totally achieved. They are guidelines and something to reflect on when making the inevitable trade-offs that occur in data management.

Now that you understand the general goals of a distributed database architecture, we will consider the major aspects of the enabling technology. First, we will look at distributed data access methods and then distributed database design. In keeping with our focus on the relational model, illustrative SQL examples are used.

Distributed data access

When data are distributed across multiple locations, the data management logic must also be distributed. The various types of distributed data access methods are considered, and a banking example is used to illustrate the differences between the methods.

Remote request

A remote request occurs when an application issues a single data request to a single remote site. Consider the case of a branch bank requesting data for a specific customer from the bank's central server located in Atlanta. The SQL command specifies the name of the server (`atlserver`), the database (`bankdb`), and the name of the table (`customer`).

```
SELECT * FROM atlserver.bankdb.account
   WHERE custcode = '12345';
```

A remote request can extract a table from the database for processing on the local database. For example, the Athens branch may download balance details of customers at the beginning of each day and handle queries locally rather than issuing a remote request. The SQL is

```
SELECT custcode, custbalance FROM atlserver.bankdb.customer
   WHERE custbranch = 'Athens';
```

Remote transaction

Multiple data requests are often necessary to execute a complete business transaction. For example, to add a new customer account might require inserting a row in two tables: one row for the account and another row in the table relating a customer to the new account. A remote transaction contains multiple data requests for a single remote location. The following example illustrates how a branch bank creates a new customer account on the central server:

```
BEGIN WORK;
INSERT INTO atlserver.bankdb.account
   (accnum, acctype)
   VALUES (789, 'C');
INSERT INTO atlserver.bankdb.cust_acct
   (custnum, accnum)
   VALUES (123, 789);
COMMIT WORK;
```

The commands BEGIN WORK and COMMIT WORK surround the SQL commands necessary to complete the transaction. The transaction is successful only if both SQL statements are successfully executed. If one of the SQL statements fails, the entire transaction fails.[2]

Paper disks

In April 2004, Toppan Printing and Sony Corporation announced development of a 25 Gbyte paper disk based on Blu-ray Disc, a technology that allows more than two hours of high-definition program recording. This system permits a high level of artistic label printing on the optical disk, which by weight is 51 percent paper.

A paper disk also provides excellent data security, because it can be simply cut up with scissors. The aim is to increase the capacity of the disk and also decrease the amount of raw material used and the manufacturing cost. In addition, because of its paper content, the disk is ecologically friendly, which is important given the world-wide production of approximately 20 billion optical disks per year.

The disk is still in development stage, and volume production technology has to be developed before paper disks will be seen in use.

Source: www.blu-ray.com/

Distributed transaction

A distributed transaction supports multiple data requests for data at multiple locations. Each request is for data on a single server. Support for distributed transactions permits a client to access tables on different servers.

Consider the case of a bank that operates in the United States and Norway and keeps details of employees on a server in the country in which they reside. The following example illustrates a revision of the database to record details of an employee who moves from the United States to Norway. The transaction copies the data for the employee from the Atlanta server to the Oslo server and then deletes the entry for that employee on the Atlanta server.

```
BEGIN WORK;
INSERT INTO osloserver.bankdb.employee
   (empcode, emplname, …)
   SELECT empcode, emplname, …
      FROM atlserver.bankdb.employee
         WHERE empcode = 123;
DELETE FROM atlserver.bankdb.employee
   WHERE empcode = 123;
COMMIT WORK;
```

---

2.   Chapter 19 covers transaction management in more detail.

As in the case of the remote transaction, the transaction is successful only if both SQL statements are successfully executed.

Distributed request

A distributed request is the most complicated form of distributed data access. It supports processing of multiple requests at multiple sites, and each request can access data on multiple sites. This means that a distributed request can handle data replicated or fragmented across multiple servers.

Let's assume the bank has had a good year and decided to give all employees a 15 percent bonus based on their annual salary and add $1,000 or 7,500 kroner to their retirement account, depending on whether the employee is based in the United States or Norway.

```
BEGIN WORK;
CREATE VIEW temp
    (empcode, empfname, emplname, empsalary)
AS
    SELECT empcode, empfname, emplname, empsalary
        FROM atlserver.bankdb.employee
    UNION
    SELECT empcode, empfname, emplname, empsalary
        FROM osloserver.bankdb.employee;
SELECT empcode, empfname, emplname, empsalary*.15 as bonus
        FROM temp;
UPDATE atlserver.bankdb.employee
    SET empusdretfund = empusdretfund + 1000;
UPDATE osloserver.bankdb.employee
    SET empkrnretfund = empkrnretfund + 7500;
COMMIT WORK;
```

The transaction first creates a view containing all employees by a union on the employee tables for both locations. This view is then used to calculate the bonus. Two SQL update commands then update the respective retirement fund records of the U.S. and Norwegian employees. Notice that retirement funds are recorded in U.S. dollars or Norwegian kroners.

Ideally, a distributed request should not require the application to know where data are physically located. A DDBMS should not require the application to specify the name of the server. So, for example, it should be possible to write the following SQL:

```
SELECT empcode, empfname, emplname, empsalary*.15 as bonus
        FROM bankdb.employee;
```

It is the responsibility of the DDBMS to determine where data are stored. In other words, the DDBMS is responsible for ensuring data location and fragmentation transparency.

Distributed database design

Designing a distributed database is a two-stage process. *First,* develop a data model using the principles discussed in Section 2. *Second*, decide how data and processing will be distributed by applying the concepts of partitioning and replication. **Partitioning** is the fragmentation of tables across servers. Tables can be fragmented horizontally, vertically, or by some combination of both. **Replication** is the duplication of tables across servers.

Horizontal fragmentation

A table is split into groups of rows when horizontally fragmented (see Figure 12-6). For example, a firm may fragment its employee table into three because it has employees in Tokyo, Sydney, and Jakarta and store the fragment on the appropriate DBMS server for each city.

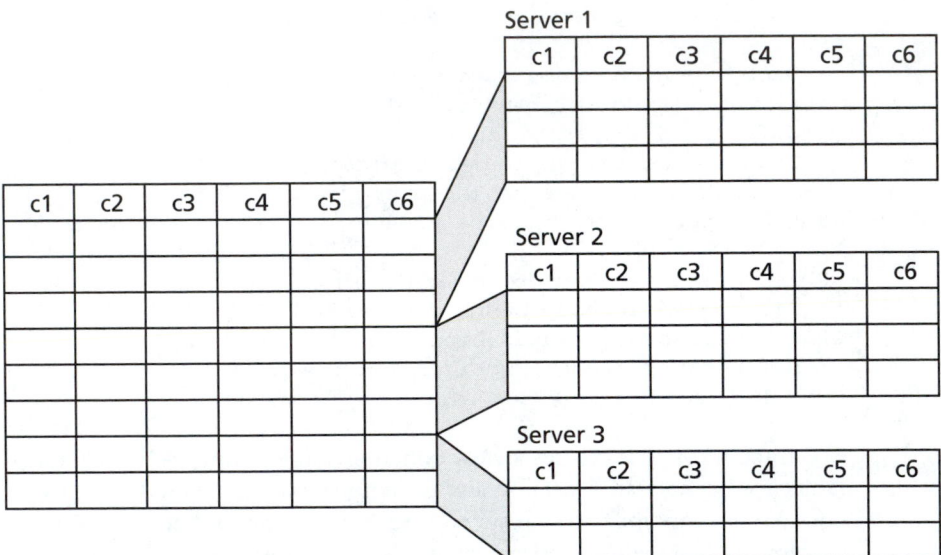

Figure 12-6. Horizontal fragmentation

Three separate employee tables would be defined. Each would have a different name (e.g., emp-syd) but exactly the same columns. To insert a new employee, the SQL code is

```
INSERT INTO table emp_syd
   SELECT * FROM new_emp
     WHERE emp_nation = 'Australia';

INSERT INTO table emp_tky
   SELECT * FROM new_emp
     WHERE emp_nation = 'Japan';
```

```
INSERT INTO table emp_jak
   SELECT * FROM new_emp
      WHERE emp_nation = 'Indonesia';
```

Vertical fragmentation

When vertically fragmented, a table is split into columns (see Figure 12-7). For example, a firm may fragment its employee table vertically to spread the processing load across servers. There could be one server to handle address lookups and another to process payroll. In this case, the columns containing address information would be stored on one server and payroll columns on the other server. Notice that the primary key column (c_1) must be stored on both servers; otherwise, the entity integrity rule is violated.

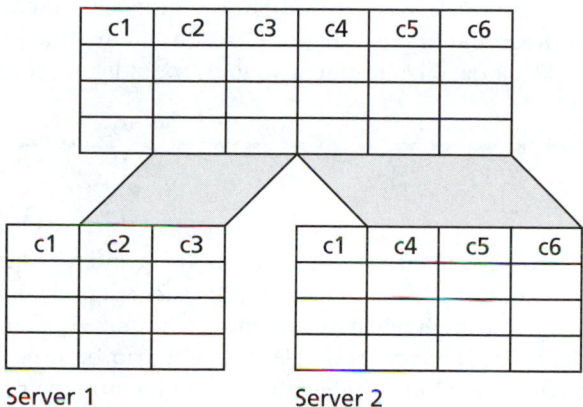

Figure 12-7. Vertical fragmentation

Hybrid fragmentation

Hybrid fragmentation is a mixture of horizontal and vertical. For example, the employee table could be first horizontally fragmented to distribute the data to where employees are located. Then some of the horizontal fragments could be vertically fragmented to split processing across servers. Thus, if Tokyo is the corporate headquarters with many employees, the Tokyo horizontal fragment of the employee database could be vertically fragmented so that separate servers could handle address and payroll processing.

Horizontal fragmentation distributes data and thus can be used to reduce communication costs by storing data where they are most likely to be needed. Vertical fragmentation is used to distribute data across servers so that the processing load can be distributed. Hybrid fragmentation can be used to distribute both data and applications across servers.

Replication

Under replication, tables can be fully or partly replicated. **Full replication** means that tables are duplicated at each of the sites. The advantages of full replication are greater data integrity (because replication is essentially mirroring) and faster processing (because it can be done locally). However, replication is expensive because of the need to synchronize inserts, updates, and deletes across the replicated tables. When one table is altered, all the replicas must also be modified. A compromise is to use **partial replication** by duplicating the indexes only. This will increase the speed of query processing. The index can be processed locally, and then the required rows retrieved from the remote database.

Skill builder

A company supplies pharmaceuticals to sheep and cattle stations[3] in outback Australia. Its agents often visit remote areas and are usually out of reach of a mobile phone network. To advise station owners. What data management strategy would you recommend for the company?

Conclusion

The two fundamental skills of data management, data modeling and data querying, are not changed by the development of a distributed data architecture such as client/server. Data modeling remains unchanged. A high-fidelity data model is required regardless of where data are stored and whichever architecture is selected. SQL can be used to query local, remote, and distributed databases. Indeed, the adoption of client/server technology has seen a widespread increase in the demand for SQL skills.

Summary

Data can be stored and processed locally or remotely. Combinations of these two options provide four basic architectures: remote job entry, host/terminal, personal database, and client/server. Under remote job entry, data are sent over a communication link to a remote computer for processing, and the output is sent back. Under host/terminal architecture, data storage and processing occur at one location. With a personal database, users store and process their data locally. Client/server supports remote storage, and data are mainly processed locally. A LAN connects computers and devices within a limited geographic area. A server is a general-purpose computer that provides and controls access to shareable resources. A file server is a central data store for users attached to a LAN. It is a relatively simple solution to data sharing on a local area network. A DBMS server, a server with a DBMS installed, does query processing so that only necessary records are transferred across a network. In a client/server architecture, the client initiates requests, and the serv-

---

3. You might think that these are places where sheep and cows can catch a train, but what North Americans call a ranch is called a station in Australian English. Some Australians might think a cowcatcher is where cows catch a train.

er responds. The client is the dominant partner because it initiates a request. Client/server exploits cost savings that result from moving processing from a mainframe to less expensive personal computers.

There are two major client/server models: two-tier and three-tier, also known as thick and thin- client technologies. Three-tier client server, particularly with the advent of Web browsers (thin clients), is becoming the dominant client/server technology.

Under distributed database architecture, a database is in more than one location but still accessible as if it were centrally located. The trade-off is lowered communication costs versus increased complexity. A hybrid architecture is a mix of data processing architectures. The concern of the IS department is to patch this hybrid together so that users see a seamless system that readily provides needed information. The fundamental principles that a hybrid architecture should satisfy are transparency, no reliance on a central site, local autonomy, continuous operation, distributed query processing, distributed transaction processing, fragmentation independence, replication independence, hardware independence, operating system independence, network independence, and DBMS independence.

There are four types of distributed data access. In order of complexity, these are remote request, remote transaction, distributed transaction, and distributed request.

Distributed database design is based on the principles of fragmentation and replication. Horizontal fragmentation splits a table by rows and reduces communication costs by placing data where they are likely to be required. Vertical fragmentation splits a table by columns and spreads the processing load across servers. Hybrid fragmentation is a combination of horizontal and vertical fragmentation. Replication is the duplication of identical tables at different sites. Partial replication involves the replication of indexes. Replication speeds up local processing at the cost of maintaining the replicas.

Key terms and concepts

Application server	Host/terminal
Client/server	Hybrid architecture
Continuous operation	Hybrid fragmentation
Data communications manager	Local area network (LAN)
Data processing	Local autonomy
Data server	Mainframe
Data storage	Network independence
Database architecture	Personal database
Database management system (DBMS)	Remote job entry
DBMS independence	Remote request
DBMS server	Remote transaction
Distributed data access	Replication
Distributed database	Replication independence
Distributed query processing	Server
Distributed request	Software independence
Distributed transaction	Supercomputer
Distributed transaction processing	Three-tier architecture
File manager	Transaction processing monitor
File server	Transparency
Fragmentation independence	Two-tier architecture
Graphical user interface (GUI)	Vertical fragmentation
Hardware independence	Workstation
Horizontal fragmentation	

References and additional readings

Bobak, Angelo R. 1993. *Distributed and multi-database systems*, Bantam professional books. New York: Bantam Books.

Morris, C. R., and C. H. Ferguson. 1993. How architecture wins technology wars. *Harvard Business Review* 71 (2):86–96.

Orfali, Robert, Dan Harkey, Jeri Edwards, and Robert Orfali. 1999. *Client/server survival guide*. 3rd ed. New York: John Wiley.

Exercises

1. How does client/server differ from host/terminal computing?
2. How have personal computers affected data architecture decisions?
3. In what situations are you likely to use remote job entry?
4. What are the disadvantages of personal databases?
5. What are the differences between two- and three-tier client/server architectures?
6. What is a potential major problem with a file server system?
7. Describe the difference between a file server and a DBMS server.
8. When is client/server likely to be a cheaper information-processing solution than host/terminal?

9. What factors are likely to inhibit a company's move from host/terminal to client/server?

10. What is a firm likely to gain when it moves from a centralized to distributed database? What are the potential costs?

11. Identify some situations where you would use two-tier over three-tier client server and vice versa.

12. In terms of a hybrid architecture, what does transparency mean?

13. In terms of a hybrid architecture, what does fragmentation independence mean?

14. In terms of a hybrid architecture, what does DBMS independence mean?

15. How does ODBC support a hybrid architecture?

16. A university professor is about to develop a large simulation model for describing the global economy. The model uses data from 65 countries to simulate alternative economic policies and their possible outcomes. In terms of volume, the data requirements are quite modest, but the mathematical model is very complex, and there are many equations that must be solved for each quarter the model is run. What data processing/data storage architecture would you recommend?

17. A large retailer is about to establish a mail-order catalog division. Initially, it plans to hire 500 people to answer telephones. The system will have a few standard transactions (e.g., take an order, query the status of the order, and check inventory). It is anticipated that within two years the database will need to maintain details of two million customers and 10,000 products. What data processing/data storage architecture would you recommend?

18. A small bank has reformulated its strategy to focus on serving the wealthiest 25 percent of the population in its reasonably affluent region. Customers will have a personal banker who will offer a wide range of services. For example, a personal banker will be able to analyze an investment portfolio, organize foreign currency transfers, and book foreign travel. The bank expects to appoint 22 personal bankers and will provide each person with extensive training in a wide range of transactions. What data processing/data storage architecture would you recommend?

19. The advertising manager of a small veterinary pharmaceutical supplier wants to track the firm's advertising in the journal and at the conference of each of the 50 U.S. state veterinary societies. Each state has one journal, which is published at most 12 times per year, and one annual conference. What data processing/data storage architecture would you recommend?

20. A multinational company has operated relatively independent organizations in 15 countries. The new CEO wants greater coordination and believes that marketing, production, and purchasing should be globally managed. As a result, the corporate IS department must work with the separate national IS departments to integrate the various national applications and databases. What are the implications for the corporate data processing and database architecture? What are the key facts you would like to know before developing an integration plan? What problems do you anticipate? What is your intuitive feeling about the key features of the new architecture?

21. Take the data model for the SQL Playbook (see page 289). Assume this company operates in three major urban areas. How might you vertically and horizontally fragment the data model to improve processing speed?

13

Object-Oriented Data Management

The goal of all inanimate objects is to resist man and ultimately to defeat him.
Russell Baker, "Observer," *The New York Times*, June 18, 1968

Learning objectives

Students completing this chapter will be able to

❖ explain the main concepts of object-orientation;
❖ compare and contrast the object-oriented model with the relational model;
❖ develop a simple object-oriented model;
❖ be abreast of current implementations of ODBMS.

Introduction

Originally, the concern of most businesses was to manage text and numeric data. Information systems have, however, moved beyond storing only numbers and text. New applications are often required to support multimedia (video, audio, and animation), CAD/CAM, economic models, document management systems, and other complex data structures, which are generally called objects. Procedural languages and relational databases were not specifically designed to manipulate and store these data forms, but object-oriented programming languages (OOPLs) and object-oriented database management systems (ODBMSs) were created with the intention of manipulating and storing objects. Thus, we need to consider the data management aspects of objects.

Information systems managers are continually searching for better ways to develop and maintain information systems. They want to deliver, on time and on budget, fully functional information systems that meet clients' needs. In recent years, object orientation (OO) has attracted considerable attention because it offers the prospect of lowering systems development and maintenance costs. OO concepts are being applied to analysis, design, programming, and database.[1]

The proponents of OO[2] maintain that an ODBMS offers several advantages over current implementations of relational database technology. They assert that the shortcomings of the relational model are the following:

1. It cannot handle complex objects, such as multimedia.
2. There is no support for general data types found in some programming languages.
3. Performance degrades when large numbers of tables must be joined to respond to a query.
4. There is a mismatch between the relational data model's set-at-a-time processing and the record-at-a-time processing of programming languages.
5. There is no support for representing and recording change, such as different versions of objects.

ODBMS technology addresses these shortcomings. We explain the concept of OO and then explore the current state of ODBMS.

UML

Marching in step with the OO approach to software development is the Unified Modeling Language (UML). Introduced in late 1997 by the Object Management Group (OMG), UML has become the common modeling language for OO software development. UML standardizes the notation for describing processes and has nine predefined diagrams (see Table 13-1). Our attention will be focused on the class diagram because of its correspondence to a data model. UML notation will be used throughout this chapter.[3] UML is widely used for process modeling, but UML's data modeling features have not displaced traditional approaches to representing data models, such as the one used in this book.

Table 13-1: UML predefined diagrams

Diagram	Purpose
Class	Describes the structure of a system by specifying classes and relationships
Object	Shows a number of object instances of a class
Statechart	Identifies possible states of a class or system and which events cause the state to change
Activity	Describes the activities and actions taking place in a system
Sequence	Illustrates one or several sequences of messages exchanged among objects

1. Tore Ørvik of Agder University College (Kristiansand, Norway) is the coauthor of this section.
2. There is some disagreement between OO and relational adherents. This chapter tries to present a balance of the two viewpoints, but in describing the OO approach, it is often easier to present the OO proponents' perspective. Also, you need to remember that we are comparing implementations of the two concepts and not the theoretical models. For example, if the domain concept of the relational model were implemented, then some deficiencies of present relational systems would disappear.
3. To learn more about UML, visit www.rational.com, which is the major provider of UML software.

Table 13-1: UML predefined diagrams (continued)

Diagram	Purpose
Collaboration	Shows collaboration among a set of objects
Use case	Depicts the top-level relationships between actors and use cases, which describe what a system should or does do
Component	Displays the physical structure of the code in terms of components
Deployment	Represents the physical architecture of a system's hardware and software

---

UML in e-business

Companies model complex software applications for the same reason they hire architects to design buildings prior to starting construction. In the long run, a detailed blueprint saves time and money and produces a better system. It allows developers to consider alternatives, select the best option, work out details, and achieve agreement before anyone starts building the application. It is much less costly to change a model than it is to modify an application after it has been built. A good model documents an application's structure and simplifies future modification. This is critical when you consider that 90 percent of the costs involved in large applications occur as they are changed, extended, and otherwise maintained.

UML is an open-standards success story of the late 1990s. In three years, a dozen object-oriented modeling methodologies were replaced by UML, which is currently supported by all major software modeling tools. The OMG drove the rapid transition to UML and continues to maintain it as the world's premier open, object-oriented analysis and design standard.

UML turns out to be a key ingredient in the new model-driven development approach to the software development and is proving to be popular with e-business developers. They use UML models to drive their designs and maintain consistency.

Source: Anonymous. 2001. Building advanced applications: UML models e-business. *Softwaremag.com*, Apr/May. www.softwaremag.com/archive/2001apr/UMLModelsEBiz.html.

Historical development

The underlying concepts of OO have been known for some time. The first OOPL, Simula, was developed in Norway in the mid-1960s. The development of the Smalltalk language at Xerox PARC in the 1970s introduced the terms *object* and *OO* and was a major step toward popularizing OO programming. In the 1980s, several existing programming languages were extended to embrace OO. Now, languages such as C++ and COBOL support OO. In addition to these languages, several pure OO languages, such as Java, were developed.

In the late 1980s, the graphical user interface (GUI), with its support for windows, icons, mouse, and pointers (WIMP), became increasingly common. OOPLs are invaluable for the development of GUI applications, which further enhanced the popularity of OO. As OO programming languages matured, OO found its way into the realms of database and systems analysis and design. UML was mainly developed by Grady Booch, James Rumbaugh, and Ivar Jacobson based on several second-generation OO representation methods. UML was approved by the OMG as a standard in 1997.

Key OO concepts

It is useful to become familiar with some key OO concepts first before examining the benefits of applying OO ideas. OO applications are created by assembling and using objects—self-contained units that can contain data and are very much like entities in data modeling. An object is something in the real world. Like an entity, it can be physical (e.g., a car) or conceptual (e.g., a job). Objects also contain the necessary instructions, the algorithm, to transform data. Thus, an object contains both data and methods, which are also known as procedures, operations, or services. Objects, therefore, can be thought of as application development building blocks. For instance, an employee object may consist of textual data (such as name, address, and phone number) and multimedia data (such as a photograph, video clip, or fingerprint image) combined with methods such as hire, transfer, or promote.

OO modeling and data modeling have a common objective of creating a representation of a real-world information system. Consequently, they frequently deal with the same concepts but use different terminology. A comparison of some of the key concepts is shown in Table 13-2.

Table 13-2: A comparison of data modeling and OO modeling terminology

Data modeling term	OO modeling term
Entity	Object class or classes
Instance	Object
Attribute	Attribute

Data abstraction

Real-world systems are very complex, and the fundamental features of a complicated system can be difficult to extract from the mass of detail. Consequently, simplified models showing the relationships between key elements are often used to reveal the essentials. **Data abstraction** is the process of creating an abstract model to enhance understanding of reality. Data modeling (see Section 2) illustrates the use of data abstraction, because a data model captures the essential elements of the relationships between entities. An organizational chart, another example of data abstraction, shows the associations between roles in an organization. A diagram of the structure of an investment portfolio is another example of data abstraction (see Figure 13-1).

The craft of data abstraction is an important skill for IS professionals. As well as learning some common data abstraction methods, such as data modeling, you also need to develop

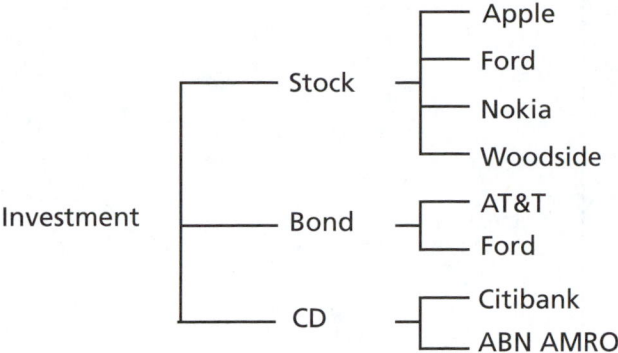

Figure 13-1. A model of an investment portfolio

the general skill of reducing complex systems to understandable models that can be readily drawn, described, and explained.

Object instances and classes

A database stores facts about objects, in ODBMS terms, or entities, in relational terms. Each single representation is called an **object instance**. Most databases contain several objects of the same type, and these are called an **object class** or, simply, class. All the instances of the same type of object are grouped into an object class. In a grading system, for example, there will be an object class, which we will call STUDENT. Individual students are instances belonging to the student object class. In the investment portfolio model, there are object instances for each of the investments (e.g., Apple is an instance of the STOCK object class).

UML represents a class by a rectangle divided into three parts (see Figure 13-2). The upper part contains the name of the class, the attributes of the class are in the middle, and the methods appear in the lower part. Because attributes and methods may need more specification detail than can fit into the available block, each block can be visualized as an expandable window that, when fully opened, shows additional detail. This will certainly be the case if we use special-purpose OO modeling software (e.g., a UML tool). In order to focus on the higher-level aspects of an OO model, however, the following examples will not always specify attributes and methods even though this additional detail is required to define an OO model fully.

The object class shown in Figure 13-2 is the familiar SHARE entity introduced in Chapter 3. Notice that, as well as including the attributes in the model, there is now a method called *yield* for calculating the yield of a share. In the relational model, yield was determined by a calculation within a view and was not shown in the data model.

Figure 13-2. The object class Share

In an object model, every instance of an object has a unique identifier, the **object identification (OID)**. The OID, used to reference an instance of an object uniquely, is comparable to the table name, row name, and primary key combination that uniquely identify a value in a relational model. OIDs are generated by the system and are not related to or derived from the data contained within the object. An OID remains constant for the life of an instance.

Encapsulation

Encapsulation means that all processing that changes the state of an object (i.e., changes the value of any of its attributes) is done within that object. Encapsulation implies that an object is shielded from interference from other objects; that is, an object cannot directly change any other objects. Encapsulation means that data and methods can be packaged together.

Message passing

Objects communicate with each other by sending and receiving messages. For example, an object may send a message to request particular data from another object. Provided a relevant method has been established for the receiving object, the requested data value is sent back to the object issuing the request. This method of communicating is usually referred to as *message passing*. A message can also trigger a change in the receiving object. Again, an appropriate method must be defined for the object receiving the message.

Generalization/specialization hierarchies

Classes can be specializations or generalizations of other classes. The STUDENT class, for example, may be viewed as a specialization, or **subclass**, of ACADEMIC PERSON. A class, might have several subclasses which, as Figure 13-3 shows, include STAFF and STUDENT. The ACADEMIC PERSON class is a generalization, or **superclass**, of the two classes, STUDENT and STAFF.

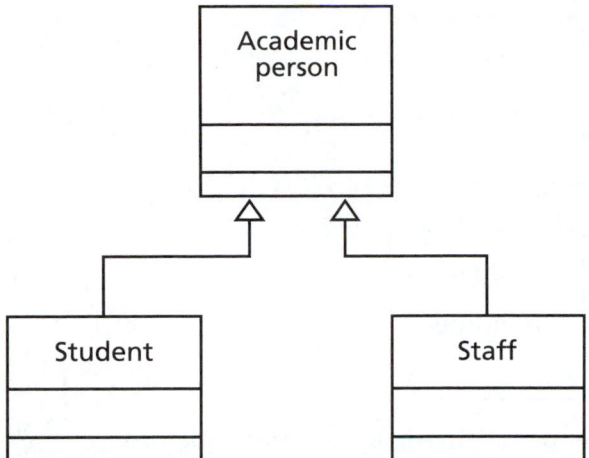

Figure 13-3. An example of a generalization/specialization hierarchy

Inheritance

An important feature of OO is that classes in a generalization/specialization hierarchy will inherit data and methods from the superclass. The ACADEMIC PERSON class in the preceding example probably will have attributes such as person name, address, and Social Security number. These attributes will be inherited by both the STUDENT and STAFF classes. In addition, we may specify some additional attributes for the STUDENT class, such as GPA and major, that are not relevant for the superclass. Inheritance simplifies specification and programming and is especially important for creating reusable objects.

The ideas of inheritance and generalization are conceptually similar to the independent/subordinate entities structure (see Figure 13-4+) of data modeling. The independent entity, ANIMAL, contains general attributes common to all subordinate entities, which have specific attributes appropriate to the entity (e.g., *fleece weight* for SHEEP). Thus, you can think of SHEEP inheriting the attributes of ANIMAL, with this inheritance occurring when the two entities are joined. Of course, there are no methods explicitly associated with this data model.

Reuse

When building new applications with OO software tools, the programmer usually looks for existing object classes to use as building blocks. The exact required class may not be found, but by creating new subclasses and using the inheritance feature, new classes can be created with little effort. For example, if you are writing a drawing program, you may avoid writing a new spelling checker by reusing the existing object class written for a word-processing program. This leads to a development strategy in which recognizing and exploiting similarities in classes is a major means of increasing programmer productivity.

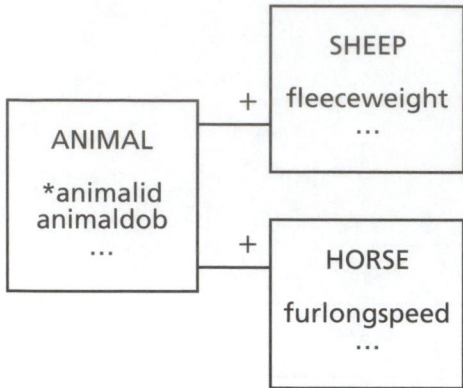

Figure 13-4. An independent/subordinate entities structure

Skill Builder

On a typical commercial flight there is a cockpit crew, cabin crew, and passengers. Draw a generalization/specialization to model the people on a flight.

Why OO?

Many organizations have a substantial backlog of applications because it takes significant resources to build new applications and maintain existing systems. The need to increase programmer productivity and reduce the cost of maintaining systems is the major reason for adopting the OO approach.

Productivity

The productivity of software development has not increased substantially over the years, maybe as little as a four- to sevenfold increase since the early 1960s. This is trivial compared to the massive increases in hardware throughput over the same period. As a result, many potential applications that are now economically feasible because of reduced hardware costs are awaiting the attention of programmers. Software productivity has not kept pace with the increase in demand for new applications. Also, many of the projects in the pipeline tend to be larger and more complex than those already undertaken.

Many problems, such as WIMP-based applications, are not easily programmed using traditional, functional languages. In most cases, the use of an OOPL makes programming easier and also produces more compact and efficient code. This in itself enhances productivity. More important, there is the possibility of creating reusable objects, which, if this feature is exploited, can precipitate significant increases in productivity.

The potential reuse of objects has stimulated widespread interest in OO. Organizations can create or purchase libraries of objects that can become an important source of objects for new applications. Consequently, application development time and cost will be reduced because significant portions of new systems can be built using existing objects.

Maintenance

The slow growth in programmer productivity is exacerbated by the massive effort required to keep operational software systems current. Some companies spend as much as 80 percent of their potential development resources on maintenance of old systems. There are five main reasons for the maintenance problem:

1. Programming is a difficult, intellectual task and one that is prone to logic errors.
2. Determining the client's true needs is a major challenge. Too often, the specified requirements do not reflect the client's real needs, and these needs sometimes do not clearly emerge until after the first version of the software is released.
3. Additional features that could not be accommodated in the original development schedule might be needed once the system is introduced.
4. The business environment changes.
5. Hardware changes as new technologies are developed.

The first two problems are strictly maintenance, and we can alleviate them by using better programming tools and by determining requirements more precisely. Items 3 and 4 are more correctly called enhancements or extensions, and we want to handle these more speedily. The fifth item, that hardware changes, we try to avoid by adhering to common architectural standards, which should result in smooth transitions when hardware is replaced.

Changing large programs is very complicated, and new errors will often be introduced in the process. Because of the tendency not to document all changes properly, the actual software and documentation become inconsistent as time passes. As developers move on to new assignments or new careers and documentation becomes outdated, it becomes increasingly complicated for maintenance programmers to get a thorough understanding of how existing programs work; therefore, it is difficult to change or correct items without introducing unwanted side effects.

As we have shown, OO can address the software crisis—slow development of new applications and expensive maintenance. Many of the claims made for adopting OO modeling echo Codd's rationale for introducing the relational model (see Chapter 9). Data modeling and the relational model are tools for increasing programmer productivity and reducing maintenance. Codd argued for the separation of data and procedures (or methods in OO terminology) to increase productivity. The OO school claims that encapsulating both in an object will improve productivity. So who is right? We believe there is still not enough evidence to make a judgment, and there probably will be no overall advantage for either approach. OO modeling may be better suited for some applications and process modeling/data modeling for others. With research and experience, we will discover when to use each approach.

Summary

Many concepts were introduced in the preceding discussion on OO modeling. Figure 13-5 maps the links between some key OO ideas. An object class, composed of individual occurrences of objects, has attributes and methods. Attributes are the facts an object remembers, and methods are the actions an object can perform. Associations describe the links between object occurrences. Objects can participate in two types of structures: generalization (*is a kind of*) and aggregation (*is part of*).

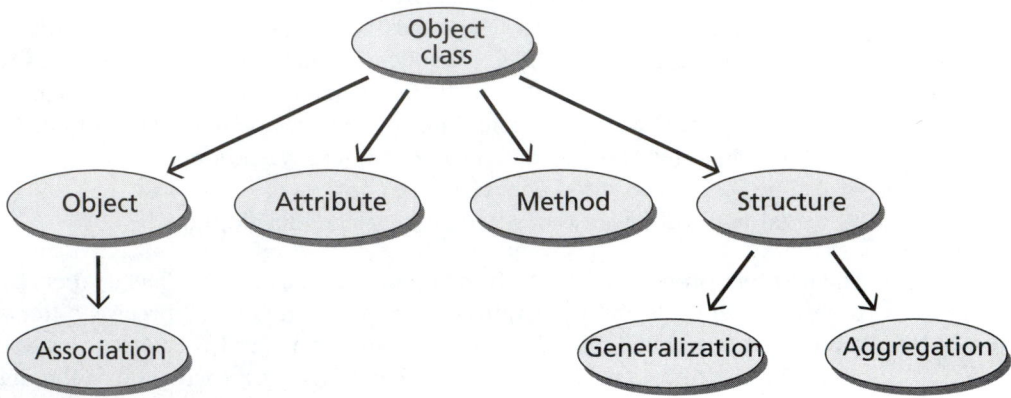

Figure 13-5. A map of OO concepts

Objects and information system modeling

Modeling, as you discovered in Section 2, is a central activity of systems development. Models allow us to describe and understand information systems and to explore possible changes to such systems without interfering with, or disrupting, the actual system. Many different modeling techniques exist. Some deal with different aspects of information systems description (e.g., procedure modeling as compared to data modeling), and some others deal with the same aspects differently (e.g., different methods of data modeling).

Models and abstraction levels

A model is by definition an abstraction of something else. When modeling, we omit some of the features or details we find in the real world and incorporate only those we find useful for the client's needs. For instance, there are many attributes necessary to describe a person completely (height, weight, shoe size, color of eyes), but we only select those that are pertinent to the current problem.

A city map is a model of some aspects of a city's streets. For the tourist, it conveys the layout of a city very concisely and effectively. It is also an abstract model of the city; many features and details are left out. Only the information that is useful for the intended purpose is depicted. As we develop software systems, we start out with quite abstract models, concentrating on understanding required functionality. As we progress, more detail is needed, and our models become more elaborate and concrete. Eventually, they become a functioning system.

The client-developer mind-frame gap

Clients frequently have problems defining what they want from an information system.[4] Even when they are reasonably certain, it is very difficult to capture all the necessary details. Modeling techniques used to capture and record details often include methods for prompting clients about their needs and ensuring that no details are overlooked. Nonetheless, if clients are not trained in data modeling techniques, their way of thinking about their information needs may not relate closely to the way the systems analysts try to model their requirements.

This communication gap between clients and systems developers is purportedly a major reason for low-quality, overdue, and over-budget projects. OO supporters assert that dealing with systems of objects, which closely resemble real-life objects, is more natural than dealing with entities, relationships, and data flows. They argue that the OO approach narrows the communication gap because it uses modeling concepts and techniques that are more closely related to the clients' way of thinking.

Data and procedures

Data modeling deals with what the system needs to remember. A data model is often called static because it tends to be fairly stable and requires little change over time. This does not mean, however, that it will never change. The procedural model describes what the system needs to do and how to do it. Often referred to as the dynamic part of an information systems model, a procedural model has two main parts: processing and control.

The **processing model** records the instructions, the algorithms, for processing data. Traditionally, this has been described using data flow diagrams (DFDs) or pseudocode (a structured English description of a procedure). The **control model** deals with sequencing and timing control of processing. It also specifies any conditions that must exist in order for processing to occur.

Imagine a simple banking system with accounts for the deposit or withdrawal of money. The processing model deals with identifying and describing processes such as establishing an account, processing a withdrawal, and depositing funds. The control model defines sequencing requirements, such as "A deposit cannot be made until after an account has been established." State transition diagrams and entity life-history diagrams are the predominant tools for control modeling.

---

4. For an excellent discussion of this problem, see Wetherbe, J. C. 1991. Executive information requirements: Getting it right. *MIS Quarterly* 15 (1):51–65.

Statics and dynamics

In OO analysis (OOA), the terms *static* and *dynamic* assume slightly different meanings from those used in other analysis methods. The static aspects are modeled in the class diagram, which shows the potential or the capabilities of the system as opposed to what the system will actually do in a given circumstance. The model is static in the sense that it shows what the objects are capable of doing and remembering (like a data model), and these are fairly stable characteristics. In this case, "static" is a relative term, and both the capability for remembering and that for doing may change over time. Methods, the capability for doing, is possibly the more volatile. The dynamic aspect of a model deals with what the system actually does for any particular event.

Scenarios

A scenario is a typical event or sequence of events in the problem domain and the related behavior of the information system. In a simple banking system, some key scenarios are a customer making a withdrawal or a deposit and a manager requesting the day's total withdrawals and deposits. Although the same classes might be involved in the different scenarios, different data and methods will be invoked, and different messages will be transmitted. For each scenario, a subset of the potential capabilities is used and combined to yield the desired system behavior. We usually start by developing the static model, which also incorporates the main methods. We gain sufficient knowledge of all the needed methods only after a thorough analysis of all relevant scenarios.

Traditional systems have an overall control structure or main application program. There is no such parallel in OO because each scenario is associated with a sequence of actions and interactions that define system behavior in that particular context.

Static OO modeling

The basic data modeling concepts learned earlier apply to OO modeling of the static part of a system. It may help to think of object classes as entities with integrated procedural rules. Like entities, object classes can be related to other object classes.

Two broad types of possible relationships are depicted in an OO model: relationships between classes and relationships between individual objects. Classification or inheritance relationships are between classes; aggregation and association relationships are between individual objects. Each of these relationships will be demonstrated with an OO modeling exercise.

Finding objects and classes

Usually the initial activity in OO analysis, finding objects and classes is, in many respects, very similar to identifying entities in data modeling. Which classes to include in a system is highly dependent on the context, the client, and the modeler. Although there is no *correct* set of classes (or entities, in the case of data modeling), the OO analyst should strive to create a high-fidelity model of the client's world. Careful questioning and looking for exceptions are key skills for an analyst. Domain area knowledge and experience also play important roles in the development of high-fidelity models.

One approach is to underline any nouns in the problem description. Most nouns are possible classes, and underlining ensures that no potential classes are overlooked. These suggestions for OO modeling also apply to data modeling. Finding entities and discovering classes are similar exercises.

We will use a four-layer model of OO analysis:

* **Class and object layer**—object classes
* **Structure layer**—structural relations between classes
* **Attribute layer**—the attributes of each class
* **Service layer**—the methods for each class

Although presented sequentially, actual analysis will usually not strictly follow such a serial pattern. The sequence does suggest a main order of activities, however, because the tendency is to work in an iterative fashion rather than finishing all the activities associated with one layer before undertaking the next.

We will now explore these concepts in more depth through an example that will gradually build the layers of an OO model using UML notation.

AFLAC's new system does not duck work

The insurance firm AFLAC has successfully re-engineered a legacy underwriting field and sales batch system into a real-time application, using Java to wrap IBM code. This conversion has sped up the processing of 2.7 million applications that arrive at AFLAC electronically (87 percent of its total applications). This means AFLAC can sell and underwrite policies in real time, processing thousands per day.

AFLAC can now process each application in a few seconds and has increased the accuracy of application processing by 50 percent, evenly distributing the workload from morning to night rather than running all night. Associates now get information back quickly, so they check applications immediately and correct errors. They were less inclined to follow up when they had to wait a day or more.

AFLAC recognized the value of extending its existing applications to new, more modern architectures despite the mismatch between Java and mainframes. The success of this project has encouraged AFLAC to undertake re-engineering other legacy systems.

Source: Havenstein, Heather. 2005. AFLAC speeds policy processing with re-engineered legacy code. *Computerworld*, Mar. 14. www.computerworld.com/managementtopics/management/story/0,10801,99974,00.html.

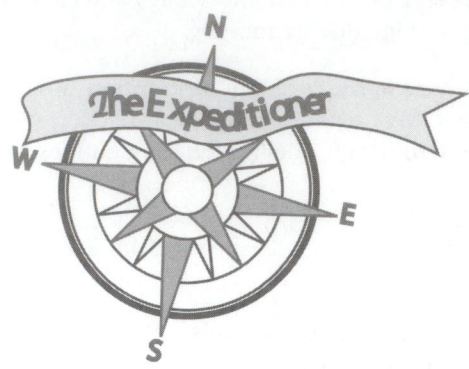

The Expeditioner has arranged many diving safaris to the Great Barrier Reef off Australia's northeast coast. The customers have been extremely pleased with these expeditions, which were handled by a local operator, Dick's Dive 'n Thrive, or DDT for short. Stories in diving magazines and word of mouth among diving devotees have generated tremendous growth for DDT. Although he is a great diver, Dick unfortunately is a poor manager. The company has been unable to handle the growth and is now in serious financial trouble. As a result, Dick has turned to one of his major customers, The Expeditioner, for help. After a thorough investigation of the business opportunities, The Expeditioner decides to take a major interest in DDT. Its management team recognizes that new business practices have to be established, especially for the rental side of DDT, which generates most of the business and is currently losing money.

The management team concludes that existing procedures need to be automated to provide better control and information for managerial decision making, and so they hire a local systems analyst to develop and install an information system. A young lad from Townsville, Bruce "Shark" Dundee,[5] is hired. Shark has had considerable success using OO concepts and decides to create an OO model of DDT's rental business. He starts by writing a statement of the business and underlining the nouns.

<u>Customers</u> can rent <u>diving equipment</u> and <u>boats</u> from <u>DDT</u>. When a <u>customer</u> has seen what is available and decided what to rent, a <u>rental agreement</u> or <u>contract</u> is produced and signed.

Class and object layer

The brief description of DDT's rental business is a starting point for modeling. By underlining the nouns, we see that customer, diving equipment, contract, and boat all are prime candidates for classes (see Figure 13-6).

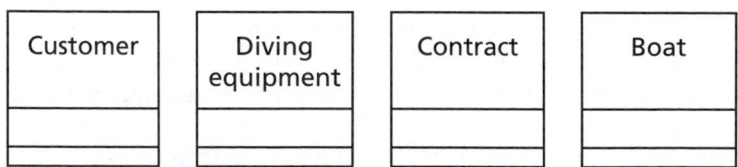

Figure 13-6. Some classes

---

5.   Although his father is a famous crocodile hunter, Shark prefers the ocean.

Structure layer

There are two types of structures: generalization and aggregation. Each of these will be discussed in turn.

Generalization

Depending on how and with which classes we start, OO modeling can be top down or bottom up. In this example, we first look at the classes[6] BOAT and DIVING EQUIPMENT, both of which may be regarded as types of rental equipment. Thus, it is useful to establish a generalized class, which we call RENTAL EQUIPMENT. The attributes and methods established for the superclass or **base class** RENTAL EQUIPMENT are inherited by the subclasses or **derived classes** DIVING EQUIPMENT and BOAT. In this case, we have done bottom-up modeling (see Figure 13-7). If we had started with RENTAL EQUIPMENT, we would have done top-down modeling.

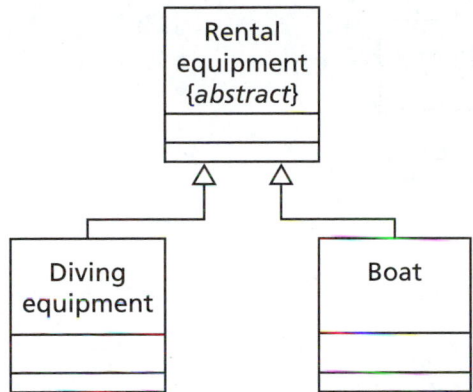

Figure 13-7. A generalization/specialization hierarchy

The RENTAL EQUIPMENT class does not contain any objects, which is why it is an *abstract* class. It serves solely as a vehicle for specifying the common attributes and methods of DIVING EQUIPMENT and BOAT.

If we look more closely at DIVING EQUIPMENT, we see that more detail may be required. DDT rents the usual diving gear such as tanks, regulators, weights, wet suits, and depth gauges, but it needs to store additional specialized information about some of this equipment. For example, diving suits are described by size, thickness, and type. Although we have not specified attributes yet, it is still necessary to think about them to determine what subclasses to create. An analyst who understands the business and the intended use of the system will soon learn the required attributes. As with data modeling, when attributes are specified, some changes in structure often occur. Thus, it makes sense to define attributes as you develop the OO model.

---

6.   The names of classes are shown in uppercase in the text.

In this case, we recognize the need for a subclass SUIT (see Figure 13-8). Later, we might have to refine DIVING EQUIPMENT, but for now it will have only one subclass. This means that all diving equipment we rent, except diving suits, will be called DIVING EQUIPMENT, with an attribute identifying the type of diving equipment (e.g., tank, regulator). DIVING EQUIPMENT contains objects (the subclass is not abstract). In addition to the services and attributes we will later specify for it, the SUIT class will inherit all specified attributes and services from DIVING EQUIPMENT and RENTAL EQUIPMENT.

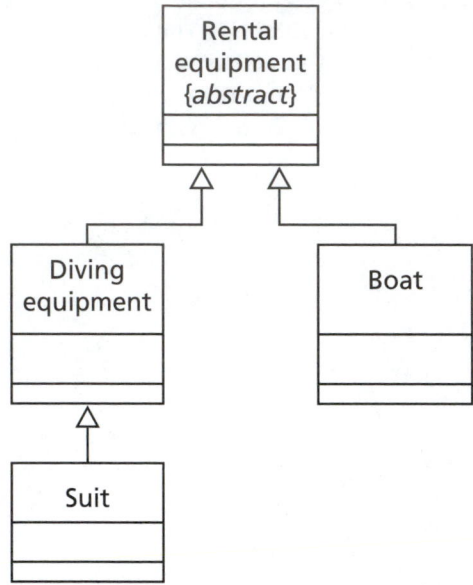

Figure 13-8. SUIT as a subclass of DIVING EQUIPMENT

We have now seen an example of generalization in which inheritance flows from the superclass to the subclass. This is sometimes referred to as an inheritance relation or an "is a kind of" relation; for instance, SUIT is a kind of DIVING EQUIPMENT. An inheritance relation is depicted by, and distinguished from, the other types of relationships by the open arrowheads shown in Figure 13-7 and Figure 13-8. We recommend placing the superclass above the subclasses to increase readability.

An inheritance relation is between classes, but inheritance is not like a relationship in data modeling. The inheritance relationship between SUIT and DIVING EQUIPMENT does not imply that a SUIT object (one specific suit) is linked to a corresponding DIVING EQUIPMENT object. Here, inheritance means SUIT has the same methods and attributes as DIVING EQUIPMENT and some other methods and attributes that are unique to SUIT.

Multiple inheritance

So far, generalization structures have been simple tree structures. Each subclass has one superclass from which it inherits methods and attributes. Multiple inheritance means that a derived class can inherit attributes and methods from more than one base class. The generalization structure then becomes more like a lattice than a tree.

Looking at DDT's customers, we see a difference (see Figure 13-9). Some customers rent boats, and others rent diving equipment. If this difference is significant in DDT's context (due to different licensing and insurance requirements, for example), we could create a class for each group.

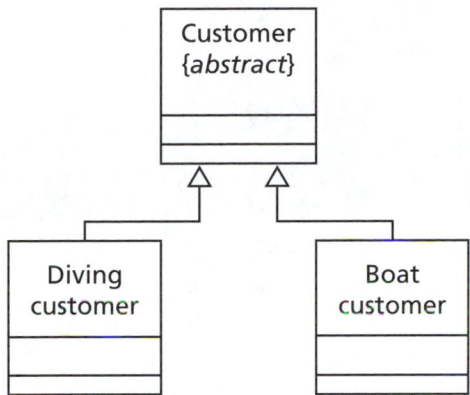

Figure 13-9. Classes of CUSTOMER

Some customers probably will be both diving customers and boat customers (see the model in Figure 13-10), so COMBINED CUSTOMER inherits methods and attributes from both DIVING CUSTOMER and BOAT CUSTOMER.

As you may anticipate, multiple inheritance can create problems when an application is executed. There may be conflicts between the inherited methods and attributes. Although there are different strategies for dealing with this problem, the issue remains unresolved. One strategy is not to support multiple inheritance, which is the approach taken by some OOPLs. In Java, for example, a class inherits from only one superclass but may implement multiple interfaces. From a modeling perspective, it is certainly possible to model multiple inheritance and defer considerations about conflict resolution until time for design. Some modelers recommend avoiding multiple inheritance altogether, especially if the software environment does not support it.

Aggregation

Now, let us now look more closely at the class BOAT. Some of DDT's boats are rented with a trailer and some with zero, one, or two motors. Trailers and motors always stay with the

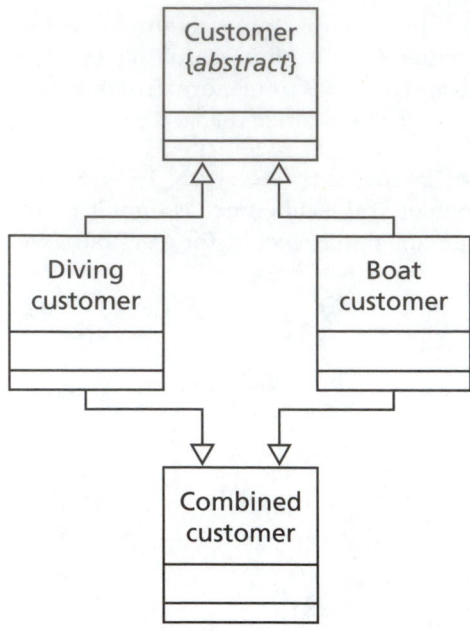

Figure 13-10. Multiple inheritance

same boats. Motors are never rented without boats or taken away from the boats to which they belong except to be serviced or replaced. We now have a BOAT ASSEMBLY which includes BOAT, TRAILER, and MOTOR classes, as shown in Figure 13-11. This is an aggregation, depicting the whole (the boat assembly) and its parts. The relationship is sometimes called a whole/part structure because a TRAILER is a *part of* BOAT ASSEMBLY. It is also sometimes called an owned relationship.

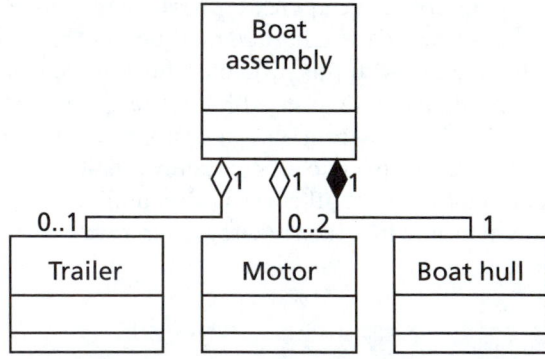

Figure 13-11. An aggregation

The **composition relationship** is distinguished from the other types of relationships by open or filled diamonds (see page 181). In this case, we have a composition aggregation between boat assembly and the boat's hull. In other words, the boat assembly exclusively owns the hull; they are inseparable. The other two aggregations are shared because a boat assembly might not always have a trailer or motor.

An OO model, like a data model, records details of the aggregation relationship. In the case of an OO model, the relationship is between objects. Because a boat assembly can have one or two motors, this must be shown on the OO model. Furthermore, a motor belongs to one and only one boat assembly at a particular time.

Read the aggregation model (Figure 13-11) as follows:

❖ A boat has zero or one trailers, and a trailer belongs to one boat.
❖ A boat has zero, one, or two motors, and a motor belongs to one boat.
❖ A boat has one hull, and one hull belongs to one boat.

We can now combine the completed pieces to illustrate the current state of our OO model (Figure 13-12). Observe that the model is incomplete at this stage because it does not include CUSTOMER or CONTRACT.

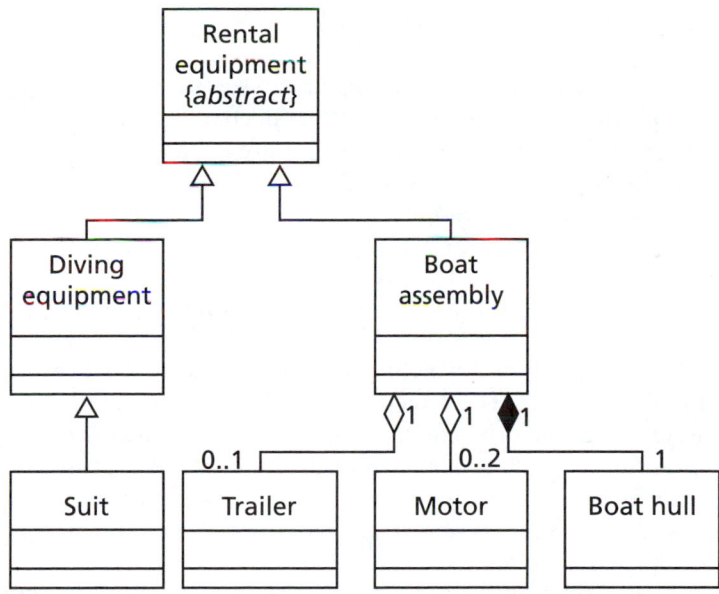

Figure 13-12. OO model—take 1

Attribute layer

The attribute layer has two purposes: specification of attributes and specification of association relationships.

Attributes

Attributes are the facts to be remembered by the object. Some OO proponents argue that the definition of attributes is not needed until physical design or implementation. We recommend that you specify attributes as you discover them. It is only by recording attributes that you really understand the nature of the object classes. As a result, you may have to revise some classes and structures to improve the fidelity of your OO model. Attribute names are listed in the middle segment in the class representation (see Figure 13-13).

Customer
Name Address Phone

Figure 13-13. Attributes of customer

As in data modeling, more information (e.g., range, length, and validation criteria) about an attribute than is provided in the model will be needed before a system can be fully described. Attribute names serve as references to more detailed descriptions that we store elsewhere, typically in a UML modeling tool database. Due to space limitations, we might also want to show aggregate attributes in the model and then completely specify them elsewhere. Address, for example, is usually an aggregate of address lines, city, state, and postal code. By specifying only "address" in the model, we avoid cluttering it with too much detail, although we still convey an impression of what is included.

When deciding which attributes to include, the same principles that are used in data modeling apply to OO modeling. The selection of attributes is based on understanding how objects are described in the problem domain, the responsibilities they will have in the information system, and what they need to remember and do. For example, a student object is unlikely to include details of hair color. Although this is an attribute of a student, this fact probably will not be used by any object and need not be remembered by the system.

If an attribute is only relevant for some of the objects in a class, another class, a specialization, might be needed. For example, diving certificate issue date may be an attribute, but it is not relevant for customers who only rent a boat assembly. We then must differentiate between different types of customers by introducing specialized classes for diving equipment customers and boat-assembly customers. To keep the model simple, attribute names are not shown in our examples except where needed for illustration purposes.

Association relationships

Association relationships, or reference relationships, depict links between occurrences of an object. Sometimes called instance connections, they are conceptually the same as relations in data modeling. For example, a specific contract or rental agreement is associated with a specific customer. A CUSTOMER can be associated with many CONTRACTs, a one-to-many association (1:m).[7] A CONTRACT is related to one and only one CUSTOMER (see Figure 13-14). A CONTRACT is also related to RENTAL EQUIPMENT because a CONTRACT describes the RENTAL EQUIPMENT rented (see Figure 13-15).

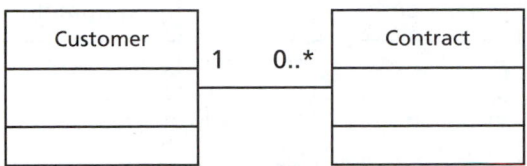

Figure 13-14. A 1:m association between CUSTOMER and CONTRACT

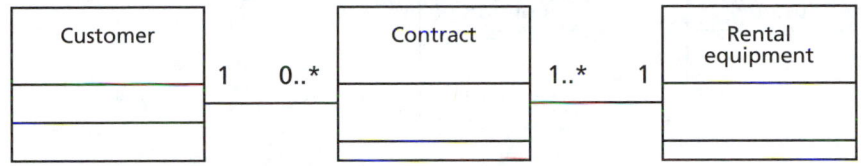

Figure 13-15. An association between CUSTOMER, CONTRACT, and RENTAL EQUIPMENT

As you can see, there is a many-to-many (m:m) association between CUSTOMER and RENTAL EQUIPMENT objects. A customer can rent many pieces of equipment, and a piece of equipment can be rented by many customers. When a customer rents equipment, a contract is created, and this typically includes many items. Because there is an m:m association between CONTRACT and RENTAL EQUIPMENT objects, the model should include another object class, CONTRACT ITEM, which is related to CONTRACT. We have shown this as an aggregation relationship because it reflects the client's thinking that an item on a contract is logically part of a contract (see Figure 13-16).

The aggregation relationship is actually a special version of the association relationship. It reflects a strong tie between objects and also resembles a fundamental way of thinking about objects in the real world: an object as part of another object. All aggregation relationships conceivably can be modeled with association relationships, although some OO proponents discard the aggregation relationship altogether. By using it, we obtain a model that is less abstract and closer to the way we usually think about objects. The final version of the model, at least as far as we will go in this text, is shown in Figure 13-17.

---

7. UML uses an asterisk (*) to indicate many.

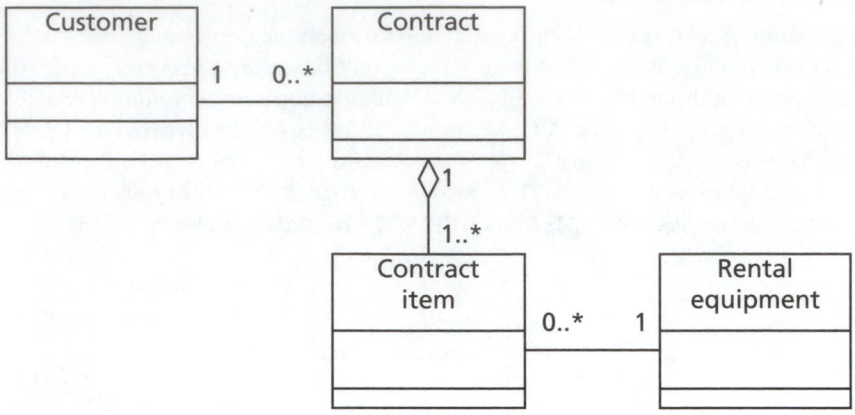

Figure 13-16. An aggregation relationship between CONTRACT and CONTRACT ITEM

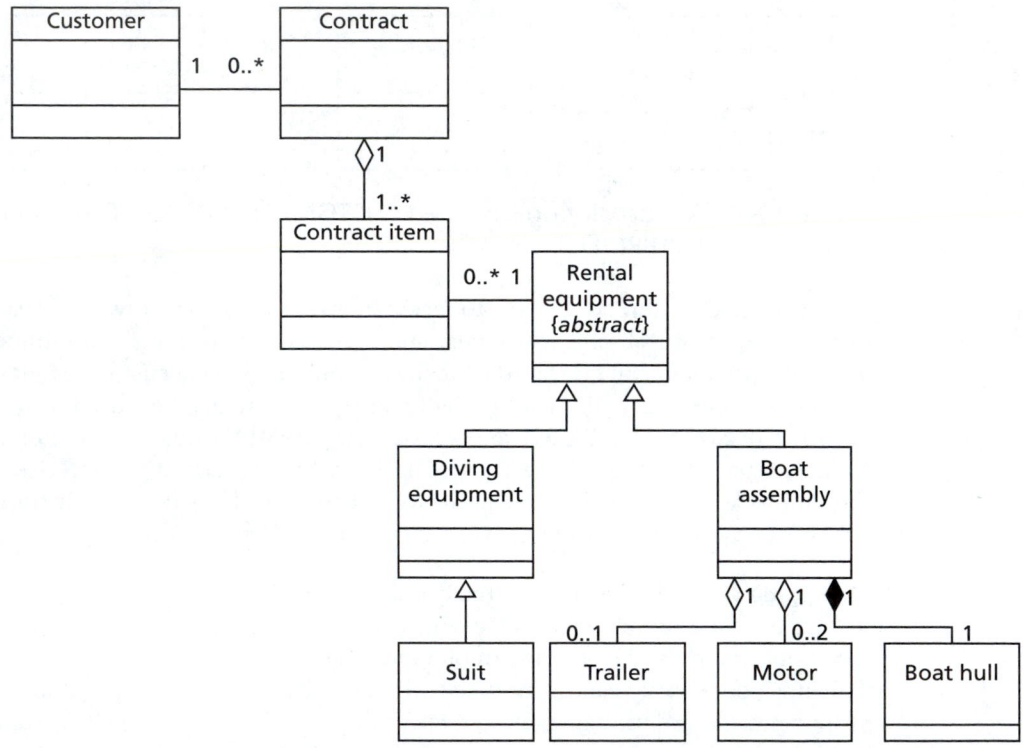

Figure 13-17. OO model—final

Service layer

The required processing for each object is specified in the service layer. Simple and complex services are distinguished. Simple services are the standard services that most objects need to be able to perform. These are usually implied as always being available and are not shown in the model. Simple services typically include create, connect, access, and release.

Complex or nonstandard services, which are shown explicitly, fall into two categories: calculate and monitor. For example, the object class CONTRACT needs to calculate a rental fee. This nonstandard service is shown in the services window (see Figure 13-18). The service name shown in the model is also a reference to a detailed specification of the rental fee calculation algorithm. The actual specification is usually deferred until the static model has stabilized after a few iterations.

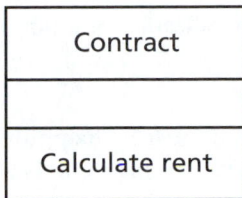

Figure 13-18. The service *Calculate rent*

This completes the first iteration of the static class and object model. You now have seen examples of the three types of relationships—inheritance, aggregation, and association, which are basic features of OO modeling.

The OO and relational paradigms

Now that you have some understanding of the fundamental ideas of OO, it is useful to review the key differences between the object and relational paradigms, which are summarized in Table 13-3.

Table 13-3: The OO and relational paradigms

	OO paradigm	Relational paradigm
Basis	Software engineering principles of coupling,[a] cohesion,[b] and encapsulation	Mathematical concepts of set theory
Goal	To improve the quality of systems, with concern for both data and processes	To improve data management
Data access	Traversing objects via relationships	Matching primary and foreign keys

a. Coupling is a measure of how cleanly the modules in a system are separated from one another.
b. Cohesion is the measure of the strength of functional relatedness of elements within a module.

In practice, the relational model reigns in data management, and the OO model dominates software engineering. Thus, there is a need to know how to transform a class diagram into a relational database so that you can translate between these major paradigms.

Mapping objects to a relational database

Mapping attributes to columns

Each attribute is mapped to zero or more columns, usually one column. Nonpersistent attributes (i.e., those that can be derived, such as the yield of a share), are not mapped. Some attributes, such as address, need to broken into their components (e.g., street, city, postal code) before mapping.

Generalization

There are three possible approaches to mapping a generalization or inheritance structure.

Vertical mapping

Each class is mapped to a separate table. The tables resulting from mapping the subclasses have the primary key of the superclass as a foreign key. This mapping is likely to be relatively slow for queries because of the frequent need to join tables corresponding to a subclass and its superclass.

Horizontal mapping

Each subclass is mapped to a different table, and the superclass is not mapped to a table. The tables resulting from mapping the subclasses have all the attributes of the corresponding class plus those inherited from the superclass. This method works well when the superclass has few attributes.

Filtered mapping

All classes are mapped to the same table. The table contains columns for all attributes in all classes with a column added to distinguish between the subclasses. This method violates normalization rules and will have many columns with a null value. It is not recommended.

In terms of preserving object-oriented and relational concepts, vertical mapping is the superior method. It should be used as the default choice unless there are compelling reasons for either horizontal or filtered mapping.

Association and aggregation

From a database perspective, the only difference between association and aggregation relationships is how tightly the objects are bound to each other. With aggregation, anything that you do to the whole in the database you almost always need to do to the parts, whereas with association that is not the case.

Associations are mapped like their corresponding data model parallels. For example, an m:m association is mapped by creating an associative entity.

Aggregation relationships are mapped in the same manner as relationships in a data model (see page 181). Physically, an aggregation might be implemented using clustering (see page 329) or a linked list (see page 338) because the whole and parts are often retrieved together.

Persistent objects

In OO programming, objects only exist for the duration of a program's execution. If we use OO for information systems, we need to be able to store details of *persistent* objects, those that last much longer. We need a database that stores objects and has facilities for accessing and executing them. What we need is an ODBMS.

Object-oriented database management systems

An ODBMS stores simple and complex objects. It also supports the creation of abstract data types, encapsulation, and inheritance. An ODBMS is the database extension of OO concepts. It stores data when the OO application is no longer executing. ODBMSs also are designed to work closely with OOPLs, and the linkage is tighter than that between a relational database management system (RDBMS) and procedural languages. Because of the consistent use of OO concepts, OO applications are more suited to managing data using ODBMS rather than RDBMS technology. As you would expect, ODBMSs also manage data sharing, concurrent data access, and recovery control, which are necessary features of any database technology.

There are some fundamental differences between ODBMS and RDBMS technology. An ODBMS has pointers, as prerelational models do, for quickly accessing data. Every object has a system-generated unique object identifier, which contains the address of the pointer to the data. This is a significant difference from the approach of the relational data model, where relationships are maintained by foreign keys. As a result, the system can directly access the required data. An ODBMS does not require joins.

The so-called impedance problem, the mismatch between RDBMS set-at-a-time processing and procedural language record-at-a-time processing, is cited as a shortcoming of relational technology. OOPLs and ODBMSs do not have this problem because all operations are at the record level. Of course, this also means the relational model advantage of set-at-a-time processing is lost. Furthermore, some procedural languages do not handle RDBMS data types and arithmetic. For example, not all procedural languages support all SQL data types, such as dates, or may store them differently, which can cause additional work when programming. There is no mismatch between ODBMS and OOPL data types.

ODBMS standards

Information systems managers are reluctant to adopt technology that ties them to a particular vendor. They seek compatibility and standardization because it gives them greater flexibility when buying new hardware and software. Consequently, OO technology vendors have established the OMG[8] to create and promulgate standards for OO technology and object interaction. The OMG is also working on ODBMS issues. Its objective is to minimize incompatibilities across various implementations of the ODBMS idea and standardize some of the features. OMG has released an object database standard,[9] which it intends to promote as an industry standard.

Directions

DBMS vendors are following two major directions. One approach is the pure ODBMS path, and the other is a hybrid object-relational model. Most major vendors have followed the hybrid road. Interest in ODBMS technology appears to have peaked. There is now far less on the topic in the computing popular press than four or five years ago, and many of the ODBMS vendors have disappeared or redefined their business. One of the major ODBMS players is Versant with its Versant Developer Suite (VDS).[10] Its revenues in 2004 were \$22.1 million. In contrast, the relational vendor Oracle reported revenues of \$10.1 billion in the same year.[11]

Hybrid technology

There are two forms of hybrid technology: object-relational and extended-relational. **Object-relational** databases try to add objects on top of relational technology. These hybrids are not full implementations of an object database model. For example, they do not support inheritance, which must be implemented with application code. **Extended-relational systems** add user-defined data types to their underlying relational structures.

Hybrid systems at their core are relational data stores. Thus, object purists criticize the hybrid approach because the DBMS must decompose objects into relational tables—rows and columns—for storage and then rebuild them into objects before delivery to the user. Requests for data objects from the database must be continually assembled and disassembled. Consequently, flexibility and performance can suffer in hybrid databases. It has been estimated that one-third of hybrid database processing time is spent translating data into objects. Hybrid database implementations represent compromises to both the object database and relational models.

SQL-99 (see page 282) standardizes the different approaches to adding OO concepts to the relational model. The failure of vendors to follow these standards will likely result in a reluctance of developers to take full advantage of the new standard because of incompatibility concerns.

If product performance meets a client's requirements, however, it does not matter whether the system is pure object or hybrid. What the product does is hidden, and unless its ar-

---

8.   www.odmg.org/
9.   Cattell, R. G. G., D. K. Barry, M. Berler, J. Eastman, D. Jordan, C. Russel, O. Schadow, T. Stanienda, and F. Velez, eds. 2000. *The object data standard: OMG 3.0.* San Francisco: Morgan Kaufmann.
10.   www.versant.com
11.   www.oracle.com

J2EE

The goal of J2EE (Java 2 Enterprise Edition) is to deliver Java's write-once, run-anywhere promise to the server. J2EE is not a single product but a series of specifications that vendors use to build products, most notably application servers. Sun recognized that the whole of Java was greater than the sum of its parts, so it started to bundle and integrate its Java products into a coherent platform, J2EE.

J2EE provides programmers with the necessary infrastructure to create new applications. Many Web applications today, particularly corporate ones, are written in Java and run on a J2EE-compliant server program such as IBM's WebSphere. What companies like is that J2EE allows them to develop highly customized applications quickly without having to start from scratch.

Features included in J2EE are Enterprise JavaBeans (EJBs), Common Object Request Broker Architecture (CORBA), XML messaging, Java Server Pages (JSP), Java servlets, Java Naming and Directory Interface (JNDI) to access directory services, Java Database Connectivity (JDBC), and Java Message Service (JMS) for asynchronous messaging.

Driving the adoption of J2EE is the acceptance of Java and the fact that developers know their code will work on any platform once an application server is certified as J2EE-compliant. To be certified as J2EE-compliant, an application server must pass a battery of 13,000 validation tests.

Source: Patrizio, A. 2001. Serving up Java 2 Enterprise Edition. *Informationweek.com*, Apr 23, www.informationweek.com/834/ooj2ee.htm.

---

chitecture interferes with maintenance and enhancement, clients should be indifferent. Experience will demonstrate whether the RDBMS vendors are successful in adapting the relational model to complex-data support.

The future of ODBMS

A question that many data managers ask is, "Will ODBMS replace RDBMS in the next five years?" Based on the slowness with which the RDBMS technology was adopted, this is unlikely. RDBMS technology first appeared in 1979, and it took many years for it to replace hierarchical and network systems. Organizations have a heavy investment in relational database systems and have learned how to build and manage such systems. They are unlikely to discard this large investment quickly. Many companies still maintain prerelational legacy systems; so, ODBMSs cannot be expected to become a dominant force in the next few years.

Relational vendors have a major advantage because the maturity of their technology enables them to handle large volumes of data efficiently. If the ODBMS vendors had the resources, it would take them some years to compete on efficiency terms in the market for very large databases. Also, the relational vendors are far more profitable and have more funds to invest in improving their products. If anything, ODBMS technology has lost momentum over the last few years, and it is less likely a competitor to relational technology.

There is no single database system that is *right* for all applications. Instead of generally adopting a single model, database designers need to consider the characteristics of the data, data structures, and the system's goals before deciding on which DBMS is appropriate. Clearly, applications that must handle complex objects are well suited to ODBMS. Our prognosis is that relational systems will continue to evolve to handle new data types.

Summary

OO has attracted considerable attention because it offers the prospect of lowering systems development and maintenance costs. OO concepts are being applied to analysis, design, programming, and database. OO modeling creates a representation of a real-world information system. An ODBMS with an OOPL can overcome some of the shortcomings of relational database technology. OOPLs are invaluable for the development of GUI applications.

OO applications are created by assembling and using objects:, self-contained units that can contain data. Objects also contain the necessary instructions to transform data. Encapsulation means that all processing that changes the state of an object is done within an object. Objects are individual occurrences, often corresponding to objects in the real world. Objects of the same type are called an object class. Objects communicate with each other by sending and receiving messages.

Classes can be specializations or generalizations of other classes. More specialized classes in a generalization hierarchy (derived classes or subclasses) will inherit data and methods from the more general class (base class or superclass). Inheritance simplifies specification and programming and is especially important for creating reusable objects. Recognizing and exploiting similarities between classes is a major means of increasing programmer productivity.

Modeling is a central activity of systems development. A model is an abstraction of something. OO supporters argue that their approach narrows the communication gap between client and analyst because it uses modeling concepts and techniques that are more closely related to the clients' ways of thinking. It is necessary to describe two aspects of an information system: data and procedures. The static part of a model shows what objects are capable of doing and remembering; the dynamic aspect deals with what the system actually does for any particular event. A scenario is a typical event or sequence of events in the problem domain and the related behavior of the information system.

Two broad types of possible relationships are shown in an OO model: relationships between classes and relationships between individual objects. Finding objects and classes is usually the initial activity in OO analysis. One approach is to underline any nouns in the problem description. A four-layer model of OO analysis includes class and object layer, structure layer, attribute layer, and service layer.

The two types of structures are generalization and aggregation. A generalization is sometimes referred to as an inheritance relation or an *is a kind of* relation. Multiple inheritance means that a class can inherit attributes and methods from more than one base class.

The attribute layer has two purposes: specification of attributes and specification of association relationships. Attributes are the facts to be remembered by the object. Association relationships depict links between actual object occurrences. They are conceptually the same as relations in data modeling. The aggregation relationship is a special version of the association relationship. The processing required for each object is specified in the service layer. Simple services are the standard services that most objects need to be able to perform. Complex or nonstandard services fall into two categories: calculate and monitor. Objects can have message connections and use relationships.

An ODBMS stores details of persistent objects; it is the database extension of OO concepts. ODBMSs have high synergy with OOPLs. ODBMSs manage data sharing, concurrent data access, and recovery control. Every object has a system-generated unique object identifier, which contains the address of the pointer to the data. All operations are at the record level. OO technology vendors have established the OMG with the goal of creating and promulgating standards for OO technology and object interaction. Relational systems are likely to continue to dominate over the next few years, especially with the release of the SQL-99 standard and its embrace of OO ideas.

Key terms and concepts

Abstract class
Aggregation
Association
Attribute
Base class
Complex objects
Complex service
Composition
Derived class
Dynamic model
Encapsulation
Extended-relational
Generalization
Hybrid technology
Impedance problem
Inheritance
Message passing
Methods
Object
Object class
Object identifier
Object Management Group (OMG)

Object relational
Object-orientation (OO)
ODBMS
OO analysis (OOA)
OO design (OOD)
OO modeling
OO programming language (OOPL)
Persistent object
Relationship
Reusable objects
Scenario
Service
Simple service
Software productivity
Specialization
Static model
Structured analysis
Subclass
Subject
Superclass
UML
Windows, icon, mouse, pointer (WIMP)

References and additional readings

Ambler, S. W. 2000. Mapping objects to relational databases: Ronin International. www.AmbySoft.com/mappingObjects.pdf.

Booch, G. 1991. *Object-oriented design with applications.* Redwood City, CA: Benjamin/Cummings.

Coad, P., and E. Yourdon. 1990. *Object-oriented analysis.* Englewood Cliffs, NJ: Prentice-Hall.

Rumbaugh, J., I. Jacobson, and G. Booch. 1999. *The Unified Modeling Language reference manual,* The Addison-Wesley object technology series. Reading, MA: Addison-Wesley.

Exercises

1. What circumstances have stimulated interest in OO concepts?
2. What is encapsulation? Why is it desirable?
3. Draw a generalization/specialization hierarchy to describe audio recording media (e.g., cassette, CD, LP).
4. Draw a generalization/specialization hierarchy to describe farm animals.
5. What are the advantages of inheritance?
6. Draw a generalization/specialization hierarchy to describe transport choices (e.g., bus, car, plane, boat). What attributes are common to all object classes? What are some unique attributes of a plane?
7. What are the advantages of the OO approach?
8. How does OO reduce maintenance costs?
9. How does a data model differ from a procedural model?
10. Why do objects pass messages?
11. What is the difference between association and aggregation relationships?
12. When is an ODBMS required?
13. How do an ODBMS and an RDBMS differ in the way they handle recording relationships?
14. What are ODBMS vendors doing to increase the likelihood of the adoption of ODBMS technology?
15. What is the likely future for ODBMS and RDBMS?
16. A travel company sells two types of trips: ship cruises and bus tours. Customers fall into two categories: group and individual. Group customers belong to an affinity group (e.g., a bird watchers' club), which will book a block of tickets on a trip. Individual customers make personal bookings. Some individual customers, because of their frequent use of the travel company, are designated *gold star travelers* and receive additional benefits when traveling. Draw a class and object layer model.
17. Night-on-the-Town offers a package deal to New York tourists. For a flat fee, a person can select a Broadway play, dinner at a fancy restaurant, and jazz at a nightclub. Night-on-the-Town offers a choice in each category, and the customer selects one from each of the three categories (i.e., the customer goes to a play, eats dinner, and then listens to jazz). Draw a class and object layer model.

18. An agent can represent many bands, but a band has only one agent. A band consists of many musicians, but a musician belongs to only one band. Model this situation using association and aggregation relationships.

19. A government treasury bond provides a guaranteed stream of future payments. The date and amount of each of these payments are known. Model this relationship first, and then add to your model the information that the BOND object can use an object called NET PRESENT VALUE to calculate the current value of this stream of payments. Show relevant attributes.

20. An educational software developer has asked you to develop a database of orchestral musical instruments. An orchestra consists of four broad classes (strings, woodwinds, brass, and percussion). What data would you store for each musical instrument? How would the data describing a drum differ from those of a violin? Draw a class and object layer model. Consider one of the microcomputer databases with which you are familiar. How suitable would it be for this database?

14

Spatial and Temporal Data Management

Nothing puzzles me more than time and space; and yet nothing troubles me less, as I never think about them.
Charles Lamb, 1810.

Learning objectives

Students completing this chapter will

❖ be able to define and use a spatial database;
❖ be familiar with the issues surrounding the management of temporal data.

Introduction

The introduction of ubiquitous networks and information appliances will lead to location-based services (see Chapter 21). Customers will be delivered information based on, among other things, where they are. For example, a person touring the historic German city of Regensburg could receive information about its buildings and parks via her mobile phone in the language of her choice. Her information appliance will determine her location and then select from a database details of her immediate environment. Data managers need to know how to manage the **spatial** data necessary to support location-based services.

Some aspect of time is an important fact to remember for many applications. Banks, for example, want to remember what dates customers made payments on their loans. Airlines need to recall for the current and future days who will occupy seats on each flight. Thus, the management of time-varying, or **temporal** data would be assisted if a database management system (DBMS) had built-in temporal support. As a result, there has been extensive research on temporal data models and DBMSs for more than a decade. The management of temporal data is another skill required of today's data management specialist.

The Open Geospatial Consortium, Inc. (OGC)[1] is a nonprofit international organization developing standards for geospatial and location based services. Its goal is to create open and extensible software application programming interfaces for geographic information systems (GIS) and other geospatial technologies. DBMS vendors (e.g., MySQL) have implemented some of OGC's recommendations for adding spatial features to SQL. MySQL is gradually adding further GIS features as it develops its DBMS.

Managing spatial data

A spatial database is a data management system for the collection, storage, manipulation, and output of spatially referenced information. Also known as a geographic information system (GIS), it is an extended form of DBMS. Geospatial modeling is based on three key concepts: theme, geographic object, and map.

A **theme** refers to data describing a particular topic (e.g., scenic lookouts, rivers, cities) and is the spatial counterpart of an entity. When a theme is presented on a screen or paper, it is commonly seen in conjunction with a **map**. Color may be used to indicate different themes (e.g., blue for rivers and black for roads). A map will usually have a scale, legend, and possibly some explanatory text.

A **geographic object** is an instance of a theme (e.g., a river). Like an instance of an entity, it has a set of attributes. In addition, it has spatial components that can describe both geometry and topology. Geometry refers to the location-based data, such as shape and length, and topology refers to spatial relationships among objects, such as adjacency. Management of spatial data requires some additional data types to represent a point, line, and region (see Table 14-1).

Table 14-1: Generic spatial data types

Data type	Dimensions	Example
Point	0	Scenic lookout
Line	1	River
Region	2	County

Consider the case where we want to create a database to store some details of political units.[2] A political unit can have many boundaries. The United States, for example, has a boundary for the continental portion, one for Alaska, and one for Hawaii. In its computer form, a boundary is represented by an ordered set of line segments (a path). These relationships are captured in the data model shown in Figure 14-1.

MySQL has data types for storing geometric data (see Table 14-2). The data model in Figure 14-1 is mapped to MySQL using the statements listed in Table 14-3. In the preceding definition of the database's tables, note two things. The boundpath column of

1.   www.opengeospatial.org
2.   Country, state, province, county, and so forth

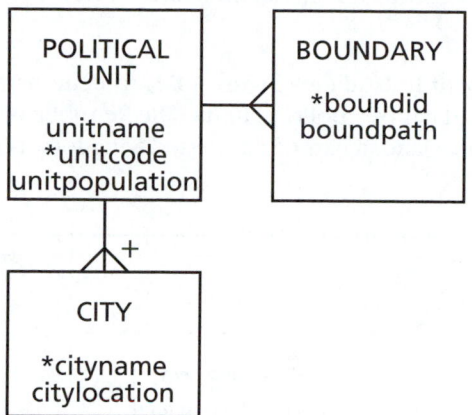

Figure 14-1. Data model for political units

Table 14-2: MySQL geometric data types

Type	Representation	Description
LineString	`LINESTRING(x₁ y₁,x₂ y₂,…)`	A sequence of points with linear interpolation between points (e.g., a road)
Point	`POINT(x y)`	A point in space (e.g., a city)
Polygon	`POLYGON((x₁ y₁,x₂ y₂,…),` `(x₁ y₁,x₂ y₂,…))`	A polygon (e.g., a boundary), which has a single exterior boundary and zero or more interior boundaries (i.e., holes)

Table 14-3: Political unit database definition

```
1  CREATE TABLE political_unit (
2    unitname      VARCHAR(30) NOT NULL,
3    unitcode      CHAR(2),
4    unitpop       DECIMAL(6,2),
5    PRIMARY KEY(unitcode));
6  CREATE TABLE boundary (
7    boundid       INTEGER,
8    boundpath     POLYGON NOT NULL,
9    unitcode      CHAR(2),
10   PRIMARY KEY(boundid),
11   CONSTRAINT fk_boundary_polunit FOREIGN KEY(unitcode)
12     REFERENCES political_unit(unitname)) TYPE MYISAM;
13 CREATE TABLE city (
14   cityname      VARCHAR(30),
15   cityloc       POINT NOT NULL,
16   unitcode      CHAR(2),
17   PRIMARY KEY(unitcode,cityname),
18   CONSTRAINT fk_city_polunit FOREIGN KEY(unitcode)
19     REFERENCES political_unit(unitname)) TYPE MYISAM;
```

boundary is defined with a data type of POLYGON {8}.[3] The cityloc column of city is defined as a POINT {15}. In MySQL, you specify the file type for tables containing geo-

---

3.   In this chapter, numbers in {} refer to line numbers in the corresponding SQL statement.

metric data, which in this case is MYISAM. Otherwise, there is little new in the set of statements to create the tables.

We now use the geographic entity of Ireland (see Figure 14-2) to demonstrate the application of spatial concepts. The island has two political units. The Republic of Ireland (Eire) governs the south, while Northern Ireland, a part of the United Kingdom, is in the north.

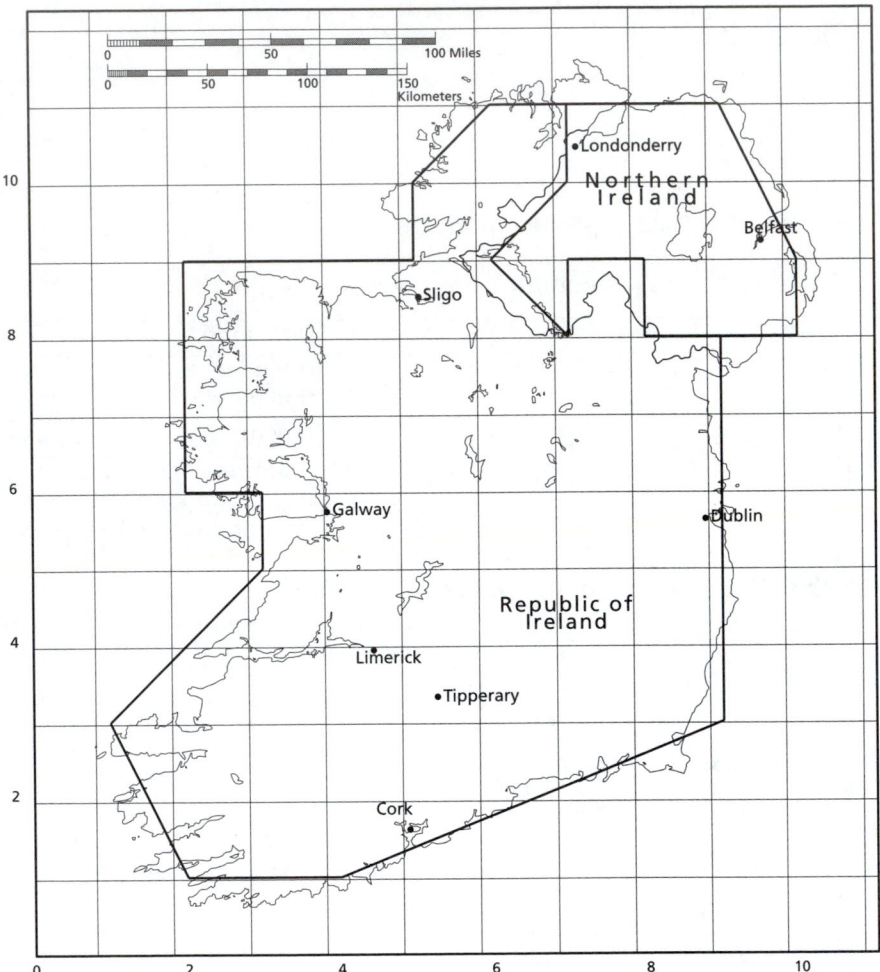

Figure 14-2. Map of Ireland

To represent these two political units within a spatial database, we need to define their boundaries. Typically, this is done by approximating the boundary by a single exterior polygon. In Figure 14-2, you see a very coarse representation of the island based on connecting intersection points of the overlay grid. The statements for populating the three tables representing the data model defined in Figure 14-1 are listed in Table 14-4.

Table 14-4: Insert statements for populating database

```
 1 INSERT INTO political_unit VALUES ('Republic of Ireland','ie', 3.9);
 2 INSERT INTO political_unit VALUES ('Northern Ireland','ni', 1.7);
 3 INSERT INTO boundary VALUES
 4   (1,GeomFromText('POLYGON((9 8, 9 3, 4 1, 2 2, 1 3, 3 5, 3 6, 2 6,
 5    2 9, 5 9, 5 10, 6 11, 7 11, 7 10, 6 9, 7 8, 7 9, 8 9, 8 8, 9 8))'),'ie');
 6 INSERT INTO boundary VALUES
 7   (2,GeomFromText('POLYGON((7 11, 9 11, 10 9, 10 8, 8 8, 8 9, 7 9,
 8    7 8, 6 9, 7 10, 7 11))'),'ni');
 9 INSERT INTO city VALUES ('Dublin',GeomFromText('POINT(9 6)'),'ie');
10 INSERT INTO city VALUES ('Cork',GeomFromText('POINT(5 2)'),'ie');
11 INSERT INTO city VALUES ('Limerick',GeomFromText('POINT(4 4)'),'ie');
12 INSERT INTO city VALUES ('Galway',GeomFromText('POINT(4 6)'),'ie');
13 INSERT INTO city VALUES ('Sligo',GeomFromText('POINT(5 8)'),'ie');
14 INSERT INTO city VALUES ('Tipperary',GeomFromText('POINT(5 3)'),'ie');
15 INSERT INTO city VALUES ('Belfast',GeomFromText('POINT(9 9)'),'ni');
16 INSERT INTO city VALUES ('Londonderry',GeomFromText('POINT(7 10)'),'ni');
```

Lines 4–5 and 7–8, respectively, define the boundaries of the Republic of Ireland and Northern Ireland. Because of the coarseness of this sample mapping, the Republic of Ireland has only one boundary. A finer-grained mapping would have multiple boundaries, such as one to include the Arran Islands off the west coast near Galway. Each city's location is defined by a point or pair of coordinates. GeomFromText is a MySQL function to convert text into a geometry data form.

- -

Skill builder

If you have access to MySQL, create the three tables for the example and insert the rows listed in Table 14-4.[4]

- -

MySQL includes a number of geometry functions and operators[5] for processing spatial data that simplify the writing of queries. For illustrative purposes, just a few of these functions are described in Table 14-5 .

Table 14-5: Some MySQL geometric functions

Function	Description
X(Point)	The x-coordinate of a point
Y(Point)	The y-coordinate of a point
GLength(LineString)	The length of a linestring
NumPoints(LineString)	The number of points in a linestring
Area(Polygon)	The area of a polygon

---

4. The create and insert statements are available on the book's web site. Click on the Tables link.
5. See dev.mysql.com/doc/mysql/en/spatial-extensions-in-mysql.html for full details.

Once the database is established, we can do some queries to gain an understanding of the additional capability provided by the spatial additions. Before starting, examine the scale on the map (Figure 14-2) and note that one grid unit is about 37.5 kilometers (23 miles). This also means that the area of one grid unit is 1406 km^2 (526 square miles).

○ **What is the area of the Republic of Ireland?**

Because we approximate the border by a polygon, we use the area function and multiply the result by 1406 to convert to square kilometers.[6]

```
SELECT AREA(boundpath)*1406
    AS "Area (km^2)" FROM political_unit, boundary
WHERE unitname = 'Republic of Ireland'
AND political_unit.unitcode = boundary.unitcode;
```

Area(km^2)
71706

○ **How far, as the crow flies,[7] is it from Sligo to Dublin?**

MySQL has not yet implemented a distance function to measure how far it is between two points. However, we can get around this limitation by using the function GLength to compute the length of a linestring. We will not get into the complications of how the linestring is created, but you should understand that a one segment linestring is created, with its end points being the locations of the two cities. Notice also that the query is based on a self-join.

```
SELECT GLENGTH(LINESTRINGFROMWKB(LINESTRING(ASBINARY(orig.cityloc),
ASBINARY(dest.cityloc))))*37.5 AS "Distance (kms)"
    FROM city orig, city dest
        WHERE orig.cityname = 'Sligo'
        AND dest.cityname = 'Dublin';
```

Distance (kms)
167.71

Assuming the distance function was implemented, the query would be

```
SELECT DISTANCE(orig.cityloc, dest.cityloc)*37.5 AS "Distance (kms)"
    FROM city orig, city dest
        WHERE orig.cityname = 'Sligo'
        AND dest.cityname = 'Dublin';
```

---

6. The actual area is 70,273 km^2, so the coarse gradation gives a good approximation.
7. An English expression to describe the shortest distance between two points.

○ **What is the closest city to Limerick?**

This query has a familiar structure. The inner query determines the minimum distance between Limerick and other cities. Notice that there is a need to exclude comparing the distance from Limerick to itself, which will be zero. In this case, we assume the distance function exists for ease of understanding the logic.

```
SELECT dest.cityname FROM city orig, city dest
WHERE orig.cityname = 'Limerick'
AND DISTANCE(orig.cityloc,dest.cityloc) =
(SELECT MIN(DISTANCE(orig.cityloc,dest.cityloc)
   FROM city orig, city dest
      WHERE orig.cityname = 'Limerick'
      AND dest.cityname <> 'Limerick');
```

cityname
Tipperary

○ **What is the westernmost city in Ireland?**

The first thing to recognize is that by convention the west is shown on the left side of the map, which means the westernmost city will have the smallest x-coordinate.

```
SELECT west.cityname FROM city west
WHERE NOT EXISTS
   (SELECT * FROM city other WHERE X(other.cityloc) < X(west.cityloc));
```

cityname
Limerick
Galway

Skill builder

1. What is the area of Northern Ireland? Because Northern Ireland is part of the United Kingdom and miles are still often used to measure distances, report the length in miles.
2. What is the direct distance from Belfast to Londonderry in miles?
3. What is the northernmost city of the Republic of Ireland?

R-tree

Conventional DBMSs were developed to handle one-dimensional data (numbers and text strings). In a spatial database, points, lines, and rectangles may be used to represent the location of retail outlets, roads, utilities, and land parcels. Such data objects are represented by sets of x, y or x, y, z coordinates. Other applications requiring the storage of spatial data include computer-aided design (CAD), robotics, and computer vision.

The B-tree (see page 335), often used to store data in one-dimensional databases, can be extended to n dimensions, where $n \geq 2$. This extension of the B-tree is called an **R-tree**. As well as storing pointers to records in the sequence set, an R-tree also stores boundary data for each object. For a two-dimensional application, the boundary data are the x and y coordinates of the lower left and upper-right corners of the *minimum bounding* rectangle, the smallest possible rectangle enclosing the object. The index set, which contains pointers to lower-level nodes as in a B-tree, also contains data for the minimum bounding rectangle enclosing the objects referenced in the node. The data in an R-tree permit answers to such problems as *Find all pizza stores within 5 miles of the dorm*.

How an R-tree stores data is illustrated in Figure 14-3, which depicts five two-dimensional objects labeled A, B, C, D, and E. Each object is represented by its minimum bounding rectangle (the objects could be some other form, such as a circle). Data about these objects is stored in the sequence set. The index set contains details of two intermediate rectangles: X and Y. X fully encloses A, B, and C. Y fully encloses D and E.

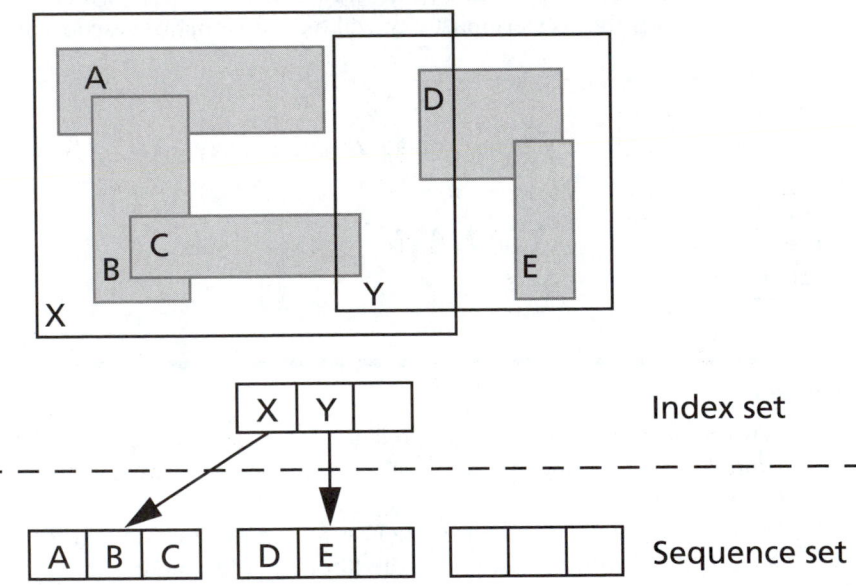

Figure 14-3. An R-tree with sample spatial data

An example demonstrates how these data are used to accelerate searching. Using a mouse, a person could outline a region on a map displayed on a screen. The minimum bounding rectangle for this region would then be calculated and the coordinates used to locate geographic objects falling within the minimum boundary. Because an R-tree is an index, geographic objects falling within a region can be found rapidly. In Figure 14-4, the drawn region (it has a bold border) completely covers object E. The R-tree software would determine that the required object falls within intermediate region Y, and thus takes the middle node at the next level of the R-tree. Then, by examining coordinates in this node, it would determine that E is the required object.

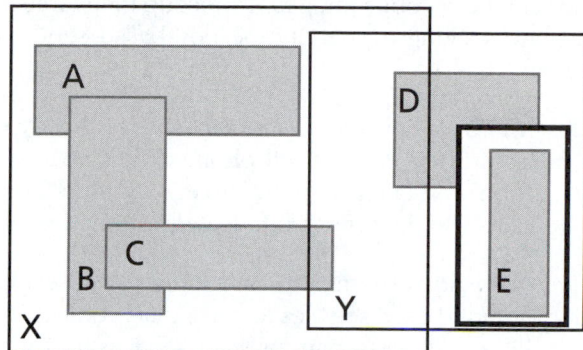

Figure 14-4. Searching an R-tree

As the preceding example illustrates, an R-tree has the same index structure as a B-tree. An R-tree stores data about *n*-dimensional objects in each node, whereas a B-tree stores data about a one-dimensional data type in each node. Both also store pointers to the next node in the tree (the index set) or the record (the sequence set).

This short introduction to spatial data has given you some idea of how the relational model can be extended to support geometric information. Most of the major RDBMS vendors have taken steps to provide management of spatial data. There is support for spatial data in Oracle 9i,[8] and IBM has DB2 Spatial Extender.[9] Microsoft seems more focused on adding spatial features to its personal productivity products.[10] Teradata has an alliance with Boeing Autometric to offer Spatial Query Server™ to its customers.[11]

Managing temporal data

With a temporal database, stored data have an associated time period indicating when the item was valid or stored in the database. By attaching a timestamp to data, it becomes possible to store and identify different database states and support queries comparing these states. Thus, you might be able to determine the number of seats booked on a flight by 3 P.M. on January 21, 2005, and compare that to the number booked by 3 P.M. on January 22, 2005.

---

8. otn.oracle.com/docs/products/oracle9i/doc_library/901_doc/appdev.901/a88805/sdo_intr.htm
9. www-3.ibm.com/software/data/spatial/
10. www.microsoft.com/office/mappoint/evaluation/infomanage.asp
11. www.autometric.com/products/index.cfm?content=sqs

Location-based services

The U.S. government has mandated that mobile phone providers will be able to determine the location of a person making an emergency call (911 in the United States). It is expected that this will cost billions for the providers to comply with this requirement. As a result, by 2005, U.S. wireless subscribers will be able to receive highly accurate location information on their mobile phones. To recoup their large investments, mobile phone companies are seeking to identify location-based services for which consumers are willing to pay.

Edmunds.com, a provider of information services to car buyers, already offers information to mobile consumers via their PDA or cell phone. It anticipates augmenting these services to provide information tailored to the driver's location. For example, a person looking to trade his car might get offers from dealers as he drives near car lots.

In Japan, where there are often no street names or addresses on secondary roads, there is a high demand for location-based services to solve this problem. The big issue is how much consumers will be willing to pay for such services and whether these services can be delivered profitably.

Betts, Mitch. 2002. Will location-based services pay-off? *Computerworld*, Dec 16, www.computerworld.com/mobiletopics/mobile/story/0,10801,76660,00.html.

To appreciate the value of a temporal database, you need to know the difference between transaction and valid time.

❖ **Transaction time** is the timestamp applied by the system when data are entered and cannot be changed by an application. It can be applied to a particular item or row. For example, when changing the price of a product, the usual approach would be to update the existing product row with the new price. The old price would be lost unless it was stored explicitly. In contrast, with a temporal database the old and new prices would automatically have separate timestamps. In effect, an additional row is inserted to store the new price and the time when the insert occurred.

❖ **Valid time** is the actual time at which an item was a valid or true value. Consider the case where a firm plans to increase its prices on a specified date. It might post new prices some time before their effective date. Valid time can be changed by an application.

Valid time records when the change takes effect, and transaction time records when the change was entered. Storing transaction time is essential for database recovery because the DMBS can roll back the database to a previous state (see page 542). Valid time provides a historical record of the state of the database. Both forms of time are necessary for a temporal database.

As you might expect, a temporal database will be somewhat larger than a traditional database because data are never discarded and new timestamped values are inserted so that there is a complete history of the values of an instance (e.g., the price of a product since it was first entered in the database). Thus, you can think of most of the databases we have dealt with previously as snapshots of a particular state of the database, whereas a temporal database is a record of all states of the database. As disk storage becomes increasingly cheaper and firms recognize the value of business intelligence (see Chapter 15), we are likely to see more attention paid to temporal database technology.

Times remembered

SQL supports several different data types for storing numeric values (e.g., integer and float), and a temporal database also needs a variety of data types for storing time values. The first level of distinction is to determine whether the time value is anchored or unanchored (see Figure 14-5). **Anchored time** has a defined starting point (e.g., October 15, 1582[12]), and **unanchored time** is a block of time with no specified start (e.g., 45 minutes).

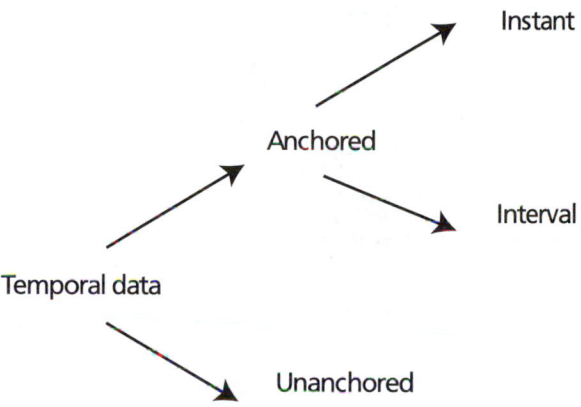

Figure 14-5. Types of temporal data

Adapted from: Goralwalla, I. A., M. T. Özsu, and D. Szafron. 1998. An object-oriented framework for temporal data models. In *Temporal databases: research and practice*, edited by O. Etzion, S. Jajoda, and S. Sripada. Berlin: Springer-Verlag.

Anchored time is further split into an instant or interval. An **instant** is a moment in time (e.g., a date and time). In SQL, an instant can be represented by a DATE, TIME, or TIMESTAMP data type. An **interval** is the time between two specified instants, and can be defined as a value or a range with an upper and lower bound instant. For example,[13] [2003-01-01, 2003-01-23] defines an interval in 2003 beginning January 1 and ending January 23.

12. When Pope Gregory XIII reformed the Julian calendar, there was an overnight jump from Oct. 4, 1582 to Oct. 15, 1582.
13. I really could have added some confusion by writing "For instance."

Interval

SQL-99 introduced the INTERVAL data type, which is a single value expressed in some unit or units of time (e.g., 6 years, 5 days, 7 hours). A small example illustrates the use of INTERVAL for time values. Consider the rotational and orbital periods of the planets (see Table 14-6). The CREATE statement for this table is[14]

```
CREATE TABLE planet (
pltname   VARCHAR(7),
pltday    INTERVAL,
pltyear   INTERVAL,
    pk_planet PRIMARY KEY(pltname));
```

Table 14-6: Planetary data

Planet	Rotational period (hours)	Orbital period (years)
Mercury	1407.51	0.24
Venus	−5832.44[a]	0.62
Earth	23.93	1.00
Mars	24.62	1.88
Jupiter	9.92	11.86
Saturn	10.66	29.45
Uranus	17.24	84.02
Neptune	16.11	164.79
Pluto	153.28	247.92

a. Rotates in the opposite direction to the other planets.

To insert the values for Mercury, you would use

```
INSERT INTO planet VALUES ('Mercury','1407.51 hours','0.24 years');
```

- -

Skill builder

Create the planet table and populate it with the values in Table 14-6.

- -

Once the table is populated, we can query it.

○ **List the length of the orbit of each planet.**

```
SELECT pltname, pltyear FROM planet;
```

---

14. This example was tested using PostgreSQL as some relational implementations do not yet support INTERVAL.

pltname	pltyear
Mercury	2 mons
Venus	7 mons
Earth	1 year
Mars	1 year 10 mons
Jupiter	11 years 10 mons
Saturn	29 years 5 mons
Uranus	84 years
Neptune	164 years 9 mons
Pluto	247 years 11 mons

Skill builder

Write SQL to report the time it takes a planet to rotate on its axis.

Modeling temporal data

You already have the tools for modeling temporal values. For example, the project management data model discussed on page 174 and reproduced in Figure 14-6 contains temporal data.

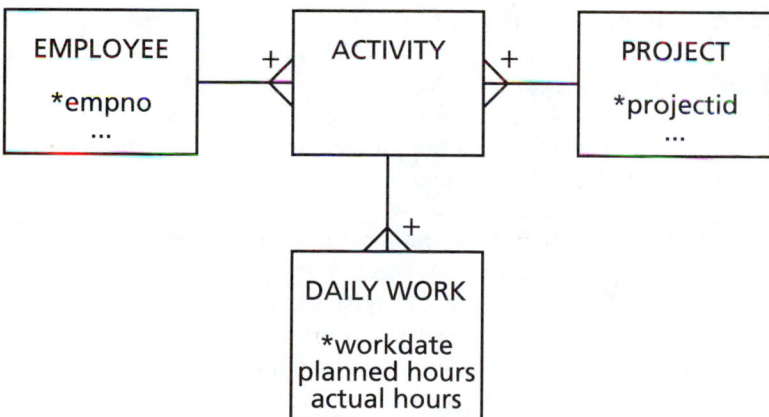

Figure 14-6. A project management data model

If we take the SHARE entity introduced very early in your data modeling experience, we can add temporal information to record the history of all values that are time-varying (i.e., price, quantity, dividend, and earnings). The data model to record temporal data is displayed in Figure 14-7. Firms pay dividends and report earnings only a few times per year, so we can associate a date with each value of dividend and earnings. Recording the history of trading transactions requires a timestamp, because a person can make multiple trades in a day. Every time a share is bought or sold, a new row is inserted containing both the transaction quantity and price. The number owned can be derived by using SUM.

Recording the share's price requires further consideration. If the intention is to record every change in price, then a time stamp is required as there will be multiple price changes in a day, and even in an hour in busy trading. If there is less interest in the volatility of the stock and only the closing price for each day is of interest, then a date would be recorded.

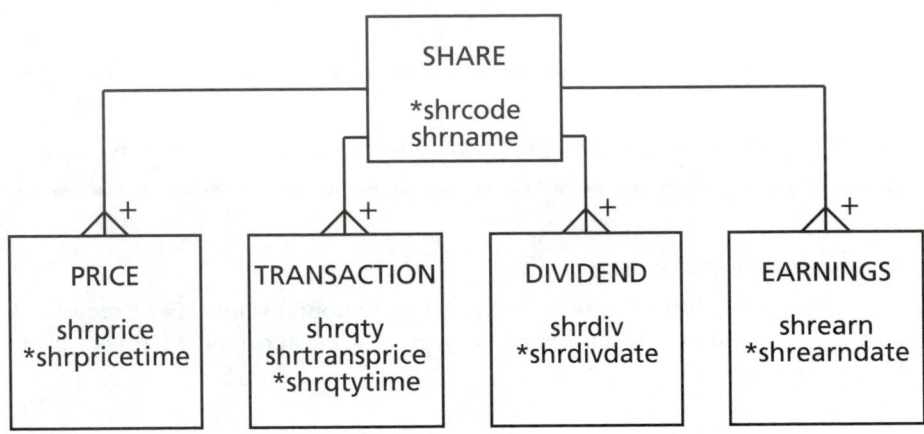

Figure 14-7. A temporal model of SHARE

You can add additional attributes to tables in a relational database to handle temporal data, but doing so does not make it a temporal database. The problem is that current relational implementations do not have built-in functions for querying time-varying data. Such queries can also be difficult to specify in SQL.

A temporal database has additional features for temporal data definition, constraint specification, data manipulation, and querying. A step in this direction is the development of TSQL (Temporal Structured Query Language). Based on SQL, TSQL supports querying of temporal databases without specifying time-varying criteria. There is a proposal to make TSQL an ANSI and ISO standard, which would do much to promote its acceptance. IBM reports that its TempDB project will enrich SQL with extensions to handle temporal data.[15] Also working on a temporal database is Microsoft.[16]

---

15. www.research.ibm.com/compsci/brochure2001/datamgmt_brochure.html
16. www.infoworld.com/articles/hn/xml/01/04/16/010416hndataman.xml

Summary

Spatial database technology stores details about items that have geometric features. It supports additional data types to describe these features, and has functions and operators to support querying. The new data types support point, line, and region values. Spatial technology is likely to develop over the next few years as organizations start to offer localized information services.

Temporal database technology provides data types and functions for managing time-varying data. Transaction time and valid time are two characteristics of temporal data. Times can be anchored or unanchored and measured as an instant or as an interval.

Key terms and concepts

Anchored time	Spatial data
Geographic object	Temporal data
Geographic information system (GIS)	Theme
Interval	Transaction time
Map	Valid time
R-tree	

References and additional readings

Gregersen, H., and C. S. Jensen. 1999. Temporal entity-relationship models—a survey. *IEEE Transactions on Knowledge and Engineering* 11 (3):464–497.

Rigaux, P., M. O. Scholl, and A. Voisard. 2002. *Spatial databases: with application to GIS*, The Morgan Kaufmann series in data management systems. San Francisco: Morgan Kaufmann Publishers.

Exercises

1. What circumstances will lead to increased use of spatial data?
2. A national tourist bureau has asked you to design a database to record details of items of interest along a scenic road. What are some of the entities you might include? How would you model a road? Draw the data model.
3. Using the map of the Iberian peninsula in Figure 14-8, populate the spatial database with details of Andorra, Portugal, and Spain. Answer the following questions.
   a. What is the direct distance, or bee line, from Lisbon to Madrid?
   b. What is the farthest Spanish city from Barcelona?
   c. Imagine you get lost in Portugal and your geographic positioning system (GPS) indicates that your coordinates are (3,9). What is the nearest city?
   d. Are there any Spanish cities west of Braga?
   e. What is the area of Portugal?
   f. What is the southernmost city of Portugal?
4. Redesign the data model for political units (Figure 14-1) assuming that your relational database does not support point and polygon data types.

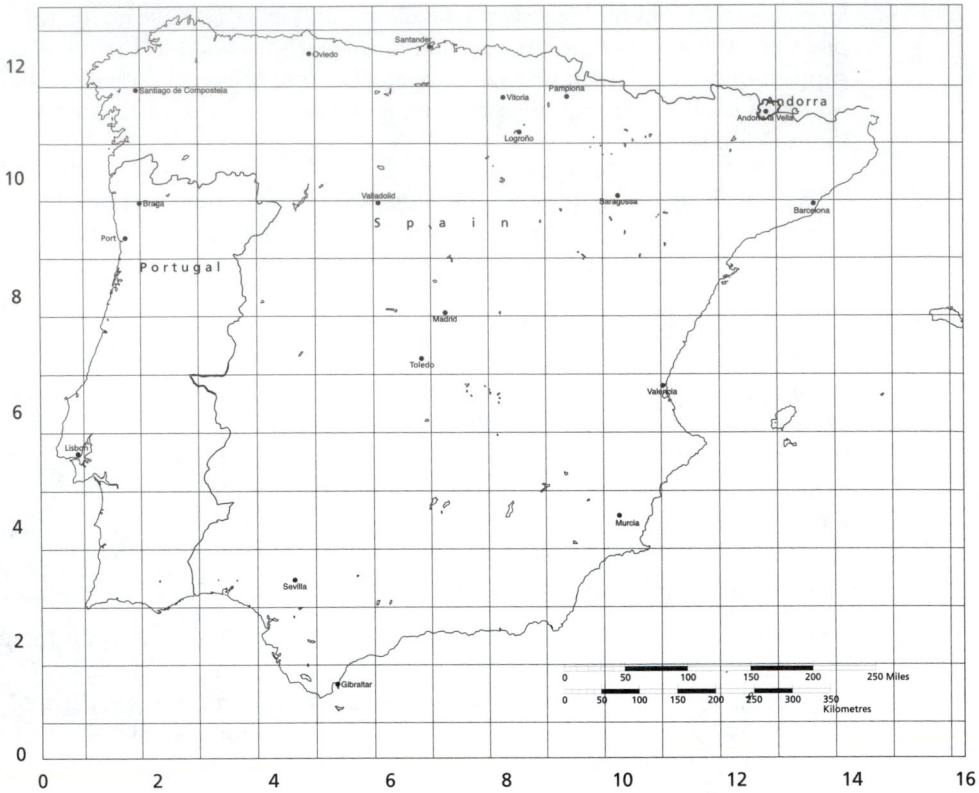

Figure 14-8. Iberian peninsula

5. For more precision and to meet universal standards, it would be better to use latitude and longitude to specify points and paths. You should also recognize that Earth is a globe and not flat. How would you enter latitude and longitude in MySQL? How do you compute the distance between two points on a globe? For some help, see www.realestate3d.com/gps/world-latlong.htm and jan.ucc.nau.edu/~cvm/latlon_formula.html.

6. When might you use transaction time and when might you use valid time?

7. Design a database to report basketball scores. How would you record time?

8. A supermarket chain has asked you to record what goods customers buy during each visit. In other words, you want details of each shopping basket. It also wants to know when each purchase was made. Design the database.

9. An online auction site wants to keep track of the bids for each item that a supplier sells. Design the database.

Section 4

Organizational Memory Technologies

Science and technology revolutionize our lives, but memory, tradition, and myth frame our response.

Arthur M. Schlesinger, Jr. "The Challenge of Change," *New York Times Magazine*, 27 July 1986

In recent years, data management has become more critical to organizational performance. Organizations have realized that they can learn a great deal from analyzing the data they collect as part of their everyday operations. They also know that they can greatly improve marketing and customer service by using the Web to interact with customers. Of course, the Web can also be used to interact with other stakeholders such as employees, suppliers, and investors. In the network economy where organizations cooperate extensively, the Internet has become a key conduit for exchanging data. However, you need more than just a high-speed communication line to exchange data; you also need a standard to describe the exchanged data so that the meaning is also shared.

Organizational intelligence is the outcome of an organization's efforts to collect, store, process, and interpret data from internal and external sources. Unfortunately, many companies have inadequate organizational intelligence systems because they make limited use of the vast amounts of data collected by their transaction processing systems. They fail to use the data to support managerial decision making because they are scattered across many systems rather than centralized in one readily accessible, integrated data store. Recently, technologies have been introduced to enable organizations to create single, vast repositories of data that can then be analyzed using special-purpose software. Technologies such as data warehousing, online analytical processing, and data mining have become increasingly important to data managers over the last few years, and these are covered in Chapter 15.

Internet technology, in particular Web browsers, has greatly enlarged the capability of organizations to capture, manage, and distribute organizational memory. Organizations are using the Internet, intranets, and extranets to share data with customers, employees, and business partners. Consequently, data managers now have a new domain. They must be concerned with managing the data stored on Web servers and making accessible, via a Web browser, data stored in existing organizational data stores. The Web has given data management a more central role because organizations now have a cost-effective and simply mastered means of making organizational memory available to a wide range of stakeholders. The relationship between Web and database management system (DBMS) technology is the theme of Chapter 16.

Java has become a popular choice for writing programs that operate on multiple operating systems. Combining the interoperability of Java with standard SQL provides software developers with an opportunity to develop applications that can run on multiple operating systems and multiple DBMSs. Thus, for a comprehensive understanding of data management, it is important to learn how Java and SQL interface.

The **Extensible Markup Language (XML)** has emerged at the beginning of this century as the standard for describing data. The arrival of this common language for data exchange adds another skill set to those that the data manager must acquire. XML will become a critical data management technology in the next few years because it is at the core of cooperation among firms. In the network economy, firms exchange high volumes of data to coordinate their activities. They need to exchange data without compromising internal operational autonomy. Firms want to cooperate while maintaining different information architectures.

As you may have surmised, the intent of this section is to broaden your understanding and knowledge of the role of data management. In our view, a data manager who focuses solely on databases is providing a poor and incomplete customer service. Data managers need to embrace the full gamut of technologies that can improve organizational performance by making better use of an organization's memory.

15

Organizational Intelligence Technologies

There are three kinds of intelligence: One kind understands things for itself, the other appreciates what others can understand, the third understands neither for itself nor through others. This first kind is excellent, the second good, and the third kind useless.

Machiavelli, *The Prince*, 1513

Learning objectives

Students completing this chapter will be able to

- ❖ understand the principles of data warehousing and organizational intelligence;
- ❖ decide whether to use verification or discovery for a given problem;
- ❖ select the appropriate data analysis technique(s) for a given situation;
- ❖ select variables to be included in a multidimensional database.

Introduction

Too many companies are *data rich* but *information poor*. They collect vast amounts of data with their transaction processing systems, but they fail to turn these data into the necessary information to support managerial decision making. Many organizations make limited use of their data because they are scattered across many systems rather than centralized in one readily accessible, integrated data store. Technologies exist to enable organizations to create single, vast repositories of data that can be then analyzed using special-purpose software.

Organizational intelligence[1] is the outcome of an organization's efforts to collect, store, process, and interpret data from internal and external sources. The conclusions or clues

---

1. *Intelligence* in this case means the gathering and distribution of information and making sense of such information.

gleaned from an organization's data stores enable it to identify problems or opportunities, which is the first stage of decision making.

An organizational intelligence system

transaction processing systems (TPSs) are a core component of organizational memory and thus an important source of data. Along with relevant external information, the various TPSs are the bedrock of an organizational intelligence system. They provide the raw facts that an organization can use to learn about itself, its competitors, and the environment. A TPS can generate huge volumes of data. In the United States, a regional telephone company may generate 200 million records per day detailing the telephone calls it has handled. The 600 million credit cards on issue in the world generate more than 100 billion transactions per year. A popular Web site can have a hundred million hits per day. TPSs are creating a massive torrent of data that potentially reveals to an organization a great deal about its business and its customers.

Unfortunately, many organizations are unable to exploit, either effectively or efficiently, the massive amount of data generated by TPSs. Data are typically scattered across a variety of systems, in different database technologies, in different operating systems, and in different locations. The fundamental problem is that organizational memory is highly fragmented. Consequently, organizations need a technology that can accumulate a considerable proportion of organizational memory into one readily accessible system. Making these data available to decision makers is crucial to improving organizational performance, providing first-class customer service, increasing revenues, cutting costs, and preparing for the future. For many organizations, their memory is a major untapped resource—*an underused intelligence system containing undetected key facts about customers*. To take advantage of the mass of available raw data, an organization first needs to organize these data into one logical collection and then use software to sift through this collection to extract meaning.

The **data warehouse**, a subject-oriented, integrated, time-variant, and nonvolatile set of data that supports decision making,[2] has emerged as the key device for harnessing organizational memory. *Subject* databases are designed around the essential entities of a business (e.g., customer) rather than applications (e.g., auto insurance). *Integrated* implies consistency in naming conventions, keys, relationships, encoding, and translation (e.g., gender is always coded as m or f in all relevant fields). *Time-variant* means that data are organized by various time periods (e.g., by months). Because a data warehouse is updated with a bulk upload, rather than as transactions occur, it contains *nonvolatile* data.

Data warehouses are enormous collections of data, often measured in terabytes, compiled by mass marketers, retailers, and service companies from the transactions of their millions of customers. Associated with a data warehouse are data management aids (e.g., data extraction), analysis tools (e.g., OLAP[3]), and applications (e.g., executive information sys-

2. Inmon, W. H. 1996. *Building the data warehouse*. 2nd ed. New York, NY: Wiley. p. 33.
3. Online analytical processing (OLAP) is discussed in detail, starting on page 442.

tem). The three aspects of the data warehouse environment, shown in Figure 15-1, are discussed in detail in the following sections.

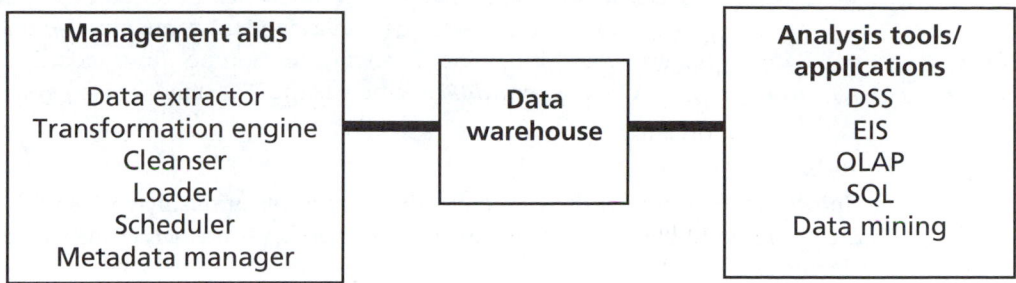

Figure 15-1. The data warehouse environment

The data warehouse

Creating and maintaining the data warehouse

A data warehouse is a snapshot of an organization at a particular time. In order to create this snapshot, data must be extracted from existing systems, transformed, cleaned, and loaded into the data warehouse. In addition, regular snapshots must be taken to maintain the usefulness of the warehouse.

Extraction

Data from the operational systems, stored in operational data stores (ODS), are the raw material of a data warehouse. Unfortunately, it is not simply a case of pulling data out of ODSs and loading them into the warehouse. Operational systems were often written many years ago at different times. There was no plan to merge these data into a single system. Each application is independent or shares little data with others. The same data may exist in different systems with different names and in different formats. The extraction of data from many different systems is time-consuming and complex. Furthermore, extraction is not a one-time process. Data must be extracted from operational systems on an ongoing basis so that analysts can work with current data.

Transformation

Transformation is part of the data extraction process. In the warehouse, data must be standardized and follow consistent coding systems. There are several types of transformation:

❖   Encoding: Non-numeric attributes must be converted to a common coding system. Gender may be coded, for instance, in a variety of ways (e.g., m/f, 1/0, or M/F) in different systems. The extraction program must transform data from each application to a single coding system (e.g., m/f).

❖ Unit of measure: Distance, volume, and weight can be recorded in varying units in different systems (e.g., centimeters or inches) and must be converted to a common system.

❖ Field: The same attribute may have different names in different applications (e.g., `sales-date`, `sdate`, or `saledate`), and a standard name must be defined.

❖ Date: Dates are stored in a variety of ways. In Europe the standard for date is *dd/mm/yy*, in the U.S. it is *mm/dd/yy*, whereas the ISO standard is *yyyy-mm-dd*.

Cleaning

Unfortunately, some of the data collected from applications may be *dirty*—they contain errors, inconsistencies, or redundancies. There are a variety of reasons why data may need cleaning:

❖ The same record is stored by several departments. For instance, both Human Resources and Production have an employee record. Duplicate records must be deleted.

❖ Multiple records for a company exist because of an acquisition. For example, the record for AT&T should be removed because it was acquired by SBC.

❖ Multiple entries for the same entity exist because there are no corporate data entry standards. For example, FedEx and Federal Express both appear in different records for the same company.

❖ Data entry fields are misused. For example, an address line field is used to record a second phone number.

Data cleaning starts with determining the dirtiness of the data. An analysis of a sample should indicate the extent of the problem and whether commercial data-cleaning tools are required. Data cleaning is unlikely to be a one-time process. All data added to the data warehouse should be validated in order to maintain the integrity of the warehouse. Cleaning can be performed using specialized software or custom-written code.

Loading

Data that have been extracted, transformed, and cleaned can be loaded into the warehouse. There are three types of data loads:

❖ **Archival:** Historical data (e.g., sales for the period 1995–1999) that is loaded once. Many organizations may elect not to load these data because of their low value relative to the cost of loading.

❖ **Current:** Data from current operational systems.

❖ **Ongoing:** Continual revision of the warehouse as operational data are generated. Managing the ongoing loading of data is the largest challenge for warehouse management. This loading is done either by completely reloading the data warehouse or by just updating it with the changes.

Scheduling

Refreshing the warehouse, which can take many hours, must be scheduled as part of a data center's regular operations. Because a data warehouse supports medium- to long-term decision making, it is unlikely that it would need to be refreshed more frequently than daily. For shorter decisions, operational systems are available. Some firms may decide to schedule less frequently after comparing the cost of each load with the cost of using data that are a few days old.

Metadata

A data dictionary is a reference repository containing *metadata* (i.e., *data about data*). It includes a description of each data type, its format, coding standards (e.g., volume in liters), and the meaning of the field. For the data warehouse setting, a data dictionary is likely to include details of which operational system created the data, transformations of the data, and the frequency of extracts. Analysts need access to metadata so that they can plan their analyses and learn about the contents of the data warehouse. If a data dictionary does not exist, it should be established and maintained as part of ensuring the integrity of the data warehouse.

Data warehouse technology

Selecting an appropriate data warehouse system is critical to support significant data mining or online analytical processing. Data analysis often requires intensive processing of large volumes of data, and large main memories are necessary for good performance. In addition, the system should be scalable so that as the demand for data analysis grows, the system can be readily upgraded. The three key building blocks of a data warehouse are the overall warehouse architecture, the server architectures, and the DBMS.

Warehouse architectures

Designing a data warehouse starts with selecting the physical and logical structure of the warehouse architecture. The fundamental physical choice is between a centralized or distributed data warehouse. A **centralized data warehouse** (see Figure 15-2) gives processing efficiency and lowers support costs.

A distributed architecture can be either federated or tiered. With a **federated data warehouse**, data are distributed by function. For example, financial data are on one DBMS server, marketing data on a different DBMS server at the same location, and manufacturing data on a DBMS server at a different location. To the analyst the data warehouse may appear as one logical structure, but, to reduce response time, it is dispersed across several related physical databases (see Figure 15-3).

A **tiered architecture** houses highly aggregated data on an analyst's workstation, with more detailed summaries on a second server, and most detailed data on a third server. The first tier handles most data requests, with the second and third tiers handling respectively fewer requests (see Figure 15-4). The workstation at the first tier is selected to handle a

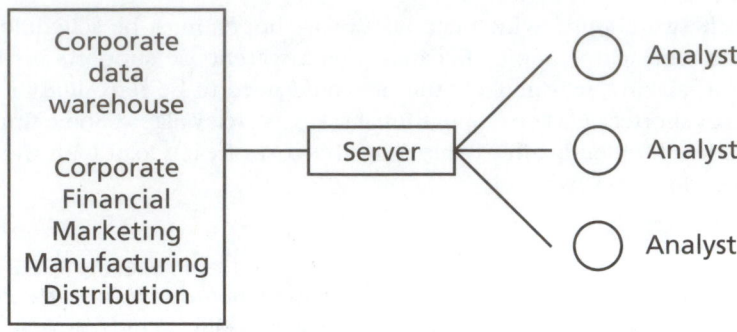

Figure 15-2. A centralized data warehouse

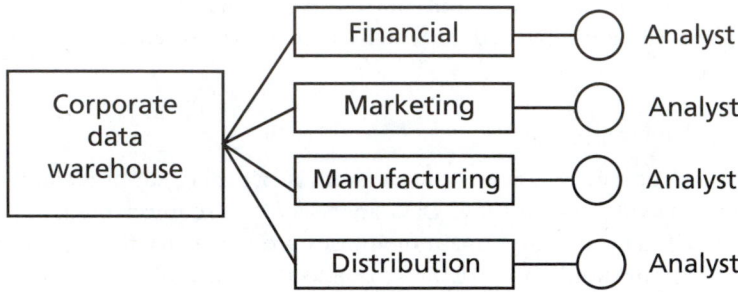

Figure 15-3. A federated data warehouse

heavy data analysis workload, while a third-tier server is chosen to handle high data volumes but a light data analysis workload. The second tier is a **data mart,** a local, single-subject database. In some situations, a data mart may be stand-alone rather than linked to the corporate data warehouse.

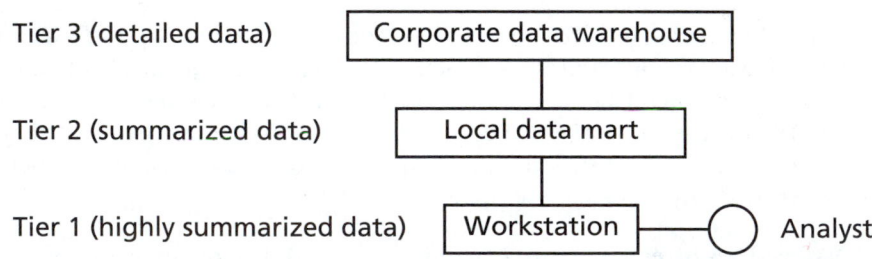

Figure 15-4. A tiered data warehouse

Server and DBMS selection

Server options

Servers hold and deliver data to analysts. The selection of the type of server is determined by an organization's need for scalability, availability of servers, and ease of management of the system. There are four options (see Figure 15-5):

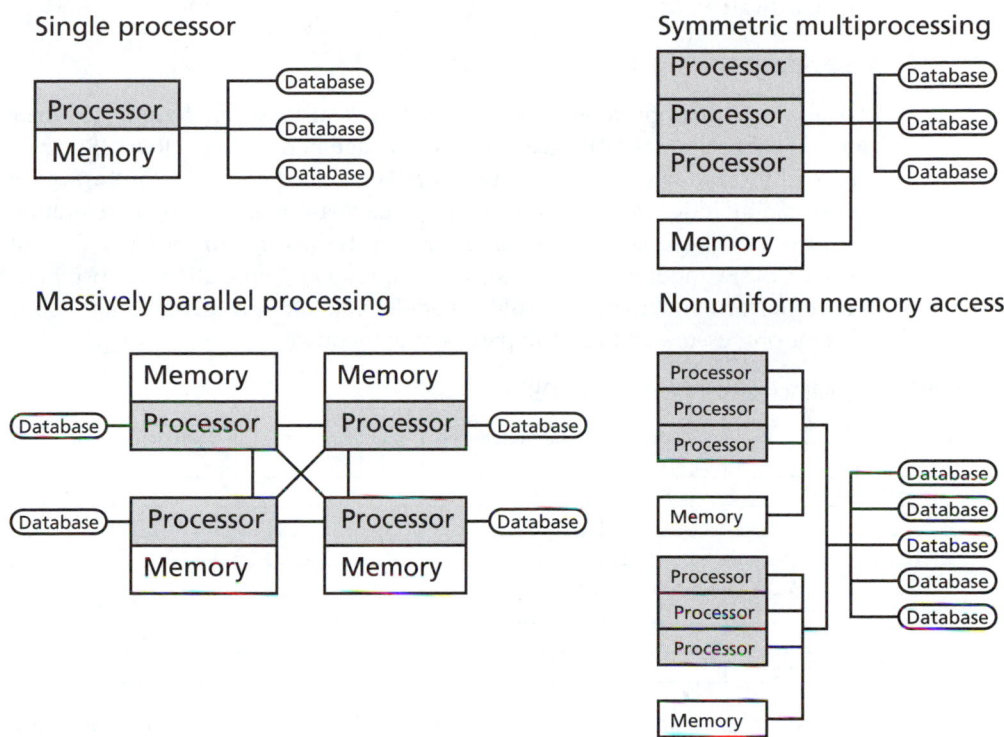

Figure 15-5. Server architectures

❖ The simplest option is a single-processor server, which is easy to manage but has limited processing power and scalability. Also, a single-server system limits reliability because when it is unavailable, so is the warehouse.

❖ A symmetric multiprocessor (SMP) has multiple servers sharing memory and disks. Because processors can be added as additional processing capacity is required, an SMP is scalable. However, as processors are added, the memory bus can become congested, and too many CPUs will slow performance. Although applications don't have to be specifically designed to run in this environment, the operating system must be designed for multiprocessing.

❖ A massively parallel processor (MPP) connects an array of processors with a high-speed, high-bandwidth link. These processors have independent memory and disks, so there is no shared memory or disk. To take advantage of parallelism, applications must be designed to work in parallel. MPP, while expensive, has the processing capacity for searching large databases using a parallel version of a DBMS.

❖ A nonuniform memory access (NUMA) machine joins multiple SMP nodes into a single, distributed memory pool with a single operating system. NUMA has the simplicity of operation of an SMP, and existing DBMSs and applications can be used without modification. The downside is that the operating system must be designed for NUMA hardware.

DBMS options

To improve responsiveness, large data warehouses often require features that are not found in a traditional relational database management system (RDBMS), and these features are seldom found within one type of database (see Table 15-1). **Super-relational systems** can include specialized hardware, a database machine, to accelerate retrievals. Performance of these systems is also improved by using join indexes, fully inverted index lists, or other indexing methods (see Chapter 11). Some RDBMSs use parallelism to improve performance. For example, a parallel version of a RDBMS might split a join across several processors and run the parts simultaneously.

Table 15-1: DBMS choices (Weldon, 1997)

Features/functions	Relational	Super-relational	Multidimensional (logical)	Multidimensional (physical)	Object-relational
Normalized data structures	✔	✔			✔
Abstract data types					✔
Parallelism	✔				
Multidimensional structures		✔	✔	✔	
Drill-down			✔	✔	✔
Rotation			✔	✔	✔
Data-dependent operations					✔

Analysts often want to see data from several dimensions (e.g., sales by region, by product line, and by division). These **multidimensional views** can be achieved by either a logical or physical **multidimensional database** (MDDB).[4] The *logical* approach uses multiple tables and pointers with an RDBMS to simulate a multidimensional structure. In the logical approach, multidimensionality is supported at a layer above the database. Providing multidimensionality at this layer is costly in terms of response performance, but there is tremendous flexibility because the underlying relational data can be tapped. The *physical* approach is based on a database technology specifically designed to support multidimensional data. In this case, multidimensionality is supported at the database layer. Consequently, physical systems respond more rapidly. However, additional implementation effort is required because the way in which clients use the database must be predetermined and data presummarized. Drill-down and rotation, features of a MDDB, are dis-

---

4.   See page 444 for details on MDDB.

cussed in detail later in this chapter. Major RDBMS vendors are likely to integrate MDDB capabilities into their products, just as they integrated object management.

If the items to be stored in a data warehouse include significant video, images, documents, and other *abstract data types*, then an object-oriented database management system (ODBMS) or **object-relational database** might be appropriate. These databases store and process objects and require specialized operators for handling abstract data types.

Hardware and software

The selection of a server architecture and DBMS are not independent decisions. Parallelism might be an option only for RDBMSs, such as DB2 Parallel and Oracle Parallel, and not available for multidimensional and object-relational technologies. The data warehouse manager has to find the best fit between hardware and data management technologies that meets the organization's goals. The data warehouse decision matrix (see Table 15-2) is a useful tool for relating the business needs to technology options. Notice that the decision is driven by the business requirements and the needs of the clients, which is what you should expect.

Table 15-2: Data warehouse decision matrix (Weldon, 1997)

For these environments ...			Choose ...		
Business requirements	Client population	Systems support	Architecture	Server	DBMS
Scope: departmental Uses: data analysis	Small; single location	Minimal local; average central	Consolidate; turn-key package	Single-processor or SMP	MDDB
Scope: departmental Uses: analysis plus informational	Large; analysis at single location; informational users dispersed	Minimal local; average central	Tiered; detail at central; summary at local	Clustered SMP for central; SP or SMP for local	RDBMS for central; MDDB for local
Scope: enterprise Uses: analysis plus informational	Large; geographically dispersed	Strong central	Centralized	Clustered SMP	Object-relational web support
Scope: departmental Uses: exploratory	Small; few sites	Strong central	Centralized	MPP	RDBMS with parallel support

The scope of the hardware/software decision can range from a department (e.g., a marketing data mart) to the enterprise data warehouse. The power and functionality of a data warehouse usually increase with its scope. Groups using standardized reports and predefined queries will require a simpler environment than business analysts using the data warehouse for decision support. In a highly volatile environment with many changes to the data warehouse, an RDBMS will be more efficient than an MDDB, which could require rebuilding after each change. These and other factors need to be carefully reviewed when selecting a hardware and data management combination. Once a data warehouse is established, the volume of data and number of users will grow. In addition, it is also likely that the complexity of queries will increase as clients learn to take full advantage of an integrated data store. Thus, it is important to select a system that is scalable across the dimensions of data volume, number of users, and query complexity.

The decision must embrace the entire data warehouse environment (see Figure 15-1). In considering the hardware and software combination, attention must also be paid to the tools that are used to manage the data warehouse and systems that will be used to analyze the stored data. The management tools, usually part of the data warehouse software, must be assessed for their ease of use and ability to perform the required functions. Some of the analysis software may already exist (e.g., current DSSs), and the ease of integration of the data warehouse and existing systems should be a key consideration.

Exploiting data stores

Two approaches to analyzing a data store (i.e., a database or data warehouse) are data mining and online analytical processing (OLAP). Before discussing each of these approaches, it is helpful to recognize the fundamentally different approaches that can be taken to exploiting a data store.

Verification and discovery

The **verification** approach to data analysis is driven by a hypothesis or conjecture about some relationship (e.g., customers with incomes in the range of $50,000–75,000 are more likely to buy minivans). The analyst then formulates a query to process the data to test the hypothesis. The resulting report will either support or disconfirm the theory. If the theory is disconfirmed, the analyst may continue to propose and test hypotheses until a target customer group of likely prospects for minivans is identified. Then, the minivan firm may market directly to this group because the likelihood of converting them to customers is higher than mass marketing to everyone. The verification approach is highly dependent on a persistent analyst eventually finding a useful relationship (i.e., who buys minivans?) by testing many hypotheses. OLAP, DSS, EIS, and SQL-based querying systems support the verification approach.

Data mining uses the **discovery** approach. It sifts through the data in search of frequently occurring patterns and trends to report generalizations about the data. Data mining tools operate with minimal guidance from the client. Data mining tools are designed to yield useful facts about business relationships efficiently from a large data store. The advantage of discovery is that it may uncover important relationships that no amount of conjecturing would have revealed and tested.

A useful analogy for thinking about the difference between verification and discovery (see Table 15-3) is the difference between conventional and open-pit gold mining. A conventional mine is worked by digging shafts and tunnels with the intention of intersecting the richest gold vein. Verification is like conventional mining—some parts of the gold deposit may never be examined. The company drills where it believes there will be gold. In open-pit mining, everything is excavated and processed. Discovery is similar to open-pit mining—everything is examined. Both verification and discovery are useful; it is not a case of selecting one or the other. Indeed, analysts should use both methods to gain as many insights as possible from the data.

OLAP

Edgar F. Codd, the father of the relational model, and colleagues (including, notably, Sharon B. Codd, his wife) proclaimed in 1993 that RDBMSs were never intended to pro-

Table 15-3: A comparison of verification and discovery queries

Verification	Discovery
What is the average sale for in-store and catalog customers?	What is the best predictor of sales?
What is the average high school GPA of students who graduate from college compared to those who do not?	What are the best predictors of college graduation?

vide powerful functions for data synthesis, analysis, and consolidation. This was the role of spreadsheets and special-purpose applications. They argued that analysts need data analysis tools that complement RDBMS technology, and they put forward the concept of **online analytical processing (OLAP):** the analysis of business operations with the intention of making timely and accurate analysis-based decisions.

Instead of rows and columns, OLAP tools provide multidimensional views of data, as well as some other differences (see Table 15-4). OLAP means fast and flexible access to large volumes of derived data whose underlying inputs may be changing continuously.

Table 15-4: Comparison of TPS and OLAP applications

TPS	OLAP
Optimized for transaction volume	Optimized for data analysis
Process a few records at a time	Process summarized data
Real-time update as transactions occur	Batch update (e.g., daily)
Based on tables	Based on hypercubes
Raw data	Aggregated data
SQL is widely used	MDX becoming a standard

For instance, an OLAP tool enables an analyst to view how many widgets were shipped to each region by each quarter in 1997. If shipments to a particular region are below budget, the analyst can find out which customers in that region are ordering less than expected. The analyst may even go as far as examining the data for a particular quarter or shipment. As this example demonstrates, the idea of OLAP is to give analysts the power to view data in a variety of ways at different levels. In the process of investigating data anomalies, the analyst may discover new relationships. The operations supported by the typical OLAP tool include

❖ Calculations and modeling across dimensions, through hierarchies, or across members
❖ Trend analysis over sequential time periods
❖ Slicing subsets for on-screen viewing
❖ Drill-down to deeper levels of consolidation
❖ Drill-through to underlying detail data
❖ Rotation to new dimensional comparisons in the viewing area

An OLAP system should give fast, flexible, shared access to analytical information. Rapid access and calculation are required if analysts are to make ad hoc queries and follow a trail of analysis. Such quick-fire analysis requires computational speed and fast access to data. It also requires powerful analytic capabilities to aggregate and order data (e.g., summarizing sales by region, ordered from most to least profitable). Flexibility is another desired feature. Data should be viewable from a variety of dimensions, and a range of analyses should be supported.

MDDB

OLAP is typically used with an MDDB, a data management system in which data are represented by a multidimensional structure. The MDDB approach is to mirror and extend some of the features found in spreadsheets by moving beyond two dimensions. These tools are built directly into the MDDB to increase the speed with which data can be retrieved and manipulated. These additional processing abilities, however, come at a cost. The dimensions of analysis must be identified prior to building the database, and changes can be costly and time-consuming. In addition, MDDBs have size limitations that RDBMSs do not have and, in general, are an order of magnitude smaller than a RDBM.

MDDB technology is optimized for analysis, whereas relational technology is optimized for the high transaction volumes of a TPS. For example, SQL queries to create summaries of product sales by region, region sales by product, and so on, could involve retrieving many of the records in a marketing database and could take hours of processing. A MDDB could handle these queries in a few seconds. TPS applications tend to process a few records at a time (e.g., processing a customer order may entail one update to the customer record, two or three updates to inventory, and the creation of an order record). In contrast, OLAP applications usually deal with summarized data.[5]

Fortunately, RDBMS vendors have standardized on SQL, and this provides a commonality that allows analysts to transfer considerable expertise from one relational system to another. Similarly, MDX, originally developed by Microsoft to support multidimensional querying of an SQL server, has been implemented by a number of vendors for interrogating an MDDB. More details are provided later in this chapter.

The current limit of MDDB technology is approximately 10 dimensions, which can be millions to trillions of data points. At this level, response is too slow. However, as MDDB technology is implemented for multiprocessor server architectures, this current limit will be extended.

ROLAP

An alternative to a physical MDDB is a *relational OLAP* (or ROLAP), in which case a multidimensional model is imposed on a relational model. As we discussed earlier, this is also known as a logical MDDB. Not surprisingly, a system designed to support OLAP should be

---

5. If you want to experience OLAP, spend some time playing with the PivotTable feature of Microsoft's Excel.

superior to trying to retrofit relational technology to a task for which it was not specifically designed.

The **star schema** is used by some MDDBs to represent multidimensional data within a relational structure. The center of the star is a table storing multidimensional *facts* derived from other tables. Linked to this central table are the *dimensions* (e.g., region) using the familiar primary-key/foreign-key approach of the relational model. Figure 15-6 depicts a star schema for an international automotive company. The advantage of the star model is that it makes use of a RDBMS, a mature technology capable of handling massive data stores and having extensive data management features (e.g., backup and recovery). However, if the fact table is very large, which is often the case, performance may be slow. A typical query is a join between the fact table and some of the dimension tables.

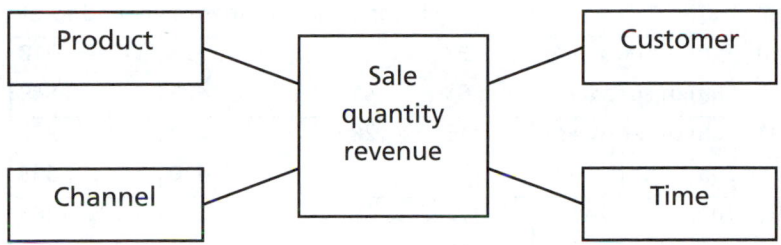

Figure 15-6. A star schema

A **snowflake schema**, more complex than a star schema, resembles a snowflake. Dimensional data are grouped into multiple tables instead of one large table. Space is saved at the expense of query performance because more joins must be executed. Unless you have good reasons, you should opt for a star over a snowflake schema.

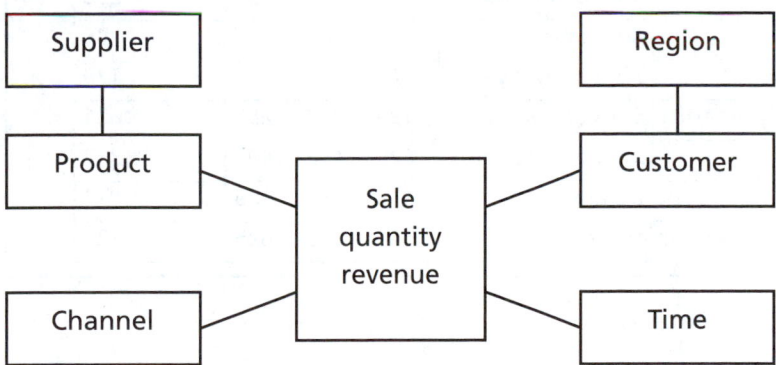

Figure 15-7. A snowflake schema

Rotation, drill-down, and drill-through

MDDB technology supports **rotation** of data objects (e.g., changing the view of the data from "by year" to "by region" as shown in Figure 15-8) and **drill-down** (e.g., reporting the details for each nation in a selected region as shown in Figure 15-9), which is also possible with a relational system. Drill-down can slice through several layers of summary data to get to finer levels of detail. The Japanese data, for instance, could be dissected by region (e.g., Tokyo region), and if the analyst wants to go further, the Tokyo region could be analyzed by store. In some systems, an analyst can **drill through** the summarized data to examine the source data within the organizational data store from which the MDDB summary data were extracted.

| Year | Data | Region | | | |
		Asia	Europe	North America	Grand total
2000	Sum of hardware	97	23	198	318
	Sum of software	83	41	425	549
2001	Sum of hardware	115	28	224	367
	Sum of software	78	65	410	553
2002	Sum of hardware	102	25	259	386
	Sum of software	55	73	497	625
Total sum of hardware		314	76	681	1,071
Total sum of software		216	179	1,332	1,727

| Region | Data | Year | | | |
		2000	2001	2002	Grand total
Asia	Sum of hardware	97	115	102	314
	Sum of software	83	78	55	216
Europe	Sum of hardware	23	28	25	76
	Sum of software	41	65	73	179
North America	Sum of hardware	198	224	259	681
	Sum of software	425	410	497	1,332
Total sum of hardware		318	367	386	1,071
Total sum of software		549	553	625	1,727

Figure 15-8. Rotation

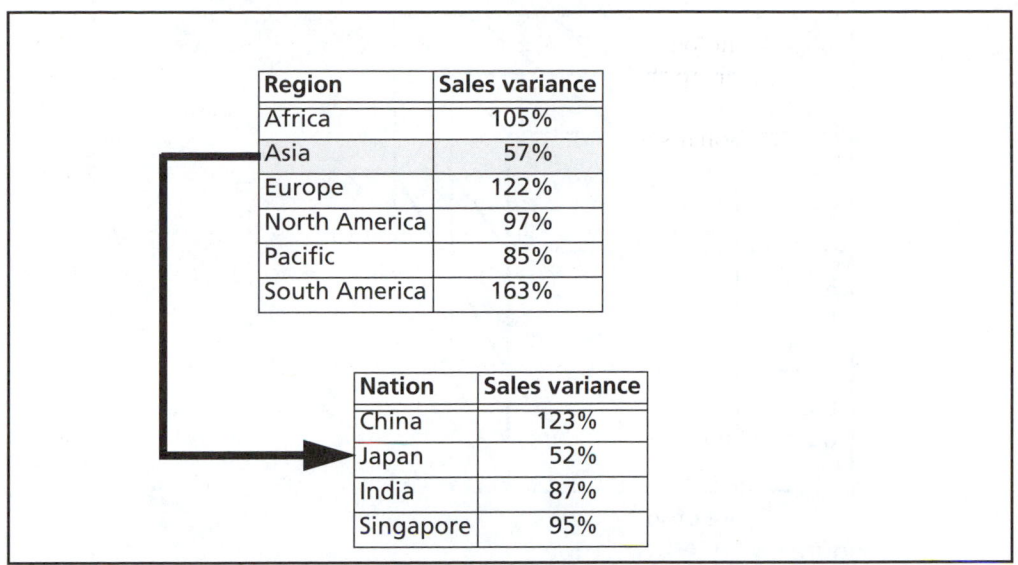

Figure 15-9. Drill-down

The hypercube

From the analyst's perspective, a fundamental difference between MDDB and RDBMS is the representation of data. As you know from data modeling, the relational model is based on tables, and analysts must think in terms of tables when they manipulate and view data. The relational world is two-dimensional. In contrast, the **hypercube** is the fundamental representational unit of a MDDB (see Figure 15-10). Analysts can move beyond two dimensions. To envisage this change, consider the difference between the two-dimensional blueprints of a house and a three-dimensional model. The additional dimension provides greater insight into the final form of the building.

Of course, on a screen or paper only two dimensions can be shown. This problem is typically overcome by selecting an attribute of one dimension (e.g., North region) and showing the other two dimensions (i.e., product sales by year). You can think of the third dimension (i.e., region in this case) as the page dimension—each page of the screen shows one region or slice of the cube (see Figure 15-11).

A hypercube can have many dimensions. Consider the case of a furniture retailer who wants to capture six dimensions of data (see Table 15-5). Although it is extremely difficult to visualize a six-dimensional hypercube, it helps to think of each cell of the cube as representing a fact (e.g., the Atlanta store sold five Mt. Airy desks to a business in January).

A six-dimensional hypercube can be represented by combining dimensions as shown in Figure 15-12. Brand and store are combined in the row dimension by showing the stores within a brand. The column dimension, which shows for each type of furniture the units

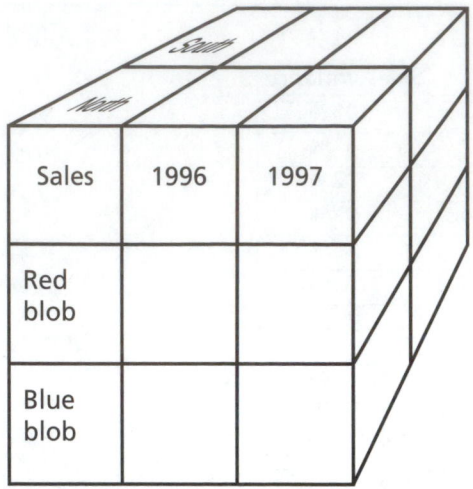

Figure 15-10. A hypercube

		Page					Columns	

Page
Region: North

Columns
Sales

	Red blob	Blue blob	Total
2001			
2002			
Total			

Rows
Year

Figure 15-11. A three-dimensional hypercube display

Table 15-5: A six-dimensional hypercube

Dimension	Example
Brand	Mt. Airy
Store	Atlanta
Customer segment	Business
Product group	Desks
Period	January
Variable	Units sold

sold and revenue, combines the product group and variable dimensions. The page, the third dimension, combines month and customer segment. Although combining dimensions enables the display of a multidimensional hypercube, it frequently has a cost. Tables can become quite large and no longer fit on one screen. As a result, the analyst is unable to see the complete picture without scrolling, and this can make the detection of patterns or anomalies more difficult.

Page						Columns	
Month Segment						Product group Variable	
	March	Business	Desks		Chairs		
			Units	Revenue	Units	Revenue	
	Carolina	Atlanta					
		Boston					
Rows	Mt. Airy	Atlanta					
Brand Store		Boston					
	Totals						

Figure 15-12. A six-dimensional hypercube display

The link between RDBMS and MDDB

A quick inspection of Table 15-4 (see page 443) reveals that relational and multidimensional database technologies are designed for very different circumstances. Thus, the two technologies should be considered as complementary, not competing, technologies. Appropriate data can be periodically extracted from an RDBMS, aggregated, and loaded into an MDDB. Ideally, this process is automated so that the MDDB is continuously updated. Because analysts sometimes want to drill down to low-level aggregations and even drill through to raw data, there must be a connection from the MDDB to the RDBMS to facilitate access to data stored in the relational system. The relationship between the two systems is illustrated in Figure 15-13.

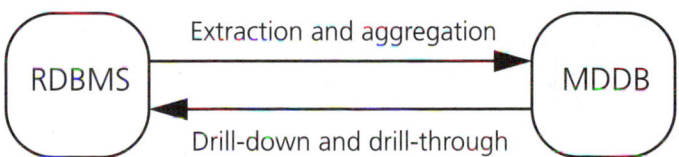

Figure 15-13. The relationship between RDBMS and MDDB

Designing a multidimensional database

The multidimensional model, based on the hypercube, requires a different design methodology from the relational model. At this stage, there is no commonly used approach, such as the entity-relationship principle of the relational model. However, the method proposed by Thomsen (1997) deserves consideration.

The starting point is to identify what must be tracked (e.g., sales for a retailer or revenue per passenger mile for a transportation firm). A collection of tracking variables is called a **variable dimension**.

The next step is to consider what types of analyses will be performed on the variable dimension. In a sales system, these may include sales by store by month, comparison of this month's sales with last month's for each product, and sales by class of customer. These types of analyses cannot be conducted unless the instances of each variable have an identifying tag. In this case, each sale must be tagged with time, store, product, and customer type. Each set of identifying factors is an **identifier dimension**. As a cross-check for identifying either type of dimension, use the six basic prompts shown in Table 15-6.

Table 15-6: Basic prompts for determining dimensions

Prompt	Example
When?	June 5, 2002
Where?	Paris
What?	Tent
How?	Catalog
Who?	Young adult woman
Outcome?	Revenue of €400

Variables and identifiers are the key concepts of MDDB design. The difference between the two is illustrated in Table 15-7. Observe that time, an identifier, follows a regular pattern, whereas sales do not. Identifiers are typically known in advance and remain constant (e.g., store name and customer type), while variables change. It is this difference that readily distinguishes between variables and identifiers. Unfortunately, when this is not the case, there is no objective method of discriminating between the two. As a result, some dimensions can be used as both identifiers and variables.

Table 15-7: A sales table

Identifier time (hour)	Variable sales (dollars)
10:00	523
11:00	789
12:00	1,256
13:00	4,128
14:00	2,634

There can be a situation when your intuitive notion of an identifier and variable is not initially correct. Consider a Web site that is counting the number of hits on a particular page. In this case, the identifier is a hit and time is the variable because the time of each hit is recorded (see Table 15-8).

The next design step is to consider the form of the dimensions. You will recall from statistics that there are three types of variables (dimensions in MDDB language): nominal, ordinal, and continuous. A nominal variable is an unordered category (e.g., region), an ordinal variable is an ordered category (e.g., age group), and a continuous variable has a numeric value (e.g., passenger miles). A hypercube is typically a combination of several types of dimensions. For instance, the identifier dimensions could be product and store

Table 15-8: A hit table

Identifier hit	Variable time (hh:mm:ss)
1	9:34:45
2	9:34:57
3	9:36:12
4	9:41:56

(both nominal), and the variable dimensions could be sales and customers. A dimension's type comes into play when analyzing relationships between identifiers and variables, which are known as independent and dependent variables in statistics (see Table 15-9). The most powerful forms of analysis are available when both dimensions are continuous. Furthermore, it is always possible to recode a continuous variable into ordinal categories. As a result, wherever feasible, data should be collected as a continuous dimension.

Table 15-9: Relationship of dimension type to possible analyses

		Identifier dimension	
		Continuous	Nominal or ordinal
Variable dimension	Continuous	Regression and curve fitting *Sales by quarter*	Analysis of variance *Sales by store*
	Nominal or ordinal	Logistic regression *Customer response (yes or no) to the level of advertising*	Contingency table analysis *Number of sales by region*

This brief introduction to multidimensionality modeling has demonstrated the importance of distinguishing between types of dimensions and considering how the form of a dimension (e.g., nominal or continuous) will affect the choice of analysis tools. Because multidimensional modeling is a relatively new concept, you can expect design concepts to evolve. If you become involved in designing an MDDB, then be sure to review carefully current design concepts. In addition, it would be wise to build some prototype systems, preferably with different vendor implementations of the multidimensional concept, to enable analysts to test the usefulness of your design.

- -

Skill builder

A national cinema chain has commissioned you to design a multidimensional database for its marketing department. What identifier and variable dimensions would you select?

- -

Multidimensional expressions (MDX)

MDX is a language for reporting data stored in a multidimensional database. On the surface, it looks like SQL because the language includes SELECT, FROM, and WHERE. The reality is that MDX is quite different. MDX works with cubes of data, and the result of an MDX query is a cube, just as SQL produces a table. The basic syntax of MDX statement is

```
SELECT {member selection} ON COLUMNS
    FROM [cube name]
```

Thus, a simple query would be

```
SELECT {[measures].[unit sales] } ON COLUMNS
FROM [sales]
```

Measures
Unit Sales
266,773

The first step in using MDX is to define a cube, which has dimensions and measures. Dimensions are the categories for reporting measures. The dimensions of product for a supermarket might be food, drink, and nonconsumable. Measures are the variables that typically measure outcomes. For the supermarket example, the measures could be unit sales, cost, and revenue. Once a cube is defined, you can write MDX queries for it. If we want to see sales broken down by the product dimensions, we would write

```
SELECT {[Measures].[Unit Sales] ON COLUMNS,
    {[Product].[All Products].[Food]} ON ROWS
    FROM [Sales]
```

In this section, we use the foodmart dataset to illustrate MDX.[6] To start simple, we just focus on a few dimensions and measures. We have a product dimension containing three members: food, drink, and nonconsumable, and we will use the measures of unit sales and store sales. Here is the code to report the data for all products.

```
SELECT {[Measures].[Unit Sales],[Measures].[Store Sales]} ON COLUMNS,
    {[Product].[All Products]} ON ROWS
    FROM [Sales]
```

	Measures	
Product	Unit Sales	Store Sales
All Products	266,773	565,238.13

---

6. Available from sourceforge.net/project/showfiles.php?group_id=35302&package_id=55863. This is a widely used dataset for illustrating MDDB and MDX principles. Ignore the old dates for the data.

To examine the unit sales and store sales by product, use the following code:

```
SELECT {[Measures].[Unit Sales], [Measures].[Store Sales]} ON COLUMNS,
    {[Product].[All Products],
    [Product].[All Products].[Drink],
    [Product].[All Products].[Food],
    [Product].[All Products].[Non-Consumable]} ON ROWS
    FROM [Sales]
```

	Measures	
Product	Unit Sales	Store Sales
All Products	266,773	565,238.13
Drink	24,597	48,836.21
Food	191,940	409,035.59
Non-Consumable	50,236	107,366.33

These few examples give you some idea of how to write an MDX query and the type of output it can produce. In practice, most people will use a GUI for defining queries. The structure of a MDDB makes it well suited to the select-and-click generation of an MDX query.

Mondrian

Mondrian[7] is a Java-based open-source OLAP that supports analysis of large relational databases. Mondrian executes queries written in the MDX language and presents the results in multidimensional format.

JPivot

JPivot[8] is an open-source Java program that provides a GUI to Mondrian. Analysts use select-and-click to define a query, which is then turned into MDX for execution by Mondrian. The start-up screen for JPivot, Figure 15-14, gives grand totals for the three measures for all products.

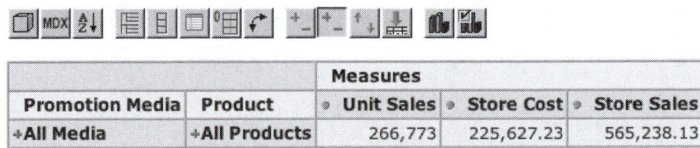

Promotion Media	Product	Measures		
		Unit Sales	Store Cost	Store Sales
+All Media	+All Products	266,773	225,627.23	565,238.13

Figure 15-14. JPivot initial screen

---

7. mondrian.sourceforge.net
8. jpivot.sourceforge.net/

To specify reporting by product type, the analyst clicks the leftmost button (OLAP navigator), as shown in Figure 15-15. With a few more clicks, the analyst has specified the re-

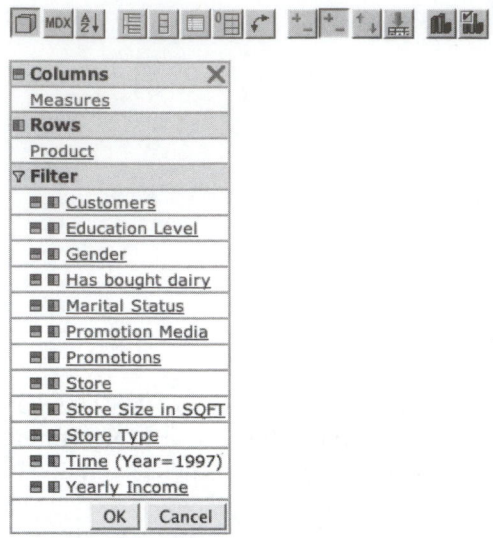

Figure 15-15. JPivot OLAP navigator

quired breakdown of sales (Figure 15-16) and the MDX command is generated to produce

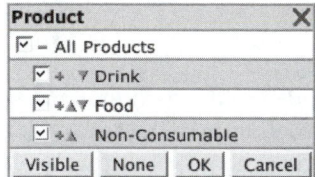

Figure 15-16. JPivot definition of product categories to report

the output shown in Figure 15-17. This is the same result as produced by the final MDX query on page 452.

Product	Measures		
	Unit Sales	Store Cost	Store Sales
All Products	266,773	225,627.23	565,238.13
+Drink	24,597	19,477.23	48,836.21
+Food	191,940	163,270.72	409,035.59
+Non-Consumable	50,236	42,879.28	107,366.33

Figure 15-17. JPivot output

Skill builder

Visit the book's Web site JPivot page,[9] and use JPivot to answer the questions posed.

Data mining

Data mining is the search for relationships and global patterns that exist in large databases but are *hidden* in the vast amounts of data. In data mining, an analyst combines knowledge of the data with advanced *machine learning* technologies to discover *nuggets* of knowledge hidden in the data. Data mining software can find meaningful relationships that might take years to find with conventional techniques. The software is designed to sift through large collections of data and, by using statistical and artificial intelligence techniques, identify hidden relationships. The mined data typically include electronic point-of-sale records, inventory, customer transactions, and customer records with matching demographics, usually obtained from an external source. Data mining does not require the presence of a data warehouse. An organization can mine data from its operational files or independent databases. However, data mining in independent files will not uncover relationships that exist between data in different files. Data mining will usually be easier and more effective when the organization accumulates as much data as possible in a single data store, such as a data warehouse. Recent advances in processing speeds and lower storage costs have made large-scale mining of corporate data a reality.

Database marketing, a common application of data mining, is also one of the best examples of the effective use of the technology. Database marketers use data mining to develop, test, implement, measure, and modify tailored marketing programs. The intention is to use data to maintain a lifelong relationship with a customer. The database marketer wants to anticipate and fulfill the customer's needs as they emerge. For example, recognizing that a customer buys a new car every three or four years and with each purchase gets an increasingly more luxurious car, the car dealer contacts the customer during the third year of the life of the current car with a special offer on its latest luxury model.

Data mining uses

There are many applications of data mining:

❖ Predicting the probability of default for consumer loan applications. Data mining can help lenders to reduce loan losses substantially by improving their ability to predict bad loans.

❖ Reducing fabrication flaws in VLSI chips. Data mining systems can sift through vast quantities of data collected during the semiconductor fabrication process to identify conditions that cause yield problems.

❖ Predicting audience share for television programs. A market-share prediction system

---

9. richardtwatson.com/dm5e/Reader/jpivot.html

allows television programming executives to arrange show schedules to maximize market share and increase advertising revenues.

❖ Predicting the probability that a cancer patient will respond to radiation therapy. By more accurately predicting the effectiveness of expensive medical procedures, health care costs can be reduced without affecting quality of care.

❖ Predicting the probability that an offshore oil well is going to produce oil. An off-shore oil well may cost $30 million. Data mining technology can increase the probability that this investment will be profitable.

❖ Identifying quasars from trillions of bytes of satellite data. This was one of the earliest applications of data mining systems, because the technology was first applied in the scientific community.

Wal-Mart prepares for good sales in bad weather

In 2004, a week ahead of Hurricane Frances's landfall, Wal-Mart's CIO requested forecasts based on what products customers rushed to buy when Hurricane Charley struck several weeks earlier. Through mining the trillions of bytes' worth of shopper history, Wal-Mart was able to stock the stores in areas near Frances's path with the right products.

Wal-Mart amasses more data about the products it sells and its shoppers' buying habits than any other company. With 3,600 stores and 100 million customers per week, Wal-Mart has 460 Tbytes of data on Teradata mainframes. The Internet has less than half as much data.

The company uses its data to push for greater efficiency at all levels of its operations, especially in regard to maintaining the right amount of inventory. Consumer data are used to determine where to build new stores. Eventually, some experts say, Wal-Mart will use its technology to institute scan-based trading, in which manufacturers own each product until it is sold. The impact will probably be felt by suppliers, but none are likely to complain, because Wal-Mart is so large and powerful.

Source: Hays, C. L. 2004. What they know about you. *New York Times*, Nov. 14, query.nytimes.com/gst/abstract.html?res=FB0C14F63D5B0C778DDDA80994DC404482&in-camp=archive:search.

Data mining functions

Based on the functions they perform, five types of data mining functions exist:

Associations

An association function identifies affinities existing among the collection of items in a given set of records. These relationships can be expressed by rules such as "72 percent of all the records that contain items A, B, and C also contain items D and E." Knowing that 85 percent of customers who buy a certain brand of wine also buy a certain type of pasta can help supermarkets improve use of shelf space and promotional offers. Discovering that fathers, on the way home on Friday, often grab a six-pack of beer after buying some diapers, enabled a supermarket to improve sales by placing beer specials next to diapers.[10]

Sequential patterns

Sequential pattern mining functions identify frequently occurring sequences from given records. For example, these functions can be used to detect the set of customers associated with certain frequent buying patterns. Data mining might discover, for example, that 32 percent of female customers within six months of ordering a red jacket also buy a gray skirt. A retailer with knowledge of this sequential pattern can then offer the red-jacket buyer a coupon or other enticement to attract the prospective gray-skirt buyer.

Classifying

Classifying divides predefined classes (e.g., types of customers) into mutually exclusive groups, such that the members of each group are as *close* as possible to one another, and different groups are as *far* as possible from one another, where distance is measured with respect to specific predefined variables. The classification of groups is done before data analysis. Thus, based on sales, customers may be first categorized as *infrequent, occasional,* and *frequent.* A classifier could be used to identify those attributes, from a given set, that discriminate among the three types of customers. For example, a classifier might identify frequent customers as those with incomes above $50,000 and having two or more children. Classification functions have been used extensively in applications such as credit risk analysis, portfolio selection, health risk analysis, and image and speech recognition. Thus, when a new customer is recruited, the firm can use the classifying function to determine the customer's sales potential and accordingly tailor its market to that person.

Clustering

Whereas classifying starts with predefined categories, clustering starts with just the data and discovers the *hidden* categories. These categories are derived from the data. Clustering divides a dataset into mutually exclusive groups such that the members of each group are as *close* as possible to one another, and different groups are as *far* as possible from one another, where distance is measured with respect to all available variables. The goal of clustering is to identify categories. Clustering could be used, for instance, to identify natural groupings of customers by processing all the available data on them. Examples of applications that can use clustering functions are market segmentation, discovering affinity groups, and defect analysis.

Prediction

Prediction calculates the future value of a variable. For example, it might be used to predict the revenue value of a new customer based on that person's demographic variables.

---

10. Brandel, M. 1995. Fermenting a new formula. *Computerworld.* June 1.

These various data mining techniques can be used together. For example, a sequence pattern analysis could identify potential customers (e.g., red jacket leads to gray skirt), and then classifying could be used to distinguish between those prospects who are converted to customers and those who are not (i.e., did not follow the sequential pattern of buying a gray skirt). This additional analysis should enable the retailer to refine its marketing strategy further to increase the conversion rate of red-jacket customers to gray-skirt purchasers.

Data mining technologies

Data miners use technologies that are based on statistical analysis and data visualization.

Decision trees

Tree-shaped structures can be used to represent decisions and rules for the classification of a dataset. As well as being easy to understand, tree-based models are suited to selecting important variables and are best when many of the predictors are irrelevant. For an example, see Figure 15-18.

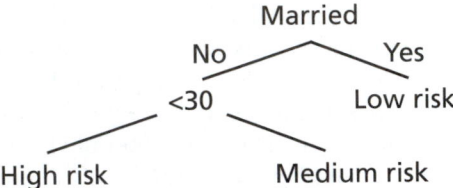

Figure 15-18. A decision tree

Genetic algorithms

Genetic algorithms are optimization techniques based on the concepts of biological evolution, use processes such as genetic combination, mutation, and natural selection. Possible solutions for a problem compete with each other. In an evolutionary struggle of the survival of the fittest, the best solution survives the battle. Genetic algorithms are suited for optimization problems with many candidate variables (e.g., candidates for a loan).

K-nearest-neighbor method

The nearest-neighbor method is used for clustering and classification. In the case of clustering, the method first plots each record in n-dimensional space, where n attributes are used in the analysis. Then, it adjusts the weights for each dimension to cluster together data points with similar goal features. For instance, if the goal is to identify customers who frequently switch phone companies, the k-nearest-neighbor method would adjust weights for relevant variables (such as monthly phone bill and percentage of non-U.S. calls) to cluster switching customers in the same neighborhood. Customers who did not switch would be clustered some distance apart.

> ### The SAS data mining method
>
> A senior statistician at SAS Institute, a large supplier of statistical analysis software, advocates a five-step process to data mining, which he calls SEMMA.
>
> Sample: Extract a portion of the dataset for data mining. This set should be large enough to contain significant data and small enough for rapid data mining.
>
> Explore: Search for unanticipated trends and relationships to gain insights to the data and ideas for further exploration.
>
> Modify: Create, select, and transform variables with the intention of building a model.
>
> Model: Specify a relationship of variables that reliably predicts a desired goal.
>
> Assess: Evaluate the practical value of the findings and the model resulting from the data mining effort.
>
> Source: SAS Institute. 1996. Data mining reveals the diamonds in your databases. *SAS Communications* 22(2): 15–21.

Neural networks

A neural network, mimicking the neurophysiology of the human brain, can learn from examples to find patterns in data and classify data. Although neural networks can be used for classification, they must first be trained to recognize patterns in a sample dataset. Once trained, a neural network can make predictions from new data. Neural networks are suited to combining information from many predictor variables; they work well when many of the predictors are partially redundant. One shortcoming of a neural network is that it can be viewed as a black box with no explanation of the results provided. Often managers are reluctant to apply models they do not understand, and this can limit the applicability of neural networks.

Data visualization

Data visualization can make it possible for the analyst to gain a deeper, intuitive understanding of data. Because they present data in a visual format, visualization tools take advantage of our capability to discern visual patterns rapidly. Data mining can enable the analyst to focus attention on important patterns and trends and explore these in depth using visualization techniques. Data mining and data visualization work especially well together.

SQL-99 and OLAP

SQL-99 includes extensions to the GROUP BY clause to support some of the data aggregation capabilities typically required for OLAP. Prior to SQL-99, the following questions required separate queries:

1. Find the total revenue.
2. Report revenue by location.
3. Report revenue by channel.
4. Report revenue by location and channel.

Skill builder

Write SQL to answer each of the four preceding queries using the EXPED table, which is a sample of 1,000 sales transactions from The Expeditioner.[11]

Writing separate queries is time-consuming for the analyst and is inefficient because it requires multiple passes of the table. SQL-99 introduced GROUPING SETS, ROLLUP, and CUBE as a means of getting multiple answers from a single query and addressing some of the aggregation requirements necessary for OLAP.

Grouping sets

The GROUPING SETS clause is used to specify multiple aggregations in a single query and can be used with all the aggregate functions (see page 99). In the following SQL statement, aggregations by location and channel are computed. In effect, it combines questions 2 and 3 of the preceding list.

```
SELECT location, channel, SUM(revenue)
FROM exped
GROUP BY GROUPING SETS (location, channel) ;
```

location	channel	revenue
null	Catalog	108762
null	Store	347537
null	Web	27166
London	null	214334
New York	null	39123
Paris	null	143303
Sydney	null	29989
Tokyo	null	56716

The query sums revenue by channel or location. The null in a cell implies that there is no associated location or channel value. Thus, the total revenue for catalog sales is 108,762, and that for Tokyo sales is 56,716.

---

11. This table is available from the book's Web site as exped.xls (an Excel file) or exped.txt (a text file with SQL commands for creating and populating the table).

Although GROUPING SETS enables multiple aggregations to be written as a single query, the resulting output is hardly elegant. It is not a relational table, and thus a view based on GROUPING SETS should not be used as a basis for further SQL queries.

Skill builder

Query the exped table to compute total revenue by location, channel, and item.

Rollup

The ROLLUP option supports aggregation across multiple columns. It can be used, for example, to crosstabulate revenue by channel and location.

```
SELECT location, channel, SUM(revenue)
FROM exped
GROUP BY ROLLUP (location, channel);
```

location	channel	revenue
null	null	483465
London	null	214334
New York	null	39123
Paris	null	143303
Sydney	null	29989
Tokyo	null	56716
London	Catalog	50310
London	Store	151015
London	Web	13009
New York	Catalog	8712
New York	Store	28060
New York	Web	2351
Paris	Catalog	32166
Paris	Store	104083
Paris	Web	7054
Sydney	Catalog	5471
Sydney	Store	21769
Sydney	Web	2749
Tokyo	Catalog	12103
Tokyo	Store	42610
Tokyo	Web	2003

In the columns with null for location and channel, the preceding query reports a total revenue of 483,465. It also reports the total revenue for each location and revenue for each combination of location and channel. For example, Tokyo Web revenue totaled 2,003.

Skill builder

Run the following query

```
SELECT channel, location, SUM(revenue)
FROM exped
GROUP BY ROLLUP (channel, location);
```

How do the results differ from those for the preceding ROLLUP query?

Cube

CUBE reports all possible values for a set of reporting variables. If SUM is used as the aggregating function, it will report a grand total, a total for each variable, and totals for all combinations of the reporting variables.

```
SELECT location, channel, SUM(revenue)
FROM exped
GROUP BY CUBE (location, channel);
```

location	channel	revenue
null	Catalog	108762
null	Store	347537
null	Web	27166
null	null	483465
London	null	214334
New York	null	39123
Paris	null	143303
Sydney	null	29989
Tokyo	null	56716
London	Catalog	50310
London	Store	151015
London	Web	13009
New York	Catalog	8712
New York	Store	28060
New York	Web	2351
Paris	Catalog	32166
Paris	Store	104083
Paris	Web	7054
Sydney	Catalog	5471
Sydney	Store	21769
Sydney	Web	2749
Tokyo	Catalog	12103
Tokyo	Store	42610
Tokyo	Web	2003

The SQL-99 extensions to GROUP BY are useful, but they certainly do not give SQL the power of a multidimensional database. If you complete the final exercise on page 466, then you will have some idea of the power of the multidimensional approach to data analysis. In addition, it would seem that CUBE could be used as the default without worrying about the differences among the three options.

MySQL implements only ROLLUP with some exceptions. The syntax is different, and the result is equivalent to CUBE. See the MySQL manual for details.[12]

Conclusion

Data management is a rapidly evolving discipline. Where once the spotlight was clearly on TPSs and the relational model, there are now multiple centers of attention. In an information economy, the knowledge to be gleaned from data collected by routine transactions can be an important source of competitive advantage. The more an organization can learn about its customers by studying their behavior, the more likely it can provide superior products and services to retain existing customers and lure prospective buyers. As a result, data managers now have the dual responsibility of administering databases that keep the organization in business today and tomorrow. They must now master the organizational intelligence technologies described in this chapter.

Summary

Organizations recognize that data are a key resource necessary for the daily operations of the business and its future success. Recent developments in hardware and software have given organizations the capability to store and process vast collections of data. Data warehouse software supports the creation and management of huge data stores. The choice of architecture, hardware, and software is critical to establishing a data warehouse. The two approaches to exploiting data are verification and discovery. DSS, EIS, and OLAP are mainly data verification methods. Data mining, a data discovery approach, uses statistical analysis techniques to discover *hidden* relationships. The relational model was not designed for OLAP, and MDDB is the appropriate data store to support OLAP. MDDB design is based on recognizing variable and identifier dimensions. MDX is a language for interrogating an MDDB. SQL-99 includes extensions to GROUP BY to improve aggregation reporting.

---

12. dev.mysql.com/doc/mysql/en/group-by-modifiers.html

Key terms and concepts

Association
Centralized data warehouse
Classifying
Cleaning
Clustering
CUBE
Continuous variable
Database marketing
Data mart
Data mining
Data visualization
Data warehouse
Decision support system (DSS)
Decision tree
Discovery
Drill-down
Drill-through
Executive information system (EIS)
Extraction
Federated data warehouse
Genetic algorithm
GROUPING SETS
Hypercube
Identifier dimension
Information systems cycle
K-nearest-neighbor method
Loading

Management information system (MIS)
Massively parallel processor (MPP)
Metadata
Multidimensional database (MDDB)
Multidimensional expressions (MDX)
Neural network
Nominal variable
Nonuniform memory access (NUMA)
Object-relational
Online analytical processing (OLAP)
Operational data store (ODS)
Ordinal variable
Organizational intelligence
Prediction
Relational OLAP (ROLAP)
ROLLUP
Rotation
Scheduling
Sequential pattern
Star model
Super-relational system
Symmetric multiprocessor (SMP)
Tiered architecture
Transaction processing system (TPS)
Transformation
Variable dimension
Verification

References

Codd, E. F., S. B. Codd, and C. T. Salley. 1993. Beyond decision support. *Computerworld*, 87–89.

Finkelstein, R. 1995. MDD: Database reaches the next dimension. *Database Programming & Design* 8 (4):27–38.

Hurwicz, M. 1997. Take your data to the cleaners. *Byte* 22 (1):97–102.

Inmon, W. H. 1996. *Building the data warehouse*. 2nd ed. New York, NY: Wiley.

Thomsen, E. 1997. *OLAP solutions: Building multidimensional information systems*. New York, NY: Wiley.

Spofford, George. 2001. *MDX solutions*. New York, NY: Wiley,

Weldon, J. L. 1997. Warehouse cornerstones. *Byte* 22 (1):85–88.

Exercises

1. Identify data captured by a TPS at your university. Estimate how much data are generated in a year.
2. What data does your university need to support decision making? Does the data come from internal or external sources?

3. What database architecture would you recommend for your university?
4. What database architecture might be appropriate for a regional telephone company?
5. What database architecture might be appropriate for a global bank?
6. What special feature must you look for in software if you select an MPP?
7. Discuss the differences between a logical and a physical MDDB.
8. If your university were to implement a data warehouse, what examples of dirty data might you expect to find?
9. How frequently do you think a university should revise its data warehouse?
10. Write five data verification questions for a university data warehouse.
11. Write five data discovery questions for a university data warehouse.
12. Imagine you work as an analyst for a major global auto manufacturer. What techniques would you use for the following questions?
    a. How do sports car buyers differ from other customers?
    b. How should the market for trucks be segmented?
    c. Where does our major competitor have its dealers?
    d. How much money is a dealer likely to make from servicing a customer who buys a luxury car?
    e. What do people who buy midsize sedans have in common?
    f. What products do customers buy within six months of buying a new car?
    g. Who are the most likely prospects to buy a luxury car?
    h. What were last year's sales of compacts in Europe by country and quarter?
    i. We know a great deal about the sort of car a customer will buy based on demographic data (e.g., age, number of children, and type of job). What is a simple visual aid we can provide to sales personnel to help them show customers the car they are most likely to buy?
13. What impact is the Web likely to have on organizational intelligence technologies?
14. Discuss the conceptual views of a database presented by the relational, object, and multidimensional models. How do you reconcile these different views? Are they likely to cause confusion for data analysts?
15. An international airline has commissioned you to design an MDDB for its marketing department. Choose identifier and variable dimensions (use Table 15-6 on page 450). List some of the analyses that could be performed against this database and the statistical techniques that might be appropriate for them.
16. A regional telephone company needs your advice on the data it should include in its MDDB. It has an extensive relational database that captures details (e.g., calling and called phone numbers, time of day, cost, length of call) of every call. As well, it has access to extensive demographic data so that it can allocate customers to one of 50 lifestyle categories. What data would you load into the MDDB? What aggregations would you use? It might help to identify initially the identifier and variable dimensions (use Table 15-6 on page 450).
17. What are the possible dangers of data mining? How might you avoid these?

18. Download the file exped.xls from the book's web site and open it with MS Excel. This file is a sample of 1,000 sales transactions for The Expeditioner. For each sale, there is a row recording when it was sold, where it was sold, what was sold, how it was sold, the quantity sold, and the sales revenue. Use the PivotTable Wizard (Data>PivotTable Report) to produce the following report:

Sum of REVENUE	HOW			
WHERE	Catalog	Store	Web	Grand total
London	50,310	151,015	13,009	214,334
New York	8,712	28,060	2,351	39,123
Paris	32,166	104,083	7,054	143,303
Sydney	5,471	21,769	2,749	29,989
Tokyo	12,103	42,610	2,003	56,716
Grand Total	108,762	347,537	27,166	483,465

Continue to use the PivotTable Wizard to answer the following questions:

    a. What was the value of catalog sales for London in the first quarter?
    b. What percent of the total were Tokyo Web sales in the fourth quarter?
    c. What percent of Sydney's annual sales were catalog sales?
    d. What was the value of catalog sales for London in January? Give details of the transactions.
    e. What was the value of camel saddle sales for Paris in 2002 by quarter?
    f. How many elephant polo sticks were sold in New York in each month of 2002?

16

The Web and Data Management

Experience is never limited, and it is never complete; it is an immense sensibility, a kind of huge spider-web of the finest silken threads suspended in the chamber of consciousness, and catching every air-borne particle in its tissue.

Henry James, *The Art of Fiction*, 1884

Learning objectives

Students completing this chapter will be able to

- ❖ understand the principles of Web site management;
- ❖ know the principal functions of a content management system (CMS) and wiki;
- ❖ create a wiki page;
- ❖ understand how a CMS and a wiki can be used for knowledge management.

Introduction

The capability of organizations to capture, manage, and distribute organizational memory has been greatly enhanced by the development of Internet technology, in particular the use of Web browsers. Data managers now have a new domain. They must be concerned with managing the data stored on Web servers and making accessible, via a Web browser, data stored in organizational data stores.

The Web has given data management a more central role because organizations now have a cost-effective and simply mastered means of making organizational memory available to a wide range of stakeholders. For example,

- ❖ A UPS customer can track the status of her parcel.
- ❖ A Vanguard investor can check the value of his mutual funds.
- ❖ A supplier to GE can browse open contracts.

❖ An amateur photographer can read Kodak's advice on composing photos and using a flash.

As organizations are increasingly reliant on clearly communicating information to a wide variety of stakeholders, data managers must be familiar with the principles of information design, Web site management, and database application development for the Web.

Literacy skills in a digital world

Students have difficulty sifting through the wealth of information available on the Web. The Educational Testing Service, the nonprofit group behind the SAT, GRE, and other college tests, has developed a new test to assess students' ability to make sound critical evaluations of the vast amount of material available to them.

The Information and Communications Technology literacy assessment is intended to measure students' ability to manage exercises like sorting e-mail messages or manipulating tables and charts, and to assess how well they organize and interpret information from many sources and in myriad forms.

There is no widespread agreement on whether such skills can be taught, much less measured in a test. However, a lucrative market is emerging for testing companies. President Bush's commitment to expanding the standardized testing mandated under the No Child Left Behind Act virtually ensures a growth market.

Source: Zeller Jr., Tom. 2005. Measuring literacy in a world gone digital. *New York Times*, Jan 17, query.nytimes.com/gst/abstract.html?res=F5071EF63E5C0C748DDDA80894DD404482.

Information presentation

Information technologies, such as a relational database management system (RDBMS) and fast server, provide rapid access to extensive volumes of information, but just because a machine can retrieve information rapidly does not mean that humans can process it speedily. Information must be meaningfully organized for human consumption.[1]

The meaningful organization of data is termed **information architecture**.[2] Instances of information architecture are an annual report, a musical composition, or a Web site. An information architecture results from the arrangement of data elements into an interrelated system. Thus, a Web site is a cohesive assembly of pages, with each page composed of related information structures (e.g., text, hyperlinks, sounds, and images). This arrangement of information structures is known as **information design**. The thoughtful arrangement of information elements on a page is called **information arts**.

---

1. This section is primarily based on Mok, C. 1966. *Designing business: multiple media, multiple disciplines*. San Jose, CA: Adobe. A beautiful, inspiring, and insightful book.
2. The term *information architecture* is sometimes used to describe an organization's information technology collection. Here it has a broader sense, which embraces information technology architecture.

Organization models

There are seven universal models (see Table 16-1) for the organization of information. Text, audio, music, images, and video can be organized using these models. A novel is a *linear* organization, because data are organized and processed sequentially. A novel is designed to be read from cover to cover. The playoff charts for a tennis competition and the NCAA basketball tournament are instances of *hierarchical* structures even though usually turned sideways. A *web* is the underlying structure of a thesaurus, because readers can jump from one word to another, particularly with an electronic thesaurus. Timetables for airlines, trains, and buses follow a *parallel* structure. Details such as time and type of service, for any route, are listed in parallel—side by side or one under the other. Most calendars show dates in *matrix* format. All the days on which Monday occurs are shown in the same column and all the days of a week in the same row. With an electronic calendar, each cell of the matrix is active, and clicking on a cell results in the display of the details for that day. The *overlay* model is often used to show levels of detail. By turning the plastic sheets of an anatomical model, the reader peels away layers of a body. Some presenters use the overlay model to reveal features on a single slide gradually. *Spatial zoom* is seen on some Web pages. Clicking on a thumbnail of an image results in the display of the object at full magnification. In the case of online analytical processing (OLAP), drill-down is magnification.

Table 16-1: Information organization models

Type	Examples
Linear	Novel
Hierarchical	Organizational chart
Web	Thesaurus
Parallel	Airline timetable
Matrix	Calendar
Overlay	X-ray
Spatial zoom	Magnification of a thumbnail image

When designing the interface to a data collection, the designer must decide which of the information organization models is appropriate at the macro and micro level. At the macro level, the designer needs to decide on the basic structure for the collection. A textbook author usually selects a linear structure for the macro level but may use many of the other structures within this overall structure. Matrix structures (tables) are a common feature of many texts. The Web page designer has more design choices and decisions, because electronic media are inherently more flexible. Thus, a designer of a CD-ROM might settle on a hierarchical structure at the macro level but then make extensive use of a web organization to link sections of the text, as well as use many of the other information organization options.

The matrix format of the relational model is likely to be a fundamental feature of many information reports for managers. However, with the emergence of the Web browser as the common interface to information systems, designers now need to think about the broader structure within which tables are presented and reports are accessed.

Skill builder

What information organization model would you choose for the following situations?

1. A photo album
2. A conference program
3. A management book review
4. An analysis of information flows between senior managers
5. A comparison of several DBMSs on multiple dimensions
6. A map of transport options within a city
7. An outline of a textbook

Information design

An information designer must understand how various information elements can work together to convey meaning. In the case of a Web site, this means comprehending how information elements support the design goals of a page and how a collection of linked pages supports the design goals of a Web site. As well, the designer must decide which information organization models are appropriate for structuring data elements. For example, should a collection of images be presented using spatial zoom within a matrix structure, as a linear sequence of full-size images, or some other structure? In many cases, the purpose of the project will determine the organizational structure and information elements. A price list, for example, is well suited to a matrix organization, with possibly spatial zoom for additional details of any item. The information designer must always remember that the purpose is to enable people to find meaningful information quickly. The combination of purpose, organizational models, and information design creates a solution.

Navigation aids

When a Web site contains many pages, there is always the danger that visitors will get lost in a maze of pages and hyperlinks. Signs are necessary to let visitors know where they are and how to get around. Metropolitan railway systems (e.g., the London Underground and Paris Métro) are good examples of navigation systems. There are large signs to tell travelers the name of the current station and maps for the various destinations. Similarly, each Web page should have signage to indicate the purpose of the current page and how to move to other pages.

The design process

The design of a Web site is a top-down process:

1. **Architecture:** The designer sketches the architecture of the site by broadly defining the content, navigation structure, and interface of the site. This means the goal

of the site must be clearly described and a general idea of what is on each page identified, the navigation signage designed, and the look-and-feel of the interface delineated.

2. **Design:** The form of each section of the Web site is clarified, where a section is a collection of closely related pages. The main output of this stage is greater detail of the content, navigation, structure, and interface of each page.

3. **Information arts:** Information elements are added to each page to provide content, navigation signage, and the interface.

Many Web sites are at the heart of a hierarchical structure. Thus, a good starting point is to use the outliner in your word processor to sketch the architecture of the site, as illustrated in Figure 16-1. As you become more involved in design, you might create a more visual representation and also include details of the files stored on the Web site.

Figure 16-1. Using an outliner for initial Web site design

```
Data management home page
   support
   revision
   exercises
      chapter 1
      chapter 2
      ...
      chapter 20
```

Consistency

Visitors to a Web site will find navigation easier if the site has a consistent layout and set of icons. This means a uniform design for each page, including standard navigation icons in the same place on each page. This does not mean that every page has exactly the same layout; rather, it means that there is an evident consistency that assists the visitor to move about the site. For instance, root-level pages may have different navigation aids from those at the second level in the Web page hierarchy, but all pages should have a very similar look and feel. A Web site management tool that supports site-level or global changes (e.g., changing the image representing the left icon on all pages) simplifies maintaining consistency and is especially valuable when a site contains hundreds of pages. Stylesheets, which you will learn about in Chapter 18, also support consistency.

A performance, not a system

Think of a Web site as a Broadway performance rather than a system. A Web site is designed to attract visitors and encourage them to browse the site. Traditional information systems are very utilitarian—information only and no pizzazz. Web sites are often entertaining and informative.

A firm's Web site often provides the most definitive impression of a company and the main conduit for communicating with a wide range of stakeholders. The combined skills of marketing and IS must be effectively combined, so that a firm's Web site conveys the desired image and communicates clearly. Marketing front-end skills must be integrated with IS back-end expertise to create the appropriate performance for each Web visitor.

This means that the front end of a Web system—what the visitor sees—may change often, just like the window display of a retail store. Marketing personnel will want to continually revise, and sometimes completely revamp, a firm's Web pages. Unchanging marketing displays and Web sites convey the image of a static company with no new products or services. Traditional IS applications change more slowly. Because a Web site is more like a performance than a system, data management is more dynamic. Thus, Web site management tools should support rapid development of a new front end.

The back end of a Web site is frequently an existing IS application system. For example, the UPS[3] parcel-tracking system relies on a database that was created prior to the development of the Web. IS has considerable experience managing these types of applications, and traditional data management tools, such as relational technology, are applicable. Linking the back end to the front end will be discussed in this chapter.

Web site management

A Web site is a collection of text (HTML code) and image files (e.g., JPEG files) and may also include audio, video, animation, and other file types. Once an organization's Web site exceeds more than a dozen pages, a data management problem emerges, and tools for managing the site are required. Web site data management software has different features from database technology, because the stored data have different characteristics. They are not as structured as data in a production planning system. Web site management tools typically have two components: page creation and site management.

Creating and maintaining HTML files

The Web is a client/server system in which the client is called a **browser**. The **server** contains files that are converted by the browser for display on a monitor. The file pulled from the server by the browser contains instructions written in **Hypertext Markup Language (HTML)**, a language for describing how a Web browser should display a file from a server, declaring hyperlinks, and defining multimedia objects included with a Web document.

HTML editors, such as Adobe GoLive and Microsoft FrontPage, accelerate the creation and maintenance of Web pages. HTML editors permit you to lay out text and images in a WYSIWYG (what you see is what you get) mode, as illustrated in Figure 16-2.

Managing a Web site

Managing the many files and links in a Web site requires appropriate software. Although there are several alternatives available, this section focuses on Adobe GoLive. Each of its major features will be discussed.

---

3. www.ups.com

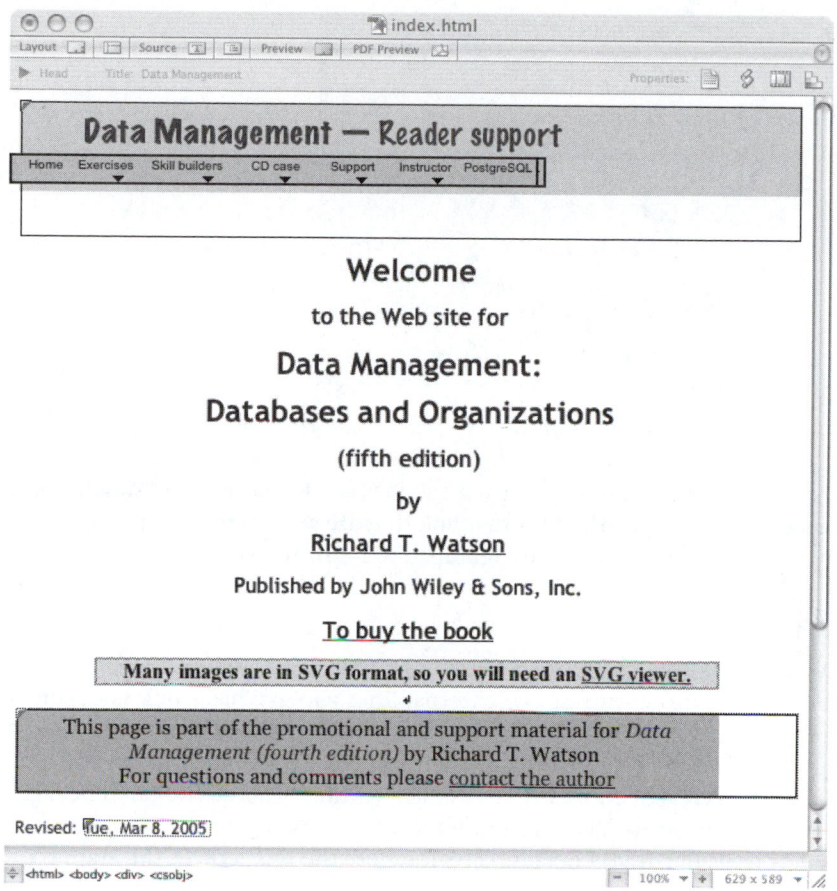

Figure 16-2. A HTML editor in WYSIWYG mode

Visual site management

Site management software will typically display the organization and layout of a Web site in a variety of ways. For example, you might want to visualize the links to and from a particular HTML file (see Figure 16-3), the hierarchical structure of the site, or a site's external links. These and other features of a site's structure are generally provided by Web site management software.

Automatic link changes

Detecting and repairing broken links in a Web site is a data management problem, because an invalid link, like a missing foreign key in a table, means that a visitor cannot access data. Instead, the visitor clicks on the link and gets the all too familiar "Error 404" message: "The file you requested was not found." This is a major source of irritation to Web visitors.

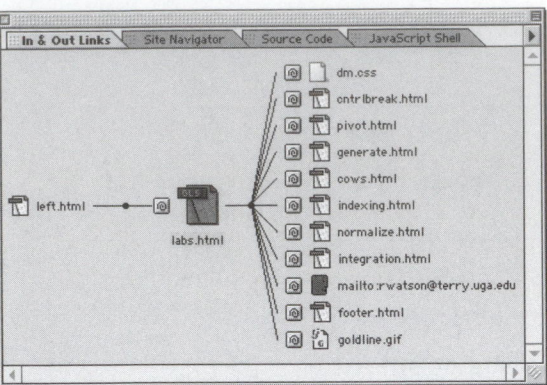

Figure 16-3. GoLive link view

Broken links are commonly caused by changes to file names. When you use GoLive to change a file name, all the files that link to it are automatically updated to reflect the file's new name. This is a very useful feature and helps to avoid the dreaded 404 message.

Link checker

A Web site has internal links and external links. Files within the site's root directory are internal links; those outside are external links. GoLive has a link checker that verifies the status of all links and reports those that are broken. The difficult task, more so for external links, is to find the link's new name if it still exists. The link checker also reports any files that are not referenced by any HTML files within the site. The link checker should be run on a regular basis to maintain the integrity of a Web site, because URLs tend to change frequently, as illustrated in Figure 16-4, where the bug icon in the Status column indicates a broken link.

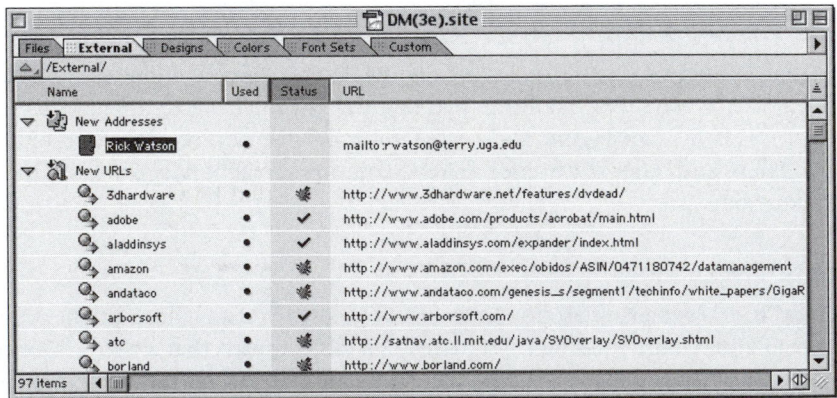

Figure 16-4. External link checking

Another requirement of broken-link prevention is to ensure that other Web sites linked to your Web site remain valid. For instance, if the support site for this book were changed to www.rickwatson.com, there would be a need to change all links that pointed to www.wiley.com/college/watson. Fortunately, finding those pages that link to another page is very easy.

Links to a particular site can be checked by using the advanced features of a search engine, such as Google. On the advanced search page of Google, you specify a page-specific search for the link www.wiley.com/college/watson. The search engine will identify all pages linked to this URL. You then need to notify the owners of each page that the URL has changed.

Web site publishing

The usual procedure is to maintain a copy of all Web site files on your personal computer and transfer these files, using FTP, to the Web server upon completion of any changes. Site management software should make uploading a site a one- or two-click process and should also upload only those pages that have changed.

Data management guidelines

Two simple guidelines greatly facilitate the management of Web site data.

All images in one file

Store all images (i.e., GIFs and JPEGs) in one file. This means you can have a single, common library of images.

Consistent naming

Some Web servers are case sensitive (e.g., they distinguish between mis/index.html and MIS/index.html). Consequently, if you spell the URL correctly, but get the case wrong, then you get the dreaded 404. To avoid this problem, many Web site developers use lowercase for all file names. This is a sensible convention to adopt.

- -

Skill builder

Mozilla,[4] an open-source browser, contains an HTML editor called Composer. Download a copy of Mozilla and investigate the features provided by Composer. Does it have Web site management features? Under what circumstance might you decide to use Composer?

- -

---

4. www.mozilla.org/

Content management systems

A content management system (or **CMS**) is a program for managing the content of Web sites, though sometimes the term is used more broadly to cover a wide range of digital material (e.g., movies, photos, and music). Our focus is on Web sites.

Content management software is a step beyond Web site management programs, such as GoLive. It provides more functionality and greater control. A CMS enables many to work collaboratively to maintain a variety of content because it incorporates controls (e.g., where the logo appears on each page) and workflow software to ensure that only validated content is published. A CMS can be used for managing public Internet sites and private intranets.

A CMS offers several advantages:

- ❖ The creation and maintenance of content can be distributed to appropriate personnel. Instead of relying on one person (e.g., the web master) for maintaining a site, those who create and understand content can be given responsibility for an appropriate portion of the Web site. For example, the public relations person could have responsibility for all pages that deal with press releases.
- ❖ Workflow software can be used to ensure control over publication. For example, a press relations officer could prepare a press release that, when completed, is automatically sent to the Vice President of Public Relations for review before being published. When the VP clicks a button indicating approval of the document, it is automatically published.
- ❖ Content versioning[5] can be applied to ensure that there is an audit trail of all revisions. The change and the person who made the change are recorded. If necessary, changes can be undone.
- ❖ A CMS can ensure that the Web site has a consistent look and feel. All pages have a similar format and layout, and editors must work within this format. This also means that a site can be redesigned with reduced effort because the overall design is altered rather than each page.
- ❖ A CMS separates design and content, so designers and content providers can work independently.
- ❖ A CMS defines roles for the various users of the site. There is typically a small set of content providers and an even small group of reviewers who check the work of content providers before it is released to the largest group, who have read access only to the site.
- ❖ Content providers do not need to know HTML.
- ❖ A CMS should incorporate good design and usability principles (e.g., compliance with U.S. electronic and information technology accessibility standards, also known as Section 508).
- ❖ Maintaining the timeliness of the site, because editing is easier. A Web site managed

---

5. A content versioning system maintains dated or numbered copies of the different versions of a content item. It makes it possible to restore a previous version of a particular piece of content.

via a CMS should be more current, and thus of greater value to both a firm's internal and external customers.

❖ A CMS typically includes a built-in search engine. Thus, all pages in the site can be searched.

❖ Many CMSs offer additional tools for adding polls, message boards, calendars, and so forth to Web sites.

There are many products that claim to manage Web content. These vary from enterprise systems (costing around $200,000) to free, open source products. We will examine one of the most popular open source products, Plone.

Plone

Plone[6] is a widely used open source CMS. Organizations such as Crédit Municipal de Paris, New York Marriott Marquis, and the U.K.'s Royal Military College of Science use Plone. Let's examine some of its features.[7]

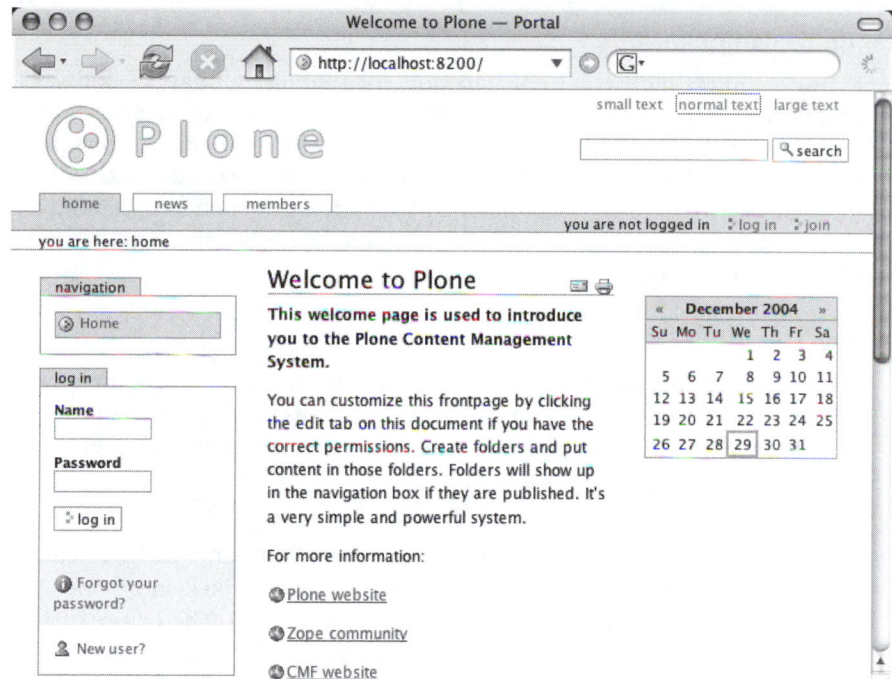

Figure 16-5. Default first page of Plone

6. www.plone.org
7. This section is based on Bollenbach, Brad. 2004. Open source content management with Plone. *ONLamp.com*, Sep. 23, http://www.onlamp.com/lpt/a/5193.

Membership

Anyone can view a Plone site, but a member has additional privileges. Members can edit and review content. Regular members create content, and reviewers approve or reject it.

Workflow

Workflow defines the steps through which a content item proceeds before publication. Workflow enables the definition of approval procedures that an item must pass through before being displayed on a site. When a document is created by a regular member, it will be automatically routed to a reviewer who can review the document prior to release for display.

Internationalization and localization

Internationalization (also known as i18n[8]) means writing a program so that it can be used in multiple languages without altering the source. Localization (l10n) is the resulting translation to a specific language. Plone supports around 40 languages.

Standards compliance

Plone complies with common standards for usability and accessibility. Plone pages are compliant with U.S. Section 508, which requires that Federal agencies' electronic and information technology be accessible to people with disabilities. It also meets the W3C's AA rating for accessibility, which is designed to make Web content accessible to people with disabilities. Plone follows best-practice Web standards such as Extensible HTML (XHTML) and Cascading Style Sheets (CSS). As a result, Plone looks the same when viewed by most of the major browsers.

Summary

Web site content is another element of the total data an organization must manage. A CMS has become a required tool for many organizations as they try to manage, efficiently and consistently, the many pages that constitute a typical enterprise's Web site.

Wiki

A wiki[9] (pronounced "wicky") is a Web site that allows any reader to edit or add material. No login is required to add or modify content. Thus, a wiki is more open than a traditional Web site, which typically restricts who can edit material. The nature of a wiki encourages the collaborative and incremental development of a Web site. Ward Cunningham, the developer of the original wiki, formulated 12 design principles (Table 16-2). His original wiki, written in 1994, is still operational.[10]

---

8. *Internationalization* starts with i, ends with n, and has 18 letters between the i and the n.
9. *Wikiwiki* is a Hawaiian word meaning fast, speedy, swift, and informal.
10. c2.com/cgi/wiki

Table 16-2: Wiki design principles (Source: c2.com/cgi/wiki?WikiDesignPrinciples)

Principle	Explanation
Open	Should a page be found to be incomplete or poorly organized, any reader can edit it.
Incremental	Pages can cite other pages, including pages that have not been written yet.
Organic	The structure and text content of the site is open to editing and evolution.
Mundane	A small number of (irregular) text conventions will provide access to the most useful page markup.
Universal	The mechanisms of editing and organizing are the same as those of writing so that any writer is automatically an editor and organizer.
Overt	The formatted (and printed) output will suggest the input required to reproduce it.
Unified	Page names will be drawn from a flat space so that no additional context is required to interpret them.
Precise	Pages will be titled with sufficient precision to avoid most name clashes, typically by forming noun phrases.
Tolerant	Interpretable (even if undesirable) behavior is preferred to error messages.
Observable	Activity within the site can be watched and reviewed by any other visitor to the site.
Convergent	Duplication can be discouraged or removed by finding and citing similar or related content.
Trust	This is at the core of wiki. Trust the people, trust the process, enable trust building.

Because a wiki is so open, it incorporates content versioning to enable tracking of revisions and reversing them as required. For every page of a wiki, there is a "history" page, which displays a list of edits made to that page. The reader can compare the differences between any two versions of the page (e.g., the version at 13:39 on 28 Dec 2004 (the current version)) with that of 08:20 25 May 2004. (see Table 16-3). Colors are typically used to show differences between versions, but in this case differences are indicated in italics.

Table 16-3: Wiki difference between pages display

Revision as of 08:20, 25 May 2004	Current revision
If these data are stored in HTML format (as in Table 3), then the meaning of the data has to be inferred by the reader. This is generally quite easy for humans, but impossible for machines. Furthermore, the presentation format is fixed and can only be altered by rewriting the HTML.	If these data are stored in HTML format (as in Table 3), then the meaning of the data has to be inferred by the reader. This is generally quite easy for humans, but impossible for machines. Furthermore, the presentation format is fixed and can only be altered by rewriting the HTML. *If you are not familiar with HTML, you should read the WikiBooks chapter on [http://en.wikibooks.org/ wiki/Programming:XHTML programming in XHTML], an extension of HTML, before reading the next chapter.*

The complete revision history means that any reader can make any prior version of the page the current version. This is very useful if there is any vandalism of a page or some serious errors introduced between versions. If vandalism is a persistent problem, the administrators of the wiki can restrict editing to a few people with logins. Some wikis go as far as requiring all editors to have logins, but generally wikis are open.

Wikipedia's untouchables

Contributors to Wikipedia are required to adopt a neutral point of view. Unfortunately, not everyone follows this directive, and the editors occasionally have to step in when objectivity seems to have become a lost cause.

In October 2004, prior to the U.S. Presidential elections, contributors were continually editing the biographies of President Bush and Senator Kerry to reflect their particular opinions of the candidates. Eventually, a Wikipedia administrator had to stop free-for-all editing until after the election. All changes had to be approved before publication, which is counter to the wiki model of letting anybody edit any entry.

Bush and Kerry joined other Wikipedia untouchables—Ariel Sharon, Osama bin Laden, Rush Limbaugh, and Salvador Allende—whose entries are also under tight control.

Of course, the controversy did not finish with the election, and disagreement about the entries for Bush and Kerry continues. For controversial topics, the normal Wiki editing protocol breaks down.

Source: Boxer, Sarah. 2004. Mudslinging weasels into online history. *The New York Times,* Nov. 10, http://www.nytimes.com/2004/11/10/arts/10wiki.html.

Wiki software has proved very useful for private and public knowledge management systems. Ease of use and openness make it very easy for anyone to add and amend knowledge. A wiki can also support collaboration, such as joint authorship and project management. In addition, wiki software usually includes a search engine to facilitate searching of all pages managed by the wiki.

Wiki uses a simple markup language. For example, to indicate that a phrase should be displayed as a level 1 heading, it is surrounded by a pair of equal (=) signs. Thus, you can quickly learn how to edit a page.

Wikipedia[11] is probably the most successful wiki. It is an open content, free encyclopedia that anyone can read and anyone can edit. The English version, started in 2001, had over 400,000 articles by the end of 2004. The concept has been extended, and Wikipedias exist in roughly 50 languages, though none has as many articles as the English version.

---

11. en.wikipedia.org

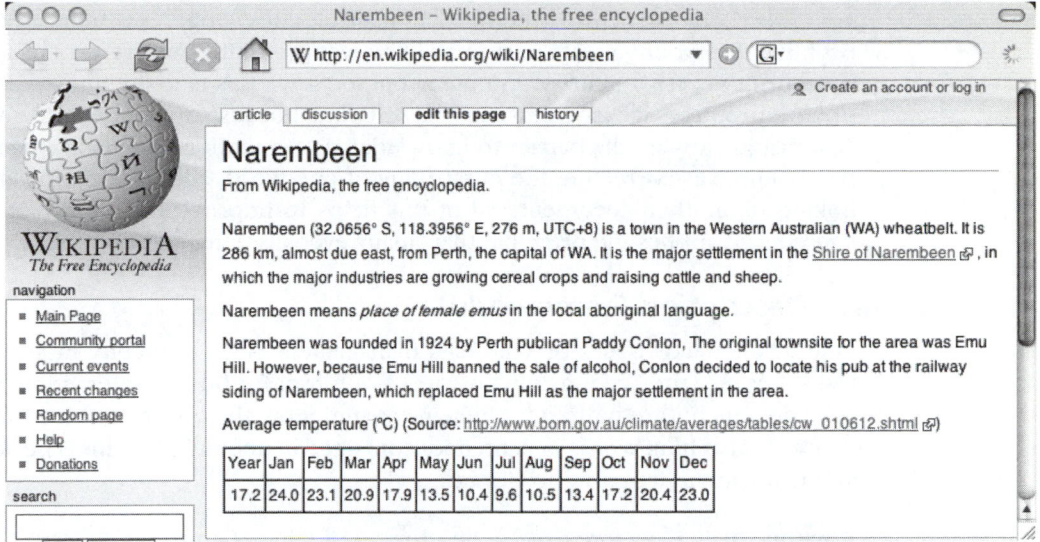

Figure 16-6. A page from Wikipedia

There are wikis for a variety of knowledge management problems. For example, Wikispecies is a directory of species that covers all forms of life. Wiktionary is an open content dictionary and thesaurus. A collection of quotations can be found in Wikiquote.

Wiki technology has also been applied to book publishing. For example, students in an advanced data management course at the University of Georgia collaborated to write an open content XML textbook.[12] This text can be freely used by other students, who are encouraged to also improve the book by adding exercises, adding examples of the use of XML, or contributing new chapters. As a result, the book is continually improved by the collaborative efforts of many professors and students.

Skill Builder

Add an entry to or edit an existing entry in ISPedia,[13] an open content information systems encyclopedia based on wiki software. Consult the help page (top right) to learn how to start a new page or edit an existing page.

---

12. en.wikibooks.org/wiki/XML
13. ispedia.terry.uga.edu

Knowledge management is an important issue for most organizations in the information age. Everybody recognizes the need to manage knowledge, but there is a fundamental problem: Everybody wants to read and few want to write. We are very pleased when we find an answer to our current problem, but too few of us take the time to document solutions to problems we have solved. Wiki software, because of its ease of use and openness, significantly lowers the barrier to knowledge dissemination. A person's contribution can be as simple as correcting the misspelling of one word, adding a clarifying sentence, or linking to another document. All of this helps to improve the quality of a knowledge source, and applies the principle that "many eyeballs detect all errors."

Resource Description Framework[14]

One of the major issues of Web data management is the difficulty in automating many tasks, because the Web mainly operates as a forum for human interaction. Because most Web documents are written for human consumption, the only available form of searching is simply matching words or sentences contained in documents. This is not very effective, and many found items are irrelevant.

What we need is a more precise description of what is on the Web. Then, we can move the Web from machine-readable to machine-understandable, which would greatly facilitate a more efficient use of the Web.

The Resource Description Framework (RDF) is a general framework for describing any Internet resource, such as a Web site and its content. An Internet resource is defined as any resource with a Uniform Resource Identifier (URI). This includes the Uniform Resource Locators (URLs) that identify entire Web sites and specific Web pages.

An RDF description can include metadata, such as the authors of the resource, date of creation or updating, the organization of the pages on a site, information that describes content in terms of audience or content rating, key words for search-engine data collection, and subject categories.

An RDF makes it possible for everyone to share a Web site and other descriptions more easily and for software developers to build products that can use the metadata to provide better search engines and directories, to act as intelligent agents, and to give Web users more control of what they are viewing. The RDF is an application of XML (see Chapter 18). A sample RDF is shown in Table 16-4.

As a device for managing data describing web resources, the RDF is another tool of which data managers should be aware. It is particularly relevant for those who manage Web sites. The RDF is a work in progress and is still not widely implemented.[15]

---

14. For a more detailed discussion, see en.wikibooks.org/wiki/RDF_-_Resource_Description_Framework
15. For more information, see www.w3.org/RDF/#overview.

Table 16-4: A sample RDF

```
<rdf:RDF xmlns:rdf="http://www.w3.org/1999/02/22-rdf-syntax-ns#"
         xmlns:dc="http://purl.org/dc/elements/1.0/">
   <rdf:Description rdf:about="http://www.wiley.com/college/watson"
      dc:creator="Richard T. Watson"
      dc:title="Data Management"
      dc:description="Support for the 5th edition of Data Management: Databases
            and Organizations by Richard T. Watson"
      dc:date="2005-07-01" />
</rdf:RDF>
```

Web browser-to-DBMS server connectivity

The Web browser has emerged as a popular interface to database applications for several important reasons. *First*, there is a one-time installation. Once a browser has been installed, all Web-based applications are accessible. Deployment of new systems is easy and fast. Client/server systems require a new client to be installed for each application. *Second*, the Web is global, and those in remote locations can easily connect to the application. *Third*, the simple, page-oriented design of Web applications makes application development relatively straightforward. *Fourth*, once people have learned how to use a browser, they have acquired most of the skills for using any new application, and training costs are lower. Consequently, it is not surprising that many organizations have adopted the Web browser as the standard interface to most applications.

Web applications are **thin-client** systems (see page 367 for a comparison of thick and thin clients). Converting legacy applications to thin-client Web applications is generally easier than converting them to fat clients, because applications expect the client to do so little. With a thin client, most of the work is done by the server, and as a result, network traffic is lower, because there is less need to exchange messages between the client and the server.

Browsers interface to a database management system (DBMS) server via a three-tier architecture (see Figure 16-7). The first tier is the browser. This tier operates with any browser. The first tier may have some application logic, for instance some JavaScript to validate an input form. The application server, the second tier, processes the bulk of the application logic, and manages security and access to the application. It also is a client to DBMS servers. It issues DBMS commands to DBMS servers, the third tier, which contain the data and referential integrity rules. The DBMS servers can be those of a variety of vendors. Briefly, the first tier handles presentation, the second processes application logic, and the third manages data.

Options

The marketplace currently provides many ways of interfacing a Web browser to a DBMS server. Nearly every DBMS vendor offers such software, and there is a variety of third-party vendors. Software developers usually prefer a vendor-independent approach or a method that works on multiple platforms.

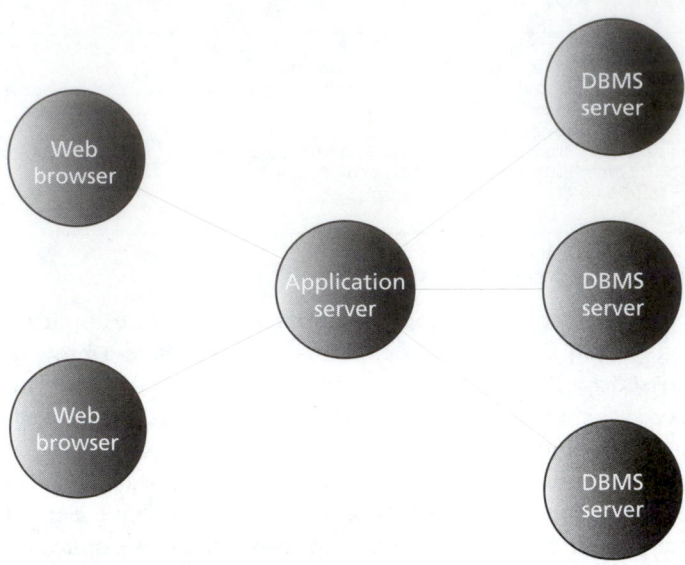

Figure 16-7. Three-tier architecture

CGI

A Common Gateway Interface (CGI) program is a gateway between the browser request and the data required. Perl is the most popular of the many languages for CGI programming. The downside of CGI is that it does not scale well to handle high transaction volumes.

ASP

Microsoft's Active Server Pages (ASP) combines HTML, scripting, and server-side components into a single file called an Active Server Page. Scripting can be in Jscript (Microsoft's version of JavaScript) or VBScript. ASP operates only with Microsoft's Web servers (i.e., IIS) on its operating systems (e.g., Windows NT), and thus portability is restricted.

With the introduction of the .NET framework, Microsoft released an environment for building, deploying, and running Web applications. It replaced ASP with ASP .NET, which is not an upgrade of ASP, but a new approach to server-side scripting. ADO .NET, which can be used with ASP .NET, is a set of classes to handle database access. The classes are very similar in functionality to those used with JDBC to support database access.

Java servlets and JSP

Java servlets and JavaServer Pages (JSP) are based on the widely used Java programming language. Sun's Java Servlet application programming interfaces (APIs) are extensions to Java to support server-side processing by Java Servlets. A JSP combines HTML, Java code, and JavaBeans components and thus is similar in concept to ASP .NET. In Chapter 17, we will cover the use of Java to access a relational database using JDBC.

PHP

PHP: Hypertext Preprocessor (PHP), developed in 1994 by Rasmus Lerdorf to track visitors to his online resume, was released in 1995 as a personal home page tool. Since then, PHP has been embraced by the Web community and has gained considerable acceptance among commercial sites because it is free and open- source. It is an alternative to Microsoft's ASP technology.

A PHP application consists of HTML and PHP script, which are executed by the server before sending a page of HTML code to the browser. Because PHP generates HTML, it works with any browser. In addition, PHP is platform independent, and versions are available for most operating systems and Web servers, including popular ones such as Apache and IIS.

Conclusion

The Web is giving database applications, and many other information systems, a new face—the browser. This new face brings with it a broader set of tools for presenting information. The table, the mainstay of the relational model, has been augmented by six other information organization models. Thus, database application design, with more choices for information presentation, becomes more complicated.

Summary

The data on a Web site must be managed. HTML editors and Web site managers are tools to support Web site creation and management. Web site designers need to create an information architecture and apply information design and information arts skills when creating a Web site. There are seven universal models for the organization of data (linear, hierarchical, web, parallel, matrix, overlay, and spatial zoom). The Web browser, a thin client, is becoming a standard interface to database applications. Three-tier architecture consists of a Web browser (first tier), application server (second tier), and DBMS server (third tier). Some Web database application development approaches are CGI, proprietary APIs, active server pages (ASP), server-side JavaScript (SSJS), Java servlets, JSP, and PHP. A content management system (CMS) is a program for managing the content of a Web site. Wiki technology can be used for Web site and knowledge management.

Key terms and concepts

Active Server Page (ASP)	JavaServer Pages (JSP)
Application server	JavaScript
Browser	Navigation aids
Content management system	Organization model
Content versioning system	.NET
Common Gateway Interface (CGI)	PHP: Hypertext Preprocessor (PHP)
Connectivity	Plone
Fat client	Server
HTML editor	Servlet
Hypertext Markup Language (HTML)	Site management
Information organization	Thin client
Information arts	Three-tier architecture
Information design	Two-tier architecture
Intranet	Wiki
Java	Wikipedia

References

Ehrenberg, D., et al. 2005. *Programming: XHTML*. WikiBooks, Jan 3, http://en.wiki-books.org/wiki/Programming:XHTML.

Leuf, B., and W. Cunningham. 2001. *The Wiki way: quick collaboration on the web*. Boston: Addison-Wesley.

Meloni, J. C. 2004. *Plone content management essential*s. Indianapolis, IN: Sams.

Mok, C. 1996. *Designing business: multiple media, multiple disciplines*. San Jose, CA: Adobe.

Wagner, C. 2004. Wiki: a technology for conversational knowledge management and group collaboration. *Communications of AIS* 13 (9):265-289.

Exercises

1. The development of a Web site requires blending the skills of IS and graphics arts professionals. What roles should each of these professionals play in information architecture, information design, and information arts? Who is likely to play the major role in each phase?
2. Surf the Web to find examples of each of the seven universal models of information organization. Which model appears to be most commonly used?
3. Design a Web page for a book store.
4. Distinguish between fat and thin clients. If you were in charge of running the computer laboratories at your university, would your prefer fat or thin clients?
5. What are the advantages and disadvantages of PHP?
6. Describe the advantages and disadvantages of database application development using Java.
7. What are the differences between Java and JavaScript?

8. Visit plone.org/about/sites and check out some of the sites created using Plone. Can you tell that they were created using Plone?

9. The Connexions Project, hosted by Rice University, is based on Plone. Why do you think Plone was selected for this site?

10. Search Wikipedia to see whether it has an article on your home town. If it does, improve the article in some way. If not, create an article for your home town. You might use Narembeen as an example.

11. Can you use a CMS to manage a wiki? Search the Web to see whether any software is available.

12. What circumstances might favor a CMS over a wiki, and vice versa?

13. Visit en.wikipedia.org/wikistats/EN/Sitemap.htm, which contains details of Wikipedia statistics. What do you conclude?

14. What is the purpose of an RDF?

17

SQL and Java

The vision for Java is to be the concrete and nails that people use to build this incredible network system that is happening all around us.
James Gosling, 2000[1]

Learning objectives

Students completing this chapter will be able to

❖ write a Java program to access and maintain a relational database;
❖ understand how SQL commands are used for transaction processing.

Introduction

Java is a platform-independent application development language. Its object-oriented nature makes it easy to create and maintain software and prototypes. These features make Java an attractive development language for many applications, including database systems.

This chapter assumes that you have completed an introductory course in Java programming. It focuses on how to embed SQL commands in a Java program to build an application. MySQL is used for all the examples, but the fundamental principles are the same for all relational databases. With a few changes, your program will work with another implementation of the relational model.

The great advantage of Java is that it provides a simple approach to the development, management, and deployment of client/server and browser applications. It is simpler because it has the good parts of C++, a popular object-oriented development language, but not the bad features. New client/server applications or modifications of existing ones are easily distributed by placing them on the server. There is no need to install a new or updated client on each machine—distribution is immediate. In addition, many vendors provide support for JDBC, which is discussed in the next section.

---

1. Inventor of Java <www.infoworld.com/articles/hn/xml/00/10/09/001009hnjg.html>.

Before discussing Java database application development, we need to cover briefly Java's three major object-oriented constructs: interface, class, and object, as illustrated in Figure 17-1. An *interface* defines fields and methods but does not contain programming statements. You can think of an interface as a specification whose implementation is left to someone else. A *class* implements the actions that objects perform by implementing methods declared in the interface or by declaring and implementing its own methods. An *object* is a run-time instance of a class.

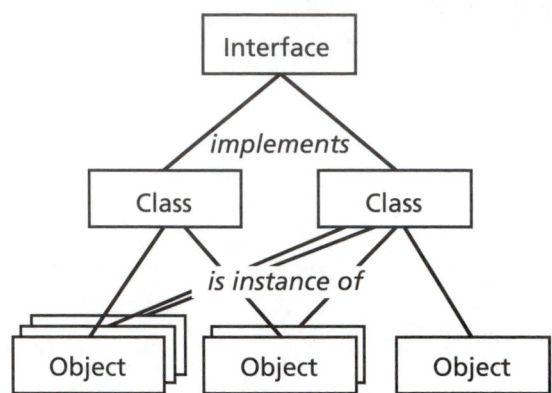

Figure 17-1. Relationship between interface, class, and object

JDBC

Java Database Connectivity (JDBC), a Java version of a portable SQL command line interface (CLI), is modeled on ODBC. JDBC enables programmers to write Java software that is both operating system and DBMS independent. As Figure 17-2 illustrates, JDBC provides two major services: an application programming interface (JDBC API) and a driver interface (JDBC driver manager). There are two approaches to implementing a Java driver. A *direct* driver sits on top of the DBMS's native interface. A *bridged* driver is built on top of an existing ODBC driver. Since JDBC is based on ODBC, the translation between protocols for a bridged driver should be very fast.

Figure 17-2. JDBC layers

Application
JDBC API
JDBC driver manager
Service provider API
Driver for DBMS server
DBMS server

The JDBC core

The JDBC core, which handles 90 percent of database programming, contains seven interfaces and two classes. The purpose of each of these is summarized in Table 17-1.

Table 17-1: JDBC core interfaces and classes

Interfaces	Description
Driver	Locates a driver for a specified database
Connection	Connects an application to a database
Statement	A container for an SQL statement
PreparedStatement	Precompiles an SQL statement and then uses it multiple times
CallableStatement	Executes a stored procedure
ResultSet	The rows returned when a query is executed
ResultSetMetaData	The number, types, and properties of the result set
Classes	
DriverManager	Loads driver objects and creates database connections
DriverPropertyInfo	Used by specialized clients

For each DBMS, implementations of these interfaces are required, because they are specific to the DBMS and not part of the Java package. For example, specific drivers are needed for PostgreSQL, DB2, Oracle, MySQL, etc. Before using JDBC, you will need to install these interfaces for the DBMS you plan to access.[2] The standard practice appears to be to refer to this set of interfaces as the driver, but the 'driver' also includes implementations of all the interfaces.

In the next section on using SQL with Java, you will need to download and install BlueJ,[3] a free integrated Java environment specifically designed for learning Java. You will need BlueJ to run the example Java applications.

Using SQL within Java

We now examine each of these major steps in processing an SQL query and, in the process, create Java methods to query a database.

Connect to the database

The `getConnection` method of the `DriverManager` specifies the URL of the database, the user identifier, and the password. The `DriverManager` locates a driver that can process the database and returns a `Connection` object.

---

2. See servlet.java.sun.com/products/jdbc/drivers for a list of drivers.
3. www.bluej.org

The first action is to establish a connection to the DBMS, which involves two steps.

1. Loading the driver
2. Making the connection

Loading the driver

One line of code is required to load the appropriate JDBC driver for the DBMS.

```
Class.forName(driver);
```

You cannot assume that loading the driver will be trouble-free. Thus, good coding practice requires that you detect and report any errors using Java's `try-catch` structure. We can put all this into a method (Table 17-2).

Table 17-2: Loading a driver

```
1 public void loadDriver(String driver) {
2   try {
3     Class.forName(driver);
4   }
5   catch (ClassNotFoundException error) {
6     System.out.println("Could not load driver: " + error.toString());
7     System.exit(1);
8   }
9 }
```

Connecting to the DBMS

The second action is to connect to the DBMS by supplying its URL and the account's login and password.

```
dbConnect = DriverManager.getConnection(url,"User", "Password");
```

The format of the `url` parameter varies with the JDBC driver, and you will need to consult the documentation for the driver. In the case of MySQL, the possible formats are

```
jdbc:mysql:database
jdbc:mysql://host/database
jdbc:mysql://host:port/database
```

The default value for host is "localhost" and, for MySQL, the default port is "3306."

For example:

```
jdbc:mysql://www.richardtwatson.com:3306/text
```

will connect to the database "text" on the host "www.richardtwatson.com" on port 3306.

User and Password have the usual meanings for any computer account. A method for connecting is illustrated in Table 17-3.

Table 17-3: Making a connection

```
1  public void connectDatabase(String db, String user, String password) {
2      try {
3          dbConnect = DriverManager.getConnection(db, user, password);
4      }
5      catch(SQLException error) {
6          System.err.println("Error connecting to database: " + error.toString());
7          System.exit(2);
8      }
9  }
```

Create an SQL statement

The createStatement method is invoked to produce a Statement object (Table 17-4). Note that the dbConnect in dbConnect.createStatement() refers to the connection created by the getConnection method.

Table 17-4: Creating an SQL statement

```
1  public void createSQL() {
2      try {
3          dbStatement = dbConnect.createStatement();
4      }
5      catch(SQLException error) {
6          System.err.println("Error creating statement: " + error.toString());
7          System.exit(3);
8      }
9  }
```

Execute a SELECT

Now, we write a method that accepts an SQL statement as input and displays it (Table 17-5). The SQL query is passed as a string by the executeSQL method of the Statement object. The results are returned in a ResultSet object by the following line of Java code

```
dbResultSet = dbStatement.executeQuery(query);
```

Table 17-5: Executing a SELECT

```
1   public void executeSQL(String query) {
2       try {
3           System.out.println(query + "\n");
4           dbResultSet = dbStatement.executeQuery(query);
5       }
6       catch(SQLException error) {
7           System.err.println("Error executing SQL: " + error.toString());
8           System.exit(4);
9       }
10  }
```

Report a SELECT

The rows in the table are processed a row at a time using the next method of the ResultSet object (Table 17-6). Columns are retrieved one at a time using a getString. In the illustrative example, all columns are treated as string data types to give a general solution to reporting the results of a query.

Table 17-6: Reporting a SELECT

```
 1 public void reportSQL() {
 2   int i;
 3   try {
 4     dbResultSetMetaData = dbResultSet.getMetaData();
 5     // Get the number of columns in the result set
 6     int numCols = dbResultSetMetaData.getColumnCount();
 7     // Fetch until end of the result set
 8     while (dbResultSet.next()) {
 9       // Loop through each column
10       for (i=1; i<=numCols; i++) {
11         if (i > 1) System.out.print("  ");
12         System.out.print(dbResultSet.getString(i));
13         System.out.println("");
14       }
15     }
16   catch(SQLException error) {
17       System.err.println("Error displaying results: " + error.toString());
18       System.exit(5);
19   }
20 }
```

Inserting a row

Here is a method for inserting a row in a table. The insert command is passed as a string by the executeUpdate method of the Statement object (Table 17-7).

Table 17-7: Inserting a row

```
 1 public void insertSQL(String sql){ {
 2   try {
 3     dbStatement = dbConnect.createStatement();
 4     int result = dbStatement.executeUpdate(sql);
 5   }
 6   catch(SQLException error) {
 7     System.err.println("Error inserting row: " + error.toString());
 8     System.exit(6);
 9   }
10 }
```

Release the Statement object

The resources associated with the Statement object are freed using close as follows:

```
dbResultSet.close();
dbStatement.close();
```

Release the Connection object

The resources associated with the Connection object are also freed using close.

```
dbConnect.close();
```

The resulting method to release the statement and connection objects is shown in Table 17-8.

Table 17-8: Closing a connection

```
 1 public void closeDatabase() {
 2   try {
 3     dbResultSet.close();
 4     dbStatement.close();
 5     dbConnect.close();
 6     }
 7   catch(SQLException error) {
 8     System.err.println("Error closing: " + error.toString());
 9     System.exit(7);
10     }
11 }
```

All the methods are now complete, and we package them into one file, DatabaseAccess.java (Table 17-9). The code for the various methods is not replicated so that you can quickly see the broad structure of the file.

We also create a test program, DatabaseTest.java (Table 17-10), to illustrate use of the various methods. Note that the `driver` and `jdbc` fields {3-4} make this program DBMS specific, MySQL in the case. You will need to change them for another DBMS.

Skill builder

1. Get from the book's supporting Web site the BlueJ packages for Database and MapCollection and the SQL for creating the tables to use with these packages.
2. Create the test table in the DBMS to which you have access.
3. Modify DatabaseTest.java for your local environment.
4. Run DatabaseTest several times to get a feel for what it does.
5. Inspect the code of DatabaseTest.java and DatabaseAccess.java to learn how you use SQL from within a Java application.[4]

BMW runs on Java

Found in BMW's 7 Series, 6 Series, and 5 Series cars, iDrive controls a car's audio system, navigation, the air conditioning, and other features of the car. Drivers can manipulate all these systems from a single knob, rather than multiple buttons.

iDrive is based on Top Level Architecture, a programming architecture for car systems. TLA was designed by Siemens VDO Automotive, a German firm. TLA is founded on Sun Microsystems' Java programming platform.

Source: Anonymous. 2004. Change the Oil, Upgrade the Software. *BusinessWeek*, Sep. 14, www.businessweek.com/technology/content/sep2004/tc20040914_2307_tc178.htm.

---

4. Both DatabaseAccess.java and DatabaseTest.java are available on the book's web site.

Table 17-9: database.java

```
1  import java.sql.*;
2  /**
3   * Methods for connecting to a database,
4   * executing SQL, and reporting the result *
5   * @author (Rick Watson)
6   * @version (2004.08.28)
7   */
8  public class DatabaseAccess {
9    // instance variables
10   private Connection dbConnect;
11   private Statement dbStatement;
12   private ResultSet dbResultSet;
13   private ResultSetMetaData dbResultSetMetaData;
14   /**
15   * Load the driver class
16   */
17   public void loadDriver(String driver) {
18        (method code)
19   }
20   /**
21   * Make a connection to a database
22   */
23   public void connectDatabase(String db, String user, String password) {
24        (method code)
25   }
26   /**
27   * Create an SQL statement
28   */
29   public void createSQL() {
30        (method code)
31   }
32   /**
33   * Execute a SELECT
34   */
35   public void executeSQL(String query) {
36        (method code)
37   }
38   /**
39   * Report a SELECT
40   */
41   public void reportSQL() {
42        (method code)
43   }
44   /**
45   * INSERT a row
46   */
47   public void insertSQL(String sql) {
48        (method code)
49   }
50
51   /**
52   * Close the connection
53   */
54   public void closeDatabase() {
55        (method code)
56   }
57  }
```

Table 17-10: databaseTest.java

```
1  public class DatabaseTest {
2    public static void main(String[] args) {
3      //Set fields
4      String driver = "com.mysql.jdbc.Driver";
5      String jdbc = "jdbc:mysql:";
6      String db = "//blaze.terry.uga.edu:3306/textbook";
7      String username = "student";
8      String password = "student";
9      String insert;
10     String query;
11     insert = args [0]; // name to insert supplied as parameter;
12     //Create database
13     database test = new database();
14     //Invoke methods
15     test.loadDriver(driver);
16     test.connectDatabase(jdbc + db,username,password);
17     test.createSQL();
18     test.insertSQL("insert into test values ('" + insert + "');");
19     test.executeSQL("select * from test");
20     test.reportSQL();
21     test.closeDatabase();
22   }
23 }
```

Map collection case

 The Expeditioner has added a new product line to meet the needs of its changing clientele. It now stocks a range of maps. The firm's data modeler has created a data model describing the situation (see Figure 17-3). A map has a scale; for example, a scale of 1:1 000 000 means that 1 unit on the map is 1,000,000 units on the ground (or 1 cm is 10 km, and 1 inch is ~16 miles). There are three types of maps: road, rail, and canal. Initially, The Expeditioner decided to stock maps for only a few European countries.

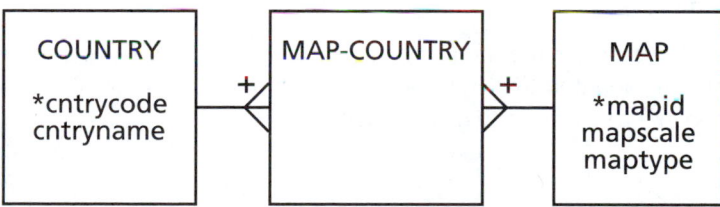

Figure 17-3. The Expeditioner's map collection data model

Data entry

Once the tables have been defined, we want to insert some records. This could be done using the Java code just created, but it would be very tedious, as we would type INSERT statements for each row (e.g., INSERT INTO map VALUES (1, 1000000, 'Rail');). A better approach is to use a data entry form, see Figure 17-4, which was developed using the NetBeans GUI tools to create the form and supporting Java code.[5]

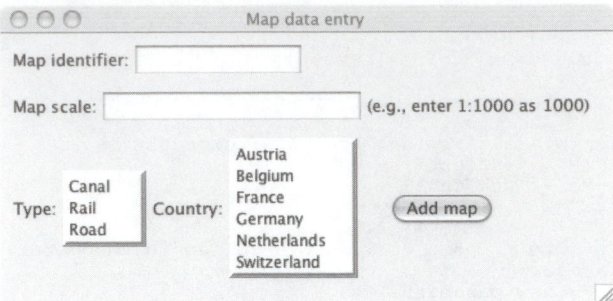

Figure 17-4. Map collection data entry form

The data entry form captures a map's identifier, scale, type, and the number of countries covered by the map. The identifier and scale are entered, and should be integer. The type of map is selected from the list, which is defined so that only one type can be selected. Multiple countries can be selected by holding down a key combination[6] when selected from the displayed list of countries.

When the "Add map" button is clicked, an event handler is alerted. The code executed by this event handler validates the input data and processes the transaction to add details of a map to the database. The necessary code for each of these actions is now discussed.

Data validation

The map identifier and scale should be integer, otherwise there will be data type mismatch when inserting a new row. The following code (Table 17-11) handles converting the input data into integer format and reporting any errors. Note that the code checks both input values and, if either is noninteger, terminates further processing of the form by executing a `return`.

This is fairly elementary error reporting; in practice, the error message would be reported on the form, but the intention in this section is to focus on the database side of a transaction and keep error reporting to a necessary minimum.

Transaction processing

A transaction is a logical unit of work. In the case of adding a map, it means inserting a row in MAP for the map and inserting one row in MAP-COUNTRY for each country on the map. All of these inserts must be executed without failure for the entire transaction to be processed. SQL has two commands for supporting transaction processing:, COMMIT and ROLLBACK. The beginning of a transaction is always implicit, and it terminates with either a COMMIT or ROLLBACK.

---

5. NetBeans <www.netbeans.org> is an open source integrated development environment (IDE).
6. Command-click on Mac OS X and Control-click on Windows.

Table 17-11: Numeric validation

```
1  dataOK = true;
2  try {
3  mapId = Integer.parseInt(jTextField2.getText());
4       }
5  catch(NumberFormatException error) {
6      System.err.println("Map identifier not an integer");
7      dataOK = false;
8       }
9  try {
10 mapScale = Integer.parseInt(jTextField1.getText());
11      }
12 catch(NumberFormatException error) {
13      System.err.println("Map scale not an integer");
14      dataOK = false;
15      }
16 if (! dataOK) {
17      return;
18 }
```

Autocommit

Before processing a transaction, you need to turn of autocommit to avoid committing each database change separately before the entire transaction is complete. The following code (Table 17-12) describes a general approach to handling autocommit. Use it by calling `autoCommit()`. It is a good idea to set the value for autocommit immediately after a successful database connection, which is what is done in this example, as you will see when you inspect the code for MapInsert.java.

Table 17-12: Autocommit

```
1  public void autoCommit(boolean commit){
2      try {
3          dbConnect.setAutoCommit(false);
4      }
5      catch (SQLException error){
6          System.out.println("Could not turn off autocommit");
7          System.exit(1);
8      }
9  }
```

Commit

The `COMMIT` command is executed when all parts of a transaction have successfully executed. It makes the changes to the database permanent. The following code (Table 17-13) describes a general approach to handling `COMMIT`. It is used by calling `dbCommit()`.

Rollback

The `ROLLBACK` command is executed when any part of a transaction fails. All changes to the database since the beginning of the transaction are reversed, and the database is restored to its state prior to transaction. The following code (Table 17-14) describes a general approach to handling `ROLLBACK`. It used by calling `dbRollback()`.

Table 17-13: Commit

```
1  public void dbCommit(){
2     try {
3        dbConnect.commit();
4        System.out.println("Transaction commit");
5     }
6     catch (SQLException error){
7        System.out.println("Could not commit");
8        System.exit(1);
9     }
10 }
```

Table 17-14: Rollback

```
1  public void dbRollback(){
2     try {
3        dbConnect.rollback();
4        System.out.println("Transaction rollback");
5     }
6     catch (SQLException error){
7        System.out.println("Could not rollback");
8        System.exit(1);
9     }
10 }
```

Inserting a new map

To insert a new row into the map table, you must first retrieve the selected type of map and convert it to a string {1}, put together the SQL INSERT {2-3}, and then execute the INSERT statement {6}. If an error is caught, a flag, transOK, is set to false to indicate the transaction failed {10} (Table 17-15).

Table 17-15: Inserting a row into the map table

```
1  mapType = mapList.getSelectedValue().toString();
2  sql = "insert into map values (" +
3     + mapId + "," + mapScale + "," + "'" + mapType + "')";
4  try {
5     dbStatement = dbConnect.createStatement();
6     int result = dbStatement.executeUpdate(sql);
7  }
8  catch(SQLException error) {
9     System.err.println("Error inserting row: " + error.toString());
10    transOK = false;
11 }
```

Inserting the countries on a map

To record the details of the countries on a map, you must first retrieve the number of countries entered {1}, and then loop through a set of statements {3-13} to insert a row for each country into MAPCOUNTRY and report any errors. The logic within the loop is similar to adding a map.If an error is caught, a flag, transOK, is set to indicate the transaction failed {12} (Table 17-16).

Table 17-16: Inserting rows into the mapCountry table

```
1  selectedIndices = nationList.getSelectedIndices();
2  i = selectedIndices.length;
3  for (j = 0; j < i; j++ ){
4    natCode = nationCode[selectedIndices[j]];
5    sql = "insert into mapCountry values (" + mapId + "," + "'" + natCode + "')";
6    try {
7      dbStatement = dbConnect.createStatement();
8      int result = dbStatement.executeUpdate(sql);
9    }
10   catch(SQLException error) {
11       System.err.println("Error inserting row: " + error.toString());
12       transOK = false;
13   }
14 }
```

Completing the transaction

The final task, to commit or roll back the transaction depending on whether any errors were detected during any of the inserts, is determined by examining `transOK`. (Table 17-17).

Table 17-17: Completing the transaction

```
1  if (transOK) {
2      dbCommit(); // all inserts successful
3  }
4  else {
5      dbRollback(); // at least one insert failed
6  }
```

Putting it all together

You have now seen all the pieces for the event handler that processes a transaction to add a map and the countries on that map. Let's look at the broad flow of the code, shown in full in Table 17-18.

1. The name of the event handler called when "Add map" is clicked {1};
2. Fields are defined and initialized as needed {2-10};
3. The value input for `mapId` is validated {11-18};
4. The value input for `mapScale` is validated {19-26};
5. If either `mapId` or `mapScale` is noninteger, the event handler is terminated {27-30};
6. A row for a map is inserted {31-42};
7. Rows for each country on the map are inserted {43-57};
8. The transaction is either committed or rolled back {58-64}.

The complete application

The Java code for the complete application can be downloaded from the book's Web site.[7] When you inspect the roughly 400 lines of code, you will notice a sprinkling of blocks be-

---

7. http://richardtwatson.com/dm4e/Reader/java.html

Table 17-18: MapInsert.java

```
1  private void jButton1MouseClicked(java.awt.event.MouseEvent evt) {
2  int mapId, mapScale;
3  int[] selectedIndices;
4  String sql, mapType, natCode;
5  String nationCode[] = {"at","be","fr","de","nl","sh"};
6  boolean transOK, dataOK;
7  mapId = 0; // initialize
8  mapScale = 0; // initialize
9  transOK = true; // initialize
10 dataOK = true; // initialize
11 // check mapId is integer
12 try {
13   mapId = Integer.parseInt(jTextField2.getText());
14 }
15 catch(NumberFormatException error) {
16   System.err.println("Map identifier not an integer");
17   dataOK = false;
18 }
19 // check mapScale is integer
20 try {
21   mapScale = Integer.parseInt(jTextField1.getText());
22 }
23 catch(NumberFormatException error) {
24   System.err.println("Map scale not an integer");
25   dataOK = false;
26 }
27 // errors for mapId or mapScale?
28 if (! dataOK) {
29   return;
30 }
31 // insert a map
32 mapType = mapList.getSelectedValue().toString();
33 sql = "insert into map values (" +
34 mapId + "," + mapScale + "," + "'" + mapType + "')";
35 try {
36   dbStatement = dbConnect.createStatement();
37   int result = dbStatement.executeUpdate(sql);
38 }
39 catch(SQLException error) {
40   System.err.println("Error inserting row: " + error.toString());
41   transOK = false;
42 }
43 // insert countries on map
44 selectedIndices = nationList.getSelectedIndices();
45 int i = selectedIndices.length;
46 for (int j = 0; j < i; j++ ){
47   natCode = nationCode[selectedIndices[j]];
48   sql = "insert into mapCountry values (" + mapId + "," + "'" + natCode + "')";
49   try {
50 dbStatement = dbConnect.createStatement();
51 int result = dbStatement.executeUpdate(sql);
52   }
53   catch(SQLException error) {
54 System.err.println("Error inserting row: " + error.toString());
55 transOK = false;
56   }
57 }
58 // commit or rollback?
59 if (transOK) {
60   dbCommit();//all inserts successful
61   }
62 else {
63   dbRollback(); //at least one insert failed
64   }
65 }
```

ginning and closed by `//GEN` with some other text. These blocks of code are generated by NetBeans' GUI form designer.

Conclusion

Java is a widely used object-oriented programming language used to develop distributed multi-tier applications. JDBC is a key technology in this environment because it enables a Java application to interact with various implementations of the relational database model (e.g., Oracle, SQL Server, MySQL). As this chapter has demonstrated, with the help of a few examples, JDBC can be readily understood and applied.

Summary

Java is a platform-independent application development language. JDBC enables programs that are DBMS independent. SQL statements can be embedded within Java programs. `COMMIT` and `ROLLBACK` are used for transaction processing.

Key terms and concepts

Autocommit	Java Database Connectivity (JDBC)
`COMMIT`	`ROLLBACK`
Java	Transaction processing

References

Barnes, D. J., and M. Kölling. 2005. *Objects first with Java : a practical introduction using Blue J.* 2nd ed. Upper Saddle River, NJ: Prentice Hall.

Exercises

1. Write a Java application to maintain the database defined by the following data model. The database keeps track of the cars sold by a salesperson in an automotive dealership. Your application should be able to add a person and the cars a person has sold. These should be separate transactions.

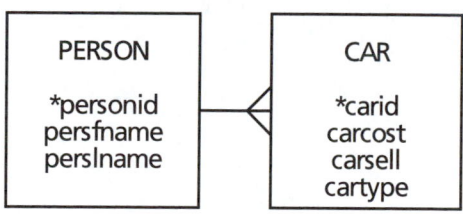

18

XML: Managing Data Exchange

Words can have no single fixed meaning. Like wayward electrons, they can spin away from their initial orbit and enter a wider magnetic field. No one owns them or has a proprietary right to dictate how they will be used.

David Lehman, *End of the Word*, 1991

Learning objectives

Students completing this chapter will be able to

❖ define the purpose of XML;
❖ create an XML schema;
❖ code data in XML format;
❖ create an XML stylesheet;
❖ discuss data management options for XML documents.

Introduction

There are four central problems in data management: capture, storage, retrieval, and exchange. The focus for most of this book has been on storage (i.e., data modeling) and retrieval (i.e., SQL). Now it is time to consider capture and exchange. Capture has always been an important issue, and the guiding principle is to capture data once in the cheapest possible manner. Likewise, data exchange has long been an issue, but the Internet has elevated the importance of this issue. Electronic Data Interchange (EDI), the traditional standard of data exchange for large organizations, is giving way to XML, which is likely to become the data exchange standard for all organizations, irrespective of size.

EDI

EDI, which has been used for more than 20 years, describes the electronic exchange of standard business documents between firms. A structured, standardized data format is used to exchange common business documents (e.g., invoices and shipping orders) between trading partners. In contrast to the free form of e-mail messages, EDI supports the exchange of repetitive, routine business transactions. Standards mean that routine electronic transactions can be concise and precise. The main standard used in the United States and Canada is known as ANSI X.12, and the major international standard is EDIFACT. Firms following the same standard can electronically share data. The majority of electronic commerce transactions are handled by EDI.

Before EDI, many standard messages between partners were generated by computer, printed, and mailed to the other party, and then data were manually entered into its computer. The main advantages of EDI are that

- ❖ Paper handling is reduced, saving time and money.
- ❖ Data are exchanged in real time.
- ❖ Data are keyed only once, resulting in fewer errors.
- ❖ Activities are better coordinated between business partners through enhanced data sharing.
- ❖ Money flows are accelerated and payments received sooner.

Most EDI traffic has been handled by value-added networks (VANs) or private networks. VANs add communication services to those provided by common carriers (e.g., Bell-South). However, these networks are too expensive for all but the largest 100,000 of the 6 million businesses in existence today in the United States. As a result, many businesses have not been able to participate in the benefits associated with EDI. However, the Internet enables smaller companies to take advantage of EDI.

Internet communication costs are typically less than those of VANs. In addition, the Internet is a global network, potentially accessible by nearly every firm. Consequently, the Internet is displacing VANs as the electronic transport path between trading partners. The simplest approach is to use the Internet as a means of replacing a VAN by using a commercially available Internet EDI package. Another approach is to reexamine the technology of data exchange; EDI was developed in the 1960s. A result of this rethinking is XML, but before considering XML, we need to learn about SGML, the parent of XML.

SGML

It is estimated that document management consumes up to 15 percent of a typical company's revenue, nearly 25 percent of its labor costs, and anywhere between 10 and 60 percent of an office worker's time. The Standard Generalized Markup Language (SGML) is designed to reduce the cost and increase the efficiency of document management.

A **markup language** embeds information about the text in the text. In Table 18-1, the markup tags indicate that the text contains CD liner notes. Note also that the titles and identifiers of the mentioned CDs are explicitly identified.

Table 18-1: Markup language

```
<cdliner>This uniquely creative collaboration between Miles Davis and
Gil Evans has already resulted in two extraordinary albums—
<cdtitle>Miles Ahead</cdtitle><cdid>CL 1041></cdid> and
<cdtitle>Porgy and Bess</cdtitle><cdid>CL 1274</cdid>.
</cdliner>
```

SGML is an International Standard (ISO 8879) that defines the structure of documents. It is a vendor-independent language that supports cross-system portability and publication for all media. Developed in 1986 to manage software documentation, SGML is widely accepted as the markup language for a number of information-intensive industries. As a metalanguage, SGML is the mother of both HTML and XML. Thus, SGML can generate both of these markup languages. SGML provides a stable platform for managing data when technology is rapidly changing. Because SGML is software- and hardware-neutral, businesses can choose *best- of- breed* tools to create, manage, retrieve, and disseminate data. This stability of SGML comes from its open-systems approach.

SGML has three major advantages for data management:

❖ **Reuse:** Information can be created once and reused over and over. By storing critical documents in SGML, firms do not need to duplicate efforts when there are changes to documents. For example, a firm might store all its legal contracts in SGML.

❖ **Flexibility**: SGML documents can be published in any medium for a wide variety of audiences. Because SGML is content-oriented, presentation decisions are delayed until the output format is known. Thus, the same content could be printed, presented on the Web in HTML, or written to a CD as PDF.

❖ **Revision**: SGML enhances control over revision and enables version control. When stored in an SGML database, original data are archived alongside any changes. That means you know exactly what the original document contained and what changes were made.

Electronic publishing does not require SGML. CD-ROMs and Web sites can be created without SGML. However, the use of SGML preserves textual information independent of how and when it is presented. SGML protects a firm's investment in documentation for the long term. Because it is now possible to display documentation using multiple media (e.g., Web and CD-ROM), firms have become sensitized to the need to store documents in a single, independent manner that can then be converted for display by a particular media.

SGML's power is derived from its recording of both text and the meaning of that text. A short section of SGML demonstrates clearly the features and strength of SGML (see Table 18-2). The tags surrounding a chunk of text describe its meaning and thus support presentation and retrieval. For example, the pair of tags <title> and </title> surrounding "XML: Managing Data Exchange" indicates that it is the chapter title.

Table 18-2: SGML code

```
<chapter>
<no>18</no>
<title>XML: Managing Data Exchange</title>
<section>
<quote><emph type = "2">Words can have no single fixed meaning. Like
wayward electrons, they can spin away from their initial orbit and
enter a wider magnetic field. No one owns them or has a proprietary
right to dictate how they will be used.</emph>
</quote>
</section>
</chapter>
```

Taking this piece of SGML, it is possible, using an appropriate stylesheet, to create a print version where the title of the chapter is displayed in Times, 16 point, bold, or a HTML version where the title is displayed in red, Georgia, 14 point, italics. Furthermore, the database in which this text is stored can be searched for any chapters that contain "exchange" in their title.

Now, consider the case where the text is stored as HTML (see Table 18-3). How do you, with complete certainty, identify the chapter title? Do you extract all text contained by <h1> and </h1> tags? You will then retrieve "18" as a possible chapter title. What happens if there is other text displayed using <h1> and </h1> tags? The problem with HTML is that it defines presentation and has very little meaning. A similar problem exists for documents prepared with a word processor.

Table 18-3: HTML code

```
<html>
<body>
<h1><b>18 </b></h1>
<h1><b>XML: Managing Data Exchange</b></h1>
<p><i>Words can have no single fixed meaning. Like wayward electrons,
they can spin away from their initial orbit and enter a wider magnetic
field. No one owns them or has a proprietary right to dictate how they
will be used.</i>
</body>
</html>
```

By using embedded tags to record meaning, SGML makes a document platform-independent and greatly improves the effectiveness of searching. However, before a firm can use SGML, it needs to determine what meaning is contained within its document. In other words, it needs to define a data model[1] and create a **Document Type Definition** (DTD). Document elements to be marked up in SGML are *mapped* to a DTD. The accuracy of an SGML mapping can then be validated using the DTD.

---

1. And you thought you had said goodbye to this beast :)

Fortunately, several industries have already developed DTDs for common documents. Today, DTDs have been designed for the aerospace, automotive, electronics manufacturing, publishing, software development, and telecommunications documentation sectors. For example, the publishing industry has defined ISO 12083 for articles, books, and serials.[2]

There are some features of SGML that are considered to make implementation difficult and that also limit the ability to create tools for information management and exchange. As a result, XML, a derivative of SGML, was developed.

XML

Extensible Markup Language (XML), a new language designed to make information self-describing, retains the core ideas of SGML. You can think of XML as SGML for electronic and mobile commerce. XML has the potential to extend the Internet beyond information delivery to many other kinds of human activity. Since the definition of XML was completed in early 1998 by the World Wide Web Consortium (W3C), this new standard has spread rapidly because it solves a critical data management problem. XML is more than a mere incremental improvement of HTML. It is a conceptual change because XML is a meta-language—a language to generate languages. XML will steadily replace HTML on many Web sites. The major differences between XML and HTML are captured in Table 18-4.

Table 18-4: XML vs. HTML

XML	HTML
Structured text	Formatted text
User-definable structure (extensible)	Predefined formats (not extensible)
Context-sensitive retrieval	Limited retrieval
Greater hypertext linking	Limited hypertext linking

HTML, an electronic-publishing language, describes how a Web browser should display text and images on a computer screen. It tells the browser nothing about the meaning of the data. For example, the browser does not know whether a piece of text represents a price, a product code, or a delivery date. Humans infer meaning from the context (e.g., August 8, 2002, is recognized as a date). Given the explosive growth of the Web, HTML clearly works well enough for exchanging data between computers and humans. It does not, however, work for exchanging data between computers, because computers are not smart enough to infer meaning from context.

Successful data exchange requires that the meaning of the exchanged data be readily determined by a computer. The XML solution is to embed tags in a file to describe the data (e.g., insert tags into an order to indicate attributes such as price, size, quantity, and color). A browser, or program for that matter, can then recognize this document as a customer order. Consequently, it can do far more than just display the price. For example,

---

2. See www.xmlxperts.com/12083.htm

it can convert all prices to another currency. More importantly, the data can be exchanged between computers.

XML consists of rules (see Table 18-5) that anyone can follow to create a markup language (e.g., a markup language for financial data). Hence, the "eXtensible" in the XML name, indicating that the language can be easily extended to include new tags. In contrast, HTML is not extensible and its set of tags is fixed, which is one of the major reasons why HTML is easy to learn. The XML rules ensure that a type of computer program known as a **parser** can process any extension or addition of new tags.

Table 18-5: XML rules

❖   Elements must have both an opening and a closing tag.
❖   Elements must follow a strict hierarchy with only one root element.
❖   Elements must not overlap other elements.
❖   Element names must obey XML naming conventions.
❖   XML is case sensitive.

Consider the credit card company that wants to send your latest statement via the Internet so that you can load it into your financial management program. Since this is a common problem for credit card companies and financial software authors, these industry groups have combined to create Open Financial Exchange (OFX),[3] a language for the exchange of financial data across the Internet.

XML has a small number of rules. Tags almost always come in pairs, as in HTML. A pair of tags surrounds each piece of data (e.g., `<price>89.12</price>`) to indicate its *meaning*, whereas in HTML they indicate how the data are *presented*. Tag pairs can be nested inside one another to multiple levels, which effectively creates a tree or hierarchical structure. Because XML uses Unicode (see page 341), it enables exchange of information not only between different computer systems, but also across language boundaries.

The differences between HTML and XML are captured in the following examples for each markup language. Note that in Table 17-6, HTML incorporates formatting instructions (i.e., the course code is bold), whereas XML describes the meaning of the data.

Table 18-6: Comparison of HTML and XML coding

HTML	XML
`<p><b>MIST7600</b>` `Data Management ` `3 credit hours</p>`	`<course>` `<code>MIST7600</code>` `<title>Data Management</title>` `<credit>3</credit>` `</course>`

---

3. www.ofx.net/

The introduction of XML will see a shift of processing from the server to the browser. At present, most processing has to be done by the server because that is where knowledge about the data is stored. The browser knows nothing about the data and therefore can only present but not process. However, when XML is implemented, the browser can take on processing that previously had to be handled by the server.

Imagine that you are selecting a shirt from a mail-order catalog. The merchant's Web server sends you data on 20 shirts (100 Kbytes of text and images) with prices in U.S. dollars. If you want to see the prices in euros, the calculation will be done by the server, and the full details for the 20 shirts retransmitted (i.e., another 100 Kbytes are sent from the server to the browser). However, once XML is in place, all that needs to be sent from the server to the browser is the conversion rate of dollars to euros and a Java program to compute the conversion at the browser end (see Table 18-7). In most cases, less data will be transmitted between a server and browser when XML is in place. Consequently, widespread adoption of XML will reduce network traffic.

Table 18-7: Execution of HTML and XML code

HTML	XML
Retrieve shirt data with prices in $U.S. Retrieve shirt data with prices in euros.	Retrieve shirt data with prices in $U.S. Retrieve conversion rate of $U.S. to euro. Retrieve Java program to convert currencies. Compute prices in euros.

XML will also make searching more efficient and effective. At present, search engines look for matching text strings, and consequently return many links that are completely irrelevant. For instance, if you are searching for details on the Nomad MP3 player, and specify "nomad" as the sought text string, you will get links to many items that are of no interest (e.g., *The Fabulous Nomads Surf Band*). Searching will be more precise when you can specify that you are looking for a product name that includes the text "nomad." The search engine can then confine its attention to text contained with the tags `<productname>` and `</productname>`, assuming these tags are the XML standard for representing product names.

The major expected gains from the introduction of XML are

❖ **Store once and format many ways**—Data stored in XML format can be extracted and reformatted for multiple presentation styles (e.g., printed report, CD-ROM).
❖ **Hardware and software independence**—One format is valid for all systems.**Capture once and exchange many times**—Data are captured as close to the source as possible and never again (i.e., no rekeying).
❖ **Accelerated targeted searching**—Searches are more precise and faster because they use XML tags.
❖ **Less network congestion**—The processing load shifts from the server to the browser.

> **Classified ads XML standard**
>
> The NAA Classified Advertising Standards Task Force of approximately 40 classified advertisers, advertising publishers, aggregators, system users, suppliers, and technology experts is designing a standard for the electronic exchange of classified ads. The standard will define a common classified advertising data structure that technology providers can use to create better tools and systems for handling these data. With standardization, advertisers, ad aggregators, and publishers can simplify their workflows and more effectively provide data sought by consumers.
>
> The task force has generated a DTD to define XML tags and their proper usage in conjunction with this standard. The DTD has a set of elements, or fields, which describe a product being listed for sale. The use of keyword tagging and standardized data fields will dramatically improve searching speed and accuracy.
>
> Source: www.naa.org/technology/clsstdtf/index.html

XML language design

XML lets developers design application-specific vocabularies. To create a new language, designers must agree on three things:

- ❖ The allowable tags
- ❖ The rules for nesting tagged elements
- ❖ Which tagged elements can be processed

The first two, the language's vocabulary and structure, are typically defined in an XML schema. When first introduced, XML adopted the DTD of SGML to define markup tags. The more recently developed XML schema is now the recommended method for defining an XML document. Programmers use the XML schema to understand the meaning of tags so they can write software to process an XML file.

XML tags describe meaning, independent of the display medium. An XML stylesheet, another set of rules, defines how an XML file is automatically formatted for various devices. This set of rules is called an Extensible Stylesheet Language (XSL). Stylesheets allow data to be rendered in a variety of ways, such as Braille or audio for visually impaired persons.

XML schema

An **XML schema** (or just *schema* for brevity) is an XML file associated with an XML document that informs an application how to interpret markup tags and valid formats for tags. The advantage of a schema is that it leads to standardization. Consistently named and defined tags create conformity and support organizational efficiency. They avoid the confusion and loss of time when the meaning of data is not clear. Also, when validation information is built into a schema, some errors are detected before data are exchanged.

XML does not require the creation of a schema. If a document is well formed, XML will interpret it correctly. A well-formed document follows XML syntax and has tags that are correctly nested. One of the strengths of XML is that browser writers have agreed to reject any XML file that is not well formed. Incorrectly specified HTML works on some browsers and not others, so using XML should result in greater consistency across browsers.

A schema is a very strict specification, and any errors will be detected when parsing. A schema defines

- ❖ The names and contents of all elements that are permissible in a certain document
- ❖ The structure of the document
- ❖ How often an element may appear
- ❖ The order in which the elements must appear
- ❖ The type of data the element can contain

DOM

The **document Object Model** (DOM) is the model underlying XML. It is based on a tree (i.e., it supports one-to-one and one-to-many, but not many-to-many relationships). A document is modeled as a hierarchical collection of nodes that have parent/child relationships. The node is the primary object and can be of different types (such as document, element, attribute, text). Each document has a single document node, which has no parent, and zero or more children that are element nodes. It is a good practice to create a visual model of the XML document and then convert this to a schema, which is XML's formal representation of the DOM.

At this point, an example is the best way to demonstrate XML, schema, and DOM concepts. We will use the familiar CD problem that was introduced in Chapter 3 (see page 83). In keeping with the style of this text, we define a minimal amount of XML to get you started, and then more features are added once you have mastered the basics.

CD library case

The CD library case gradually develops, over several chapters, a data model for recording details of a CD collection, culminating in the model on page 152. Unfortunately, we cannot quickly convert this final model to an XML document model, because a DOM is based on a tree model. Thus, we must start afresh.

The model (see Figure 18-1), in this case, is based on the observation that a CD library has many CDs, and a CD has many tracks.

A model is then mapped into a schema using the following procedure.

- ❖ Each entity becomes a complex element type.
- ❖ Each data model attribute[4] becomes a simple element type.
- ❖ The one-to-many (1:m) relationship is recorded as a sequence.

---

4. XML also has the notion of an attribute, and so we need to be precise when talking about attributes.

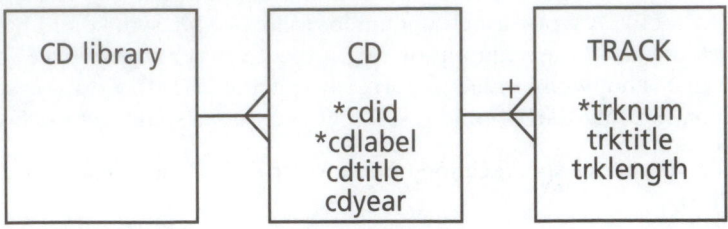

Figure 18-1. CD library tree data model

The schema for the CD library is shown in Table 18-8. For convenience of exposition, the source code lines have been numbered, but these numbers are not part of a schema.

Table 18-8: Schema for CD library (cdlib.xsd)

```
 1 <?xml version="1.0" encoding="UTF-8"?>
 2 <xsd:schema xmlns:xsd='http://www.w3.org/2001/XMLSchema'>
 3 <!--CD library-->
 4   <xsd:element name="cdlibrary">
 5     <xsd:complexType>
 6       <xsd:sequence>
 7         <xsd:element name="cd" type="cdType" minOccurs="1"
 8           maxOccurs="unbounded"/>
 9       </xsd:sequence>
10     </xsd:complexType>
11   </xsd:element>
12 <!--CD-->
13   <xsd:complexType name="cdType">
14     <xsd:sequence>
15       <xsd:element name="cdid" type="xsd:string"/>
16       <xsd:element name="cdlabel" type="xsd:string"/>
17       <xsd:element name="cdtitle" type="xsd:string"/>
18       <xsd:element name="cdyear" type="xsd:integer"/>
19       <xsd:element name="track" type="trackType" minOccurs="1"
20         maxOccurs="unbounded"/>
21     </xsd:sequence>
22   </xsd:complexType>
23 <!--Track-->
24   <xsd:complexType name="trackType">
25     <xsd:sequence>
26       <xsd:element name="trknum" type="xsd:integer"/>
27       <xsd:element name="trktitle" type="xsd:string"/>
28       <xsd:element name="trklen" type="xsd:time"/>
29     </xsd:sequence>
30   </xsd:complexType>
31 </xsd:schema>
```

There are several things to observe about the schema.

❖   All XML documents begin with an XML declaration {1}.[5] The encoding attribute (i.e., `encoding="UTF-8"`) specifies what form of Unicode is used (in this case the 8-bit form; see page 341)).

❖   The XSD Schema namespace is declared {2}.[6]

---

5. In this chapter, numbers in {} refer to line numbers in the corresponding XML code.

- ❖ Comments are placed inside the tag pair < ! -- and --> {3}.
- ❖ The CD library is defined {4-10} as a complex element type, which essentially means that it can have embedded elements, which are a sequence of CDs in this case.
- ❖ A sequence is a series of child elements embedded in a parent, as illustrated by a CD library containing a sequence of CDs {7}, and a CD containing elements of CD identifier, label, and so forth {15-20}. The order of a sequence must be maintained by any XML document based on the schema.
- ❖ A sequence can have a specified range of elements. In this case, there must be at least one CD (minOccurs="1") but there is no upper limit (maxOccurs= "unbounded") on how many CDs there can be in the library {7}.
- ❖ An element that has a child (e.g., cdlibrary, which is at the 1 end of a 1:m) or possesses attributes (e.g., track) is termed a complex element type.
- ❖ A CD is represented by a complex element type {13-20}, and has the name cdType {13}.
- ❖ The element cd is defined by specifying the name of the complex type (i.e., cdType) containing its specification {7}.
- ❖ A track is represented by a complex type because it contains elements of track number, title, and length {24-30}. The name of this complex type is trackType {24}.
- ❖ Notice the reference within the definition of cd to the complex type trackType, used to specify the element track {19}.
- ❖ Simple types (e.g., cdid and cdyear) do not contain any elements, and thus the type of data they store must be defined. Thus, cdid is a text string and cdyear is an integer.

The purpose of a schema is to define the contents and structure of an XML file. It is also used to verify that an XML file has a valid structure and that all elements in the XML file are defined in the schema.

Some common data types are shown in Table 18-9. The meaning is obvious in most cases for those familiar with SQL, except for uriReference. A Uniform Resource Identifier (URI) is a generalization of the URL concept.[7]

Table 18-9: Some common data types

string
boolean
anyURI
decimal
float
integer
time
date

---

6. A namespace is a collection of names of attributes, types, and elements. That's all you need to know for now.
7. See the Glossary for an extended definition.

We can now use the recently defined `cdlibrary` schema to describe a small CD library containing the CD information given in Table 17-10.

Table 18-10: Data for a small CD library

Id	A2 1325		D136705	
Label	Atlantic		Verve	
Title	Pyramid		Ella Fitzgerald	
Year	1960		2000	
Track	Title	Length	Title	Length
1	Vendome	2:30	A tisket, a tasket	2:37
2	Pyramid	10:46	Vote for Mr. Rhythm	2:25
3			Betcha nickel	2:52

The XML for describing the CD library is displayed in Table 18-11. There are several things to observe:

❖   All XML documents begin with an XML declaration {1}.
❖   The declaration immediately following the XML declaration identifies the root element of the document (i.e., `cdlibrary`) and the schema[8] (i.e., cdlib.xsd) {2–3}.
❖   The definition of the first CD and its tracks {4–19}.
❖   The definition of the first track on the first CD {9–13}.

As you now realize, the definition of an XML document is relatively straightforward. It is a bit tedious with all the typing of tags to surround each data element. Fortunately, there are XML editors that relieve this tedium.[9]

- -

Skill builder

1.   Use a browser (e.g., Firefox or Internet Explorer) to access this book's Web site, link to the Support > XML section, and click on <u>cdlib.xml</u>. You will see how the browser displays XML. Investigate what happens when you click minus (–) and then plus (+).

2.   Save the XML code (File > Save As >) displayed by your browser and paste it into a text editor or word processor. Notice that line 2 as displayed by your browser might be different from that of the original XML file.

Now, add details of the CD[10] displayed in Table 18-12 to this XML code, save it as cdlibv2.xml, and open it with your browser.

- -

---

8.   Your browser might not validate an XML file against its schema.
9.   See www.xmlsoftware.com/editors.html for more information on XML editors.
10.   The CD actually has 16 tracks, but let's settle for entering 5 tracks.

Table 18-11: XML for describing a CD (cdlib.xml)

```
1  <?xml version="1.0" encoding="UTF-8"?>
2  <cdlibrary xmlns:xsi="http://www.w3.org/2001/XMLSchema-instance"
3    xsi:noNamespaceSchemaLocation="cdlib.xsd">
4      <cd>
5          <cdid>A2 1325</cdid>
6          <cdlabel>Atlantic</cdlabel>
7          <cdtitle>Pyramid</cdtitle>
8          <cdyear>1960</cdyear>
9          <track>
10             <trknum>1</trknum>
11             <trktitle>Vendome</trktitle>
12             <trklen>00:02:30</trklen>
13         </track>
14         <track>
15             <trknum>2</trknum>
16             <trktitle>Pyramid</trktitle>
17             <trklen>00:10:46</trklen>
18         </track>
19     </cd>
20     <cd>
21         <cdid>D136705</cdid>
22         <cdlabel>Verve</cdlabel>
23         <cdtitle>Ella Fitzgerald</cdtitle>
24         <cdyear>2000</cdyear>
25         <track>
26             <trknum>1</trknum>
27             <trktitle>A tisket, a tasket</trktitle>
28             <trklen>00:02:37</trklen>
29         </track>
30         <track>
31             <trknum>2</trknum>
32             <trktitle>Vote for Mr. Rhythm</trktitle>
33             <trklen>00:02:25</trklen>
34         </track>
35         <track>
36             <trknum>3</trknum>
37             <trktitle>Betcha nickel</trktitle>
38             <trklen>00:02:52</trklen>
39         </track>
40     </cd>
41 </cdlibrary>
```

Table 18-12: CD data

Id	314 517 173-2	
Label	Verve	
Title	The essential Charlie Parker	
Year	1992	
Track	Title	Length
1	Now's the time	3:01
2	If I should lose you	2:46
3	Mango mangue	2:53
4	Bloomdido	3:24
5	Star eyes	3:28

XSL

As you now know from the prior exercise, the browser display of XML is not particularly usable. What is missing is a *stylesheet* that tells the browser how to display an XML file. The **eXtensible Stylesheet Language (XSL)** is a language for defining the rendering of an XML file. An XSL document defines the rules for presenting an XML document's data. XSL is an application of XML, and an XSL file is also an XML file.

The power of XSL is demonstrated by applying the stylesheet shown in Table 18-13 to the XML displayed in Table 18-11 to produce Figure 18-2.

```
Complete List of Songs
Pyramid, Atlantic, 1960.5 [A2 1325]
1 Vendome 00:02:30
2 Pyramid 00:10:46

Ella Fitzgerald, Verve, 2000 [D136705]
1 A tisket, a tasket 00:02:37
2 Vote for Mr. Rhythm 00:02:25
3 Betcha nickel 00:02:52
```

Figure 18-2. Result of applying a stylesheet to CD data

To use a stylesheet with an XML file, you must add a line of code to point to the stylesheet file. In this case, you add the following:

```
<?xml-stylesheet type="text/xsl" href="cdlib.xsl" media="screen"?>
```

as the second line of cdlib.xml (i.e., it appears before <cdlibrary ... >). The added line of code points to cdlib.xsl as the stylesheet. This means that when the browser loads cdlib.xml, it uses the contents of cdlib.xsl to determine how to render the contents of cdlib.xml.

We now need to examine the contents of cdlib.xsl so that you can learn some basics of creating XSL commands. You will soon notice that all XSL commands are preceded by xsl:.

❖ Tell the browser it is processing an XML file {1}.

❖ Specify that the file is a stylesheet {2}.

❖ Specify a template, which identifies which elements should be processed and how they are processed. The match attribute {4} indicates the template applies to the source node. Process the template {11} defined in the file {15–45}. A stylesheet can specify multiple templates to produce different reports from the same XML input.

❖ Specify a template to be applied when the XSL processor encounters the <cdlibrary> node {15}.

❖ Create an outer loop for processing each CD {16–44}.

❖ Define the values to be reported for each CD (i.e., title, label, year, and id) {19, 21, 23, 25}. The respective XSL commands select the values. For example, <xsl:value-of select="cdtitle" /> specifies selection of cdtitle.

Table 18-13: Stylesheet for displaying an XML file of CD data (cdlib.xsl)

```
1  <?xml version="1.0" encoding="UTF-8"?>
2  <xsl:stylesheet version="1.0"
           xmlns:xsl="http://www.w3.org/1999/XSL/Transform">
3    <xsl:output encoding="UTF-8" indent="yes" method="html" version="1.0" />
4    <xsl:template match="/">
5    <html>
6      <head>
7        <title> Complete List of Songs </title>
8      </head>
9    <body>
10     <h1> Complete List of Songs </h1>
11     <xsl:apply-templates select="cdlibrary" />
12     </body>
13     </html>
14   </xsl:template>
15   <xsl:template match="cdlibrary">
16     <xsl:for-each select="cd">
17       <br/>
18       <font color="maroon">
19         <xsl:value-of select="cdtitle" />
20         ,
21         <xsl:value-of select="cdlabel" />
22         ,
23         <xsl:value-of select="cdyear" />
24         [
25         <xsl:value-of select="cdid" />
26         ] </font>
27       <br/>
28       <table>
29         <xsl:for-each select="track">
30           <tr>
31             <td align="left">
32               <xsl:value-of select="trknum" />
33             </td>
34             <td>
35               <xsl:value-of select="trktitle" />
36             </td>
37             <td align="center">
38               <xsl:value-of select="trklen" />
39             </td>
40           </tr>
41         </xsl:for-each>
42       </table>
43       <br/>
44     </xsl:for-each>
45   </xsl:template>
46 </xsl:stylesheet>
```

❖ Create an inner loop for processing the tracks on a particular CD {29–41}.
❖ Present the track data in tabular form using HTML table commands interspersed with XSL {28–42}.

Skill builder

1. Use a browser (Firefox or IE) to access this book's Web site, link to the XML section, and download cdlib.xsl into a directory on your machine.
2. Edit a copy of cdlib.xml by inserting the following as the second line of cdlib.xml:
   `<?xml-stylesheet type="text/xsl" href="cdlib.xsl" media="screen"?>`.

3. Save the file as cdlibv3.xml in the same directory as cdlib.xsl and open it with your browser.
4. Make a similar change to cdlibv2.xml and open it with your browser.

Converting XML

There are occasions when there is a need to convert an XML file:

- **Transformation**—conversion from one XML vocabulary to another (e.g., between financial languages FPML and finML)
- **Manipulation**—reordering, filtering, or sorting parts of a document
- **Rendering in another language**—rendering the XML file using another format, such as Wireless Access Protocol (WAP)

You have already seen how XSL can be used to transform XML for rendering as HTML. The original XSL has been split into three languages:

- XSLT for transformation and manipulation
- XSLT for rendition
- XPath for accessing the structure of an XML file

For a data management course, this is as far as you need to go with learning about XSL. Just remember that you have only touched the surface. To become proficient in XML, you will need an entire course on the topic.

XML and databases

XML is more than a document-processing technology. It is also a powerful tool for data management. For database developers, XML is likely to be used to facilitate middle-tier data integration and schemas. Most of the current major DBMS producers are developing XML-centric extensions to their product lines.

Many XML documents are stored for the long term, because they are an important repository of organizational memory. A data exchange language, XML is a means of moving data between databases, which means a need for tools for exporting and importing XML.

XML documents can be stored in the same format as you would store a word processing or HTML file: You just place them in an appropriately named folder. File systems, however, have limitations that become particularly apparent when a large number of files need to be stored, as in the corporate setting.

What is needed is a DBMS for storing, retrieving, and manipulating XML documents. Such a DBMS should

- Be able to store a large number of documents
- Be able to store large documents

❖ Support access to portions of a document (e.g., the data for a single CD in a library of 20,000 CDs)

❖ Enable concurrent access to a document but provide locking mechanisms to prevent the *lost update problem* (see page 533)

❖ Keep track of different versions of a document

❖ Integrate data from other sources (e.g., insert the results of an SQL query formatted as an XML fragment into an XML document)

There are several possible solutions for XML document management: relational database management system (RDBMS), object-oriented database management system (ODBMS), or an XML database.

RDBMS

An XML document could be stored within an RDBMS. Storing an intact XML document as a CLOB (see page 257) is a sensible strategy if the XML document contains static content that will only be updated by replacing the entire document. Examples include written text such as articles, advertisements, books, or legal contracts. These *document-centric* files[11] (e.g., articles and legal contracts) are retrieved and updated in their entirety.

For more dynamic *data-centric* XML files[12] (e.g., orders, price lists, airline schedules), the RDBMS must be extended to support the structure of the data so that portions of the document (e.g., elements) can be retrieved and updated. The object-relational extensions of most major databases provide the wherewithal to capture the structure of an XML document. For example, Oracle's XML SQL utility can store an XML document by mapping it to an object-relational format. The same utility can then retrieve the data as an XML document.

You can expect most RDBMS vendors to offer extensions for supporting storage and retrieval of both document- and data-centric XML files. Some of them are likely to release XML servers that are built on underlying relational technology.

Another issue is the conversion of existing relational data to XML. Products such as DB2XML, are already emerging.

DB2XML

Some sources estimate that more than 75 percent of current Web pages are generated from database data. These data are typically converted into HTML by a server-side script. An alternative is to convert relational data to XML and, with an appropriate stylesheet, let the browser generate the presentation. This approach has the advantage of reducing the complexity of applications by separating SQL and server-side scripting code. DB2XML[13] is an example of a tool for converting relational data to XML.

---

11. Document-centric files have low structure (i.e., a few elements and mainly text).
12. Data-centric files have high structure (i.e., many elements, often repeated).
13. www.informatik.fh-wiesbaden.de/~turau/DB2XML/

DB2XML has three main functions:

- ❖ It transforms the results of a query into an XML document.
- ❖ It generates a schema for the XML.
- ❖ It transforms the XML using a stylesheet.

Skill builder

Use your browser to access www.informatik.fh-wiesbaden.de/~turau/DB2XML/demo/ db2xmlxslservlet.html and execute one of the demonstrations. Inspect the stylesheet and XML document.

A DBMS is designed to store data, and XML is designed for data interchange. Thus, we need tools, such as DB2XML, for converting data extracted from a database into a format that can be exchanged. However, it is not clear at this point which path data presentation should follow: SQL and server-side scripting or XML and stylesheets. As tools are developed to support both of these paths, this uncertainty should be resolved.

ODBMS

ODBMS vendors can also use their technology for storing XML documents, and the ODBMS model might be a better candidate for managing XML documents than the relational model. However, at this point, most ODBMS vendors have done little more than store entire XML documents as objects. This is not surprising, as ODBMS vendors do not have the market size of RDBMS vendors and hence have less resources to invest in creating advanced XML-handling features.

XML database

A third approach is to build a special-purpose XML database. Tamino is an example of such an approach, and you can expect others to emerge in the near future. Because this is such a new area, this textbook can do little more than make you aware of the technology and urge you to monitor the development of XML databases.

Skill builder

1. Visit the web site for Tamino[14] and review its benefits and architecture.
2. Search the Tamino site or the computer press[15] to learn who has adopted Tamino.
3. What conclusions do you reach about the usefulness of an XML database?

---

14. www.softwareag.com/tamino platform/introduction.htm
15. For example, computerworld.com/

XML in government

The UK's e-Government Interoperability Framework (e-GIF) sets out the government's technical policies and standards for achieving interoperability and information systems conformity across the public sector. It defines the essential prerequisite for linked, Web-enabled government, and is a key policy in the overall e-government strategy.

The main thrust is to adopt Internet and Web standards for all government systems. The e-GIF also adopts standards that are well supported in the marketplace. It is a pragmatic strategy that aims to reduce costs and risks for government systems while aligning them to the global Internet revolution.

The government policy is to use XML and XML schemas for data integration; UML, RDF, and XML for data modeling and description language; and XSL, DOM, and XML for data presentation. XML products will be written so as to comply with W3C's recommendations.

e-GIF is a key plank in the government's drive to get all its services online by 2005 and cut bureaucracy within the public sector. There are two main benefits the policy will bring: creating 24-hour one-stop government and banishing bureaucracy in government by moving the public sector away from traditional paper-based ways of working by electronically integrating information across a range of government departments and organizations.

The government has launched the UK GovTalk initiative. This is a Cabinet Office–led, joint government and industry forum for generating and agreeing on XML data schemas for use throughout the public sector. The GovTalk Group will manage the acceptance, publication, and any subsequent change requests for the schema. The initiative helps developers by providing information, best practice guidance, and toolkits for conversion of legacy data. It is intended to make adoption of the e-GIF policies and standards simple, attractive, and cost-effective.

Source: www.e-envoy.gov.uk/oee/oee.nsf/sections/briefings-top/$file/interoperability.htm

---

Conclusion

XML is a significant technological development, and its importance and value will be increasingly apparent. It is clear that its main role will be to facilitate the exchange of data between organizations and within those organizations that do not have integrated systems. XML will achieve much of what was promised by EDI in that it will significantly lower the cost of transactions by accelerating the transfer of information from paper to bits.

Whether XML will become dominant in data presentation and storage is undecided. There are acceptable alternatives for data presentation (e.g. server-side scripting and Java), and the superiority of XSL is not obvious. Similarly, relational technology can be successfully extended to store and process XML documents. Thus, the case for pure XML database technology is also not obvious.

New technologies inevitably generate a lot of excitement and speculation about the downfall of prior technology. XML certainly has a role in the management of organizational data. Although the size and extent of this role is unclear, it is certain that all data managers must have some knowledge of XML.

Mastery of XML is well beyond the scope of a single chapter. Indeed, it is a book-length topic, and more than 100 books have already been written on this relatively recent technology. It is important to remember that the prime goal of XML is to support data interchange. If you would like to continue learning about XML, then consider the open content textbook (en.wikibooks.org/wiki/XML), which was created by students and is under continual revision. You might want to contribute to this book.

The tags on retail

The Association for Retail Technology Standards (ARTS), the standards arm of the National Retail Federation, has compiled a dictionary of XML tags. These tags are a prerequisite for exchanging business information online in XML and are essential if business-to-business (B2B) electronic commerce is to expand.

These tags are plain English words and not computer codes. They are used to define data in an XML file. For example, a brand name in an XML document would be flanked by the tags `<BrandName>`. By having a standard data dictionary, XML messages can be transmitted without confusion in their interpretation.

The retail industry has not had an XML data dictionary until now. Currently, there are several in the works. The Uniform Code Council is compiling one as part of its UCCnet B2B exchange and data-synchronization initiative. The National Association of Convenience Stores (NACS) is developing a data dictionary for the convenience store and petroleum retailing industries.

There are two versions of the ARTS data dictionary. The standard, public-domain version is accessible at www.nrf-arts.org. It contains 2,298 tags for the retail industry with explanations for each tag.

Source: Anonymous. 2000. ARTS publishes XML retail data dictionary. *Chain Store Age* 76 (11):108.

Summary

Electronic data exchange has become more important with the widespread use of the Internet. EDI, which penetrated mainly the major organizations, is being replaced by XML.

SGML, a precursor of XML, defines the structure of documents. SGML's value derives from its reusability, flexibility, and support for revision. XML, a derivative of SGML, is designed to support electronic commerce and overcome some of the shortcomings of SGML. XML supports data exchange by making information self-describing. It is a metalanguage because it is a language for generating other languages (e.g., finML). It promises substantial gains for the management and distribution of data.

The XML language consists of an XML schema, DOM, and XSL. A schema defines the structure of a document and how an application should interpret XML markup tags. The DOM is a tree-based data model of an XML document. XSL is used to specify a stylesheet for displaying an XML document.

XML documents can be stored in either a RDBMS, ODBMS, or XML database. There are tools for converting relational data to XML format and vice versa. XML is a significant technological development that will facilitate the exchange of data between and within organizations.

Key terms and concepts

Document Object Model (DOM)	Markup language
Document Type Definition (DTD)	Occurrence indicators
Electronic Data Interchange (EDI)	Standard Generalized Markup Language
Extensible Markup Language (XML)	(SGML)
Extensible Stylesheet Language (XSL)	XML database
Hypertext Markup Language (HTML)	XML schema

References

Anderson, R. 2000. *Professional XML*. Birmingham, UK; Chicago: Wrox Press.

Watson, R. T., and others. 2004. *XML: managing data exchange:* Wikibooks, wikibooks.org/wiki/XML.

Exercises

1. A business has a telephone directory that records the first and last name, telephone number, and e-mail address of everyone working in the firm. Departments are the main organizing unit of the firm, so the telephone directory is typically displayed in department order, and shows for each department the contact phone and fax numbers and e-mail address.
    a. Create a hierarchical data model for this problem.
    b. Define the schema.
    c. Create an XML file containing some directory data.
    d. Create an XSL file containing a stylesheet.
2. Create a schema for your university or college's course bulletin.
3. Create a schema for a credit card statement.
4. Take a page in a dictionary and do the following:
    a. Create a hierarchical data model for this problem.

  b. Define the schema.
  c. Create an XML file containing some dictionary data.
  d. Create an XSL file containing a stylesheet.
5. Search the Web to identify an XML standard for an industry. What do you observe about the standard? How detailed is it (e.g., how many elements)? Is the industry adopting the standard?

Case: A conference support system

An ideal conference support system would record all conference data (e.g., accepted articles, timetable, attendees) in SGML in a conference information repository. Then, using the data in the repository, reports could be generated from multiple contexts (e.g., text on a PDA, synthesized voice on a cell phone, and XML on a browser). The essence of the system is captured in Figure 18-3.

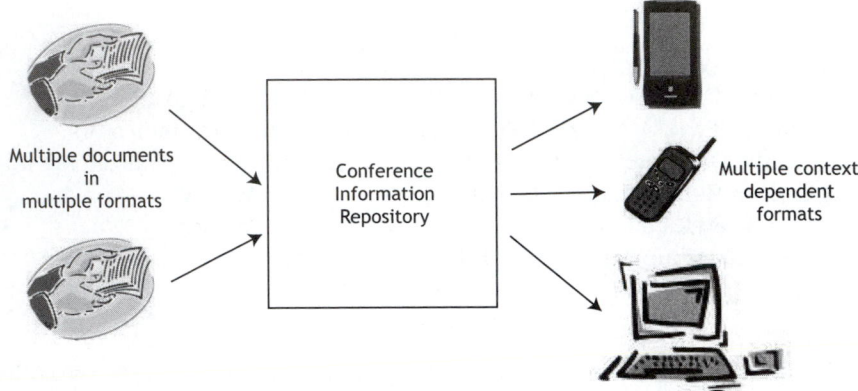

Figure 18-3. The conference support system

The major aspects of the data management problem are that the multiple documents of the conference information repository are prepared using a variety of word processors. Furthermore, authors use different stylesheets and some use none. Consequently, the current system makes it almost impossible to convert accepted articles into a standard content-recording language, such as SGML or XML.

Answer the following questions:

1. What system might you implement for getting authors to create documents that can be readily converted to XML? Don't try to be too fancy; it is probably sufficient to capture heading levels as well as the body text.
2. What technology would you select for the conference information repository?
3. What technologies exist for transforming XML for different devices (e.g., PDAs)?
4. Design the XML schema.

Section 5

Managing Organizational Memory

Everyone complains of his memory, none of his judgment.
François Duc de La Rochefoucauld "Sentences et Maximes," Morales No. 89 1678

As you now realize, organizational memory is an important resource requiring management. An inaccurate memory can result in bad decisions and poor customer service. Some aspects of organizational memory (e.g., chemical formulae, marketing strategy, and R&D plans) are critical to the well-being of an organization. The financial consequences can be extremely significant if these memories are lost or fall into the hands of competitors. Consequently, organizations must develop and implement procedures for maintaining data integrity. They need policies to protect the existence of data, maintain its quality, and ensure its confidentiality. Some of these procedures may be embedded in organizational memory technology, and others may be performed by data management staff. Data integrity (Chapter 19) is the first issue addressed in this section.

When organizations recognize a resource as important to their long-term viability, they typically create a formal mechanism to manage it. For example, most companies have a human resources department, responsible for activities such as compensation, recruiting, training, and employee counseling. People are the major resource of nearly every company, and the human resources department manages this resource. Similarly, the finance department manages a company's financial assets.

In the information age, data—the raw material of information—need to be managed. Consequently, data administration has become a formal organizational structure in many enterprises. Data administration is the focus of Chapter 20.

19

Data Integrity

Integrity without knowledge is weak and useless, and knowledge without integrity is dangerous and dreadful.

Samuel Johnson, *Rasselas*, 1759

Learning objectives

After completing this chapter, you will

- ❖ understand the three major data integrity outcomes;
- ❖ understand the strategies for achieving each of the data integrity outcomes;
- ❖ understand the possible threats to data integrity and how to deal with them;
- ❖ understand the principles of transaction management;
- ❖ realize that successful data management requires making data available and maintaining data integrity.

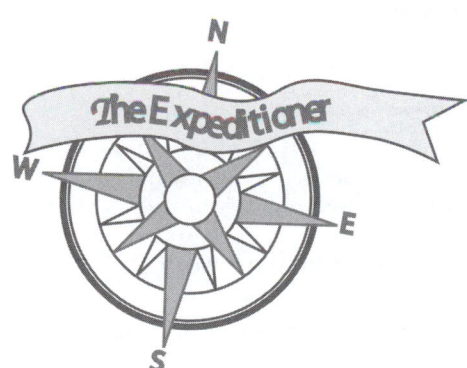

The Expeditioner has become very dependent on its databases. The day-to-day operations of the company would be adversely affected if the major operational databases were lost. Indeed, The Expeditioner may not be able to survive a major data loss. Recently, there have also been a few minor problems with the quality and confidentiality of some of the databases. A part-time salesperson was discovered making a query about staff salaries. A major order was nearly lost when it was shipped to the wrong address because the complete shipping address had not been entered when the order was taken. The sales database had been offline for 30 minutes last Monday morning because of a disk sector read error.

The Expeditioner had spent much time and money creating an extremely effective and efficient management system. It became clear, however, that more attention needed to be paid to maintaining the system and ensuring that high-quality data were continuously available to authorized users.

Introduction

The management of data is driven by two goals: availability and integrity. **Availability** deals with making data available to whoever needs it, whenever and wherever he or she needs it, and in a meaningful form. As illustrated in Figure 19-1, availability concerns the creation, interrogation, and update of data stores. Although most of the book, thus far, has dealt with making data available, a database is of little use to anyone unless it has integrity. Maintaining data integrity implies three goals:[1]

1. Protecting existence: Data are available when needed.
2. Maintaining quality: Data are accurate, complete, and current.
3. Ensuring confidentiality: Data are accessed only by those authorized to do so.

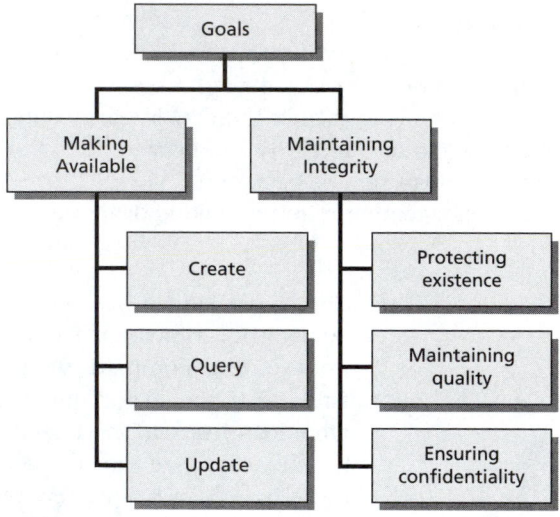

Figure 19-1. Goals of managing organizational memory

This chapter considers the three types of strategies for maintaining data integrity:

❖ **Legal** strategies are externally imposed laws, rules, and regulations. Privacy laws are an example.

---

1. To the author's knowledge, Gordon C. Everest was the first to define integrity in terms of these three goals. See Everest, G., 1986. *Database management: objectives, systems functions, and administration*. New York, NY: McGraw-Hill.

❖ **Administrative** strategies are organizational policies and procedures. An example is a standard operating procedure of storing all backup files in a locked vault.

❖ **Technical** strategies are those incorporated in the computer system (e.g., database management system [DBMS], application program, or operating system). An example is the inclusion of validation rules (e.g., NOT NULL) in a database definition that are used to ensure data quality when a database is updated.

A **consistent database** is one in which all data integrity constraints are satisfied.

Our focus is on data stored in multiuser computer databases and technical and administrative strategies for maintaining integrity.[2] The term **database integrity** is commonly used to denote data integrity in computer system environments. More and more, organizational memories are being captured in computerized databases. From an integrity perspective, this is a very positive development. Computers offer some excellent mechanisms for controlling data integrity, but this does not eliminate the need for administrative strategies. Both administrative and technical strategies are still needed.

Who is responsible for database integrity? Some would say the data users, others the database administrator (see Chapter 20). Both groups are right; database integrity is a shared responsibility, and the way it is managed may differ across organizations. Our focus is on the tools and strategies for maintaining data integrity, regardless of who is responsible.

The strategies for achieving the three integrity outcomes are summarized in Table 19-1. We will cover the strategies for protecting existence, followed by those for maintaining integrity, and finally those used to ensure confidentiality. Before considering each of these goals, we need to examine the general issue of transaction management.

Table 19-1: Strategies for maintaining database integrity

Database integrity outcome	Strategies for achieving the outcome
Protecting existence	Isolation (preventive) Database backup and recovery (curative)
Maintaining quality	Update authorization Integrity constraints/data validation Concurrent update control
Ensuring confidentiality	Access control Encryption

Transaction management

Transaction management focuses on ensuring that transactions are correctly recorded in the database. The **transaction manager** is the element of a DBMS that processes transactions. A **transaction** is a series of actions to be taken on the database such that they must be entirely completed or entirely aborted. A transaction is a **logical unit of work**. All its elements must be processed; otherwise, the database will be incorrect. For exam-

---

2.   Many of the concepts presented are also applicable to noncomputerized data stores.

ple, with a sale of a product, the transaction consists of at least two parts: an update to the inventory on hand, and an update to the customer information for the items sold in order to bill the customer later. Updating only the inventory or only the customer information would create a database without integrity, or an inconsistent database.

Transaction managers are designed to accomplish the **ACID** (atomicity, consistency, isolation, and durability) concept. These attributes are

- ❖ **Atomicity:** If a transaction has two or more discrete pieces of information, either all of the pieces are committed or none are.
- ❖ **Consistency:** Either a transaction creates a valid new database state, or, if any failure occurs, the transaction manager returns the database to its prior state.
- ❖ **Isolation:** A transaction in process and not yet committed must remain isolated from any other transaction.
- ❖ **Durability:** Committed data are saved by the DBMS so that, in the event of a failure and system recovery, these data are available in their correct state.

Transaction atomicity requires that all transactions are processed on an **all-or-nothing** basis and that any collection of transactions is **serializable**. When a transaction is executed, either all its changes to the database are completed or none of the changes are performed. In other words, the entire unit of work must be completed. If a transaction is terminated before it is completed, the transaction manager must undo the executed actions to restore the database to its state before the transaction commenced (the consistency concept). Once a transaction is successfully completed, it does not need to be undone. For efficiency reasons, transactions should be no larger than necessary to ensure the integrity of the database. For example, in an accounting system, a debit and credit would be an appropriate transaction, because this is the minimum amount of work needed to keep the books in balance.

Serializability relates to the effect of the execution of a set of transactions. An interleaved execution schedule (i.e., the elements of different transactions are intermixed) is serializable if its outcome is equivalent to a noninterleaved (i.e., serial) schedule. Interleaved operations are often used to increase the efficiency of computing resources, so it is not unusual for the components of multiple transactions to be interleaved. Interleaved transactions cause problems when they interfere with each other and, as a result, compromise the correctness of the database.

The ACID concept is critical to concurrent update control and recovery after a transaction failure.

Concurrent update control

When updating a database, most users implicitly assume that their actions do not interfere with any other users' actions. If the DBMS is a single-user system, then a lack of interference is guaranteed. Most DBMSs, however, are multiuser systems, where many can be accessing a given database at the same time. When two or more transactions are allowed to update a database concurrently, the integrity of the database is threatened. For example, multiple agents selling airline tickets should not be able to sell the same seat twice. Similarly, inconsistent results can be obtained by a retrieval transaction when retrievals are being made simultaneously with updates. This gives the appearance of a loss of database integrity. We will first discuss the integrity problems caused by concurrent updates and then show how to control them to ensure database quality.

Lost update

Uncontrolled concurrent updates can result in the *lost-update* or *phantom-record* problem. To illustrate the lost-update problem, suppose two concurrent update transactions simultaneously want to update the same record in an inventory file. Both want to update the quantity-on-hand field (`quantity`). Assume `quantity` has a current value of 40. One update transaction wants to add 80 units (a delivery) to `quantity`, while the other transaction wants to subtract 20 units (a sale).

Suppose the transactions have concurrent access to the record; that is, each transaction is able to read the record from the database before a previous transaction has been committed. This sequence is depicted in Figure 19-2. Note that the first transaction, A, has not updated the database when the second transaction, B, reads the same record. Thus, both A and B read in a value of 40 for `quantity`. Both make their calculations, then A writes the value of 120 to disk, followed by B promptly overwriting the 120 with 20. The result is that the delivery of 80 units, transaction A, is *lost* during the update process.

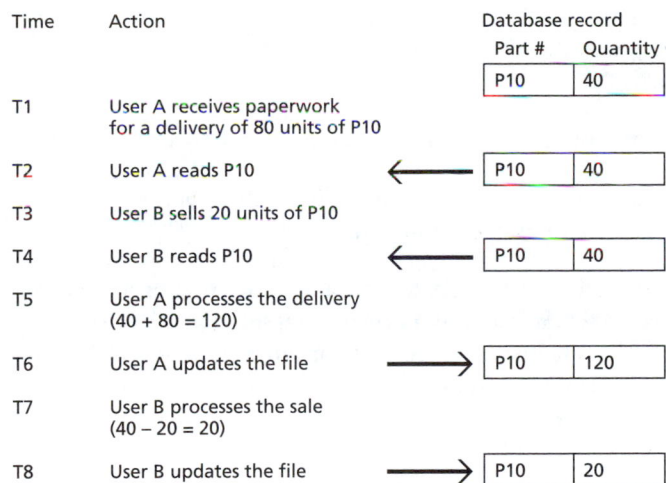

Figure 19-2. Lost update when concurrent accessing is allowed

Inconsistent retrievals occur when a transaction calculates some aggregate function (e.g., sum) over a set of data while other transactions are updating the same data. The problem is that the retrieval may read some data before they are changed and other data after they are changed, thereby yielding inconsistent results.

The solution: locking

To prevent lost updates and inconsistent retrieval results, the DBMS must incorporate a resource **lock**, a basic tool of transaction management to ensure correct transaction behavior. Any data retrieved by one user with the intent of updating must be locked out or denied access by other users until the update is completed (or aborted).

There are two types of locks: **Slocks** (shared or read locks) and **XLocks** (exclusive or write locks). Here are some key points to understand about these types of locks:

❖ When a transaction has a Slock on a database item, other transactions can issue Slocks on the same item, but there can be no Xlocks on that item.
❖ Before a transaction can read a database item, it must be granted a Slock or Xlock on that item.
❖ When a transaction has an Xlock on a database item, no other transaction can issue either a Slock or Xlock on that item.
❖ Before a transaction can write to a database item, it must be granted an Xlock on that item.

Consider the example used previously. When A accesses the record for update, the DBMS must refuse all further accesses to that record until transaction A is complete (i.e., an XLock). As Figure 19-3 shows, B's first attempt to access the record is denied until transaction A is finished. As a result, database integrity is maintained. Unless the DBMS controls concurrent access, a multiuser database environment can create both data and retrieval integrity problems.

To administer locking procedures, a DBMS requires two pieces of information:

1.   Whether a particular transaction will update the database;
2.   Where the transaction begins and ends.

Usually, the data required by an update transaction are locked when the transaction begins and then released when the transaction is completed (i.e., committed to the database) or aborted. Locking mechanisms can operate at different levels of **locking granularity**: database, table, page, row, or data element. At the most precise level, a DBMS can lock individual data elements so that different update transactions can update different items in the same record concurrently. This approach increases processing overhead but provides the fewest resource conflicts. At the other end of the continuum, the DBMS can lock the entire database for each update. If there were many update transactions to process, this would be very unacceptable because of the long waiting times. Locking at the record level is the most common approach taken by DBMSs.

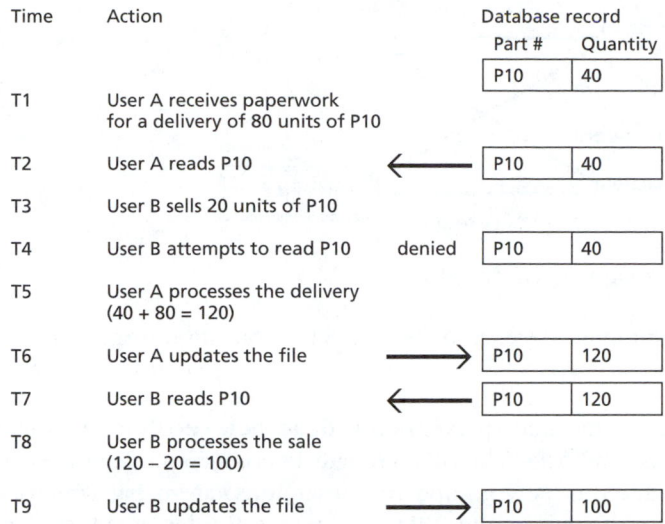

Time	Action		Database record	
			Part #	Quantity
			P10	40
T1	User A receives paperwork for a delivery of 80 units of P10			
T2	User A reads P10	←	P10	40
T3	User B sells 20 units of P10			
T4	User B attempts to read P10	denied	P10	40
T5	User A processes the delivery (40 + 80 = 120)			
T6	User A updates the file	→	P10	120
T7	User B reads P10	←	P10	120
T8	User B processes the sale (120 – 20 = 100)			
T9	User B updates the file	→	P10	100

Figure 19-3. Valid update when concurrent accessing is not allowed

In most situations, users are not concerned with locking, because it is handled entirely by the DBMS. But in some DBMSs, choices are provided to the user. These are primarily limited to programming language interfaces.

Resource locking solves some data and retrieval integrity problems, but it may lead to another problem, referred to as **deadlock** or the **deadly embrace**. Deadlock is an impasse that occurs because two users lock certain resources, then request resources locked by each other. Figure 19-4 illustrates a deadlock situation. Both transactions require records 1 and 2. Transaction A first accesses record 1 and locks it. Then transaction B accesses record 2 and locks it. Next, B's attempt to access record 1 is denied, so the application waits for the record to be released. Finally, A's attempt to access record 2 is denied, so the application waits for the record to be released. Thus, user A's update transaction is waiting for record 2 (locked by user B), and user B is waiting for record 1 (locked by user A). Unless the DBMS intervenes, both users will wait indefinitely.

There are two ways to resolve deadlock: prevention and resolution. **Deadlock prevention** requires users to lock in advance all records they will require. User B would have to lock both records 1 and 2 (in Figure 19-4) before processing the transaction. If these records are locked, B would have to wait.

The **two-phase locking protocol** is a simple approach to preventing deadlocks. It operates on the notion that a transaction has a growing phase followed by a shrinking phase. During the growing phase, locks can be requested. The shrinking phase is initiated by a release statement, which means no additional locks can be requested. A release statement

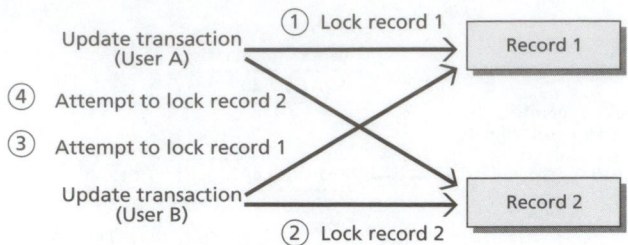

Figure 19-4. An example of deadlock

enables the programmer to signal to the DBMS the transition from requesting locks to releasing locks.

Another approach to deadlock prevention is **deadlock resolution,** whereby the DBMS detects and breaks deadlocks. The DBMS usually keeps a resource usage matrix, which instantly reflects which users (e.g., update transactions) are using which resources (e.g., rows). By scanning the matrix, the DBMS can detect deadlocks as they occur. The DBMS then resolves the deadlock by backing out one of the deadlocked transactions. For example, the DBMS might release user A's lock on record 1, thus allowing user B to proceed. Any changes made by user A up to that time (e.g., updates to record 1) would be rolled back. User A's transaction would be restarted when the required resources became available.

Transaction failure and recovery

When a transaction fails, there is the danger of an inconsistent database. Transactions can fail for a variety of reasons, including

❖   Program error (e.g., a logic error in the code)
❖   Action by the transaction manager (e.g., resolution of a deadlock)
❖   Self-abort (e.g., an error in the transaction data means it cannot be completed)
❖   System failure (e.g., an operating-system bug)

If a transaction fails for any reason, then the DBMS must be able to restore the database to a correct state. To do this, two statements are required: an **end of transaction (EOT)** and **commit**. EOT indicates the physical end of the transaction, the last statement. Commit, an explicit statement, must occur in the transaction code before the EOT statement. The only statements that should occur between commit and EOT are database writes and lock releases.

When a transaction issues a commit, the transaction manager checks that all the necessary write-record locks for statements following the commit have been established. If these locks are not in place, the transaction is terminated. Otherwise, the transaction is committed, and it proceeds to execute the database writes and release locks. Once a transaction is committed, a system problem is the only failure to which it is susceptible.

When a transaction fails, the transaction manager must take one of two corrective actions:

❖ If the transaction has not been committed, the transaction manager must return the database to its state prior to the transaction. That is, it must perform a **rollback** of the database to its most recent valid state.

❖ If the transaction has been committed, the transaction manager must ensure that the database is established at the correct post-transaction state. It must check that all write statements executed by the transaction and those appearing between commit and EOT have been applied. The DBMS may have to redo some writes.

Protecting existence

One of the three database integrity outcomes is protecting the existence of the database—ensuring data are available when needed. Two strategies for protecting existence are isolation and database backup and recovery. **Isolation** is a preventive strategy that involves administrative procedures to insulate the physical database from destruction. Some mechanisms for doing this are keeping data in safe places, such as in vaults or underground; having multiple installations; or having security systems. For example, one organization keeps backup copies of important databases on removable magnetic disks. These are stored in a vault that is always guarded. To gain access to the vault, employees need a badge with an encoded personal voice print. Many companies are building total-backup computer centers, which contain duplicate databases and documentation for system operation. If something should happen at the main center (e.g., a flood), they can be up and running at their backup center in a few hours, or even minutes in some highly critical situations. What isolation strategies do you use to protect the backup medium of your personal computer? Do you make backup files?

A study of 429 disaster declarations reported to a major international provider of disaster recovery services provides some insights as to the frequency and effects of different IT disasters. These data cover the period 1981–2000 and identify the most frequent disasters (Table 19-2) and statistics on the length of the disruption (Table 19-3).[3]

Table 19-2: Most frequent IT disasters

Category	Description
Disruptive act	Strikes and other intentional human acts, such as bombs or civil unrest, that are designed to interrupt normal organizational processes
Fire	Electrical or natural fires
IT failure	Hardware, software, or network problems
IT move/upgrade	Data center moves and CPU upgrades
Natural event	Earthquakes, hurricanes, severe weather
Power outage	Loss of power
Water leakage	Unintended escape of contained water (e.g., pipe leaks, main breaks)

3. Source: Lewis Jr., W., R. T. Watson, and A. Pickren. 2003. An empirical assessment of IT disaster probabilities. *Communications of the ACM* 46 (9):201-206.

Table 19-3: Days of disruption per year

Category	Number	Minimum	Maximum	Mean
Natural event	122	0	85	6.38
IT failure	98	1	61	6.89
Power outage	67	1	20	4.94
Disruptive act	29	1	97	23.93
Water leakage	28	0	17	6.07
Fire	22	1	124	13.31
IT move/upgrade	14	1	204	20.93
Environmental	6	1	183	65.67
Miscellaneous	5	1	416	92.80
IT capacity	2	4	8	6.00
Theft	2	1	3	2.00
Construction	1	2	2	2.00
Flood	1	13	13	13.00
IT user error	1	1	1	1.00

Backup and recovery

Database backup and recovery is a curative strategy to protect the existence of a physical database and to recreate or recover the data, whenever loss or destruction occurs. The possibility of loss always exists. The use of, and choice among, backup and recovery procedures depends upon an assessment of the risk of loss and the cost of applying recovery procedures. The procedures in this case are carried out by the computer system, usually the DBMS. Data loss and damage should be anticipated. No matter how small the probability of such events, there should be a detailed plan for data recovery.

There are several possible causes for data loss or damage, which can be grouped into three categories.

Storage-medium destruction

In this situation, a portion or all of the database is unreadable as a result of catastrophes such as power or air-conditioning failure, fire, flood, theft, sabotage, and the overwriting of disks or tapes by mistake. A more frequent cause is a disk failure. Some of the disk blocks may be unreadable as a consequence of a read or write malfunction, such as a head crash.

Abnormal termination of an update transaction

In this case, a transaction fails part way through execution, leaving the database partially updated. The database will be inconsistent because it does not accurately reflect the current state of the business. The primary causes of an abnormal termination are a transaction error or system failure. Some operation in the transaction, such as division by zero, may cause it to fail. A hardware or software failure will usually result in one or more active programs being aborted. If these programs were updating the database, integrity problems could result.

Incorrect data discovered

In this situation, an update program or transaction incorrectly updated the database. This usually happens because a logic error was not detected during program testing.

Because most organizations rely heavily on their databases, a DBMS must provide the following three mechanisms for restoring a database quickly and accurately after loss or damage:

1. **Backup facilities**, which create duplicate copies of the database
2. **Journaling facilities**, which provide backup copies or an audit trail of transactions or database changes
3. A **recovery facility** within the DBMS that restores the database to a consistent state and restarts the processing of transactions.

Before discussing each of these mechanisms in more depth, let us review the steps involved in updating a database and how backup and journaling facilities might be integrated into this process.

An overview of the database update process is captured in Figure 19-5. The process can be viewed as a series of database state changes. The initial database, state 1, is modified by an update transaction, such as deleting customer Jones, creating a new state (state 2). State 1 reflects the state of the organization with Jones as a customer, while state 2 reflects the organization without this customer. Each update transaction changes the state of the database to reflect changes in organizational data. Periodically, the database is copied or backed up, possibly onto a different storage medium and stored in a secure location. In Figure 19-5, the backup is made when the database is in state 2.

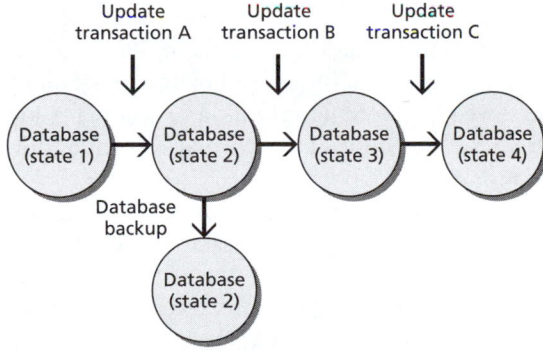

Figure 19-5. Database update procedures

A more detailed illustration of database update procedures and the incorporation of back-up facilities is shown in Figure 19-6. The updating of a single record is described in the following steps.

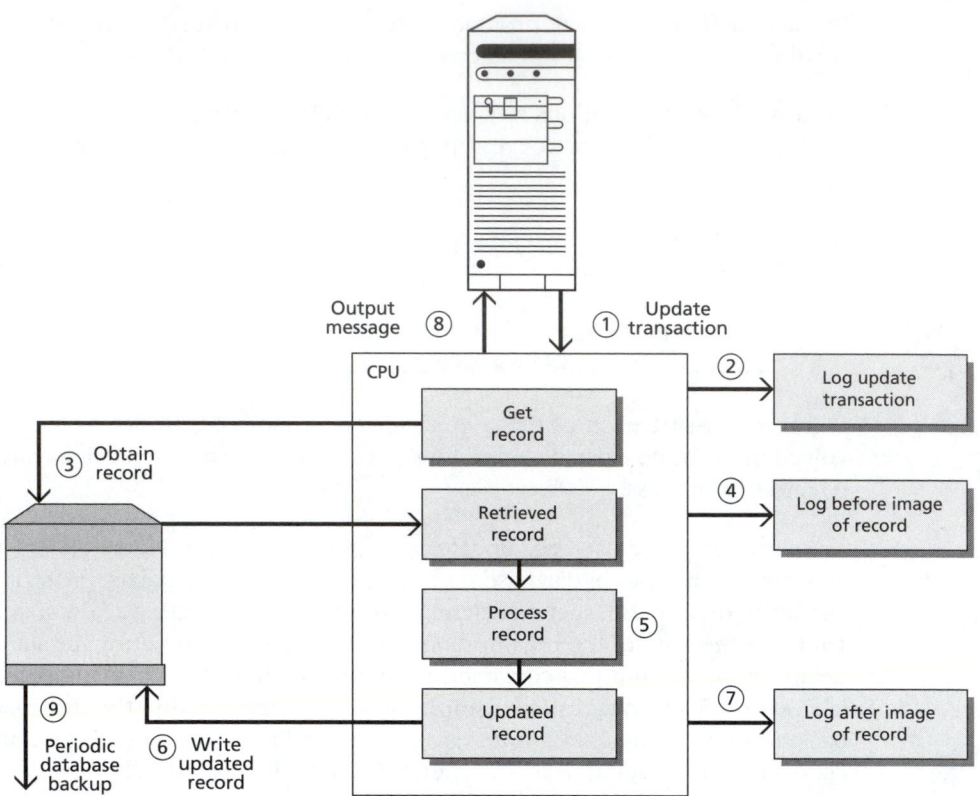

Figure 19-6. Possible procedures for a database update

1.   The user submits an update transaction from a workstation.
2.   The transaction is edited and validated by an application program or the DBMS. If it is valid, it is logged or stored in the transaction log or journal. A journal or log is a special database or file that stores information for backup and recovery.
3.   The DBMS obtains the record to be updated.
4.   A copy of the retrieved record is logged to the journal file. This copy is referred to as the *before image*, because it is a copy of the database record before the transaction changes it.
5.   The transaction is processed by changing the affected data items in the record.
6.   The DBMS writes the updated record to the database.

7. A copy of the updated record is written to the journal. This copy is referred to as the *after image*, because it is a copy of the database record after the transaction has updated it.
8. An output message tells the user that the update has been successfully completed.
9. The database is copied periodically. This backup copy reflects all updates to the database up to the time when the copy was made. An alternative strategy to periodic copying is to maintain multiple (usually two) complete copies of the database online and update them simultaneously. This technique, known as *mirroring*, is discussed in Chapter 11.

In order to recover from data loss or damage, it is necessary to store backup data, such as a complete copy of the database or the necessary data to restore the accuracy of a database. Preferably, backup data should be stored on another medium and kept separate from the primary database. As the description of the update process indicates, there are several options for backup data (see Table 19-4), depending on the objective of the backup procedure.

Table 19-4: Backup options

Objective	Action
Complete copy of database	Dual recording of data (mirroring)
Past states of the database (also known as database dumps)	Database backup
Changes to the database	Before-image log or journal After-image log or journal
Transactions that caused a change in the state of the database	Transaction log or journal

Data stored for backup and recovery are generally some combination of periodic database backups, transaction logs, and before- and after-image logs. Different recovery strategies use different combinations of backup data to recover a database.

The recovery method is highly dependent on the backup strategy. The database administrator selects a backup strategy based on a trade-off between ease of recovery from data loss or damage and the cost of performing backup operations. For example, keeping a mirror database is more expensive then keeping periodic database backups, but a mirroring strategy is useful when recovery is needed very quickly, say in seconds or minutes. An airline reservations system would probably use mirroring to ensure fast and reliable recovery. In general, the cost of keeping backup data is measured in terms of interruption of database availability (e.g., time the system is out of operation when a database is being restored), storage of redundant data, and degradation of update efficiency (e.g., extra time taken in update processing to save before or after images).

Recovery strategies

The type of recovery strategy or procedure used in a given situation depends on the nature of the data loss, the type of backup data available, and the sophistication of the DBMS's recovery facilities. The following discussion outlines the four major recovery strategies: switch to a duplicate database; backward recovery or rollback; forward recovery or roll forward; and reprocessing transactions.

The recovery procedure of switching to a duplicate database requires the maintenance of the mirror copy. The other three strategies assume a periodic dumping or backing up of the database. Periodic dumps may be made on a regular schedule, triggered automatically by the DBMS, or triggered externally by personnel. The schedule may be determined by time (hourly, daily, weekly) or by event (the number of transactions since the last backup).

Switching to a duplicate database

This recovery procedure requires maintaining at least two copies of the database and updating both simultaneously. When there is a problem with one database, access is switched to the duplicate. This strategy is particularly useful when recovery must be accomplished in seconds or minutes. This procedure offers good protection against certain storage-medium destruction problems, such as disk failures, but none against events that damage or make both databases unavailable, such as a power failure or a faulty update program. This strategy entails additional costs in terms of doubling online storage capacity. It can also be implemented with dual computer processors, where each computer updates its copy of the database. This duplexed configuration offers greater backup protection at a greater cost.

Backward recovery or rollback

Backward recovery (also called rollback or rolling back) is used to back out or undo unwanted changes to the database. For example, Figure 19-5 shows three updates (A, B, and C) to a database. Let's say that update B terminated abnormally, leaving the database, now in state 3, inconsistent. What we need to do is return the database to state 2 by applying the before images to the database. Thus, we would perform a rollback by changing the database to state 2 with the before images of the records updated by transaction B.

Backward recovery reverses the changes made when a transaction abnormally terminates or produces erroneous results. To illustrate the need for rollback, consider the example of a budget transfer of $1,000 between two departments.

1. The program reads the account record for Department X and subtracts $1,000 from the account balance and updates the database.
2. The program then reads the record for Department Y and adds $1,000 to the account balance, but while attempting to update the database, the program encounters a disk error and cannot write the record.

Now the database is inconsistent. Department X has been updated, but Department Y has not. Thus, the transaction must be aborted and the database recovered. The DBMS would apply the before image to Department X to restore the account balance to its original value. The DBMS may then restart the transaction and make another attempt to update the database.

Forward recovery or roll forward

Forward recovery (also called roll forward or bringing forward) involves recreating a database using a prior database state. Returning to the example in Figure 19-5, suppose that state 4 of the database was destroyed and that we need to recover it. We would take the last database dump or backup (state 2) and then apply the after-image records created by update transactions B and C. This would return the database to state 4. Thus, roll forward starts with an earlier copy of the database, and by applying after images (the results of good transactions), the backup copy of the database is moved forward to a later state.

Reprocessing transactions

Although similar to forward recovery, this procedure uses update transactions instead of after images. Taking the same example shown in Figure 19-5, assume the database is destroyed in state 4. We would take the last database backup (state 2) and then reprocess update transactions B and C to return the database to state 4. The main advantage of using this method is its simplicity. The DBMS does not need to create an after-image journal, and there are no special restart procedures. The one major disadvantage, however, is the length of time to reprocess transactions. Depending on the frequency of database backups and the time needed to get transactions into the identical sequence as previous updates, several hours of reprocessing may be required. Processing new transactions must be delayed until the database recovery is complete.

Table 19-5 reviews the three types of data losses and the corresponding recovery strategies one could use. The major problem is to recreate a database using a backup copy, a previous state of organizational memory. Recovery is done through forward recovery, reprocessing, or switching to a duplicate database if one is available. With abnormal termination or incorrect data, the preferred strategy is backward recovery, but other procedures could be used.

Table 19-5: What to do when data loss occurs

Problem	Recovery procedures
Storage medium destruction (database is unreadable)	* Switch to a duplicate database—this can be transparent with RAID Forward recovery Reprocessing transactions
Abnormal termination of an update transaction (transaction error or system failure)	* Backward recovery Forward recovery or reprocessing transactions— bring forward to the state just before termination of the transaction

Table 19-5: What to do when data loss occurs (continued)

Problem	Recovery procedures

Incorrect data detected (database has been incorrectly updated)	* Backward recovery
	Reprocessing transactions
	  (excluding those from the update program
	  that created the incorrect data)

* Preferred strategy

Use of recovery procedures

Usually the person doing a query or an update is not concerned with backup and recovery. Database administration personnel often implement strategies that are automatically carried out by the DBMS. ANSI has defined standards governing SQL processing of database transactions that relate to recovery. Transaction support is provided through the use of the two SQL statements: COMMIT and ROLLBACK. These commands are employed when a procedural programming language such as Java is used to update a database. Consider the program segment in Figure 19-7, which contains the SQL commands to execute an update transaction.

```
MAIN
* If an error occurs, perform undo code block.
1 EXEC SQL WHENEVER SQL ERROR PERFORM UNDO
* Insert a single row in table A.
2 EXEC SQL INSERT
* Update a row in table B.
3 EXEC SQL UPDATE
* Successful transaction, all changes are now permanent.
4 EXEC SQL COMMIT WORK
5 PERFORM FINISH
UNDO
* Unsuccessful transaction, perform rollback of the transaction.
6 EXEC SQL ROLLBACK WORK
FINISH
 EXIT
```

Figure 19-7. Use of COMMIT and ROLLBACK

The programmer wants the two update actions (statements 2 and 3) to be considered as a transaction. If both update actions are not successfully completed, the database would be inconsistent.

In the example, the programmer issues a COMMIT WORK command to the DBMS (or the transaction processing portion of the DBMS) if the program completes the two updates successfully, which will commit the changes to the database and make them permanent. If anything goes wrong, however, the program issues the ROLLBACK WORK command to undo any changes made so far. The ROLLBACK WORK command works just like the backward recovery procedure previously discussed.

Skill builder

A Internet bank with more than 10 million customers has asked for your advice on developing procedures for protecting the existence of its data. What would you recommend?.

Maintaining data quality

The second integrity goal is to maintain data quality, which typically means keeping data accurate, complete, and current. *Data are high-quality if they fit their intended uses in operations, decision making, and planning. They are fit for use if they are free of defects and possess desired features.*[4] The preceding definition implicitly recognizes that data quality is determined by the customer. It also implies that data quality is relative to a task. Data could be high-quality for one task and low-quality for another. The data provided by a flight-tracking system[5] are very useful when you are planning to meet someone at the airport, but not particularly helpful for selecting a vacation spot. Defect-free data are accessible, accurate, timely, complete, and consistent with other sources. Desirable features include relevance, comprehensiveness, appropriate level of detail, easy-to-navigate source, high readability, and absence of ambiguity.

Poor-quality data have several detrimental effects. Customer service decreases when there is dissatisfaction with poor and inaccurate information or a lack of appropriate information. For many customers, information is the heart of customer service, and they lose confidence in firms that can't or don't provide relevant information. Bad data interrupt information processing because they need to be corrected before processing can continue. Poor-quality data can lead to the wrong decision because inaccurate inferences and conclusions are made.

As we have stated previously, data quality varies with circumstances, and the model in Figure 19-8 will help you to understand this linkage. By considering variations in a customer's uncertainty about a firm's products and a firm's ability to deliver consistently, we arrive at four fundamental strategies for customer-oriented data quality.

❖ **Transaction processing:** When customers know what they want and firms can deliver consistently, customers simply want fast and accurate transactions and data confirming details of the transaction. Most banking services fall into this category. Customers know they can withdraw and deposit money, and banks can perform reliably.

❖ **Expert system:** In some circumstances, customers are uncertain of their needs. For instance, Vanguard[6] offers personal investors a choice from more than 150 mutual funds. Most prospective investors are confused by such a range of choices, and

---

4. Redman, T. C. 2001. *Data quality: the field guide.* Boston: Digital Press. p. 73.
5. www.fboweb.com/cob/aero1.asp
6. personal.vanguard.com/

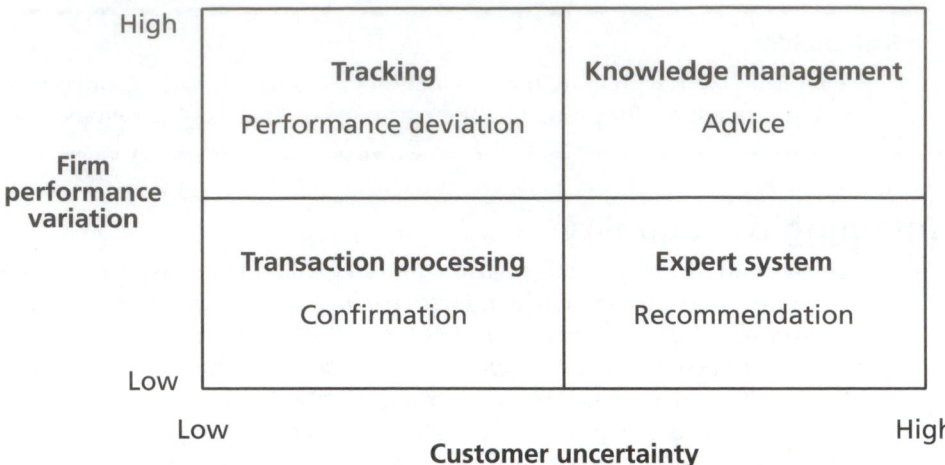

Figure 19-8. Customer-oriented data quality strategies

Vanguard, by asking a series of questions, helps prospective investors to narrow their choices and recommends a small subset of its funds. A firm's recommendation will vary little over time because the characteristics of a mutual fund (e.g., intermediate tax-exempt bond) do not change.

❖ **Tracking:** Some firms operate in environments where they don't have a lot of control over all the factors that affect performance. Handling more than 2,500 take-offs and landings and nearly 225,000 passengers per day,[7] Atlanta's Hartsfield Airport becomes congested when bad weather, such as a summer thunderstorm, slows down operations. Passengers clearly know what they want—data on flight delays and their consequences. They assess data quality in terms of how well data tracks delays and notifies them of alternative travel arrangements.

❖ **Knowledge management:** When customers are uncertain about their needs for products delivered by firms that don't perform consistently, they seek advice from knowledgeable people and organizations. Data quality is judged by the soundness of the advice received. Thus, a woman wanting a custom-built house would likely seek the advice of an architect to select the site, design the house, and supervise its construction, because architects are skilled in eliciting clients' needs and knowledgeable about the building industry.

An organization's first step toward improving data quality is to determine in which quadrant it operates so it can identify the critical information customers expect. Of course, data quality in many situations will be a mix of expectations. The mutual fund will be expected to confirm fund addition and deletion transactions. However, a firm must meet its dominant goal to attract and retain customers.

---

7.   August 2002 data.

A firm will also need to consider its dominant data quality strategy for its internal customers, and the same general principles illustrated by Figure 19-8 can be applied. In the case of internal customers, there can be varying degrees of uncertainty as to what other organizational units can do for them, and these units will vary in their ability to perform consistently for internal customers. For example, consulting firms develop centers of excellence as repositories of knowledge on a particular topic to provide their employees with a source of expertise. These are the internal equivalent of knowledge centers for external customers.

Once they have settled on a dominant data quality strategy, organizations need a corporate-wide approach to data quality, just like product and service quality. There are three generations of data quality:

❖ **First generation**: Errors in existing data stores are found and corrected. This data cleansing is necessary when much of the data is captured by manual systems.
❖ **Second generation**: Errors are prevented at the source. Procedures are put in place to capture high-quality data so that there is no need to cleanse it later. As more data are born digital, this approach becomes more feasible. Thus, when customers enter their own data or barcodes are scanned, the data should be higher-quality than when entered by a data-processing operator.
❖ **Third generation**: Defects are highly unlikely. Data capture systems meet six-sigma standards (3.4 defects per million), and data quality is no longer an issue.

Skill builder

1. A consumer electronics company with a well-respected brand offers a wide range of products. For example, it offers nine world-band radios and seven televisions. What data quality strategy would you recommend?
2. What data quality focus would you recommend for a regulated natural gas utility?
3. A telephone company has problems in estimating how long it takes to install DSL in homes. Sometimes it takes less than an hour and other times much longer. Customers are given a scheduled appointment and many have to make special arrangements so that they are home when the installation person arrives. What data might these customers expect from the telephone company, and how would they judge data quality?

Dimensions

The many writers on quality all agree on one thing—quality is multidimensional. Data quality also has many facets, and these are presented in Table 19-6. The list also provides data managers with a checklist for evaluating overall high-quality data. Organizations should aim for a balanced performance across all dimensions because failure in one area is likely to diminish overall data quality.

Table 19-6: The dimensions of data quality

Dimension	Conditions for high-quality data
Accuracy	Data values agree with known correct values.
Completeness	Values for all reasonably expected attributes are available.
Representation consistency	Values for a particular attribute have the same representation across all tables (e.g., dates).
Organizational consistency	There is one organizationwide table for each entity and one organizationwide domain for each attribute.
Row consistency	The values in a row are internally consistent (e.g., a home phone number's area code is consistent with a city's location).
Timeliness	A value's recentness matches the needs of the most time-critical application requiring it.
Stewardship	Responsibility has been assigned for managing data.
Sharing	Data sharing is widespread across organizational units.
Fitness	The format and presentation of data fit each task for which they are required.
Interpretation	Clients correctly interpret the meaning of data elements.
Flexibility	The content and format of presentations can be readily altered to meet changing circumstances.
Precision	Data values can be conveniently formatted to the required degree of accuracy.
International	Data values can be displayed in the measurement unit of choice (e.g., kilometers or miles).
Accessibility	Authorized users can readily access data values through a variety of devices from a variety of locations.
Security and privacy	Data are appropriately protected from unauthorized access.
Continuity	The organization continues to operate in spite of major disruptive events.
Granularity	Data are represented at the lowest level necessary to support all uses (e.g., hourly sales).
Metadata	There is ready access to accurate data about data.

Skill builder

1. What level of granularity of sales data would you recommend for an online retailer?
2. What level of data quality completeness might you expect for a university's student table?

DBMS and data quality

To assist data quality, functions are needed within the DBMS to ensure that update and insert actions are performed by authorized persons in accordance with stated rules or integrity constraints, and that the results are properly recorded. These functions are accomplished by update authorization, data validation using integrity constraints, and concurrent update control. Each of these functions is discussed in turn.

Update authorization

Without proper controls, update transactions can diminish the quality of a database. Unauthorized users could sabotage a database by entering erroneous values. The first step is to ensure that anyone who wants to update a database is authorized to do so. Some responsible person—usually the database owner or database administrator—must tell the DBMS who is permitted to initiate particular database operations. The DBMS must then check every transaction to ensure that it is authorized. Unauthorized access to a database exposes an organization to many risks, including fraud and sabotage.

Update authorization is accomplished through the same access mechanism used to protect confidentiality. We will discuss access control more thoroughly later in this chapter. In SQL, access control is implemented through the GRANT, which gives a user a privilege, and REVOKE, which removes a privilege. (These commands are discussed in Chapter 10.) A control mechanism may lump all update actions into a single privilege or separate them for greater control. In SQL, they are separated as follows:

❖ UPDATE (privilege to change field values using UPDATE; this can be column specific)
❖ DELETE (privilege to delete records from a table)
❖ INSERT (privilege to insert records into a table)

Separate privileges for each of the update commands allow tighter controls on certain update actions, such as updating a salary field or deleting records.

Data validation using integrity constraints

Once the update process has been authorized, the DBMS must ensure that a database is accurate and complete before any updates are applied. Consequently, the DBMS needs to be aware of any integrity constraints or rules that apply to the data. For example, the qdel table in the relational database described previously (see page 289) would have constraints such as

❖ Delivery number (delno) must be unique, numeric, and in the range 1–99999.
❖ Delivered quantity (delqty) must be nonzero.
❖ Item name (itemname) must appear in the qitem table.
❖ Supplier code (splno) must appear in the qspl table.

Once integrity constraints are specified, the DBMS must monitor or validate all insert and update operations to ensure that they do not violate any of the constraints or rules.

The key to updating data validation is a clear definition of valid and invalid data. Data validation cannot be performed without integrity constraints or rules. A person or the DBMS must know acceptable data format, valid values, and procedures to invoke to determine validity. All data validation is based on a prior expression of integrity constraints.

Data validation may not always produce error-free data, however. Sometimes integrity constraints are unknown or are not well defined. In other cases, the DBMS does provide a convenient means for expressing and performing validation checks. Sometimes, the costs of implementing the constraints are too high. Certain checks may take too long or require the storage and management of too much extra data. For example, to validate American state codes, you need to create a table containing the correct codes for all 50 states and Washington, DC. This is not very expensive to establish. But what if you decided to validate all ZIP codes? Like most design decisions, establishing integrity constraints involves trade-offs.

Based on how integrity constraints have been defined, data validation can be performed outside the DBMS by people or within the DBMS itself. External validation is usually done by reviewing input documents before they are entered into the system and by checking system outputs to ensure that the database was updated correctly. Maintaining data quality is of paramount importance, and data validation preferably should be handled by the DBMS as much as possible rather than by the application, which should handle the exceptions and respond to any failed data validation checks.

Integrity constraints are usually specified as part of the database definition supplied to the DBMS. For example, the primary-key uniqueness and referential integrity constraints can be specified within the SQL CREATE statement. DBMSs generally permit some constraints to be stored as part of the database schema and are used by the DBMS to monitor all update operations and perform appropriate data validation checks. Any given database is likely to be subject to a very large number of constraints, but not all of these can be automatically enforced by the DBMS. Some will need to be handled by application programs.

The general types of constraints applied to a data item are outlined in Table 19-7. Not all of these necessarily would be supported by a DBMS, and a particular database may not use all types.

Table 19-7: Types of data items in integrity constraints

Type of Integrity constraint	Explanation	Example
type	Validating a data item value against a specified data type	Supplier number is numeric.
size	Defining and validating the minimum and maximum size of a data item	Delivery number must be at least 3 digits, and at most 5.
values	Providing a list of acceptable values for a data item	Item colors must match the list provided.
range	Providing one or more ranges within which the data item must lie	Employee numbers must be in the range 1–100.

Table 19-7: Types of data items in integrity constraints (continued)

Type of Integrity constraint	Explanation	Example
pattern	Providing a pattern of allowable characters that define permissible formats for data values	Department phone number must be of the form 542-nnnn (stands for exactly four decimal digits).
procedure	Providing a procedure to be invoked to validate data items	A delivery must have valid item name, department, and supplier values before it can be added to the database (tables are checked for valid entries).
Conditional	Providing one or more conditions to apply against data values	If item type is "Y," then color is null.
Not null (mandatory)	Indicating whether the data item value is mandatory (not null) or optional; the not-null option is required for primary keys	Employee number is mandatory.
Unique	Indicating whether stored values for this data item must be compared to other values of the item within the same table	Supplier number is unique.

As mentioned, integrity constraints are usually specified as part of the database definition supplied to the DBMS. Table 19-8 contains some typical specifications of integrity constraints for a relational DBMS.

Table 19-8: Examples of integrity constraints

Examples	Explanation
```CREATE TABLE stock (stkcode CHAR(3), ..., natcode CHAR(3), PRIMARY KEY(stkcode), CONSTRAINT fk_stock_nation FOREIGN KEY(natcode) REFERENCES nation(natcode) ON DELETE RESTRICT);```	Column `stkcode` must always have 3 or fewer alphanumeric characters, and `stkcode` must be unique because it is a primary key. Column `natcode` must be assigned a value of 3 or less alphanumeric characters and must exist as the primary key of the `nation`. Do not allow the deletion of a row in `nation` while there still exist rows in `stock` containing the corresponding value of `natcode`.

Data quality control does not end with the application of integrity constraints. Whenever an error or unusual situation is detected by the DBMS, some form of response is required. Response rules need to be given to the DBMS along with the integrity constraints. The responses can take many different forms, such as abort the entire program, reject entire update transaction, display a message and continue processing, or let the DBMS attempt to correct the error. The response may vary depending on the type of integrity constraint violated. If the DBMS does not allow the specification of response rules, then it must take a default action when an error is detected. For example, if alphabetic data are entered in a numeric field, most DBMSs will have a default response and message (e.g., nonnumeric data entered in numeric field). In the case of application programs, an error code is passed to the program from the DBMS. The program would then use this error code to execute an error-handling procedure.

Ensuring confidentiality

Thus far, we have discussed how the first two goals of data integrity can be accomplished: Data are available when needed (protecting existence); data are accurate, complete, and current (maintaining quality). This section deals with the final goal: ensuring confidentiality or data security. Two DBMS functions—access control and encryption—are the primary means of ensuring that the data are accessed only by those authorized to do so. We begin by discussing an overall model of data security.

General model of data security

Figure 19-9 depicts the two functions for ensuring data confidentiality: access control and encryption. Access control consists of two basic steps—identification and authorization. Once past access control, the user is permitted to access the database. Access control is applied only to the established avenues of entry to a database. Clever people, however, may be able to circumvent the controls and gain unauthorized access. To counteract this possibility, it is often desirable to hide the meaning of stored data by encrypting them, so that it is impossible to interpret their meaning. Encrypted data are stored in a transformed or coded format that can be decrypted and read only by those with the appropriate key.

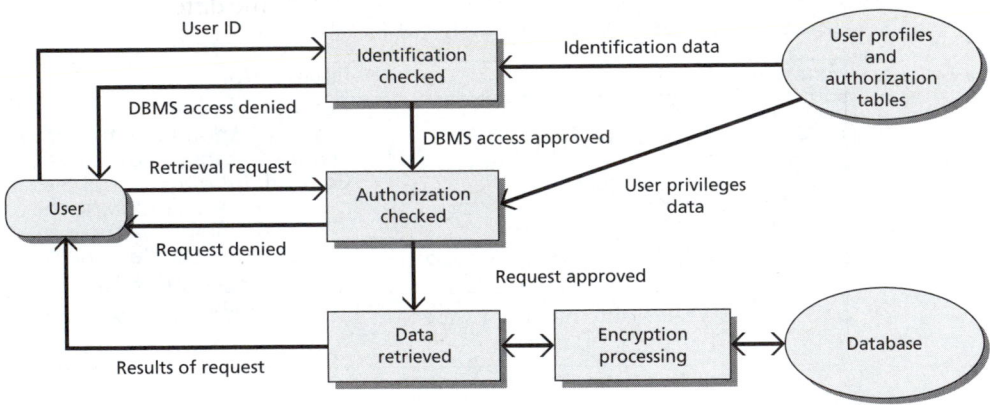

Figure 19-9. A general model of data security

Now let us walk through Figure 19-9 in detail.

❖   A user must be identified and provide additional information required to authenticate this identification (e.g., a userid and password). User profile information (e.g., a password or a voice print) is used to verify or authenticate a user.

❖ Having authenticated the user, the authorization step is initiated by a user request (retrieve or update database). The previously stored user authorization rules (what data each user can access and the authorized actions on those data) are checked to determine whether the user has the right or privilege to access the requested data. (The previously stored user privileges are created and maintained by an authorized person, database owner, or administrator.) A decision is made to permit or deny the execution of the user's request. If access is permitted, the user's transaction is processed against the database.

❖ Data are encrypted before storage, and retrieved data are decrypted before presentation.

Data access control

Data access control begins with some identification of the user or subject, an organizational entity that can access the database. Examples are individuals, departments, groups of people, transactions, terminals, and application programs. Valid combinations may be required, for example, a particular person entering a certain transaction at a particular terminal. A user identification (often called *userid*) is the first piece of data the DBMS receives from the subject. It may be a name or number. The user identification enables the DBMS to locate the corresponding entry in the stored user profiles and authorization tables (see Figure 19-9).

Taking this information, the DBMS goes through the process of authentication. The system attempts to match additional information supplied by the intended user with the information previously stored in the user profile. The system may perform multiple matches to ensure the identity of the user (see Table 19-9 for the different types). If all tests are successful, the DBMS assumes that the subject is an authenticated user.

Table 19-9: Authenticating mechanisms[a]

Class	Examples
Something a person knows: **remembered information**	Name, account number, password
Something the person has: **possessed object**	Badge, plastic card, key
Something the person is: **personal characteristic**	Fingerprint, voiceprint, signature, hand size

a.   Adapted from Everest, *Data management*, op. cit.

Many systems use remembered information to control access. The problem with remembered information is that it does not positively identify the user. Passwords have been the most widely used form of access control. If used correctly, they can be very effective. Unfortunately, people leave them around where others can pick them up, allowing unauthorized people to gain access to databases.

To deal with this problem, organizations are moving toward using personal characteristics and combinations of authenticating mechanisms to protect sensitive data. Collectively, these mechanisms can provide even greater security. For example, access to a large firm's very valuable marketing database requires a smart card and a fingerprint, a combination of personal characteristic and a possessed object. The database can be accessed through only a few terminals in specific locations, an isolation strategy. Once the smart card test is passed, the DBMS requests entry of other remembered information—password and account number—before granting access.

Data access authorization is the process of permitting users whose identity has been authenticated to perform certain operations on certain data objects in a shared database. The authorization process is driven by rules incorporated into the DBMS. Authorization rules are readily shown in a table that includes subjects, objects, actions, and constraints for a given database. An example of such a table is shown in Table 19-10. Each row of the table indicates that a particular subject is authorized to take a certain action on a database object, perhaps subject to some constraint. For example, the last entry of the table indicates that Brier is authorized to delete supplier records with no restrictions.

We have already discussed subjects, but not objects, actions, and constraints. Objects are database entities protected by the DBMS. Examples are databases, views, files, tables, and data items. In Table 19-10, the objects are all tables. A view is another form of security. It restricts the user's access to a database. Any data not included in a view are unknown to the user. Although views promote security, several persons may share a view or unauthorized persons may gain access. Thus, a view is another object to be included in the authorization process. Typical actions on objects are shown in Table 19-10: read, insert, modify, and delete. Constraints are particular rules that apply to a subject-action-object relationship.

Table 19-10: Sample authorization table

Subject/Client	Action	Object	Constraint
Accounting department	Insert	Supplier table	None
Purchase department clerk	Insert	Supplier table	If quantity < 200
Purchase department supervisor	Insert	Delivery table	If quantity >= 200
Production department	Read	Delivery table	None
Todd	Modify	Item table	Type and color only
Order-processing program	Modify	Sale table	None
Brier	Delete	Supplier table	None

Implementing authorization rules

Most contemporary DBMSs do not implement the complete authorization table shown in Table 19-10. Usually, they implement a simplified version. The most common form is an authorization table for subjects with limited applications of the constraint column. Let us take the granting of table privileges, which are needed in order to authorize subjects to perform operations on both tables and views (see Table 19-11).

Table 19-11: Authorization commands

SQL Command	Result
SELECT	Permission to retrieve data
UPDATE	Permission to change data; can be column specific
DELETE	Permission to delete records or tables
INSERT	Permission to add records or tables

The GRANT and REVOKE SQL commands discussed in Chapter 10 are used to define and delete authorization rules. Some examples:

```
GRANT SELECT ON qspl TO vikki;
GRANT SELECT, UPDATE (splname) ON qspl TO huang;
GRANT ALL PRIVILEGES ON qitem TO vikki;
GRANT SELECT ON qitem TO huang;
```

The GRANT commands have essentially created two authorization tables, one for user Huang and the other for user Vikki. These tables, shown in Table 19-12, illustrate how most current systems create authorization tables for subjects using a limited set of objects (e.g., tables) and constraints.

Table 19-12: A sample authorization table

Client	Object (table)	Action	Constraint
vikki	qspl	SELECT	None
vikki	qitem	UPDATE	None
vikki	qitem	INSERT	None
vikki	qitem	DELETE	None
vikki	qitem	SELECT	None
huang	qspl	SELECT	None
huang	qspl	UPDATE	splname only
huang	qitem	SELECT	None

Because authorization tables contain highly sensitive data, they must be protected by stringent security rules and encryption. Normally, only selected persons in data administration have authority to access and modify them.

Encryption

Encryption techniques complement access control. As Figure 19-9 illustrates, access control applies only to established avenues of access to a database. There is always the possibility that people will circumvent these controls and gain unauthorized access to a database. To counteract this possibility, encryption can be used to obscure or hide the meaning of data. Encrypted data cannot be read by an intruder unless that person knows the method of encryption and has the key. Encryption is any transformation applied to data that makes it difficult to extract meaning. Encryption transforms data to cipher text, and decryption reconstructs the original data from cipher text.

Public-key encryption is based on a pair of private and public keys. A person's public key can be freely distributed because it is quite separate from his or her private key. To send and receive messages, communicators first need to create private and public keys and then exchange their public keys. The sender encodes a message with the intended receiver's public key, and upon receiving the message, the receiver applies her private key (see Figure 19-10). The receiver's private key, the only one that can decode the message, must be kept secret to provide secure message exchanging.

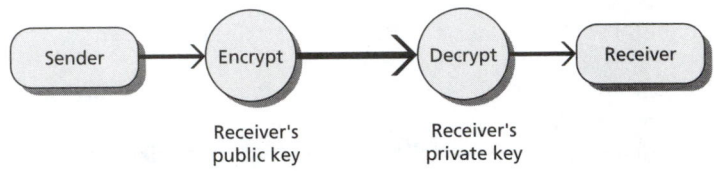

Figure 19-10. Public-key encryption

In a DBMS environment, encryption techniques can be applied to transmitted data sent over communication lines to and from terminals, or between computers, and to all highly sensitive stored data in active databases or their backup versions. Some DBMS products include encryption routines that automatically encrypt sensitive data when they are stored or transmitted over communication channels. Other DBMS products provide exits that allow users to code their own encryption routines. Encrypted data may also take less storage space because they are often compressed.

Skill builder

A university has decided that it will e-mail students their results at the end of each semester. What procedures would you establish to ensure that only the designated student opened and viewed the e-mail?

Monitoring activity

Sometimes no single activity will be detected as an example of misuse of a system. However, examination of a pattern of behavior may reveal undesirable behavior (e.g., persistent attempts to log into a system with a variety of userids and passwords). Many systems now monitor all activity using **audit trail analysis**. A time- and date-stamped audit trail of all system actions (e.g., database accesses) is maintained. This audit log is dynamically analyzed to detect unusual behavior patterns and alert security personnel to possible misuse.

A form of misuse can occur when an authorized user violates privacy rules by using a series of authorized queries to gain access to private data. For example, some systems aim to protect individual privacy by restricting authorized queries to aggregate functions (e.g., AVG and COUNT). Since it is impossible to do nonaggregate queries, this approach should prevent access to individual-level data, which it does at the single-query level. However, multiple queries can be constructed to circumvent this restriction.

Assume we know that a professor in the IS department is aged 40 to 50, is single, and attended the University of Minnesota. Consider the results of the following set of queries.[8]

```
SELECT COUNT(*) FROM faculty
    WHERE dept = 'MIS'
    AND age >= 40 AND age <= 50;
```

10

```
SELECT COUNT(*) FROM faculty
    WHERE dept = 'MIS'
    AND age >= 40 AND age <= 50
    AND degree_from = 'Minnesota';
```

2

```
SELECT COUNT(*) FROM faculty
    WHERE dept = 'MIS'
    AND age >= 40 AND age <= 50;
    AND degree_from = 'Minnesota'
    AND marital_status = 'S';
```

1

```
SELECT AVG(salary) FROM faculty
    WHERE dept = 'MIS'
    AND age >= 40 AND age <= 50
    AND degree_from = 'Minnesota'
    AND marital_status = 'S';
```

85000

The preceding set of queries, while all at the aggregate level, enables one to deduce the salary of the professor. This is an invasion of privacy and counter to the spirit of the re-

---

8.   Adapted from Helman, P. 1994. *The science of data management*. Burr Ridge, IL: Irwin. p. 434.

striction queries to aggregate functions. An audit trail should detect such **tracker queries**, one or more authorized queries that collectively violate privacy. One approach to preventing tracker queries is to set a lower bound on the number of rows on which a query can report.

Summary

The management of organizational data is driven by the joint goals of availability and integrity. Availability deals with making data available to whoever needs them, whenever and wherever they need them, and in a meaningful form. Maintaining integrity implies protecting existence, maintaining quality, and ensuring confidentiality. There are three strategies for maintaining data integrity: legal, administrative, and technical. A consistent database is one in which all data integrity constraints are satisfied.

A transaction must be entirely completed or aborted before there is any effect on the database. Transactions are processed as logical units of work to ensure data integrity. The transaction manager is responsible for ensuring that transactions are correctly recorded.

Concurrent update control focuses on making sure updated results are correctly recorded in a database. To prevent loss of updates and inconsistent retrieval results, a DBMS must incorporate a resource-locking mechanism. Deadlock is an impasse that occurs because two users lock certain resources, then request resources locked by each other. Deadlock prevention requires applications to lock all required records at the beginning of the transaction. Deadlock resolution uses the DBMS to detect and break deadlocks.

Isolation is a preventive strategy that involves administrative procedures to insulate the physical database from destruction. Database backup and recovery is a curative strategy that protects an existing database and recreates or recovers the data whenever loss or destruction occurs. A DBMS needs to provide backup, journaling, and recovery facilities to restore a database to a consistent state and restart the processing of transactions. A journal or log is a special database or file that stores information for backup and recovery. A before image is a copy of a database record before a transaction changes the record. An after image is a copy of a database record after a transaction has updated the record.

In order to recover from data loss or damage, it is necessary to store redundant, backup data. The recovery method is highly dependent on the backup strategy. The cost of keeping backup data is measured in terms of interruption of database availability, storage of redundant data, and degradation of update efficiency. The four major recovery strategies are switching to a duplicate database, backward recovery or rollback, forward recovery or roll forward, and reprocessing transactions. Database administration personnel often implement recovery strategies automatically carried out by the DBMS. The SQL statements COMMIT and ROLLBACK are used with a procedural programming language for implementing recovery procedures.

Maintaining quality implies keeping data accurate, complete, and current. The first step is to ensure that anyone wanting to update a database is required to have authorization. In

---

It is electronically elementary, my dear Watson

Stop! Don't write that check without first considering the personal information you are divulging to a possible stranger. Does your check contain your name, address, telephone number, Social Security number, or driver's license number? Consider what students at the University of Alabama at Birmingham discovered about their instructor, with just his name, as part of a class project on Privacy Issues.

First, they went to the offices of the Tax Assessor and Collector at the courthouse in the county where the instructor lived. These offices provided the students with the information the government had on the properties (in this case, a house and two cars) on which he paid taxes. In fact, the offices gave them photocopies and duplicates of the tax bills and other information (e.g., location of the house, amount of mortgage, the seller, the lien holder, and the valuation and description of the properties). This information is in the public domain and is available to anybody in the United States. Included among the documents found at the courthouse was the professor's Social Security number, which, along with his name and address, provided enough information for the students to get his credit report.

Having obtained his license plate numbers from the courthouse, the students then called the Department of Motor Vehicles, which proceeded to give them his entire driving record. In addition, they went to the university library and looked up his employment record. The instructor being a state employee, his salary, rank, position, and date of employment are public information. At this point, the students stopped, but they could have obtained further public-domain information about his marital and criminal history.

The students gathered all the information in about a week. These aspiring Sherlock Holmeses used the following two books as a guideline:

Culligan, J. J. 1993. *You, too, can find anybody: a reference manual*. Miami, FL: Hallmark.

Gunderson, T. L. 1989. *How to locate anyone anywhere without leaving home*. New York, NY: Dutton.

Electronic tracking services are readily available at low cost. For example, Find a Friend (findafriend.com) charges $20.00 to find the address of the owner of a Social Security number.

Contributed by Dr. Sanjay Singh, Department of Management, The University of Alabama. Birmingham.

SQL, access control is implemented through GRANT and REVOKE. Data validation cannot be performed without integrity constraints or rules. Data validation can be performed external to the DBMS by personnel or within the DBMS based on defined integrity constraints. Because maintaining data quality is of paramount importance, it is desirable that the DBMS handle data validation rather than the application. Error response rules need to be given to the DBMS along with the integrity constraints.

Two DBMS functions, access control and encryption, are the primary mechanisms for ensuring that the data are accessed only by authorized persons. Access control consists of identification and authorization. Data access authorization is the process of permitting user whose identities have been authenticated to perform certain operations on certain data objects. Encrypted data cannot be read by an intruder unless that person knows the method of encryption and has the key. In a DBMS environment, encryption can be applied to data sent over communication lines between computers and data storage devices.

Database activity is monitored to detect patterns of activity indicating misuse of the system. An audit trail is maintained of all system actions. A tracker query is a series of aggregate function queries designed to reveal individual-level data.

Key terms and concepts

ACID	Integrity constraint
Administrative strategies	Isolation
After image	Journal
All-or-nothing rule	Legal strategies
Atomicity	Locking
Audit trail analysis	Maintaining quality
Authentication	Private key
Authorization	Protecting existence
Backup	Public-key encryption
Before image	Recovery
COMMIT	Reprocessing
Concurrent update control	REVOKE
Consistency	Roll forward
Data access control	ROLLBACK
Data availability	Rollback
Data quality	Serializability
Data security	Slock
Database integrity	Technical strategies
Deadlock prevention	Tracker query
Deadlock resolution	Transaction
Deadly embrace	Transaction atomicity
Decryption	Transaction manager
Durability	Two-phase locking protocol
Encryption	Validation
Ensuring confidentiality	Xlock
GRANT	

References and additional readings

Clarke, R. A. 1988. Information technology and dataveillance. *Communications of the ACM* 31 (5):498–512.

Culnan, M. J. 1993. "How did they get my name?": An exploratory investigation of consumer attitudes toward secondary information use. *MIS Quarterly* 17 (3):341–363.

Exercises

1. What are the three goals of maintaining organizational memory integrity?
2. What strategies are available for maintaining data integrity?
3. A large corporation needs to operate its computer systems continuously to remain viable. It currently has data centers in Miami and San Francisco. Do you have any advice for the CIO?
4. An investment company operates out of a single office in Boston. Its business is based on many years of high-quality service, honesty, and reliability. The CEO is concerned that the firm has become too dependent on its computer system. If some disaster should occur and the firm's databases were lost, its reputation for reliability would disappear overnight and so would many of its customers in this highly competitive business. What should the firm do?
5. What mechanisms should a DBMS provide to support backup and recovery?
6. What is the difference between a before image and an after image?
7. A large organization has asked you to advise on backup and recovery procedures for its weekly, batch payroll system. They want reliable recovery at the lowest cost. What would you recommend?
8. An online information service operates globally and prides itself on its uptime of 99.98 percent. What sort of backup and recovery scheme is this firm likely to use? Describe some of the levels of redundancy you would expect to find.
9. The information systems manager of a small manufacturing company is considering the backup strategy for a new production planning database. The database is used every evening to create a plan for the next day's production. As long as the production plan is prepared before 6 A.M. the next day, there is no impact upon plant efficiency. The database is currently 200 Mbytes and growing about 2 percent per year. What backup strategy would you recommend and why?
10. How do backward recovery and forward recovery differ?
11. What are the advantages and disadvantages of reprocessing transactions?
12. When would you use ROLLBACK in an application program?
13. When would you use COMMIT in an application program?
14. Give three examples of data integrity constraints.
15. What is the purpose of locking?
16. What is the likely effect on performance between locking at a row compared to locking at a page?
17. What is a deadly embrace? How can it be avoided?
18. What are three types of authenticating mechanisms?
19. Assume that you want to discover the grade point average of a fellow student. You know the following details of this person. She is a Norwegian citizen who is majoring in IS and minoring in philosophy. Write one or more aggregate queries that should enable you to determine her GPA.
20. What is encryption?

21. What are the disadvantages of the data encryption standard (DES)?
22. What are the advantages of public-key encryption?
23. A national stock exchange requires listed companies to transmit quarterly reports to its computer center electronically. Recently, a hacker intercepted some of the transmissions and made several hundred thousand dollars because of advance knowledge of one firm's unexpectedly high quarterly profits. How could the stock exchange reduce the likelihood of this event?

20

Data Administration

Bad administration, to be sure, can destroy good policy; but good administration can never save bad policy.

Adlai Stevenson, speech given in Los Angeles, September 11, 1952

Learning objectives

Students completing this chapter will

- ❖ understand the importance and role of data administration;
- ❖ understand how system-level data administration functions are used to manage a database environment successfully;
- ❖ understand how project-level data administration activities support the development of a database system;
- ❖ understand what skills data administration requires and why it needs a balance of people, technical, and business skills to carry out its roles effectively;
- ❖ understand how computer-based tools can be used to support data administration activities;
- ❖ understand the management issues involved in initiating, staffing, and locating data administration organizationally.

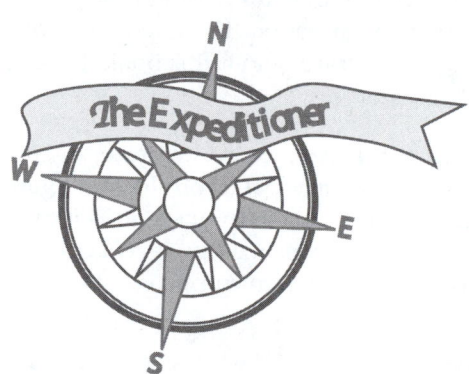

The Tahiti tourist resort had been an outstanding success for The Expeditioner. Located 40 minutes from Papeete, the capital city, on a stretch of tropical forest and golden sand, the resort had soon become the favorite meeting place for The Expeditioner's board. No one objected to the long flight to French Polynesia. The destination was well worth the journey, and The Expeditioner had historic ties to that part of the South Pacific. Early visitors to Tahiti, James Cook and William Bligh, had been famous customers of The

Expeditioner in the eighteenth century. Before Paul Gauguin embarked on his journey to paint scenes of Tahiti, he had purchased supplies from L'Explorateur, now the French division of The Expeditioner.

Although The Expeditioner is very successful, there are always problems for the board to address. A number of board members are very concerned by the seeming lack of control over the various database systems that are vital to the firm's profitability. Recently there had been a number of incidents that had underscored the problem. Purchasing had made several poor decisions. For example, it had ordered too many parkas for the North American stores and had to discount them heavily to sell all the stock. The problem was traced to poor data standards and policies within Sales. In another case, Personnel and Marketing had been squabbling for some time over access to the personnel database. Personnel claimed ownership of the data and was reluctant to share data with Marketing, which wanted access to some of the data to support its new incentive program. In yet another incident, a new database project for the Travel Division had been seriously delayed when it was discovered that the Travel Division's development team was planning to implement a system incompatible with The Expeditioner's existing hardware and software.

After the usual exchange of greetings and a presentation of the monthly financial report, Alice forthrightly raised the database problem. "We all know that we depend on information technology to manage The Expeditioner," she began as she glanced at her notes on her personal digital assistant. "The Information Systems department does a great job running the computers, building new systems, and providing us with excellent service, but," she stressed, "we seem to be focusing on managing the wrong things. We should be managing what really matters: the data we need to run the business. Data errors, internecine[1] fighting over data, and project delays are costly. Our present system for managing data is fragmented. We don't have anyone or any group who manages data centrally. It is critical that we develop an action plan for the organizational management of data." Pointing to Bob, she continued, "I have invited Bob to brief us on data administration and present his proposal for solving our data management problem. It's all yours, Bob."

Introduction

In the information age, data are the lifeblood of every organization and need to be properly managed to retain their value to the organization. The importance of data as a key organizational resource has been emphasized throughout this book. Data administration is the management of organizational data stores.

Information technology permits organizations to capture, organize, and maintain a greater variety of data. These data can be hard (e.g., financial or production figures) or soft (e.g., management reports, correspondence, voice conversations, and video). If these data are to be used in the organization, they must be managed just as diligently as accounting information. *Data administration* is the common term applied to the task of managing or-

---

1. She had certainly waited a long time to use this word, learned when studying for the university admission exam.

ganizational memory. Although common, basic management principles apply to most kinds of organizational data stores, the discussion in this chapter refers primarily to databases.

CERN's grid computer

Geneva-based CERN, the world's biggest particle physics center, assists scientists to figure out what constitutes matter and what holds it together. Engineers are building a giant grid to store and process the vast amounts of data the Large Hadron Collider (LHC) is expected to produce when it begins operations in mid-2007. The computing network encompasses more than 100 sites in 31 countries, most likely the world's largest international scientific grid. An estimated 15 TBytes of data will be produced each year. The grid links a vast network of computing and storage systems and provides scientists with access to the data and processing power when they need it.

Virtually no suitable commercial tools were available to build the grid. Therefore, CERN had to produce its own software using components and tools from many different sources. CERN must also come up with a framework that ensures that data and computing resources are available when needed but gives the various institutions independence to run their own projects and applications.

The grid currently has only about 5 percent of the processing capacity it will eventually need. CERN expects to reach 100 percent by adding new sites, by adding new resources at existing sites, and through improved processor speed and disk storage capacity.

Source: Niccolai, J. 2005. CERN readies world's biggest science grid. *Computerworld*, Mar. 21, www.computerworld.com/databasetopics/data/story/0,10801,100543,00.html.

Why manage data?

Data are constantly generated in every act and utterance of every stakeholder (employee, shareholder, customer, or supplier) in relation to the organization. Some of these data are formal and structured, such as invoices, grade sheets, or bank withdrawals. A large amount of relatively unstructured data is generated too, such as feedback from customers. Much of the unstructured data generated in organizations, while potentially useful, are never captured and recorded.

Organizations typically begin maintaining systematic records for data most likely to impinge on their performance. Often, different departments or individuals would like to maintain records for the same data. For instance, you may have experienced completing multiple-copy forms, perhaps forms with half a dozen copies. Each copy was required by a different functional group or department. The same data may be used in different ways by each department, and so each department may adopt a different system of organizing the data. Over time, an organization accumulates a great deal of redundant data, which demands considerable, needless administrative overhead for its maintenance. Inconsistencies may begin to emerge between the various forms of the same data. A department may incorrectly enter some data, which could result in embarrassment at best or a serious financial loss for the organization at worst.

When data are fragmented across several departments or individuals, and especially when there is personnel turnover, data may not be accessible when most needed. This is nearly as serious a problem as not having any data. Yet another motivation is that effective data management can greatly simplify and assist in the identification of new information system application development opportunities. Also, poor data management can result in breaches of security. Valuable information may be revealed to competitors or antagonists.

In summary, the problems arising from poor data management are the following:

❖ The same data may be represented through multiple, inconsistent definitions.
❖ There may be inconsistencies among different representations.
❖ Essential data may be missing from the database.
❖ Data may be inaccurate or incomplete.
❖ Some data may never be entered into the database and thus are effectively lost to the organization.
❖ There may be no way of knowing how to locate data when they are needed.

The overall goal of data administration is to prevent the occurrence of these problems by enabling users to access the data they need in the format most suitable for achieving their organizational goals and by ensuring the integrity of organizational databases.

Management of the database environment

In many large organizations, there is a formal data administration function to manage corporate data. The relationship between these components is shown in Figure 20-1.

Databases

A database management system (DBMS) can manage multiple databases covering different aspects of an organization's activities. When a database has multiple users, it may be designed to meet all their requirements, even though a specific user may need only a portion of the data contained within the database. For instance, a finished-goods database may be accessed by Production and Finance, as well as Marketing. It may contain cost information that is accessible by Production and Finance but not by Marketing. It may contain pricing information that is accessible by Finance and Marketing but not by Production.

Interface

The user interface consists of screen formats, menus, icons, and command languages that enable users to direct the system to manipulate data. Users may range from casual novices, who need to be insulated from the underlying complexity of the data, to expert applica-

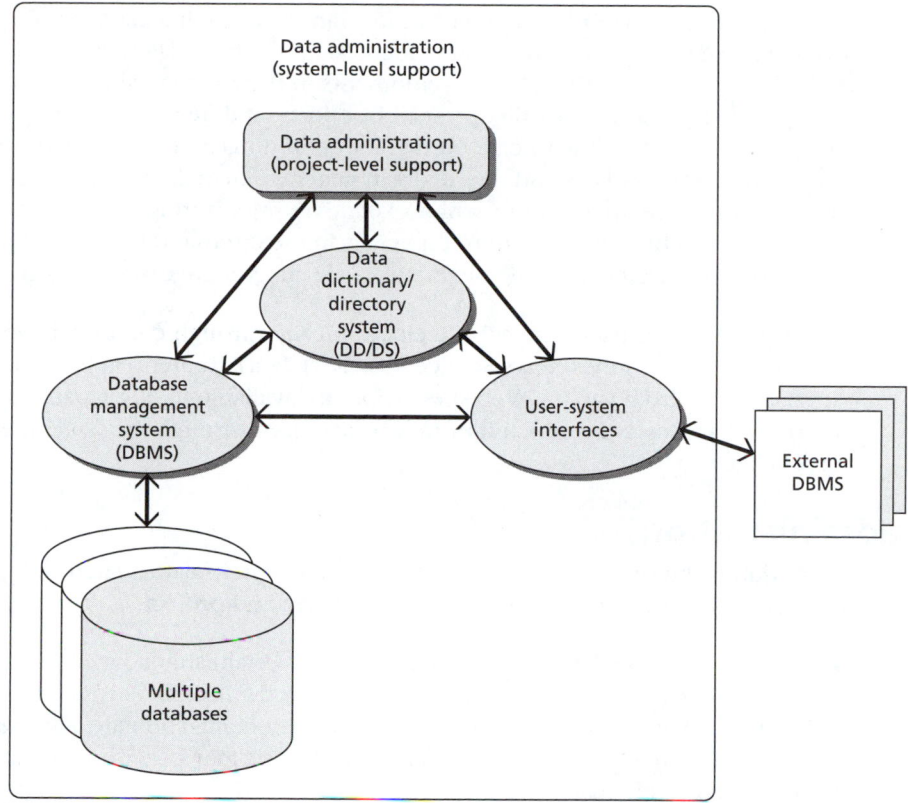

Figure 20-1. Management of the database environment

tion developers, who manipulate the data using programming languages or other data-handling tools.

Data dictionary

A data dictionary is a reference repository containing *metadata* (i.e., *data about data*) that is stored in the database. Among other things, the data dictionary contains a list of all the databases; their component parts and detailed descriptions such as field sizes, data types, and data validation information for data entry purposes; authorized users and their access privileges; and ownership details.

A data dictionary is a map of the data in organizational data stores. It permits the data administration staff and users to document the database, design new applications, and redesign the database if necessary. The data dictionary/directory system (DD/DS), itself a DBMS, is software for managing the data dictionary.

External databases

For organizations to remain competitive in a rapidly changing marketplace, access to data from external sources is becoming increasingly critical. Research and development groups need access to the latest developments in their technical fields and need to track information such as patents filed, research reports, and new product releases. Marketing departments need access to data on market conditions and competitive situations as reported in various surveys and the media in general. Financial data regarding competitors and customers are important to senior executives. Monitoring political situations may be critical to many business decisions, especially in the international business arena. Such external data are often delivered to executives via an executive information system (EIS).

Extensive external data are available electronically through commercial information services such as Dow Jones News Service (financial data), Reuters (news), and LEXIS-NEXIS (legal data), or from various Web sites. Tools are available to download external data into internal databases, from which they may be accessed through the same interface as for internal data.

Data administration

Data administration is responsible for the management of data-related activities. There are two levels of data administration activities: system and project.

System-level administration is concerned with establishing overall policies and procedures for the management and use of data in the organization. Formulating a data strategy and specifying an information architecture for the organization are also system-level data administration functions. System-level responsibilities may cover both electronic and non-electronic corporate data.

Project-level administration deals more with the specifics, such as optimizing specific databases for operational efficiency, establishing and implementing database access rights, creating new databases, and monitoring database use.

In general, the system-level function takes a broader perspective of the role played by data in achieving business objectives, while the project-level function is more concerned with the actual mechanics of database implementation and operation. We use the term *data administration* to refer to both functional levels.

Data administration functions and roles

The functions of data administration may be accomplished through multiple roles or job titles such as database administrator, database developer, database consultant, and database analyst, collectively referred to as the data administration staff. A single role could be responsible for both system and project levels of data administration, or responsibility may be distributed among several persons, depending on the size of the organization, the number of database applications, and the number of users.

In addition, data administration could be carried out entirely in a client department. For instance, a client could be the data steward responsible for managing all corporate data for some critical business-related entity or activity (e.g., a customer, a production facility, a supplier, a division, a project, or a product) regardless of the purpose for which the data are used. **Data stewards** coordinate planning of the data for which they are responsible. Tasks include data definition, quality control and improvement, security, and access authorization. The data steward's role is especially important today because of the growing emphasis on customer satisfaction and cross-functional teams. Data stewardship seeks to align data management with organizational strategy.

Database levels

Databases may be maintained at several levels of use: personal, workgroup (e.g., project team or department), and organizational. The more users, the greater the complexity of both the database and its management.

Personal databases in the form of diaries, planners, and name and address books have existed for a long time. The availability of notebook computers and personal digital assistants (PDAs) has made it convenient to maintain electronic personal databases. Personal databases may not require a sophisticated DBMS. Indeed, versatile software tools known as personal information managers (PIMs) are often better suited for the task of storing personal information.

Workgroup databases cannot be as idiosyncratic, because they are shared by many people. Managing them requires more planning and coordination to ensure that all users' needs are addressed and data integrity is maintained. Organizational databases are the most complex in terms of both structure and need for administration. All databases, regardless of scope or level, require administration.

Managing a personal database is relatively simple. Typically, the user of the database is also its developer and administrator. Issues such as access rights and security are settled quite easily, perhaps by the user locking the computer when away from the desk. Managing workgroup databases is more complex. Controls almost certainly will be needed to restrict access to certain data. On the other hand, some data will need to be available to many group members. Also, responsibility for backup and recovery must be established. Small workgroups may jointly perform both system- and project-level data administration activities. Meetings may be a way to coordinate system-level data administration activities, and project-level activities may be distributed among different workgroup members. Larger groups may have a designated data administrator, who is also a group member.

Managing organizational databases is typically a full-time job requiring special skills to work with complex database environments. In large corporations, several persons may handle data administration, each carrying out different data administration activities. System-level data administration activities may be carried out by a committee led by a senior IS executive (who may be a full- or part-time data administrator), while project-level data administration activities may be delegated to individual data administration staff members.

System-level data administration functions

System-level data administration functions, which may be performed by one or more persons, are summarized in Table 20-1.

Table 20-1: System-level data administration functions

Planning
Developing data standards and policies
Defining XML data schemas
Maintaining data integrity
Resolving data conflict
Managing the DBMS
Establishing and maintaining the data dictionary
Selecting hardware and software
Managing external databases
Benchmarking
Internal marketing

Planning

Because data are a strategic corporate resource, planning is perhaps the most critical data administration function. A key planning activity is creating an organization's information architecture, which includes all the major data entities and the relationships between them. It indicates which business functions and applications access which entities. An information architecture also may address issues such as how data will be transmitted and where they will be stored. Since an information architecture is an organization's overall strategy for data and applications, it should dovetail with the organization's long-term plans and objectives.

Developing data standards and policies

Whenever data are used by more than one person, there must be standards to govern their use. Data standards become especially critical in organizations using heterogeneous hardware and software environments. Why could this become a problem? For historical reasons, different departments may use different names and field sizes for the same data item. These differences can cause confusion and misunderstanding. For example, "sale date" may have different meanings for the legal department (e.g., the date the contract was signed) and the sales department (e.g., the date of the sales call). Furthermore, the legal department may store data in the form *yyyy-mm-dd* and the sales department as *dd-mm-yy*. Data administration's task is to develop and publish data standards so that field names are clearly defined, and a field's size and format are consistent across the enterprise.

Furthermore, some data items may be more important to certain departments or divisions. For instance, customer data are often critical to the marketing department. It is useful in such cases to appoint a data steward from the appropriate functional area as custodian for these data items.

Policies need to be established regarding who can access and manipulate which data, when, and from where. For instance, should employees using their home computers be allowed to access corporate data? If such access is permitted, then data security and risk exposure must be considered and adequate data safeguards implemented.

Defining XML data schemas

Data administration is responsible for defining data schemas for data exchange within the organization and among business partners. This is a new role that will be more important in the next few years as organizations adopt XML as the data exchange standard. Data administration is also responsible for keeping abreast of industry schema standards so that the organization is in conformance with common practice. Advanced adopters of XML may even work on defining a data schema for an industry.

Maintaining data integrity

Data must be made available when needed, but only to authorized users. The data management aspects of data integrity are discussed at length in Chapter 19.

Resolving data conflict

Data administration involves the custodianship of data *owned* or originating in various organizational departments or functions, and conflicts are bound to arise at some point. For instance, one department may be concerned about a loss of security when another department is allowed access to its data. In another instance, one group may feel that another is contaminating a commonly used data pool because of inadequate data validation practices. Incidents like these, and many others, require management intervention and settlement through a formal or informal process of discussion and negotiation in which all parties are assured of a fair hearing. Data administration facilitates negotiation and mediates dispute resolution.

Managing the DBMS

While project-level data administration is concerned more directly with the DBMS, the performance and characteristics of the DBMS ultimately impinge on the effectiveness of the system-level data administration function. It is, therefore, important to monitor characteristics of the DBMS. Over a period, benchmark statistics for different projects or applications will need to be compiled. These statistics are especially useful for addressing user complaints regarding the performance of the DBMS, which may then lead to design changes, tuning of the DBMS, or additional hardware.

Database technology is rapidly advancing. For example, relational DBMSs are continually being extended. Keeping track of developments, evaluating their benefits, and deciding on converting to new database environments are critical system-level data administration functions that can have strategic implications for the corporation.

Establishing and maintaining the data dictionary

A data dictionary is a key data administration tool that provides details of data in the organizational database and how they are used (e.g., by various application programs). If modifications are planned for the database (e.g., changing the size of a column in a table), the data dictionary helps to determine which applications will be affected by the proposed changes.

More sophisticated data dictionary systems are closely integrated with specific database products. They are updated automatically whenever the structure of the underlying database is changed.

Selecting hardware and software

Evaluating and selecting the appropriate hardware and software for an organizational database are critical responsibilities with strategic organizational implications. These are not easy tasks, because of the dynamic nature of the database industry, the continually changing variety of available hardware and software products, and the rapid pace of change within many organizations. Today's excellent choice might become tomorrow's nightmare if, for instance, the vendor of a key database component goes out of business or ceases product development.

Extensive experience and knowledge of the database software business and technological progress in the field are essential to making effective database hardware and software decisions. The current and future needs of the organization need to be assessed in terms of capacity as well as features. Relevant questions include the following:

❖ How many users will simultaneously access the database?
❖ Will the database need to be geographically distributed? If so, what is the degree to which the database will be replicated, and what is the nature of database replication that is supported?
❖ What is the maximum size of the database?
❖ How many transactions per second can the DBMS handle?
❖ What kind of support for online transaction processing is available?
❖ What are the initial and ongoing costs of using the product?
❖ Can the database be extended to include new data types?
❖ What is the extent of training required, who can provide it, and what are the associated costs?

DBMS selection should cover technical, operational, and financial considerations. An organization's selection criteria are often specified in a request for proposal (RFP). This document is sent to a short list of potential vendors, who are invited to respond with a software or hardware/software proposal outlining how their product or service meets each criterion in the RFP. Visits to current user sites are usually desirable to gain confirming evidence of a vendor's claims. The final decision should be based on the manner and degree to which each vendor's proposal satisfies these criteria.

Skill builder

A small nonprofit organization has asked for your help in selecting a relational database management system (RDBMS) for general-purpose management tasks. Because of budget limitations, it is very keen to adopt an open source RDBMS. Search the Web to find at least two open source RDBMSs, compare the two systems, and make a recommendation to the organization.

Benchmarking

Benchmarking, the comparison of alternative hardware and software combinations, is an important step in the selection phase. Because benchmarking is an activity performed by many IS units, the IS community gains if there is one group that specializes in rigorous benchmarking of a wide range of systems. The Transaction Processing Council (TPC)[2] is the IS profession's Consumer Union. TPC has established benchmarks for a variety of business situations. Here we consider four benchmarks that are useful for data managers.

TPC-C

Many data managers are concerned with the efficiency of transaction processing systems. The TPC-C test simulates the principal transactions of an order-entry environment. These transactions include entering and delivering orders, recording payments, checking the status of orders, and monitoring the level of stock at warehouses. TPC-C test results are measured in transactions per minute (tpm). A benchmark provides precise information for a clearly specified hardware/software combination.

TPC-H

The TPC-H (ad-*h*oc, decision support) benchmark describes a decision support environment where there is no prior knowledge of the queries to be executed. Given their unplanned nature, optimization of these queries cannot be built into the DBMS system, and query execution times can be very long.

TPC-R

TPC-R is a business *r*eporting and decision support benchmark. It assesses an environment where clients run a standard set of queries against a database system. Pre-knowledge of the queries is assumed, and the DBMS system can be optimized to run these standard queries very rapidly.

---

2. www.tpc.org

TPC-W

In late 1998, TPC introduced a Web Commerce benchmark (TPC-W) designed to represent any business (e.g., a retail store, airline reservation) that markets and sells over the Web. It also represents intranet environments that use Web-based transactions for internal operations. The benchmark is designed to measure the performance of systems supporting customers browsing, ordering, and conducting transaction-oriented business activities.

Executive tool-kit

The consulting firm Bain & Co. continually tracks the tools used by executives. Currently, managers are very keen on tools that help them get closer to customers. Many claim that "insufficient customer insight" is a major problem. Thus, it is not surprising that customer relationship management (CRM) is number two on the list of most popular tools. Top is strategic planning, and number three is benchmarking.

The biggest change in recent years has been the rise of tools that depend on information technology, such as CRM, supply chain management, and knowledge management. Underpinning all these tools is database technology, which is increasingly required to handle larger databases and higher transaction volumes.

Source: Anonymous. 2005. The cart pulling the horse. *The Economist* 375 (8421):53.

Managing external databases

Providing access to external databases has increased the level of complexity of data administration, which now has the additional responsibility of identifying information services that meet existing or potential managerial needs. Data administration must determine the quality of such data and the means by which they can be channeled into the organization's existing information delivery system. Costs of data may vary among vendors. Some may charge a flat monthly or annual fee, while others may have a usage charge. Data may arrive in a variety of formats, and data administration may need to make them adhere to corporate standards. Data from different vendors and sources may need to be integrated and presented in a unified format and on common screens, perhaps including them in an EIS.

Monitoring external data sources is critical because data quality may vary over time. Data administration must determine whether user needs are continuing to be met and data quality is being maintained. If they are not, a subscription may be canceled and an alternative vendor sought. Security is another critical problem. When corporate databases are connected to external communication links, there is a threat of hackers breaking into the system and gaining unauthorized access to confidential internal data. Also, corporate data may be contaminated by spurious data or even by viruses entering from external sources. Data administration must be cautious when incorporating external data into the database.

Internal marketing

Because IS applications can have a major impact on organizational performance, the IS function is becoming more proactive in initiating the development of new applications. Many users are not aware of what is possible with newly emergent technologies, and hence do not see opportunities to exploit these developments. Also, as custodian of organizational data, data administration needs to communicate its goals and responsibilities throughout the organization. People and departments need to be persuaded to share data that may be of value to other parts of the organization. There may be resistance to change when people are asked to switch to newly set data standards. In all these instances, data administration must be presented in a positive light to lessen resistance to change. Data administration needs to market internally its products and services to its customers.

Project-level data administration

At the project level, data administration focuses on the detailed needs of individual users and applications. It supports the development and use of a specific database system.

Systems development life cycle (SDLC)

Database development follows a fairly predictable sequence of steps or phases similar to the systems development life cycle for applications. This sequence is called the database development life cycle (DDLC). The database and application development life cycles together constitute the systems development life cycle (SDLC) described in Table 20-2.

Table 20-2: Systems development life cycle (SDLC)

Application development life cycle (ADLC)	Database development life cycle (DDLC)
Project planning	Project planning
Requirements definition	Requirements definition
Application design	Database design
Application construction	
Application testing	Database testing
Application implementation	Database implementation
Operations	Database usage
Maintenance	Database evolution

Application development involves the eight phases shown in Table 20-2. It commences with project planning, which, among other things, involves determining project feasibility and allocating the necessary personnel and material resources for the project. This is followed by requirements definition, which involves considerable interaction with clients to clearly specify the system. These specifications become the basis for a conceptual application design, which is then constructed through program coding and tested. Once the system is thoroughly tested, it is installed and user operations begin. Over time, changes may be needed to upgrade or repair the system, and this is called system maintenance.

The database development phases parallel application development. Data administration is responsible for the DDLC. Data are the focus of database development, rather than procedures or processes. Database construction is folded into the testing phase because database testing typically involves minimal effort. In systems with integrated data dictionaries, the process of constructing the data dictionary also creates the database shell (i.e., tables without data). While the sequence of phases in the cycle as presented is generally followed, there is often a number of iterations within and between steps. Data modeling is iterative, and the final database design evolves from many data modeling sessions. A previously unforeseen requirement may surface during the database design phase, and this may prompt a revision of the specifications completed in the earlier phase.

System development may proceed in three different ways:

1.   The database may be developed independently of applications, following only the DDLC steps.
2.   Applications may be developed for existing databases, following only the ADLC steps.
3.   Application and database development may proceed in parallel, with both simultaneously stepping through the ADLC and DDLC.

Consider each of these possibilities.

Database development may proceed independently of application development for a number of reasons. The database may be created for storing information that later may be used by an application or for ad hoc queries using a built-in query language. In another case, an existing database may undergo changes to meet changed business requirements. In such situations, the developer goes through the appropriate stages of the DDLC.

Application development may proceed based on an existing database. For instance, a personnel database may already exist to serve a set of applications, such as payroll. This database could be used as the basis for a new personnel benefits application, which must go through all the phases of the ADLC.

A new system requires both application and database development. Frequently, a new system will require creation of both a new database and applications. For instance, a computer manufacturer may start a new Web-based order sales division and wish to monitor its performance. The vice-president in charge of the division may be interested in receiving daily sales reports by product and by customer as well as a weekly moving sales trend analysis for the prior 10 weeks. This requires both the development of a new sales database as well as a new application for sales reporting. Here, the ADLC and DDLC are both used to manage development of the new system.

Database development roles

Database development involves several roles, chiefly those of developer, end user, and data administrator. The roles and their responsibilities are outlined in Table 20-3.

The database developer shoulders the bulk of the responsibility for developing data models and implementing the database. This can be seen in Table 20-3, where most of the cells in the database developer column are labeled "Does." The database developer does project planning, requirements definition, database design, database testing, and database implementation, and in addition, is responsible for database evolution.

The client's role is to establish the goals of a specific database project, provide the database developers with access to all information needed for project development, and review and regularly scrutinize the developer's work.

The data administrator's prime responsibilities are implementing and controlling, but the person also may be required to perform activities and consult. In some situations, the database developer is not part of the data administration staff and may be located in a user department, or may be an analyst from an IS project team. In these cases, the data administrator advises the developer on organizational standards and policies as well as provides specific technical guidelines for successful construction of a database. When the database developer is part of the data administration staff, developer and data administration activities may be carried out by the same person, or by the person(s) occupying the data administration role. In all cases, the data administrator should understand the larger business context in which the database will be used and should be able to relate business needs to specific technical capabilities and requirements.

Database development life cycle (DDLC)

Previously, we discussed the various roles involved in database development and how they may be assigned to different persons. In this section, we will assume that administration and development are carried out by the data administration staff, since this is the typical situation encountered in many organizations. The activities of developer and administrator, shown in the first two columns of Table 20-3, are assumed to be performed by data administration staff.

Table 20-3: Database development roles

Database development phase	Database developer	Data administrator	Client
Project planning	Does	Consults	Provides information
Requirements definition	Does	Consults	Provides requirements
Database design	Does	Consults Data integrity	Validates data models
Database testing	System and client testing	Consults Data integrity	Testing
Database implementation	System-related activities	Consults Data integrity	Client activities
Database usage	Consults	Data integrity monitoring	Uses
Database evolution	Does	Change control	Provides additional requirements

Now, let us consider data administration project-level support activities in detail (see Figure 20-2). These activities are discussed in terms of the DDLC phase they support.

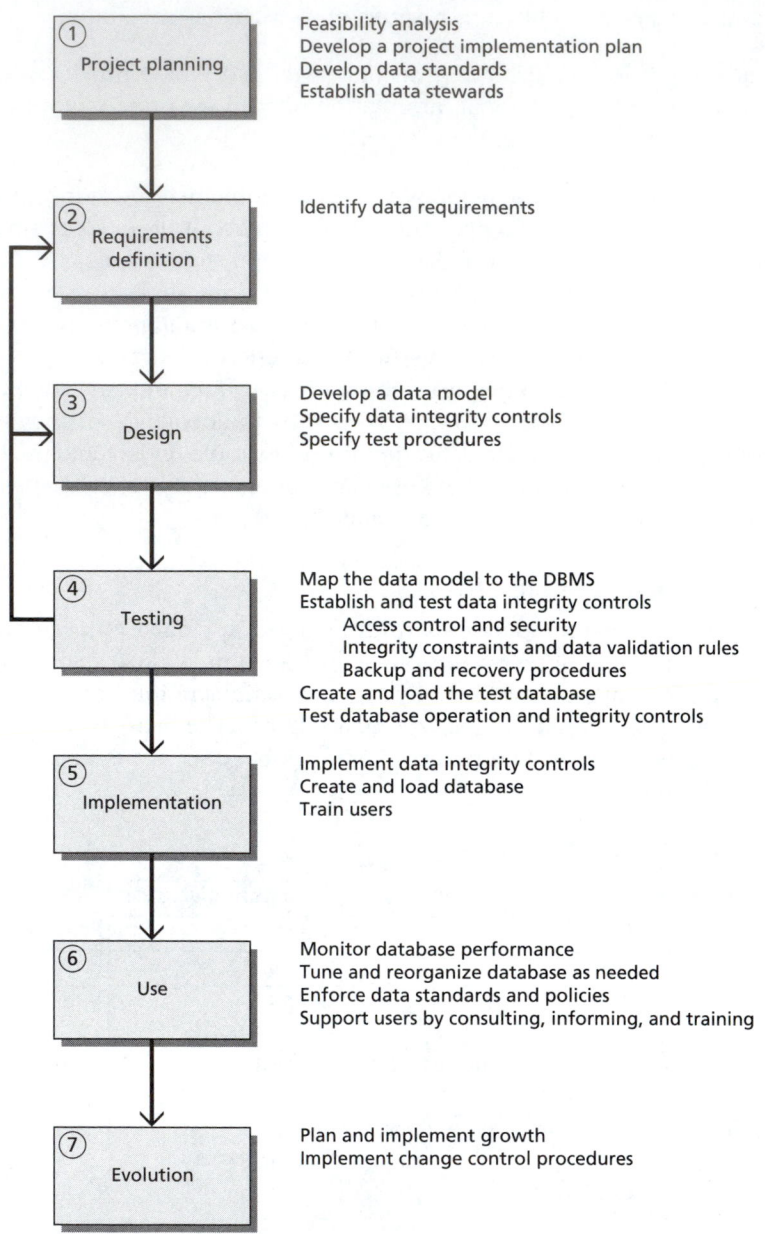

Figure 20-2. Database development life cycle

Database *project planning*

Database project planning includes establishing project goals, determining project feasibility (financial, technical, and operational), creating an implementation plan and schedule, assigning project responsibilities (including data stewards), and establishing standards. All project stakeholders, including users, senior management, and developers, are involved in planning. They are included for their knowledge as well as to gain their commitment to the project.

Requirements *definition*

During requirements definition, users and developers establish requirements and develop a mutual understanding of what the new system will deliver. Data are defined and the resulting definitions stored in the data dictionary. Requirements definition generates documentation that should serve as an unambiguous reference for database development. Although in theory the users are expected to *sign-off* on the specifications and accept the developed database as is, users' needs may actually change in practice. Users may gain greater understanding of their requirements, and business conditions may change. Consequently, the original specifications may require revision. In Figure 20-2, the arrows connecting phase 4 (testing) and phase 3 (design) to phase 2 (requirements definition) indicate that modeling and testing may identify revisions to the database specification, and these amendments are then incorporated into the design.

Database *design*

Conceptual and internal models of the database are developed during database design. Conceptual design, or data modeling, is discussed extensively in Section 2 of this book. Database design should also include specification of procedures for testing the database. Any additional controls for ensuring data integrity are also specified. The external model should be checked and validated by the user.

Database *testing*

Database testing requires previously developed specifications and models to be tested using the intended DBMS. Users are often asked to provide operational data to support testing the database with realistic transactions. Testing should address a number of key questions.

- ❖ Does the DBMS support all the operational and security requirements?
- ❖ Is the system able to handle the expected number of transactions per second?
- ❖ How long does it take to process a realistic mix of queries?

Testing assists in making early decisions regarding the suitability of the selected DBMS. Another critical aspect of database testing is verifying data integrity controls. Testing may include checking backup and recovery procedures, access control, and data validation rules.

Database implementation

Testing is complete when the users and developers are extremely confident the system meets specified needs. Data integrity controls are implemented, operational data are loaded (including historical data, if necessary), and database documentation is finalized. Users are then trained to operate the system.

Database use

Users may need considerable support as they learn and adapt to the system. Monitoring database performance is critical to keeping users satisfied; enables the data administrator to anticipate problems even before the users begin to notice and complain about them, and tune the system to meet users' needs; and also helps to enforce data standards and policies during the initial stages of database implementation.

Database evolution

Since organizations cannot afford to stand still in today's dynamic business environment, business needs are bound to change over time, perhaps even after a few months. Data administration should be prepared to meet the challenge of change. Minor changes, such as changes in display formats, or performance improvements, may be continually requested. These have to be attended to on an ongoing basis. Other evolutionary changes may emerge from constant monitoring of database use by the data administration staff. Implementing these evolutionary changes involves repeating phases 3 to 6 of Figure 20-2. Significant business changes may merit a radical redesign of the database. Major redesign may require repeating all phases of the DDLC.

Data administration interfaces

Data administration is increasingly a key corporate function, and it requires the existence of established channels of communication with various organizational groups. The key data administration interfaces are with clients, management, development staff, and computer operations. The central position of the data administration staff in Figure 20-3 reflects the liaison role that it plays in managing databases. Each of the groups has a different focus and different terminology and jargon. Data administration should be able to communicate effectively with all participants. For instance, operations staff will tend to focus on technical, day-to-day issues, to which management is likely to pay less attention. These different focuses can, and frequently do, lead to conflicting views and expectations among the different groups. Good interpersonal skills are a must for data administration staff in order to deal with a variety of conflict-laden situations. Data administration, therefore, needs a balance of people, technical, and business skills for effective execution of its tasks.

Data administration probably will communicate most frequently with computer operations and development staff, somewhat less frequently with users, and least frequently with management. These differences, however, have little to do with the relative importance of communicating with each group. The interactions between the data administration staff and each of the four groups are discussed next.

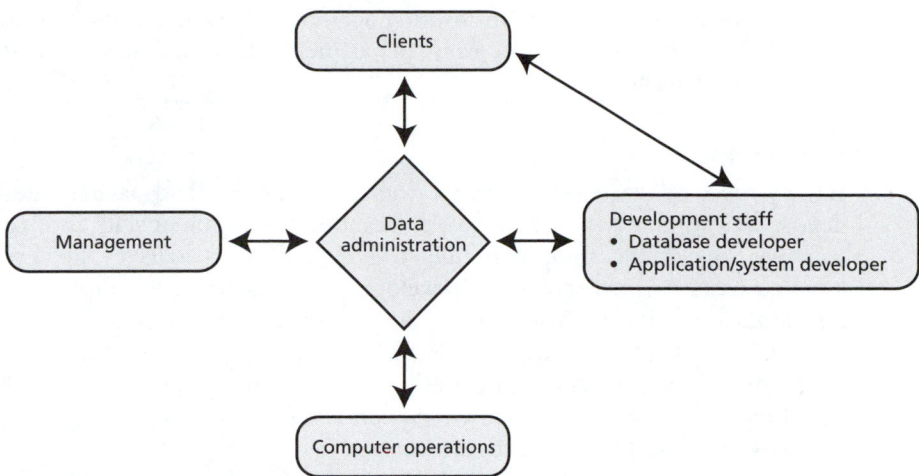

Figure 20-3. Major data administration interfaces

Management

Management sets the overall business agenda for data administration, which must ensure that its actions directly contribute to the achievement of organizational goals. In particular, management establishes overall policy guidelines, approves data administration budgets, evaluates proposals, and champions major changes. For instance, if the data administration staff is interested in introducing new technology, management may request a formal report on the anticipated benefits of the proposed expenditure.

Interactions between the data administration staff and management may focus on establishing and evolving the information architecture for the organization. In some instances, this may involve the introduction of a new technology that could fundamentally transform the organization. For example, Lotus Notes was introduced into a management consulting company on an enterprisewide basis. The introduction of Notes was a strategic technology decision that transformed the company's information architecture because it allowed consultants around the world to exchange information and gain fast access to in-house expertise. This capability became a significant source of competitive advantage. Such technological change never would have occurred without management's approval and wholehearted support.

Clients

On an ongoing basis, most clients will be less concerned with architectural issues and will focus on their personal needs. Data administration must determine what data should be collected and stored, how they should be validated to ensure integrity, and in what form and frequency they should be made available. For instance, the chief financial officer may use the existing EIS to access financial data from external data vendors.

Typically, the data administration staff is responsible for managing the database, while the data supplier is responsible for ensuring accuracy. This may cause conflict, however, if there are multiple users from separate departments. If conflict does arise, data administration has to arbitrate.

Development staff

Having received strategic directions from management, and having determined clients' needs, data administration next works with the development staff, both application and database developers, in order to fulfill the organization's goals for the new system. On an ongoing basis, this may consist of developing specifications for implementation. Data administration works on an advisory basis with systems development, providing inputs on the database aspects. For instance, data administration is responsible for establishing standards for program/database interfaces and making developers aware of these standards. Developers may need to be told which commands may be used in their application programs and which databases they can access.

In many organizations, database development is part of data administration, and it has a very direct role in database design and implementation. In such instances, communication between data administration and database development is within the group. In other organizations, database development is not part of data administration, and communication is between groups.

Computer operations

The focus of computer operations is on the physical hardware, procedures, schedules and shifts, staff assignments, physical security of data, and execution of programs. Data administration responsibilities include establishing and monitoring procedures for operating the database. The data administration staff needs to establish and communicate database backup, recovery, and archiving procedures to computer operations. Also, the scheduling of new database and application installations needs to be coordinated with computer operations personnel.

Computer operations provide data administration with operational statistics and exception reports. These data are used by data administration to ensure that corporate database objectives are being fulfilled.

Communication

The diverse parties with which data administration communicates often see things differently. This can lead to misunderstandings and results in systems that fail to meet requirements. Part of the problem arises from a difference in perspective and approaches to viewing database technology.

Management is interested in understanding how implementing database technology will contribute to strategic goals. In contrast, users are interested in how the proposed database and accompanying applications will affect their daily work. Developers are concerned with translating management and clients' needs into conceptual models and converting these into tables and applications. Operations staff are concerned primarily with efficient daily management of DBMS, computer hardware, and software.

Data models can serve as a common language for bridging the varying goals of users, developers, management, and operational staff. A data model can reduce the ambiguity inherent in verbal communications and thereby ensure that users' needs are more closely met and all parties are satisfied with the results. A data model provides a common meeting point and language for understanding the needs of each group.

Data administration does not work in isolation. It must communicate successfully with all its constituents in order to be successful. The capacity to understand and correctly translate the needs of each stakeholder group is the key to competent data administration.[3]

Data administration tools

Several computer-based tools have emerged to support data administration. There are five major classes of tools: data dictionary, DBMS, performance monitoring, computer-aided software engineering (CASE), and groupware tools. Each of these tools is now examined and its role in supporting data administration considered. We focus on how these tools support the DDLC (see Figure 20-2). Note, however, that groupware is not shown in Table 20-4 because it is useful in all phases of the life cycle.

Table 20-4: Data administration tool use during the DDLC

Database development phase	Data dictionary (DD)	DBMS	Performance monitoring	Case tools
1. Project planning tools	Document Data map Design aid			Estimation
2. Requirements definition	Document Design aid			Document Design aid
3. Database design	Document Data map Design aid Schema generator			Document Design aid Data map
4. Database testing	Data map Design aid Schema generator	Define, create, test, data integrity	Impact analysis	Data generator Design aid
5. Database implementation	Document Change control	Data integrity Implement Design	Monitor Tune	

3. For a more extensive discussion and guidance on improving your interpersonal skills in relation to IS development, see Bostrom (1989), Cause and Weinberg (1989), and Weinberg (1986). There are many books that discuss communication skills and serve as a useful source for self-development. Some of these are Doyle and Strauss (1976) and Kayser (1990). Full details are provided at the end of the chapter.

Table 20-4: Data administration tool use during the DDLC (continued)

Database development phase	Data dictionary (DD)	DBMS	Performance monitoring	Case tools
6. Database usage	Document Data map Schema generator Change control	Provide tools for retrieval and update Enforce integrity controls and procedures	Monitor Tune	
7. Database evolution	Document Data map Change control	Redefine	Impact analysis	

Data administration staff, users, and computer operations all require information about organizational databases. Ideally, such information should be stored in one central repository. This is the role of the DD/DS, perhaps the main data administration tool. Thus, we start our discussion with this tool.

Data dictionary/directory system (DD/DS)

The DD/DS, a database application that manages the data dictionary, is an essential tool for data administration. The DD/DS is the repository for organizational metadata, such as data definitions, relationships, and privileges. The DBMS manages data, and the DD/DS manages data about data. The DD/DS also uses the data dictionary to generate table definitions or schema required by the DBMS and application programs to access databases.

Users and data administration can utilize the DD/DS to ask questions about characteristics of data stored in organizational databases such as

❖ What are the names of all tables for which the user Todd has delete privileges?
❖ Where does the data item *customer number* appear or is used?

The report for the second query could include the names and tables, transactions, reports, display screens, users' names, and application programs.

In some systems, such as a relational DBMS, the catalog (see page 279) performs some of the functions of a DD/DS, although the catalog does not contain the same level of detail. The catalog essentially contains data about tables, columns, and owners of tables, whereas the DD/DS can include data about applications, forms, transactions, and many other aspects of the system. Consequently, a DD/DS is of greater value to data administration.

Although there is no standard format for data stored in a data dictionary, several features are common across systems. For example, a data dictionary for a typical relational database environment would contain descriptions of the following:

❖ All columns that are defined in all tables of all databases. The data dictionary stores specific data characteristics such as name, data type, display format, internal storage format, validation rules, and integrity constraints. It indicates where a column is used and by whom.

❖ All relationships among data elements, what elements are involved, and characteristics of relationships, such as cardinality and degree.

❖ All defined databases, including who created each database, the date of creation, and where the database is located.

❖ All tables defined in all databases. The data dictionary is likely to store details of who created the table, the date of creation, primary key, and the number of columns.

❖ All indexes defined for each of the database tables. For each of the indexes, the DBMS stores data such as the index name, location, specific index characteristics, and creation date.

❖ All users and their access authorizations for various databases.

❖ All programs that access the database, including screen formats, report formats, application programs, and SQL queries.

A data dictionary can be useful for both systems and project level data administration activities. The five major uses of a data dictionary are the following:

1. Documentation support: recording, classifying, and reporting metadata.
2. Data maps: a map of available data for data administration staff and users. A data map allows users to discover what data exist, what they mean, where they are stored, and how they are accessed.
3. Design aid: documenting the relationships between data entities and performing impact analysis.
4. Schema generation: automatic generation of data definition statements needed by software systems such as the DBMS and application programs.
5. Change control: setting and enforcing standards, evaluating the impact of proposed changes, and implementing amendments, such as adding new data items.

Database management systems (DBMSs)

The DBMS is the primary tool for maintaining database integrity and making data available to users. Availability means making data accessible to whoever needs them, when and where they need them, and in a meaningful form. Maintaining database integrity implies the implementation of control procedures to achieve the three goals discussed in Chapter 19: protecting existence, maintaining quality, and ensuring confidentiality. In terms of the DDLC life cycle (see Figure 20-2), data administration uses, or helps others to use, the DBMS to create and test new databases, define data integrity controls, modify existing database definitions, and provide tools for users to retrieve and update databases. Since much of this book has been devoted to DBMS functions, we limit our discussion to reviewing its role as a data administration tool.

Performance monitoring tools

Monitoring the performance of DBMS and database operations by gathering usage statistics is essential to improving performance, enhancing availability, and promoting database evolution. As shown in Table 20-4, monitoring tools are used to collect statistics and improve database performance during the implementation and use stages of the DDLC. Monitoring tools can also be used to collect data to evaluate design choices during testing.

Many database factors can be monitored and a variety of statistics gathered. Monitoring growth in the number of rows in each table can reveal trends that are helpful in projecting future needs for physical storage space. Database access patterns can be scrutinized to record data such as

- ❖ Type of function requested: query, insert, update, or delete
- ❖ Response time (elapsed time from query to response)
- ❖ Number of disk accesses
- ❖ Identification of user
- ❖ Identification of error conditions

The observed patterns help to determine performance enhancements. For example, these statistics could be used to determine which tables or files should be indexed. Since gathering statistics can result in some degradation of overall performance, it should be possible to turn the monitoring function on or off with regard to selected statistics.

CASE tools

A CASE tool, as broadly defined, provides automated assistance for systems development, maintenance, and project management activities. Data administration may use project management tools to coordinate all phases within the DDLC. The dictionary provided by CASE systems can be used to supplement the DD/DS, especially where the database development effort is part of a systems development project.

One of the most important components of a CASE tool is an extensive dictionary that tracks all objects created by systems designers. Database and application developers can use the CASE dictionary to store descriptions of data elements, application processes, screens, reports, and other relevant information. Thus, during the first three phases of the life cycle (see Figure 20-2), the CASE dictionary performs functions similar to a DD/DS. During stages 4 and 5, data from the CASE dictionary would be transferred, usually automatically, to the DD/DS.

Groupware

Groupware can be applied by data administration to support any of the DDLC phases shown in Figure 20-2. Groupware supports communication between people and thus enhances access to organizational memory residing within humans. As we have pointed out, data administration interfaces with four major groups during the DDLC: management, users, developers, and computer operations. Groupware supports interactions with all of these groups.

Data administration is a complex task involving a variety of technologies and the need to interact with, and satisfy the needs of, a diverse range of users. Managing such a complex environment demands the use of computer-based tools, which make data administration more manageable and effective. Software tools, such as CASE and groupware, can improve data administration.

Data integration

A common problem for many organizations is a lack of data integration, which can manifest in a number of ways:

❖ Different identifiers for the same instance of an entity (e.g., the same product with different codes in different divisions)

❖ The same, or what should be the same, data stored in multiple systems (e.g., a customer's name and address)

❖ Data for, or related to, a key entity stored in different databases (e.g., a customer's transaction history and profile stored in different databases)

❖ Different rules for computing the same business indicator (e.g., the Australian office computes net profit differently from the U.S. office)[4]

In Table 20-5, we see an example of a firm that practices data integration. Different divisions use the same numbers for parts, the same identifiers for customers, and have a common definition of sales date. In contrast, Table 20-6 shows the case of a firm where there is a lack of data integration. The different divisions have different identifiers for the same part and different codes for the same customer, as well as different definitions for the sales date. Imagine the problems this nonintegrated firm would have in trying to determine how much it sold to each of its customers in the last six months.

Table 20-5: Firm with data integration

	Red division	Blue division
partnumber (code for green widget)	27	27
customerid (code for UPS)	53	53
Definition of salesdate	The date the customer signs the order	The date the customer signs the order

Table 20-6: Firm without data integration

	Red division	Blue division
partnumber (code for green widget)	27	10056
customerid (code for UPS)	53	613
Definition of salesdate	The date the customer signs the order	The date the customer receives the order

---

4. For an excellent report on how Microsoft remedied some of its data integration problems, see Herbold, Robert J. 2002. Inside Microsoft: Balancing creativity and discipline. *Harvard Business Review* 80 (1):72–79.

Skill builder

Complete the data integration lab exercise described on the book's Web site (Lab exercises > Data integration).

Not surprisingly, many organizations seek to increase their degree of data integration so that they can improve the accuracy of managerial reporting, reduce the cost of managing data, and improve customer service by having a single view of the customer.

There are several goals of data integration:

1. A standard meaning for all data elements within the organization (e.g., customer acquisition date is the date on which the customer first purchased a product)
2. A standard format for each and every data element (e.g., all dates are stored in the format yyyymmdd and reported in the format yyyy-mm-dd)
3. A standard coding system (e.g., female is coded "f" and male is coded "m")
4. A standard measurement system (e.g., all measurements are stored in metric format and reported in the client's preferred system)
5. A single corporate data model, or a least a single data model for each major business entity

These are challenging goals for many organizations and sometimes take years to achieve. Many organizations are still striving to achieve the fifth, and most difficult, goal of a single corporate data model. Sometimes, however, data integration might not be a goal worth pursuing if the costs outweigh the benefits.[5]

The two major factors that determine the desirable degree of data integration between organizational units are unit interdependence and environmental turbulence. There is a high level of interdependence between organizational units when they affect each other's success (for example, the output of one unit is used by the other). As a result of the commonality of some of their goals, these units will gain from sharing standardized information. Data integration will make it easier for them to coordinate their activities and manage their operations. Essentially, data integration means that they will speak a common information language. When there is low interdependence between two organizational units, then the gains from data integration are usually outweighed by the bureaucratic costs and delays of trying to enforce standards. If two units have different approaches to marketing and manufacturing, then a high level of data integration is unlikely to be beneficial. They gain little from sharing data because they have so little in common.

When organizational units operate in highly turbulent environments, they need flexibility to be able to handle rapid change. They will often need to change their information sys-

---

5. This discussion is based on Goodhue, D. L., M. D. Wybo, and L. J. Kirsch. 1992. The impact of data integration on the costs and benefits of information systems. *MIS Quarterly* 16 (3):293–311.

tems quickly to respond to new competitive challenges. Forcing such units to comply with organizational data integration standards will slow down their ability to create new systems and thus threaten their ability to respond in a timely fashion.

Firms have three basic data integration strategies based on the level of organizational unit interdependence and environmental turbulence (see Figure 20-4).When unit interdependence is low and environmental turbulence high, a unit should settle for a low level of data integration, such as common financial reporting and human resources systems. Moderate data integration might mean going beyond the standard financial reporting and human resources system to include a common customer database. If unit independence is high and turbulence high, then moderate data integration would further extend to those areas where the units overlap (e.g., if they share a manufacturing system, this would be a target for data integration). A high level of data integration, a desirable target when unit interdependence is high and environmental turbulence low, means targeting common systems for both units.

		Unit interdependence	
		Low	High
Environmental	High	Low	Moderate
turbulence	Low	Moderate	High

Figure 20-4. Target level of data integration between organizational units

Skill builder

1. Global Electronics has nine factories in the United States and Asia producing components for the computer industry, and each has its own information systems. Although there is some specialization, production of any item can be moved to another factory, if required. What level of data integration should the company seek, and what systems should be targeted for integration?

2. European Radio, the owner of 15 FM radio stations throughout Europe, has just purchased an electronics retailing chain of 50 stores in Brazil. What level of data integration should the company seek, and what systems should be targeted for integration?

3. Australian Leather operates several tanneries in Thailand,[6] two leather goods manufacturing plants in Vietnam, and a chain of leather retailers in Australia and New Zealand. Recently, it purchased an entertainment park in Singapore. The various units have been assembled over the last five years, and many still operate their original information systems. What level of data integration should the company seek, and what systems should be targeted for integration?

---

6. A tannery converts raw animal hides into leather.

Organizing data administration

Data administration is essential to ensuring the availability and integrity of shared databases. To ensure that this function is properly performed, its importance must first be recognized. Then the necessary steps must be taken to integrate data administration formally into the organization. These steps include establishment of a data administration function, assigning data administration roles, and locating data administration in the formal organization. These steps are not necessarily carried out in sequence; indeed, there may be value in performing all three simultaneously. In most large organizations, all three steps have already been undertaken. Many smaller organizations, however, may have yet to embark on them. Even where all three steps have been completed, the second and third are continually monitored and reviewed because of rapid changes in current information technologies.

The mainframe-oriented, centralized database architecture of the past is being supplanted by Web-browser-based computing based on a distributed architecture. Both computing power and databases are being spread throughout the organization rather than being controlled by a central IS group. In many instances, databases are becoming locally managed by individual workgroups or departments. This transformation creates a need for data administration to be performed where workgroup or departmental databases are located rather than centrally. Where users and databases are linked by local area networks, there is a need for both local and central data administration. Central data administration is responsible for coordinating the functioning of the separate local database administrators.

Initiating data administration

Initially, the need for data administration is unlikely to be recognized by senior management; more likely, it is major data users or someone in the IS function who first recognizes the need for data administration. Establishing data administration typically involves convincing management of the importance of data administration and the need for a formal organizational function with assigned roles. A survey of data needs and practices in the organization is one approach to justifying establishment of data administration.

Data administration typically possesses very little organizational power. The power that it has derives from the extent to which senior management recognizes its importance. Management support is crucial because the function affects the generators and users of data throughout the organization.

Selecting data administration staff

If data administration is to be performed as an additional responsibility of existing IS or user staff, the nature and scope of duties must be detailed and clearly assigned to the nominated staff. If data administration requires full-time responsibility, either a data administrator is hired or someone from within the organization is reassigned. An internal hire may be more familiar with organizational needs but may not possess the necessary skills, and thus requires additional training. An external hire may have the necessary experience and skills to transform the organization but will have to learn how the organization operates.

An effective data administrator should possess a variety of interpersonal, business, and technical skills. For system-level support, there is a relatively greater emphasis on managerial and business skills. At the project level, a greater degree of technical ability is needed. In both cases, interpersonal and communication skills are essential.

Locating data administration in the organization

Throughout this chapter, we have spoken of data administration as a function or set of activities rather than as a department to emphasize that organizations can choose to locate the function in a variety of ways. The most common location for data administration is in the IS department. Where data administration is considered highly critical, there may be a separate data administration manager who reports to the CIO. The data administration staff is organized within this group (see Figure 20-5).

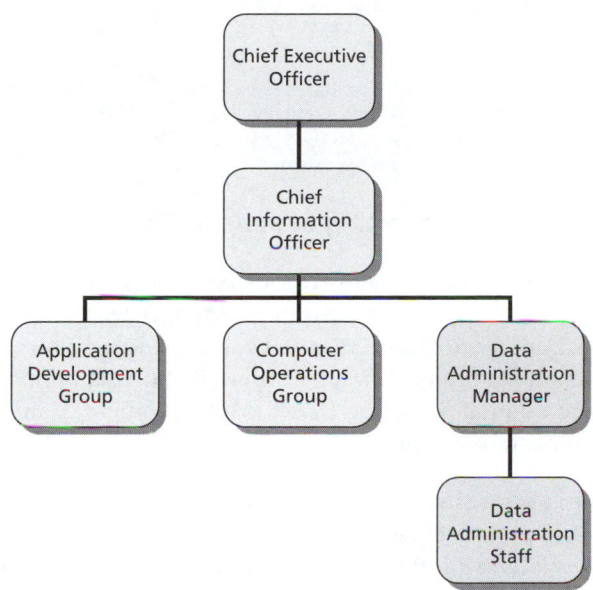

Figure 20-5. Data administration reporting to the CIO

In some organizations, data administration may be included as part of a larger group, such as support services, which may include the information center and help desk staff (see Figure 20-6). The data administration staff also could be located in application development, computer operations, or some other group reporting to the CIO.

A matrix organization, a very different approach from the structures described previously, is another choice for the location of data administration (see Figure 20-7). In a matrix organization, data administration staff belong to the data administration group in terms of the functions performed but are also members of specific project teams. Staff members

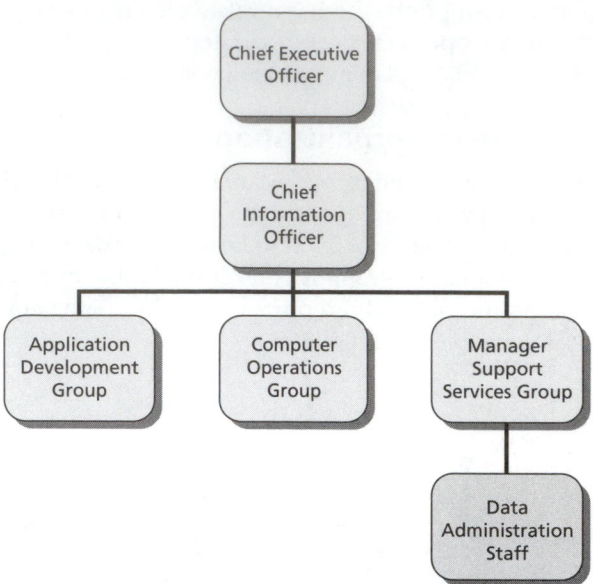

Figure 20-6. Data administration reporting to Support Services

are responsible to the project leader for all project-specific responsibilities and deliverables. At the same time, there is a data administration manager who coordinates the performance of data administration activities across all projects, and monitors and supervises data administration staff on all projects. Data administration staff report to individual project leaders for the duration of a specific DDLC while also being administratively supervised by the data administration manager.

A major benefit of a matrix organization is that data administration members are in close communication with other project personnel, and, consequently, the resulting database may be more closely integrated with the system under development and hence more effectively satisfy user needs. Furthermore, the data administration member may be able to draw on more resources when needed (from the manager and perhaps from other projects) because of the additional relationships outside of the project. Not all organizations, however, prefer to use this structure. A data administration member has, in effect, two supervisors, and this situation potentially can result in conflicts and affect performance and productivity.

In some instances, data administration is a staff function within the office of the CIO performed by an advisory committee drawn from within the IS function and user departments (Figure 20-8). This committee is concerned typically with system-level data administration issues. Within the IS department, the advisory committee may serve to advise and coordinate the data administration activities of project database staff. If the database technology is new to the organization, the committee may undertake database architectural planning

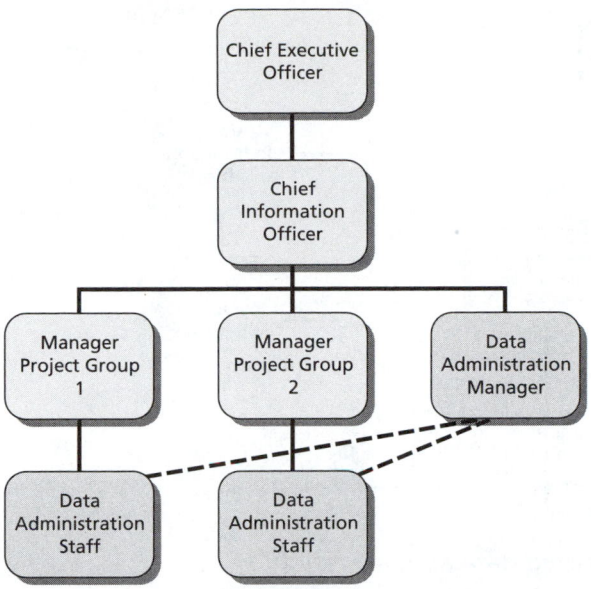

Figure 20-7. Matrix structure for data administration

and data administration policy development. Once a DBMS is implemented, a more formal and operational organizational structure is typically adopted. In workgroups or user departments, a data administration staff advisory committee helps to manage local databases in distributed database environments.

In decentralized database environments, data administration responsibilities also may be distributed among various departments, divisions, or workgroups. Local data administration reports to its respective workgroup heads while coordinating its relevant activities via a data administration manager located in the IS function (Figure 20-8). There are two different possibilities here. In one instance, perhaps in multiple relatively independent divisions, local data administration is fully responsible for local data administration, and the staff manager is mainly a consultant who coordinates the development and enforcement of organizational standards and provides expert advice to local staff when requested. In another instance (say, multiple offices within a single campus), local data administration may actually report to the staff data administration manager, who plans all local data administration activity together with local staff. In this case, the involvement and local responsibility of the data administration manager is far greater. The latter instance is an example of a true matrix organization, whereas in the former, the extradepartmental relationship is purely consultative.

The organizational designs described are encountered quite frequently but are not the only ways to organize data administration. Each situation demands a different way to organize, and the particular needs of the organization need to be fully considered before

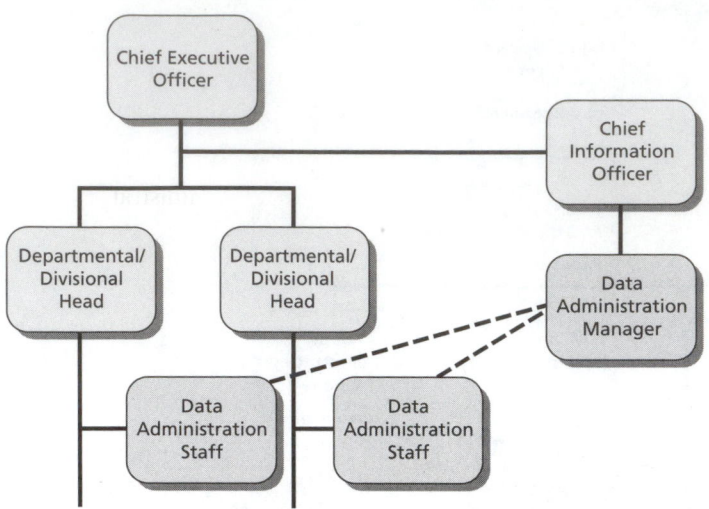

Figure 20-8. Decentralized data administration

adopting any particular structure. In most organizations, the nature, importance, and location of data administration change over time and are influenced by new technologies, organizational growth, and evolving patterns of database usage. It is important to remain alert to such changes and reorganize data administration when necessary to ensure that the organization's data requirements are constantly satisfied.

Summary

Data administration is the task of managing that part of organizational memory that involves electronically available data. Managing electronic data stores is important because key organizational decisions are based on information drawn from it, and it is necessary to ensure that reliable data are available when needed. Data administration is carried out at both the system level, which involves overall policies and alignment with organizational goals, and the project level, where the specific details of each database are handled. Key modules in data administration are the DBMS, the DD/DS, user interfaces, and external databases.

Data administration is a function performed by those with assigned organizational roles. Data administration may be carried out by a variety of persons either within the IS department or in user departments. Also, this function may occur at the personal, workgroup or organizational level.

Data administration involves communication with management, users, developers, and computer operations staff. It needs the cooperation of all four groups to perform its functions effectively. Since each group may hold very different perspectives, which could lead to conflicts and misunderstandings, it is important for data administration staff to possess superior communication skills. Successful data administration requires a combination of interpersonal, technical, and business skills.

Data administration is complex, and its success partly depends on a range of computer-based tools. Available tools include DD/DS, DBMS, performance monitoring tools, CASE tools, and groupware.

A variety of options are available for organizing data administration, and a choice has to be made based on the prevailing organizational context.

Key terms and concepts

Application development life cycle (ADLC)
Benchmark
Change agent
Computer-aided software engineering (CASE)
Data administration
Data dictionary
Data dictionary/directory system (DD/DS)
Data integrity
Data steward
Database administrator
Database developer

Database development life cycle (DDLC)
Database management system (DBMS)
External database
Groupware
Matrix organization
Performance monitoring
Project-level data administration
Request for proposal (RFP)
System-level data administration
Systems development life cycle (SDLC)
Transaction Processing Council (TPC)
User interface

References and additional readings

Bostrom, R. P. 1989. Successful application of communication techniques to improve the systems development process. *Information & Management* 16:279–295.

Cause, D. E., and G. M. Weinberg. 1989. *Exploring requirements: Quality before design*. New York, NY: Dorset House.

Davenport, T. H., R. G. Eccles, and L. Prusak. 1992. Information politics. *Sloan Management Review* 34 (1):53–65.

Doyle, M., and D. Strauss. 1976. *How to make meetings work: The new interaction method*. New York, NY: Jove.

Goodhue, D. L., J. A. Quillard, and J. F. Rockart. 1988. Managing the data resource: A contingency perspective. *MIS Quarterly* 12 (3):373–391.

Goodhue, D. L., M. D. Wybo, and L. J. Kirsch. 1992. The impact of data integration on the costs and benefits of information systems. *MIS Quarterly* 16 (3):293–311.

Kayser, T. A. 1990. *Mining group gold*. El Segundo, CA: Serif.

Loshin, D. 2001. *Enterprise knowledge management: The data quality approach*. San Diego, CA: Morgan Kaufmann.

Redman, T. C. 2001. *Data quality: The field guide*. Boston: Digital Press.

Weinberg, G. M. 1986. *Becoming a technical leader: An organic problem solving approach*. New York, NY: Dorset House.

Exercises

1. Why do organizations need to manage data?
2. What problems can arise because of poor data administration?
3. What is the purpose of a data dictionary?
4. Do you think a data dictionary should be part of a DBMS or a separate package?
5. How does the management of external databases differ from internal databases?
6. What is the difference between system- and project-level data administration?
7. What is a data steward? What is the purpose of this role?
8. What is the difference between workgroups and organizational databases? What are the implications for data administration?
9. What is an information architecture?
10. Why do organizations need data standards? Give some examples of typical data items that may require standardization.
11. You have been asked to advise a firm on the capacity of its database system. Describe the procedures you would use to estimate the size of the database and the number of transactions per second it will have to handle.
12. Why would a company issue an RFP?
13. How do the roles of database developer and data administrator differ?
14. What do you think is the most critical task for the user during database development?
15. A medium-sized manufacturing company is about to establish a data administration group within the IS department. What software tools would you recommend that group acquire?
16. What is a stakeholder? Why should stakeholders be involved in database project planning?
17. What support do CASE tools provide for the DDLC?
18. How can groupware support the DDLC?
19. A large international corporation has typically operated in a very decentralized manner with regional managers having considerable autonomy. How would you recommend the corporation establish its data administration function?
20. Describe the personality of a successful data administration manager. Compare your assessment to the personality appropriate for a database technical adviser.
21. Write a job advertisement for a data administrator for your university.
22. What types of organizations are likely to have data administration reporting directly to the CIO?
23. What do you think are the most critical phases of the DDLC? Justify your decision.
24. When might application development and database development proceed independently?
25. Why is database monitoring important? What data would you ask for in a database monitoring report?
26. Get the TPC-D Benchmark report from the TPC Web site (www.tpc.com), and answer the following questions:
    a. What are the smallest and largest databases benchmarked?
    b. How is the database populated?

        c. Why does the report specify the SQL for each query?

27. Get the TPC-C Benchmark report from the TPC Web site (www.tpc.org), and report how the SQL queries differ from those of TPC-D. Why is this so?

28. Create a benchmark for your personal computer DBMS by doing the following:
    a. Create the TPC-D database.
    b. Use Excel to generate test data and import them into your test database.
    c. Run several of the TPC-D queries.
    d. Investigate the effect of database size.

21

U-Commerce and Data Management

The only way to predict the future is to have the power to shape the future.
Eric Hoffer, *The Passionate State of Mind*, 1954

Learning objectives

Students completing this chapter will be able to

❖ understand the information technology developments supporting the emergence of u-commerce;
❖ discuss the data management implications of u-commerce;
❖ understand how networks are changing the delivery of customer service.

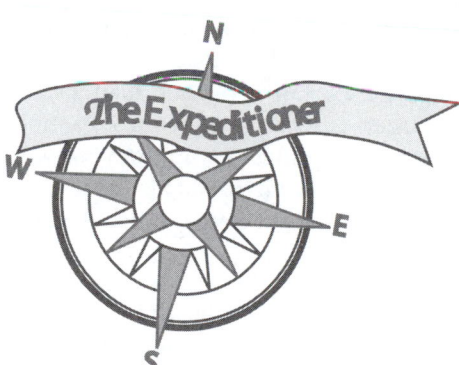

Annually, The Expeditioner's management team spends two days contemplating the firm's future. Increasingly, the interplay between business success and information technology has dominated discussions at these retreats, which are usually held at an exotic destination. The team has asked Sophie to find speakers to address two topics, the future of e-commerce and customer service technology, that the team believe are critical to the firm's future.

For this year's meeting in the Seychelles, Alice has two guest speakers. Leyland, an internationally renowned futurist who is a frequent speaker at some of the best business schools in the world, will speak on the future of e-commerce. Kathryn, the leader of a team investigating customer service technology, will report on her group's field research in major service firms. Alice knows that it is not enough for the team to listen passively to the speakers. She has assigned each person on the management team to report on the implications of the speakers' view for their functional areas.

Introduction

A firm's ability to serve its customers' needs determines its success. Initially, firms needed to meet face-to-face to satisfy most of their customers' needs, but with the development of information technology, the requirement for face-to-face interaction has gradually declined. The Internet opened up a new channel for firm-customer interaction that has significantly changed the customer relationship equation. Now, cell phone networks are enabling m-commerce and a further change in the firm-customer dynamic. In this chapter, we consider the ultimate direction of network-supported commerce and, in particular, its impact on customer service. These developments have important implications for data management, and so these are discussed and analyzed.

U-commerce[1]

Traditionally, business has been biased by geography and located near rivers, roads, and other transport services so that the costs of being reached by customers or reaching customers is lowered. Now, business is increasingly using electronic networks (e.g., the Internet and mobile phone networks) to interact with customers. Thus, in the next few years, it is likely that we will see the emergence of *u-commerce,* where the *u* stands for ubiquitous, universal, unique, and unison. **U-commerce** is *the use of ubiquitous networks to support personalized and uninterrupted communications and transactions between a firm and its various stakeholders to provide a level of value over, above, and beyond traditional commerce.* Each of the elements of u-commerce requires some more explanation.

Ubiquitous

Networked computers will soon be everywhere. Low-cost microprocessors and network connections will be embedded in all consumer durable devices. Already, a car has somewhere between 30 and 40 processors. The Korean appliance manufacturer LG (Lucky Goldstar) is advertising home air conditioners that can be called from a mobile phone and timed to switch on to a particular temperature setting. The ubiquity, or omnipresence, of computer chips means not only that they are everywhere but also that they are in a sense "nowhere", for they become invisible as we no longer notice them. The mobile phone is a good early example of ubiquity.

Real ubiquity of computer chips means that they are not just in durable devices but, indeed, everywhere. It is feasible that one day, very low-cost silicon flakes will be in every manufactured object, not to do advanced processing but simply to make every object part of the ubiquitous network and carry out a few simple but critical tasks.

---

1.   Watson, R. T., L. F. Pitt, P. Berthon, and G. M. Zinkhan. 2002. U-commerce: Expanding the universe of marketing. *Journal of the Academy of Marketing Science* 30 (4):329–343.

When firms started to use the Web for e-commerce, there was a massive increase in the volume of data to be managed, because many more transactions were born digital, and a great deal of data needed to be put online for customers to browse. When customers can always reach firms because networks are ubiquitous, there will be more electronic customer transactions and more demand for data that can be accessed in real time from anywhere, provided customers have the right device. U-commerce will see an increase in the volume of data an organization must manage.

Microsoft's global radio network

Microsoft intends to build a global network to support the smart watches and other devices based on its Smart Personal Objects Technology (SPOT). In the United States it has already created a network of more than 100 FM radio stations to broadcast precise time information and personalized data to the watches. Customers can sign up to receive tailored information such as sports scores, weather, or traffic information.

Source: Brewin, B. 2003. Microsoft eyes global radio network to support smart devices. *Computerworld*, Jan 10, www.computerworld.com/mobiletopics/mobile/story/0,10801,77442,00.html?nas=AM-77442.

Universal

Some information appliances are limited in their usefulness because they are not universally usable. For example, a U.S. cell phone is unlikely to work in Europe because of different standards and network frequencies. An Australian mobile phone that does not work on Japanese cell networks is excess baggage. In the future, consumers will have a universal information appliance, probably some combination of phone and PDA, that will enable them to stay connected wherever they are.[2]

The Internet has also become universal in another way, by being even more portable than a laptop or PDA. One can travel to most places that have Internet access nowadays and still access one's "own" Internet. Simply by using someone else's machine, travelers can access their e-mail or bank without physically carrying anything with them. Most airline business-class lounges and many hotels offer Internet access today, and many firms and institutions have facilities for visitors.

Universal devices increase the value of ubiquitous networks because consumers always have a means of accessing the network. Hence, there will be a further increase in the volume of data to be managed.

---

2. The SonyEricsson T68i <www.sonyericsson.com/us/> is a good example of a phone that is approaching universality. Also, its many features make it far more than a phone—it is an information appliance.

Unique

Uniqueness in its full bloom means that consumers will receive information that is dependent on the person's location, time of day, and current role or multiplicity of roles (e.g., tourist, parent, commuter, manager) and their expressed or learned preferences (i.e., learned by the systems providing the service).

Information can easily be customized to the current context and particular needs of each person. For example, insurance companies might require auto policyholders to have their vehicles fitted with a GPS. Premiums will then be charged based not on the traditional variables, such as age and place of residence, which have been presumed to determine risk, but on factors such as how often the car is used, how fast it is driven, and where it is driven, which arguably are more precise determinants of accident risk.

To support uniqueness, databases will need to be redesigned to store personal preference data. A system cannot recommend a particular restaurant unless it knows the customer's food preference by time of day (e.g., toast for breakfast, pizza for lunch, and fish for dinner). Databases will become larger in terms of tables, columns, and number of rows.

J-NAVI is a service in Japan (the first country to use third-generation mobile technology) that lets users enter a phone number, address, or landmark and then searches the area within a 500-meter (1,640 feet) radius. This makes it possible to find the subway station nearest to a particular shop, or a particular restaurant within walking distance of a specific office building. Users of the service can download a full-color map. At launch in May 2000, J-NAVI was expected to handle 100,000 hits per day. By day 3, it already had 1.6 million hits. Now, it has 2 million hits a day, and 50,000 users a day request a map.

Source: Looking for the pot of gold. 2001. *The Economist*, Oct. 11.

Unison

When consumers have complete agreement between their phone book, calendar, "to-do" list, and other such files across a range of information appliances (i.e., cell phone, computer, and PDA), they have unison. Unison means that a person's phone book on a desktop computer matches that on her cell phone, PDA, laptop, and so forth. A change in one phone book is synchronized to all others with complete transparency to the owner. The same is true for address books, diaries, and to-do lists, as well as links to Web sites and Wireless Access Protocol (WAP) sites. Specified files will be kept in unison so that location becomes irrelevant. The required information will always be available irrespective of the device and location. Unison means the integration of various communication systems so that there is a single interface or connection point. Apple released iSync in 10.2 of its operating system, a feature that uses Bluetooth[3] to synchronize files between a person's personal computer and all digital devices, including MP3 players.

To achieve unison, some major information appliance suppliers[4] are sponsoring the development and adoption of SyncML. This synchronization language is an open standard designed to establish a language for communications between devices, applications, and networks. It ensures that a consistent set of data are always available on any device or application, at any time. SyncML is based on XML and supports a wide variety of transport protocols (e.g., HTTP and WAP).

Data synchronization, or unison in u-commerce terms, is the process of making two sets of data identical. Because mobile users might not always be connected to a network or because it might be too costly to stay permanently connected, mobile users retrieve data from a server database and store it on their mobile devices. As they move around, they access and manipulate local copies of data. Periodically, they reconnect with the network to send any local changes back to the server database, and, at the same time, they will receive updates made to the server database while they were disconnected. There is also a need to resolve conflicts among the updates made to the server database.

Unison also describes the case where a team decides that it needs to share certain files and keep these synchronized. For example, a project team might have several people working on the same reports. When one person updates a report, the revised version is sent to all team members automatically. The team's work files are kept in unison.

As you would expect, unison has implications for data management. It will increase the availability of data to employees, customers, and other key stakeholders. All employees are mobile to some extent. At a minimum, they travel to and from an office, and others are on the road much of the day. Unison will make data available to employees where they need it, such as at a customer's office or on the factory floor. With the spreading of data across so many devices, data security will be a greater concern. Data managers will need to develop procedures for ensuring that sensitive data on thousands of mobile devices are protected.

A conceptual framework for u-commerce

U-space, the new arena of interaction between an organization and its customers, has two dimensions. Time-space specificity, the first dimension, ranges from the unique (time-space specific, localized) to ubiquitous (time-space unspecific, everywhere). Thus, for the consumer, technology can be either unique (i.e., localized in time and space) or ubiquitous (i.e., dispersed in time and space and everywhere). The second dimension, awareness, ranges from the unconscious (behind or out of consciousness) to ultraconscious (extension or enhancement of awareness). Technology can amplify or attenuate consciousness. *First,* it can extend or enhance a consumer's ordinary awareness (i.e., make

---

3.   Bluetooth is a short-range wireless technology for connecting electronic devices.
4.   Ericsson, IBM, Lotus, Matsushita, Motorola, Nokia, Openwave, Starfish Software, and Symbian.

the customer ultraconscious). *Second*, it can take something that once occupied a consumer's conscious awareness and perform it automatically (i.e., render it an unconscious task for the consumer). U-space delineates four types of commerce: the hyper-real, the post-human, the matrix, and the node (see Figure 21-1).

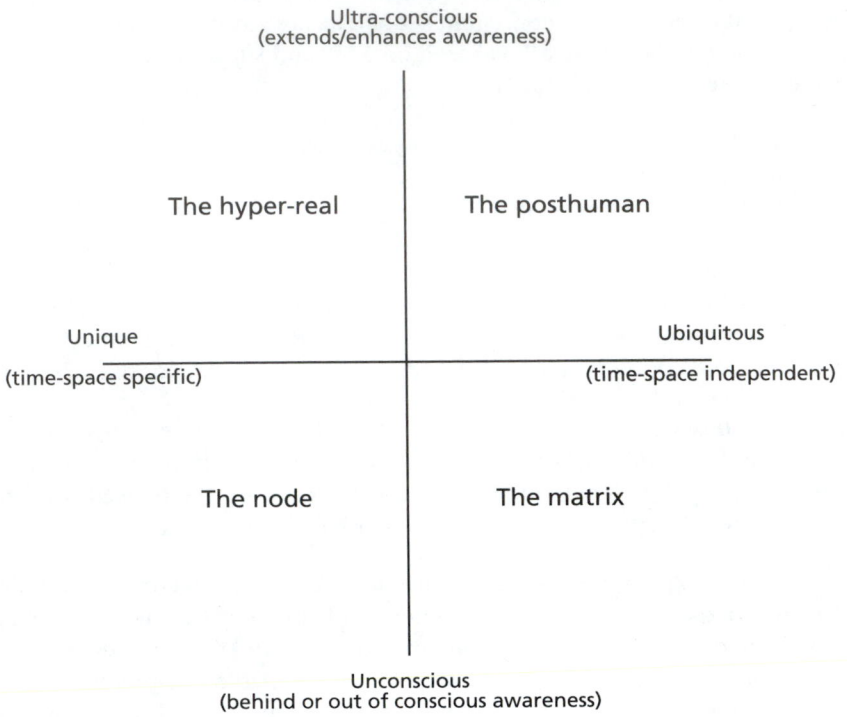

Figure 21-1. U-space

The hyper-real (ultraconscious, unique)

When technology creates value by extending normal conscious experience to unique contexts, we enter the realm of the *hyper-real*. Everyday experiences are enriched and expanded. In the future, this quadrant will increasingly comprise manufactured experience (e.g., virtual worlds) that enhance experience.

This is an entirely new world of data management for most companies. They will probably have to learn from the gaming (e.g., Nintendo) and simulation companies (such as Electronic Arts) that have experience in creating and managing virtual worlds.

The posthuman (ultraconscious, ubiquitous)

When technology delivers value by extending the consumers' normal conscious experience ubiquitously (i.e., across time and space), then we enter the domain of the *posthu-*

man. This includes processes that are always "on," always present independent of a person's location. This results in a permanent enhancement of human faculties. The progression is likely to be from enhancement of information storage and processing (the present) to advanced prosthetics and genetic enrichment of the cyberhuman.

The posthuman quadrant includes features that combine enhancement of an individual's conscious interaction with the world by transcending specific time-space locations (e.g., contact lens and education). On the software level, mind-machine interfaces (via neural grafting) will allow electronic implants that will facilitate the enhancement of memory, computation, and communication. On a hardware level, examples of the posthuman include biomachinery, advanced cybernetic prosthetics, and genetic engineering.

> A professor in the UK underwent an operation to surgically implant a silicon chip transponder in his forearm. He can operate doors, lights, heaters and other computers without lifting a finger. The technology has the capability to transform human life in ways portrayed in science fiction.
>
> Source: www.kevinwarwick.org/

We might well see bio-data management emerging as a new discipline that is concerned with linking bionic devices and data management technology to support the posthuman. Of course, a lot of this sounds like science fiction, but when viewed from several decades ago, much of today's technology has the wizardry of science fiction.

The matrix (unconscious, ubiquitous)

In the matrix quadrant, technology removes and performs tasks outside or behind awareness and ubiquitously (i.e., across time and space). This quadrant is dominated by omnipresent network infrastructure technologies (e.g., Internet, cell phone, GPS, Wi-Fi, Iridium, Bluetooth, sensornets). A current example is provided by the SIM chip in GSM phones, which handles billing and roaming charges across networks and continents.

The matrix is dominated by the need for data synchronization, and the comments made about data management with respect to unison apply. We will see single devices that are a merge of technologies. An information appliance, for instance, might have GPS, phone, PDA, camera, and MP3 capabilities. A herald of this type of appliance is the SonyEricsson P800.[5]

The node (unconscious, unique)

In the node quadrant, technology creates value by performing tasks outside or behind awareness in specific time-space locations (e.g., electronic toll collection). It is the marketplace of traditional subscription services. The purchase of the local newspaper, cable TV,

---

5. See www.sonyericsson.com/cebit/

and some utilities, for example, involves unconscious, unique consumption. Consumers did make a decision at one point to initiate the consumption; now, renewal is automatic or routine. We will purchase self-diagnosing, self-reporting products that interact with their original suppliers to a far greater extent than they do with their owners.

> Turbines made by GE are equipped with sensors that allow the firm to tell its customers online how efficiently their machinery is operating. Indeed, it is even possible for GE to spot a potential problem on a GE machine and dispatch someone to deal with it before the problem actually occurs, and before the customer is even aware of it.
>
> Source: Siegele, L. 2002. How about now? A survey of the real-time economy. *The Economist* 362 (8258):1-20.

In many advanced countries, we don't think of a consumer decision when we switch on a light or ignite a gas jet. Yet, these kinds of activities are quite significant, in terms of consumer resources. However, there are less-advanced economies where these can be conscious decisions (e.g., putting another coin in the gas heater slot).

Skill builder

Identify current or future products or services in each of the four quadrants of u-space.

Organizations will need to manage data for each customer-information appliance relationship. In other words, databases will need to support a many-to-many (m:m) relationship between customer and information appliance, which we might call something like ownership, service, or subscription. This entity will store details of all the episodes of this relationship, as illustrated by the generic data model in Figure 21-2. Clearly, this additional relationship will increase the number of transactions the database server must process and the volume of data to be managed.

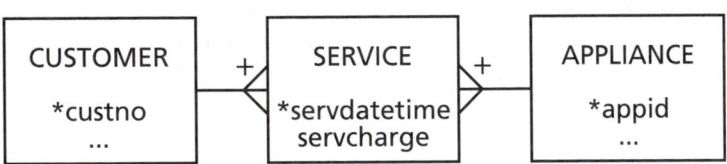

Figure 21-2. Generic data model for node quadrant

Implications

Humans are five-channel information processors (see, hear, feel, smell, touch), and it is perception, through the combination and interaction of these five senses, that determines the quality of a product or service. For example, a customer's perception of a car is based on its design, the sound of the engine, the feel of the highway, the smell of the interior, and the touch of the accelerator. We engage all of our senses in the assessment of any object or event. At its core, business is about the delivery of information, because it is concerned with engaging the consumer's information-processing capability to create a favorable impression or encourage certain behavior.

The important transformations in the human condition have largely resulted from those innovations that significantly altered our capacity to process information. Digitization, which is the driving force of the current period, started with the telegraph and Morse code in the mid-1800s. Prior revolutions, such as the alphabet, have had profound effects on society. Revolutions take time to accelerate and reach their terminal speed because of the compounding effect of innovations flowing from the breakthrough invention. We are still on the upward slope of the digitization revolution. Some input channels have recently been digitized (e.g., sound). Digitization of the senses of touch and taste is on the drawing boards at the time of writing.

U-commerce will increase the importance of data management. There will be more data to manage and more relationships to maintain. Firms will need to be able to supply information to their customers wherever they might be and keep records of their customers' interactions with their many devices—from toasters to information appliances. Data will be central to competition because it is the raw material of information, and information is what customers, and the products they own, consume in the information age.

Major innovations in our ability to process information have been the bedrock of cultural, social, political, and economic change. Ubiquitous connectivity to information and computer processing power will be a profound change, and it represents the ultimate consummation of the digitization revolution that started more than a century ago.

Summary

U-commerce, the ultimate form of commerce, is explained in terms of the concepts of ubiquitous, universal, unique, unison, ultraconscious, and unconscious. The interaction of these concepts leads to u-space and four forums for commerce: the hyper-real, posthuman, matrix, and node. U-commerce will increase the importance of data management, as there will be more data to store and more data to deliver to customers wherever they might be.

Wal-Mart plays tag

In late 2003, Wal-Mart mandated that its top 100 suppliers place radio-frequency identification (RFID) tags on certain shipments by January1, 2005. An RFID is a small, 25-cent tag containing a chip, an antenna, and product information that is scanned in the warehouse and store. RFID may be the most important technological development for retailers since the bar code. Potential savings for retailers and their suppliers are tremendous. Labor costs to take inventory can be significantly reduced, and tagging every product can curb both shoplifting and theft en route to the warehouse.

While most suppliers have lived up to the letter of the mandate, they are not embracing RFIDs. Many have simply tagged the minimum required shipments and hoped for the best —"slap-and-ship" is what the industry calls it. The costs for suppliers are huge, and many companies think that Wal-Mart reaps all the benefits. As one analyst commented: "It's just a higher-cost bar code." Another problem is that the technology is still new, and few retail suppliers are fond of using cutting-edge technology. Other retailers have learned from Wal-Mart's experience and changed the approach and been more open to collaboration with suppliers.

Most still buy the ultimate RFID vision, but they say it's at least a decade off. One way or another, RFID will become common. It's just a question of who takes advantage of the technology—and when.

Source: Lacy, S. 2005. RFID: Plenty of mixed signals. *BusinessWeek*, Jan 31, www.businessweek.com/technology/content/jan2005/tc20050131_5897_tc024.htm.

Key terms and concepts

Information appliance	Ultraconscious
Hyper-real	Unconscious
Matrix	Unique
Node	Unison
Posthuman	Universal
Ubiquitous	U-space
U-commerce	

References and additional readings

Watson, R. T., L. F. Pitt, P. Berthon, and G. M. Zinkhan. 2002. U-commerce: Expanding the universe of marketing. *Journal of the Academy of Marketing Science* 30 (4):329-343. Tokyo's Nomura Research Institute (NRI) is the leading Japanese think tank. Several papers are available from its Web site (www.nri.co.jp/english/), and these are most easily found by entering "ubiquitous" in the search box window.

Implications

Exercises

1. How will u-commerce change data management?
2. What data management technologies are likely to become more important as u-commerce emerges?
3. Is the universal information appliance more likely to come from a cell phone company (e.g., Nokia or Ericsson), a PDA firm (e.g., Palm or Handspring), or somewhere else?
4. Discuss some occupations where unison across information appliances would enhance productivity.
5. Consider in turn each of the four quadrants of Figure 21-1 and identify some current or future products or services in that quadrant.
6. Visit xmradio.com or sirius.com and identify which u-factors (ubiquity, universal, unique, or unison) these services satisfy.
7. Visit apple.com/ipod and determine which u-factors the iPod satisfies.
8. On November 17, 2002, Microsoft's Bill Gates introduced SPOT. To which quadrant or quadrants of u-space is this aimed?[6]

---

6. See www.microsoft.com/presspass/features/2002/nov02/11-17SPOT.asp

Photo Credits

Index